D0829765

The Catholic
University of America
A Centennial History

His Holiness, Pope Leo XIII (1810–1903), papal founder of The Catholic University of America, in reproduction in Carrara marble of a statue from his golden jubilee exposition, presented to the university in 1891 by Joseph Loubat of New York, who became a papal count, and placed in McMahon Hall in 1895. Giuseppi Luchetti was the sculptor.

The Catholic University of America

A Centennial History

C. Joseph Nuesse
Professor of Sociology Emeritus and
Provost Emeritus

The Catholic University of America Press
Washington, D.C.

Copyright © 1990
The Catholic University of America Press
All rights reserved

LIBRARY OF CONGRESS CATALOGING-IN-PUBLICATION DATA

Nuesse, C. Joseph, 1913–
    The Catholic University of America : a centennial history /
by C. Joseph Nuesse.
        p.   cm.
    Includes bibliographical references.
    1. Catholic University of America—History. I. Title.
LD838.N84 1990
378.753—dc20   89-29649
ISBN 0-8132-0722-3
ISBN 0-8132-0736-3 (pbk.)

To My Wife, Margaret O'Donoghue Nuesse

Contents

Illustrations

Abbreviations

Abbreviations are used in the footnotes of this work in order to designate economically (a) the archival collections in which documents are deposited, (b) the documentary sources, (c) encyclopedias, and (d) serial publications, except newspapers, with titles of more than a single word.

Most of the documents that are cited are to be found in the archives of The Catholic University of America. Only when they are not is the archival location identified. In citations from intra-campus correspondence, no place of writing is given since it is obvious.

Abbreviations for a university office are maintained continuously despite changes in its title. Thus, the abbreviation for Office of the Rector (OR) is used for items dated after as well as before 1968, when the title of the chief executive officer was changed to president. Similarly, the abbreviation for Office of the Vice Rector (OVR) is used throughout, although the title of the officer and sometimes the duties have been changed several times, to Executive Vice Rector (1966–68), Executive Vice President and Provost (1968–79), Executive Vice President (1979–81), Provost (1979–83), and Executive Vice President (1983 to date).

It should be noted also that a single abbreviation, AR, is used for the published annual report of the rector, which, except for a few years, appeared under slightly varying but similar titles from 1890 to 1967. Further, since 1983 there has been publication of extensive statistical data under the title "President's Annual Report." The academic and fiscal year for which each report is made is shown in parentheses.

Archives

AAB	Archdiocese of Baltimore
AACi	Archdiocese of Cincinnati
AAD	Archdiocese of Detroit
AANY	Archdiocese of New York
AAO	Archdiocese of Omaha
ACHC	College of the Holy Cross

Abbreviations

ACHS	The Catholic Historical Society of St. Paul
ACSP	Paulist Fathers Archives
ACUA	The Catholic University of America
ADB	Diocese of Buffalo
ADR	Diocese of Richmond
AGU	Georgetown University
AMHS	Minnesota Historical Society
APF	Sacra Congregazione per L'Evangelizzione dei Popoli o "de Propaganda Fide"
ASJU	St. Joseph's University
ASV	Archivio Segreto Vaticano
ASVA	St. Vincent Archabbey and College
AUND	University of Notre Dame

Documentary Sources

AA	Alumni Association
ABC	Administration and Budget Committee
AS	Academic Senate
BD	Board of Deans
BT	Board of Trustees
DA	Delegazione Apostolica negli Stati Uniti
EC	Executive Committee
exh	Exhibits attached to minutes
FSS	Fondo Segretariato di Stato
GSAS	Graduate School of Arts and Sciences
mm	Minutes of meetings
OR	Office of the Rector
OVR	Office of the Vice Rector
PC	President's Council
SL	School of Law
SP	School of Philosophy
SOCG	Scritture Originali riferite nella Congregazione generali
SRC	Scritture riferite nei Congressi (APF)
SSS	School of Sacred Sciences
SSoS	School of Social Science

Encyclopedias

CE	*Catholic Encyclopedia* (15 vols. & suppl.; New York: Robert Appleton, 1907–50).
DAB	*Dictionary of American Biography* (20 vols.; New York: Charles Scribner's Sons, 1929–36).
EB	*Encyclopedia Britannica* (24 vols.; Chicago: Encyclopedia Britannica, 1956).
NCE	*New Catholic Encyclopedia* (15 vols. & suppl.; New York: McGraw-Hill, 1967–89).

Serial Publications

AA	*American Archivist*
AAS	*Acta Apostolicae Sedis*

AAUP	American Association of University Professors *Bulletin*
AB	"Administrative Bulletin"
ACQR	*American Catholic Quarterly Review*
AEIM	American Enterprise Institute *Memorandum*
AER	*American Ecclesiastical Review*
AM	*Ave Maria*
AR	*Annual Report of the Rector*
ASS	*Acta Sanctae Sedis*
BQR	*Brownson's Quarterly Review*
CA	*Catholic Action*
CBN	*Catholic Book News*
CBSJ	*Central Blatt and Social Justice*
CCICA	Catholic Commission on Intellectual and Cultural Affairs "Annual"
CER	*Catholic Educational Review*
CGSC	Council of Graduate Schools in the U.S. *Communicator*
CHE	*Chronicle of Higher Education*
CHR	*Catholic Historical Review*
CLW	*Catholic Library World*
CUAM	CUA *Magazine*
CUB	*Catholic University Bulletin*
CULR	*Catholic University Law Review*
CW	*Catholic World*
DM	*Donohue's Magazine*
DR	*Dublin Review*
END	*Education and National Defense Series*
ER	*Educational Record*
FJ	*Freeman's Journal*
HE	*Higher Education*
HRS	*Historical Records and Studies*
IW	*Irish World*
JR	*Journal of Religion*
MLR	*Monthly Labor Review*
NCAQ	*North Central Association Quarterly*
NCEA	National Catholic Educational Association *Bulletin*
NCWC	National Catholic Welfare Conference *Bulletin*
NO	*Nursing Outlook*
NS	*The New Scholasticism*
RACHS	*Records of the American Catholic Historical Society*
ST	*Social Thought*
TS	*Theological Studies*
USCH	*U.S. Catholic Historian*
USNWR	*U.S. News and World Report*
WL	*Woodstock Letters*

Preface

The Catholic University of America had been open only five years when its first rector, on December 2, 1894, announced that he had appointed Thomas O'Gorman, a professor of ecclesiastical history, to be its annalist and to write its history. Within fourteen months, however, the appointee, who was a priest of the archdiocese of St. Paul, was named the second bishop of Sioux Falls, South Dakota. The annalist's position that he vacated seems never to have been filled again.

The rector, dismissed from his own office soon after, took care to pen a personal account of how the institution had been begun. Then historians among the professors were relied upon to lend their talents, sometimes to provide only sketches commemorating anniversaries and at other times to examine in scholarly detail one phase or another of the university's past. Particularly deserving of mention among them are Peter Guilday, who was a prolific historian of the American Church, and Richard J. Purcell, the second occupant of the Knights of Columbus chair of American history. Systematic critical presentation, however, had to await the early research of John Tracy Ellis that is reported in his volume, *The Formative Years of the Catholic University of America*, published by the American Catholic Historical Association in 1946.

This work was continued by students. Three uncommonly fine master's dissertations directed by Monsignor Ellis were published by The Catholic University of America Press: Patrick Henry Ahern, *The Catholic University of America, 1887–1896: the Rectorship of John J. Keane*, in 1948; Peter E. Hogan, S.S.J., *The Catholic University of America, 1896–1903: the Rectorship of Thomas J. Conaty*, in 1949; and Colman J. Barry, O.S.B., *The Catholic University of America, 1903–1909: the Rectorship of Denis J. O'Connell*, in 1950. Immediately succeeding administrations became the subjects of two doctoral dissertations reproduced by University Microfilms in 1972: Blase Dixon, T.O.R., "The Catholic University of America, 1909–1928: the Rectorship of Thomas Joseph Shahan," and H. Warren Willis, "The Reorganization of The Catholic University of America during the Rectorship of James Hugh Ryan (1928–1935)."

That this previous historical work has been of enormous advantage to me, I am glad to acknowledge here and in appropriate citations in the text that follows. I, nevertheless, have attempted a fresh exploration of the sources and have made interpretations for which I alone can be held responsible.

The preparation of this history in view of the university's approaching centennial was suggested to me by Edmund D. Pellegrino during his presidency of the university (1978–82) and has been generously supported by his successor, the Reverend William J. Byron, S.J. (1982 to date). I can never fully express my gratitude for the opportunity to undertake this study that they extended to me.

Gratitude for supplementary funding is owed to the Robert Schalkenbach Foundation of New York City, which allowed me to extend the use of its grant for research in Roman archives to the examination of records relevant to this history in the collections of the Roman congregation for the evangelization of peoples (Propaganda Fide) and in those of the secret archives of the Vatican. At the time, May of 1983, the latest documents open to scholars were those from the pontificate of Leo XIII (1878–1903). These had been made accessible in 1978. When, subsequently, in 1986, documents from the pontificates of St. Pius X (1903–1914) and Benedict XV (1914–1922) were opened, the university supported my return to Rome during October of 1987 for the perusal of records that could be made available at the time, namely, those of the apostolic delegation to the United States. I am particularly indebted for the invaluable assistance on these occasions of the Very Reverend Josef Metzler, O.M.I., prefect of the Vatican archives since 1985, who previously was archivist at Propaganda Fide, and of the Reverend Monsignor Charles Burns. The use of these archives of the Holy See is a particular contribution of this history.

When Monsignor Ellis wrote *The Formative Years of the Catholic University of America* in the wake of the university's golden jubilee celebration, he expressed the hope that it would serve as "an introduction" to a definitive history that it was then too early to write. It may be too early still to write a comprehensive history. Perhaps at some time in the future a multi-volume treatment will be undertaken. At present, however, in my judgment, what is needed most is an attempt to place the course of the institution in the perspective of what has been happening in American higher education during the past century. The selection of material for inclusion, therefore, has had to be of vital concern. Many episodes or facets of the university's history are deserving of presentation in much more detail than I have been able to include, but probably most readers will want to follow only the decisive institutional developments bearing upon the historic academic mission outlined by the founders. I trust that my selection and interpretation of the developments will be found to be fully supported by the facts and sources that I cite.

I have pursued archival research as nearly as possible down to the present, but necessarily in Part V, which treats of recent decades, with due regard for restrictions imposed upon files of recent administrations, for developments that have not yet run their course, and for possibilities of personal bias that may be rooted in my own experience in instructional positions beginning in 1945 and in central administration from 1967 until 1981. This part of the university's history, which is the contemporary period for most of its living alumni, will be treated comprehensively by historians only at some later time. In interpreting earlier periods, it has been especially interesting for me to examine documents from the hands of professors who had been on the campus more than forty years when I first met them after becoming a member of the department of sociology in 1945. Seeing the university through their correspondence and that of so many others whom I later came to know has deepened whatever awareness I had at the outset that a century is not a long time in the history of an institution.

I know that the presentation of any history is apt to suggest what the novelist John Updike has indicted as "the tyranny of a plan." If there appears to be such in what follows, I would like to believe that it has emerged from what might in turn be called the tyranny of the facts. Necessarily, however, it is indeed "perceived reality—reality in the eyes of the beholder," as George F. Kennan has called it, that is reconstructed in these pages.

The chapters that outline developments as they occurred during the successive administrations of the university are arranged in five parts, according to my perception of phases in institutional development that can be distinguished. These are phases in the maturing of ideas and structures as they appear retrospectively. Distinguishing them serves chronology, obviously, but it is helpful also in emphasizing the saving dualism between the administration and the professoriate that is found in a university. Institutional leadership is as necessary on a university campus as in any other organization and it can be not only competent but creative. At the same time, happily, there can reside in the faculties a capacity to preserve essential academic values even when administrative leadership is wanting.

From its earliest days, certain aspects of institutional character have been prominent in the life of The Catholic University of America. The institution has been shaped by, as in turn it has helped to shape, developments in the Church in the United States. The corporate commitment of the bishops to be its sponsors has given it at once unique promise and unique limits, perhaps not so much doctrinally, as might be thought, as materially. Yet its dedication to advanced study from the first has given it academic as well as ecclesiastical singularity and has afforded to it a more explicit sense of mission than most institutions can claim.

My purpose is to present a serious, critical study that will hold the interest not only of historians but also of all those in whom affection for the university abides, among whom are some whose duty it is to reflect upon its policies. The principle by which I have tried to be guided has been stated succinctly in a letter of October 31, 1983, on Martin Luther, admittedly a much vaster subject, by His Holiness, Pope John Paul II: "Only by placing ourselves unreservedly in an attitude of purification by means of the truth can we find a shared interpretation of the past and at the same time reach a new point of departure for the dialogue of today."

A dialogue with their age and with America, it should become clear, was what the founders of The Catholic University of America had in mind. Evangelization was certainly always their goal—many, indeed, had imbibed the hopes of Isaac Hecker, called "the Yankee Paul" by a biographer of the community that he founded—but the integrity of the university's own work as a prerequisite for evangelization was never inpugned by the leaders. The capacity to engage in dialogue at the highest intellectual level in every essential field was what they thought they were cultivating and what they intended should be the criterion of their institution's success, as indeed it still must be when judgment is rendered upon either its past or its future.

Dialogue can lead to controversy; controversy does not necessarily lead to dialogue. Since neither academics nor ecclesiastics are noted for moderation in disputes, it should not be surprising that disagreeable exchanges have characterized developments rather frequently during the university's first century. Walter Elliot, a pioneer Paulist whose biography of his founder was producing a storm in the wake of its translation and adaptation for a French audience, took note of them during the controversies that preceded the papal condemnation of "Americanism" in 1899. Writing to the priest who was later to become the university's third rector, he remarked ruefully, "Holy Church rolls along in her chariot, but sometimes the wheels creak; and then the wheel grease is nothing less than the blood of the Church's best friends & servants." His respondent himself and the university's first rector might already have served him as examples; others in administrative or professorial positions in later years would come to know his meaning. Sometimes indeed aptness can be found in Randall Jarrell's bitter inversion of a familiar scriptural injunction, "It is necessary that good come, but woe to him by whom it cometh." Yet controversies and, for that matter, all other events must be kept in perspective in any truthful account.

To help me to maintain perspective, I have had the benefit of readings of my manuscript by the Reverend Monsignor John Tracy Ellis, dean of American Catholic church historians, and Professor Philip Gleason, active historian of American Catholicism at the University of Notre Dame.

Dr. Anthony Zito, archivist of The Catholic University of America, has also read the entire manuscript with particular care for my utilization of archival collections. With his assistant, Sister Anne Crowley, S.S.N.D., he has rendered invaluable assistance to me from the beginning of this project. So too have members of the staff of the John K. Mullen of Denver Library on the campus.

The Reverend Peter E. Hogan, S.S.J., archivist of the Josephite Fathers, has assisted me by reading Chapter IV in draft. Other archivists of many dioceses and institutions who have helped me in using collections are remembered gratefully as well but are not named here because of their number, except that I cannot fail to single out Sister Mary Felicitas Powers, R.S.M., former archivist of the archdiocese of Baltimore, who in that capacity had custody of many records of the university's founding and of its life until the conclusion of World War II.

There are others who by correspondence or interview have provided information in response to my inquiries: E. Catherine Dunn, professor emerita and former head of the department of English; the Reverend John Whitney Evans, of the department of history of the College of St. Scholastica in Duluth, Minnesota; the late Paul J. FitzPatrick, professor emeritus and former head of the department of economics; the Reverend Monsignor Paul Hanly Furfey, professor emeritus and former head of the department of sociology; Regina Flannery Herzfeld, professor emerita and former head of the department of anthropology; the Reverend Monsignor James A. Magner, who as procurator and later as a vice president had charge of administration and finance from 1940 until 1968; the Reverend Bernard G. Mulvaney, C.S.V., a former colleague in the department of sociology; J. Kerby Neill, professor emeritus of

English; the late George D. Rock, professor emeritus of physics, former dean of the graduate school of arts and sciences, and former secretary general of the university; the Reverend Walter J. Schmitz, S.S., professor emeritus and former dean of the school of sacred theology; and John K. Zeender, professor emeritus of history.

Finally, I owe to David J. McGonagle, director of The Catholic University of America Press, deep gratitude for arranging for the final typing of the manuscript, for assistance in the selection of illustrations, and for supervision of the production of this book.

C. *Joseph Nuesse*

PART ONE

The Aims of the Founders

Since in setting forth, explaining, and defending the history and doctrines of the Church the intellect is the instrument we use, it is important that this instrument should be brought to the highest possible effectiveness. And since this culture of mind, in our day especially, is an insidious and dangerous foe of religion, it is our urgent duty to form men who will be able to make it also its serviceable ally. — *John Lancaster Spalding, "The Catholic Priesthood," address at silver jubilee of St. Francis Seminary, Milwaukee, Wisconsin, June 30, 1881, in* Lectures and Discourses *(New York: Catholic Publication Society, 1882), 156.*

CHAPTER I

The Idea of an American Catholic University

The word "university" was in the air in the middle years of the nineteenth century, as the first president of The Johns Hopkins University was able to recall in relating how his institution had been begun with no prescriptive mandate other than this word in the will of its Quaker founder.[1] What he was able to look back upon with justifiable pride was the emergence in Baltimore, in 1876, of a new type of institution that had already begun to shape a creative movement in university education. A social historian of no mean repute has gone so far as to call the achievement "the single, most decisive event in the history of learning in the Western hemisphere."[2] Roman Catholics as well as other Americans were to be among its beneficiaries. Their participation, however, had its beginnings in an independent development in their own circles that resulted in the foundation of The Catholic University of America.

Undoubtedly, Catholics of the time would not have been able to define any more precisely than their fellow citizens the word that was in the air. But when their leaders gave thought to establishing a university, they had a distinctive intellectual heritage within which to search for the meaning and promise that such an institution might have. The first principle of this heritage and at the same time the instrument of its continuity was the religious faith that they professed. True, the rebuke that Jesus had addressed to Martha, "Only one thing is necessary,"[3] could be applied to men and women with intellectual concerns no less

---

1. Daniel Coit Gilman, *The Launching of a University* (New York: Dodd, Mead, 1906), 5–6, 128.

2. Edward Shils, "The Order of Learning in the United States: The Ascendancy of the University," in Alexandra Oleson and John Voss (eds.), *The Organization of Knowledge in Modern America, 1860–1920* (Baltimore: The Johns Hopkins University Press, 1979), 28.

3. Luke 10:12.

than to others. The first Christians, certainly, had come to appreciate learning only gradually. Their intention had been to extend the revealed religion that had been preached to them. But in encounters with the theological and philosophical ideas of their contemporaries they were soon led to formulate apologies for their belief and to give these apologies systematic form. Beyond this, those who were educated had to address critically the perennial human questions. Already in the second century, St. Justin Martyr was observing that "the truths which men in all lands have rightly spoken belong to us Christians."[4] Within the next hundred years there were expressed views that ranged from the virtual rejection of all ancient philosophy by Tertullian, who found in it "little more than the foolishness of this world," to the exaltation of the same philosophy by Clement of Alexandria as "a gift of God, a means of educating the pagan world for Christ."[5] Happily, in the further development of Christian thought, in spite of recurring echoes of Tertullian, the position of Justin and Clement became dominant within Roman Catholic tradition.

Accordingly, in response to the needs of successive ages and diverse European cultures, the liberal arts and philosophy together with religion were taught first in the monastic and then in the cathedral and palace schools that were established after the decay of classical civilization. The Church provided the milieu for the scholastic revival that began in the eleventh century and flowered in the foundation of universities during the thirteenth. In the latter, as a historian has concisely summarized the matter, "the men of the Middle Ages established in the mind of the western world the principle that the preservation and perpetuation of theoretical knowledge is properly entrusted to a special institution . . . which is a permanent association of scholars and students and which is largely self-governing and mainly self-perpetuating." The medieval founders recognized, too, that the university institution should embrace "the whole of knowledge other than traditional handicraft skills."[6] Thus was established the universal range in which, according to St. Anselm's earlier theological formulation, faith would seek understanding.

The medieval institution—the *studium generale,* as it was known

---

4. "The Second Apology of Justin to the Roman Senate in Behalf of the Christians," Chap. XIII, in Thomas B. Falls (ed.), *Saint Justin Martyr* (Fathers of the Church, VI; Washington, D.C.: The Catholic University of America Press, 1948), 133–34.

5. Frederick Copleston, S.J., *A History of Philosophy,* II (Westminster, Md.: Newman Press, 1960), 15. See Gerard L. Ellspermann, O.S.B., *The Attitude of the Early Christian Latin Writers Toward Pagan Literature and Learning* (Washington, D.C.: The Catholic University of America Press, 1949).

6. Paul Farmer, "Nineteenth Century Ideas of the University—Continental Europe," in Margaret A. Clapp (ed.), *The Modern University* (Ithaca: Cornell University Press, 1950), 3.

originally—was buffeted by changing fortunes during the eventful centuries from the thirteenth to the nineteenth. Beginning in the sixteenth
century, it fell into a general decline. On the Catholic side, there was
no encouraging development until the reopening in 1834 of the Catholic
University of Louvain in Belgium, which had been founded in 1425 but
which French republican armies had suppressed in 1797. This success
was for a long time a singular one. Within the English-speaking world,
only Saint Patrick's College at Maynooth in Ireland, founded in 1795,
was offering advanced courses in theology, but it was not a university.[7]
John Henry Newman, of course, contributed what was to become an
educational classic when he published *The Idea of a University* in 1852,
but his concept, sadly, could not be given concrete reality in the
Catholic University of Ireland which he was then planning with the
Irish bishops and which he served as rector from its opening in 1854
until his withdrawal four years later. Twenty years or so afterward, an
attempt of the English bishops to establish a Catholic university was a
worse failure.[8]

By the beginning of the nineteenth century, the continental universities were almost everywhere regarded as creations of the state and
expressions of the national spirit. In France, universities had been
abolished altogether in 1793 and then, by a decree of Napoleon in
1806, specialized schools and independent faculties were centralized
into one system with the entire structure of public education. Not
until after 1875 were the French bishops free to establish the Catholic
"institutes" that now exist, and under the anti-clerical legislation of the
succeeding years they could not even designate them as universities. In
Germany, early campaigns to establish an institution on the model of
Louvain produced only meager funds and ended completely after the
Prussian unification of the country and the *Kulturkampf* of Bismarck.
The modern state had come into its own.

The German universities, however, were developing a new concept
of purpose that was destined to revitalize the traditional institution and
to have a notable influence in the United States, where private as well
as public institutions could make it their own. To the received purposes
of the conservation and transmission of knowledge the Germans were
adding what has since become the distinguishing mark of the modern
university, that is, the advancement of knowledge through research.

---

7. John Healy, *Maynooth College, Its Centenary History* (Dublin: Brown & Nolan,
1895), Chap. XI.
8. John Tracy Ellis, *The Formative Years of the Catholic University of America* (Washington, D.C.: American Catholic Historical Association, 1946), 26–41, reviews these

Previously this function had been accomplished only through independent scholarship or in specialized academies. Instructionally, within the
German system, the university was for students who had completed
their general or liberal education before entry and who thenceforth
would concentrate upon work for the doctorate. Today, in its more
recent American form, which combines certain features of both English
and German institutions, and which is increasingly dominant internationally, the university has come to be appraised as, together with the
research complex, "the most critical single feature of the developing
structure of modern societies."[9] In one important particular, through
the graduate education that it offers, it trains those upon whom the
continuity of scholarship in the basic fields of knowledge depends and
thus it forms "an intellectually self-sustaining order."[10]

Catholic leaders may have been a little slower than some other
Americans to perceive the significance of the developing triadic definition of purpose. The research function of the university, however, was
not widely accepted in any country other than Germany until the last
quarter of the nineteenth century. Catholic scholars everywhere were
more likely to be concerned about the apparent decline of classical and
humanistic and of philosophical and theological studies. Science was
ascendant. Specialization was proceeding and the traditional ideal of
the "learned man" was being supplanted by that of the research scholar,
the pursuer of what in another context altogether the young William
Butler Yeats in Ireland was characterizing as "Grey Truth."[11]

The university, in these circumstances, rapidly became more than
ever before the institutional means through which intellectual developments could be related to Christian concerns. It was the place for
the systematic examination of, for example, the evolutionary theories
of Charles Darwin and Herbert Spencer that were then abroad. So,
although he was not the first to place his hope in its establishment,
John Lancaster Spalding (1840–1916), a product of Louvain, long
before he became the foremost proponent of an American Catholic
university, was assessing the revolutionary character of the contemporary scientific progress in the best Catholic tradition when he wrote

---

developments. This work provides the full historical account of the foundation that is the
subject of this chapter and the succeeding one.

9. Talcott Parsons and Gerald M. Platt, The American University (Cambridge: Harvard
University Press, 1973), vi. For a historical view of the rise of the university to dominance
in the world of knowledge, see Shils, op. cit., 19–47.

10. John Higham, "The Matrix of Specialization," in Oleson and Voss, op. cit., 25.

11. "The Song of the Happy Shepherd," in The Wanderings of Oisin and Other Poems
(1889).

as a young priest that "the great intellectual work in the church in our day is to show that theology which is the science of God's revelation as interpreted by the church, is not only not in contradiction with, but is the essential and central point of union of the whole scientific group."[12]

This intellectual purpose radiated from the papacy itself after the accession of Leo XIII in 1878. The new pope, according to a prudent estimate, "would have taken a position as a statesman of the first rank had he held office in any secular government."[13] Comparing him with his predecessor, Isaac Thomas Hecker (1819–88), the nationally known convert, founder of the Paulists, and inspiration of many who became devoted to the university cause, editorialized with satisfaction that the dominant note of Leo's policy was intellectual as that of Pius IX had been emotional.[14] Declaring the improvement of theological training to be his first objective and desiring to encourage not only the theological but also the humanistic education of priests, Leo, in his encyclical *Aeterni Patris*, had promulgated officially the revival of Thomism in philosophy and theology that had already begun. This intellectual movement, which was to gain momentum in the next century, spread into artistic, literary, political and other realms. Scholars found also in Leo's opening of the Vatican archives in 1883 a mark of approbation for their work and ground for renewed confidence in its compatibility with religion.

It was hardly surprising, therefore, that after initial attention to opposing views, the Holy Father became receptive to the proposal for the foundation of a Catholic university that emanated from the Third Plenary [*i.e.*, national] Council of the American bishops in 1884. Indeed, he took a personal interest in the project, from which Bishop John J. Keane, the first rector, perhaps too readily inferred that the pope had a "deep conviction that the church in America is to exercise a dominant influence in the world's future, and that this influence must rest on intellectual superiority." The frequency and ardor of Leo's references to the university project in various audiences supported Keane's impression "that the great enterprise is as much his own as ours, and that his heart is set on its realization."[15]

12. *The Life of the Most Reverend M. J. Spalding, D.D., Archbishop of Baltimore* (New York: Christian Press Association, 1873), 316n.

13. A. W. Huddleston, "Leo XIII," *EB*, XIII, 929.

14. "Leo XIII," *CW*, XLVI (Dec., 1887), 294. James Hennesey, S.J., "Leo XIII's Thomistic Revival: A Political and Philosophical Event," *JR*, LVIII (Suppl., 1978), S185–97, provides historical perspective.

15. "Leo XIII and the Catholic University of America," *CW*, XLVI (Nov., 1887), 150, 146. A contemporary editor had earlier remarked that to papal eyes at the time

Fittingly, by virtue of his approval of its canonical institution, Pope Leo XIII became the official founder of The Catholic University of America.

The First Proposals

Seemingly the first to propose an ecclesiastical institution of this kind in the United States had been Robert Browne, an unruly Irish-born Augustinian priest serving in Charleston, South Carolina, and Augusta, Georgia. About 1820, Browne was reporting, at the request of the Roman congregation for the propagation of the faith, on means to reduce the widespread dissension that then existed in the American Church. At this early date, when Catholic Americans numbered only about 200,000 in a national population approaching ten million, Browne believed that there was a need for a national ecclesiastical college that would be authentically American. He did not consider Georgetown College in the District of Columbia and St. Mary's Seminary in Baltimore, already chartered as universities, to qualify as such, but wanted a foundation in the national capital that would be under the direction of the Holy See, presided over by a local bishop, and supported by annual collections.[16] His contribution, however, can best be regarded as the first of several proposals for a national seminary of quality.

There seem to have been no subsequent concrete proposals from Catholics while developments toward advanced work were being initiated during the 1820s and again during the 1840s and early 1850s at Harvard, Yale, Brown, Michigan, and other institutions.[17] Catholic colleges, beginning early in the nineteenth century, were occasionally conferring the master's degree for mere residence or experience as prevailing custom allowed, and even their formal organization of graduate programs, attempted at Georgetown College in 1877 and soon thereafter by a few other Jesuit institutions, was described, as one historian aptly distinguishes, "in quantitative rather than qualitative language."[18]

What was foremost in the minds of the bishops with respect to higher education had been revealed in their preparation for the First Plenary

America was "the ultimate boundary of an immense European emigration." *DM*, X (Nov., 1883), 562.

16. APF, SRC, 1st Series, America Centrale, V, fol. 682–94, Carolina, "Causa di Browne e Gallagher che appelano alla S. Sede" (in Italian).

17. Richard J. Storr, *The Beginnings of Graduate Education in America* (Chicago: University of Chicago Press, 1953), provides an interesting account of proposals for a national university and of institutional developments.

18. Edward J. Power, *Catholic Higher Education in America* (New York: Appleton-Century-Crofts, 1972), 335. A history of the ventures in question is presented on pp. 334–52.

Council of Baltimore, which was convened in 1852. Inquiring if it was "expedient and practicable to found a Catholic University," Archbishop American John B. Purcell of Cincinnati had wondered how, if it was not, the Catholic bishops could "otherwise efficiently provide for the education of such a University Clergy as the peculiar circumstances of the Country require."[19] The efforts for the establishment of Catholic universities in England and Ireland were being followed closely and in the customary pastoral letter that they issued following their council the bishops identified the Irish project as "an undertaking in the success of which we necessarily feel a deep interest, and which, as having been suggested by the Sovereign Pontiff, powerfully appeals to the sympathies of the whole Catholic world."[20] Writing in 1859, the hardy, pioneering Abbot Boniface Wimmer, O.S.B., founder of St. Vincent's Archabbey in Pennsylvania and of American Benedictinism, passed on a report that the American bishops were "planning to build a university in the East and another in the West,"[21] but he did not cite his sources. Almost two decades later, Bishop Bernard J. McQuaid of Rochester, writing to his close friend and metropolitan, Archbishop Michael A. Corrigan of New York, referred to an "original idea of three Universities, one for the East, one for the West, and one for the Pacific Coast," also without further attribution of the authors of the "idea."[22] During the last years of the antebellum decade, Orestes Brownson, the brilliant convert, had pleaded for a thorough Catholic educational reform in which a university established by the American episcopate or by the papacy would lead American Catholics to "the commanding position in the modern world" to which, in his estimation, their heritage entitled them.[23]

19. AAB, Francis Patrick Kenrick Papers, 31-B-4, Purcell to Kenrick, n.p., Nov. 20, 1851.

20. Hugh J. Nolan (ed.), *Pastoral Letters of the United States Catholic Bishops* (4 vols.; Washington, D.C.: United States Catholic Conference, 1983), I, 180. "Intense agitation" and the "most spirited and intelligent support" of the Irish university were recalled by Herman J. Heuser in "American Catholics and the Proposed University," ACQR, X (Oct., 1885), 637. Almost 28 percent of the £58,071 that were collected for the Catholic University of Ireland between 1850 and 1855 came from the United States, as reported in John Henry Newman, *My Campaign in Ireland*, ed. William P. Neville (Aberdeen: A. King, 1896), 435.

21. ASVA, *Annalen der Verbreitung des Glaubens durch den Ludwig Missionsverein*, XXVIII (1860), 61–62, reprinting Wimmer to Gregory Scherr, O.S.B., archbishop of Munich and Freising, Latrobe, Pa., Dec. 10, 1859 (in German). Supplied by courtesy of Brother Philip Hurley, O.S.B., assistant archivist.

22. AANY, Michael Augustine Corrigan Papers, Rochester, July 14, 1887.

23. "Present Catholic Dangers," BQR, New York Series, II (July, 1857), 362. See James M. McDonnell, Jr., "Orestes Brownson and Nineteenth Century Catholic Education" (unpublished doctoral dissertation, University of Notre Dame, 1975), especially Chap. IV. Brownson repeated his plea in the year before his death in "Our Colleges," BQR, Last Series, III (April, 1875), 254–55.

Hierarchical initiative first became manifest at the close of the Civil War when Archbishop Martin John Spalding, the uncle of John Lancaster Spalding, soon after his translation to Baltimore, the first American see, included the project of a university in the planning he was called upon to do for the Second Plenary Council. Previously, as bishop of Louisville from 1850 until 1864, he had shown a keen interest in the training of the clergy and in Catholic education generally. In 1855, he had been a leader in the First Provincial Council of Cincinnati, which had petitioned the Holy See, unsuccessfully, to erect the recently founded Mount St. Mary's Seminary of the West as a pontifical institution with the right to confer doctorates in philosophy and theology. With Peter P. Lefevre, coadjutor bishop of Detroit, he had been instrumental in founding, in 1857, the American College at Louvain even before the bishops, in 1859, established as a residence for their priests the North American College in Rome. Corresponding with Bishop John Timon, C.M., of Buffalo, in preparation for the council, Spalding asked, on August 23, 1865, "Why should we not have a Catholic University? It would be a great thing, if we could only agree as to the location and arrangement."[24]

From an exchange of letters with Archbishop John McCloskey of New York, if not otherwise, Spalding was aware that there would be "considerable diversity even divergence of opinion" about a university project when the council met in 1866.[25] Although the nephew, who was present during the conciliar deliberations, later reported that his uncle had repudiated any implied threat to the two American Catholic foundations in Europe and also "the opinion of those who hold that an university should not be created, but should grow into being and form," the preoccupation of the bishops with the finances of their Roman college was given as a sufficient reason for postponement of the university project. In the council plan for expanded seminary studies, however, the younger Spalding thought that he saw indicated "the urgent want of a Catholic university in this country."[26] Archbishop Spalding himself probably wrote the final paragraph of the council's chapter, *De Universitate Literarum Fundanda*, which read:

Would that in this region it were permissible to have a great college or university which would embrace the advantages and the usefulness of all

24. AAB, Martin John Spalding Papers, Letterpress of Archbishop Spalding, 150 (copy). See also Ellis, *op. cit.*, 43–50; and, for biographies, J. L. Spalding, *op. cit.*; and Thomas W. Spalding, C.F.X., *Martin John Spalding: American Churchman* (Washington, D.C.: The Catholic University of America Press, 1973).

25. AAB, Spalding Papers, 35-E-10, McCloskey to Spalding, New York, May 14, 1866.

26. *Life of M. J. Spalding*, 314, 315.

those colleges whether domestic or foreign; in which, namely, all the letters and sciences, both sacred and profane, could be taught! Whether or not the time for founding such a university has arrived, we leave it to the judgment of the Fathers, that they may examine the whole matter more maturely hereafter.[27]

The seed had been planted and the ensuing years proved to be favorable for its germination. The period from 1865 to 1876 saw great forward thrusts in university organization at Cornell, Harvard, Columbia, and Michigan, and, with the opening of The Johns Hopkins University, the first attempt at a primarily graduate foundation. Noting the expansive philanthropy that was making these efforts possible, Hecker, whom Archbishop Spalding was soon to designate as a personal theologian at the First Vatican Council, called for a Catholic congress so that, among other things, after discussions such as had been held at similar congresses in Germany, Catholic millionaires might be persuaded to endow a Catholic university.[28] Subsequently, in the Paulist organ that he had founded, he was able to elucidate a concept and a rationale for a university as no one had before him.[29]

About the same time, in the Louisville diocesan press, from which articles were often reprinted in other Catholic papers, there appeared editorial proposals written by John Lancaster Spalding,[30] then hardly more than thirty years of age, which were soon followed by observations on the university idea both in the abstract and in reference to the council proposal of 1866.[31] On the eve of his appointment as the first bishop of Peoria, Illinois, in unsigned articles in the *Catholic World* during 1876, he pleaded for "Catholic universities . . . which in time will grow to be intellectual centers in which the best minds of the church in this country may receive the culture and training that will enable them to work in harmony for the furtherance of Catholic ends."[32]

27. *Concilii Plenarii Baltimorensis II., in Ecclesia Metropolitana Baltimorensi . . . Decreta* (Baltimore: John Murphy, 1868), 228, trans. Ellis, *op. cit.*, 49, where the suggestion of authorship may be found.

28. "Shall We Have a Catholic Congress?" *CW*, VIII (Nov., 1868), 224–28.

29. "On the Higher Education," *ibid.*, XII (Mar., 1871), 721–31, and XIII (Apr., 1871), 115–24.

30. Louisville *Catholic Advocate*, Jan. 28, 1871, and, by way of comment on Hecker's article, Mar. 11, 1871 and Apr. 1, 1871, quoted in Ellis, *op. cit.*, 51–57. Spalding was at the time secretary to the bishop of Louisville and temporary editor of the paper. His authorship is established by his use of identical passages in other writings and correspondence. See David F. Sweeney, O.F.M., *The Life of John Lancaster Spalding, First Bishop of Peoria, 1840–1916* (New York: Herder & Herder, 1965), 128n.

31. These are included in *Life of M. J. Spalding*, 314–16.

32. "The Catholic Church in the United States 1776–1876," *CW*, XXIII (July, 1876), 451. See also, "The Next Phase of Catholicity in the United States," *ibid.*, XXIII (Aug., 1876), 577–92.

In 1876 also, in a review of a work by Newman, there came from a convert member of the hierarchy, Thomas A. Becker, first bishop of Wilmington, Delaware, a carefully reasoned proposal and plan.[33] The Baltimore *Catholic Mirror,* among others, urged that it should be supported, remarking, "Assuredly, the bishops of the country are the proper persons to break the ground."[34] Brother Azarias, F.S.C. (Patrick Francis Mullany), an influential Catholic educator, anticipating "a glorious success," could assert, "The Church in the United States is on the eve of establishing a Catholic university."[35]

During this same decade, as Hecker recognized, German Catholics on their own were advancing proposals that were limited in effect by linguistic and cultural barriers. Theirs were in fact proposals for a German Catholic university in the United States. The earliest appeared in a petition from a Wisconsin delegate to the German Roman Catholic Central Verein of North America, meeting in Louisville, in 1870.[36] It and kindred proposals were the subject of discussions in succeeding annual meetings of the organization and of vigorous endorsements from leaders whose educational efforts in the extremely active Central Verein were marked particularly by enthusiasm for higher education.[37] When the plans of these German Catholics did not materialize, some of their enthusiasm was given, first to support, then, in the wake of inter-ethnic conflict, to denounce The Catholic University of America.[38]

33. "Shall We Have a University?" *ACQR,* I (Apr., 1876), 230–53, and "A Plan for the Proposed Catholic University," *ibid.*, I (Oct., 1876), 655–79. See Thomas J. Peterman, "Thomas Andrew Becker, the First Catholic Bishop of Wilmington, Delaware and Sixth Bishop of Savannah, Georgia, 1831–1899" (unpublished doctoral dissertation, The Catholic University of America, 1982), published as *The Cutting Edge: The Life of Thomas Andrew Becker* (Devon, Pa.: William T. Cooke, 1982).

34. Nov. 11, 1876; see Ellis, *op. cit.*, 63–66, for a review of this and subsequent editorials.

35. "The Catholic University Question in Ireland and England," *ACQR,* III (Oct., 1878), 577.

36. Frederick P. Kenkel, "An Extraordinary Project," *CBSJ,* XVIII (Dec., 1925), 305–8.

37. Sister Mary Liguori Brophy, B.V.M., *The Social Thought of the German Roman Catholic Central Verein* (Washington, D.C.: The Catholic University of America Press, 1941), 57. See Leo F. Miller *et al.*, *Monsignor Joseph Jessing (1836–1899)* (Columbus, Oh.: Carroll Press, 1936), 152–53, for the efforts of the editor of the widely circulated *Ohio Waisenfreund* and founder of the Pontifical College Josephinum; Georg Timpe (ed.), *Katholisches Deutschtum in den Vereinigten Staaten von Amerika* (Freiburg im Breisgau: Herder, 1937), 151, for those of Joseph Salzmann, founder of the Holy Family Teachers College near Milwaukee; and Frederick P. Kenkel, "On Fr. F. X. Weninger, S.J.," *CBSJ,* XVIII (Dec., 1925), 308, for those of "perhaps the most influential and beloved" of the missionaries who worked among German immigrants. On the latter, see the entry of F. X. Curran, *NCE,* XIV, 874–75.

38. Philip Gleason, *The Conservative Reformers: German-American Catholics and the Social Order* (Notre Dame: University of Notre Dame Press, 1968), 42–44, summarizes the rise of the opposition to The Catholic University of America.

Isaac Thomas Hecker, C.S.P. (1819–88), founder of the Congregation of St. Paul in 1858, who sought to give shape to a new spirit in the American Church.

The Leadership of John Lancaster Spalding

The bishop of Peoria, an old-line American of independent mind and bearing, became the catalyst in the university cause. Friend and foe alike were to testify to his influence, of which, for lack of his personal correspondence, only a partial record is extant. His was largely a personal attainment but one with deep familial as well as intellectual roots. The optimism that he projected was strongly, somewhat stoically Christian—a reproach to those who acted "as though this were a devil's world, and not the eternal God's"[39]—and at the same time fervently

39. "University Education," address at the laying of the cornerstone of Caldwell Hall, May 24, 1888, in *Education and the Higher Life* (Chicago: A. C. McClurg, 1891), 187.

American, for he had faith that "not the most visionary dreamer" could even suspect "to what an extent the fate of the whole human race is bound up with the work which we here in America are doing."[40] To a contemporary literateur and diplomat who knew him well it seemed that "all the circumstances of life had taught him to command, and to look on ordinary obstacles as mere trifles."[41]

Born into a slave-holding family of rural Kentucky, Spalding was descended directly on both sides from English Catholics who had settled in southern Maryland two centuries earlier. As the favorite nephew of Martin John Spalding, he, after completing his studies for the priesthood at Louvain, had been able to enjoy a year of travel and study in Germany and Rome. At thirty-six, following service in the diocesan chancery and in the founding of the first parish for Negroes in Louisville, and after preparing his uncle's biography and assisting for four years amid the Irish immigrants of St. Michael's parish in New York City—"practical experience as a working priest" that a disdainful brother bishop was later to dismiss as *nil*[42]—he had been appointed to a newly established diocese in northern Illinois. There, while complaining that it was "very difficult to write anything worthwhile in the midst of the labors and cares in which a missionary bishop finds himself,"[43] he was writing and lecturing constantly, promoting movements for Irish-Catholic colonization, temperance, and the like, composing essays and poems, and, not least, attaining standing as "the leading Catholic educator in the period between the Civil War and the World War."[44] Indeed there still is no challenge to the estimate of a historian that, so far as intellectual leadership in the episcopate is concerned, "twentieth century Catholicism has not produced his counterpart."[45] On all occasions, he showed

40. "The Catholic Priesthood," address at the silver jubilee of St. Francis Seminary, Milwaukee, Wisconsin, June 30, 1881, in *Lectures and Discourses* (New York: Catholic Publication Society, 1882), 159.

41. Maurice Francis Egan, *Recollections of a Happy Life* (New York: George H. Doran, 1924), 183.

42. McQuaid to Richard Gilmour, Rochester, Feb. 27, 1883, quoted in Frederick J. Zwierlein, *The Life and Letters of Bishop McQuaid* (3 vols.; Rochester, N.Y.: Art Print Shop, 1925–27), II, 290. McQuaid wrote to the Holy See that Spalding was "a man of talent, but young and with *very little experience*, his forte being restricted entirely to literary works." Quoted by Cardinal Giovanni Battista Franzelin, S.J., "Circa la presenta condizione della Chiesa Cattolica negli Stati Uniti di America," APF, *Acta* (1883), CCLII, fol. 1081–1108, Par. 31 (in Italian).

43. AAB, James Gibbons Papers, 76-A-8, Spalding to Gibbons, Peoria, July 18, 1882.

44. Merle Curti, *The Social Ideas of American Educators* (2nd ed.; Paterson, N.J.: Pageant Books, 1951), 348. Honorary doctorates conferred upon Spalding by Columbia University (1902) and Western Reserve University (1904) were marks of his standing, as was his appointment by President Theodore Roosevelt to the latter's commission on the anthracite coal strike in 1902.

45. Thomas T. McAvoy, C.S.C., "Bishop John Lancaster Spalding and the Catholic Minority (1877–1908)," in *The Image of Man, A Review of Politics Reader*, ed. M. A.

*John Lancaster Spalding (1840–1916), in a bust donated by
his nephew, the Reverend Martin J. Spalding, in 1936, that is
an exact copy in Carrara marble of one approved by the
bishop for the Spalding Council of the Knights of Columbus in
Peoria, Illinois. Priests of the diocese who were serving in the
faculties had proposed a memorial some years earlier.*

supreme confidence that, as he told the bishops assembled in the council, "if intellectualism is often the foe of religious truth, there is no good reason why it should not also be its ally."[46]

Spalding was to follow academic affairs sufficiently to observe that American progress in university education was "one of the most real,

Fitzsimons, Thomas T. McAvoy, and Frank O'Malley (Notre Dame: University of Notre Dame Press, 1955), 392. See also, John Tracy Ellis, *John Lancaster Spalding, First Bishop of Peoria, American Educator* (Milwaukee: Bruce, 1961); Sister Agnes Claire Schroll, O.S.B., *The Social Thought of John Lancaster Spalding, D.D.* (Washington, D.C.: The Catholic University of America Press, 1944), to which a bibliography of Spalding's works is appended; and Sweeney, *op. cit.*

46. *University Education Considered in its Bearing on the Higher Education of Priests* (Baltimore: John Murphy, 1884), 12.

and potent influences in shaping our national character and destiny."[47]
But unlike Hecker and Becker, he never outlined a plan for an institution, nor, apparently, was his sight set consistently on a university
instead of a higher seminary. In 1880, he solicited the interest of the
coadjutor archbishop of Cincinnati, who was contending with financial
disaster, in what he portrayed as the "opportunity to make a beginning
towards founding a Catholic University" by proposing the sale of Mount
Saint Mary's Seminary of the West to the bishops for use as a national
"theological high school."[48] The next year, in his notable sermon on
the silver jubilee of St. Francis Seminary in Milwaukee, he proposed a
"High School of Philosophy and Theology" as, compared with a university, "something far simpler, less expensive, and . . . better fitted to
supply the most pressing want of American Catholics."[49] Individuals
such as Bishops Richard Gilmour of Cleveland and Thomas Grace,
O.P., of St. Paul expressed their support for this idea, but it was not
received favorably in the more important centers of Milwaukee and
New York.[50] Bishop McQuaid made his opposition explicit in a pastoral
letter that he issued in 1882 to promote his own seminary collection.[51]

Probably a university was always Spalding's ultimate goal. Returning
from Rome in 1883, he told the press that it would be "a product of
time and development rather than a creation of money" and that the
first step would be agreement of the bishops on some plan for the higher
education of the clergy.[52] From Rome he had written that the Holy
Father and all to whom he had spoken had "received with great favor

47. "Women and the Higher Education," address under the auspices of the Auxiliary
Board of Trinity College, Jan. 16, 1899, in *Opportunity and Other Essays and Addresses*
(Chicago: A. C. McClurg, 1900), 63. For an account of this benefit lecture, see Sister
Columba Mullaly, S.N.D. de N., *Trinity College, Washington, D.C.; The First Eighty Years
1897–1977* (Westminster, Md.: Christian Classics, 1987), 50–55.

48. AACi, William Henry Elder Papers, Spalding to Elder, Peoria, Aug. 29, 1880.
The reference is to the German *hochschule*, not the American high school. Copies of all
cited materials from the archdiocese of Cincinnati have been supplied through the courtesy
of the Reverend Gerard Hiland, archivist.

49. *Lectures and Discourses*, 154.

50. Grace's interest in "at least one famous center of theology" is recounted in Francis
P. Cassidy, "Catholic Education in the Third Plenary Council of Baltimore," CHR,
XXXIV (Oct., 1948), 272–73. Spalding himself acknowledged that he was inspired by
Grace, writing that since Grace was "a holy man" he thought that the attempt to found
a university "might be the will of God." AACi, Elder Papers, Spalding to Elder, Sept.
16, 1880.

51. Zwierlein, *op. cit.*, II, 321–22.

52. *Michigan Catholic*, June 16, 1883. Cardinal Franzelin reported in Rome that
Spalding, "acknowledging with praiseworthy frankness the mediocrity of the education
of the clergy (including some bishops), thought of founding a great Catholic university
in the United States; however, being aware that the other bishops were little favorable
to his project, he limited himself to proposing a seminary for advanced study." *Op. cit.*,
Par. 30.

the project of a university College of Philosophy and Theology," and
that as the money was "already promised"—presumably by Mary Gwendoline Caldwell, who became the initial university donor—he did not
see "why the project should not become a fact."[53] At the Baltimore
council, certainly, although his declared concern was for the higher
education of priests and his specific proposal was for a "national school
of philosophy and theology," he left no doubt that in his mind this was
only a beginning around which the other faculties would "take their
places, in due course of time," so that there would be "an American
university, where our young men, in the atmosphere of faith and purity,
of high thinking and plain living," would become more "intimately
conscious of the truth of their religion and of the genius of their
country."[54]

When the cornerstone of the university's first building had been laid,
Hecker remarked that, "figuratively speaking," the ground had been
broken in Spalding's Milwaukee address.[55] All thereafter would testify
that the institution was born of his "intelligent understanding of the
needs of the times and his zeal in meeting those needs," as his friend
Archbishop John Ireland of St. Paul declared on the occasion of Spalding's silver anniversary in the episcopate,[56] and as Archbishop John J.
Glennon of St. Louis and Monsignor Thomas J. Shahan, fourth rector
of the university, attested in different words when Spalding celebrated
the fiftieth anniversary of his ordination to the priesthood.[57] Cardinal
Gibbons later remarked aptly, "With his wonderful intuitionary power,
he took in all the meaning of the present and the future of the Church
in America."[58]

The Case for a University

No other advocate was as able as Spalding to convey eloquently and
convincingly the significance of a university for the Church's evangelical
mission. His premises were stated in many a public forum. Thus, to
Robert Ingersoll, the implacable foe of organized religion who was more
than his equal in prominence, Spalding could calmly explain that

53. AMHS, John Ireland Papers, Spalding to Ireland, Rome, Jan. 21, 1883.

54. *University Education Considered*, 31–32.

55. "The Present Standing of the Catholic University," *CW*, XLVII (Aug., 1888),
579.

56. *Souvenir of the Episcopal Silver Jubilee of the Rt. Rev. J. L. Spalding, D.D., Bishop of
Peoria* (Chicago: Hollister Bros., 1903), 77.

57. *Ceremonies of the Golden Sacerdotal Jubilee of His Grace John Lancaster Spalding,
Titular Archbishop of Scitopolis* (Peoria, Il.: Fred J. Ringley, 1913), 19, 44.

58. "Address on the Occasion of the Silver Jubilee of the Catholic University," in *A
Retrospect of Fifty Years* (2 vols.; Baltimore: John Murphy, 1916), II, 195.

"the fundamental conception of Christianity is that of progress in the knowledge of God and His universe. The increasing intelligence of mankind is the gradual revelation of the Divine Mind."[59] It seemed to him to follow that "a right education, together with religion, is the chief and highest instrument for the reformation and elevation of mankind."[60]

The bishop often elaborated the theme of the compatibility of faith and learning along lines that at the time may have been in eclipse. "The apparent antagonism," he remarked, "lies in our apprehensions and not in things themselves, and consequently . . . reconcilement is to be sought for through the help of thoroughly trained minds."[61] Such minds would be curious; "There is no hope," he said, "for a man who knows enough."[62] At Milwaukee, identifying "patient research" as a "divine service,"[63] he suggested a theological elucidation of the distinguishing university purpose that was coming to the fore, and later, at the laying of the cornerstone of the university's first building, he put the pertinent question squarely to his hearers:

Since the prosperity of the Church is left subject to human influence, shall the Son of Man find faith on earth when he comes if the most potent instrument God has given to man is abandoned to those who know not Christ? Why should we who reckon it a part of the glory of the Church in the past that she labored to civilize barbarians, to emancipate slaves, to elevate woman, to preserve the classical writings, to foster music, painting, sculpture, architecture, poetry and eloquence, think it no part of her mission now to encourage scientific research?[64]

To its proponents, a Catholic university, which seemed to be required in principle, was needed especially to cope with changes in the American scene that they could identify. "The real issue," Spalding maintained in his sermons, lectures, and writings, was "not between the Church

---

59. "God in the Constitution—A Reply to Colonel Ingersoll," in *Religion, Agnosticism, and Education* (Chicago: A. C. McClurg, 1902), 120.

60. *Lectures and Discourses*, 145.

61. *University Education Considered*, 9.

62. *Lectures and Discourses*, 158.

63. *Ibid.*, 156–57.

64. *Education and the Higher Life*, 184. This address was the subject of complaints to Rome, from Archbishop Elder of Cincinnati, to whom it suggested "liberalism," and from Archbishop Corrigan of New York who thought that it exemplified "rationalism." APF, Lettere e Decreti, 1889, CCCLXXXV, fol. 21, Elder to Cardinal Giovanni Simeoni, Cincinnati, Jan. 14, 1889, and fol. 229, Corrigan to Simeoni, New York, Apr. 18, 1889 (both in Italian). Corrigan sent on an unsigned critique by "a theologian" of his archdiocese who suggested that the address should be referred to the Holy Office. APF, SOCG, Second Series, MXXXVII (1890), fol. 383–405. Corrigan's vicar general, the convert Monsignor Thomas S. Preston, asserting that "no one bishop is opposed to the University" but that there was fear of "Bp. Keane & the clique which commands them," remarked of Spalding's address, "One thing is sure this clique does not understand philosophy, ethics & sociology." ACUA, Microfilm Collection, Bernard Smith Papers, Preston to Smith, New York, Dec. 18, 1888.

and the sects, but between the Church and infidelity."[65] He knew that
agnosticism and atheism had begun to gain ground during his lifetime.
Addressing the National Education Association and willing to praise as
unparalleled in history "the work which has been accomplished in the
last fifty years in organizing a great system of schools in which free
elementary education is offered to all," he warned gravely that "the
result . . . of our present educational methods and means can hardly be
other than a general religious atrophy."[66] Brother Azarias, on the same
theme, observed that the efforts of the Church could "only be partially
successful unless she had control of education in its highest phases."[67]

John Gilmary Shea, the first major historian of American Catholicism, was another who found a university essential, all the more "because, though the earlier colleges in the country were under religious
control, and sustained mainly by some denomination, the later colleges
and universities are not only secularized, but, besides ignoring religion,
affect to follow the modern infidel schools of science, and in the study
of history, ancient and modern, obey the same guidance." Seeing the
federal government even then as seeking to control the schools, he
predicted that "its influence will be of the same character."[68] Of course,
it was taken for granted by all that Catholic institutions would never
go the way of the earlier denominational foundations.

These apologetic considerations were sometimes expressed stridently.
The rhetoric of the day was defensive, and it was evoked often by
recurring nativist movements in the country and by the popular prejudice to which Catholics were then and later almost everywhere subjected. There was, moreover, a perception that American society was
becoming consciously secular. When the council approved the establishment of a university, Shea expressed his own brand of conservatism by
writing, "The Church, an active living body, an army set in array,
created the universities as her auxiliaries, and, age by age, equips them
to meet the foe before her."[69] He had earlier pointed to the need to
"take issue at once with all the erroneous theories of the day so ably
that the students will feel that they are on the victorious side."[70] Even

65. "Religion and Culture," ACQR, IV (July, 1879), 410. On the subject, see James
Turner, *Without God, Without Creed; The Origins of Unbelief in America* (Baltimore: The
Johns Hopkins University Press, 1986).
66. "Progress in Education," in *Religion, Agnosticism and Education*, 216, 227.
67. *Op. cit.*, 579.
68. "The Progress of the Church in the United States from the First Provincial Council
to the Third Plenary Council of Baltimore," ACQR, IX (July, 1884), 487.
69. "The Proposed American Catholic University," *ibid.*, X (Apr., 1885), 313.
70. "The Rapid Increase of the Dangerous Classes in the United States," *ibid.*, IV
(Apr., 1879), 267.

the first rector referred to the university he was appointed to head as an "arsenal of learning."[71]

Anxiety that coming generations would be lost to the faith contributed to this militancy. Catholic leaders were generally optimistic about the progress that the Church had made but their estimates of previous losses and their fears for the future were sometimes exaggerated. Dwelling on such fears among people for whom religion was still imbedded in an ethnic language and culture and among whom there were aggressive agnostic and socialist influences, the petitioner to the Central Verein presented the establishment of a German Catholic university as a matter of immediate urgency, pleading that "our sons will no longer have a mind for it."[72] Maurice Francis Egan, when a professor of English at the University of Notre Dame, before moving to The Catholic University of America, asserted very directly, "We cannot keep our own without higher education; the highest is not too high."[73]

The existing institutions were not regarded as equal to the task before the Catholics of the country. In 1866, there had been seven Catholic institutions with university charters and sixty Catholic colleges; by 1875 the number of institutions had risen to seventy-four.[74] All were small, even by the standards of the day, and in their offerings were, even more than other American colleges, much like the classical secondary schools of Europe. In his Louisville editorial of 1871, Spalding had written scathingly of some which were hardly advanced enough to be collegiate: "If a young man, upon leaving one of their institutions, has sufficient education to enable him to construe words grammatically, we must be satisfied."[75] Shea deplored that not a few of the graduates of Catholic institutions seemed to be "moral cowards enough to be laughed out of

71. "The Roman Universities," *CW*, XLVI (Dec., 1887), 320.

72. Quoted in Kenkel, *CBSJ*, XVIII, 306.

73. "A New Departure in Catholic College Discipline," *CW*, L (Feb., 1890), 573.

74. Brother Agatho Zimmer, F.S.C., *Changing Concepts of Higher Education in America Since 1700* (Washington, D.C.: The Catholic University of America Press, 1938), 96. See pp. 102–4 for the author's listing of the arguments advanced in support of a Catholic university.

75. Louisville *Catholic Advocate*, Jan. 28, 1871, quoted in Ellis, *op. cit.*, 53. See also Spalding's castigations of a decade later in "The Position of Catholics in the United States," *DR*, 3d Series, V (Jan. 1881), 101. Toward the end of the century, a serious writer estimated that there were 180,000 students, including those in preparatory departments, in 634 non-Catholic colleges or universities, of which not one hundred deserved the name, and that there were 4,764 regular collegiate students in 80 Catholic colleges, of which those few really worthy of the name had 973 collegiate and 1,693 preparatory students. Austin O'Malley, "Catholic Collegiate Education in the United States," *CW*, LXVII (June, 1898), 289–304. John T. Murphy, C.S.Sp., in "The New Catholic University and the Existing Colleges," *ibid.*, L (Dec., 1889), 302–6, was to point out the correspondence of the Catholic colleges with the French *lycées* and *petit séminaires*, the German *Gymnasien* and the English public schools.

their faith, or at least out of the practice of religion."[76] Becker, who was kinder in his judgments, nevertheless found "no excuse for the prevalent neglect of study" and would do no more than mention "the utter superficiality of many of the younger members of the clergy."[77]

The most immediate expectation from the establishment of a university was of course the improvement of clerical education. "For the priest," said Spalding in Milwaukee, quoting St. Francis de Sales, "knowledge is the eighth sacrament and the greatest misfortunes have come upon the Church whenever the ark of science has been permitted to fall from the hands of the Levites."[78] The oldest American Catholic institution, Georgetown University, had received from Pope Gregory XVI in 1833 authority for doctoral offerings in philosophy and theology, but these had been interrupted by the Civil War and by transfers of the Jesuit scholasticate and were to be resumed only in the academic year 1889–90.[79] St. Mary's Seminary at Baltimore had been empowered to confer pontifical degrees, but it was recognized that it and other seminaries had to be occupied fully with the preparation of pastors. There were needed institutions "of a higher grade than any that the Church has yet possessed in this country," as Shea asserted.[80] Although outstanding candidates were being sent to Rome or Louvain, Spalding, soon after studying in both places, had noted that "men of great wisdom and experience . . . make very serious objections to the practice of educating the future priests of this country in the various schools of theology of Europe."[81] Hecker before him had proposed that "a thorough university course, in which all the instruction preparatory to theology should be finished, would give a more complete and thorough education to young ecclesiastics, fit them much better for their professional studies, and prepare them much more efficaciously for the high position which belongs, by all divine

76. ACQR, IV, 267.

77. "Vocations to the Priesthood," ACQR, V (Jan., 1880), 38.

78. *Lectures and Discourses*, 148.

79. James Hennesey, S.J., *American Catholics: A History of the Roman Catholic Community in the United States* (New York: Oxford University Press, 1981), 105, remarks that the granting of the pontifical charter a year before the resurrection of Louvain "could have been the key to creation in the nation's capital of a Catholic university, but that broad level of vision was beyond Georgetown." That the papal charter had been considered to accompany the transfer of the Jesuit scholasticate from Washington to Woodstock in 1869 is shown in Edmund G. Ryan, S.J., "An Academic History of Woodstock College in Maryland (1869–1944): The First Jesuit Seminary in North America" (unpublished doctoral dissertation, The Catholic University of America, 1964), 142–43.

80. "The Pastoral Letters of the Third Plenary Council of Baltimore," ACQR, X (Jan., 1885), 10.

81. Louisville *Catholic Advocate*, Jan. 28, 1871, quoted in Ellis, *Formative Years*, 53–4.

and human right, to the priesthood."[82] Even McQuaid, who became a resolute and unremitting opponent of the contemporary proposals for a university, was at this time ready to concede that a school for higher studies in theology might be feasible if the necessary diocesan seminaries could be first established.[83]

Associated with the apologetic motives and pastoral concern for higher education was an expectation of Catholic mobility through the education of an elite. Spalding attributed to his uncle, who had gloried in "the grand old University of Louvain," the opinion that Catholic education was "the essential condition of any real growth of the church in the United States," and that, although primary education was the most fundamental of the several levels, it was imperative that the standard of higher education should be raised.[84] Hecker, alert to "the immense advantage to be gained of bringing up together and binding into one intellectual brotherhood our most highly educated Catholic youth," foresaw "a body of alumni who would intellectually exert a great influence over the Catholic community throughout the United States, and make themselves respected by all classes of educated men."[85] Similarly, Shea desired "a great Catholic University that will give us what we lack, a class of thoroughly educated and truly Catholic young men, who will inspire Catholic life in the upper classes and by example and influence act on the lower class."[86] The bishop of Peoria surmised all too optimistically that "American parents, whether the descendants of the old Catholic settlers or those who have embraced the faith in later years, instead of sending their sons to Yale or Harvard, to France or Germany, would much prefer to have them educated at home in a university where their religion would be neither a scoff nor an obstacle in the way of their preferment."[87] Father Daniel E. Hudson, C.S.C., reputed to be a friend of Henry Wadsworth Longfellow, writing in the devotional weekly of the Congregation of the Holy Cross that he edited,

82. *CW*, XII, 121.

83. Pastoral letter, Aug. 20, 1882, quoted in Zwierlein, *op. cit.*, II, 322. Five years later McQuaid reiterated his opinion that "the most that can be done in many years to come, if not ever, will be to establish a higher seminary." ADR, Denis J. O'Connell Papers, McQuaid to O'Connell, Hemlock Lake, N.Y., June 28, 1887.

84. *Life of M. J. Spalding*, 170, 443.

85. *CW*, XII, 122–23.

86. *ACQR*, IV, 267–68.

87. *CW*, XXIII, 584. Father Joseph Havens Richards, S.J., president of Georgetown College, later wrote more realistically of the "disloyal spirit which sends hundreds of Catholic youths to non-Catholic Colleges for the sake of social advancement and worldly profit," adding, "That these advantages generally prove imaginary [might] be considered a just retribution." "An Explanation in Reply to Some Recent Strictures," *WL*, XXVI, No. 1 (1897), 153.

summed it all up in one sentence, "It means a *status* in this country, which, to be frank, Catholics have not yet attained."[88]

It was expected that a university would stimulate the intellectual and cultural growth required for the attainment of apologetic and social purposes and, indeed, for full Catholic life. In his Louisville editorials, Spalding had insisted that "the existence of a first class university, by creating a demand for talent, would call it forth" to remedy the "deplorable, indeed the declining state of Catholic literary culture."[89] Of his uncle, he wrote that, observing the church to have become "an ubiquitous fact," he had wanted it to have "a great central seat of Catholic learning" that would help "to create an American Catholic literature, irreproachable both in thought and style, which would deal with all the living problems of the age," and a Catholic press that would reach "a position and a power which no efforts that have hitherto been made have been able to attain for it."[90]

Looking toward an emerging structure, Hecker had noted that "a concentration of the endowments, the instructors, and the pupils in one grand institution, makes it possible to give a much better and higher kind of education, and saves a great deal of labor besides." He thought that, without suppressing any, a university would "reign as a queen among lesser institutions, giving tone, character, and uniformity to the scientific and literary community of Catholic scholars throughout the country."[91] Becker expected a university to "consolidate our educational forces so far as the higher mental culture is concerned."[92] John Lancaster Spalding saw it as the "crown of all other institutions of learning" without which no system of education could be complete, and therefore necessary to provide to Catholic educational effort "a more thorough organization."[93]

The Decision of the Bishops

It was ultimately to the bishops of the United States that the argument for an American Catholic university had to be directed. Theirs was the authority with the Holy See, which from time immemorial had exercised as a prerogative of sovereignty the right to grant academic titles in ecclesiastical foundations. In reviewing precedents from the thirteenth to the nineteenth centuries, Spalding had earlier stated the controlling

88. "A Word Concerning the New University," AM, XXIX (Aug. 3, 1889), 110.
89. Louisville *Catholic Advocate*, Jan. 28, 1871, quoted in Ellis, *Formative Years*, 54.
90. *Life of M. J. Spalding*, 82, 313.
91. CW, XII, 122, 124.
92. ACQR, I, 234.
93. *Life of M. J. Spalding*, 316; CW, XXIII, 451.

principle that "since public instruction intimately concerns faith and morals, and has a direct influence upon the welfare and peace of the church, Catholics have always held that the intervention of the ecclesiastical authority is required for the foundation of a university."[94] The bishops had to be the leaders, as Keane later remarked, "as the chief pastors are in every great work of every religious organization."[95] Actually, of course, the leadership in the Catholic university movement was in any case almost entirely clerical.

It was taken for granted by all proponents that the institution would, "before all other requirements, be Catholic to the core."[96] As the bishops were preparing for the council that opened on November 9, 1884, a Jesuit writer on education emphasized that even a university confined to "only secular sciences and arts" would be subject to the Church because the aid of theology would be needed in all fields to "keep them in check within their proper boundary."[97] Magisterial responsibility was never in question. On the level of practicality, it was clear that no single diocese or ecclesiastical province was in a position to undertake the project as it was being conceived. It had to be assumed from the outset that the university should be a national institution.

The fourteen archbishops and fifty-seven bishops who, with others, were called upon to address the question were not themselves academic men, although about two dozen had once been seminary teachers or administrators. In their varying circumstances of birth, education, and responsibility, they exemplified the notable cultural diversity within the American Church which, with more than six million souls in 1880, had long since become a sizeable immigrant body—the largest single denomination—in a nation of more than fifty million. Scarcely more than a third of the prelates were native-born. More than a fourth had immigrated from Ireland, about half that proportion from Germany, and nearly the other half of the same proportion from France. Sixteen had had an exclusively European or French Canadian seminary experience; twenty-eight others had taken at least a part of their seminary studies abroad.[98]

Two of the bishops, during their student years, had been enrolled in

94. *Life of M. J. Spalding*, 314.

95. Letter to the Editor, New York *Independent*, Sept. 3, 1888.

96. Becker, ACQR, I, 677.

97. James Conway, S.J., "The Rights and Duties of the Church in Regard to Education," *ACQR*, IX (Oct., 1884), 664.

98. Joseph B. Code (comp.), *Dictionary of the American Hierarchy, 1789–1964* (2nd ed.; New York: J. F. Wagner, 1964), provides the brief biographical entries from which these tabulations have been made.

The Third Plenary Council of Baltimore, meeting at St. Mary's Seminary, Baltimore during November and December, 1884, decreed the foundation of The Catholic University of America.

the theological faculty of Munich, twelve had attended institutions in Rome, and seven had been at the American College of Louvain. Given the state of ecclesiastical education in the period, only the latter, in a church historian's considered judgment, had been "put in touch with real university traditions as they were taking shape at the mid-century and the years that followed."[99] One half or more of the bishops had been trained in ecclesiastical seminaries exclusively. Another third or so had studied in American Catholic colleges in which laymen were enrolled. A few, such as the converts Becker of Wilmington and Edgar Wadhams of Ogdensburg, New York, had had some personal experience in American state or private non-Catholic institutions.

All things considered, although in Rome the American hierarchy was being portrayed as poorly formed and poorly chosen and inferior to the antebellum episcopate,[100] the bishops attending the council were not without learning nor even without some cosmopolitanism. Those representing major sees were virtually all in their prime, men who would continue in ecclesiastical leadership until after the turn of the century. The body was especially fortunate in having as its presiding officer Archbishop James Gibbons of Baltimore, who was appointed apostolic delegate by Pope Leo XIII because the ranking American prelate, the archbishop of New York, who had become the first American cardinal in 1875, was too feeble to attend the council and an Italian prelate was deemed unacceptable. Gibbons was then an emerging leader with an uncommon talent for conciliation and persuasion. His abilities were soon to be recognized by his own elevation to cardinalitial rank. Far from committed to the university cause by personal conviction, he subsequently came to give it progressively greater support out of a sense of duty to the Holy See and to the decision reached in the council and out of characteristic loyalty to his friends, especially to the first rector, Bishop Keane.[101]

During the preparation for the council, which was to surpass all preceding councils in its attention to education,[102] Gibbons received reports from bishops that suggested that there would be more support for seminary improvement or for a seminary for advanced study than there would be for a university. That the bishops generally did not perceive the establishment of a national university to be the pressing

99. Ellis, *Formative Years*, 26.
100. Franzelin, *op. cit.*, Par. 12, 24–29.
101. John Tracy Ellis, *The Life of James Cardinal Gibbons, Archbishop of Baltimore, 1834–1921* (2 vols.; Milwaukee: Bruce, 1952) I, 110.
102. Cassidy, *op. cit.*, XXXIV (Oct., 1948; Jan., 1949), 257–305, 414–36.

matter its proponents considered it to be can be inferred from the fact that, in spite of its inclusion in the council agenda of 1866 and the public discussion during the intervening years, the question did not appear in the preliminary schema for the Third Plenary Council.[103] Even after it was placed on the agenda, it might have been postponed again, as it had been in 1866, in the face of the strong opposition that developed and in view of the many other issues before the council. Spalding had been active in Rome and in the United States but his supporters were for the most part, like himself, bishops of new or small dioceses, and even one so convinced of the university cause as Becker appears to have refrained from active support because he was not confident of its practicability or of Spalding's prudence.[104]

Undoubtedly, it was the offer of a founding gift by a Spalding protégé that forced the issue. The donor was Mary Gwendoline Caldwell[105] of Newport, Rhode Island, then twenty-one years of age, who, with her younger sister, Mary Elizabeth, had inherited the fortune of William Shakespeare Caldwell, a generous Virginian who had moved first to Louisville—where the Caldwells and Spaldings had become family friends—and afterward to New York, where he had entered the Church before his death in 1874. Spalding, then living in New York, had come to know the daughters as students at an academy. The gift of $300,000 that was offered to the bishops and soon accepted by them was later claimed by the elder daughter to be a little less than one-third of the share of the fortune that had been left to her. At the time of the claim, having, with her sister, denounced Spalding and left the Church, she recalled that the motive of her earlier generosity had been to do "some-

---

103. To prepare for the council, the archbishops of the United States were called to Rome late in 1883. Archbishop Corrigan reported to Cardinal McCloskey that Pope Leo had ordered the holding of a council (AANY, Rome, Nov. 12, 1883, and London, Dec. 24, 1883) and that because of the opposition of Simeoni, prefect of Propaganda, the university project was not included in the schema (AANY, Rome, Dec. 10, 1883). Gibbons mistakenly retained a "strong impression" that the project had been recommended (AANY, Gibbons to Corrigan, Baltimore, Nov. 4, 1886, cited in Ellis, *Gibbons*, I, 401–2). Keane recalled that Gibbons had been "astounded" when Corrigan reported to the university committee that this project was looked on with disfavor by the Propaganda (ADR, O'Connell Papers, Keane to O'Connell, Richmond, May 20, 1886). The translated "Minutes of Rome Meetings Preparatory to the III Plenary Council of Baltimore," *Jurist*, XI (1951), 121–33, 302–12, 417–24, 538–47, contain no reference to the university.

104. AAB, Gibbons Papers, 83-H-2, Benjamin J. Keiley to Gibbons, Atlanta, Aug. 18, 1887. At least one powerful archbishop regarded Becker as "a crank." ADR, O'Connell Papers, Ireland to O'Connell, St. Paul, Aug. 18, 1888. Bishop John J. Kain noted Becker's "difficult nature." APF, SOCG, MVI, 329–30, Kain to Cardinal Alessandro Franchi, Wheeling, Feb. 6, 1877 (in Latin), trans. in Peterman, "Becker," 465.

105. John J. Keane Papers, "Sketch of the C. University—May 1895," gives the name as Mary Gwendolen Byrd Caldwell.

thing to lift the church from the lowly position which it occupied in America" by providing "a university or higher school, where its clergy could be educated, and if possible, refined." In all of this she maintained that she had been "greatly influenced by Bishop Spalding of Peoria, who represented it to me as one of the greatest works of the day."[106] She was later quoted as remarking, perhaps not unjustly, that the acceptance of her gift "from so young and inexperienced a girl would itself have justified profound criticism."[107]

Miss Caldwell's terms, which undoubtedly were Spalding's, were outlined in a statement that she presented a few days after the council began, on November 13:

> I hereby offer the sum of three hundred thousand dollars ($300,000) to the Bishops of the Third Plenary Council, for the purpose of founding a National Catholic School of Philosophy and Theology. This offer is made subject to the following conditions: 1st. This school is to be established in the United States. 2nd. It is to be under the control of a committee of Bishops representing the

---

106. *New York Times*, Nov. 16, 1904.

107. *Washington Post*, Oct. 6, 1907. Five years before her renunciation, the University of Notre Dame had bestowed its Laetare Medal upon "the foundress of the Catholic University" because, in the words of the esteemed John Zahm, C.S.C., "she deserved it better than any other person in America for she has done more than anyone else to break through the refractories." ADR, O'Connell Papers, Zahm to O'Connell, Notre Dame, Mar. 30, 1899. That her regard for Spalding had not been steadily maintained can be inferred from a reference to their "restored friendship" in a letter of the first rector. OR, Keane to Philip J. Garrigan, Rome, Feb. 2, 1899. Spalding had been appointed, with the United States Trust Company of New York, a cotrustee of the father's estate when the original trustee, Eugene Kelly, resigned in 1895, but apparently he was never active in this office, from which he resigned in 1905. Sweeney, *op. cit.*, 211n, 348n. Meanwhile, in 1902, Mary Elizabeth Caldwell, the Baroness von Zedowitz following her marriage, denounced Spalding to the Holy See on the basis of accusations of immoral conduct heard from her sister. She had renounced the Church the year before. Robert N. Barger, "John Lancaster Spalding: Catholic Educator and Social Emissary" (unpublished doctoral dissertation, University of Illinois, 1976), 25–26, and Sweeney, *op. cit.*, 308–9, appendix, review the documents in APF. Mary Gwendoline, who had become the Marquise des Monstiers-Merinville after her marriage in 1896, was separated from her husband. She had written in 1900 "that Rome last winter did for me what it has done for many an honest soul before me, made me *Protestant*." ADR, O'Connell Papers, Caldwell to O'Connell, Paris, Nov. 9, 1900. Later, however, she was planning with the same correspondent, when he became the third rector of the university, to build a university church—"at least to give $100,000 towards it . . . to be my memorial." OR, Caldwell to O'Connell, New York, Feb. 19, 1904. Subsequently, the front-page story of the *New York Times* mentioned her protracted illness; her earlier letter to O'Connell from Paris had mentioned a "psychical crisis," and her companion had reported that she was suffering "increasing depression." *Ibid.*, M. L. Donnelly to O'Connell, New York, Dec. 16, 1903. More than two years after her public renunciation she described Spalding to a lapsed priest as a "whited sepulchre" and "a very atheist and infidel" whom she used to know "*intimately*" (her emphasis); the letter from Rome, dated Apr. 11, 1907, is in Jeremiah J. Crowley, *Romanism a Menace to the Nation* (Cincinnati: published by the author, c. 1912), 38. Perhaps relying upon his previous experience at the apostolic delegation in Washington, Bishop Frederick Z. Rooker, writing to Denis J. O'Connell, then in Rome, had called Spalding "a brazen villain." OR, Jero, Philippine Islands, Sept. 30, 1904.

Catholic Episcopate of the United States. 3rd. It is to be a separate institution, and not affiliated to any other institution. 4th. Only ecclesiastics who have completed their elementary course of Philosophy and Theology are to be received into this institution. 5th. This institution is never to be under the control of any religious order, and its chairs are to be filled in preference by professors chosen from the secular clergy and laity. 6th. Other faculties may be affiliated to this institution with a view to form a Catholic University. 7th. This fund shall never be diverted from the purpose for which it is given, and the site once chosen shall not be changed without the greatest reasons. 8th. In consideration of this donation I am to be considered the founder of this institution.[108]

The Caldwell offer provided an effective backdrop for the sermon that Spalding had been invited to preach in Benjamin Henry Latrobe's Cathedral of the Assumption on the evening of November 16. "Ah surely," he asserted, "as to whether an American Catholic university is desirable there cannot be two opinions among enlightened men."[109] He supported this confidence with a rather lengthy marshalling of arguments that were not new, emphasizing the invaluable service of a trained clergy to the Church, the inherent narrowness of the professional training that seminaries exist to provide, and the necessity of a university to offer the advanced education required for intellectual attainment. There was only the practical question, "But is it feasible?" About this Spalding could now be optimistic.

Although the minutes of the council are not informative concerning the arguments advanced for and against the proposal, it is clear that agreement was obtained only with difficulty and then somewhat ambiguously. The agenda provided for discussion of *De Seminario Principali* and the references in the documentation are to a "principal seminary" rather than a university. The minutes of the opening session of the debate are as enlightening as those of any that followed:

Although many of the speakers favored the proposal of the Schema, some thought it best that there should be given a longer and more perfect course of studies in theological seminaries, for there could not be obtained a supply of money and persons for founding the principal seminary.[110]

To this discussion, which took place on November 25, there was

108. AAB, Gibbons Papers, 78-T-6.

109. *University Education Considered*, 32.

110. *Acta et Decreta Concilii Plenarii Baltimorensis Tertii* (Baltimore: John Murphy, 1884), lvii, trans. Ellis, *Formative Years*, 102. This 1884 edition is more inclusive than that published in 1886. The debates were later interpreted by the university's first professor as showing that the bishops, "having come down to *brass tacks* decided to give up the idea of a University." Thus he could refer to "the *dream* of Bp. Spalding of a house of higher studies with no well defined *purpose* or plan of systematic training." Henri Hyvernat Papers, Hyvernat to Sebastian G. Messmer, Washington, Dec. 27, 1917 (copy).

added the following morning a report of twelve professional theologians who had been deputed to examine subjects concerning clerical education. Disagreeing among themselves, they recommended that the university question should be referred to a special committee. This recommendation carried after the failure—by only three votes—of a motion to expunge the proposal altogether or to defer it until the next plenary council. The committee that was appointed reported favorably on December 2, and its recommendations were accepted, as follows:

1. A Seminary is to be erected like the Dunboyne in Ireland or Louvain in Belgium, from which as from a seed the University is to grow. 2. It is to be erected near a large and populous city. 3. A very respectable lady has promised that she will give $300,000 for the erection and endowment of the Seminary. 4. A commission is to be formed of five or seven prelates and some laymen to whom is to be given the care of erecting and administering the Seminary.[111]

Gibbons had already asked Miss Caldwell to name those whom she wished to have appointed to the commission or permanent committee and on December 6 her selections were approved, with a proviso for the addition of others by the bishops, after her letter offering $300,000 for the beginning of the institution was read into the record. Thus, the bishops decided "that in these states there should exist a distinguished center of learning where youths excelling in talent and virtue, after finishing the usual course of studies, may be able to devote three or four years to theological disciplines, or canon law, or philosophy along with the natural and other sciences which are becoming to clergymen of our day, so that, once such a seminary were started, there would be a nucleus or seed from which, God's grace favoring, there would blossom forth in its time a perfect university of studies."[112]

The Decision in Context

In the context of American Catholic history, the decision of the hierarchy and the Holy See to establish The Catholic University of America—the first pontifical university in an English-speaking country since the Reformation—was the culmination of what was, in effect, a long first phase of a discussion about Catholic intellectual attainments that is still continuing. Even in the nineteenth century, the limited participation of Catholics in American intellectual life was a subject of concern. During the late colonial period and the early years of the Republic, individual Catholics had attained prominence in public life

111. *Ibid.*, lxxix, trans. *ibid.*, 110.
112. *Ibid.*, 54–55, trans. *ibid.*, 111–12.

without, in most instances, espousing distinctively Catholic positions.[113]
By the last quarter of the nineteenth century, when Catholics had
become far more numerous, but also more polyglot, diffuse dissatisfaction with their intellectual level was common among their leaders,
divided as they were in their expectations. The public sessions of the
council of 1884 included, in addition to Spalding's sermon on university
education, also one by Becker on the promotion of learning, neither of
them a topic otherwise frequently addressed in American episcopal
assemblies.

It seemed to some at the time that only converts, educated under
other than Catholic auspices, were able to champion the Catholic cause
respectably. Hecker, of course, was conspicuous and the memory of his
friend Brownson was still fresh. The Spaldings, both uncle and nephew,
in successive generations, were on record deploring the decline of Catholic literary talent.[114] Denis J. O'Connell, a future rector, then the head
of the North American College in Rome, expressed his disgust with
"even indifference to the University" when he beheld "the immense
intellectual inferiority of Catholics my travels revealed to me, and the
numbers of Universities Protestants possess."[115]

The university was acclaimed as the vehicle of ascent. To Father
Hudson at Notre Dame, it was "a means of remedying all defects in
Catholic educational training."[116] Sharing the *raison d'être* of Catholic
education at all levels, the university, by its unique dedication to
advanced work, would exemplify the highest levels of Catholic purpose
and achievement. It could be taken on papal authority that in the
university "the forces of revelation and reason combined should form
an invincible bulwark of faith."[117] The first rector was to give succinct
form to what was in the minds of the earlier proponents when he praised
the institution as "a living embodiment and illustration of the harmony

---

113. See C. J. Nuesse, *The Social Thought of American Catholics, 1634–1829* (Westminster, Md.: Newman Bookshop, 1945).

114. John Lancaster Spalding wrote, for his uncle as well as himself, "It is humiliating
to consider how much of what is best in our English and American Catholic literature is
the work of men who were educated outside of the church." *Life of M. J. Spalding*, 313.
A later effort to endow a university chair in Brownson's name was judged "most proper."
OR, George T. Montgomery, bishop of Monterey-Los Angeles, to Keane, San Francisco,
Feb. 10, 1896. On the other hand, as Donna Merwick asserts, it is probably true that
most converts to Catholicism "were never accepted by the local clergy. And if they had
been, their writings would simply have added to the growing conviction that Catholicism
had nothing whatsoever to learn from Protestantism." *Boston Priests, 1848–1910: A Study
of Social and Intellectual Change* (Cambridge: Harvard University Press, 1973), 97.

115. OR, O'Connell to Keane, New York, June 4, 1890.

116. *Op. cit.*

117. Leo XIII, *Quod in novissimo conventu*, Apr. 10, 1887. Official translation. AAB,
Gibbons Papers, 82-P-10/1.

between reason and revelation, between science and religion, between the genius of America and the church of Christ."[118] Catholic yearning for this result was international. Informed of the bishops' decision by an anonymous friend, Cardinal Newman wrote from England, in a letter read with one from the pope when the university committee met on November 11, 1885, "At a time when there is so much in this part of the world to depress and trouble us as to our religious prospects, the tidings . . . of the actual commencement of so great an undertaking on the other side of the ocean on the part of the church will rejoice the hearts of all educated Catholics in these Islands."[119]

Indeed, the decision of the bishops in 1884 was applauded as a bold step. Seeking their votes, Spalding had urged, "though the event be less than our hope, though even failure be the outcome, is it not better to fail than not to attempt a worthy work which might be ours?"[120] John Boyle O'Reilly, editor of the Boston *Pilot*, who was later the only layman to speak at the university's opening, predicted that what the bishops had established would be "a fountainhead of strength and a focus of light for the whole Church in America" because "the genius of the two peoples," the Irish and the German, that were predominant in the Catholic population of the time would guarantee its success.[121]

Later, after classes had opened, the archbishop of San Francisco declared forthrightly that the Church of the United States would be "forever disgraced should the work fall to the ground—or not realize the expectations that have been aroused, through the apathy of the Bishops."[122] Gibbons, whose appreciation of the significance of the venture was to be gained at the cost of more "anxiety and tension of spirit" than any of his other duties or cares would impose, became able to defend it, in the perspective of its first quarter century, as "the most important work ever undertaken for Catholic education in our country."[123]

What the bishops had grasped, even in their division, was a general problem with a general solution. The tradition of which they were the official teachers recognized the need of faith constantly to seek

118. Quoted in the *Washington Star*, Oct. 14, 1897, from Keane's response at a testimonial dinner in his honor.

119. OR, Newman to Gibbons, n.p., Oct. 10, 1885.

120. *University Education Considered*, 34.

121. Boston *Pilot*, Sept. 12, 1885. For the poem read by O'Reilly at the dedicatory banquet, "From the Heights," see *Solemnities of the Dedication and Opening of The Catholic University of America, November 13, 1889. Official Report* (Baltimore: John Murphy, 1890), 36–38.

122. OR, Patrick W. Riordan to Keane, San Francisco, Feb. 4, 1890.

123. *Op. cit.*, II, 191, 204.

James Gibbons (1834–1921), cardinal priest of the Holy Roman Church, archbishop of Baltimore, and first chancellor of The Catholic University of America, once called by President Theodore Roosevelt the nation's most beloved citizen.

understanding and in the late nineteenth century the expansion of the world of knowledge must have appeared to them to have gone very far indeed. But their understanding of higher degrees was limited, especially since the licentiate and the doctorate in theology had had their origins, as the first faculty was to remind them, "back in the time when theological research had not yet come into existence," and therefore stood, in the late nineteenth century, not so much for specialized knowledge, as for "a general, yet profound training in the whole field of theology."[124] The bishops, like most other people, were hardly aware that the specialized model was in the making.

124. Hyvernat Papers, "A Memoir on the Catholic University of America submitted to His Excellency the Most Reverend John Bonzano, Archbishop of Melitene, Apostolic

That a national Catholic university was being brought into being by those with markedly American antecedents, whether in consequence of lineage or persuasion, rather than by those preoccupied with the immediately pressing problems of episcopal ministry, may not have been any more apparent. The rapid increase of immigrant numbers that was swelling their flocks undoubtedly deflected the interest of most bishops from higher education. They had churches and schools to build and nettlesome questions to decide; secret societies, socialism, and temperance were among the moral issues of the day. But none could quarrel with Spalding's desire to bring Catholic intellects to the highest possible effectiveness. Some leaders who were more intellectually inclined, more activist, more restlessly American than the others were sharing Hecker's earlier premonitions of "an approaching conflict between the society of the nineteeth century and the Church," a conflict which he thought had "already begun" and would be possibly "more threatening than that of the sixteenth century."[125] To meet the needs of the age as they saw them, they were seeking with Hecker to recognize the "Divine Expansion" at work in their individualistic society "by accentuating, developing and fortifying the internal action of the Holy Spirit in the soul and stimulating personal initiative and courage."[126] Their spiritual master, in the last year of his life, more optimistically irenic than before, was hoping that the university that was being founded would "tend to shape the expression of doctrines in such wise as to assimilate them to American intelligence" so that its work would "precede the conversion of the country."[127]

Delegate to the United States of America, Washington, D.C." (Dec., 1922), 40 (copy).

125. ACSP, Isaac Hecker Papers, "Notes on Interior States while abroad in 1874–75," Aug. 1, 1875.

126. *Ibid.*, Nancy, Sept. 4, 1875. See Joseph P. Chinnici, *Devotion to the Holy Spirit in American Catholicism* (New York: Paulist Press, 1985), for the context of Hecker's statements.

127. "The Things That Make for Unity," *CW*, XLVII (Apr., 1888), 108. The influence of Hecker and the Paulists upon the university was immediately through Bishop Keane, the first rector, whose ecclesiology, according to a recent student, was virtually identical with Hecker's. See Margaret Mary Reher, "Leo XIII and 'Americanism,'" *TS*, XXXII (Dec., 1973), 680. Keane had once sought to join Hecker's congregation. O'Connell called him "Father Hecker's spiritual child in everything." ACSP, Felix Klein Papers, O'Connell to Klein, Rome, Oct. 27, 1897. A Paulist biographer of Hecker called Keane "our old prophet's foremost disciple." ADR, O'Connell Papers, Walter Elliott, C.S.P., to O'Connell, New York, Jan. 25, 1898. Hecker's influence was of course widespread. On the friendly Archbishop Ireland, see Dennis J. Dease, "The Theological Influence of Orestes Brownson and Isaac Hecker on John Ireland's Americanist Ecclesiology" (unpublished doctoral dissertation, The Catholic University of America, 1978). Also, it should be recalled that the vocation of Cardinal Gibbons had been decided by his hearing of a sermon in New Orleans by the pioneer Paulist missioner, Clarence Walworth. See Ellis, *Gibbons*, I, 28.

CHAPTER II

The Development of the Pontifical Project

The initial meeting of the committee on the university that the bishops established at Baltimore was convened by "a legal quorum" of six members who were attending the dedication of the Church of St. Paul in New York City on January 25, 1885, and who were disposed to take "whatever steps" might be necessary and in their power "to carry out the intentions of the Fathers of the Plenary Council."[1] Present were Archbishop Patrick Ryan of Philadelphia, who presided, Monsignor John Murphy Farley of New York (the future cardinal archbishop), who acted as secretary, Coadjutor Archbishop Michael Corrigan of New York, Bishops Ireland and Spalding, and Eugene Kelly, a philanthropic self-made banker whose second wife was a niece of John Hughes, Cardinal McCloskey's predecessor as archbishop of New York. Miss Caldwell had also named Gibbons, Coadjutor Archbishop Michael Heiss of Milwaukee, Archbishop John J. Williams of Boston, the convert benefactor Reuben Springer of Cincinnati, and Francis Anthony Drexel of Philadelphia, the devout and charitable senior brother administering the far-flung Drexel family interests.

Those present formally accepted the gift of the donor under the conditions specified by her. It was quickly decided, on the motion of Ireland, that the new institution should be named The Catholic University of America, and also that a lawyer should be consulted about the method to be pursued in incorporation, that the donor should be requested to transfer her money to the trustees, and that the property of Seton Hall College of South Orange, New Jersey, should be purchased for conversion into the university, provided that Miss Caldwell was first consulted. There was extended discussion of the endowment of professorships that would be needed and of the means for obtaining the necessary funds.

1. BT, mm, Jan. 26, 1885. (The minutes of the university committee are included with those of the board as the official record.)

The second but first planned meeting of the committee was held in Baltimore on May 7, 1885. Gibbons, Corrigan, Ryan, Ireland, Spalding, and Farley were present. It was at this meeting that Washington, D.C., was selected as the location for the university, instead of Seton Hall, and that measures were taken for the first purchases of the site of the university near the Soldiers' Home.[2] Ireland had proposed location in Washington at the first meeting and Spalding, after a visit, had become convinced that it was "neither a Northern nor Southern nor Western city, but common ground upon which we can all meet to establish a national institution."[3] The change was a cause of contention for some time. The *New York Times*, however, which had earlier editorialized that there was "no reason why a Roman Catholic university should be founded in order to teach purely secular branches of study,"[4] now took note of "evidence that the prelates of the Church of Rome in this country recognize the changed and rapidly changing character of the capital city and its promise for the future."[5]

Miss Caldwell had elaborated her purpose to indicate that no more than $200,000 of her gift should be spent on buildings and grounds and that $100,000 should be used to endow professorships. Later she wrote to restrain use of her gift altogether until there would be raised "a sufficient sum to secure the full endowment of the university."[6] Spalding was asked to draft an appeal for funds that could be used nationally.[7]

---

2. This initial acquisition for $29,500 embraced "Sidney," advertised as a "Beautiful Country Seat" of 57.32 acres in possession of Ellen R. Middleton, widow of Erasmus J. Middleton, Sr., and an additional 8.75 acres from a larger "Turkey Thicket" tract that was owned by Mary Virginia Middleton, the only heir of her deceased brother, Erasmus J. Middleton, Jr. "Sidney" had been owned by Henry Duley, who had died intestate prior to 1802, leaving as heirs at law ten children from whom Samuel Harrison Smith, a pioneer newspaperman, acquired the property in 1804 under a title that was finally cleared only after suit by the university in the Supreme Court of the District of Columbia (*James Gibbons v. David Duley et al.*). A description of the property and of the visits of the Thomas Jeffersons, James Madisons, Henry Clays, and others may be found in *The First Forty Years of Washington Society in the Family Letters of Margaret Bayard Smith*, ed. Gaillard Hunt (New York: Frederick Ungar, 1906). Smith sold the property in 1839. The Middletons purchased it from a Mr. France in 1844. The house, which was three minutes' walk from Brooks' Station on the Metropolitan Branch Railroad, became the first residence of the Paulist Fathers at the university and was renamed St. Thomas Aquinas College. It was occupied by the Paulists until 1913. After continuous use in various capacities as St. Thomas Hall, it was razed in 1970, although as early as 1930 a rector had recommended its demolition. For additional details of the early period, see Walter J. Bonner and David I. Gale, "The Campus in Washington's History," *CUB*, N.S., XVI, No. 6 (May, 1949), 2–3.

3. BT, mm, Jan. 27, 1885, appendix, Spalding to Ryan, Peoria, Feb. 8, 1885 (copy).

4. Dec. 13, 1884.

5. May 11, 1885.

6. BT, mm, May 7, 1885, and AAB, Gibbons Papers, 86-L–2, Caldwell to Gibbons, Newport, R.I., Sept. 4, 1889.

7. Miscellanea, III, *An Appeal to the Catholics of the United States in behalf of the*

St. Thomas Aquinas College, in which the Paulist Fathers incorporated the Middleton home as the first house of studies of religious at the university, which they occupied until 1913. Later, as St. Thomas Hall, the building was used first as a residence hall for undergraduates and then for various administrative and faculty offices until its demolition in 1970.

At this meeting, since Drexel and Springer had died before they could serve, Bernard N. Farren of Philadelphia, who remained for only two years, and Michael Jenkins, an outstanding Baltimore banker, business magnate, and philanthropist, were elected to replace them. The committee was enlarged by the election of Bishops John J. Keane of Richmond, Virginia, and Martin Marty, O.S.B., vicar apostolic of the Dakota Territory, the Reverend Fathers Placide L. Chapelle of Washington and John S. Foley and Thomas S. Lee of Baltimore, all pastors, and Thomas Ennalls Waggaman, a real estate broker of Washington.

Before the committee met again, in Baltimore, on November 11, 1885, Pope Leo XIII had given his private approval to the idea of an American Catholic university and various promises of funds had been received.[8] More systematic canvassing seemed to be indicated, however, and Spalding, Ireland, Keane, and Marty were authorized to approach all dioceses for the collection of funds. Waggaman was given charge over the Washington property that had been acquired, Williams over

---

University which the late Council of Baltimore resolved to Create (New York: Catholic Publication Society, 1885).

8. BT, mm, Nov. 11, 1885.

the planning of the first building. It was agreed that all members present would meet in Washington on the following day to sign the petition of incorporation. This petition, which had been drafted by Attorney Martin F. Morris of Washington, was not filed until April 19, 1887, after formal papal approval for the university project had been announced.[9]

Opposition to the University

Even as the university committee began its work, it became clear that the institution was to remain an object of controversy. Scarcely more than three months after the hierarchy's decision, the publishers of the *American Catholic Quarterly Review* were requesting from Gibbons an article that would respond to critics.[10] The opposition that became manifest proved to be deep-rooted, far-reaching, and enduring in its consequences.

That within the episcopate was most conspicuous and most damaging. Its center was in the powerful ecclesiastical province of New York. Cardinal McCloskey, of course, had earlier indicated his reserve when the agenda for the Second Plenary Council was being prepared and again when Spalding had proposed the purchase of Mount St. Mary's Seminary of the West. His coadjutor and successor, Archbishop Corrigan, was revealed as an opponent while he was serving on the university committee, in which his membership was recognized on both sides as essential for the appearance of hierarchical unity. But the most caustic adversary by far was Corrigan's former teacher and closest friend, McQuaid, who was advising Hecker that "gumption is worth more than all the virtues when dealing with those outside the church"[11] and was hardly hesitating to exhibit the same vaunted quality when dealing with those within. His feelings but also those of some others deepened in intensity with the progress of the university project.

Differences about specific matters such as the site of the institution, its scope, and its administration could not have been unexpected. Washington, as noted, was not a popular choice as the site, partly

9. The applicable law at the time was a General Incorporation Act of Congress of May 3, 1870, for the District of Columbia. Its first section provided for the incorporation of institutions of learning. Martin S. Quigley, "A Study of the Political Dimension of Private Higher Education: Government Relations of Five Universities and a Consortium in Washington, D.C." (unpublished doctoral dissertation, Columbia University, 1977), 54, finds it "strange" that a Congressional charter was not sought. It was not required. In 1928, a necessary Act of Congress was obtained to amend the certificate of incorporation (*infra*, Chap. VI).

10. AAB, Gibbons Papers, 79-F–11, Hardy & Mahony to Gibbons, Philadelphia, Mar. 10, 1885.

11. ACSP, Hecker Papers, McQuaid to Hecker, Rochester, Mar. 10, 1885.

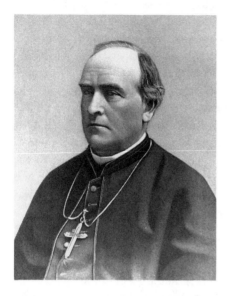

Bernard Joseph John McQuaid (1823–1909), first bishop of Rochester, New York, the most colorful and perhaps the best-informed opponent of the university cause. He had been the first president of Seton Hall College and one of the minority opposing the definition of papal infallibility at Vatican Council I.

because it was regarded as removed from the centers of Catholic population, partly because it was seen as "a corrupt *political* center" to which young clerics should not be exposed.[12] There was even an obvious residue of sectional feeling in McQuaid's derisive reference to "the *Grand American* Catholic University for the *Southern States*"[13] and his subsequent argument that the university had become "a Southern affair, with a majority of Southerners to control it" and was therefore "destined to ultimate failure for that reason, if for no other."[14] But, in their nature, such differences would have been of transitory significance.

12. Corrigan to McQuaid, New York, Oct. 9, 1886, in Frederick J. Zwierlein (ed.), *Letters of Archbishop Corrigan to Bishop McQuaid and Allied Documents* (Rochester: Art Print Shop, 1946), 86, recounting arguments against the university used in a memorandum to the prefect of Propaganda. McQuaid thought Washington "the worst place that could be chosen." AANY, Corrigan Papers, McQuaid to Corrigan, Rochester, June 17 and 23, 1887. Similar objections were raised by Archbishop Elder of Cincinnati (*ibid.*, Elder to Corrigan, Cincinnati, Mar. 20, 1885) and Bishop Gilmour of Cleveland. Elder reported that Gibbons had written to him that he did not want the university in either Washington or Baltimore and that Williams also opposed Washington. *Ibid.*, Rome, Dec. 5, 1885. See Ellis, *Formative Years*, 135, and "The Formation of the American Priest: An Historical Perspective," in John Tracy Ellis (ed.), *The Catholic Priest in the United States: Historical Investigations* (Collegeville, Minn.: St. John's University Press, 1971), 79. At an early board meeting, Spalding himself opposed a proposal for popular lecturers partly to "save the students from dangerous contacts with a promiscuous audience." BT, mm, Sept. 7, 1887.

13. McQuaid to Corrigan, Rochester, June 20, 1885, quoted in Ellis, *Formative Years*, 156.

14. McQuaid to Gilmour, Rochester, Jan. 31, 1897, in Zwierlein, *Life and Letters*, III, 391.

More serious in their effects were the divisions within the episcopate in what was proving to be one of the most critical periods in the history of the American Church. These divisions arose from ethnic allegiances and from differences about policies to be adopted in response to recurring nativism, the growth of secret societies, the emergence of labor unionism, the temperance movement, and the like. The relation of the university project to positions taken on these issues was never more than tenuous but was often assumed to be otherwise. Inevitably, conflicts of personalities assumed importance. Observing from Rome, a contemporary to whom Pope Leo was allowing unrestrained access to the Vatican correspondence noted that virtually every discrete issue was "not looked upon as an object to be promoted this or another way according to the ideologies and judgments of either party, but rather as another opportunity to measure one's strength by those engaged in the struggle for supremacy."[15]

When the early reservations about the university, the reports of individual participants in the council, and the later developments are probed and considered together, proponents and opponents of the university cause appear to have differed most in their respective judgments about the priority to be assigned to higher education, the prospective effects of the new foundation upon existing institutions, the availability of funding, and, more generally, the readiness of the Catholic population to support a university. Disagreement on the first of these questions, the allocation of resources, should not have been surprising. McQuaid was on record as holding that antecedent to any kind of institution for advanced study was the need for "the establishing of Diocesan seminaries to answer the ordinary and usual wants of a Diocese, and to serve as feeders to the higher school."[16] In this opinion he was joined by James McMaster, convert editor of the *Freeman's Journal* of New York, who also gave priority to "the need of good parochial schools," although he withheld no resentment later when Monsignor Thomas J. Capel, who had bungled an attempt to found a Catholic university college in England, undertook to advise American Catholics to strengthen their elementary schools in order to attain Protestant standards before establishing a university.[17] Of course, Martin John Spalding had made the necessary distinction decades before, and now Shea pointed out that it was for the young men who were already graduating from Georgetown,

15. AUND, Eduardo Soderini, "Leo XIII & the U. S. of America," tr. F. Terras (unpublished manuscript), 19.

16. Pastoral letter, Aug. 20, 1882, *op. cit.*

17. Editorials, Oct. 21, 1882; Feb. 21, 1885.

Mount St. Mary's, Fordham, Notre Dame, St. Louis, and other Catholic colleges that the faithful had to be concerned.[18]

Whether these potential "feeders of the university" were sufficient in number and quality was disputed. Shea had earlier noted that "colleges and universities cannot thrive unless the preparatory schools exist in greater number."[19] Augustine J. Thébaud, S.J., the former Kentucky missioner from France who had baptized John Lancaster Spalding and had later been president of St. John's College (now Fordham University), had been skeptical about the feasibility of a university for want of the "previous link required between colleges, such as we have them, and that highest degree of universal knowledge."[20] Father Herman J. Heuser of Philadelphia, founder and longtime editor of the *American Ecclesiastical Review*, in defending the university project, recognized as a source of difficulty "the uneven character, the indefinite scope, and the incompleteness on the whole" of the existing collegiate institutions.[21]

The most blatant of the attempts to protect the interests of the latter occurred during the Baltimore council in an intemperate attack by Father Robert Fulton, S.J., a former president of Boston College who was present as the superior of the New York–Maryland province of the Society of Jesus. A fellow theologian who later became the bishop of Nashville remembered Fulton as arguing "that the Diocesan Clergy were not intended to be an educated clergy or at least a learned and erudite body; that they were ordained to do the ordinary work of a parish and that the proper custodians, cultivators, and representatives of learning in the Church were the Religious Orders to whom alone universities should be entrusted."[22] The proposal before the council, of course, which was to win approval, eventually from the pope, was to maintain the university under the authority of the bishops (never, according to Miss Caldwell's document, "under the control of any religious order"). Archbishop Corrigan, for one, nevertheless continued to believe that a university should be established in New York under the Jesuits, and, in submitting his objections to the bishops' project

---

18. ACQR, X, 321–22.

19. "Converts—Their Influence and Work in This Country," *ibid.*, VIII (July, 1883), 528.

20. "Superior Instruction in Our Colleges," *ibid.*, VII (Oct., 1882), 696. For a biographical sketch, see V. C. Hopkins, NCE, XIV, 6–7.

21. ACQR, X, 650. Heuser's review was known as the *Ecclesiastical Review* from 1905 to 1943, and was not consistently titled. For a biographical sketch see B. F. Fair, NCE, IV, 1091–92.

22. Thomas S. Byrne to Sister Mary Agnes McCann, Dec. 3, 1917, quoted in Ellis, *Formative Years*, 104.

at the invitation of the cardinal prefect of the congregation for the propagation of the faith, he followed suggestions prepared for him by Fulton, noting that a foundation under a religious order was a possible alternative to the university that the bishops had already approved.[23]

Roman authorities were specific in their inquiries about the probable effects of the new institution upon the Jesuits' Georgetown University, which was then offering only undergraduate and professional, not graduate, instruction. If there was not concerted opposition to the university from the Society of Jesus, there were well-founded suspicions that it was being encountered then and later not only in Washington and elsewhere in the United States but also in Rome, through the Jesuit organ *Civiltà Cattolica*, being edited by Father Salvatore Brandi, who, while in exile from Italy, had taught theology at Woodstock College, and in the person of the recently elevated Jesuit Cardinal Camillo Mazzella, who, exiled from the Kingdom of Naples, had gone first to Georgetown in 1867 and then to Woodstock when it was opened in 1869 and had become a naturalized American citizen before being recalled in 1878 to teach at the Gregorian University. Any opposition was publicly denied by both sides, and individual Jesuits, including J. Havens Richards, president of Georgetown from 1888 to 1898, took pains either to remain objective or to befriend the university cause.[24] In his first interview upon returning from Rome after his appointment as rector, Keane was reported as emphasizing that the university would not "be a rival of any existing college,"[25] and two years later, preaching at its formal opening, Gilmour, a

23. Zwierlein, *Letters of Corrigan*, 87; Ellis, *Formative Years*, 178, 186. Keane and Ireland, reporting on their Roman negotiations to the trustees, described the pope as "very emphatic" in asserting "that, though he highly esteemed the religious orders, he would never consent that any one of them should have under its control this chief institution for the education of the people, and especially the clergy of our country—that the University must absolutely be organized, as the Church was, under the government of the Hierarchy." BT, mm, Sept. 7, 1887, exh. For a subsequent report of this position by Keane, see *CUB*, XI (Apr., 1905), 268–69.

24. John J. Keane, "A Chat about the Catholic University," *CW*, XLVIII (Nov., 1888), 216–26, and "Note to Article on the Catholic University," *ibid.*, L (Dec., 1889), 413–14. Keane's correspondence, with press clippings of the day, reveals the suspicions, as does Richards's extensive correspondence. The latter, notably successful as a president, prepared an account for the Jesuit father general in which he outlined the policy which he had "deliberately adopted from the first" to "make no opposition in any point to the new University, but on the contrary to show cordial friendship and cooperation in its work" but to "not on account of the presence of that University curtail in any way the progress and development of our own University." "Father Joseph Havens Richards' Notes on Georgetown and the Catholic University," ed. E. J. Burrus, S.J., *WL*, LXXXIII (1954), 86.

25. "Bishop Keane and the Situation," *FJ*, XLVIII, No. 17 (June 18, 1887), 4.

friend of McQuaid's, looked ahead to caution, "Above all, let no narrowness seek to make this the only Catholic University in this country."[26]

In the matter of funding, it was acknowledged in all proposals and in recorded discussion that the university would have to be supported by income from endowment, to be supplemented by gifts. An unidentified writer in the *American Catholic Quarterly Review* in 1882 had asked, "Among whom has the idea of endowment been better understood in the past than among Catholics?"[27] McQuaid, successful in producing and selling altar wine for the support of his seminary, knew the basic case and stated it with reference to his own institution:

A Seminary to be successful needs to be independent. This means that it should be financially strong. If a Seminary has to court the favor of patrons or students it will not be able to do the best work, nor will undesirable candidates be kept out of the priesthood. . . .[28]

Like John Carroll, the first American bishop, in his pastoral letter of 1792, the bishops collectively in 1884 appealed to "those among our Catholic people to whom God has been pleased to give wealth" especially for the founding of scholarships, although, tellingly, they did not then associate this need with the institution that they had just decided to establish.[29] Brother Azarias anticipated the "slow growth" of a university institution that would require "considerable endowment" before "its alumni will be able to speak for it, and its necessity shall have imperceptibly grown upon the people."[30] Hecker had earlier stated a deeper principle, holding that "education ought to be made cheap and accessible to boys and youths of all classes." He had added, "This cannot be done without large endowments and revenues."[31]

Comparisons were unavoidable. The benefactions of Ezra Cornell, Cornelius Vanderbilt, Johns Hopkins, Leland Stanford, Jonas Clark, and others were changing the face of higher education in America. Hecker had sighed, "Let us have one-twentieth part of the money expended on education by other religious or learned societies, and we will show again what we did in former ages."[32] His purpose in proposing

26. *Solemnities*, 17. Gilmour had earlier commented, "I fear the university is a bigger task than was at first believed." ADR, O'Connell Papers, Gilmour to O'Connell, Cleveland, Mar. 9, 1888.

27. "What is the Outlook for our Colleges?" VII (July, 1882), 395.

28. AUND, Daniel E. Hudson, C.S.C. Papers, McQuaid to Hudson, Rochester, Oct. 24, 1901.

29. Nolan, *op. cit.*, I, 220.

30. *Op. cit.*, 580.

31. "Duties of the Rich in Christian Society," CW, XV (July, 1872), 516.

32. CW, XII, 123.

43

a congress had been to produce a "united, powerful body of Catholics" that he thought would meet the challenge.[33] In his Milwaukee sermon of 1881, Spalding had estimated that $500,000 would be sufficient to build the institution that he then had in mind and to provide the endowment for its first chairs; this he called "a paltry sum in a country in which a single individual will not infrequently give a million or several million dollars to establish a centre of education."[34] At the council, with the Caldwell offer in hand, he observed simply, "Money is necessary, and this, I am persuaded, we may have. A noble cause will find or make generous hearts."[35] Shea found it difficult to believe that wealthy Catholics could "be so different from their Protestant neighbors that they cannot be interested in education."[36]

Others were more skeptical and perhaps more realistic. Thébaud was observing that Catholics, "who in general have been so lavish of their means for the building of churches and the support of charitable institutions, have not yet appeared to feel that superior instruction is at least of equal importance."[37] There was a similar theme in McQuaid's pastoral letter of 1882. Finding among Catholics "no inclination to rival non-Catholics by endowing educational institutions," he thought it possible only to "wait and pray for a change . . . before the dream of a Catholic University, except in name, can be realized."[38] The bishop was to have many occasions on which to feel vindicated, and when the university committee failed to raise funds for endowment as easily as it had anticipated he predicted accurately enough that an annual collection in the dioceses would soon be proposed.[39] Relying upon his interpretation that the council had authorized only "a higher course of theology, equivalent to a university course," he wrote to Gibbons at length to place his views on record "so that my reasons for withholding co-operation shall appear in after years."[40]

The readiness of Catholics for the task at hand was the underlying question. Heuser called attention to it, finding "that even in the circles of the better educated there is no clear understanding as to the precise aim and nature of such an institution."[41] This could have been said of the Third Plenary Council itself, since probably only Becker and Spal-

33. *Ibid.*, VIII, 227.
34. *Lectures and Discourses*, 157.
35. *University Education Considered*, 33.
36. ACQR, VIII, 529.
37. *Ibid.*, VII, 682.
38. *Op. cit.*
39. McQuaid to Gilmour, Rochester, Jan. 31, 1887, *ibid.*, II, 392.
40. June 11, 1887, *ibid.*, 393.
41. ACQR, X, 637.

ding on one side and McQuaid on the other had "thought through the distinction between a higher seminary and a university,"[42] and then only in terms that were soon to be outmoded. Spalding, however, was seeing the university not only as an end but also as a means, and counseling his brother bishops that "so long as we look rather to the multiplying of schools and seminaries than to the creation of a real university, our progress will be slow and uncertain, because a university is the great ordinary means to the best cultivation of mind."[43]

There was seeming plausibility in a general objection that Fulton had raised in the council "heaping ridicule upon the idea of setting up a University, saying it was foolish to attempt to do so; that universities were not created, but grew out of small beginnings."[44] Spalding had long since anticipated this line of argument, crediting to his uncle the view that "with a primitive people, institutions grow up; among a highly cultivated and civilized people, they are created."[45] With sociological insight, he had concluded that nothing any longer would be "allowed to take its way" but would instead be "forced and evolved with conscious purpose," so that, like anything else, a university would no more grow up organically in the late nineteenth century than would a new language.[46] The new university in neighboring Baltimore was in fact such a creation, and Gibbons was correct in a sense beyond that which he intended when he observed that success in Washington would depend upon the selection of "a rector who would devote all his energies to the work in the way that President Daniel Coit Gilman was doing for the Johns Hopkins University."[47]

One of Hecker's original band, also a convert to the Church, dismissed the contemporary "objections and forebodings" as "only the refrain of an old song we heard thirty years ago when the project of a university was first talked about, and which we then feared would result in nothing else but talk."[48] Yet, with the decision taken, the familiar refrain continued to be heard because, it would seem, what was being created was so little understood by the bishops generally and by the

42. Ellis, *Formative Years*, 115.

43. *University Education Considered*, 27.

44. Byrne, *op. cit.* Intellectuals of the period were making much of the contrast between what William Graham Sumner, a social Darwinist, was distinguishing as crescive and enacted institutions. *Folkways* (Boston: Ginn, 1907), Par. 61.

45. *Life of M. J. Spalding*, 314.

46. *The Religious Mission of the Irish People and Catholic Colonization* (New York: Catholic Publication Society, 1880), 133–35.

47. ADR, O'Connell Papers, Keane to O'Connell, Richmond, May 20, 1886.

48. Augustine F. Hewit, C.S.P., "The American Catholic University," CW, XLII (Nov., 1885), 226.

Catholic body they were leading that a weakness of collective will was being disclosed. The opposition of a McQuaid or even a Corrigan could be placed in the perspective of the Church's system of governance, which in more matters than is popularly realized guarantees autonomy even to woeful intransigence. But in the council the bishops had been persuaded to declare themselves for learning and to harbor expectations for an institution of the first rank without having had to confront what their high goals would later demand of them. A generation later, responding at length to an apostolic delegate's request for his view of the university, the veteran professor Henri Hyvernat attributed to the majority in the council feelings of self-congratulation because "neither as a body nor individually had they assumed the slightest financial responsibility." Instead, "as a body they had reserved for themselves the right of supervision and had incurred correlative duties, but they had managed to shift that burden to a self-recruiting Commission [later the trustees], to which nobody in particular was obliged to belong."[49]

In spite of the cogency of the case made by Spalding and other proponents, events of the succeeding years showed that some leading laymen as well as ecclesiastics had not been convinced. The preacher at the episcopal ordination of the second rector of the university was to deem it necessary to address "not a few who say that we do not need a specifically Catholic University."[50] Evidently not all the grounds for such an opinion or the consequences of its prevalence had been explored carefully by the founders. One painful dilemma, for example, to which they seem not to have adverted, was revealed when, responding to an inquiry from the first rector, who was seeking to recruit the strongest faculty that he could, an outstanding anatomist and surgeon—and a true Boston blueblood—was led to ask whether his presence at Harvard was "not more useful to the cause at large than one more among many would be at Washington."[51] Another reservation was expressed when a Washington banker and benefactor reported stating candidly to the first rector and to others his "doubts as to the University becoming an Institution for the laity—of ever being a true University," even his "doubts whether it should be so, as at present ruled."[52]

49. Hyvernat Papers, "Memoir," 6–7.

50. Thomas J. Shahan, *On the Great Need of a Catholic University* (Washington, D.C.: New Century, 1901), 23. Pointing to Louvain, Shahan asked, "Were it not for that great school, would not the huge Catholic majority of Belgium be today like the Catholic majorities of Italy and France and Spain, a dumb, helpless thing dominated by the higher intellect of its enemies?" *Ibid.*, 25.

51. OR, Thomas Dwight to Keane, Nahant, Mass., May 31, 1891. On Dwight (1843–1911), who published, among other works, *Thoughts of a Catholic Anatomist* (New York: Longmans, 1911), see J. L. Morrison, NCE, IV, 1129.

52. OR, E. Francis Riggs to O'Connell, Washington, Jan. 23, 1906.

Some laymen apparently saw no purpose at all in the institution, attributing what they perceived as "lethargy on the part of the Catholic public" to the "inutility and impracticability" of the project, especially if it would produce clerics who could be castigated as "idealists, theorists, or nonsensical, transcendentalist philosophers."[53] Higher education was still generally understood as embracing only undergraduate and professional studies. George E. Hamilton, who was to become the university's attorney, missed the distinction between undergraduate and graduate work when he undertook to express to a representative of the apostolic delegate, as reported, "the conviction and feeling not only of himself, but of the entire body of Catholic laymen in all parts of the country . . . that the placing of the Catholic University at Washington, where we already had a venerable and honored university, strong in the affections of all educated Catholics in the country, respected and even loved by non-Catholics, and making rapid progress in all its departments, was a very great mistake."[54] But others were suggesting, well before the university began to offer its own undergraduate programs, that "to attract the class of Catholic young men who go to Harvard and Yale, what we need is a popular, fashionable college."[55] Certainly the foremost families were reluctant to accept the promise of a new institution as a substitute for the quality and the social prestige for which they had already turned to the Ivy League. Richards, writing in 1896 to the American assistant to the Jesuit father general, explained as he had earlier the attitudes that were a part of the contemporary situation:

Harvard alone had more than 300 Catholic students three years ago in her *college classes*, without counting Law or Medicine. This is double the number of students at that time in the corresponding four years of any Catholic college in the United States. Moreover, there is a very decided tendency among many secular priests not only to approve but to advise parents to send their sons to Non-Catholic universities. Now even if the parents should resist, the young men would go where they wished; for this is almost universally the case with us; the parents always yield to the sons' determination in this matter. But the parents themselves are generally most anxious to send their sons to non-Catholic universities, for the sake of the social advancement which they expect them to obtain thereby.[56]

53. AGU, clipping, J. DeSilver, St. Louis, Mo., to Editor, *Sun*, Sept. 21, n.p., n.d.
54. AGU, Rector's letterbook, Richards to Rudolph Meyer, S.J., Washington D.C., Feb. 18, 1894.
55. Thomas P. Kernan, "The Catholic Layman in Higher Education," CW, LXXI (June, 1900), 384. Kernan, of Syracuse, son of Francis Kernan, a prominent political figure, had thought of the priesthood with a parish in Niagara in mind. ADR, O'Connell Papers, Kernan to O'Connell, Soussac, France, Mar. 19, 1888.
56. AGU, Rector's letterbook, Richards to Meyer, Washington D.C., Feb. 5, 1896.

The fatefulness of these questions was to become apparent in the university's second decade when no less a rigorist than McQuaid, still objecting to what he considered to be the premature foundation of a Catholic university—"this abortion," he had called it[57]—and strictly forbidding Catholics from his diocese to attend Cornell University, which was within his jurisdiction, nevertheless felt compelled to establish a Catholic hall of high quality at the same institution in order "to assume religious care of the 250 young Catholic men and women . . . whose bishops had failed to keep their diocesans away from a non-Catholic university."[58] He wondered then, as he probably had earlier, how Catholics could "even enter into serious competition with the numberless non-Catholic childless millionaires."[59] Indeed, at the time that papal approval and civil incorporation had been obtained, McQuaid was writing to a friend that, never having believed "in the possibility of a university in the true sense of the word," he was "growing incredulous with regard to the practicality of even a higher seminary."[60] Later, while he was the third rector, Denis O'Connell attributed McQuaid's opposition to the institution itself to a conviction "that the solution was to be found elsewhere, namely, in building the Catholic Hall by the side of the non–Catholic university."[61] Indeed, although confidences seem to have been maintained, McQuaid was to express himself in this vein forthrightly to the archbishops of the country.[62] If doubts and preferences such as these were unvoiced and even hidden during the university's formative period, their expression during its early years suggests that they were present from the beginning and were, of their nature, genuinely inhibitory. On this account, Hyvernat could write later that the university was suffering "from an insufficient period of gestation" and needed to "be born again."[63]

57. To Corrigan, Rochester, Jan. 26, 1887, in Zwierlein, *Life and Letters*, III, 392.

58. AUND, Hudson Papers, McQuaid to Hudson, Rochester, Apr. 21, 1907; see also letters of May 30, 1907, and Sept. 12, 1908, and John Whitney Evans, *The Newman Movement* (Notre Dame: University of Notre Dame Press, 1980), 29.

59. AUND, Hudson Papers, McQuaid to Hudson, Rochester, May 30, 1907.

60. To Gilmour, Rochester, June 28, 1887, in Zwierlein, *Life and Letters*, III, 391.

61. OR, O'Connell to Sebastian G. Messmer, Washington, Jan. 7, 1907; also O'Connell to John J. Farrell, Washington, Jan. 7, 1907. Messmer was archbishop of Milwaukee, Farrell chaplain to Catholic students at Harvard. In view of O'Connell's recollections, the historian of the diocese of Rochester considers it "quite likely" that McQuaid had been "theorizing" along these lines in the 1880s. Robert F. McNamara, *The Diocese of Rochester 1868–1968* (Rochester, N.Y.: Diocese of Rochester, 1968), 565.

62. At their meeting of Apr. 26, 1906, the archbishops received a reminder from McQuaid that the problem of higher education was urgent; he noted that he favored Catholic colleges associated with secular universities that would be staffed by Catholic professors and supported, if possible, from state funds. AAB, Gibbons Papers, 103-L–5, mm.

63. Hyvernat Papers, "Memoir," v.

The approval of the Holy See required formal review of what the bishops had proposed with attention to its feasibility and its conformity with Roman requirements for the ecclesiastical degrees that would be conferred in the name of the pope. At the time, because the United States was still classified as mission territory, responsibility for the review rested with Propaganda Fide.

The congregation's earlier review of the decrees of the Third Plenary Council had altered the passages on the "principal seminary" in only two significant respects. One of the changes had been made to reserve the decisions on university governance and on final approval for the establishment of the institution itself until papal approval of a constitution and program of studies was obtained. This safeguarded the rights of the Holy See in the matter. The other, of lesser relevance, had served to protect the financial support that the colleges in Rome and Louvain, residences for priests pursuing university studies, were receiving from American Catholics. Subsequently, however, the concerns of the American opposition were reflected in the inquiries of curial officials, whom the American proponents usually found less friendly to their cause than the pope himself.[64] After the council, Leo XIII had not only sent his private letter of encouragement to Gibbons but, to assist in funding the university, had suspended temporarily a request that he had previously made of the American bishops for support of the missions of the East.[65] He was reported by journalists to be following the university project in detail.[66]

A report on the progress being made with a view to presentation of a plan for formal approval by the Holy See was decided upon at the meeting of the university committee during May, 1886. At this meeting, also, in addition to receiving reports on the title to the Washington

64. See BT, mm, Sept. 7, 1887, exh., for the report on their Roman meetings by Keane and Ireland. Roman doubts at the time were encountered also by Hyvernat who, before accepting appointment to the faculty, sought advice from English-speaking ecclesiastics in Rome. "Card. Howard," he found, "as behooves a Cardinal was reserved. Mgr. O'Callaghan (later Bp) rector of the English College with whom I was quite intimate urged me to refuse. He did not believe that the American Hierarchy as he knew it would unite to support the new university. . . . 'It will be a fiasco, he said just like the University of Dublin.' " Hyvernat Papers, "Notes on C.U."

65. Ellis, *Formative Years*, 166–67.

66. Bernard O'Reilly, New York *Sun*, reprinted in *FJ*, July 24, 1886, quoted in *ibid.*, 179–80. Later, thanking Monsignor James McMahon for the gift that had made possible the erection of the hall bearing his name, the first apostolic delegate to the United States, Archbishop Francesco Satolli, remarked that the pope, "in a manner," considered "as bestowed upon himself the donations and bequests that are made for the advancement of this institution." Quoted in Boston *Pilot*, Sept 23, 1894.

property and the funds collected by the episcopal committee, the members awarded prizes for plans submitted by architectural firms (which proved to be of "no practical use"[67]), authorized negotiations with the Sulpician Fathers for the supervision of priest students, and, most importantly, selected a rector of the university to be proposed to the Holy See.

Although virtually everyone had expected Spalding to be named to the office, and although he had earlier declared that it would be his "greatest happiness to . . . devote the rest of my life" to the higher education of priests,[68] he declined to accept the position when it was offered to him by the four archbishops designated by the committee to make the choice, just as on several occasions he declined to leave Peoria for promotion to major sees.[69] Keane, on whom the choice fell, was told by Spalding "that, for years to come, the post would practically be that of the President of a Seminary, a post which he could in no way be induced to fill."[70] This statement was hardly consistent with Spalding's earlier professions, but it revealed that doubts of some weight were in his mind.[71] Keane reported that he had yielded in obedience only because Gibbons had impressed upon him "that I must accept the position or that the whole project must fall through."[72] Thus, although

67. Keane Papers, "Chronicles of the Catholic University of America from 1885" (unpublished manuscript), 23.

68. Spalding to Gibbons, Peoria, July 18, 1882, quoted in Sweeney, *op. cit.*, 139.

69. Sweeney, *op. cit.*, cites Spalding's consideration for Newark (133–34), San Francisco (134–35, 152), Philadelphia (155n), Milwaukee (113–18), and St. Louis (212n). Richards reported a general supposition that Spalding was regarded as too much influenced by German philosophy and as insufficiently grounded in scholasticism (*op. cit.*, 83), and Becker had earlier reported to Rome that Spalding held philosophical views that had been condemned at Louvain (APF, *Acta*, 1875, CCXLIII, fol. 25, Becker to Franchi, Sept. 14, 1874)—an accusation that he later retracted—but it appears to be entirely clear that the decisions were Spalding's own. When Spalding was considered for Chicago, Father John A. Conway, S.J., of Georgetown University, responded to the inquiry of Archbishop Sebastian Martinelli, the apostolic delegate, by noting, among other things, Spalding's frequent absences from his diocese, his public association "with his lady friend," and "a ring about his public utterances and written productions that savors of the school of modern philosophy." ASV, DA, IV, No. 54, fols. 21–22.

70. "Chronicles," 8–9.

71. It seems likely that, aware of how skeptically some bishops regarded his theology and his prudence, and recalling the divisions in the council discussions, Spalding may have felt himself to be too much of an episcopal isolate to obtain the support for the university that he knew it would need. Also, awareness of Miss Caldwell's personal instability and of his own vulnerability could have entered into his motives. Perhaps he knew that Archbishop Ryan entertained fears that his selection as rector would mean that Caldwell would be "constantly there, and attract much comment." AANY, Ryan to Corrigan, Philadelphia, June 4, 1885.

72. "Chronicles," 9. Keane's talents had been utilized by McCloskey and Gibbons in 1879 in appealing to the bishops to relieve the financial crisis of the archdiocese of Cincinnati.

his selection could not be divulged for many months, there was placed upon him immediately the task of leadership. He began, according to the committee's decision, by preparing two letters, one for the pope and one for the cardinal prefect of the Propaganda, which he and Ireland could present in Rome.

These letters were approved at the eighth meeting of the university committee on October 27, 1886. They set forth the plans of the committee and provided the basis for the papal approbation that was to come. In addressing the Holy Father, the bishops acknowledged with compliments the pontiff's intellectual thrust and recalled his approval of the conciliar decrees in which, giving attention to education at all levels, the fathers had sought to provide for the higher education that they knew to be close to his heart by undertaking to found a principal seminary to which other faculties could be added. As the committee charged with the task of foundation, confident that the theological faculty would be endowed *in perpetuum,* they petitioned for approval of their project. They included the complete direction of the university by the hierarchy, not by a religious order; the recruitment of faculty in the sacred sciences from religious as well as diocesan clergy; the supervision of clerical students by the Society of St. Sulpice; the location of the university in Washington, where it would always hold primacy; a prohibition against the foundation of another pontifical university until the next plenary council; and the confirmation of the choice of Keane as rector, with his relief from responsibility for the diocese of Richmond, especially in view of "the judgment of the people that the Rector should be a Bishop."[73] There were assurances, too, that attendance at the North American College in Rome would be maintained.

The letter to the prefect of the congregation differed from that to the pope principally in its emphasis upon certain practical matters. It looked ahead to providing a place for Catholics who otherwise might attend non-Catholic institutions in which their faith would be endangered. It portrayed funding as so assured that only the wealthy would need to be approached for support, allowing the resources of the faithful in general to be devoted to parochial education. It gave as the reason why the first rector, "for the present at least," should be a bishop "the common opinion that no priest, although otherwise suitable, would be a proper person for an undertaking of such importance."[74] It made it clear that the question of location was secondary, in case there should be objection

73. OR, Letter to His Holiness, Pope Leo XIII, Baltimore, Oct. 27, 1886 (copy).
74. *Ibid.*, Letter to Cardinal Simeoni, Baltimore, Oct. 25, 1886 (copy).

to Washington. Finally, it asked for the necessary faculties to accord to the principal seminary the ordinary privileges of a university and gave assurances that the regulations of the proposed university would be submitted at the proper time to the Holy See.

In presenting these letters in Rome, Keane and Ireland encountered questions, prompted by their opponents at home, as to whether the favorable vote of the bishops represented an actual commitment to the university. Pope Leo delayed decision until the arrival of Gibbons for the public consistory of newly created cardinals in March. Gibbons, sufficiently discouraged at one point to suggest abandonment of the project, had his back stiffened by Ireland, but he prudently decided to canvas the American bishops before seeking approval of the Holy See for the Washington site and meanwhile asked for formal papal approval of the university. This took the form of a papal brief issued on Easter Sunday, April 10, 1887, providing that the university "must remain under the authority and protection of all the Bishops of the country, in such a way that its whole administration shall be directed by them through certain Bishops selected for that purpose, whose right and duty it shall be to regulate the system of study, to make rules of discipline, to select the professors and other officials of the University, and to ordain whatever else pertains to its best government."[75] The action of the pope allowed the notarization and filing of the certificate of incorporation to which signatures had been affixed in Washington seventeen months earlier. The university committee thereupon became the first board of trustees (often addressed in the early decades as the board of directors).

The board, meeting on September 7, 1887, was free to proceed with the formal appointment of Keane as rector and with the confirmation of Washington as the permanent location, thirty-three of the fifty-three bishops voting having cast their ballots for the national capital. Keane thought that the property already purchased—three miles out—was too remote from the central city to facilitate the public lectures that he considered important, but he was unsuccessful in moving for a change of site. Archbishop Williams continued as chairman of the building committee that was appointed. It was empowered to proceed with a plan that Keane had formed after visits to other institutions and which E. J. Baldwin of the Baltimore firm of Baldwin and Pennington had put into shape. Another committee was appointed to develop statutes and

---

75. AAB, Gibbons Papers, 82-P–10–11, *Quod in novissimo conventu*. The anniversary is currently commemorated as Founders' Day. BT, mm, July 26–27, 1968.

a course of studies and to enter into contracts with professors. The committee of collectors was expanded and a separate committee on investments appointed. Keane was charged with drafting a letter to be sent to all the bishops urging their assistance to the collectors. Responsibility in all matters was really in his hands.

To further understanding of the university project, the rector published in the *Catholic World* during the next months a series of articles using the statements of Leo XIII and accounts of the Catholic universities of Rome, France, Louvain, and Strassburg (then a German city) as contexts for presentation of his case. He had visited these and other institutions after he and Ireland had concluded their Roman mission, and even before his prospective appointment was publicly announced he had visited Harvard and Laval Universities and the Roman Catholic seminaries of Boston and Montreal to hold, as he put it, "conferences with all the long-headed clerics and laics whom I could find, capable of giving advice on the University question."[76] While in Rome, at the urgent suggestion of the Holy Father, he had consulted with Monsignor Désiré Mercier, later the revered cardinal archbishop of Malines, who was then seeking to establish a philosophical institute at Louvain, and also with Monsignor Francesco Satolli, whom the pope had brought from Perugia to assist in the Thomistic revival and who later, as the first apostolic delegate to the United States, would initially regard Keane with favor and then press for his dismissal as rector. There can be, certainly, no dispute as to the diligence and the sagacity with which Keane educated himself in the changing university world during the three years between his selection as rector and the opening of the institution on November 13, 1889.

The collections for the university fund did not reach expectations. By exaggerating the amounts being sought and otherwise printing irresponsible reports, some newspapers had generated confusion and mistrust. Bishops who received favorably the circular appeal from Gibbons often had few Catholics of means in their dioceses. In the more affluent New York area, not only McQuaid upstate, but his close friend Corrigan, who almost two years earlier had undermined Keane's first efforts in the metropolis, refused to allow solicitations by the appointed committee. Corrigan, moreover, resigned from the university committee, even after Gibbons pleaded with him to remain, although he returned about a year later, at the meeting of November 13, 1888.[77] His relations with Gib-

76. *Ibid.*, 81-R-9, Keane to Gibbons, Fortress Monroe, Va., Aug. 12, 1886.
77. *Ibid.*, 83-T-6, Corrigan to Gibbons, New York, Nov. 28, 1887; AANY, Corrigan Papers, Gibbons to Corrigan, Baltimore, Dec. 3, 1887; AAB, Gibbons Papers, 83-V-4,

bons had deteriorated markedly during 1887, for reasons that objectively had little to do with the university,[78] but both he and McQuaid were piqued and agitated because Ireland, Keane, and Spalding had appealed to the priests of the United States directly and not through the bishops.[79]

Successes in Baltimore and Washington added sufficiently to the initial benefactions for the university to allow the building committee to begin construction early in 1888. The laying of the cornerstone of what is now Caldwell Hall was scheduled for May 24. Elaborate ceremonies were held in spite of a heavy downpour. Cardinal Gibbons presided. President Grover Cleveland and members of his cabinet, some thirty bishops, distinguished guests, and a large gathering were in attendance. Spalding's address on the occasion, reported unfavorably to Rome but received favorably throughout the country, was characteristic in his exaltation of the opportunities afforded to the Church in the United States and his confidence in its capacity to adapt to the changing realities introduced by modern science. A gold medal from the Holy Father was presented to the founding donor.

All the archbishops and bishops present at the laying of the cornerstone were invited to attend the meeting of the board that followed the ceremony. The resignation of Corrigan, when presented, was not accepted and action concerning it was deferred to the next meeting (at which he was to return to the board). It was decided that vacancies that might occur in positions occupied by laymen in the board should be filled by laymen. The rector's financial report provided cause for optimism, since $600,000 had been collected or pledged to augment the original benefaction of $300,000. Subsidies were authorized to prepare for the faculty Edward A. Pace, a priest of the diocese of St. Augustine who was studying in Europe, and Hyvernat, a French specialist in Assyriology and Egyptology who was teaching at the Apollinaris (the Roman seminary). The rector was instructed to open negotiations for a statue of Orestes Brownson to be the first of several that would commemorate visibly on the campus great men who had rendered distinguished service to the Church in the United States. All accepted with enthusiasm Gibbons's proposal that the formal opening of the university should be a part of the centennial celebration of the foundation of the American hierarchy in the autumn of 1889.[80]

Corrigan to Gibbons, New York, Dec. 17, 1887; and, 84-R-10, John M. Farley to Gibbons, New York, July 8, 1888, cited in Ellis, *Formative Years,* 261–62, 300.

78. Robert Emmett Curran, S.J., *Michael Augustine Corrigan and the Shaping of Conservative Catholicism in America, 1878–1902* (New York: Arno Press, 1978), 263–64.

79. AANY, Corrigan Papers, McQuaid to Corrigan, Rochester, Dec. 26, 1887.

80. BT, mm, May 24, 1888. Ireland, unaccountably, went so far as to report optimisti-

Philip M. Garrigan (1840–
1919), first vice rector, who had
been director of the provincial
seminary at Troy, New York, for
three years and pastor of St.
Bernard's Church at Fitchburg,
Massachusetts, for fourteen years
before his appointment in
1888. He served until he was
named bishop of Sioux City, Iowa
in 1902.

That summer, while Keane was in New England, acting on the advice
of Gibbons that he should seek a vice rector in the region, he chose for
the position, as a result of inquiries that he made among bishops and
clergy, Philip J. Garrigan, pastor of St. Bernard's Church in Fitchburg,
Massachusetts, who previously had been rector of St. Joseph's Seminary
at Troy, New York. The selection was disclosed prematurely in *The Pilot*
of Boston on July 21, 1888, but the mail ballot of 'the trustees was
nevertheless favorable to the appointment. Garrigan, who like himself
was Irish-born, was described by Keane as "a model priest, a polished
gentleman, an earnest student, an excellent administrator."[81] He became a friend in whom Keane placed complete confidence for the day-
to-day operation of the university and he gave his assistance as well to
Keane's successor until his own appointment as the first bishop of Sioux
City, Iowa, in 1902.

Keane spent the months from August to October at the University
of Notre Dame drafting what were to become the first constitutions of
the university. The trustees made only minor changes in the drafts of
the two documents (one applicable to the university in general, the
other to only the faculty of sacred science). In preparing a letter of
submission in the name of the board, Keane wrote that the trustees had

cally, "The University is to be a great success—money without end." ADR, O'Connell
Papers, Ireland to O'Connell, St. Paul, Aug. 18, 1888.
    81. AANY, John M. Farley Papers, Keane to Farley, Notre Dame, Aug. 18, 1888.

"aimed at giving only the fundamental laws, guided by the points already decided by the Holy Father in his Apostolic Letter . . . and also by the statutes of the other Catholic Universities already approved, and by their long experience in directing Christian education and their intimate acquaintance with the character and needs of the American people." The matters of detail, such as programs of study and examinations, were "left to be decided, year after year, by the Commission of Archbishops and Bishops and the University Senate, in conformity with the Statutes as approved by the Holy See, and according to the condition of the studies and of the students each year."[82] Among the statutes that Keane had used were those in effect at Louvain, Laval, Paris, Lille, and Strassburg.

The First Faculty

The proposed "constitutions" were approved by the board on November 13, 1888. Keane sailed for Europe immediately thereafter to obtain papal approval for the opening of the university and to recruit professors. Sailing with him was Thomas J. Shahan, recently chancellor of the diocese of Hartford, who, like Pace, previously selected, was to remain in Europe to prepare himself for the faculty. Negotiations with Europeans were clouded by a disputed interpretation of a congressional act of 1885 by which, at the urging of the nascent labor movement, immigrants under contract to labor were to be denied entry into the country. An outcome exempting the university's professors was not obtained until July of 1889, but Keane had been able to return to Washington in May with the feeling that his mission had been accomplished. He had to respond to critics from outside the Church who maintained that only Americans should have been selected for the faculty,[83] which he did in

---

82. OR, "A Statement of the facts connected with the establishment of the Catholic University of America." Ten years later, when a committee of the academic senate was reporting on the constitutionality of certain legislation, it noted that it was guided in part by "the Constitution of the University of Lille which was used as a model for ours, to the extent that many articles have been taken bodily into our Constitution." AS, mm, May 20, 1898.

83. "Bishop Keane and the Catholic University," Washington *Church News*, May 19, 1889, reprinting communication to the Baltimore *Sun*, cited in Ellis, *Formative Years*, 358–60. The New York *Commercial Advertiser*, May 6, 1889, carried a headline, "A Foreign Faculty. No Americanism in the Catholic University," cited in Patrick H. Ahern, *The Life of John J. Keane, Educator and Archbishop, 1839–1918* (Milwaukee: Bruce, 1954), 99n. Charles G. Herberman took pains to refute nativist criticism in "The Faculty of the Catholic University," ACQR, XIV (Oct., 1889), 701–15. A disgruntled priest later wrote to complain that "home talent was overlooked." OR, A. Heiter to Gibbons, Buffalo, N.Y., Nov. 26, 1892. Keane, however, had written of Pace and Shahan, "Would that I could fill every chair with Americans like yourselves." Thomas Joseph Shahan Papers, Keane to Shahan, Louvain, Aug. 23 [1889].

the spirit of Leo XIII's earlier admonition that, as Keane reported it, "the university should be founded by American means, and . . . conducted by American brains; and if at first you have to call in the help of foreign talent in your faculties, it must be with the view of developing home intellect, of training professors who will gradually form indigenous faculties worthy of the name the university bears."[84]

Keane had cause for satisfaction with the small band that he was able to recruit for the first faculty, even if the efforts that he made to attract some of the most eminent European scholars did not meet with success.[85] The trustees had limited the number of appointments to six.[86] Monsignor James A. Corcoran, an esteemed professor at St. Charles Seminary of the archdiocese of Philadelphia and editor of the *American Catholic Quarterly Review*, was the first to be invited to join the faculty, but he declined for reasons of age and health.[87] The first to be appointed was Hyvernat, who had been recommended by his mentor, the Abbé Fulcran Vigouroux, S.S., a renowned scripture scholar; he thus became the founder of the present department of Semitic and Egyptian languages and literatures, specializing in Christian Arabic studies, and he contributed lustre to the university until his death in 1941.[88]

Two theologians were obtained who had been exiled from Germany during the *Kulturkampf*. Both were to return to their homeland in the wake of the bitter American controversies of the 1890s. The Very Reverend Monsignor Joseph Schroeder, about forty years of age, after teaching in Liège, Belgium, and returning as a pastor, had just been appointed to teach at Cologne, but had obtained the consent of his archbishop to accept Keane's invitation. His sympathies with German ethnic causes and his involvement in the "school controversy" of 1891 and thereafter, on the side opposite from the rector and other colleagues, were to lead to his resignation under pressure in 1897.[89] Joseph Pohle, four years younger, also Roman-educated, had taught in Switzerland and at Leeds and was in the seminary at Fulda when he accepted Keane's

84. "Leo XIII and the Catholic University of America," CW, XLVI (Nov., 1887), 150; see also Keane, "Chronicles," 14, and Soderini, *op. cit.*, 18.

85. For an ample account, see Patrick Henry Ahern, *The Catholic University of America, 1887–1896: The Rectorship of John J. Keane* (Washington, D.C.: The Catholic University of America Press, 1948), 3–30. Cardinal Manning was said to have remarked nastily—and unjustly—that "Bishop Keane could have found enough mediocrities in his own country without going across the Atlantic for others." Egan, *Recollections*, 185.

86. BT, mm, Nov. 13, 1888.

87. Washington *Church News*, May 12, 1889, cited by Ahern, *op. cit.*, 5.

88. Theodore C. Peterson, C.S.P., "Professor Henry Hyvernat," CW, CLIII (Sept., 1941), 653–66; NCE, VII, 309.

89. John P. Whalen, NCE, XII, 1180–81.

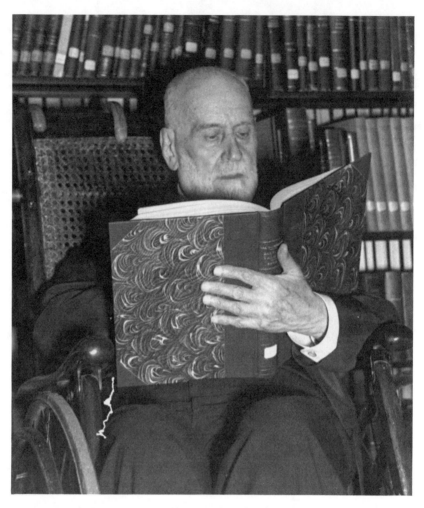

Henri Hyvernat (1858–1941), professor of Semitic and Egyptian languages and literatures, first professor to be appointed, who had a long, productive, and internationally celebrated career, and whose pastoral interest paved the way for the establishment of St. Anthony's Church in the vicinity of the university.

invitation to teach Thomistic philosophy. He was to resign in 1894 to accept a chair of dogmatic theology in the Catholic academy at Münster.[90] Also Germanic in sympathy was Swiss-born Sebastian G. Messmer, who had taught theology at Seton Hall, and who had accepted appointment to teach canon law. He had spent his first year in Rome

90. John F. Wippel, *NCE*, XI, 466.

preparing for the task, but was to find himself appointed in 1891 bishop of Green Bay, Wisconsin (and, in 1903, archbishop of Milwaukee).[91]

The remaining theologian, on whom Keane and most of the faculty came to rely heavily, was Thomas Joseph Bouquillon, a Roman-educated moralist who, after teaching in the seminary of his diocese at Bruges and as the first occupant of the chair of moral theology at the Catholic Institute of Lille, had retired to the abbey of Maredsous to revise his manual of moral theology, the first edition of which had been received with much acclaim. Bouquillon remained as a member of the faculty until his untimely death in 1902.[92] Also teaching was Charles Warren Stoddard, a convert then in high repute as a lecturer and an author who had taught English literature at the University of Notre Dame during the year 1885–86. A bachelor, he lived for several years with priests of the faculty and students in Caldwell Hall and associated with prominent families and literati in Washington until his resignation was requested in 1901. His chronic ill health, consequent absences, and the assertion of his department that his services were not needed led to the request.[93] Also associated with the faculty as lecturers were two Paulist priests, members of the first religious institute to establish a house of study at the university, Augustine F. Hewit in church history and George M. Searle, later appointed director of the observatory, in astronomy and physics. The Sulpician, John B. Hogan, who had left his position as rector of St. John's Seminary in the archdiocese of Boston to become director of Divinity College, the corporate name for the priest students in residence, lectured in ascetical theology.[94] His assistant director, Alexis Orban, S.S., served also as librarian and as a private teacher of geology. Joseph Graf, a German priest who had been at the Baltimore cathedral for eight years, was appointed to be musical director.

91. Peter Leo Johnson, NCE, IX, 721–22. According to a correspondent, Keane had not been permitted "to entertain the thought of bringing over a native Roman canonist." ADR, O'Connell Papers, William Maher to O'Connell, Hartford, Conn., May 22, 1888.

92. William J. Kerby, CE, II, 715–16; and DAB, II, 481–82; John P. Whalen, NCE, II, 731; also C. Joseph Nuesse, "Thomas Joseph Bouquillon (1840–1902), Moral Theologian and Precursor of the Social Sciences at The Catholic University of America," CHR, LXXII (Oct., 1986), 601–19.

93. M. J. Flaherty, CE, XIV, 298–99; and AS, mm, Oct. 5, 1900; Nov. 12, 1901; OR, Stoddard to Conaty, Washington, Nov. 18, 1901. See Carl G. Stroven, DAB, XVIII, 52, who credits Stoddard with "a wider friendship among literary folk than any one else in his day."

94. Hogan had been suggested "as most suitable for Rector of the new University" at the first meeting of the university committee. BT, mm, Jan. 27, 1885. Austin Dowling, an early student who later became bishop of Des Moines and then archbishop of St. Paul, noted Hogan's "rare gift of filling the student's mind with the unrest of inquiry." Quoted in Ellis, *Catholic Priest in the United States*, 52. On Hogan's scholarly contributions, see Francis J. Connell, C.Ss.R., "The Theological School in America," in Roy J. Deferrari

Before these appointments were concluded, Pope Leo XIII had approved, with amendments, the statutes that had been submitted for review. Two amendments proposed by the curial review commission had revealed differences in perceptions of the character of the university between the American petitioners and the Roman congregation. Cardinal Mazzella, the chairman of the commission, had objected to the concept of an exclusively graduate institution and had claimed the support of Cardinal Simeoni and the Holy Father on this point. In the light of this insistence, Keane undertook to speak for the bishops among the trustees as "thankful for permission from the Holy See to derogate from the Council in this matter" and to agree that they "would see, according to circumstances, whether it would be wise for them to do so." (It was not until the university's second decade that the board decided to offer programs for undergraduate study.) A more felicitous solution was found with respect to the second problem, which was the insistence of the commission upon requirements for graduation that would be uniform with Roman institutions. Since the Americans, from the outset, were aspiring to higher standards, it was not difficult for Keane to agree that "our conditions for graduation should be at least equal to those demanded in Rome."[95]

The apostolic letter *Magni Nobis gaudii*, given on March 7, 1889, noted that the opening of the university would be a "perpetual memorial" of the centennial of the American hierarchy and endowed the institution "with the rights proper to a lawfully-constituted University," including the power to confer pontifical degrees. The office of chancellor was conferred upon the archbishop of Baltimore and his successors. Approval of programs of study, "especially in so far as they relate to philosophy and theology," was reserved to the Holy See. The admission of those "who wish to begin or to continue their studies" was included, as was the affiliation with the university of "seminaries, colleges, and other Catholic institutions, according to the plan suggested in the Constitution, in such a manner, however, as not to destroy their auton-

---

(ed.), *Essays on Catholic Education in the United States* (Washington, D.C.: The Catholic University of America Press, 1942), 219–33.

95. "Chronicles," 18–19, 20. Mazella's initial reaction to the American proposal had been reported by Keane and Ireland as "amazement that anyone could think of alleging Georgetown College as an argument against the establishment of the University in Washington, since it was evident that the scope of the two institutions was very different and that they ought to be reciprocally helpful rather than prejudicial." BT, mm, Sept. 7, 1887, exh. But, as Hyvernat was to recall for Bonzano's benefit, it had been the Roman congregation's insistence upon the admission of "beginners" that had earlier delayed the canonical erection of the Catholic Institute of Paris from 1882 until 1889. Hyvernat Papers, "Memoir," 8–9.

omy." It was decreed also "that no other institution of this nature shall be undertaken by anyone without consulting the Apostolic See."[96] On the latter point, especially in view of his earlier experience with Corrigan, Keane did not rest until he had received a clarifying rescript to the effect that the clause was meant to exclude any other comparable foundations "until all the ordinary faculties have been established in the University at Washington, and unless, before anything whatever has been done in the matter, the Holy See has been consulted."[97]

The formal opening of the pontifically chartered university on November 13, 1889, was an auspicious occasion in spite of rain the equal of that which had fallen during the laying of the cornerstone. Keane had not wanted to rival Georgetown's celebration of its centennial earlier in the year; he had instructed the vice rector to plan something "stately and grand—but, I think, not too *loud.*"[98] The ceremonies followed the three-day Baltimore celebration of the hierarchy's centennial that had begun with a solemn mass and had included a controversial two-day congress of the laity.[99] The solemn mass of dedication was celebrated by the papal delegate for the occasion, Archbishop Satolli. While Bishop Gilmour was preaching, those who could not be accommodated in the small chapel of Caldwell Hall heard a discourse entitled "The Vitality of the Church a Manifestation of God" that was delivered by the convert and prominent Passionist preacher, Father Fidelis of the Cross (James Kent Stone). An apologetic emphasis and tone that would be excessive to late-twentieth-century ears characterized much that was said during the day.[100] President Benjamin Harrison attended the dinner following the inaugural program, as did members of his cabinet. The messages of congratulation and gifts that were received were tokens of the hopes of the entire Catholic world in the new institution. At the end of the day, faculty and students began their great venture by entering into a spiritual retreat.

96. ASS, XXI (1888), 517–19, trans. *Constitutions of the Catholic University of America translated from the Latin* (Washington, D.C.: The Catholic University of America [1899]), 1–3.
97. Simeoni to Keane, Rome, Mar. 23, 1889, *ibid.*, 4.
98. OR, Keane to Garrigan, Rome, Mar. 11, 1889.
99. See William H. Hughes, *Souvenir Volume Illustrated. Three Great Events in the History of the Catholic Church in the United States. (1) The Centenary Celebration, (2) Proceedings of the First American Catholic Congress, and (3) Dedication of the Catholic University* (Detroit: W. H. Hughes, 1890), and Vincent J. Donovan, "The First American Catholic Lay Congress held at Baltimore, November 11–12, 1889" (unpublished master's dissertation, The Catholic University of America, 1940).
100. See *Solemnities, passim.* When the chapel of Caldwell Hall was blessed, it was placed under the patronage of St. Paul, who had been chosen, with the approbation of the Holy See, as the patron of the faculty of divinity.

The Founders' Concept in Retrospect

Specificity about academic aims and the organization of the university could hardly have been expected from the founding bishops. It was clear enough, as Hecker had put it, that even a "well-conducted college for undergraduates is not a university, though it is often dignified with that name; but is merely one of the principal constituent parts of a university."[101] What were regarded as certain false starts were similarly excluded, for example, "the endeavor to annex a post graduate course to every one of our colleges,"[102] or attempts at a "collection or association of independent schools,"[103] of law and medicine, mainly, which would have made a university "a machine expected to turn out professional men merely."[104] There was, in fact, no clear contemporary image upon which to draw and no Catholic leaders were professional students of higher education. Writing from his own experience and reflection in the year that The Johns Hopkins University was to open, Becker could assert flatly, "There is not *to-day*, in the entire country, a single institution, Catholic, Protestant (of any shade) or non-descriptive, entitled to the name of university in the European sense of the word."[105]

Two elements of the traditional concept were clearly in the minds of the founders. One of these was mainly a matter of scale and level, as in Hecker's formal definition: "A university is a corporation of learned and studious men who are devoted to the acquisition and communication of science and art in all their higher branches."[106] A similar definition was given by an apologetic writer who, emphasizing breadth, saw the university as "an educational institution in which all the sciences which constitute a liberal and professional education are taught."[107] Indeed, this had been an explicit aspiration of the council of 1866. Becker, distinguishing between a college and a university, emphasized "the extent and thoroughness of the latter," which would have "special professors for each branch."[108] John Lancaster Spalding put it eloquently:

---

101. CW, VIII, 232.
102. Thébaud, *op. cit.*, 697.
103. Shea, ACQR, X, 321.
104. Heuser, *ibid.*, 656.
105. ACQR, I, 232. The National Teachers Association had made a similar judgment in 1869 when, meeting in Trenton, it had declared, "We have, as yet, no near approach to a real university in America." United States Commissioner of Education, *Annual Report, 1870* (Washington, D.C.: Government Printing Office, 1870), 418. James Bryce, at the time that The Catholic University of America was preparing to open, thought that he could identify eight to twelve true universities in the country. *The American Commonwealth* (2 vols.; New York: Macmillan, 1889), II, 529.
106. CW, VIII, 119.
107. James Conway, *op. cit.*, 663.
108. ACQR, I, 239, 232.

"The idea of a university is that of an institution whose soul life is the intercommunion and mutual connection of all the sciences."[109]

In this, a second, more substantive element can be found. Clearly, it was advancement in liberal learning, especially among priests, that the early advocates of a Catholic university were seeking most of all. In accord with their understanding of what a university was, they were interested in the formation of learned men, not specialists. There was an expectation that, as Shea counseled, "the university should be homogeneous in all its parts, activated by one spirit and one consensus of ideas."[110] Like Hecker, who emphasized the importance of a "permanent body of learned men residing within its precincts,"[111] Becker found "advantages of university education, as contrasted with collegiate, in the formation of character, imparting of knowledge, and preparation of the student for life."[112] To Brother Azarias, who was a proponent of "prolonged study," one of the main objects was, "under the guidance of representative exponents of modern thought and modern science, to discipline the mind into habits of correct thinking, and accustom the senses to accurate observation."[113] In all, as Becker saw it, there would "soon establish itself, as inseparable from the place, a recognized standard, both of Catholic thought and practice, to have been subject to which would in itself be a *liberal education,* and one infinitely more important than that other culture (momentous though it be), to attain which was the prime object in matriculating."[114]

These were aspirations for advanced study that did not include the emphasis upon research and disciplinary development that were to characterize graduate offerings in the United States in the wake of the Johns Hopkins influence. This influence itself was instructional, but the object of the bishops was still, as the first professor later recounted, "not so much to give young men an opportunity to obtain a higher education for their own private benefit, as to furnish the church with an elite of highly trained men for the general good and advantage of the church . . . in which doing the Bishops were convinced that they would serve, at the same time, the cause of the nation and contribute to the advancement of science."[115] Even if it is not possible to discern any

109. *Life of M. J. Spalding,* 316.
110. ACQR, X, 321.
111. CW, XIII, 120.
112. ACQR, I, 239.
113. ACQR, III, 579, 588.
114. *Ibid.,* I, 240.
115. Hyvernat Papers, "Documents Relating to the Constitution of the Catholic University of America," 3–4.

direct influence, what all were seeking was closer to an advanced version of Newman's concept of a university education and the English pattern that was his context than to the continental and particularly the German developments that were then being incorporated into American higher education.

There was in fact Catholic opposition to the new developments. The pioneer historian Shea took it for granted that "it is not the province of the university to stimulate invention or discovery"[116] even after President Gilman at Hopkins had made "investigation . . . the duty of every leading professor."[117] To some Catholic observers it appeared that in the new foundation at Baltimore there was "an institution shaped exactly on the programme advocated by the anti-classical party"[118] that was being identified with President Charles W. Eliot's fateful introduction of the elective system into the undergraduate curriculum at Harvard. Their instincts may have been sound in so far as the cause of liberal education was concerned, but the American university that was taking shape was in a way the "elective principle writ large."[119] American higher education, which some had once thought should be crowned by a national university, had already evolved toward a multiplicity of universities. Seen in retrospect, the concept held by the bishops was a static one which would not have accommodated the expansion of learning that was taking place. Although they could not have foreseen it, the institution that they were founding was to be led in the direction of the newer model. The word university was being attached to the emerging American reality.

116. ACQR, X, 316.
117. *Op. cit.*, 135.
118. Thomas Hughes, S.J., "What is a Liberal Education?" ACQR, X (Jan, 1885), 19.
119. Oleson and Voss, *op. cit.*, x.

PART TWO

The Troubled Beginnings of the Academic Community, 1887-1909

Happily we can point, even now and in this country, to individual Catholics whose scientific attainments command a merited respect. Within a limited sphere they personify, no doubt, that union of knowledge and belief for which we are striving. But at best they are isolated, and the larger world knows them as scientists only. Scattered here and there through the land, with no visible organizing hand, they certainly do not exercise the influence they would have if their efforts were united. Let men of this stamp be formed into a body; and without weakening in the least their ardor of investigation, they will be palpable proof of our Catholic sympathy with progress. – "The Work of the University," *Year-Book of the Catholic University of America*, 1893–94.

CHAPTER III

Implanting Academic Tradition and the Research Ideal

The translation of the founders' broad aims into participation in the nascent graduate school movement, which came to emphasize original research, began in the course of the first rector's survey of appropriate institutional models in Europe and America. He was subject inevitably to significant European influences, on the one hand in Rome and through the ecclesiastical system in which the university was established, and, on the other, in his dependence for practical guidance upon the European scholars whom he was able to recruit for the first faculty and the American priests who were being sent to European institutions to prepare for professorial positions. In turning to Europe in the first instance, he was of course by no means alone among American university presidents of his day. It was some time, in fact, before the university could aspire to prepare its own faculty, although its board of trustees early resolved to do so in voting unanimously to accord "preference to our own men whenever we had able candidates for such positions."[1] In subsequent decades this aspiration would soon come to be frowned upon as "inbreeding," so fast was the development of the American university movement.

As the date for the opening of the university neared, the friendly successor of Hecker as superior general of the Paulist Fathers observed that Keane had been impressed "more favorably with the German methods than the English."[2] At Baltimore the bishops had agreed that only those should be admitted to the university who had already completed a collegiate or a seminary curriculum. The Roman amendments had not changed this resolve. The rector went even further in publicly committing the institution to "making specialists, who alone can be

1. BT, mm, Nov. 12, 1902.
2. [Augustine F. Hewit, C.S.P.], "The Catholic University and Its Constitutions," CW, LXIX (July, 1889), 429.

accurate or profound scholars."[3] He had in mind that the students should be "made to appreciate the differences between the text-book recitations of the Seminary & the personal research which was to be the chief characteristic of University work."[4] In this linking of teaching with research, there was an unmistakable mark of influence from abroad, although what became a distinctly American academic milieu was then already being fashioned by Johns Hopkins, Michigan, Chicago, and similar institutions, also with visible dependence upon contemporary images of German precedents. Indeed, the latest of Gilman's successors at Johns Hopkins has attributed "not the reform, but the creation of the American university" to the discovery in the Prussian system of "an institution committed to two dominant concepts: freedom of scientific inquiry, and unity of teaching and research."[5] The Catholic University of America began "in close touch" with this neighbor in Baltimore that was exercising leadership. There were "many friendships that grew up between the administrators and faculty members of the two institutions."[6] European influence became evident, too, in the pattern of collegial governance that took root within The Catholic University of America.

The newness of the direction which the university took in its beginnings could not possibly have been foreseen by the founders. Few among them, or among their successors for that matter, had sufficient familiarity with higher education to appraise adequately what was being attempted. The period was in general one of change and invention in American higher education. Existing Catholic institutions, whether or not they were called universities, were still adjusting their organization and offerings to the American four-year college pattern (a task in which the new university was to give them practical assistance for at least half a century). As the center of graduate education that it set out to be, however, the university soon became the first and, until after World War II, the only American institution under Catholic auspices to offer doctoral work on a recognized significant scale. Among all institutions nationally, if "genuine entry" into graduate education can be measured by a criterion employed in one authoritative study, *i.e.*, an annual volume of one per cent or more of all doctorates awarded, it was to become one of twenty American institutions that were able to attain standing in this respect

3. CW, XLVIII, 219.
4. "Chronicles," 48.
5. Steven Muller, quoted in CHE, XXX (May 29, 1985), 29.
6. Roy J. Deferrari, "The Origin and Development of Graduate Studies under Catholic Auspices," in *Essays on Catholic Education in the United States*, ed. Roy J. Deferrari (Washington: The Catholic University of America Press, 1942), 200–201.

John Joseph Keane (1839–1918), bishop of Richmond (1878–88), first rector of The Catholic University of America (1888–96), archbishop of Dubuque (1900–1911).

before 1925.[7] Historians acknowledge that it became "the principal channel through which the methods and spirit of modern university work were diffused into the world of Catholic higher education" in the United States.[8]

Thus, in the lengthening perspective of the institution's first century, even with due deference to a seasoned judgment of its pioneer professor that the university's administrations, "beginning with the first rector,"

7. Bernard Berelson, *Graduate Education in the United States* (New York: McGraw-Hill, 1960), 93.
8. Philip Gleason, "American Catholic Higher Education: A Historical Perspective," in Robert Hassenger (ed.), *The Shape of Catholic Higher Education* (Chicago: University of Chicago Press, 1967), 41.

were always wanting in "professionalism,"[9] the achievement of its initial leadership must be admired. One can hardly do better than to echo a sentiment expressed by Cardinal Gibbons when the university was celebrating the twenty-fifth anniversary of its opening. On that occasion, he thanked God that there was at its beginning, in the person of his good friend, Bishop Keane, "a *man* whose soul, filled with a holy creative enthusiasm, would quicken the project into living reality and make its life breathe and pulsate in every Catholic heart."[10] In these words Gibbons was certainly exaggerating the response that Keane's efforts had received, but he was eminently just in praising the efforts themselves. They had been directed, by no means faultlessly, but faithfully, intelligently, and energetically toward bringing into being in Washington the kind of "community of scholars" that ever since the thirteenth century has defined a university.

The traditional phrase continues to have particular resonance for academic men and women. Implicit in it, even if perceived in ways that are often incompatible, are ideals of academic autonomy, liberal learning, and collegial relationships according to which the best institutions and their standards are measured. It is, after all, the academic community that provides the indispensable atmosphere for the encouragement of research and teaching. The implanting of the requisite ideals can never be an easy task. During the last quarter of the nineteenth century, the organization of an American institution committed to graduate instruction was truly pioneer work. Much more so was bound to be an attempt to embody in a national institution an expression of the Catholic mind in the United States. The trials of the new community that were experienced during the administrations of Keane and his first two successors, Thomas J. Conaty and Denis J. O'Connell, stand in evidence.[11]

The First Rector (1887–96)

John Joseph Keane (1839–1918) had been born in Ireland and brought to the United States as a child. Conaty and O'Connell were like him in their foreign birth. Until 1978, in fact, every one of Keane's successors was to be of Irish lineage, although only the ninth rector,

9. Hyvernat Papers, "Notes on C. U."

10. *Op. cit.*, II, 194.

11. The narrative accounts of these administrations will be found in Ahern, *Catholic University*; Peter E. Hogan, S.S.J., *The Catholic University of America, 1896–1903; The Rectorship of Thomas J. Conaty* (Washington: The Catholic University of America Press, 1949); and Colman J. Barry, O.S.B., *The Catholic University of America, 1903–1909; the Rectorship of Denis J. O'Connell* (Washington: The Catholic University of America Press, 1950).

the only one after O'Connell who was born abroad, had completed his
seminary education in Ireland before coming to the United States.
Keane grew up in Baltimore and worked commercially for three years
after high school before he began to study for the priesthood under the
Sulpician Fathers. His only archdiocesan assignment after his ordination
in 1866 was as an assistant to a beloved pastor, Jacob A. Walter, at St.
Patrick's Church, Washington, D.C. Then, in 1878, after notable
success with youth organizations and temperance societies and as a
lecturer, and after having been refused permission to leave the archdiocese to join the Paulist congregation, he was appointed bishop of Richmond.[12] At the Baltimore council, in 1884, he declined the first invitation extended to him to serve on the university committee because he
thought that he would feel "out of place."[13] Later, with unassailable
logic, he "pleaded that it was simply absurd for a man to undertake to
organize and run a university who had never been in a university in his
life."[14] Yet before the doors of Caldwell Hall were opened officially,
Keane was leading his little community not only along well-marked
paths but into the new ones that were gaining primacy.[15]

On meeting Keane, Georgetown's president surmised that he "had
very little practical knowledge of educational matters."[16] On campus,
his daily companions sometimes grew tired of what one called his "fatal
fluency,"[17] but they could not fail to observe also that he was "a miracle
of zeal, of hopefulness, of enthusiasm and fervour."[18] During the ten
years between his selection for the office of rector in 1886 and the
autumn of 1896, when he was compelled to accept his abrupt dismissal,
albeit with unswerving loyalty and awesome humility, Keane redirected
his talents to educate himself in the affairs of universities, constructed
the first building, learned the processes of institutional formation and
academic governance, obtained the approval of the board of trustees
and the Holy See for the constitutional documents that he drafted, led
efforts to raise funds across the nation, recruited the first professors and
students of the faculty of theology and lived with them in Caldwell Hall,

12. When named, assuring the Paulist founder of his "lasting affection," Keane ventured
to him the hope "that, in my endeavors to accomplish the holy will of God, you and your
associates may yet be my greatest auxiliaries." ACSP, Hecker Papers, Keane to Hecker,
Ellicott City, Md., Aug. 3, 1878.
13. "Chronicles," 4.
14. ADR, O'Connell Papers, Keane to O'Connell, Richmond, May 20, 1886.
15. See Ahern, *Catholic University* and *Life* and, for a brief account, NCE, VII, 139–
40. Thomas E. Wangler, "A Bibliography of the Writings of Archbishop John J. Keane,"
RACHS, XXCIX (1978), 60–73, may be of interest.
16. Richards, *op. cit.*, 84.
17. Charles Warren Stoddard Diaries, Oct. 3, 1892.
18. Egan, *Recollections*, 180.

Keane Hall, erected in 1896 and opened in 1897, renamed Albert Hall in 1906 in recognition of a benefaction from Captain Albert F. Ryan, shown here at the time of President Woodrow Wilson's inauguration in 1913.

brought into affiliation the first houses of study of religious communities, expanded instruction into the arts and sciences and professional fields, and built McMahon Hall for the new classes and Keane Hall (later renamed, on his own motion, Albert) as a residence for the first laymen to be enrolled. He was found to be honest and forthright in his dealings, his writings pleased general readers, his style of speaking earned the praises of even a professor of elocution,[19] and he used seemingly every opportunity in which he thought that his influence could serve the good of the university and the Church.

Keane came to know well prominent American academic leaders who were themselves engaged in pioneer efforts: Gilman; G. Stanley Hall, the German-trained father of psychology in the United States, whom Gilman had recruited for his faculty but later lost to the presidency of Clark; Andrew D. White, renowned both as a champion of science against theology and as the founding president of Cornell; and Eliot, the president under whom Harvard was being rejuvenated. Somewhat

19. OR, T. C. Trueblood to Keane, Ann Arbor, June 10, 1891. Ahern, *Life*, 109–11, gives other examples.

like them, although necessarily in his own way, Keane had to become "a special kind of university president," peculiarly American, "not the leading scholar but the persuasive executive."[20] In his day, of course, it was easy for a president to maintain first-hand contact with every aspect of campus life. It was his variously termed liberal and Americanist predilections that were to make his efforts suspect in ways that he, who was reputed to be "void of suspicion," perhaps did not understand.[21] After leaving the campus, he was in a kind of exile, briefly in California and then in Rome, until his restoration was made evident by his appointment, in 1900, as archbishop of Dubuque. But under his leadership The Catholic University of America had identified itself at the outset as what is now termed a research-oriented institution.

The University in the Developing Catholic Subculture

The trials faced by Keane and his next two sucessors were not academic but ecclesiastical and financial. Given the nature of the institution and the divisions concerning it that were evident at the outset, the ecclesiastical challenges were fundamental. The leaders in the university venture soon learned that, the corporate decision of the sponsors notwithstanding, the necessary support from the sponsors individually would not always be forthcoming. On the intellectual plane, the leaders had been confident in the unity of truth and apparently had never doubted that their highest academic ideals would be sustained and even deepened through free inquiry joined with free submission to ecclesiastical authority within a community of Catholic faith. Spalding was urging his coreligionists that it was "more necessary that they should think than that they should think alike."[22] It was taken for granted that a thoroughly Catholic university could and would be an equal participant—or, if possible, another Harvard—in American academic life and in society generally. Indeed, the leaders' presentation of what they were about gained credence for their assumptions in circles that otherwise would have remained skeptical, if not downright hostile. Fair Harvard itself, its prestige long established, not only invited Keane to give its Dudleian lecture in 1890, but conferred an honorary doctorate upon him three years later.[23]

20. G. W. Pierson, "Nineteenth Century Ideas of the University: United States," in Clapp, *op. cit.*, 81. See also Joseph F. Kauffman, *At the Pleasure of the Board* (Washington, D.C.: American Council on Education, 1980).

21. William Macon Coleman to Editor, *Washington Post*, June 5, 1899. Coleman was a feature writer on the *Post's* staff.

22. "The University: A Nursery of the Higher Life," *CUB*, V (Oct., 1899), 466.

23. See Ahern, *op. cit.*, 62–63, 67. The lecture had been founded by Judge Paul Dudley in 1750 to expose the "damnable heresies" of the Roman Catholic Church, but for some

On the practical level, what the leaders seem not to have foreseen was that the young university community would not be protected from and often would be drawn into—by their own actions as well as by those of their antagonists—the ecclesiastical and social crises of their time. Although they were far from holding the views that had been censored in the Syllabus of Errors in 1864 and, sometimes, as in Spalding's case, were too quickly labeled as liberal only because they were seeking an authentically American expression of their Catholicism, their fortunes were fated to ebb before a powerful conservative ascendancy. Noting it, a youthful recruit to the faculty tried to explain to his brother that a conservative "constantly repeats principles absolutely true and denied by no one Catholic" and then "insinuates that the Liberal denies those principles."[24] Already, the university seemingly had become "the head-quarters of the assimilated liberal elite of Catholic America."[25] In Rome, which was still in reaction against the French Revolution and continental thought, it was being seen as "a true fortress of Catholic intellectual liberalism and, as such, subject to continuous criticism by those who were opposed to such ideology."[26]

On the domestic scene, unwittingly but perhaps even necessarily, the same council of bishops that had decided upon the establishment of the university had in other regulations drawn up what has been called in retrospect "the blueprint for the Catholic subculture that would be institutionalized in the next few decades and would constitute the ghetto, setting Catholics apart from American society."[27] Separation among religious bodies was then the rule, of course, and by no means only on the Catholic side. Incidents of the university's first years could not do other than impress the fact of Catholic separatism upon Keane. Even before he received negative reactions to his Dudleian lecture, he had been compelled to retract his acceptance of an invitation to address a Catholic group at Cornell University because to the ordinary, Bishop McQuaid, his appearance there would have been "equivalent to an

---

decades the institution had tempered this objective. Keane, who lectured on "The Obviousness of Christianity," was criticized by Catholics for appearing in his prelatial robes and for imparting his episcopal blessing upon the non-Catholic audience.

24. Thomas O'Gorman Papers, William J. Kerby to Edward Kerby, Louvain, Apr. 9, 1897.

25. Robert C. Ayers, "The Americanists and Franz Xaver Kraus: An Historical Analysis of an International Liberal Catholic Combination, 1897–1898" (unpublished dissertation, Syracuse University, 1982), 7.

26. Soderini, *op. cit.*, 115. The most comprehensive survey of the domestic conserva-tive–liberal polarization is presented in Robert D. Cross, *The Emergence of Liberal Catholi-cism in America* (Cambridge: Harvard University Press, 1958).

27. Curran, *op. cit.*, 114.

approval of membership in said university by Catholics."[28] McQuaid's communication was hardly civil, but his position was not singular. Seventeen years afterward, a priest who had been appointed to minister to the Catholic students at Harvard confided to Keane's second successor that in his own mind he was still "sailing between Scylla and Charybdis, and would much prefer to put back to port" were it not that he was "acting with the fullest approval" of his archbishop.[29]

All the while, the walls of the intellectual ghetto were being not just reinforced but heightened by curial policies in Rome. A new instrumentality—a normal one in papal diplomacy—became available when the apostolic delegation to the United States was established, on January 14, 1893. Archbishop Satolli, the first incumbent, was the Thomistic philosopher who had been consulted by Keane on the foundation of the university and who had been the pope's representative on the occasion of its opening. Pace, who had studied under Satolli, writing from Europe at the time, had called him "about the best man they could send" and had looked forward enough to predict that "certainly *Cardinal* Satolli, either in the Propaganda or in the Congregation of Studies, will wield a mighty influence for, or against, the Catholic University."[30] Returning to the United States as a special delegate for several months in 1892 before the establishment of the delegation was announced, and in the face of general American episcopal opposition to its establishment at all, he resided in Caldwell Hall, lectured on Thomistic philosophy, utilized the advice of the professors, decided cases—notably in the "school controversy" and in the reconciliation of the New York pastor Edward McGlynn—in ways that pleased the "Americanizers" and the "liberals," and became the first honorary member of the faculty.[31] But by 1895 he had moved to the support of the conservatives and the Germans in current American controversies, and his influence in Rome after his elevation to the cardinalate and his return there in 1896 was consistently opposed to what initially he had seemed to support.[32]

28. OR, McQuaid to Keane, Rochester, Feb. 25, 1890.
29. *Ibid.*, John J. Farrell to O'Connell, Cambridge, Jan. 16, 1907.
30. *Ibid.*, Pace to Keane, Leipzig, Oct. 4, 1889.
31. BT, mm, Apr. 11, 1893, approving a recommendation of the faculty of sacred sciences, in *AR* (1892–93), 30.
32. Soon after Satolli's arrival on the campus, Schroeder was reporting to Corrigan his "disturbingly sympathetic attitude toward Ireland and his friends." AANY, Schroeder to Corrigan, Washington, Oct. 15, 1892, in "Private Record," 283, quoted in Curran, *op. cit.*, 370. Richards at Georgetown first believed Satolli to be "entirely under the control and influence of the clique who seem to have brought him over to accomplish their own ends" (AGU, Rector's letterbook, Richards to Brandi, Washington, Jan. 9, 1893), but after a dinner conversation with the delegate surmised that "if he were freed from the influences which surround him at present, he would be perfectly sound in two weeks" (*ibid.*, Richards to Thomas J. Campbell, S.J., Washington, Feb. 26, 1893).

Caldwell Hall, the university's first building, opened in 1889 as Divinity Hall to provide administrative offices, classrooms for the faculty of sacred sciences, and housing for faculty and students. It was referred to as Caldwell Hall, its present name, as early as 1898.

Much as American institutions were admired in some quarters in Rome, and much as the pope's personal interest in the university was evident, curial officials found it difficult to understand that American liberalism, unlike what the Church was fighting in Europe, "was carried by a much more positive and religious attitude" and "was full of optimism, based upon religious faith."[33] They tended to be extremely fearful that the claims of the one true faith were being compromised. Early in a series of decisions and proclamations that revealed their triumphs was a reaction to Catholic participation in the Parliament of Religions held in connection with the World's Columbian Exposition in Chicago during 1893. Keane had been cast in the role of initiator because, after preliminary approaches to him by the organizers, he had asked the archbishops of the country, "Can the Catholic Church afford not to be there?"[34] The archbishops had appointed him to represent them in the preparatory work, but Roman vigilance, alert to agitation for a similar

33. Soderini, *op. cit.*, 2.
34. AAB, Gibbons Papers, 90-P-6, Keane to the Most Reverend the Board of Archbishops of the United States, Washington, Nov. 12, 1892 (italics omitted).

gathering in France, had led Satolli to suggest and the pope to advise that henceforth Catholics should "hold their assemblies apart."[35]

By this time, "Americanizers" such as Keane had had some cause for mild disappointment in the tone of an apostolic letter, *Longinqua oceani*, addressed by the Holy Father to the bishops of the United States on January 6, 1895. Its principal burden was to leave no doubt as to the papal intent with respect to the apostolic delegation. The university, one of whose professors had been involved in the drafting, was strongly supported. But it was made clear also that the successful separation of church and state in the country should not be taken as an ideal for the Church universally.[36] Then a few months later, Denis O'Connell, prominent "Americanist" who had been the rector of the North American College in Rome for ten years, was asked to resign from his strategic post.[37] He had served in that capacity as the agent for many American bishops, especially for the "liberal" wing, and three years before had been Satolli's guide in the United States. In little more than a year, Keane also was to be relieved of his office.

Satolli, who had become prefect of the congregation of studies, was reported to have regarded Keane as "without a deep philosophical training and education."[38] He had remarked acidly after an address that Keane had delivered before Unitarians that it contained "nothing which

35. Leo XIII to Satolli, Rome, Sept. 18, 1895, quoted in Zwierlein, *Life and Letters*, III, 238. Satolli's request of Aug. 12, 1895, is cited by Soderini, *op. cit.* See James F. Cleary, "Catholic Participation in the World's Parliament of Religions, Chicago, 1893," *CHR*, LV (Jan., 1970), 585–609. Although praising Keane's handling of the situation, Satolli criticized Catholic participation from the beginning because the president was a Protestant, all sorts of religious errors were heard, and bishops feared that religious indifferentism might be a result. APF, N.S., Rubric 5, 1894, XXXI, fol. 89–90, Satolli to Cardinal Mieceslaus Ledochowski, Washington, Oct. 6, 1893 (in Italian). Spalding's impression that Catholic participation had favorable consequences was mentioned by Corrigan, *ibid.*, Rubric 153, 1895, LXXIV, fol. 524–25, Corrigan to Ledochowski, New York, Dec. 22, 1893.

36. ASS, XXVII (1894–95), 387–99 (in Latin), translated in John J. Wynne, S.J., *The Great Encyclical Letters of Pope Leo XIII* (New York: Benziger Bros., 1903), 320–25. See Ellis, *Gibbons*, I, 647–48. Thomas O'Gorman, professor of church history from 1890 to 1895, prepared notes for Pope Leo XIII while in Rome during the summer of 1894.

37. Barry, *op. cit.*, 19, and Gerald P. Fogarty, S.J., *The Vatican and the Americanist Crisis: Denis J. O'Connell, American Agent in Rome, 1885–1903* (Rome: Universita Gregoriana Editrice, 1974), 251–56. At Georgetown, Father Richards, son of a convert Episcopal clergyman, had taken note of the Americanist agitation and had remarked slyly, with pride in his own lineage, "I have long been thinking of joining the Sons of the American Revolution. It would be a quiet card against the foreign-born Americanizers." AGU, Rector's letterbook, Richards to Campbell, Georgetown, Apr. 17, 1893.

38. *Washington Post*, Oct. 6, 1896. According to a companion who was disgruntled with the university, Satolli, listening to Keane discuss philosophy before an audience in New Orleans, "was not able to prevent a show of impatience and resentment" and "chose to leave the platform quietly under pretext of the advanced hour." Colman J. Barry, O.S.B. (ed.), "Tour of His Eminence Cardinal Francesco Satolli, Pro-Apostolic Delegate,

any non-Catholic might not have said."[39] Archbishop Patrick Riordan of San Francisco, when inquiring of Satolli as to the reason for Keane's dismissal, was told that his speeches were contrary to the teaching of the Syllabus of Errors.[40] Spalding, finding "a more disgusting state of things than our ecclesiastical situation" to be "hardly conceivable," reported that the impression in Rome was that the pope had given "a death blow to the University," and he avowed a complete loss of patience with Keane's reaction, remarking, "If the Pope had him down on all fours kicking him, each time he lifted his foot, the enthusiastic bishop would shout;—see how the Holy Father honors me."[41]

These adversities were soon to be dwarfed by world-wide theological controversies that necessarily had their effects upon the university. First there appeared, in 1899, precipitated by a French translation and adaptation of Walter Elliot's life of Isaac Hecker and ensuing exchanges, a papal encyclical or letter to the universal church, *Testem benevolentiae*, condemning a vaguely defined "Americanism."[42] In the wake of the dismissals of O'Connell and Keane, the document was hardly necessary to halt within the United States the advance of any "incipient ecclesiology" that might have exalted American Catholicism as "a paradigm for the future of the Universal Church."[43] European manifestations were of concern, however, and a little more than a year after the encyclical appeared, Archbishop Ireland could fend off a questioner by saying that the pope had told him jocularly that it had "no application except in a few dioceses in France."[44]

---

through the United States (of the North) from 12 February to 13 March 1896," *HRS*, XLIII (1955), 46. Soderini in Rome thought that the action was taken "because of a certain lack of firmness of character and for not having a degree." *Op. cit.*, Notes, 7. The new rector of the North American College, William Henry O'Connell, for whom Satolli was a powerful ally, attributed Keane's problems to his "exuberant nature" and a faulty "knowledge of fundamental theology and philosophy" that revealed "his lack of thorough training in the seminary." To an unidentified bishop, Rome, Dec. 20, 1896, quoted in Robert A. O'Leary, "William Henry Cardinal O'Connell: A Social and Intellectual Biography" (unpublished doctoral dissertation, Tufts University, 1980), 55.

39. Richards, *op. cit.*, 90.

40. AANY, "Private Record," 460, citing James Connolly, secretary to Archbishop Corrigan, as source, quoted in Curran, *op. cit.*, 469.

41. AUND, Hudson Papers, Spalding to Hudson, Peoria, Dec. 6, 1896.

42. See Thomas T. McAvoy, C.S.C., *The Great Crisis in American Catholic History, 1895–1900* (Chicago: Henry Regnery, 1957); Ayers, *op. cit.*; Ellis, *Gibbons*, II, Chap. XVI; and Fogarty, *Vatican and Americanist Crisis, passim*, and *The Vatican and the American Hierarchy, 1870–1965* (Stuttgart: Anton Hieresmann, 1982), Chaps. VI–VII. For the Latin text, *ASS*, XXXI (1888–99), 470–79, and sympathetic commentaries, Condé B. Pallen, *CE*, XIV, 537–38, and Joseph C. Fenton, "The Teachings of the *Testem Benevolentiae*," *AER*, LXXIX (Aug., 1953), 124–33.

43. Dease, *op. cit.*, 1.

44. Ireland to Maria Longworth Storer, Rome, Aug. 5, 1900, in Maria Longworth Storer, *In Memoriam Bellamy Storer* (Boston: privately printed, 1923), 46.

Even before *Testem benevolentiae*, the Roman curia had made clear how skeptically it regarded not only the Americanist ecclesiological tendencies but also the current interest in scientific progress. Father John Zahm, C.S.C., a friend of the university from the beginning who had risen to high office in his congregation, found that those whom he liked to call "the refractories" had obtained a decree prohibiting the reading of his book, *Evolution and Dogma* (Chicago: D. H. McBride, 1896). Although papal intervention prevented publication of the decree, Corrigan in New York reportedly told his seminarians "that he had positive information that Dr. Zahm would soon be condemned."[45]

The climax of the several Roman developments took the form of an encyclical issued in 1907 by Leo's successor, St. Pius X, to condemn the theological modernism that had gained a foothold in Europe.[46] After the new pope's election, the noted Harvard philosopher Josiah Royce had speculated that he would "undertake to bring to a pause the . . . tendencies towards a reform of Catholic philosophy, and towards an era of good feeling between Catholic and non-Catholic science and scholarship" that had been in evidence.[47] The university's rector, the third by then, was O'Connell. His apparent change of course had restored him to Satolli's favor but had disappointed the faculty soon after his appointment to the university. There was little he could do but call "the attention of the Senate to the Syllabus and the encyclical," adding that "naturally these two documents shall henceforth constitute a norm in this University."[48] In any case, there was no widespread modernism in the United States, even if Americanism had been perceived in Rome as an element in the modernist movement, as the encyclical itself indicated.[49]

45. ADR, O'Connell Papers, Zahm to O'Connell, Notre Dame, Mar. 30, 1899. See also same to same, Sept. 28, 1898; Oct. 20, 1898; and Oct. 31, 1898; Ireland to O'Connell, St. Paul, Oct. 27, 1898; and ASV, FSS, 1903, Rubric 43, fasc. 2, fol. 166, Cardinal Mariano Rampolla to Ireland, Rome, Nov. 26, 1898, with information on suspension of the decree. On Zahm, see R. E. Weber, *NCE*, XIV, 1109.

46. *Pascendi dominici gregis*, ASS, XL (1907), 593–650, trans. in V. A. Yzermans, *All Things in Christ* (Westminster, Md.: Newman Press, 1954), 89–132. See also, Lester Kurtz, *The Politics of Heresy: The Modernist Crisis in Roman Catholicism* (Berkeley: University of California Press, 1986). For a summary, J. F. Heaney, *NCE*, IX, 991–95.

47. Boston *Evening Transcript*, July 29, 1903, quoted by William M. Halsey, *The Survival of American Innocence: Catholicism in an Era of Disillusionment, 1920–1940* (Notre Dame: University of Notre Dame Press, 1980), 141.

48. AS, mm, Nov. 12, 1907. On Jan. 22, 1908, the senate was informed of the acknowledgement by Cardinal Raffaele Merry del Val, papal secretary of state, of Gibbons's formal expression of the university's adhesion to the encyclical teaching. The trustees regarded compliance with the teaching as entirely a matter for the chancellor. BT, mm, May 6, 1908, exh.

49. Hennesey, *American Catholics*, 197, portrays modernism as "contiguous rather than continuous" with Americanism.

Any kind of "liberalism" was suspect, however. Individuals were able to contribute significantly to scientific and social advances, but generally, as has been remarked, "the American Catholic Church lapsed into an intellectual slumber from which it did not awaken until the 1940s."[50] There was a strengthening of hierarchical authority, insistence upon Roman training for clerics thought to have prospects for advancement, and adamant resistance to efforts to develop policies and plans on a national rather than a diocesan scale. Conjecturally, adherence to the encyclical may have cut off "Catholic participation in an evolving process by which many other Americans began to question and criticize the presuppositions of their cultural myths."[51]

In such circumstances, the university had to navigate in narrowed straits. It was hemmed in, beset with internal problems, almost swamped financially, and slowed, of course. Institutionally, however, it was able to hold to its academic ideals and even to provide within the coalescing Catholic subculture important means for the *rapprochement* with scientific and professional developments that the intellectuals among the founders had ardently desired. It was evident to the sympathetic Roman observer that, in spite of occasional lapses in prudence, "the 'liberal' Catholics took up various social and moral tasks with enthusiasm, whereas the 'intransigents' stayed aside, or watched such activities with hostility."[52] Out of what the founders intended, although bishops might withhold their financial support and, along with religious congregations, direct their energies and their funds into multiplying seminaries unwisely, there emerged, as Georgetown's president among others had foreseen that there might, an institution that became "an immense influence in elevating and coordinating Catholic education in the United States."[53]

The Importance of Collegial Governance

This result was facilitated by a collegial form of governance that was uncommon in the United States at the time. The general constitutions and the special constitutions of the school of sacred sciences that Keane had drafted and that, after revision, Pope Leo had approved were to

50. Fogarty, *Vatican and American Hierarchy*, 193, and for a summary of the American manifestations, Ellis, *Catholic Priest in the United States*, especially the essay by Michael V. Gannon, "Before and After Modernism: The Intellectual Isolation of the American Priest," 293–384.

51. Halsey, *op. cit.*, 128.

52. Soderini, *op. cit.*, 109.

53. Richards, *op. cit.*, 86. Comments to this effect from an address by Richards were quoted in "Note to Article on the Catholic University," *op. cit.*, 413–14.

remain in effect until 1926.[54] The principle of self-governance imbedded in them and in successor instruments had been established with the birth of universities as medieval guilds and had been retained through various permutations in the old world. On the American scene, the early colleges had inherited from Oxford and Cambridge the concept of institutional autonomy. Self-governance, however, could give rise to frequent difficulties and sometimes the principle itself was viewed as inconsistent with ecclesiastical order. In the typical American setting, moreover, collegiality had become subordinated to a corporate structure and trustees were learning only gradually that the essential work of universities could not be administered hierarchically because, in contrast to what transpires in most other organizations, "rational organization . . . requires leaving the professor alone rather than coordinating his efforts."[55] The first faculty of The Catholic University of America, European in origin, was steeped in the older tradition and its use of the statutes of European Catholic universities as models allowed it scope.

In the first article of the general constitutions, the institution's mission was stated no less broadly than had been the intent of the founders: "The purpose of the Catholic University of America shall ever be to afford to the youth of our country an opportunity for pursuing higher studies in the most important branches of learning under the inspiration of Catholic truth" (Chap. I, Par. 1). Any ambiguity that might have remained from the bishops' reference to a *seminarium principale* was removed in the provision that "in the beginning the University shall consist of a Faculty of Theology, but in the course of time shall embrace all Faculties pertaining to a complete University" (Chap. I, Par. 6). In other publications, the public was being promised that "the Faculties for the laity" would be opened "within a few years," and informed also that admission to them would be restricted to the graduate level in spite of the inclusion of beginning students in the authorizing papal documents.[56] As the general constitutions enjoined that the courses of study were to be "such in quality and grade as befit a real University" (Chap. VIII, Par. 1), the vice rector, with pride shared by others, could emphasize that "the average grade of knowledge demanded for entering

54. *Constitutiones Catholicae Universitatis Americae a Sancta Sede Approbatae cum Documentis Annexis* (Rome: Sacra Congregatione Propaganda Fide, 1889). Quotations are from the official translation previously cited.

55. Henry L. Mason, *College and University Government; A Handbook of Principle and Practice* (New Orleans: Tulane University, 1972), 1. See pp. 1–6 for a brief elaboration of the concepts and distinctions that have been introduced.

56. *The Catholic University of America. Official Announcements. September, 1889*; also, *CUB*, XI (Apr., 1905), 268–69.

the university is above that which is exacted at most of the European centers, unless we except Louvain and some of the German Universities."[57]

The declaration that the university should "always be under the government of the Bishops" (Chap. I, Par. 3) gave effect to the corporate commitment made at Baltimore in 1884, to the name given to the institution, and to the pertinent provision of the apostolic brief of April 10, 1887. "Under the supreme authority of the Apostolic See," to be represented by the chancellor in the conferral of degrees and in the annual approval of courses and examinations (Chap. III), to the bishops was given "full jurisdiction in those things which pertain to laws of discipline and to the method and order of studies" (Chap. II, Par. 1). As the original donor had provided, the university was never to "become subject to the authority of any order or particular institute" (Chap. I, Par. 7); the pope himself had insisted that the university should be conducted by the bishops. So was it to remain, in Gibbons's words, the "sacred trust"[58] of the episcopate, even if, in the course of its first century, other Catholic institutions would open their own graduate schools.

Episcopal authority was expressly delegated to a board of trustees to consist of "Bishops and others elected to such office in a Plenary Council or in a like assembly of Bishops," although in any interim between such meetings the board itself was empowered "to fill vacancies occurring among its members, by the appointment of other Bishops or prudent men, or also, if it deem it expedient, to increase its membership" (Chap. II, Par. 2). In this respect, probably because the board membership was expected to be overwhelmingly episcopal, attention seems not to have been given to divergences between the civil and pontifical founding documents or to problems that might have been inherent in the delegation of authority itself. The selection of the first board of seventeen members, which had obtained civil incorporation, had been conducted in the manner prescribed and this board had legal authority and responsibility. In practice, it became self-perpetuating from the time that the first vacancies occurred.[59] The difficulties in its composition that were soon presented were far from insuperable but they were forerunners of deeper conflicts.

The issue that was the first to arise was in the ecclesial rather than

---

57. Philip J. Garrigan, "Present Aspect of the Catholic University," *AER,* I (Aug., 1889), 292.

58. *Op. cit.,* II, 193.

59. OVR, George Dougherty to John G. Bowman, Washington, Sept. 11, 1907.

the civil order and concerned the number of laymen to be appointed to the board. Soon this was fixed at four.[60] The maintenance and increase of lay support was of obvious concern, but lay membership in the board was to remain numerically minimal until 1968. Legal questions were raised when Keane proposed that the board should be enlarged to include all the archbishops of the country—to mobilize ecclesiastical support— and also representatives of the disciplines being taught in the university. The change would have been allowed by the general constitutions but it was deemed by counsel to be inconsistent with the certificate of incorporation. The archbishops were then accorded status as an advisory body. Ten years later, after the adoption of bylaws for its conduct that were considered to give it the opportunity it had sought, the board, instead of extending membership to all archbishops, increased the number of trustees from seventeen to twenty-five.[61] The bylaws, in fact, were so restricted that when a faculty committee resorted to them in seeking to resolve questions of the rector's authority, it found that "the information contained therein is very meagre."[62] And in subsequent years it took the prodding of the founding donor to bring the university to comply with a simple legal requirement for the filing of annual corporate reports to the District of Columbia.[63]

More important by far, constitutionally and functionally, were the effects upon the board of the decentralized system of diocesan governance in the Church. Keane's biographer has noted that the members "were so preoccupied with the responsibilities of their own dioceses that they had little time to give to the business of a university."[64] Keane himself knew that the problem was deeper and he wrote frankly to the board that the necessary success in fund-raising would "largely depend upon the friendly and active encouragement of the local authorities," acknowledging as would the forthright among all his successors that "more than once has a lack of such encouragement been alleged as an argument or as a pretence against appeals in behalf of the University."[65]

60. BT, mm, May 24, 1888, and Oct. 1, 1895.

61. *Ibid.*, Apr. 4, 1894, Oct. 1, 1895, Nov. 8–9, 1905, and Apr. 25, 1906; also, OR, George E. Hamilton to Keane, Washington, Aug. 8, 1895, and Hamilton to Conaty, Washington, Nov. 24, 1897. A prominent archbishop later complained, "I often wondered what in the world is meant by the statement in the Catholic Directory that 'all the Archbishops of U.S. are ipso facto members of the *Advisory* Board of the University.' And yet we know absolutely nothing of what is doing or needed at the University." Hyvernat Papers, Messmer to Hyvernat, Milwaukee, Dec. 11, 1905.

62. BT, mm, May 3, 1905, exh., John J. Griffin to Camillus P. Maes, Washington, Jan. 16, 1905. The bylaws were approved on Nov. 11, 1899. A second edition was printed by the Church News Publishing Company of Washington in 1900.

63. *Ibid.*, Apr. 25, 1906.

64. Ahern, *Life*, 104.

65. AR (1892–93), 7.

As will be seen, this inherent problem, aggravated by the contemporary cleavages in the sponsoring body, was sapping the will to give the support to the fledgling institution that, in accord with American concepts of trusteeship, was the board's responsibility.

The board was organized effectively for its regular work through the close working relationships that Keane maintained with it, in part, no doubt, because he had participated in the university project almost from the beginning.[66] Matters were considered by three standing committees, at first on studies, discipline, and finance, later through the combination of the first two and the addition of a committee on organization. An executive committee of five members was authorized in 1895.[67] Each committee maintained liaison with appropriate officers of the small institution and reported in such a manner as to allow a substantial part of each board meeting to be devoted to discussion of its findings. Keane assumed a vigorous role in these meetings and wrote frankly in his published annual reports. He had the advantage of relations with Gibbons—who was both chancellor and, as senior prelate, chairman of the board—that were the product of genuine friendship as well as of frequent association. Although he had been so honest with his friend as to confront him with Roman perceptions of him as "uncertain and vacillating" when the fate of the university project had been in question,[68] he had never had cause to doubt Gibbons' support, and, on the occasion of Keane's dismissal, Gibbons was quoted as saying, "I am a hard man to move, but today I am moved with the most profound sorrow I have ever felt in a long life full of sorrow."[69]

The action of the Holy See in removing Keane was an unexpected manifestation of its "supreme authority." Although the board was unanimous in retaining Keane in the capacity of trustee, an attempt made at the time to express at least "its regret, that because of the great commotion caused in this country, such action had not been communicated through the Board," was not advanced when it became clear that not all members would support it.[70] The papal letter informing Keane that, his term of office not being fixed constitutionally, it seemed best to revert to the ecclesiastical custom of limited terms indicated the course to be followed in the future.[71] Until 1968, in fact, Keane's successors were appointed for definite terms, specified at first as six and later as

66. BT, mm, July 23, 1890.
67. *Ibid.*, Oct. 1, 1895.
68. AAB, Gibbons Papers, 82-J-4, Keane to Gibbons, Rome, Dec. 29, 1886.
69. New York *Irish World*, Oct. 10, 1896.
70. BT, mm, Oct. 21, 1896.
71. Reprinted in *CUB*, II (Oct. 1896), 583 and elsewhere.

five years, without prejudice to their reappointment.[72] In the appointments and reappointments, in spite of the provision of the general constitutions that the rector was to be "elected by the Board of Trustees and approved by the Holy See" (Chap. IV, Par. 1), the submission of a *terna* of three names in order of preference for papal appointment was sometimes insisted upon.

When Keane left office immediately upon notification of his dismissal, he protested only that he "was always conscious that my best was far from being up to the requirements of the case,"[73] and in the California home of his friend and benefactor, Myles Poore O'Connor, he set down his "Chronicles" of the institution he had served. The priest students, meanwhile, declared that they were "desolate from the loss of a father guide and ever-gracious and kind friend."[74] A year later the *Washington Post*, reporting a testimonial dinner that was attended by a majority of President William McKinley's cabinet, observed that in Washington Keane had become "endeared to all classes through his Christian character, his broad and intelligent mind, and, above all, his intense patriotism."[75]

Even if Keane had been less identified with such leaders in the hierarchy as Gibbons and Ireland, the duties of his office would have placed him in the midst of every storm affecting the university. The constitutions required the rector to be a priest and a doctor of sacred theology. His duty internally was all-encompassing: "to govern the University according to the Constitutions and the rulings laid down by the Board of Trustees" (Chap. IV, Par. 2). To enable him to discharge this duty, he was made a member of the board *ex officio* and the presiding officer of the academic senate and, if he chose, of all faculty and other university meetings. All enactments of university bodies except those of the board were subject to his approval, all appointments except those reserved to the board were his to make (Pars. 3, 4). How these broad powers were to be exercised, to the satisfaction of the board on the one hand and the faculty on the other, was of decisive importance.

Keane seldom if ever portrayed his problems as constitutional in character. He carried his authority easily. The tone that he set was that of a ready champion of the leading founders, optimistically maintaining that "such a vocation as our country evidently has among the nations

72. BT, mm, Oct. 25, 1896, approving six-year term with unlimited eligibility for reelection.
73. OR, Keane to Gibbons, San Jose, Nov. 5, 1896.
74. BT, mm, Oct. 21, 1896, exh.
75. Oct. 14, 1897.

of the earth can be reached in no other way than by intellectual pre-eminence." The faculty was bound to be pleased with his conviction that, although the Germans might have gone too far in the matter, "more freedom than is usually accorded to professors, even in institutions which aim at occupying the highest rank, is assuredly necessary for the formation of specialists and great scholars."[76] Those on the campus would have been even more pleased, some years later, if they had known that as an archbishop he was warning his successor at the university against a board committee's tendency "to make economy and retrench-ment the permanent and almost exclusive consideration to be had in view," when such criteria could be applicable only to the extent that they were "consistent with what all proprieties demand of the University as a University."[77] Two years later he complained to the man who was to be the third rector that the university was "a case of arrested development," in the hands of men whose "*primary* concern" was "fi-nancial economy."[78]

Administration required few subordinate offices during the early years. The general constitutions made provision for two (Chap. V). One officer, the vice rector, was charged with general management and supervision of the plant and internal finances. He had to report the state of the latter to the academic senate every three months and to the board at least annually. The board, through the treasurer, who was one of its members, retained responsibility for the general funds of the university. The vice rector was to be a priest and a doctor of sacred theology who would be selected by the rector in consultation with the senate and confirmed by the board. Garrigan, whom Keane had selected in 1888 and whom he later described as "the university's sheet-anchor" for his "solid, steady, faithful, self-sacrificing devotedness,"[79] remained in the position until he was named to a see within Keane's ecclesiastical province at the end of Conaty's term.

After 1902, during the O'Connell administration, the office was filled in only one year, 1905–6, when Charles P. Grannan, a scripture scholar, agreed to the senate's proviso that his acceptance of the position would carry with it "no increase in salary and no release from class duties."[80] About the same time, by amending its bylaws, the board relieved the office of the duty of financial reporting and, agreeing to allow the

76. "The University of Strassburg," CW, XLVI (Feb., 1888), 646, 649.
77. OR, Keane to Conaty, Dubuque, Oct. 29, 1900.
78. ADR, O'Connell Papers, Keane to O'Connell, Dubuque, Sept. 26, 1902.
79. OR, Keane to Garrigan, Rome, May 24, 1898.
80. AS, mm, May 3, 1905.

treasurer to select his own assistant, appointed as assistant treasurer George Dougherty, a priest of the archdiocese of Baltimore,[81] who was O'Connell's secretary and chief assistant, and who became vice rector under O'Connell's successor.

The other office of central administration, that of general secretary, was not filled by Keane. Records were kept by a registrar. As the faculty grew, Keane's successor presented to the board the senate's recommendation that its secretary, Daniel W. Shea, professor of physics, should be appointed. The recommendation was approved.[82] As general secretary from 1898 until 1907, he retained all his other duties in the university.

The principal instrument of collegiality was the academic senate, established by the general constitutions (Chap. VI) long before bodies of the type became "the decisive institution-wide agent of faculty participation" in American institutions of higher education.[83] The provisions were broad and somewhat vague, except that the membership was to consist of "the Rector as presiding officer, the Vice Rector, the General Secretary, the Presidents of the Colleges [*i.e.*, the residential halls] . . . the Deans of the different Faculties, and besides of two Professors from each Faculty" who would retire from their biennial terms in alternate years (Par. 1). Special invitations were extended initially to Pohle as "sole representative of our future Faculty of Philosophy" and to Hewit, as superior of the Paulist house.[84] Keane, recalling that "all were eager to put things in the best shape," noted that "as the organization of our work had to be studied and regulated in all its details, the meetings of the Senate were not only monthly, as required by law, but almost weekly throughout the year."[85] The minutes of the body for these early years, unfortunately, seem to have been lost.[86]

Keane informed the board that at its first meeting the senate had unanimously adopted three principles that were considered to embody the intentions of the American hierarchy and to be the foundation and criteria for judgment of the university's work:

First, was laid down the paramount principle that the teaching of the University should be faithfully Catholic, conformed in all things to the creed of the Church and the decisions of the Holy See.

81. BT, mm, May 3, 1905.
82. *Ibid.*, Oct. 14, 1898.
83. Mason, *op. cit.*, 70.
84. AR (1889–90), 1–2.
85. "Chronicles," 45.
86. AS, mm, Nov. 2, 1917.

Secondly, it was decreed with no less heartiness that the spirit and action of the University must be thoroughly American, cordially in harmony with our country's institutions.

Thirdly, it was emphatically agreed that, in all the teaching of the Professors, and all the moulding of the students, regard must be had always to the actual needs of our age and country, so that the character and work of the University may not only embody the wisdom of the past, but be eminently adapted to the intellectual requirements of the present.[87]

The senate gave attention to almost every aspect of university life, but especially to the admission of students, faculty appointments and salaries, confirmation of committee appointments and election results, appointments of fellows, copy for official announcements, financial reports, and the like. Before ten years were completed, there were demands for digests of the enactments.[88] By this time Keane's successors were discovering that, even in a small institution, "to handle a senate in the non-hierarchical milieu of the university is a far more challenging task for an administrator than to sit on top of a hierarchical structure and merely tend to the chains of command."[89] That not all the faculty had patience with the system was revealed in a commentary written by the dean of the school of the social sciences (soon to be founding dean of the school of law) during 1897 and early 1898 and later given to the rector urging "that progress in the sound development of the University is impossible unless its lawful Head and Leader exercises his constitutional authority and is loyally supported by all the other members of the institution."[90] Although the second rector, Conaty, always maintained the dignity of his office even when vexed by Keane's precedents, the third, O'Connell, was to come into disruptive conflict with the senate and, winning a victory in the board, to realize nevertheless that he could not regain standing on the campus. After 1895, of course, the rectors were dealing with more than the single faculty with which the university had begun.

The Organization of the First Faculty

The academic distinctions and procedures prescribed by the general constitutions were American adaptations of European practices. There

87. AR (1889–90), 2.
88. AS, mm, Oct. 10, 1899, record that the general secretary and secretary of the senate would prepare such a digest; on Dec. 12, 1899, a committee was appointed to reconsider the enactments and codify those continuing in force; on Feb. 10, 1903, a digest was ordered to be submitted in proof to each member; by Oct. 10, 1905, a board committee was requesting "that a continuous text of all the legislation of the senate and faculties be prepared for presentation" to it.
89. Mason, *op. cit.*, 71.
90. OR, William C. Robinson to O'Connell, Laconia, N.H., Aug. 3, 1904. Discontent

were provisions for three academic ranks (Chap. VII, Pars. 5–8). To the board was reserved appointment to full professorial rank, the occupants of which are to this day accorded the European title, uncommon in the United States, of ordinary professor. Previous consultation was required, however, by the board of the academic senate and by the latter body of the cognizant faculty. Associate professors might be appointed by the senate after consultation with the faculty, and instructors might be employed when circumstances required. Time was to bring more differentiation. The deanship, too, originally limited according to European usage (Par. 2), was to become more demanding. Each faculty was empowered to elect its own dean and vice-dean for two-year terms, subject to confirmation by the senate, without restriction upon re-election (Par. 1). Each faculty was empowered also to elect its own secretary (Par. 4).

Somewhat more exacting requirements were specified in the special constitution for the school of sacred sciences which, it was decreed, "in the rank and scope of its teaching should excel all other seminaries and schools" (Chap. I, Par. 1). The ordinary professors were to be clerics "commended by the integrity of their life and their reputation for learning" (Chap. III, Par. 1). Their appointment and removal were made prerogatives of "the Bishops after consultation with the Senate and the Corps of Doctors" (Par. 2), but in practice it was the trustees who exercised the authority. The few lay members of the board apparently deferred readily to the ecclesiastics, especially in matters having theological or ecclesiastical import.[91] A "corps of doctors" peculiar to this faculty included the chancellor, rector, and adjunct teachers "on the condition that they shall never be more numerous than the Ordinary Professors" (Chap. III, Par. 1). It was empowered to elect the dean, subject to the approval of the bishops, as well as the vice-dean and secretary (Par. 2).

When the university opened, the financial support of the faculty seemed to Keane to be assured. He had been able to report concerning

---

with the senate became a principal theme of faculty complaints during the Conaty and O'Connell administrations. See Chap. IV.

91. The board did not approve a proposal to limit voting on religious matters to its ecclesiastical members (BT, mm, Oct. 1, 1895), but earlier, for example, when Eugene Kelly was asked to vote on a proposal for the appointment of St. George Jackson Mivart to the faculty, he responded to Keane, "While I quite appreciate the force of your observations as to the advantage which would accrue to the University from having a gentleman of such prestige among the Faculty, at the same time I do not believe that this is a question on which a layman is fitted to decide." OR, Kelly to Keane, New York, Aug. 7, 1889. On Mivart, a convert who attempted to reconcile science and revelation as understood in his day, see J. W. Gruber, NCE, IX, 984–85, and John D. Root, "The Final Apostasy of St. George Jackson Mivart," CHR, LXXI (Jan., 1985), 1–25.

the founding, "The funds already received for the purpose not only suffice to pay entirely for the ground and the structure, but constitute a capital, safely invested, the income of which suffices to support in *perpetuum* the officials and professors of the Faculty of Theology."[92] Endowment for chairs, which had been discussed at length in the very first meeting of the university committee, had been obtained for five: the Shakespeare Caldwell chair of dogmatic theology and the Elizabeth Breckenridge Caldwell chair of philosophy, given in 1885 to memorialize the parents of the founding donor; the Francis A. Drexel chair of moral theology, endowed in 1888 by the daughters of the deceased prominent member of the original university committee; and the Eugene Kelly chair of ecclesiastical history and Margaret Hughes Kelly chair of holy scripture, established by the trustee in 1889. Within three years there were added, according to the announcements for 1892–93, the Myles Poore O'Connor chair of canon law from the generous friend of Gibbons and Keane who had prospered in California and, although not all the funds had as yet been received, the Patrick Quinn chair of ecclesiastical history, based upon a sizable bequest, and the Thomas Francis Andrews chair of scriptural archaeology, donated by the daughters of a European-educated Norfolk physician.[93]

The professorial chair, which could then be supported from a principal of $50,000, was inherited conceptually from Europe. It was already being transformed to provide the basis for the departmentalization that soon became characteristic of American universities. This development followed logically from the acceptance of research, which entails specialization, as the primary task of the university. Indeed, after six weeks, with only four professors in the single faculty, the senate, in order to provide elective options for the thirty-two students who were first enrolled, "after mature discussion, divided the studies into the four Departments . . . of Dogmatic, Moral, Scriptural, and Historical Studies."[94] Some years later, a faculty committee explained for the benefit of the board that it "treated the Department or 'chair' as the academic unit of the University."[95] Soon, promotion to full professorial rank would be open to more than one member of a department and a single department might be endowed with more than one chair.

All the first professors of the faculty, as already noted, were European

92. "A Statement of the facts . . ."
93. The donors of the Andrews chair may have been persuaded to make their gift by Father William Clarke, S.J. See Richards, *op. cit.*, 87.
94. Keane, "Chronicles," 46.
95. BT, mm, Apr. 25, 1906.

The first faculty. Back row: Hyvernat, Stoddard, Hogan, Keane, and Schroeder. Front row: Bouquillon, Orban, Garrigan, Hewit, Pohle, and Graf.

priests. When they met for the first time, they elected a German, Schroeder, as dean and the Belgian, Bouquillon, as vice-dean.[96] They took seriously what Gibbons was to recall as their "grave obligation of shaping at its inception a work which held in itself the promises and the hopes of religion present and future."[97] Within a few years, unfortunately, although Bishop Becker had long before observed that none could claim "that science is of any special country,"[98] differences about contemporary issues of ecclesiastical policy introduced what some perceived as "the discord which would inevitably arise among such a

96. SSS, *Acta*, Nov. 15, 1889.
97. *Op. cit.*, II, 194.
98. ACQR, I, 250.

heterogeneous class of learned professors of different nationalities."[99] Some historians have found in the early professorial rivalries a significant reason for loss of institutional support.[100]

At the beginning of the second year, there were two new incumbents of chairs, Messmer, who had just returned from Rome, and Thomas O'Gorman, formerly of the archdiocesan seminary in St. Paul, who was expected to begin his course in ecclesiastical history with Pope Boniface VIII and develop "the analogy between the politico-religious problems of that epoch and those of the present day."[101] When Messmer was appointed bishop, Ireland wrote with emphasis to Keane, "You must educate your professors, and then hold on to them—making bishops only of those who are not worth keeping as professors."[102] Only a few years later, however, on Ireland's own insistence, O'Gorman was appointed to the diocese of Sioux Falls, South Dakota, on which occasion, upon his request, he was granted the title doctor emeritus allowed by the constitutions.[103]

Keane, who had early determined "to meet personally those who were to be invited to professor's [sic] chairs,"[104] showed his eagerness to prepare American priests for the faculty. Pace, for example, after being counseled to "pray hard, and *pull every wire*"[105] to obtain his release for the university from the reluctant bishop of St. Augustine, was working with Mercier at Louvain and especially with Wilhelm Wundt, the pioneer experimental psychologist, at Leipzig to prepare himself for appointment to the faculty in 1891, in anticipation of the establishment of the school of philosophy, which occurred in 1895. Even while abroad, he was a prolific source of suggestions for development. Shahan, after beginning in canon law in Rome, was pursuing ecclesiastical history in Berlin, and reflecting to Keane, "I hope that you will be able to base the life of the University on mutual love, and high self-respect, and common devotion to the noblest of causes: so the iron, inferior words of rule, prohibition, etc., with their hints of force, fear, suspicion, will be unknown."[106] Grannan, of the archdiocese of New York, who had been teaching at Mount St. Mary's College, Emmitsburg, Maryland, was studying scripture

99. Coleman, *op. cit.*
100. See McAvoy, *Images of Man*, 405.
101. AR (1889–90), 16.
102. OR, Ireland to Keane, Rome, Apr. 26, 1892.
103. SSS, *Acta*, Mar. 21, 1896. See APF, N.S. XCVII (1896), Rubric 153, fol. 615–16, 633–34, Ireland to Ledochowski, St. Paul, Mar. 18 and Oct. 17, 1895 (in French). On O'Gorman, see Colman Barry, O.S.B., NCE, X, 659–60.
104. BT, mm, Nov. 13, 1888.
105. OR, Keane to Pace, Richmond, Oct. 15, 1887.
106. *Ibid.*, Shahan to Keane, Berlin, Jan. 8, 1890.

at Bonn and Leipzig. Although he did not attend lectures by the Old Catholics, he noted that when a member of the Catholic faculty at Bonn had objected to his attendance at the lectures of the Protestant professors "the other Profs. quietly sat down on him as they recognized the propriety of it in my case."[107] All three began teaching in 1891.

Problems of collegiality came to the fore, first when the initial harmony among the professors was disturbed by their association with the opposing factions in current ecclesiastical politics, and then when questions of proper academic procedure were presented. The first serious division was provoked by the so-called "school controversy" that began late in 1891. Bouquillon, when the *American Catholic Quarterly Review* declined to publish a paper that he had prepared on the subject, followed the advice of Gibbons in presenting in pamphlet form a theoretical analysis of the rights of the state in education, especially with respect to compulsory schooling. He accorded to the state rights that the church had never passed on and that seem unexceptional in the light of subsequent Catholic teaching, but that at the time more American Catholic leaders than not were quite unwilling to recognize. At the heart of the matter was opposition to proposals of Archbishop Ireland for public support of Catholic schools in Faribault and Stillwater, Minnesota. Corrigan and McQuaid and many American and Roman Jesuits led the opposition. The conservative–liberal, German–Irish, and other rivalries intersected to the extent that the controversy was continued even after the Holy See declared that Ireland's plans could not be condemned.[108]

Almost concurrently, the university was blamed again when Archbishop Satolli, his appointment as apostolic delegate still unannounced, used the special authority that had been delegated to him to reinstate the excommunicated New York pastor, Edward McGlynn, who was a disciple of Henry George. Satolli acted on the advice of four professors who were unable to find anything contrary to Catholic belief in McGlynn's defense of his position. Archbishop Corrigan, offended, reported "confidential" (but erroneous) information that McGlynn "would be made a Professor in the University" and that many were "beginning to see a 'conspiracy' in this whole movement."[109]

107. *Ibid.*, Grannan to Keane, Bonn, Oct. 30, 1890.

108. For the historical account, see Daniel F. Reilly, O.P., *The School Controversy (1891–1893)* (Washington: The Catholic University of America Press, 1943). Bouquillon's pamphlet, the ostensible object of controversy, was entitled *Education: To Whom Does It Belong?* (Baltimore: John Murphy, 1891). On Ireland, see Marvin R. O'Connell, *John Ireland and the American Catholic Church* (St. Paul: Minnesota Historical Society Press, 1989).

109. Corrigan to McQuaid, New York, Dec. 28, 1892, in Zwierlein, *Letters of Corrigan*, 138–39. On the McGlynn affair, see Fogarty, *Vatican and American Hierarchy*, Chap. IV.

Schroeder became a focal issue in the faculty. He thought that Bouquillon, who had disclaimed any other than a theoretical objective, was insensitive to the realities of the school controversy.[110] On his part, Schroeder saw events through the eyes of German-Americans who resented the preponderantly Irish spokesmen for liberals in the hierarchy. His teaching came under criticism to the extent that the board's committee on studies directed him to treat subjects more properly belonging to the field of dogmatic theology for which he had been appointed than to ecclesiology, which seemed to interest him more.[111] Complaints to Rome could be suspected when the apostolic delegate, still friendly but acting in response to a curial request that he attributed to enemies of the institution, had to ask each professor to give an exposition of his teaching from the opening of the university.[112] Pohle soon declared that the "unfortunate dispute" was his reason for returning to Germany since the antagonism toward Schroeder had destroyed "the once so delightful atmosphere of our community life."[113] Schroeder did not hesitate to protest to Rome that, with the knowledge of Keane, several professors were teaching modernist heresy.[114] The Americanists campaigned systematically for his dismissal.[115] Eventually a divided board concluded that his usefulness had come to an end. Assisted by papal intervention, he was able to postpone resignation until the end of December, 1897, after the Prussian government had announced his appointment to the Catholic Academy of Münster.[116]

Procedural questions arose in the case of Georges Peries, a French

110. AUND, Archdiocese of Philadelphia Papers, Schroeder to Heuser, Washington, Feb. 10, 1892 (in German).

111. BT, mm, Apr. 27, 1892.

112. ASV, DA, XVII, No. 2, fol. 3, Rampolla to Satolli, Rome, July 10, 1893, conveys the Holy Father's request for an accurate report on the university. See OR, Keane to Bouquillon, Aug. 11, 1893; SSS, *Acta*, Nov. 5, 1893.

113. OR, Pohle to Ryan, Washington, Mar. 26, 1894 (printed). Archbishop Ryan was chairman of the cognizant trustee committee.

114. ASV, FSS, Rubric 43 (1903), fasc. 2, fol. 78–95, Schroeder to Rampolla, Washington, June 18, 1895, a lengthy account that begins with a dispute over a thesis directed by Grannan and reviews the positions of all the members of the faculty and of some individual trustees.

115. *Ibid.*, fasc. 1, fol. 189–90, and fasc. 2, folios 1–151, contain lengthy letters to Rampolla from Gibbons, Ireland, Keane, and John Zahm, C.S.C., as well as notarized allegations of Schroeder's misconduct in Washington saloons that were presented by O'Connell. In defense of Schroeder, the apostolic delegate, Archbishop Sebastian Martinelli, O.S.A., complained of false accusations, as did Cardinal Andreas Steinhuber, S.J., who reported also attestations of the good accomplished by Schroeder that had been given by Satolli and Propaganda Fide. Ayers, *op. cit.*, 153–55, describes the plans developed by the Americanists at Fribourg in 1897.

116. See Hogan, *op. cit.*, 153–56, for a convenient summary, and OR, Record Group 1-A, Box 3, for documents and clippings, especially from German-American Catholic newspapers.

priest whose three-year appointment in 1893 was not renewed. He maintained that his occupancy of the chair of canon law entitled him to permanent tenure. Returning to Paris after insistent but unsuccessful appeals to the chancellor and the apostolic delegate, he sought his revenge in the pages of *La Verité* and in other ways during the Americanism controversy.[117] In another case, attempting to fill the chair of apologetics after it was vacated by Pohle, the board offered it to Hogan without consulting the faculty—which had recommended Grannan— and the academic senate. In consequence, the offended Hogan returned to his former position as rector of the Boston archdiocesan seminary and was replaced by Francis Louis Dumont, S.S., who had been president of St. Charles College at Catonsville, Maryland. Charles Aiken, who had earned his doctorate at the university, was sent to Europe to prepare for the faculty position.[118]

A similar lapse occurred later during O'Connell's administration when Henry A. Poels, a native of the Netherlands, was appointed an associate professor of the Old Testament without the required consultations.[119] Poels then became the victim of a serious injustice that was chargeable to a deplorable confusion of identity in its beginning and to administrative weakness thereafter. Visiting Rome in 1907, Poels had obtained an audience with the pope to explain a personal dilemma. Unable to accept the decision of the pontifical biblical commission in 1906 that Moses had to be held to be the sole author of the Pentateuch, he was continuing to teach conscientiously only because he thought that he had been directed by the pope to follow a course of action advised by two eminent biblical scholars. But when, in 1908, O'Connell, with Grannan in mind, complained to the pope of a professor who, raising all the difficulties, left students with the impression that they could not be solved, the pope thought that the reference was to Poels and held that termination was in order. O'Connell never cleared up the confusion and neither his successor nor Gibbons took steps to do so. Worse, all, and eventually the board, too, showed themselves timidly compliant in the face of papal and curial measures against modernism. Poels' contract was not renewed.[120]

117. See Ahern, *Catholic University*, 153–56; Curran, *op. cit.*, 468–69. Peries described in *La Verité* a meeting of "the leading men of Washington" at the Carroll Institute "as composed of heretics of all denominations and unbelievers, of ignorant Catholics, low people, and loafers." Coleman, *op. cit.*

118. Ahern, *Catholic University*, 55–56. See Hyvernat Papers, Bouquillon to Hyvernat, Brussels, July 15, 1894, (in French), for a detailed account.

119. OR, Grannan to Board of Trustees, Washington, Apr. 13, 1904.

120. BT, mm, Apr. 6, 1910. ASV, DA, XVII, No. 41, fol. 1–29 contains documents in the case. Poels's account, privately printed in 1910, has been reprinted, *A Vindication*

There were advantages in beginning the new institution with the faculty of sacred sciences because, although the university was indeed as Keane portrayed it, "untrammeled by any traditions of mere routine and red tape," it could use "the experience of the able men composing our Faculty,"[121] who were thoroughly familiar with the established Roman patterns in fields that the sponsors of the university had themselves studied. The divisions of the offerings were conventional and the first courses in each field were surveys on an advanced level. Specialization was manifest, however, in the courses as announced and as later summarized in the annual reports of the dean. First, following a general course, each professor offered courses dealing with selected topics. Bouquillon, for example, followed general lectures in moral theology that he gave during the first academic year with a course during the second that included "law, rights, and obligations in general, natural law and international law under their different aspects, as well as civil law, the object and binding force of which have been examined in connection with taxation, penalties, liberties, etc.; the right of property, its subject, its limit, its basis, its matter, and its inviolability, giving also a vindication of it against Communism."[122] Second, the specialized character of university work was made explicit in the appointment of the scholar in oriental languages, Hyvernat, who recognized that, as far as the founders were concerned, "what exactly the teaching of Oriental Languages meant or implied they surely did not know too well," but who, in trying to make clear to Keane initially that he "needed about ten more years of hard work to achieve a mastery that would put me on a par with the best non Catholic Orientalists," was told that he "could never be specialist enough to suit the need of America."[123] Hyvernat's later work on the organization of Coptic manuscripts for the J. Pierpont Morgan Library, from 1911 until 1925, was to be only the most illustrious of his contributions.

At one of its first meetings, the faculty decided that each professor

---

of My Honor, ed. Frans Neirynck ("Annua Nuntia Lovaniensa," XXV; Leuven: Leuven University Press, 1982). Returning to the Netherlands, Poels was active in Catholic social movements until his death in 1948. During this time, at the suggestion of the dean of the school of social science, the vice rector of the university, then Patrick J. McCormick, who had known Poels personally, was able to offer him an appointment as a research professor, but Poels thought that he could not accept the invitation under war-time conditions. OR, McCormick to Poels, Washington, Mar. 3, 1941 (copy); Poels to McCormick, Lugano, Switzerland, June 3, 1941. For a full discussion of the Poels case, see Gerald P. Fogarty, S.J., *American Catholic Biblical Scholarship: A History from the Early Republic to Vatican II* (San Francisco: Harper & Row, 1989), Chaps. V–VI.

121. "Chronicles," 45.
122. Report of the Dean, in AR (1890–91), 5–6.
123. "Notes on C. U."

should lecture for four hours each week,[124] and soon it was determined
"that three of these should be devoted to the treatment of new matter
and one to a practical review." Then to the lectures were added a
weekly "brief informal disputation" and a monthly "more formal public
disputation" that were intended "for the better training of the students
in scientific disputation and in the use of the Latin tongue, as well as
in acquiring a more perfect mastery of the matters treated in their
classes."[125] The teaching load was considered as heavy "as is consistent
with the exceptional preparation which genuine University requires."[126] By 1896, however, the faculty was notified by the acting
rector that the academic senate had judged that five-hour loads should
be required, with one hour, if desired, devoted to "academy or circle
work" as the seminar was then called.[127]

The seminar, described later by Pace as "simply the application of
laboratory methods to lines of study which have books and documents
for their apparatus,"[128] was emphasized almost from the beginning.
Bouquillon proposed its inauguration in a meeting of the faculty on June
6, 1890[129] and a year later proudly reported that his seminar on suicide
during the second academic year was "the first seminar in moral theology
in any Catholic university anywhere."[130] Several paragraphs in the
annual announcements of courses were devoted to its explanation and
importance, including the aspiration that "this system, so fruitful in
every other field, will, it is hoped, produce like results in Theology, by
training the ecclesiastic to seek the truth and uphold it in a manner
worthy of science and worthy of the Church."[131]

Much of the time of the faculty, especially during the first year, had
to be spent in discussion of requirements for degrees and of the courses,
dissertations, and examinations intended for their pursuit. A student
matriculating for a degree was expected to follow at least two courses,
accepting as obligatory the courses and examinations in his field of
specialization and attending other courses, if so inclined, without re-

124. SSS, *Acta*, Nov. 16, 1889.
125. AR (1889–90), 3, 17.
126. Report of the Dean, AR (1890–91), 4.
127. AS, Records to 1907, Garrigan to Faculty, Nov. 12, 1896. After "academy" and
"seminary," the word "seminar" was voted as the proper "general University expression."
AS, mm, Mar. 25, 1898.
128. "The McMahon Hall of Philosophy," *CUB*, I (Jan., 1895), 58.
129. SSS, *Acta*.
130. OR, "Séminaire de Morale" (in French).
131. *Official Announcements for the Scholastic Year 1892–93*, 12. Keane had assured
Shahan, completing his European studies, that Bouquillon had shown that the seminar
"works well," so that it would not be "a new thing when you establish it in your course."
Shahan Papers, Keane to Shahan, Washington, Mar. 27, 1891.

sponsibility for examination.[132] The final examination was decisive, to the extent that an extern might present himself "on exactly the same conditions"[133] as an enrolled student, provided that he could claim to have followed courses "equivalent to those of the University."[134] Similarly, "no merely honorary degrees" were to be conferred;[135] the degrees doctor of philosophy and doctor of letters granted without examination to Searle and Stoddard respectively in 1896 were "solely in due recognition of distinguished knowledge possessed and work done in the very lines indicated by the degrees conferred."[136] Conaty later declined honorary degrees from other institutions because he did not want to be "in a position to be misunderstood in university circles."[137]

On the same principle, a student matriculating in the faculty of sacred sciences who did not hold the degree of bachelor of sacred theology could sit for examination for this degree at the end of the first year of study following a four-hour written and a one-hour oral examination in the matter required for admission. This degree was conferred upon thirteen successful candidates at the first commencement in 1890. For higher degrees, the Roman pattern of examination on previously selected theses was followed. A candidate for the licentiate was examined orally on fifty theses; a dissertation replaced the written examination. The theses of one candidate in 1895 revealed apologetic concerns with, among other things, positivism, skepticism, agnosticism, utilitarianism, the Inquisition, the Galileo case, and the theories of John Stuart Mill, Herbert Spencer, and August Comte.[138] The licentiate was conferred for the first time in 1891, when there were six candidates. Two years of study after the licentiate, a dissertation contributing to knowledge, and the defense of seventy-five theses in a public examination of six hours were required for the doctorate. The first two candidates to earn this degree, in 1895, were Edmund Dublanchy, S.M., of the Marist house of studies (which had been the home of the Brooks family that gave its name to Brookland), and George L. Lucas of the diocese of Scranton.

Until 1895, of course, virtually the entire academic community,

132. *Ibid.*, 8.
133. *Official Announcements, 1890–91.*
134. OR, Keane to Conaty, Dubuque, Oct. 29, 1900.
135. *Official Announcements, 1890–91.*
136. AR (1895–96), 10.
137. OR, Conaty to C. Gillespie, S.J., Washington, Nov. 9, 1901.
138. The candidate was George V. Leahy of the archdiocese of Boston, whose handwritten "University Recollections" were used in Henry J. Browne, "Pioneer Days at the Catholic University of America," *CER,* XLVIII (Jan.–Feb., 1950), 29–38, 96–103, as were the reminiscences of the only other survivor of the Class of 1895 at the time, Edward Rengel of the diocese of Buffalo.

except for the Paulists and the Marists, resided in Caldwell Hall. The Sulpician seminary routine that was established had the complete sup- port of the hierarchy. As the reputedly liberal Ireland saw it,

The object of the University is to form model priests, and in such piety is as much needed as intellect. We do not want to reproduce in America the levity and tepidity of European universities.[139]

The day from rising at 5:30 a.m. until "lights out" and silence at 10:00 p.m. was scheduled to include spiritual exercises as well as study, meals, and recreation.[140] Keane himself was to report of the students that several "were imbued with the notion that the University should be totally different from a Seminary in regard to rule" and that "some of the Professors rather shared the conviction of the students."[141] The administration and trustees remained firm and students themselves could recognize with respect to a superior like Hogan that they would "not often see his equal in his many sided merit."[142]

Other problems to which attention had to be given included responsibility for temporal as well as spiritual care of the students; the irregularity of the students in leaving before vacations and returning afterwards, for which bishops were often to be blamed; and, after Hogan's departure, his successor's "inability rightly to express himself in the English language."[143] Noting that "many prelates contend that the spiritual training of the students of Divinity is suffering," the board threatened to rescind its agreement with the Sulpicians if the provincial superior would not accede to its request "to remove the present incumbents and to replace them by intelligent and more efficient men, able to interest the young priests in their conferences to form and strengthen their character."[144] Dumont, however, remained in his position. Faculty residents presented more problems that led a board committee to ask if it would not be "a good and desirable thing to have even professors under such mild and priestly control as the Sulpicians exercise."[145] Until 1905, board and room in Caldwell Hall was a benefit added to the salary of a priest professor. Beginning in 1893, the "domestic department" was entrusted to the Sisters of Providence of Covington, Kentucky, who maintained

139. OR, Ireland to Keane, St. Paul, Dec. 7, 1889.

140. *Rules of the Divinity College of the Catholic University of America* (Boston: Cashman, Keating, 1890).

141. "Chronicles," 48–49.

142. Philip J. Garrigan Papers, William J. Kerby to Garrigan, Dubuque, Sept. 17, 1894.

143. BT, mm, Apr. 9, 1902, exh.

144. BT, mm, May 3, 1905.

145. *Ibid.*, Nov. 8, 1905, exh.

all the dining halls of the university until their withdrawal, in 1943 from that for lay students and in 1957 from those of Caldwell and Curley Halls.

The priest students—"all young men of mature character and familiar with the rudiments of the sacred sciences"—were stimulated in their surroundings. One described the courses in theology as devoted only to "the principal and living issues of the sacred science . . . the intention being to stimulate intellectual life, shed new light on old doctrines, and make the hearers not only collectors of theoretical data, but above all accurate, and, so far as may be, original thinkers." The chapel, in which thirteen masses could be celebrated simultaneously, seemed quite extraordinary. "Where in this young republic," the student asked, "will you find anything to be compared with it?" And on pleasant Sunday afternoons, "an average of five thousand persons" reportedly came out to visit the grounds.[146]

The Uniting Academic Values

In short, once the university was opened, within the framework provided by the governing documents and in spite of the ecclesiastical controversies that could only embitter both faculty and students, the formal organization that had been established became the matrix in which a new academic community began to grow. It was small, so small that community virtually was forced upon the members. The boundaries set by the institution, partly physical and partly sociological, placed scholars and students in daily interaction in their pursuit of the advancement and dissemination of knowledge, so that they could come to identify and to nurture their academic and institutional bonds.

At the outset—and not less in all the years since—the values that united the diverse people included high aspirations. These had certainly been evident in the movement for the establishment of the university. Many of the faithful, indeed many within the narrowing influences of the Catholic subculture, had found the idea of a national Catholic university with a papal mandate to be appealing. Support was received from the outside since the university movement in the country was growing.[147] The academic objective, however, was ill-defined, even by the predominantly Irish, Americanizing, liberal wing of the hierarchy on whom leadership depended. Keane and Ireland had paid tribute to

146. Thomas C. McGolrick, "Student Life at the Catholic University," *CW*, LI (June, 1890), 358–59, 362.

147. As Storr, *op. cit.*, 129 remarks, the course of American developments in higher education generally had already produced a "tradition of aspiration and experimentation."

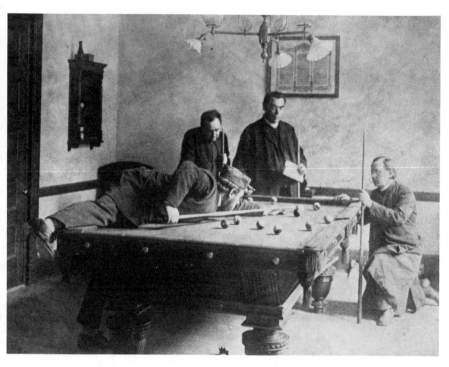

The first faculty at play in the recreation room of Caldwell Hall.

ideals but hardly to solid scholarship when, in reporting on their Roman experience before the university's founding documents were drafted, they had urged the trustees that "in the free field of our new world, the course of higher studies should be so organized that, while the intellectual work of the past should be in no wise neglected, the intellectual needs of the present and the future should be principally and always kept in view."[148] Gibbons, at the commencement exercises of 1896, when the first laymen were among the candidates for degrees, was more than a little premature in expressing gratitude that Catholics at last had an institution "ready to take the brightest college graduate and lead him along the higher paths of scientific investigation."[149]

By a fortunate historical conjunction, however, the aspirations of the leaders, vague as they were, opened them to suggestions from the educational movements that were shaping the modern university. Keane as rector was more than content—he was anxious—to follow the advice of his small band of professors in order to establish what would be

148. BT, mm, Sept. 7, 1887, exh.
149. CUB, II (July, 1896), 451.

recognized as a true university. A generation later, recalling for the current chancellor the pressures upon Keane and the shortcomings of the professors ("some of whom could not understand or speak a word of English"), Hyvernat wrote, "Upon the advice and cooperation of men so manifoldly handicapped did he . . . depend to help him make up for the sins of omission and neglect of the Hierarchy."[150] These academic men, however, had settled convictions rooted in traditions with a long history. Their scholarly interests were parts of themselves that were not likely to be comprehended by laymen, not even by those charged with trusteeship, but were nevertheless resources for mutual understanding and collegial action through which they could protect what they required for their individual specialized work and for the initiation of others in it. What was being done at The Johns Hopkins University and other institutions was proof for them of the vitality of the traditions that they were seeking to implant. They were aware, as others perhaps could not be, of the beginnings of the expansion of knowledge that, a century later, has come to be labeled an explosion. Theirs were the operative organizing values.

Consultation, the key to successful collegial administration, was easy for Keane, especially since his intuitive approach to leadership was reinforced by his consciousness of his own lack of first-hand acquaintance with the university institution. The implications of the favorable beginning in shared governance that he made were to be profound, first of all in shaping institutional aims. Although all would have accepted the traditional view enunciated by Spalding—as by Newman before him, with undergraduates in mind—that "the primary and essential aim" of a university is "to form men, not scholars,"[151] all were agreed that scholarship had to be the means to the intellectual and moral formation that was to be expected from advanced study. Excellence was thus established as a goal and with it a hint toward modernity also. Not only was the purchase of the first typewriter for the rector a sign that the university was "keeping abreast of the times."[152] This was evident more fundamentally in the dedication of the specialists who were the faculty to keeping abreast of developments in their fields and in the university world at large. No intellectual conversion on their part was required for their adherence to the emerging graduate school movement.

Collegiality, of course, is not a synonym for congeniality. Communi-

150. AAB, Michael Joseph Curley Papers, Hyvernat to Curley, Washington, Feb. 3, 1923, *Personal and Confidential.*
151. CUB, V (Oct., 1899), 465.
152. OR, Ireland to Keane, St. Paul, Mar. 3, 1890.

ties, academic or other, are not without tension and conflict. Differences within the hierarchy and the continuing antagonism of powerful prelates to the university were generally known. The so-called "school question," which on the campus became the Schroeder question, alienated many, especially among German Catholics. Spalding became so alarmed that he complained to the pope directly against Ireland, charging that, among many other things, he was making the university "a center of agitation for his ideas" and was thus threatening "the total ruin" of the institution.[153] Messmer, German in his sympathies, went so far as to seek to prevent Pace from lecturing in the Columbian Catholic Summer School conducted in Madison, Wisconsin, on the ground that "whatever each one's private opinion may be, the fact cannot be denied that the Catholic University and its Professors and Rector are not looked upon with favor by many of our Catholics." He more than implied that Pace might advance positions not "in full harmony with the commonly accepted Catholic Science."[154] Yet, as Pace's colleague Shahan pointed out in deploring such attacks, Pace was "perfectly safe in his teaching" and, by virtue of his training and pioneering in experimental psychology, "an orthodox man who can tell us what the enemy is doing, and *au besoin* can refute him in his own tongue and with his own arguments."[155]

Academic freedom in a more precise sense was not an issue during the early years. In 1892, R. W. Shufeldt of the Smithsonian Institution, who offered four of the public lectures that Keane valued so highly, complained that his account of the history of biology and of the prospects for its growth and influence had brought denunciations from students and had been subjected to censorship or curtailment in the Catholic papers of Baltimore and Washington, but he considered the university to be "an institution which promises to be in its methods and aims one of the broadest seats of learning throughout all this broad land."[156] Carroll D. Wright, United States Commissioner of Labor, who was one of the lecturers and later became a part-time teacher in the department of economics until he succeeded Hall at Clark University, reportedly said "that the Catholic University was the only educational institution in the country where he was free, provided he did not touch on theology

153. APF, N. S., Rubric 153, 1895, LXXIV, fol. 278–82, Spalding to Leo XIII, Peoria, Jan. 11, 1893 (in French).
154. Edward A. Pace Papers, Messmer to Pace, Green Bay, Jan. 20, 1896. See also, O'Gorman Papers, Messmer to O'Gorman, Green Bay, Jan. 20 and Feb. 20, 1896.
155. ADR, O'Connell Papers, Shahan to O'Connell, Washington, Feb. 14, 1897.
156. The lectures were reprinted from *The American Field*, XLI (June 30, 1894), 610–12, and XLII (July 7–Aug. 25, 1894), 6–8, 31–33, 55–56, 78–79, 104–5, 128–29, 151–53, 177–78.

or philosophy in the metaphysical sense, to teach what he chose."[157] Echoing what Spalding and Keane had said before him, Charles Bonaparte, distinguished Baltimore lawyer, future trustee, and first secretary of the navy and then attorney general under Theodore Roosevelt, enjoined his audience at the laying of the cornerstone of McMahon Hall to "let it show, so that no man may misread the lesson, that the Church of God need not and does not fear the truth."[158]

It was the failure of the academic community to grow in size that was taken by critics as a portent of doom. During the academic year 1895–96, Keane's final year, there were seven professors and only 115 students. Of the latter, thirty-four were diocesan priests—hardly more than had come to the university at its founding—and forty-five religious; thirty-six were laymen, for whom studies were being offered for the first time.[159] Keane attributed the low enrollment to such factors as "lack of appreciation of the life-long advantages which every earnest and fairly intelligent priest could derive from a couple of years of serious University study and training" and lack of recognition of how the results of such study would compensate the dioceses for the temporary deprivations that they would suffer and, more pointedly, to the deplorable oversight by the bishops of "the fact that the University belongs to them, and that their proprietorship in it ought to make them eager to cooperate for its success."[160] It was not long before he was removed from the scene. It was a long time, however, before enrollment grew substantially, in spite of the expansion of the institution that he initiated.

157. Egan, *Recollections,* 184.
158. *Official Announcements,* 1892–93, 36. For a biographical account, see F. W. O'Brien, *NCE,* II, 657.
159. AR (1895–96), 4–5.
160. AR (1891–92), 4–5.

CHAPTER IV

The Expansion of the University in the Early Decades

The expansion that Keane undertook was only an initial step—although perhaps a bold one—toward the completion of the plan of the founders. At the university's opening, he had declared that it would "begin at the earliest possible day, the organization of . . . a Faculty of Philosophy and Letters" which, like the faculty of sacred sciences then being inaugurated, would have to be established "without debt on the buildings, and with the Professorial Chairs endowed."[1] It was, however, not necessary for him to wait to begin what he called "a sort of 'University Extension,' running parallel with the more serious work of the University,"[2] which had been recommended to him in Rome by a former professor of the Sorbonne.[3]

This was an outreach intended to serve the community at large. Free public lectures were scheduled in the city and sometimes on the campus, "first, to train the students in popular treatment of important philosophical, scientific or historical themes; secondly, to give the public of the city of Washington an opportunity to hear important questions treated from a Catholic standpoint."[4] The talent presented was from both the campus and the city, and the topics in any one year might range, as they did in 1894, from "The Two World-Philosophies" expounded by Keane himself to "Belgian Life and Activities" recounted by a former American commissioner general to the international exposition at Antwerp.

After Keane's departure, the academic senate and its committees discussed these public lectures, their location, their number, and the like, but usually preferred to leave decisions about them "to the Rt.

---

1. *Solemnities*, 98.
2. OR, Keane to W. W. Willoughby, Washington, Nov. 8, 1893.
3. BT, mm, Sept. 7, 1887, exh.
4. AR (1889–90), 10–11.

Rev. Rector and the Advisory Board."[5] In 1899 the senate accepted the proposal of Keane's successor that the regularly enrolled students should be required to follow what were then being called "culture-lectures" as "an offset to specialization and as a practical means of promoting general information among the entire student body as well as utilizing the afternoon hours."[6] The faculty was informed that the theme of the lectures that year would be "the work of the century just closing" and that each professor should "be prepared to speak of the development and progress of his science."[7] Widespread Catholic interest in extension work was being seen as opening to priests "a new door to higher ecclesiastical knowledge."[8] At the second rector's suggestion, Shahan surveyed the conduct of extension work by the University of Chicago, the University of Wisconsin, and the University of the State of New York, and summarized the recommendations of the professional associations for such work.[9] A central program of public lectures of one kind or another was continued until World War II.

Keane had to deal with an unanticipated move toward expansion when, on the campus where he was still a guest, the newly appointed apostolic delegate, seemingly without communicating with the head of either institution, proposed to transfer to the university the faculties of law and medicine of Georgetown. He informed the dean of the Georgetown medical faculty, George L. Magruder, according to the latter's report, that the Holy Father was anxious for the transfer and that the Jesuit Cardinal Mazzella had thought that his confreres at Georgetown would accept the proposal because they were "chiefly interested in the college." Georgetown's president, Richards, relating Magruder's report to his provincial superior, was at first inclined to accept the proposal under specified conditions on the grounds that Jesuit "consent would show a disinterested desire on our part to do whatever the Holy Father may think best for Catholic education in this country, and at the same time would open the way for the university itself to be transferred to us at some future time."[10]

5. AS, mm, Oct 9, 1902.

6. AS, mm, Oct. 10, 1899.

7. OVR, typescript; see Joseph H. McMahon, "University Extension for Catholics," *CUB*, III (Apr., 1897), 171–76.

8. Charlotte McIlvain Moore, "University Extension," *CW*, LVII (Apr., 1893), 27–35.

9. OR, "University Extension" (typescript).

10. AGU, Rector's letterbook, Richards to William Pardow, S.J., Washington, Nov. 24, 1893. Cf. Joseph T. Durkin, S.J., *Georgetown University: The Middle Years (1840–1900)* (Washington, D.C.: Georgetown University Press, 1963), Chap. XII. The original proposal and subsequent correspondence are in ASV, FSS, 1903, Rubric 43, fol. 37–48, especially Satolli to Rampolla, Washington, Nov. 24, 1893; Rampolla to Satolli, Rome,

Previously, according to his own report, Richards had declared to his provincial "that Georgetown ought either to be developed energetically by the Society, so that it might be a university in the fullest sense of the word . . . or all its university character should be abandoned and the Medical and Law Departments turned over to the Catholic University or otherwise disposed of."[11] Four years before, he had reported an impression "both among those not connected with us and some of our best and most devoted friends, that our professors are not, as a rule, able men," confessing that "the truth has been much worse than they suppose."[12] In what he held was "by no means an isolated case," he had refused to accept an applicant for admission "because he knew far more than my professor."[13] But he was strong to defend Georgetown to the father general in Rome as "the only Catholic college that is developing rapidly on university lines,"[14] citing its congressional charter of 1815 and the papal brief of 1833, from which he had earlier concluded, on dubious grounds, that Georgetown had "all the powers enjoyed by the new University" so that there would be "not the slightest disloyalty to any authority in our exercising our rights."[15]

According to Keane, Satolli thought that the relation of the two Georgetown faculties to Georgetown College "was the chief plea for the rivalry between the two institutions" and that "the Jesuits had no right to have such Schools according to their rules, and that the transfer to our University would put all things in order and assure peace."[16] Satolli's official letter to the deans was sent under date of March 1, 1894.[17] In reply, George E. Hamilton, who was the executive officer of the law faculty, and Magruder both noted the irregularity of the line of communication and refused compliance outright, repudiating the idea of "sectarian" professional schools and threatening to organize independently

---

Dec. 12, 1893, noting referral of the proposal to the Jesuit father general, Louis Martin, S.J., and the pope's desire for a favorable response; Martin to Rampolla, Fiesole, Dec. 16, 1893, consenting to the transfer; Satolli to Rampolla, Washington, Jan 27, 1894, supplying requested information; and Rampolla to Satolli, Rome, Feb. 3, 1894, informing him of Martin's consent; and in *ibid.*, DA, XVII, No. 2, fol. 5, Rampolla to Satolli, Rome, Dec. 18, 1893, conveying Leo XIII's desire for the transfer; fol. 11–16, Martin to Rampolla, Rome, Jan. 27, 1894, reporting on the status of the faculties at Georgetown. A copy of Rampolla's first letter to Satolli is among the Bouquillon Papers.

11. *Op. cit.*, 91.

12. AGU, Rector's letterbook, Richards to Campbell, Washington, May 6, 1889.

13. *Ibid.*, Oct 12, 1890.

14. *Ibid.*, Richards [to Meyer, Washington, Oct. 30, 1893].

15. *Ibid.*, Richards to Campbell, Washington, Feb. 26, 1890. See E. G. Ryan, *op. cit.*

16. "Chronicles," Addendum, Oct. 25, 1896.

17. ASV, DA, XVII, No. 2, fol. 27–30, draft and typescript; OR, "Letter of the Most Rev. Apostolic Delegate to Deans of Law and Medicine Faculties of Georgetown University, March 1, 1894" (copy).

if they were severed from Georgetown.[18] Keane expressed relief and some pleasure in the revelation of Georgetown's tenuous relations with its professional schools but recognized that "the odium of the attempt will be surely thrown on us by the Jesuits and their friends."[19]

The New Faculties

Keane, in his exuberance, originally estimated that within four years after the laying of the cornerstone of Caldwell Hall the university could provide "the highest education which can be offered by the science of the nineteenth century" to the prospective lawyer, physician, politician, merchant, civil engineer, journalist, or man of "elegant leisure," all of whom, as the *Catholic World* reported, would "learn how to hold their own as practical Christians and be at the same time men among men of these critical times."[20] Soon he was able to acknowledge "a Providential encouragement" in the form of a proffered gift of New York real estate, valued at $400,000, from James McMahon, infirm pastor of St. Andrew's Church in the metropolis, who in return for his gift of the land was allowed to reside at the university for life.[21] Keane expected that two years spent in "securing the Faculty and providing a suitable building"[22] would allow an opening in the fall of 1893, but two postponements were necessary before the university's expansion into the arts and sciences and professions and the dedication of McMahon Hall, named for the donor, in 1895.

Apparently these developments did not please the apostolic delegate, who made his views known to the papal secretary of state.[23] Nine years later, after a visit to the university in his capacity as cardinal prefect of the congregation of studies, Satolli explained the basis for his opposition to the expansion. In contrast with the position that had been implied in his earlier attempt to transfer the Georgetown schools across the city, he had come to accept what he called the "original idea" of the university as limited to "an Atheneum for the advanced studies of Philosophy, Theology and Law" for "a select portion of the young Clergy of the United States." Further, in his assessment, he argued that experience had shown "how great is the present impossibility of competing with

18. ASV, DA, XVII, No. 2, fol. 31–33, Hamilton to Satolli, Washington, Mar. 6, 1894, and fol. 37–39, Magruder to Satolli, Washington, Mar. 12, 1894; OR, for copies.

19. ADR, O'Connell Papers, Keane to O'Connell, Washington, Apr. 13, 1894.

20. "The Present Standing of the Catholic University," CW, XLIV (Aug., 1888), 584.

21. BT, mm, Apr. 8, 1891; OR, Keane to McMahon, Washington, Apr. 9, 1891.

22. AR (1890–91), 27.

23. ASV, FSS, 1895, Rubric 8, Satolli to Rampolla, Washington, Oct. 4, 1895.

McMahon Hall, opened in 1895 for the school of philosophy, embracing the arts and sciences, and the school of the social sciences, including law, to which some administrative offices were moved.

and of meriting scientific preference to the other Universities at present existing in America," so that he found it necessary to ask "how we can presume that the young Catholic Laymen will leave these Universities and become attached to this?"[24]

The plans for the faculty of philosophy—designated so in accord with European precedents—proved to be open to change. At first, Keane had projected "a School of Philosophy, a School of Science, a School of Social Sciences, and a School of Letters," each conferring the bachelor's, master's, and doctor's degrees (the bachelor's on the same principle as in the school of sacred sciences, not as the end of an undergraduate program), with the school of science offering also "courses preparing for Diplomas in Civil, Mechanical, and Electrical Engineering." Raising the endowment needed was recognized as "a problem of great magnitude and of no small difficulty." Keane begged the board unsuccessfully to see "whether something cannot be done besides my individual endeavors, which can hardly be adequate to such a task."[25] After the second

24. ASV, DA, XVII, No. 1a, June 21, 1904, not forwarded until Nov. 16, 1904; also in AAB, Gibbons Papers. The original is hand-written in Italian. Quotations are from a translation read to the BT, mm, Nov. 17, 1904.
25. AR (1892–93), 10, 12.

postponement of the inauguration, he advised the board of the senate's judgment that an opening in 1895 "could not be longer delayed without injury to the reputation of the University,"[26] and he was authorized to proceed "with as many chairs as the finances will justify."[27]

A committee of professors under Keane as chairman was appointed by the board to propose a provisional plan of organization. Meeting late in 1894, its recommendations, which the academic senate approved, included the opening of two departmentalized schools and the erection of each as a faculty. Thus, on October 1, 1895, with the formal dedication of McMahon Hall, there were inaugurated the school of philosophy and the school of the social sciences. In the former, with Pace as dean, were departments of philosophy, letters, mathematics, physics, chemistry, and biology; in the latter, with William Callyhan Robinson, formerly of the Yale Law School, as dean, departments of economics, political science, sociology, and law.[28] In each department, the senior professor was charged with oversight and reporting to the dean. The contracts of professors were to be of indefinite duration.

The staffing of these departments exemplified the aspirations of the new institution but also, alas, the limiting realities. Georgetown's Richards referred to the school of philosophy as "Bishop Keane's Miscellaneous Department."[29] The young dean, trained in Rome, Paris, Louvain, and Leipzig, had a keen mind that his colleague Shahan had early observed to inhabit "a calm serene region."[30] He was to have a long future in the university as a professor of psychology and philosophy and as a dean (1895–99, 1906–14, 1934–35), director of studies (1913–25), general secretary (1917–25), vice rector (1925–36), and not least as a leader in the editing of the *Catholic Encyclopedia* (1907–12). Both ecclesiastical and professional recognition were accorded to him, although even after earlier opposition had faded there was rumored to be in Rome a movement to oust him from the university. A significant admirer, however, deemed this not "even *thinkable*, much less practical."[31]

Steeping himself in the new experimental psychology, in which as he was studying he saw "a sort of short way of summing up some dozen

26. AR (1893–94), 8.
27. BT, mm, Apr. 4, 1894.
28. AR (1894–95), 10–11; AR (1895–96), 26. See C. Joseph Nuesse, "The Introduction of the Social Sciences in the Catholic University of America, 1895–1909," ST, XII (Spring, 1986), 30–43.
29. AGU, Rector's letterbook, Richards to Meyer, Washington, Feb. 11, 1895.
30. OR, Shahan to Keane, Berlin, Oct. 10, 1889.
31. *Ibid.*, Edward J. Hanna to O'Connell, Rochester, n.d. [ca. 1903].

Edward Aloysius Pace (1861–1938), pioneer professor of psychology (1891–94) and of philosophy (1894–1935), dean (1895–99, 1906–14, 1934–35), general secretary (1917–25) and vice rector (1925–36), who found in the relation between clergy and laity "the great hope of the University that strong bonds of sympathy may soon unite all the members of the Catholic body in the manly struggle for higher citizenship, more refined tastes, purer social conditions, more enlightened and more durable spirituality of life."

branches of science," Pace proposed in a detailed memorandum that philosophers should "take a course of science on the same level with the scientists" and pursue philosophical study "parallel in each year with the scientific work." To respond to the challenge of the time, he was convinced that the Church should "produce specialists in various branches of science whose first aim would be to secure a scientific reputation and then throw their influence on the right side of the philosophical fight."[32] The psychological laboratory that he established on the campus in 1899 was the second of its kind in the United States and the first in any Catholic institution, preceded only by that of Hall at Johns Hopkins, which had opened in 1884. Their German mentor, Wundt, had opened his only in 1879.

32. *Ibid.*, "Notes on Philosophical Institute," Pace to Keane, Ingenbohl, Switzerland, Sept. 2, 1890. On Pace, see J. K. Ryan, NCE, X, 850–51. For a detailed study see William P. Braun, C.S.C., "Monsignor Edward A. Pace, Educator and Philosopher" (unpublished doctoral dissertation, The Catholic University of America, 1968).

With Pace in philosophy proper was Edmund T. Shanahan, a Boston priest who had been studying in Rome when he accepted appointment as an associate professor of metaphysics. He was then sent by the university to Louvain for the semester before the opening of the new school. Later, seeking permission to accept, with the approval of the archbishop of Philadelphia, an invitation to give a course in medieval philosophy at the University of Pennsylvania, he saw an opportunity to advance that university's good but had to consider, "Would the cry of 'Liberalism' be taken up afresh?"[33] In 1898 he accepted the invitation of the school of sacred sciences to become professor of dogmatic theology and he later served as its dean. William J. Kerby, a priest of Dubuque (after 1902, of Sioux City) who had studied under Bouquillon for a year, was listed in the announcements to offer ethics but was still pursuing his doctorate at Louvain in preparation for the position in sociology that he began to occupy in 1897. The active lecturer in ethics was Frederick Z. Rooker of New York, a former student and a good friend of Satolli who was attached to the apostolic delegation and who resigned from the university with some acrimony in 1902.[34]

The department of letters had Hyvernat and Stoddard from the original faculty. The latter was joined in teaching English literature by Maurice Francis Egan, who had worked with McMaster on the New York *Freeman's Journal* and was known as a romantic and victorian critic. Although he had moved reluctantly from Notre Dame, he found Washington life to his liking, but his service to the university was terminated in 1907 when he was appointed by Theodore Roosevelt to be minister to Denmark.[35] Egan and Stoddard had been called by a hypercritical Philadelphia editor "the only literary men in the Catholic Church in this country."[36] Greek was added and put in the charge of Daniel Quinn, a priest who had been teaching at Mount St. Mary's College and had been studying on university stipends at Berlin and Athens. He left after his second year in a highly publicized resignation, bitter in part because his brother was not appointed to assist him in a field that had no more than three students.[37]

The scientific departments had the advantage of popular attention.

33. OR, Shanahan to Conaty, Jan. 22, 1898.

34. Rooker served as a bishop in the Philippines from 1903 until his death in 1907.

35. See Egan's autobiography, *op. cit.*; C. W. Bernardin, NCE, V, 188; and Alan Westcott, *DAB*, VI, 49–50.

36. William Henry Thorne in *The Globe*, IX (Mar., 1899), 123, quoted in James A. White, *The Era of Good Intentions: A Survey of American Catholics' Writing between the Years 1880–1915* (New York: Arno Press, 1978), 253.

37. OR, Conaty to Gibbons, Washington, Dec. 4, 1897. In later years, Quinn combined teaching at Antioch College with a pastorate in Ohio.

Even before the university project was truly under way, the university had received from a Pennsylvanian who was pleased that the sciences would be taught in a Catholic institution more than seventy-five volumes of the geological survey of his state.[38] During the planning, the trustees' committee on organization proposed that scientific instruction should "be made the most prominent in the new course."[39] On the inside, as Egan noted, "the first two rectors looked with awe on 'science,' of which they knew very little," so that "the scientific people, rather sure that they would not be interfered with, managed to do as they pleased, and secured more money than anybody else."[40] (It could not have been much.)

John J. Griffin, a priest with a doctorate from Johns Hopkins, was appointed professor of chemistry and later served in various administrative capacities as well. In physics, Shea, with his bachelor's and master's degrees from Harvard and a doctorate from Berlin, had obtained his release from a position he held at the University of Illinois, "certain that the Catholic University has a glorious future before it" and that he "could be of more use to the world" in Washington than in Urbana.[41] He served for the remainder of his career in professorial and administrative positions. Most prominent was a convert who was a former Episcopal clergyman, Edward Lee Greene. He had been at the University of California for ten years and in 1893 had been president of the International Congress of Botanists at the Chicago exposition. Greene boasted that his one-man department of botany, through the specimens and the library that he had brought to it at his own expense, "found itself more thoroughly and more strongly equipped than was ever any other academic institution in all history, at its inception." Yet, to his chagrin, when hard financial questions had to be faced by the faculty, he found this—"of all universities in the world"—to be unconvinced about the "utility of retaining" botanical studies and he moved to the Smithsonian Institution.[42]

To these departments there was attached an institute of technology with Shea as director. Since its inclusion in the school of philosophy appeared to be incongruous, it was given independent existence, as

38. OVR, Joseph Willcox to Placide Chapelle, Media, Pa., June 9, 1885, expressing the hope that the donation would "fill a deficiency long endured in Catholic Colleges."
39. BT, mm, Apr. 11, 1893.
40. *Recollections,* 189.
41. OR, Shea to Keane, Urbana, Feb. 20, 1895.
42. *Ibid.,* A Report to Members of the Faculty of Philosophy, Catholic University of America, as to its Department of Botany, Mar. 12, 1902. For Greene's obituary, see *Science,* N.S., XLII (Nov. 19, 1915), 722.

were similar institutes at other institutions at the time. The degrees of engineer and master of engineering were offered in civil, electrical, and mechanical engineering. Albert Zahm was appointed as associate professor of mechanics in 1895 while he was completing his doctorate at Johns Hopkins. His brother John, who had at Notre Dame what he considered to be "the most complete collection of acoustic apparatus in the United States," had lectured on the campus during 1891 and 1892.[43] In 1901, Albert built at the university the first scientific wind tunnel laboratory in the United States, but he was dismissed at the end of the academic year 1907–8 because of financial considerations.[44] There was consistent trustee interest in technology, but only small funding,[45] and therefore also consistent anxiety among the informed that the university was "inviting to its work a scientific class of young men, who, in later years of their development, will demand requirements which we are not in a position to give."[46]

The problems of the somewhat haphazard expansion were evident. Pace emphasized immediately that "the work of the Departments actually in operation cannot be satisfactory so long as any principal branch is omitted."[47] In his second report as dean, pointing to the lack of instruction in history, romance languages, and biological sciences other than botany, he observed how "the lack of instruction in Biology is a serious drawback to the investigation of fundamental problems in Philosophy, and without a department of History the efficiency both of the Divinity School and of the School of the Social Sciences is considerably impaired."[48] Moreover, he noted that all departments were handicapped by "the inability of many students to handle the literature on their special subjects of study," much of which was in foreign publications. This made collegiate courses in French and German desirable.[49] The rector added that months often had to be spent "in repairing defects in undergraduate work . . . in order that the University classes may be followed with any kind of success."[50]

---

43. OR, J. A. Zahm, C.S.C. to Keane, Notre Dame, Jan. 7, 1891.

44. N. H. Randers-Pehrson, *Pioneer Wind Tunnels* (Smithsonian Miscellaneous Collections, XCIII, No. 4; Washington, D.C.: Smithsonian Institute, 1935), 911. At the end of a long career, the Guggenheim Chair at the Library of Congress was created for Zahm and he occupied it from 1930 to 1946. See Karl F. Herzfeld, *NCE*, XIV, 1109.

45. BT, mm, Oct. 10, 1900 and Nov. 20, 1901. Note OR, Ryan to O'Connell, Philadelphia, May 23, 1903, citing "so many Catholic parents, not rich enough to educate their children for professions, who can afford to have them trained as engineers."

46. Conaty, *AR* (1899–1900), 10.

47. Report of the Dean, *AR* (1895–96), 28.

48. *Ibid.*, *AR* (1896–97), 32.

49. *Ibid.*, 35.

50. *Ibid.*, 11.

The school of the social sciences was called upon to face uncertainties of its own. Keane had begun to plan for its establishment during the spring of 1891 after a personal interview with Robinson, a Dartmouth alumnus and, like Greene, a convert from the Episcopal ministry, who had been for twenty years or more a distinguished professor of law at Yale. Robinson drafted comprehensive but meliorative proposals that Bouquillon, when consulted, found lacking in theoretical depth.[51] He became the first dean of the school, in which twenty-three students enrolled, all but two in law. He became also the first incumbent of the James Whiteford chair of common law, endowed by the will of the widow and still the only endowed chair in civil law. Keane presented to the trustees "the necessity of balancing the study of the Law with sufficient study of the other Social Sciences related thereto" as "a problem far from fully solved."[52]

Indeed, there were few who could be called upon to work toward its solution. Kerby was still at Louvain and Bouquillon undertook to direct the lone student enrolled in sociology. Robinson did the same for the single student in political science, William Tecumseh Sherman Jackson, a Washington Negro and graduate of Amherst, who on December 8, 1896, was awarded the first degree in the social sciences conferred by the university (bachelor of social science).[53] There were no students in economics because two women applicants teaching in the District of Columbia were refused admission when the board, in spite of the recommendation of the faculty, could not bring itself to decide in favor of coeducation, even at the graduate level.[54]

A new trustee, Joseph Banigan of Providence, Rhode Island, whose fortune had been made in rubber, endowed a chair in the department of economics as well as a library fund. Charles P. Neill, a Georgetown alumnus and candidate for the doctorate at Johns Hopkins, who had had ten years of banking experience, was appointed to teach economics. He served until 1905 when he was appointed to succeed the lecturer Wright as United States Commissioner of Labor.[55]

Robinson quickly concluded that the organization of the school, "originally merely tentative in character, became in its two years of

51. William C. Robinson Papers, Bouquillon to Keane, n.d.; OR, Robinson to Keane, Laconia, N.H., Aug 14, 1891, and New Haven, Oct. 22, 1891. On Robinson, see J. L. Morrison, NCE, XII, 538–39.
52. AR (1895–96), 9–10.
53. Jackson was subsequently recommended by the rector for the principalship of the Manual Training School for Colored People in Washington. OR, Conaty to whom it may concern, Washington, Dec. 5, 1899 (copy).
54. AR (1895–96), 34–37.
55. J. L. Morrison, NCE, X, 316.

practical administration of doubtful utility."[56] Allegedly, he had complained that law was being "buried" under the name of the school.[57] He recommended to the rector and the senate, without consultation in his own faculty, that the department of sociology, seen as theoretical in its concerns, should be transferred to the school of philosophy and that the departments of economics and political science, seen as "practical fields," should be absorbed into a school of law.[58] Although this recommendation was approved by the academic senate, the reorganization was broadened on February 8, 1898, when all fields outside the sacred sciences and law were placed in the faculty of philosophy, which was divided into schools of philosophy, letters, physical sciences, biological sciences, and social sciences.[59] The school of law became a faculty in its own right.[60]

The Second Rector (1896–1903)

The identity of the university that had been established during Keane's administration was maintained during that of his successor, Thomas James Conaty (1847–1915), a priest of the diocese of Springfield in Massachusetts. Keane had earlier pointed out that Conaty had never "made himself a specialist in any direction,"[61] and, like Keane himself, for that matter, had never attended a university. Conaty had become "an exception among his own peers" in the priesthood whose apologetic and pastoral zeal in most instances had led them apparently either to see "nothing purposive in knowledge" or, much more frequently, as a critical student has remarked, to identify "entering new fields of knowledge" with "learning how to enlarge a parish plant."[62]

Reared in Taunton, Conaty had been educated for the priesthood in Montreal at the *petit séminaire* and—after a two-year interval permitting his graduation from the College of the Holy Cross in Worcester—the *grand séminaire*. Following his ordination in 1872, he served in the parochial ministry and became a close friend of his fellow-diocesan Garrigan. He was able to claim as another "intimate friend" the future cardinal archbishop of Boston, William Henry O'Connell, at the time

56. Report of the Dean, *AR* (1895–96), 38.
57. AS, General to 1907, "Documentary History of the School of Social Sciences," unsigned but almost certainly written by Neill.
58. Report of the Dean, *AR* (1896–97), 38–39.
59. Report of the Dean, *AR* (1897–98), 24.
60. See C. Joseph Nuesse, "The Thrust of Legal Education at The Catholic University of America, 1895–1954," *CULR*, XXXV (Fall, 1985), 33–37.
61. Robinson Papers, Keane to Robinson, Washington, Dec. 18, 1894.
62. Merwick, *op. cit.*, 97.

Thomas James Conaty (1847–1915), second rector of The Catholic University of America (1896–1903), bishop of Monterey-Los Angeles (1903–1915).

rector of the North American College in Rome.[63] Pope Leo appointed Conaty in December, 1896, as the first choice of the trustees. Probably the decisive consideration in his selection was, as was generally surmised, his independence of the factions among the bishops. In this and in other respects, he seemed to be an "admirable choice."[64] Before his appointment, however, Keane had urged Gibbons, on the advice of Garrigan, who had thought that Maes of Covington would accept the position, that "not to have a Bishop for Rector will hopelessly lower the

63. OR, Conaty to Albert H. Chafee, Washington, May 8, 1899.
64. Hogan, *op. cit.*, 13, and *NCE*, IV, 102; also, William J. Kerby, *DAB*, IV, 337–38.

University to the level of a mere college or seminary."[65] Conaty was soon elevated, in 1897, to the rank of domestic prelate and, in 1901, to a titular see. In 1903, upon leaving the university, he became bishop of Monterey-Los Angeles.

Although Spalding in Peoria seemingly accepted the negative impressions of James Kent Stone, who had attended Conaty's inauguration,[66] Denis O'Connell reported from Rome that the new rector's inaugural address had been well received in the papal curia.[67] He had described himself as "the servant of the University idea."[68] Shahan, who had "seen much of him" since boyhood and who did not "fear for his honesty and frankness," soon reported, "The new Rector is doing excellently, and threatens to be a man of spirit and of insight."[69] At the end of the year, the youthful Kerby could relay from Europe the professors' view that Conaty was "a splendid man—following Bishop Keane's policy in all things."[70] However uneasy he may have been in the academic environment for which he had not been prepared, Conaty relied upon able advisers and dealt firmly in disagreeable cases, such as Schroeder's, even when he confronted divisions among the trustees. Later, as a trustee, Keane recalled that within the board Conaty "really *bossed* our every meeting, and we were all glad that he did, for it was the only way to have deliberation and action strictly *ad rem.*"[71] His firmness on campus was typified by his announcement at the beginning of the academic year 1898–99 that he intended "to visit every class in the University, in order to know exactly what work is being done, and what the needs of the departments are."[72]

Conaty's main contribution and the one which he was best fitted to make was to guide the institution into a path of educational service and leadership that was to widen steadily during the next decades. His pastoral experience had convinced him that "so thoroughly has the intellectual idea possessed the Catholic church, especially in our own country, that there is no avenue into which it does not enter."[73] Education and the temperance movement, in which he had come to know Keane, had been his major interests. As a pastor in Worcester, he had

---

65. AAB, Gibbons Papers, 94-Y-2, Keane to Gibbons, Washington, n.d.
66. AUND, Hudson Papers, Spalding to Hudson, Peoria, Feb. 7, 1897.
67. OR, O'Connell to Conaty, Rome, Feb. 22, 1897.
68. *Chronicle*, I (Jan.–Feb., 1897), 13.
69. ADR, O'Connell Papers, [Shahan] to O'Connell, Washington, Feb. 14, 1897.
70. O'Gorman Papers, Kerby to Mrs. R. J. McHugh, Louvain, June 13, 1897.
71. OR, Keane to O'Connell, Dubuque, Apr. 2, 1906.
72. AS, mm, Oct. 14, 1898.
73. OR, "The Roman Catholic Church in the Educational Movement of Today," address to Pan American Congress, Toronto, July 23, 1895 (typescript).

been active in the boards of the public schools and the public library. A larger project of which he had been one of the organizers and soon the president was the Catholic Summer School, begun in 1892 at New London, Connecticut, and continued thereafter until 1941 at Cliff Haven, on the New York side of Lake Champlain. This was a kind of Catholic chautauqua but it offered some accredited courses given by professors of the university. It was notably popular, not least among members of the hierarchy, including, while he lived, Archbishop Corrigan. The idea was adopted in other Catholic summer or winter schools at Madison, Wisconsin, New Orleans, Louisiana, and in Maryland. With similar projects, it foreshadowed the summer sessions of colleges and universities that were to become almost universal. Satolli seems to have been charmed when he visited Cliff Haven in 1895 and was reported to have announced, on the eve of his departure from the United States in the fall of 1896, that Conaty was his choice to succeed Keane.[74]

Partly because of his personal qualities, partly by virtue of his position as rector, Conaty's leadership was soon recognized beyond the campus. In 1898, he was elected first vice president of the Association of Colleges of the Middle States and Maryland. During the same year he convened at St. Joseph's Seminary, Dunwoodie, New York, a conference of ten seminary presidents that was intended to lead to a permanent organization of presidents and faculties. This was, he said, in response to "a consciousness that the work is being done by independent and individual units, without that cohesiveness which comes from the unity of purpose and the harmony of parts."[75] On the same principle, he announced not only a second meeting of the same group to be held in Philadelphia the next year, but a similar meeting of Catholic college representatives, the proceedings of which he later pointed to as "the first educational document in collegiate work in the country which has been issued in the interest of Catholic education."[76] Although the seminary conferences lapsed after the two meetings, the Association of Catholic Colleges gained in attendance each year and received high praise from all quarters, beginning with Pope Leo himself. In his last report to the trustees, Conaty could mention also a meeting of twenty-three diocesan representatives of parochial schools held at Philadelphia during November, 1902. With himself as president, "it was determined to organize permanently for the purpose of considering the needs of the system and the

---

74. Baltimore *Sun*, Nov. 20, 1896.
75. "Educational Conference of Seminary Presidents," *CUB*, IV (July, 1898), 399.
76. AR (1898–99), 8.

methods of unification."[77] In 1904, Conaty's successor was able to bring the parochial, collegiate, and seminary developments together into a single, departmentalized Catholic Educational Association.

This was a path that Catholics of the time were evidently ready to follow since it led to perceptible advantages and posed no threats to faith or to institutional standing. Georgetown's president was characterizing the state of Catholic collegiate education as "almost chaotic"[78] and Conaty's perception, shared by many others, was that "heavily endowed and well organized institutions" were behind a "tide that is strongly set in the direction of other than Catholic schools."[79] The high school movement was then well under way. Opening the third annual college conference Conaty observed that state control was establishing "a mighty machine of secularized instruction, which threatens to destroy all private effort either on the part of individuals or the Church," making it important "to meet unification with unification." Of the delegates of the forty-two institutions represented, Conaty asked that they "perfect our collegiate work and allow the University to attend to the graduate work" with a prospective "strengthening of the entire system."[80] Earlier a keen and friendly sister had assured him that he was making even "a conquest of all the S.J.'s."[81]

Conaty took a particular interest in the foundation of Trinity College near the university, in which the vice rector, Garrigan, was to be credited with being "perhaps the strongest figure in shaping its plans and carrying them to their happy realization."[82] The question of Catholic higher education for women came before the trustees a second time as they discussed the implications of the expansion of the university for the affiliation of other institutions with it. The School Sisters of Notre Dame, having established their Collegiate Institute of Notre Dame in Maryland, respectfully asked of the University "the same measure of recognition accorded to Colleges for men."[83] Gibbons, however, urged that the Sisters of Notre Dame de Namur should have prior consider-

77. AR (1901–1902), 8. See James H. Plough, "Catholic Colleges and the Catholic Educational Association: The Foundation and Early Years of the CEA, 1899–1919" (unpublished doctoral dissertation, University of Notre Dame, 1967). As Plough remarks, the Association of Catholic Colleges was founded in response to the reform work of the university "and developed in part in opposition to it" (iv).

78. OR, Richards to Conaty, Washington, Aug. 5, 1897.

79. AR (1898–99), 9.

80. AS, General to 1907, press release, Apr. 10, 1901.

81. OR, Sister Julia, S.N.D., to Conaty, Cincinnati, May 9, 1900.

82. James J. Keane, "Tribute to the Late Bishop Garrigan," *CUB*, XXVI (Jan., 1920), 17. For the history of Trinity College, see Mullaly, *op. cit.*

83. OR, School Sisters of Notre Dame to Conaty, Baltimore, Oct. 9, 1899.

ation in any extension of privileges "on account of the sacrifices they
had made in the establishment of Trinity College near the University
and the great opposition they had met with in its foundation."[84] He had
had to calm the fears of Satolli when the apostolic delegate had learned
that a woman's college would be located near the university.[85] The trials
of the sisters were illustrated in a plea of one of their number to Conaty
that he intervene with a superior who was hesitating at the prospect of
debt because "circumstances out of her control have brought the College
before the public too soon, and so have awakened public anticipation
before she was able to satisfy it." The fact, she remarked, "does not
change the situation, and for eighteen months those interested have
vainly looked for some realization of the work."[86] At the dedication,
Spalding proclaimed, "A woman's heart founded the University, and
women will upbuild and maintain Trinity College."[87] William Torrey
Harris, United States Commissioner of Education, wrote to Conaty, "I
rejoice much in the establishment of the new college for women—
Trinity College—just as I have from the beginning rejoiced in the
establishment of the Catholic University of America."[88]

As its leadership role within Catholic circles was being developed,
the primary identity of the university among academicians received
advantageous visibility when, in 1900, it was invited to join other
research-oriented and prestigious institutions in the founding of the
Association of American Universities. The presidents of California,
Chicago, Columbia, Harvard, and Johns Hopkins had signed a call to
discuss the state of graduate education and the requirements for the
doctorate in particular. The inclusion of The Catholic University of
America in the organizational meeting was urged forcefully by President
Hall of Clark when it, with his own institution, was omitted from the
original list.[89] Georgetown's vice president, fearful of the developments
that he had been following, expressed to Conaty his conviction "that
it is the determination of the men who are managing our big universities
to crowd out all minor institutions, which would include practically
all our Catholic institutions except the Catholic University."[90] The
academic senate, when consulted, advised the rector to accept the

84. BT, mm, Oct. 11, 1899.
85. AAB, Gibbons Papers, 95-S-9, Gibbons to Satolli, Baltimore, Sept. 5, 1897
(copy).
86. OR, Sister Mary Euphrasia, S.N.D., to Conaty, Washington, Nov. 9, 1898.
87. "Women and Higher Education," *Opportunity*, 60.
88. OR, Harris to Conaty, Washington, Nov. 22, 1900.
89. *Ibid.*, Hall to Conaty, Worcester, Jan. 15 and 30, 1900.
90. *Ibid.*, James P. Fagan, S.J., to Conaty, Washington, Feb. 22, 1900.

invitation, giving it priority over all other engagements, and chose Pace and Shea as delegates to accompany him to Chicago.[91] When on his return Conaty reported to a convocation that inclusion in the conference had given "the cachet of approval to the Catholic University, as being one of the great universities engaged in graduate studies," he noted with satisfaction that "in some respects we were in advance of all other universities in some of our requirements for the doctoral degree, while we were on a level with them in everything else."[92] Conaty himself was appointed to the committee charged with drafting the constitution of the new organization and was one of the speakers at the banquet held during the second meeting.

On the campus, where community was still in the making, the qualities of the pioneer professors continued to encourage the highest hopes. The visiting Beatrice Potter Webb, even though already a Fabian, found them not only "a welcome relief from congressmen and senators," but "far more attractive as individuals than most Americans," especially in their understanding—which she sensed might have been derived from their Catholicism—of "assumptions alternative to their own." Only students were lacking![93] But Conaty was soon enough perplexed by the problems of collegial governing, particularly in defining the respective spheres of authority of the rector and the senate. Earlier, in 1893, the constitutions had been supplemented by instructions and bylaws of the faculty of the social sciences that had been patterned after instruments in use at Louvain and Paris.[94] At the beginning of 1898, Conaty forwarded to the faculties a draft of a commentary on the constitutions intended eventually for Propaganda Fide, noting that it would be a first step toward making the university's "organic character" well understood.[95] The translation of the constitutions into English was authorized by the senate.[96] The latter body appointed a committee on the constitutionality of certain previous enactments which interpreted its mandate broadly to defend the "actual share in the government of the University" given to it.[97]

But the disquiet on the campus could not be denied. At the beginning of the university one who wrote in its praise had singled out its "greatest

91. AS, mm, Feb. 24, 1900.

92. OR, "Convocation Notes," Mar. 7, 1900.

93. *Beatrice Webb's American Diary 1898*, ed. David A. Shannon (Madison: University of Wisconsin Press, 1963), 39–40, entry for April 21.

94. *Yearbook of the Catholic University of America, 1894–95*, 12–13.

95. AS, General to 1907, circular letter to faculties, Jan. 18, 1898.

96. AS, mm, Apr. 28 and May 10, 1898. Printing was authorized on June 2, 1899.

97. *Ibid.*, May 20, 1898.

disadvantage of all," as he saw it: "too many exorbitant expectations are forming respecting it, as if, forsooth, it will not have to achieve its destiny on its own merits, like everybody else, or as if within its walls, by some magic process, the 'higher learning' will be gulped down at a draught."[98] However widespread the expectations were, they did not result in increased enrollment. The lag for which Keane was criticized was not remedied in Conaty's time nor, for that matter, in his successor's. For a brief period, Conaty had thought that the law school might become "the largest section of the University,"[99] but this hope was soon dashed. Robinson, who devised any number of degree programs to entice students, had been dismayed by the trustee decision to offer training for the bar in addition to graduate programs, but it is of interest to note that during the sixteen years of his deanship 68 per cent of those who enrolled for such training already had college degrees.[100] There is in this statistic a suggestion of an ambiguity in what would today be called the university's "image." It represented for the public a thrust for specialized scholarship and a demand for high attainment from students, and at the same time it was identified with a Catholic population that did not relate its pressing practical needs to scholarly ideals.

There was an illustration of this conflict in the attempt to affiliate diocesan seminaries with the university. Keane, urged by Bishop James O'Connor of Omaha to have the university supervise seminary education, had secured authorization for some form of affiliation in the papal brief approving the university's constitutions.[101] The St. Paul Seminary was affiliated at an early date under a plan giving the faculty of theology control over the examinations that it would administer for the degree bachelor of sacred theology.[102] Progress was impeded, however, even after a senate committee recommended that the university should make "every concession that the civil and the canon law will permit, while at the same time, taking full advantage of the opportunities" for academic pressure upon the seminaries that would be offered.[103] But the faculty of sacred sciences held that since degrees in the sacred sciences were recognized as having the same value throughout the Catholic world, and since canonists held that the right to confer such degrees resided

Expansion of the University

98. James F. Loughlin, "The Higher and Lower Education of the American Priesthood," *ACQR*, XV (Jan., 1890), 118.

99. *AR* (1896–97), 7.

100. OR, John M. Fox to James H. Ryan, Washington, Apr. 28, 1933, citing a compilation prepared by R. Everitt.

101. "Chronicles," 29.

102. BT, mm, Oct. 20, 1897.

103. AS, General to 1907, Affiliation, typescript.

primarily in the pope, the university could not "sub-delegate" the authority granted to it to bestow such degrees.[104] Seminary affiliation was not arranged until the Shahan administration.

In another field, continuous recommendations from Pace and his own familiarity with the need for trained teachers in Catholic schools prompted Conaty to urge the addition of pedagogy to the curriculum, but he was not able to persuade the board to establish a department of education. Somewhat paradoxically, approval was given to the conduct of an institute of pedagogy in New York City that was registered with the regents of the state to offer courses leading to the bachelor's and master's degrees in pedagogy. Joseph H. McMahon, the New York pastor appointed as local manager, emphasized that "the main idea" of the 160 teachers who enrolled was "to have all they do count toward their promotion."[105] The project was urged by Spalding and other members of the board despite warnings based upon quarrels that McMahon had had with the Catholic Summer School[106] and despite the judgment of the academic senate that the university could not "undertake this work in a way that would ensure its success."[107] Pace as dean found that it was extremely difficult to identify Catholic instructors in New York— "probably due to the fact that Catholics have hitherto paid but little attention to the scientific aspect of pedagogies"—and maintained that continuing staffing from Washington was an impossibility.[108] Instruction was suspended in 1904, after two years of operation, despite the desire of the archdiocese to see the institute continued.[109] An institute of scientific study in New York was later "affiliated" with the university as a kind of "continuation of the School of Pedagogy."[110]

The institute of pedagogy had seemed to the board to be "a very efficient way to bring the work of the Catholic University and of its financial needs to the notice of the public."[111] A special committee that had arrived at this conclusion had been charged with examining "the actual condition, financial and academic," of the university. Its perception of dissatisfaction was instigated in part by agitation begun by the

---

104. *Ibid.*, "Has the University the right to sub-delegate its Power to confer Degrees in Theology?" (typescript).

105. OVR, McMahon to Conaty, New York, May 7, 1902.

106. OR, J. J. Donlan to Conaty, Brooklyn, Feb. 23, 1902, and John Talbot Smith to Shahan, New York, Mar. 14 [1902].

107. AS, mm, Mar. 14, 1902, also, Mar. 5, 11, and 12, 1902.

108. OR, "Supplementary Report on the Institute of Pedagogy," Nov. 8, 1902.

109. OR, Patrick Hayes to O'Connell, New York, Oct. 18, 1904.

110. BT, mm, Nov 13, 1907; Nov. 18, 1908, exh., O'Connell to Matthew Harkins, Washington, Nov. 3, 1908; Pace to William B. Martin, Washington, Nov. 25, 1908.

111. BT, mm, Apr. 9, 1902.

professor of scripture, Grannan, during 1901 and promoted through Denis O'Connell in Rome and his powerful supporters among the trustees.[112] The members of the special committee, Archbishop Keane and Bishops Maes and Spalding, spent six days in interviewing singly each faculty member. They were apprised, for example, that "the University seems to have grown up at haphazard and out of proportion with itself," that there was required of professors "too much work of a non-Academic character," that "both Theology and Philosophy should be developed more than heretofore," and that if there was to be retrenchment it should be "in the departments which can not so easily be brought into necessary correlation with the spirit and scope of the rest of the Institution."[113] Grannan had complained at length that "the Faculty of the University and the centre of the entire thing" had been neglected long enough and that if theology "had been amply and thoroughly endowed . . . before any other faculties were attempted" it would have room "for 20 or 30 Professors . . . without either ever encroaching on the sphere of work of any of the others."[114] The problem of enrollment he left unmentioned.

In submitting its recommendations, the special committee observed that "a chief object of a University is to foster and confirm habits of method, order and self-activity, and its power to do this must be derived in a large measure, from the wisdom, zeal, enlightenment and courage of its Rector, who should be at once the head and the heart of the whole organization." Its report gave priority in academic development to completion of the faculty of philosophy and endorsed establishment of a chair of pedagogy and the endowment of fellowships for the training of men competent to fill professorial chairs in all fields. It undertook to recommend numerous adjustments in programs and even in individual salaries, some of which the board in turn left to the judgment of the rector. In its wrestling with financial realities that were not yet fully apprehended, the committee admonished that "if we permit the belief in the sovereign power of Mammon to pervert our minds and hearts, we shall not only fail, but we shall make the Catholic world understand that it had been better had we never attempted a task to which we shall have proven ourselves unequal." Perhaps some criticism of Conaty's activities was implied in the statement that "the Rector's time should be given exclusively to the interests of the University."[115] Undoubtedly

112. Barry, *Catholic University*, Chap. I.
113. BT, mm, Apr. 9, 1902, exh., unsigned reports.
114. *Ibid.*, memorandum to faculty of sacred sciences, Jan. 6, 1902.
115. *Ibid.*

the discontents of the faculty weighed heavily in the committee and in the board. As Conaty's term was drawing to its close, the machinations of Grannan succeeded in undermining him further, with, it must be noted, the complicity of the man who became his successor. Conaty maintained his dignity throughout and left the campus for California, where his metropolitan was soon to find him "a splendid Bishop."[116]

The Third Rector (1903–9)

As it turned out, the administration of Denis Joseph O'Connell (1849–1927) was also to be limited to a single term of six years. It had been expected of him that, compared to Conaty, "with his education and diplomatic experiences he could better offer leadership in bringing the University into its own."[117] One of his friends, an Ohio pastor who later became the bishop of Columbus, waxed enthusiastic because, he wrote, "The bright American boy with his Roman training is the peer of any man in the ecclesiastical world."[118] O'Connell's childhood and adolescence had been spent in Columbia, South Carolina, where he had two uncles serving as missionary priests. Gibbons, as vicar apostolic, had encouraged his vocation. He had studied at St. Charles College in Ellicott City, Maryland, and at the North American College in Rome where he was ordained, in 1877, for the diocese of Richmond. Although Gibbons was translated to Baltimore in the same year, he often called upon his talented protégé for special assignments, especially in preparing for the council of 1884, which O'Connell served as a secretary. It was not surprising that in 1885 the young priest was appointed rector of his Roman alma mater.

O'Connell has been judged as natively that institution's most gifted rector during its first century.[119] Administratively, his duties included the collection of funds from alumni and friends for the virtual rebuilding of the plant that he undertook. Countless revering seminarians who later wrote to him as priests seemingly never forgot that he had treated them as men. His reputation for hospitality and charm was spread far and wide and even after he was removed as rector of the North American College, his Roman apartment was a gathering place for prominent clerics and lay persons dedicated to the modernization of the church.[120]

116. AAB, Gibbons Papers, 106-L-1, Riordan to Gibbons, San Francisco, Nov. 4, 1908. For Satolli's *ponenza* with respect to the diocesan appointment, APF, N.S., 274 (1903), fol. 216–24.

117. Barry, *Catholic University*, 35.

118. OR, James J. Hartley to O'Connell, Steubenville, Mar. 16, 1903.

119. Robert F. McNamara, *The American College in Rome, 1855–1955* (Rochester, N.Y.: Christopher Press, 1956), 290.

120. Fogarty, *Vatican and Americanist Crisis*, 236–37.

He may have been the principal strategist of "Americanism."[121] That he was resourceful can be inferred from a report that Spalding, who was his friend, called him "a little Machiavelli"; Ireland later confided to him directly, "between ourselves, Machiavelli was no fool."[122] He had long before incurred the displeasure of the conservatives to which was now added that of their ally, Satolli. For eight years after 1895 he remained in exile in Rome as vicar of Gibbons's titular church of Santa Maria in Trastevere.

O'Connell's close friend Grannan encountered no serious obstacles in campaigning for his appointment as rector of the university. The dominant figures among the bishop-trustees were O'Connell's friends. More surprisingly, Satolli, as prefect of the controlling congregation, revealed that O'Connell was his choice for the position and O'Connell himself was able to report this change of heart to those who were highly placed.[123] On the day of O'Connell's appointment, the pope approved the transfer of the university from the jurisdiction of Propaganda to Satolli's congregation.[124] Garrigan, however, now a diocesan bishop, found in the impending appointment only "the old story repeated." "The University's friends," he warned, "have always been its worst enemies!"[125] Later, a California Jesuit could attribute only to the "very strong pull" of Gibbons the fact that O'Connell, "coming from retirement," could get "such a nice job" at the university.[126]

Before the office was his, O'Connell had expressed his conviction of the "absolute need" of the university, believing even "that the University of Washingon should be the University of the Catholic Church at large." He had acknowledged, moreover, that "it would be impossible for a Rector to do anything except with the sympathy and support of a united faculty."[127] But on assuming office he was sorely pressed by developments and unexpectedly solitary in dealing with them. He had been warned at the start that "work in silence" should be his motto,[128]

121. This is the contention of Ayers, *op. cit.* O'Connell himself thought that the "failure" of "the campaign against Americanism" had shown that it was impossible "to down the onwardness of civilization." John William Spensely Papers, O'Connell to Spensely, Rome, July 19, 1900.

122. ADR, O'Connell Papers, John Moore to O'Connell, Chicago, Sept. 20, 1893, and Ireland to O'Connell, St. Paul, Dec. 3, 1897.

123. *Ibid.*, Gibbons to O'Connell, Baltimore, Sept. 1, 1902; Ireland to O'Connell, St. Paul, Sept. 7, 1902; Gerald P. Coghlan to O'Connell, Philadelphia, Oct. 17, 1902. See Barry, *Catholic University*, Chap. I.

124. AS, mm, Apr. 22, 1903; *CUB*, IX (July, 1903), 436–38.

125. Shahan Papers, Garrigan to Shahan, Sioux City, Nov. 11, 1902.

126. *Ibid.*, S. S. P. Gallagher, S.J., to Shahan, Santa Clara, Feb. 12, 1903.

127. *Ibid.*, O'Connell to Shahan, Rome, Nov. 29, 1902.

128. OR, Riordan to O'Connell, San Francisco, Dec. 4, 1903.

Denis Joseph O'Connell (1849–1927), third rector of The Catholic University of America (1903–9), auxiliary bishop of San Francisco (1909–12), bishop of Richmond (1912–26).

but neither he nor the trustees knew that the financial problems of which they were then becoming aware would almost immediately lead to a crisis of the gravest proportions. Nor would anyone have predicted that his approach to academic issues would soon arouse massive discontent in the faculties. On the outside, friends all over Europe and America continued to hold him in high regard. He maintained an enormous correspondence and was an obvious target for requests to address letters of introduction or pleas for special favors to Roman ecclesiastics. He was a joiner of associations for scholarly, civic, and, notably, ecumenical aims.

Most important externally for the institution that he served was

O'Connell's successful leadership of the Catholic Educational Association. Building upon the foundations that Conaty had laid, he could soon report to the trustees that what had formerly been separate conferences were "united by the union of the supreme officers of each into one Supreme Council, and all placed under the leadership of the Catholic University."[129] The blood brother of Brother Azarias, a Syracuse pastor who was also a writer on education, believing that the necessary "variety in unity and unity in variety" could be accomplished with "no interfering with teaching communities," counseled "that if the University means anything, it should dominate our entire educational system."[130] After a few years O'Connell himself could express to the association's faithful first secretary, who many years later became the bishop of Covington, gratification that the organization had "leaped in a bound into a position of great power and importance."[131] This was no mean achievement, because in retrospect the Catholic Educational Association appears to have been "a prerequisite to further educational reforms." At the time, a historian has concluded, "it overcame the isolation that had previously paralyzed concerted action; it stimulated the entire body of Catholic educators; and it provided the organizational vehicle for tackling the complex problems of articulation between the various levels of Catholic education."[132]

Inauguration of a department of education on the campus was, it seems, a more difficult task than the national organizational effort. It was not until 1907 that board approval was given to the step and then only on an assumption of "no extra expense being involved."[133] Conaty had recommended it in 1898 and in every annual report that he wrote thereafter. Pace, who knew from his New York experience that "to secure Catholic instructors who possess the requisite qualifications" was no easy task, believed that the need of "a central teachers' college" should be evident.[134] Not only Pace but other observers were dismayed that Catholic teachers, including religious, were being exposed in state institutions to instruction and materials that could be denounced as "a disgrace to all believers in revealed religion."[135]

In 1904, Pace and Thomas Edward Shields, who had come from the

---

129. *Ibid.*, Notes [1904].

130. *Ibid.*, John F. Mullany to O'Connell, Syracuse, Apr. 6 and 10, 1903.

131. *Ibid.*, O'Connell to Francis W. Howard, Washington, Apr. 17, 1907.

132. Gleason, in Hassenger, *op cit.*, 37.

133. BT, mm, Nov. 13, 1907. See Harold A. Buetow, "The Teaching of Education at The Catholic University, 1889–1966," CER, LXV (Jan., 1967), 120.

134. AR (1900–1901), Appendix, "Supplementary Report on the Institute of Pedagogy."

135. Mullany, *op. cit.*, 488.

St. Paul Seminary two years before to teach biology, began to offer courses in the philosophy, psychology, and history of education. Shields's own elementary schooling had been delayed until late adolescence because of preconceptions that had labeled him as a dullard, but after ordination to the priesthood he had earned a doctorate in biology at Johns Hopkins and had begun to collaborate with Pace, who had sought to obtain his services for the university as early as 1895.[136] His projects as head of the department until his death in 1921 became, as they were called by a student and subsequent colleague, "the turning point in the progress of our schools."[137] In 1906, the appointment of another St. Paul priest, the philosopher William Turner, added a sympathetic friend.

Academically, nonetheless, the most far-reaching event of the O'Connell administration was the inauguration, in 1904, of programs leading to undergraduate degrees. It was a departure from the founders' aims that affected identity profoundly. A movement in this direction had been building up within the faculties in response to academic problems, lagging enrollment, and financial difficulties. The trustees were not hesitant when the step was proposed to them, even if some might have shared the view of the archbishop of San Francisco that "when a ship is sinking there is no wisdom in taking on more cargo."[138] O'Connell himself, however, was accused by Shahan of being "always opposed to it" and, even after the formal action of the trustees, of scandalous criticism of the step, "at least implicitly, by a series of detailed acts and speeches that cover a period of one year."[139] With board approval a foregone conclusion, O'Connell attempted to establish a constituent undergraduate college in Albert Hall and place it in charge of the Congregation of Holy Cross.[140] Perhaps an adaptation of English

136. *The Making and the Unmaking of a Dullard* (Washington, D.C.: Catholic Education Press, 1909) is autobiographical; Justine Ward, *Thomas Edward Shields* (New York: Charles Scribner's Sons, 1947), is a biography by an admiring collaborator. See also, Richard J. Purcell, *DAB*, XVIII, 107–108. OR, Ireland to Keane, St. Paul, July 23, 1895, explains that, conscious of his "deep obligations" to James J. Hill, who had built and endowed the St. Paul Seminary, Ireland felt that he had to "give at once a large place in our programme to Science" and could not expect Hill to forgive him if he were to part with Shields as requested. He gave permission seven years later.

137. George Johnson, "Thomas Edward Shields: 1862–1921," *CER*, XXVII (Jan., 1929), 4.

138. OR, Riordan to O'Connell, Greenwich, Conn., June 9 [1904]. For the history, see the present author's "Undergraduate Education at The Catholic University of America: The First Decades, 1889–1930," *USCH*, VII (Fall, 1988), 429–49. For the "affectionate reminiscences" of the first freshman to enroll in the fall of 1904, see Frank Kuntz, *Undergraduate Days 1904–1908* (Washington, D.C.: The Catholic University of America Press, 1958).

139. BT, mm, May 3, 1905, exh.

140. *Ibid.*, Apr. 13, 1904, exh.

university organization might have resulted. A powerful supporter of the idea changed his mind, however, recalling in correspondence with the Holy Cross provincial that he had discovered an "original mistake" inasmuch as "members of the faculty were allowed to believe that the school would be under their original direction instead of being placed under that of an independent community."[141]

Before the trustees had decided to offer undergraduate programs, the second dean of the faculty of philosophy had reminded them not to forget "that the people upon whom we depend for support measure our success by the number of our students."[142] The faculty by then had found cause for alarm in the failure of enrollment to increase as expected. Tabulations that were made during the fifth year of the Conaty administration had made it plain, as everyone knew, that diocesan priests in the school of sacred sciences were hardly more numerous than they had been when the university opened. The approximately equal number of students from religious communities was composed mostly of auditors. Laymen in other schools were approximately as many as the total number of clerics. But during the academic year 1900–1901 all the students together, including special students and auditors, were only 155, down from the peak of 176 during the previous year. There was, on the average, one professor or instructor for every five students and the annual cost per student was calculated as $453. This was by far the highest per capita cost among all Catholic institutions reporting to the United States Commissioner for Education. Georgetown across the city was spending $190 per student. The financial as well as popular implications of low enrollment were thus revealed.

The tabulations showed also that of 225 degrees conferred by the university from 1890 to 1900, inclusive, 125 were bachelor's degrees, most by far in theology, but 25 in law. It was true that, except for the latter, these had been conferred in recognition of work considered to have been accomplished before entrance into the university or tested by examination in the course of programs for higher degrees. But other Catholic institutions found cause to protest. Earlier, the authorities at Georgetown had raised the question with Keane and prominent episcopal trustees in 1895 when the announcements of the schools of philosophy and of the social sciences allowed admission to law without a degree—which was the common practice at the time—and to the school of philosophy provided that the degree could be taken within a short

141. OR, Ireland to Zahm, St. Paul, Oct. 23, 1905, forwarded by Zahm to O'Connell, Notre Dame, n.d.
142. John J. Griffin, in AR (1914–15), 28.

time.[143] The only student to receive the bachelor's degree in the school of philosophy (in 1897), however, was Ivar Tidestrom, who had followed his patron, Greene, from the University of California and who later became a distinguished botanist in his own right.[144] Zahm, as provincial superior of the Holy Cross Fathers, with an earned standing as a friend, wrote that if undergraduate programs were to be established, "such action would ruin the Catholic University as a University, it would no longer have any *raison d'être.*"[145] When the university was expanded in 1895, Pace as dean had declared, "It is our intention to leave undergraduate studies where they belong,"[146] but it was generally known that the papal charter allowed a different course. Cardinal Mazzella's fear that an exclusively graduate institution would not attract a sufficient number of students was being confirmed in experience.

It seems impossible to identify precisely the source of the earliest initiative for expansion into undergraduate education. Shahan avowedly, and perhaps others, had opposed the idea of an exclusively graduate institution from the start and had persistently campaigned for the change.[147] In the faculty committee that had advised the rector on the organization of the new schools in 1894, Shahan had favored "an out-and-out declaration" that the university would give undergraduate courses, while Bouquillon and Pace had wanted "so to word our announcements as to lay stress on the superior quality of our teaching, without however, frightening away students by loudly insisting on 'post-graduate' work."[148]

The first formal proposal was presented in a meeting of the trustees on October 10, 1900, but action was deferred in view of the general understanding that the university would confine itself to graduate work and in view of the success of the rector in organizing Catholic colleges at the time.[149] By 1902, however, Conaty himself asked the board if it might not be wise for the university "to broaden its work as other post-graduate institutions have seen fit to do."[150] A poll he had taken revealed

143. AGU, Rectors' letterbook, Richards to Pardow, Washington, May 16 and 28 and June 19, 1895; Richards to Corrigan, Washington, Sept. 2, 1895; Richards to Father General, Washington, Jan. 12, 1896.

144. OR, Greene, *op. cit.*

145. *Ibid.*, Zahm to Conaty, Notre Dame, Feb. 15, 1898.

146. AR (1895–96), 30.

147. Shahan Papers, Shahan to Keane, Washington, Mar. 12, 1904 (copy).

148. Pace Papers, handwritten report to the rector, Dec. 16, 1894.

149. BT, mm, Oct. 10, 1900. On another matter, O'Gorman had advised his archbishop, "You can't get the University into a fight with the Jesuits just now, because Conaty is arranging for a meeting of College Presidents and wants the Jesuits in that meeting." ADR, O'Connell Papers, O'Gorman to Ireland, Washington, Mar. 13, 1899.

150. AR (1901–1902), 11.

the faculty to be generally in favor of undergraduate programs.[151] Soon after O'Connell's assumption of office, the academic senate authorized a committee to consider the matter and before the end of the academic year it approved unanimously a proposal for transmission to the board. No time was lost. Board approval was given on April 13, 1904, then suspended because of the intervening revelation of the university's financial crisis, and then immediately reaffirmed on November 17, 1904, because of the faculty's insistence that only undergraduate programs could ensure financial viability.

From the first, granting that O'Connell must have been preoccupied with the financial crisis confronting the university, he showed himself strangely unable to understand academic collegial governance. He was not in office a year before the faculties and the academic senate were presenting grievances to the board.[152] Satolli's attempt to strengthen the rector's position, which O'Connell was suspected of prompting, was nullified by his proposal to exclude the laity from the institution.[153] The next spring virtually all the professors, Grannan included, with Shahan as their spokesman, asked to be heard by the entire board. It was said that O'Connell was embittered against the academic senate and "habitually listless" in its meetings, "cold and apathetic" and completely uncommunicative in relations with professors, indifferent toward "the larger, graver more immediate academical business of the University," and that experience precluded "hope for any improvement in his conduct as far as the main points of complaint are concerned."[154] The senate had previously voted to petition the board to appoint a trustee committee "to look into the academic needs of the University"[155] and at the conclusion of Shahan's presentation the chancellor appointed such a committee "to examine all charges, to hear suggestions, and to report in November on the Status of the University."[156]

O'Connell seems to have sought to appeal again to Satolli and, having been forbidden by Gibbons to travel to Rome, had his assistant draft a letter complaining that "the professors still continue to be the head of the University."[157] The trustee committee admitted not only "serious estrangement" but "almost open conflict" that could be remedied only

151. See AS, General to 1907, for Conaty's questionnaire and responses.
152. BT, mm, Apr. 13, 1904.
153. "Pro Memoria," *op. cit.*; BT, mm, Nov. 17, 1904; May 3, 1905, exh.
154. BT, mm, May 3, 1905, exh.
155. AS, mm, May 1, 1905.
156. *Ibid.*, May 4, 1905.
157. OVR, Dougherty to Satolli, draft, n.d., and notes for letter, n.d.; Satolli to Dougherty, Rome, July 25, 1905.

by "accurately defining the organic character of the university, the meaning of its Constitution, and . . . giving an authoritative interpretation of certain of its provisions the meaning of which is called into question."[158] Resort was had to the document that had been prepared more than six years previously by Robinson but had not been printed.[159] Its burden was that the senate had no legislative authority whatever and was no more than a consultative body. A committee named by the trustees inquired in detail into the meaning of the rector's signature on the minutes of the body. O'Connell maintained that the signature was only an attestation of the record and did not constitute approval of the senate's enactments. The committee report in support of this view was signed by only three of the five members, Robinson, Hyvernat, and Creagh. Grannan and Shea dissented, not only from the report, but from the majority's draft of "Regulations Enacted by the Board of Trustees for the Government of The Catholic University of America."[160] Although the board gave the rector its support, little was changed and the academic senate was virtually reduced to formalities.

By the fall meeting of 1907, the trustees had appointed a "committee on revision." Ireland, its chairman, wrote to O'Connell, "The salvation of the institution will depend on the work done by this Committee."[161] The report made the following spring was warmly commendatory of professors and students but reviewed in detail the situation in each school, suggesting fields for appointments (e.g., sacramental theology, biology, general history, eloquence), discontinuance of offerings (e.g., the professional courses in law, engineering), reorganization of undergraduate studies and of the *Bulletin,* and similar matters. It recommended that the positions of vice rector and general secretary be filled, that seminaries should be affiliated to the university, and that a permanent trustee visiting committee should be constituted.[162] When new trustees were elected, they included two especially prominent laymen, Richard C. Kerens of St. Louis, a long-time Republican national committeeman and close friend of President Benjamin Harrison, and Walter George Smith of Philadelphia, a lawyer, progressive, internationalist, and ecumenical fervent Catholic.[163] Meanwhile, O'Connell had been elevated to a titular bishopric, late in 1907, and was informing the appropriate

---

158. BT, mm, Nov. 8, 1905.
159. *The Organic Character of the Catholic University* (Baltimore: J. H. Furst, 1904).
160. OVR, printed, n.p., n.d.
161. OR, St. Paul, Sept. 28, 1907.
162. BT, mm, May 6, 1908, exh.
163. BT, mm, Nov. 13, 1907. On Smith, see Thomas A. Bryson, *Walter George Smith* (Washington, D.C.: The Catholic University of America Press, 1977).

ecclesiastical authorities that he was anxious to leave the campus. He remained aloof from proceedings in the board with respect to his re-election or replacement and accepted appointment as an auxiliary to the archbishop of San Francisco.[164] In 1912, he became bishop of Richmond.

The Financial Threat to the Academic Community

The "worthy work" of establishing a university community that Spalding had insisted was due even at the risk of failure had been severely limited from the start by financial considerations. Within the first fifteen years, it was threatened with complete disaster. The funding principle that had been declared at the outset was sound and Keane had repeated it often. His vice rector, acknowledging to a prospective donor organization that "all respectable Catholic institutions may make some money," had explained that a university could "never Grow that way" because in its nature "its sole means of support is by endowment."[165]

In an article that he had published earlier, Garrigan had offered assurance that the university would maintain the high standard it was setting orginally because it had been "wisely started upon a financial basis which will not make it dependent for success or failure upon the number of students who may support it."[166] Tuition fees had not been charged to the diocesan priest-students in the early years and soon religious from the nearby houses of study also had been admitted to courses without charge.[167] But the enrollment of diocesan priests did not grow. During the year 1904–5, in fact, there were only twenty-three enrolled. The board did no more than resolve that each bishop member should promise to send regularly at least one student and that all other bishops should be requested to do likewise.[168] When the new faculties were added in 1895, tuition and other fees began to be charged for instruction in them. The need for fellowships and scholarships thus became evident. But the enrollment of laymen did not increase rapidly

164. Shahan Papers, Riordan to Shahan, Sept. 3 [1905], and Locarno, Sept. 24, 1905, report O'Connell's resistance to resigning and, on the assumption that he would explain his administration satisfactorily to the trustees, his willingness to accept promotion to a vacant diocese; see further, AASF, LB-27 (369–370), Riordan to Bonaventura Ceretti, San Francisco, Nov. 2, 1908 (copy), quoted by James P. Gaffey, *Citizen of No Mean City: Archbishop Patrick Riordan of San Francisco (1841–1914)* (Wilmington, N.C.: Consortium Press, 1976), 553–54. Ceretti was then the auditor of the apostolic delegation.

165. OVR, Garrigan to Thomas H. Cannon, Washington, Aug. 8, 1899. Cannon was High Court Ranger of the Catholic Order of Foresters in Chicago.

166. *Op. cit.*, 293.

167. BT, mm, Apr. 27, 1892. Keane had proposed such admission in AR (1891–92), 9.

168. BT, mm, May 6, 1908, exh.

"Plan of the Grounds," published in the Washington Evening Star, November 9, 1899, showing buildings "grouped about a central park," but evidently prepared when the present Caldwell Hall, designated as the "div. dept.," was the only building that had been erected.

either. During 1904–5, total enrollment in the university fell to ninety-five students. Seeing state institutions burgeoning, the second rector had predicted that in any case reliance upon tuition income would be illusory in view of "the opportunities given on all sides for free instruction."[169]

Endowment was being obtained much more slowly than had been anticipated. Even from the first, there were operating deficits ($29,000 in the first year). On joining the board of trustees, after studying the

169. AR (1899–1900), 8.

annual reports, the Chicago packer Michael Cudahay decided that rather than endow a chair with a gift of $50,000, he would contribute an equal sum to pay off indebtedness and to cover current expenses.[170] The rectors were called upon to be tireless in fund raising. On one of his trips, wishing that he could be "at home," Keane had expressed himself as "resigned to be a tramp, even with the scanty returns to be expected at present."[171] When Satolli had tried to persuade the deans of Georgetown's professional schools that "ample funds and the influence of all the Bishops and clergy in the United States would be available" to the university,[172] he was failing to consider the inroads that were being made by economic depression, not to mention the animosities in the hierarchy and the uncertainties about the university cause.

One midwestern pastor, for example, wondered if he should not be sending his $1,000 gift to the Negro missions in the South, since the university's needs would eventually be met, he thought, "if from no other motives, at least from mere human pride in such a magnificent Institution."[173] A southern pastor whose Catholics would not be "able to take advantage of higher education" was asking why they should "contribute to the education of the sons of the rich."[174] There were the vast distances that made California seem to be a "Foreign Country."[175] Two giants among the founders, Spalding and Ireland, seeing rosy prospects in other places, warned their friend Keane that their own dioceses were poor.[176] After his own appointment to Dubuque, Keane himself found it "impossible to enthuse these hog and corn people of the West."[177] "Mere human pride" was of course without effect in the ecclesiastical province of New York, although the appointment of John Murphy Farley to succeed Corrigan in 1902 placed at the head of that metropolitan see a member of the original university committee and a staunch friend of the university.

Fund-raising campaigns were initiated by the trustees to supplement the efforts of the rectors. When Keane was called back from his exile

170. OR, Conaty to Keane, Washington, Dec. 11, 1900. Ten years later the Board named a Michael Cudahay chair of mathematics in his honor. *Ibid.*, Shahan to Cudahay, Washington, May 2, 1910.

171. OVR, Keane to Garrigan, Kansas City, Mo., Nov. 21, 1890.

172. AGU, Rector's letterbook, Magruder to Satolli, Washington, Mar. 12, 1894 (copy).

173. OR, P. F. Pettit to Keane, Madison, Wis., Jan. 15, 1892.

174. *Ibid.*, N. F. Vandegaer to O'Connell, Vidalia, La., May 22, 1904.

175. *Ibid.*, Riordan to O'Connell, San Francisco, Dec. 4, 1903.

176. *Ibid.*, Ireland to Keane, St. Paul, Feb. 20, 1890, and Spalding to Keane, Peoria, Dec. 5, 1890.

177. *Ibid.*, Keane to O'Connell, Dubuque, Dec. 17 [1903].

in Rome he kept meticulous accounts of contributions and pledges that he received for the university during 1899 and 1900, but could only report, "I have done an enormous amount of preaching, lecturing, talking—; let us hope the seed will not be wasted."[178] The offer of a lecturer to seek funds with a commission as recompense proved that this "sole means" of his "enthusiasm" and his "absolute trust in the appreciation of our people of the magnificence of the cause" were not sufficient.[179] During 1901 and 1902, when the university's endowment amounted to nearly $900,000 and its indebtedness of $160,000 had been assumed by trustees and interested bishops, an attempt was made to raise the additional $1,000,000 that was then deemed necessary to "forever place the University upon a foundation which would enable it every year by the regular revenue to take care of the ordinary expenses."[180] But Joseph McMahon, to whom the work was entrusted, found "great difficulties in persuading priests and people of the practical utility of the University's work" and in Milwaukee, for example, had to spend most of his time "discussing the elementary question as to whether a university was needed in this country."[181]

As early as 1891, Keane was noting the suggestion "that if one general collection were ordered by the Bishops of the country, say on the first Sunday of Advent, there would be a willing and generous response from the masses of the people."[182] The trustees had acted on this suggestion five years later and had presented their recommendation to the archbishops of the country.[183] Garrigan, addressing the bishops during the interim between the Keane and Conaty administrations and citing as a precedent the Belgian collections for Louvain, used as the principal reason for the proposed collection "the fact that, owing to the continued business depression all over the country, the endowments promised for the new schools, which were opened for lay students in October, 1895, have not been paid in and, as a consequence, this Institution, like all others depending upon the general prosperity, has felt and still feels the strain of the hard times."[184] From Rome, with a national special collection in mind, Keane counseled his successor, "Do not let any diocese escape."[185] Then, after a presentation by O'Connell upon his assumption

178. *Ibid.*, Keane to Garrigan, Detroit, May 21, 1900.
179. *Ibid.*, Henry Austin Adams to Conaty, Brooklyn, Apr. 5, 1900.
180. *Ibid.*, Conaty, circular letter, June 10, 1902.
181. *Ibid.*, McMahon to Trustees, Nov. 11, 1902.
182. AR (1900–1901), 29.
183. BT, mm, Apr. 15, 1896.
184. OR, circular letter, Dec. 23, 1896.
185. *Ibid.*, Keane to Conaty, Rome, Mar. 31, 1898.

of the rector's office and subsequent discussion, the board took the historic step of deciding unanimously to petition the Holy Father "to order, for a period of ten years, an annual collection in every Diocese of the United States for the benefit of the Catholic University of America on the first Sunday of Advent."[186] Authorization was granted.

The action could not have been more timely as a financial crisis of the first order was about to break. The endowment fund of the university had been entrusted—in effect, loaned—by the trustees to Waggaman, their elected treasurer, known as "one of the most charitable Catholic gentlemen in the country,"[187] with interest at six per cent per annum. Keane reported this as "the most profitable, the safest, the most convenient, and in every way the most satisfactory" system.[188] But by 1902 some of the trustees had had questions to raise. As chairman of the special committee on "the actual condition, financial and academic, of the University," Spalding was asking for "a schedule of the securities in which our money has been invested" and finding discrepancies between notes held by Waggaman and the university's records.[189] Inquiries revealed that Waggaman had given notes to the university for the funds that had been entrusted to him, on which he was paying interest at the rate agreed upon; that he had used a large portion of the funds to purchase real estate in the name of his firm in the Woodley Park area of the District of Columbia; and that the security he could offer to the university was hopelessly inadequate. The board decided that the rector and the dean of the school of law should examine the securities in detail and have the funds "permanently and safely invested in the Corporate name of the University as soon as possible."[190]

By May of 1904 it was determined that the funds at stake amounted to $876,168.96 and George E. Hamilton had been employed as counsel to advise the trustees of the steps that were appropriate for them. These involved the obtaining of a deed of trust on the Woodley Park property, which was later declared void by the courts, and, after unsuccessful

186. BT, mm, Apr. 22, 1903. Bishop Benjamin Keiley did not consider the papal letter to be an order, did not take up the collection, and argued that "the only hope for the University" would be "to place it under the care of a Religious Society—and by preference, the Jesuits." ASV, DA, XVIII, No. 9, fol. 26–29, Keiley to Diomede Falconio, Savannah, Jan. 3 and 22, 1904; fol. 32, Falconio to Keiley, Washington, Jan. 26, 1904 (copy).

187. AGU, Rector's letterbook, Richards to Edward Purbrick, S.J., Washington, Oct. 30, 1897.

188. AR (1894–95), 8.

189. OR, Spalding to Conaty, Peoria, Mar. 5 and 30, 1902.

190. BT, mm, Apr. 9, 1902. For the details of the crisis, see Barry, *Catholic University*, Chap. III.

attempts to prevent other creditors from having Waggaman declared bankrupt, suits brought by the university or filed against it before a final settlement could be made. On the eve of the crisis, Ireland counseled, "The loss of interest we can bear. The public scandal we cannot bear. Do everything to avoid publicity."[191] The Waggaman bankruptcy put Gibbons temporarily "in a most pitiful condition."[192] Spalding thought it "doubtful whether it is wise to open the University this year."[193] But Gibbons, with two highly respected Baltimoreans, trustees Bonaparte and Jenkins, recovered determination and earned the accolades of many like a future archbishop of San Francisco who wrote, "Your willingness to sacrifice all you have to further the Institution ought to be an example and an inspiration to others."[194] O'Connell saw his duty as simply "one of waiting for kind oblivion to cover recent disclosures in the public mind with the marble of time."[195] After six years, the settlement recommended by Hamilton and accepted by the board yielded $373,135.32, about 40 per cent of Waggaman's indebtedness to the university. A heavy price had been paid for reliance upon "implicit confidence" instead of business methods to safeguard the invested funds. The latter, too depleted to provide the income to cover the expenditures for which they were intended, were destined to be reduced further by the inflation of later decades. The price of the loss for the university was a continuing one embracing dependence upon annual collections in the dioceses of the country and upon tuition revenues.

Assessment from Within

Not long before the disaster broke, after lecturing on the campus, the poet Yeats, whose international reputation was rising, thanked the hosts who had entertained him graciously by remarking, "You have a great university and I wish we had its like in Ireland."[196] He had had reason to be impressed favorably by the scholars whom he had met. They had their admirers at home, also. But, unfortunately, outside restricted circles, there was little understanding and much less recognition of what they were bringing together in their corporate effort.

On several occasions, as they sought to identify the obstacles to institutional progress with which they were obligated to deal, the trustees had invited members of the faculties to summarize for them their

191. OR, Ireland to O'Connell, St. Paul, May 25, 1904.
192. *Ibid.*, Dougherty to O'Connell, Baltimore, Aug. 28, 1904.
193. *Ibid.*, Spalding to Gibbons, Peoria, Sept. 22, 1904.
194. *Ibid.*, Hanna to Gibbons, Rochester, Nov. 21, 1904.
195. Spensely Papers, O'Connell to Spensely, Washington, Sept. 14, 1904.
196. Shahan Papers, Yeats to Shahan, New York, Mar. 8, 1904.

perceptions of the university's problems. The visiting committee in
1905 collected letters from virtually every professor.[197] But a particularly
interesting memorandum of the early years was prepared some years
later, almost a decade after the third rector had left office, by Pace, who
had become general secretary and was already the academic man *par
excellence* in the eyes of his colleagues.[198] His cosmopolitanism, his
European training, his academic pioneering, his first-hand knowledge
of what had transpired in every administration of the university, and
the responsibilities that he carried gave him a perspective that lent
authority to his views.

Not surprisingly, the young institution's lack of adequate funding
figured prominently, sometimes as cause, sometimes as effect, in Pace's
analysis. His recurring theme, however, was the lack of understanding,
even among the sponsors, to which the lack of funding often had to be
attributed. Seemingly, the bishops did not know what it was that they
had established. Although, as in the case of the development of the
Catholic Educational Association, the organizational services to the
Church that the university was rendering may have been evident to
most, and although most might even have agreed vaguely that the
university was indeed their "major intellectual resource,"[199] as Pace
undertook to demonstrate, there was a wide gulf between such a vague
understanding and the way in which the scholars who had been brought
together understood their task.

Pace began by citing certain conditions differentiating American
Catholicism from its European antecedents which were presenting
difficulties that in his view were "far greater than those which the
Church met with in the twelfth and thirteen[th] centuries." There
were missing, in the first place, as others before him had noted, the
intellectual and cultural traditions of Europe. Rather, it could be said
that in the United States any such traditions were to be found only
among Protestants, who controlled wealth and power. American Catholics had developed, to their credit, a remarkable institution in the
parochial school, but the circumstances in which this had been done
had encouraged them to regard "the whole work of Catholic education
. . . as purely ecclesiastical" and not a project of the laity. When
American Catholics became rich, therefore, "though they gave gener-

197. OVR, Faculty Criticism.
198. Pace Papers, "The Development of the Catholic University of America, 1889–
1917" (typescript).
199. Philip Gleason, "Baltimore III and Education," *USCH*, IV, Nos. 3–4 (1985),
275.

ously to all kinds of charity, they did not, in the early days, give large sums to education." There was even a tendency to expend money on "such outward display as the building of costly cathedrals, or the holding of great public celebrations," as if those of the old world that were being imitated had not long since become "simply monuments of the past, with little meaning or influence" upon the current generation because education there had "passed out of the hands of the Church."

It was Pace's impression that it was the school controversy that had interrupted the momentum of financial support that previously had been increasing rapidly since the inception of the university. Through this controversy "the division in the hierarchy became more marked, the University was represented as a dangerous place for Catholic students and the German people, always strong for the parochial school, were alienated from an institution which, with their support, might have become as powerful as any of the universities in their own Fatherland."[200] There were accusations of "liberalism" and even of "materialism." It did not seem to matter that, "dealing constantly with other institutions and doctrines and scholars" with different aims, the university had always been recognized as "genuinely Catholic" and had "suffered not a little for that very reason." Support had slackened as it had become known that some bishops—some of the most influential, in fact—were opposed to the university. The impression was given "that the University no longer enjoyed the favor of the Holy See." Distrust became pervasive and was naturally increased when the Waggaman failure prompted people to ask if the university was "competent to handle its funds." As enrollment fell off, its decline had provided in turn further reason for reluctance in giving, so that undergraduate programs had had to be added.

All the while, non-Catholic institutions of higher education had become increasingly attractive to Catholics, even as they seemed to be developing a unity of their own uncongenial to the faith. So far had this gone that "while some of the bishops refused the sacraments to Catholic parents who sent their children to public schools, some of our Catholic college men made a public protest against Harvard University because it refused to admit their (Catholic) graduates to its courses without an examination!" By 1917, when Pace wrote, there were twen-

200. Earlier, Messmer had written to Hyvernat, "I hate to see our German papers write about the University as they do lately again. The trouble is I can not, in my position, come out as I wish against them. Still I wait any opportunity. At the same time I must say a good deal will depend on Msgr. O'Connell's own conduct and doings." Hyvernat Papers, Green Bay, Feb. 6, 1904.

ty-two Catholic institutions denominated as universities, although he thought that the "majority of them" even then could be said to "scarcely deserve the name of college" and that "all of them put together would not equal one of the older universities." In accord with what Rome had urged, Pace wanted "*one* first-class university"—more could not be afforded—that would be "equal and even superior, in every respect, to the strongest non-Catholic institutions." As a center for the training of teachers, such an institution, in his view, could be expected to bring about the rapid improvement of Catholic colleges.

His own institution had many particular problems. No department was "fully organized." It was difficult to obtain Catholic professors, partly because so few Catholic young men were following scholarly or scientific careers, partly because it was impossible to pay the Catholic laymen who were holding positions in non-Catholic institutions and would "gladly" have come to the university "if they could have [had] the same salary." "Without professors of distinction and adequate equipment," Pace explained, "it is useless to expect that students will come." But "the most serious defect" to which he could point, the one to which he had pointed "to every Rector since the beginning" was "the lack of a definite plan of development." He was never to see this lack filled, neither in the peaceful administration of the fourth rector for whom he was writing nor later.

What Pace was spelling out in some detail were the limitations that, as a result of its troubled beginnings, were placing the university almost from its start in a position of peripherality among its sister institutions in the Association of American Universities.[201] The founders had not wished it so. By 1896, Keane had brought together in the ranks of the small faculties some men of uncommon ability, yet the academic community of which they were a part was never to be able to match the constellations of strength that were being assembled in some other private and public institutions. These institutions were garnering and allocating the resources that would give them centrality and even some of them, like Johns Hopkins itself, especially after failures in its railroad investments, would eventually have to yield to others in resources and

---

201. The rise of the sixteen outstanding institutions is the subject of Roger L. Geiger, *To Advance Knowledge: The Growth of American Research Universities, 1900–1940* (New York: Oxford University Press, 1986). As noted by David S. Webster, *Academic Quality Rankings of American Colleges and Universities* (Springfield, Ill.: Charles C. Thomas, 1986), 14, "The academic pecking order of the best American research universities . . . has remained remarkably stable throughout the 20th century." See also, pp. 35 and 173 on the decline of The Catholic University of America "in academic reputation relative to other AAU members."

prestige. American Catholics were not only exceedingly slow to supply to higher education the resources that would have been required by the aspirations of the founders, but their leaders were also being profligate in scattering among a multiplicity of institutions the scarce resources that they were able to amass. It is perhaps significant that some histories of graduate education in the United States, which necessarily recognize the primacy of The Johns Hopkins University in the field, point also to Clark University as the second to be founded for graduate study, but overlook entirely The Catholic University of America, which opened its doors in the same year as Clark.[202] Yet it was through this institution that the bishops had agreed to sponsor and that they were maintaining in spite of all its difficulties that Catholics were being introduced to graduate education in the country.

202. Lawrence R. Veysey, *The Emergence of the American University* (Chicago: University of Chicago Press, 1965), 166, regards Clark University as "the first and only important all graduate institution in the United States" because, while The Catholic University of America in the same years was also all-graduate, Clark was "the only such university without a pervasive religious affiliation."

PART THREE

The Projection of Identity, 1909-1928

Here, too, as in the Middle Ages when faith was strong and the Holy See supreme among the nations, theology and philosophy and the sciences of nature are harmoniously combined; clergy and laity alike have their share in government and instruction; laymen and clerics, in one student body, pursue their several courses of study. Thus, partly at least, the University within twenty-five years has realized the intention of Leo XIII and the desire of his successors. – *Thomas J. Shahan, "Fifty Years of Catholic Education," CW, CI (Apr., 1915), 27.*

CHAPTER V

The Promotion of Visibility

The priest who was called upon to lead the academic community out
of the turmoil of its first two decades had been identified as a likely
rector as early as 1902, when the trustees had placed the name of
Thomas Joseph Shahan (1857–1932) third after those of Conaty and
O'Connell in proposing their *terna* to Rome. Not long after, although
he could not have known how literally he was forecasting the course of
an administration that might never have been begun, a colleague wrote
complimentarily of Shahan that he was "always building."[1] Still, it was
a surprise to everyone when early in 1909 the university's professor
of church history was appointed its acting rector through the direct
intervention of the Holy See.

The board had proposed that Bishop John P. Carroll of Helena,
Montana, should succeed O'Connell but the pope, St. Pius X, had
declined to release the bishop from his diocese. When Shahan's appointment was announced, there was on the campus a minority effort led by
Grannan, ever a maverick, to suggest that Rome had really intended to
appoint the theologian Shanahan and had confused the names.[2] The
papal secretary of state informed Gibbons that there had been no confusion. When the board met again to propose the *terna* that Rome had
requested (despite the constitutional provisions for election by the
board), Shahan's name was the first on the list.[3] No votes were cast for

1. Shahan Papers, reprint, Maurice Francis Egan, "Bishop Shahan, A Retrospect,"
CBN (Nov. 1, 1905).

2. The Baltimore *Sun* had reported Shahan's name as Edmund Thomas, which was
Shanahan's given name. ASV, DA, XVII, No. 42, E. R. Dyer, S.S., to Diomede
Falconio, Baltimore, Jan. 26, 1909. Grannan, Griffin, and Shanahan himself wrote letters
to assure Satolli, as prefect of the congregation of studies, that Shanahan was a Thomist.
Copies are in OR. Charges of no merit were circulated against Shahan, based in part
upon his severely impaired hearing. See Blase Dixon, T.O.R. "The Catholic University of
America, 1909–1928; The Rectorship of Thomas Joseph Shahan" (unpublished doctoral
dissertation, The Catholic University of America, 1972), 52–64. Dixon's work provides
biographical data and a record of the Shahan administration. For brief biographical
accounts, see Roy J. Deferrari, NCE, XIII, 156–57, and Richard J. Purcell, DAB, XVII,
16–17.

3. BT, mm, Apr. 21, 1909. See exh. for Gibbons's correspondence with the Holy See.

Thomas Joseph Shahan (1857–1932), fourth rector of The Catholic University of America and founder of the National Shrine of the Immaculate Conception, after his ordination as titular bishop of Germanicopolis in 1914.

Shanahan. Later in the year, after the formal appointment for a six-year term had been made, the academic senate recorded its pleasure that the university had been "honored by the promotion to so great a dignity of one of its distinguished professors."[4]

The hope placed in Shahan was apparent to a visiting long-time rector of the Catholic Institute of Paris who was later to be elevated to cardinalitial dignity. In his judgment, the young host institution was weak in comparison with the European Catholic universities that he knew. He could not help but notice its failure to attract students. There

4. AS, mm, Nov. 10, 1909.

was, he thought, a nationwide reluctance for advanced study. Catholics
seemed to share in it disproportionately. The American Catholic minority was obviously lacking in resources and in leisure and was preoccupied
with religious problems. Its leading families seldom separated themselves
from their class and milieu, even when the faith of their children was
placed at risk in non-Catholic educational institutions. Ecclesiastics
were absorbed by the tasks that they faced in the expanding country.
The university was a focus of ethnic rivalry. Its first rectors had not
themselves had a university formation. In this respect, however, and in
some others as well, the fourth rector seemed to him to be better
prepared for leadership.[5]

Shahan, of course, was of the founding generation. Relevant scholarship had been his personal ambition. He has been called the "most
learned" of the university's rectors[6] or, short of that, one who was able
to recognize and appreciate genuine scholarship even if he personally
was not "very productive."[7] To admirers who wrote to congratulate him
upon his administrative appointment he protested that he was "a man
of books."[8] According to his own account, he might have come to the
university as a graduate student had Keane not selected him for the
faculty.[9] A native of Salem, Massachusetts, he had begun his seminary
years with the Sulpicians at Montreal and completed them in Rome.
There, at the North American College, he had been a fellow student
with Pace and O'Connell and also with Edward J. Hanna of Rochester,
destined to be the third archbishop of San Francisco. He had obtained
not only a doctorate in divinity but also a licentiate in canon and civil
law. After his ordination in 1882 and brief service as a curate, he had
served for five years as secretary to the bishop and chancellor of the
diocese of Hartford while its cathedral was being built.

When he returned to Rome in 1889 for advanced preparation in
canon law, he reported that he could find no one there who had "made
its history a serious study, with a view to teaching it," but that a different
"atmosphere" in Germany about which he had heard would be "more
like what we hope to make it at home."[10] Soon he was confronted with

5. Alfred Baudrillart, *Les Universités Catholiques de France et de l'Étranger* (Paris: Librairie Poussielgue, 1909), 43–49.
6. Ellis, *Catholic Bishops*, 24.
7. Roy J. Deferrari, *Memoirs of the Catholic University of America, 1918–1960* (Boston: Daughters of St. Paul, 1962), 400.
8. Shahan Papers, Shahan to Mary Ahern "and All the Girls," Washington, Jan. 24, 1909 (copy).
9. *The Voice*, IX, No. 7 (Apr., 1932), 11, citing Shahan's words at a banquet in his honor, Apr. 11, 1928.
10. OR, Shahan to Keane, Rome, May 29, 1889.

Keane's proposal that he pursue church history instead of canon law. Responding, he echoed the aims of the university's founders in asking, while he was seeking to identify the best scholars, "how shall we meet these men's disciples in America if we do not go to the same sources, and know all about their methods?"[11] Believing that to succeed it was necessary "to watch the intellectual tides, and journey with them, not after them," and acknowledging that no people in the century "began to treat history nobly so soon as the Germans," he went to Berlin to study with Adolf von Harnack, Heinrich von Treitschke, and others.[12] From there he urged Keane to "interest men in all these new sciences, the first materials for which were collected by Catholics." He was confident that "the spirit of research, aided by our experience, even mistakes, will bring forth great men in the future."[13] Finally, before returning to the United States, he followed a suggestion of Bouquillon that he study in Paris with Louis Duchesne, a historian of the first rank who had been inspired by John Baptist de Rossi, the founder of modern Christian archaeology, a man whom Shahan never ceased to admire.

At the university to which he came in 1891, Shahan was given opportunities to promote Catholic scholarship broadly. Within three years after he began to teach, he was engaged in the planning with Keane of the *Catholic University Bulletin* as a learned journal. Its publication began in 1895 with Shahan, as editor, writing many of the reviews. There were complaints that Hyvernat, Pohle, and Schroeder had been excluded from the project and the participation of Schroeder was won only when Gibbons interceded with him. For Shahan, ecclesiastical controversies were hard to bear; having come, he wrote, "from a provincial city, for the pure love of knowledge," and finding his teaching "ever mixed up with politics," he had been "tempted to tear up the whole plant . . . and go back to some little mission." Life in Caldwell Hall seemed to him "very wearing in many ways."[14] He, Pace, and Shanahan took a house off campus.

As a member of the faculty, Shahan proved his commitment as well as his versatility by agreeing to preach the 1897 Lenten series at St. Patrick's Cathedral in New York because it was "an opening for the University before the people."[15] A Philadelphia pastor observed that he was "adding to his reputation every day all over the country."[16] Natu-

11. *Ibid.*, Freiburg im B., Aug. 28, 1889.
12. *Ibid.*, Berlin, Jan. 8, 1890.
13. *Ibid.*, Jan. 25, 1890.
14. ADR, O'Connell Papers, Shahan to O'Connell, Washington, Feb. 14, 1897.
15. *Ibid.*
16. *Ibid.*, Gerald S. Coghlan to O'Connell, Philadelphia, July 23, 1897.

rally, however, sole responsibility for the *Bulletin* soon became burdensome and in the fall of 1898 he proposed a reorganization. Before he became rector, further reorganization was mandated by the trustees on the assumption, bolstered by accelerating Catholic aspirations, that the articles in the *Bulletin* were not "evidence of the high standard of the scholarship which is maintained in our great institution of learning."[17] At the beginning of 1915, Shahan transformed the journal into "a news publication." He was then looking forward to the appearance of the *Catholic Historical Review,* the first of several specialized publications that were begun during his administration in which he found "an index of the solid growth and of the wider influence of the University."[18]

Meanwhile, beginning in 1903, Shahan had become deeply engaged in the monumental project of producing and publishing the *Catholic Encyclopedia,* "the lasting creation" of its era, as one student has called it.[19] He and Pace from the university, with Charles G. Herbermann, professor of Latin and librarian at the City College of New York, Condé B. Pallen, former editor of the St. Louis *Church Progress,* and John J. Wynne, S.J., editor of the Jesuit *Messenger* and subsequently founder of *America,* constituted the editorial board. The first of the fifteen volumes in the set appeared in 1907, the last in 1912. Two supplements were published in later years. The original 1,452 contributors from forty-three countries were acknowledged for showing "in a concrete way the intellectual forces that the Church [had] developed and animated with her spirit."[20] Among them were at least twenty-seven members of the faculties of what was still a very small university.

Shahan had not been rector for a year when it was reported from the campus that "the Dove of Peace" was "hovering over the University more persistently than ever before in its history."[21] Although earlier when the institution was beset by controversies he had declared that he and his colleagues were ready "to hit every body that hits us,"[22] Shahan was seen to live by a maxim that he had once recalled for Keane, "What we cannot accomplish by love is not worth accomplishing by other means."[23] Yet he took his responsibilities seriously. As a member of the faculty who was a friend of O'Connell, he had not worked to unseat

17. BT, mm, May 6, 1908, exh.
18. *CUB,* XXI (Jan., 1915), 2.
19. White, *Era of Good Intentions,* 345.
20. *The Catholic Encyclopedia and Its Makers* (New York: Encyclopedia Press, 1917), vi.
21. OVR, [George A. Dougherty] to John M. Farley, Washington, Feb. 1, 1910 (copy).
22. ADR, O'Connell Papers, Shahan to O'Connell, Washington, Dec. 19, 1897.
23. OR, Shahan to Keane, Berlin, Jan. 8, 1890.

Conaty, nor had he hesitated to add his name to the petition of his colleagues and to serve as their spokesman when he as well as they had become disenchanted with O'Connell.[24]

Recognition, ecclesiastical and other, soon followed his assumption of the duties of rector. He was first invested with the title of domestic prelate. At the ceremony Hyvernat described the rank as "not so much a reward as it is an encouragement to the officer who now appears before the public, clothed so to speak in the authority of the Holy See."[25] Before the end of his first term, Shahan was raised to episcopal dignity.[26] Upon his retirement, he was named an assistant at the pontifical throne. By votes of the faculty, senate, and trustees, he was given the title of honorary professor.[27] Academic honors were bestowed on him because, as a former student and trustee put it when he retired, he had placed himself "in the forefront of every progressive educational movement in the Church in this country."[28] The Catholic University of Louvain conferred an honorary doctorate upon him in 1923, Georgetown University in 1928. In 1926 he was elected one of the first thirty fellows of the Medieval Academy of America.

It was characteristic of Shahan that after the beginning of his second term as rector he was still able to write, "Whoever knows me is aware that I have never spoken of the University except in terms of sincere optimism."[29] Fault was mixed with virtue in this boast but for many years, at least, it seems always to have been overshadowed by the affection that Shahan was able to inspire during his tenure, the longest of any incumbent of its chief executive office during the university's first century. Another former student who had risen to high ecclesiastical position was the eulogist at Shahan's funeral in 1932 and justly named him "the Apostle of Encouragement."[30] Shahan had used the art successfully to personify the institution that he led.

The Financial Base

Certainly no one should have envied Shahan his task as rector. He began, however, with two important fiscal advantages inherited from

---

24. BT, mm, May 3, 1905, exh.

25. "Investiture of Monsignor Shahan," *CUB*, XVI (Jan., 1910), 83–84.

26. "Consecration of Rt. Rev. Thomas J. Shahan as Bishop of Germanicopolis," *CUB*, XX (Dec., 1914), 659–72.

27. AS, mm, Apr. 8, 1929; BT, mm, Apr. 10, 1929. Shahan had retained the Kelly chair in ecclesiastical history.

28. NCWC, Annual Meetings, mm, Sept. 15, 1927, resolution proposed by Archbishop Austin Dowling of St. Paul.

29. OR, Shahan to M. J. Fallon, Washington, July 8, 1916 (copy).

30. John T. McNicholas, O.P., archbishop of Cincinnati, N.C.W.C. press release, Mar. 14, 1932.

the unhappy administration of his predecessor. The most decisive undoubtedly was the annual diocesan collection that had been begun
in 1903. Its yield was by no means sufficient to relieve either the
administration or the trustees of anxiety about finances, but as a substitute for the depleted institutional endowment it was of critical importance and was to prove to be so, not only in the short run but also in
the long. The other advantage had its origins in the decision to offer
undergraduate programs, something that Shahan himself had favored
from the beginning. In 1908, the trustees were still struggling to persuade
even each bishop in their own body to send students to the university.
The situation did not change rapidly but enrollment grew steadily during
Shahan's three terms and undergraduates made the difference. During
the 1920s they were often two-thirds of all students currently enrolled
in degree programs. During Shahan's last year, 1927–28, the registrar
reported 892 matriculated students and of these 522 were undergraduates.

There was an important academic basis for this undergraduate growth
in the caliber of the faculties that had been selected during the early
years. Evidence can be found in a report of 1912 to which the United
States Bureau of Education gave only restricted circulation, since it was
ordered suppressed by President William Howard Taft. The Bureau's
specialist in higher education had been asked to classify all colleges
and universities in the country with respect to the adequacy of their
preparation of undergraduates for graduate or professional schools. The
Catholic University of America was the only Catholic institution that
he placed among the fifty-nine in the first group "whose graduates would
ordinarily be able to take masters' degrees at any of the larger graduate
schools in one year . . . without doing more than the amount of work
regularly prescribed for such higher degree."[31] Undergraduates at the
university were then benefiting, as they have since, from the original
orientation of the institution toward graduate work.

But there had to be, continuing from former years, a dual emphasis
in fiscal policy that was implicit in the name of what the trustees'
secretary called the revenue and economy committee when it was appointed in 1916. The board repeatedly examined "the receipts and
expenditures of the various departments of the University with a view
to the increase of income and the reduction of expenses and the adoption
of a better system of fees wherever possible."[32] Salaries remained embar-

31. Kendrick C. Babcock, "A Classification of Universities and Colleges with Reference to Bachelor's Degrees," in *Report of the Commissioner of Education for the Year Ended
June 30, 1911* (2 vols.; Washington D.C.: U.S. Bureau of Education, 1912), II, 43–44.
32. BT, mm, May 3, 1916.

rassingly low, indebtedness had to be incurred, and it was even deemed necessary to invade the meager endowment to finance construction. Near the end of his third term, when Shahan announced his intention to retire from office, he acknowledged that the university still "found itself in serious financial condition." His remedy, however, then as before, was simply "confidence that God would provide in the future, as he had in the past."[33] Soon after, when the academic senate was asked to enumerate the qualifications that should be sought in a successor, it was unanimous in informing the board that "beyond all doubt or question the University's greatest need is money."[34]

It is not easy to reconstruct the finances of the university during the Shahan years, in part because capital expenditures for the several buildings that were erected were not consistently separated from current operating expenditures. An inference about the crucial importance of the diocesan collections, however, can be drawn from the increases in their volume. During the year 1909–10, the amount received was $94,665. By 1919–20 it was $164,759, five years later $240,799, and in the last year of the Shahan administration $275,795. Some of this increase must be discounted in view of the inflation associated with World War I and the boom of the 1920s. Undoubtedly the annual yield "was comparatively a pittance" so that "the University lived truly a hand-to-mouth existence."[35] It was, however, 61 per cent of all operating revenues during Shahan's first year and after 1914–15, by which time other sources of income were being tapped, it provided approximately 30 per cent annually. This was usually enough to cover all salary payments which, during these decades, were from 33 to 43 per cent of total expenditures.[36] Receipts from the collections were segregated and then drawn upon to cover the deficits that would have been incurred without them. Thus, although Gibbon's successor as chancellor was only acknowledging what he and the other trustees saw as a painful fact, that the university was "running at a tremendous loss,"[37] it would appear from the treasurer's reports that in every year except two of the nineteen that Shahan served—the exceptions were in 1914–15 and 1924–25— the receipts from the collections exceeded the deficiencies in other operating income.

33. *Ibid.*, Sept. 13, 1927.
34. OR, Joseph Dunn, secretary to BT, n.d., reporting meetings of Mar. 21, 23, and 27, 1928.
35. Deferrari, *Memoirs*, 398.
36. The data are derived from the reports of the treasurer attached to each annual report of the rector. A summary of receipts from the annual collections by year is found in the report for 1927–28.
37. AAB, Curley Papers, F 7, Curley to Ethel Fairall, Baltimore, Sept. 4, 1927 (copy).

Even before Shahan took office, the permanent visiting committee that in 1908 had replaced the earlier standing committees of the trustees was recommending "that, if possible, the Annual Collection for the University be continued indefinitely."[38] Five years before, fearful that events in the O'Connell administration might lead to the "sure ruin" of the new source of funding, Shahan had asked the bishop who had recruited him originally, "Who has prayed and hoped and labored more than I have for the establishment of a general collection?"[39] During his own rectorship, recommendations from the trustees to the archbishops or the bishops generally and from them to the pope led to renewed authorization of the collection for a second and then a third ten-year period. Gibbons, in his last year, appealing for continuing support, was to remark that he "could have no greater happiness . . . than to know that the Catholic University of America was placed on a solid basis for the present, in keeping with its admitted needs, with its encouraging growth and progress, and with the educational interest of our Catholic people."[40] His successor as chancellor was to urge that the institution "never had, even when it had but one building and four professors, any localized limits" but was to be regarded as "the treasured possession of every Bishop and every diocese in America."[41]

Archbishop Michael J. Curley (1879–1947), when accounting for the indifference of some bishops to the university, observed that the hierarchy had "left the matter completely in the hands of the Cardinal and he in turn left it in the hands of the Rector."[42] But he did not absolve the board as he knew it, for it seemed that whenever anything was decided "the carrying into effect of the plan was left in the hands of Bishop Shahan who, as a rule, did the work viva voce with those with whom he had to confer" and allowed the rest to know "no more about it."[43] The trustees, it has been remarked, "had not yet learned to consider the University their joint responsibility."[44] Of Shahan himself,

38. BT, mm, Apr. 21, 1909, exh.
39. Shahan Papers, Shahan to Keane, Washington, Mar. 12, 1904 (copy).
40. OR, circular letter, Baltimore, Oct. 15, 1920.
41. *Ibid.*, Michael J. Curley, "The Holy See and the Catholic University of America, An Appeal to the Catholics of the United States," Dec. 8, 1922.
42. AAB, Curley Papers, B 483, Curley to W. A. Baumert, Baltimore, Apr. 4, 1928 (copy).
43. *Ibid.*, M 596, Curley to Clarence E. Martin, Baltimore, Feb. 28, 1929 (copy). Hyvernat had earlier observed that the board had indeed "soon lost interest in its orphan ward, 'questa povera figlia nota storpia' as Cardinal Martinelli, while Apostolic Delegate, used to call her, and more and more relied on the Rector for the discharge of its duties. As often as not the Rector passed the buck to the Academic Senate, or simply let everybody do as he pleased, provided he created no scandal and did not bother the Administration." "Memoir," 12.
44. Deferrari, *Memoirs*, 397.

it was said that he would readily acknowledge that he had "no business ability" and knew "nothing about money."[45]

The evidence was at hand in confusing variations in the financial reports, in excesses of expenditure beyond authorized amounts, in the mingling of the sizable capital expenditures with operating expenditures, and especially in the invasion of endowment. A compilation at the end of 1926 showed an institutional indebtedness of $678,496, of which $270,646 was for construction of the National Shrine of the Immaculate Conception, then included in the university's statement. It was only toward the end of Shahan's administration, after a committee had been appointed "to make a thorough investigation of the financial management of the university and to study how best to balance the budget," that a system of annual budgeting was established by the board.[46] Effective control of budgeted expenditures was still some years in the future.

The success of the annual collection was acknowledged to be too modest. It had been conceived, not only to cover deficiencies in operating income, but, after the Waggaman loss, to develop what Gibbons had presented as "the people's endowment."[47] In Shahan's first term, the board resolved that the collection should be supplemented and that the rector should "start as soon as possible on a tour of the country to collect funds for the permanent endowment fund and subscriptions to pay the debt."[48] Four years later, it was ready to grant him leave for two years "for the purpose of visiting different parts of the country and making the needs and claims of the University better known and collecting funds to carry on its work."[49] In 1918, it was decided that the annual receipts should be divided among the university's needs in systematic fashion and that the goal for the collection should be set at $200,000 and apportioned "pro rata among the dioceses."[50] In 1920, the bishops were asked to consider a national "drive" for the university and other nationwide Catholic activities,[51] but they did not adopt the plan. Curley was well aware that it might be counter-productive "to push the members of the Hierarchy too much."[52] Finally, concern about the invasion of

---

45. AAB, Curley Papers, D 1187, Curley to Denis J. Dougherty, archbishop of Philadelphia, Baltimore, Apr. 16, 1928 (copy).
46. BT, mm, Sept. 14, 1926 and Apr. 27, 1927.
47. OR, circular letter, Gibbons to hierarchy of the United States, Baltimore, Oct. 24, 1905.
48. BT, mm, Apr. 17, 1912.
49. *Ibid.*, May 3, 1916.
50. *Ibid.*, Apr. 10, 1918, exh.
51. *Ibid.*, Sept. 21, 1920.
52. AAB, Curley Papers, L 806, Curley to Thomas F. Lillis, bishop of Kansas City, Mo., Baltimore, May 2, 1925 (copy).

endowment for capital expenditures that had been expressed in meetings of the board led to a decision that the endowment fund had to "remain intact for the future" and that any funds that had been diverted should be "returned to the Fund at the earliest possible moment."[53] This, also, was some years in the realization.

No more than in earlier years could it be assumed that the responses of bishops to appeals for their university would be always favorable. Geographic distance, ethnic alienation, suspicions of liberalism—these and other factors continued to be obstacles. Although there were no dissenting votes when the bishops were asked to request the first extension of papal permission for the annual collection, only thirty-five of sixty troubled themselves to send in affirmative replies.[54] The alumnus who was then archbishop of St. Paul reported that his predecessor, Ireland, for all his fervent advocacy of the university, had "publicly said that he didn't much care what was given to the C. U. collection," so that he was finding it "hard now to make the priests take it seriously."[55] In upstate New York, the bishop of Ogdensburg reported that his priests were disgruntled because a bequest of Theodore B. Basselin of Croghan, "who had made all his money in this part of the country and had promised to remember our own institutions in his will," had been "diverted entirely to Washington."[56]

Even more seriously, the university was seen by some as subordinate to other causes. In Milwaukee, for example, Archbishop Messmer informed his suffragans that until further notice the collection "should be applied to our Wisconsin University chapel."[57] As late as 1921, in a public letter dated November 15 of that year, Messmer avowed that the obligation of supporting the Madison chapel, a pioneer undertaking in the Newman movement, was "nearer to us than the duty of helping the Catholic University at Washington."[58] In Chicago, Archbishop (later Cardinal) George Mundelein, who previously as auxiliary bishop of Brooklyn had diverted the donor of the university's chair of the Immaculate Conception from his original plan of assistance,[59] first doubled the

53. BT, mm, Sept. 14, 1926.
54. BT, mm, Apr. 26 and Oct. 12, 1911.
55. OR, Dowling to Shahan, St. Paul, Mar. 16, 1922.
56. *Ibid.*, Henry Gabriels to Shahan, Clifton Springs, N.Y., Oct. 29, 1916.
57. *Ibid.*, Joseph J. Fox to Gibbons, Green Bay, May 20, 1911.
58. Quoted in Benjamin J. Blied, *The Archbishops of Milwaukee* (Milwaukee: published by the author, 1955), 110. Three years later, Shahan was able to report, "Milwaukee took up the collection on 1st Sunday of Advent . . . Green Bay has sent in $1,200 the first since 1908." AAB, Curley Papers, S 885, Shahan to Curley, Washington, Jan. 7, 1924. See Evans, *Newman Movement*, 28–29, 31.
59. OR, George Logan Duval to Shahan, New York, Oct. 30, 1925.

archdiocesan contribution to $8,000 in 1920, while he was reported willing to cooperate for the university even if he was "very pessimistic about its future,"[60] but then incorporated the university collection into a general collection for Catholic higher education and froze the allocation at the 1920 amount. Later, while remaining a member of the board but blaming officers of the university for intervening in Rome against his grandiose plan to develop his Seminary of Our Lady of the Lake into a major pontifical university of the west, he reduced Chicago's contributions even further.[61]

A trustee who was bishop of Buffalo, and who had previously taught philosophy at the university from 1906 until 1919, found meetings of the board "disheartening," because the efforts that Curley was making as a new chancellor were being offset by familiar parliamentary devices such as burial in committees. He wrote, "They will not help you in your efforts for the University. They will leave you high and dry, and afterwards blame you for not having accomplished the program which you so generously and unselfishly undertook."[62] In reply, Curley acknowledged that some of his episcopal colleagues were "actuated by their own selfish motives and cared absolutely nothing for the larger and wider interest of the Church, outside their own diocese or archdiocese as the case [might] be."[63]

The problems associated with dependence upon the annual diocesan collections made the assessment of tuition fees increasingly attractive. Only 15 per cent of the university's total income was obtained from this source during 1909–10, Shahan's first year, but tuition income was to supply 21 per cent during 1914–15, 26 percent during 1919–20, 34 per cent during 1924–25, and 38 per cent during 1927–28. It was equivalent to 14 per cent of the salary outlay in the first of these years and to 64 per cent in the last. These changes signified changes in fiscal concepts,

60. AAB, Curley Papers, S 813, William Turner to Curley, Buffalo, Dec. 23, 1921.
61. For reports of the Roman "lobbying" of Shahan and his vice rector, AAB, Curley Papers, P 34, Pace to Curley, Rome, Feb. 18, 1925; P 23, Pace to Curley, Rome, Feb. 25, 1925; S 903, Shahan to Curley, Rome, Mar. 9, 1925. Between 1932, when only one dollar was sent to the university from Chicago, and 1938, when the $8,000 level was restored, Mundelein contributed $6,000 annually. He died in 1939. See Edward R. Kantowicz, *Corporation Sole: Cardinal Mundelein and Chicago Catholicism* (Notre Dame: University of Notre Dame Press, 1983), 102, 108–9, 265n, and Harry Koenig, "University and Seminary of St. Mary of the Lake" (unpublished manuscript, Feehan Memorial Library, St. Mary of the Lake Seminary, n.d.), 70–71. The minutes of the trustees do not provide evidence that in either 1924 or 1928 Mundelein proposed that the university should be closed and transferred to Chicago. For Curley's report to this effect, see Ellis, *Catholic Bishops*, 17, and James P. Gaffey, *Francis Clement Kelley and the American Catholic Dream* (2 vols.; Bensenville, Ill.: Heritage Foundation, 1980), I, 339.
62. AAB, Curley Papers, T 825, Turner to Curley, Buffalo, June 22, 1923.
63. *Ibid.*, T 826, Curley to Turner, Baltimore, June 25, 1923 (copy).

both in general and in relation to clerics and religious in particular.
Conaty had urged that the university "should be so endowed that the
question of remuneration for the professor will depend upon the nature
of the work that he is able to do, and the question for the student upon
his ability to undertake advanced studies."[64] There was general assent,
however, that, as the permanent visiting committee had recommended,
"undergraduate students should pay a tuition fee."[65] Tuition income, it
must be remembered, had figured largely in the rationale that the faculty
had originally offered for undergraduate programs. Tuition charges were
applied to clerics and religious for the first time during Shahan's second
term when he was delegated by the board "to confer with the religious
communities affiliated with the University to ascertain whether they
would volunteer to pay an annual tuition fee of fifty dollars for each of
their members attending the University to help to overcome the annual
deficit."[66] This was still the charge when he left office.

In view of these developments, Shahan pressed upon the board the
need of scholarships for lay students who without such aid would not
have been able to attend the university. It was imperative, he said, not
only because of "the example of non-Catholic universities," but as "an
old Catholic form of educational generosity, one largely responsible for
the great number of University students in pre-Reformation days."[67]
The board, sometimes on advice from counsel, was alert to the need for
definite agreements with donors and with recipients "so that the general
fund of the University be safeguarded against financial burdens."[68]

For all his confessed lack of financial ability, Shahan seems to have
had what a perceptive professor later discerned as "a certain Puritan
shrewdness."[69] He is reported to have said "that if you have an unfinished
building on your campus, you have a very strong talking point for
soliciting more funds."[70] Fortunately, in spite of the aura of poor
management and insolvency that had emanated from the Waggaman
crisis, the university continued to receive gifts, endowments, and bequests. Invested funds, which were $1,124,445 in 1910, increased to
$3,106,682 by 1925.[71] Only one endowed chair was added, however,
that of the Immaculate Conception, in 1918, for the study and teaching

64. AR (1899–1900), 8.
65. BT, mm, Nov. 17, 1909.
66. *Ibid.*, Nov. 15, 1916.
67. AR (1910–11), in *CUB*, XVII (Nov., 1911), 11.
68. BT, mm, Nov. 20, 1912; also, Apr. 14, 1915, exh., Hamilton to Shahan,
Washington, Apr. 10, 1915.
69. Purcell, *op. cit.*
70. Deferrari, *Memoirs*, 399.
71. [J. Harvey Cain], "Synopsis of the History of Endowments," Feb. 1, 1935.

A Shahan plan for the campus, probably designed by Frederick Vernon Murphy, reflecting the preference of the fourth rector for collegiate Gothic.

of Mariology. Its donor, George Logan Duval of New York, had offices also in various cities of Chile and Peru. The endowment of fellowships for graduate study took on much larger proportions when, early in 1914, the Knights of Columbus, who had previously donated the chair of American history, were able to transfer to the university $500,000 that had been raised in a campaign begun in 1908. These Knights of Columbus grants have remained the most attractive fellowships under the control of the university despite drastic reductions in their number due to the effects of inflation upon university charges for tuition, board, and room.[72]

Even more substantial but limited to the education of aspirants for the priesthood was the bequest of Basselin, who had heard Curley preach during his Florida years. It, too, was accepted in 1914. The estate was in lumber, a pulp mill, and farms. Litigation concerning the will delayed the opening of "Basselin College" until 1923, by which time the fund bequeathed had grown to approximately $900,000. Its income, by the donor's intention, continues to support, with special attention to training in preaching, the last two collegiate years and the first graduate year of seminarians who are selected for Basselin scholarships in the school of philosophy. Another bequest, the John B. Manning Fund of $50,000, received in 1925, was assigned to be used for the same purpose. Still another significant gift during this period was from the estate of the convert diplomat, Frederick Courtland Penfield, of New York, who died in 1922. The Catholic University of America, New York University, and the University of Pennsylvania each received from him $80,000 for fellowships in diplomacy, international affairs, and belles-lettres. These fellowships have often been used to support the preparation or advanced work of junior faculty at institutions in the United States and abroad.

The University and the National Shrine

Shahan's deficiencies in financial management did not interfere with what became his monumental project for the erection of the National Shrine of the Immaculate Conception. Nothing, of course, had resulted

72. Christopher J. Kauffman, *Faith and Fraternalism: The History of the Knights of Columbus, 1882–1982* (New York: Harper & Row, 1982), 146–52. See "The Chair of American History," *CUB*, X (July, 1904), 371–85, reprinted from the *Columbiad*, and Charles H. McCarthy, "The Chair of American History," *ibid.*, XIV (May, 1908) 456–60; also, "Cardinal Gibbons and the Knights of Columbus Endowment," *ibid.*, XIV (Oct. 1908), 723–26. The Charles H. McCarthy Papers include suggestions for publicizing the fellowships and improving conditions for the fellows. Pace reported to the board of deans (mm, Nov. 18, 1926) the agreement of the Knights of Columbus that the number of fellowships awarded annually should be no greater than the income from the endowment would support.

from an early impulse of Mary Gwendoline Caldwell to build a university church. But about the time that it was being expressed Shahan was pleading on his own for an edifice to enhance the city, the religious life of professors and students, the annual meetings of archbishops and trustees, the priests studying at the university, the academic ceremonies, and all who would visit.[73] When he succeeded O'Connell, he was merely "anxious to build a respectable little wooden Church" to serve as "a center of religious life for our students, particularly our numerous lay students."[74] The original chapel in Caldwell Hall had already become too small and a basement chapel in the residence hall that he was planning—which became the Cardinal Gibbons Memorial Hall—was foreseen as no more than a temporary substitute. (It served as a chapel until 1988.)

Shahan's first proposal of the need to the board was referred back to the permanent visiting committee through which he had acted. Soon he and Gibbons were approving fund-raising efforts in New York City that led to the formation of a National Organization of Catholic Women and the initiation of a movement to erect the church in honor of the patroness of the nation and the university, the Blessed Virgin Mary under her title of the Immaculate Conception.[75] In 1915 Shahan obtained the services of a secretary, Bernard McKenna of the archdiocese of Philadelphia, who was appointed also to the faculty of theology.[76] Together they pursued Shahan's dream. Almost at once plaster models of a proposed structure in an English Gothic style were on exhibit in New York and San Francisco. They showed a crypt church that would accomodate a thousand students. A year later a promotional periodical entitled *Salve Regina,* edited by McKenna, began appearing. Shahan was telling the board, "It is not easy to imagine any single edifice which would more rapidly promote the success of the University than this noble and beautiful church once it were thrown open to public worship."[77]

When a special committee of the board appointed in 1917 reported, it proposed that, in a petition for approval to the Holy See, the church should be designated as the National Basilica of Mary Immaculate, that

73. "Who Will Build the University Church?" *CUB*, IX (Oct., 1903), 509–10.

74. OR, Shahan to Mrs. Charles J. Bonaparte, Washington, Aug. 11, 1910 (copy).

75. OR, Gibbons to Mrs. Francis Burrall Hoffman, Washington, Apr. 6, 1912 (copy); also, Shahan to M. J. Foley, Washington, Oct. 15, 1913 (copy). Shahan's national appeal was printed in *CUB*, XIX (Apr., 1913), 349.

76. Shahan Papers, Shahan to McKenna, Washington, June 5, 1915 (copy). See *Memoirs of the First Director of the National Shrine of the Immaculate Conception, Washington, D.C. by Rt. Reverend Monsignor Bernard A. McKenna, D.D., LL.D., 1915–1933* (privately printed, 1959).

77. AR (1915–16), 7.

it should be monumental in a Romanesque style, that the architect
should be selected by the university trustees, and that every diocese
should be invited to assist in the erection of "our first National tribute
to the Mother of God."[78] A year later the committee recommended
Charles Maginnis of Maginnis and Walsh as the architect.[79] Frederick
Vernon Murphy, who had founded the university's department of architecture in 1911, became associate architect. Pope Benedict XV's approval was expressed in a letter hoping that the National Shrine, as the
church was now called, would be "a special sanctuary" to attract "not
only the students of the University, actual and prospective, but also the
Catholic people of the whole United States."[80]

At this point, the committee on the university church was dissolved
and a new "Catholic University of America Committee of the National
Shrine of the Immaculate Conception" appointed. Archbishop Dennis
J. Dougherty of Philadelphia, soon to be named a cardinal, became its
chairman. Plans were presented to the bishops of the United States in
September, 1919, and were subsequently approved by the university's
trustees.[81] Work on the foundation was begun in 1920 by the Charles
J. Cassidy Company of Washington. The project was not universally
popular; it was even reported to have been the object of a "mean attack"
by Cardinal O'Connell.[82] Inevitably, it competed with the university
for support. When Curley took office he tried to impress this upon
Shahan, suggesting that Shrine affairs be left as much as possible in the
hands of McKenna, since there was evidence of "quite some dissatisfaction amongst the members of the University Staff about the Shrine
absorbing more attention than the Institution's academic life."[83] Later
in the same year Curley could report from Rome that the recently
elected Pope Pius XI "spoke very kindly about the Shrine" but did not
"expect to see it realized in a few years" and was urging that meanwhile
the university should "perfect the organization" of its schools and "go
forward."[84] Shahan, however, did not change his course.

Masses in the crypt church began to be celebrated in 1924. It was
ready for daily use during the academic year 1926–27 and began to be
used for ceremonial occasions as, toward the end of the year, the
university community and the diplomatic corps first gathered to cele-

78. BT, mm, Apr. 10, 1918.
79. *Ibid.*, Feb. 21, 1919.
80. AAS, XI (May, 1919), 173 (in Latin), trans. CUB XXV (June, 1919), 217–20.
81. BT, mm, Dec. 9, 1919.
82. OR, Dowling to Shahan, St. Paul, Mar. 16, 1922.
83. AAB, Curley Papers, S 831, Curley to Shahan, Baltimore, Apr. 10, 1922, (copy).
84. OR, Curley to Shahan, Rome, Aug. 2, 1922.

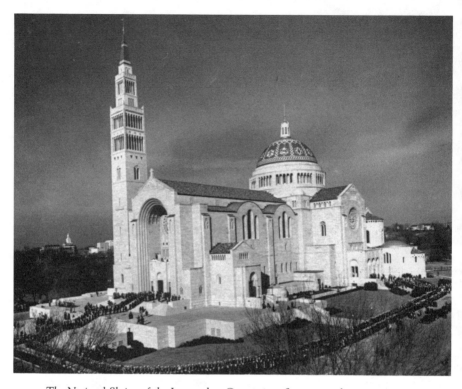

The National Shrine of the Immaculate Conception, first proposed as a university church in 1912, approved for construction by Pope Benedict XV in 1919, opened as a crypt church in 1926, separately incorporated in 1948, completed in 1959, shown here with an academic procession entering.

brate the fifth anniversary of the pope's coronation.[85] Administration of the Shrine had now been enlarged but, although limits upon expenditures and indebtedness had been placed upon the Shrine committee in 1921, and although it was then and later proposed that the Shrine should be separately incorporated, the university trustees continued to have responsibility.[86] Upon his retirement as rector, Shahan continued in the position of director of the Shrine. When he died, Archbishop Curley summarized the history ironically:

85. *Ibid.*, Curley to Shahan, Baltimore, May 12, 1927.

86. BT, mm, Apr., 1921; Apr. 18, 1928. Curley explained to Shahan, "Whilst the Shrine is on University grounds and is University property, the fact is however that it is a unit that might very well be separated from the University as such. The moneys that come to the Shrine, come as a rule, from sources from which we get very little for the University proper." AAB, Curley Papers, S 937, Curley to Shahan, Baltimore, Dec. 15, 1927 (copy). On the recommendation of its EC (mm, Oct. 6, 1948), the BT later approved separate incorporation (mm, Nov. 16, 1948).

During all the years of Bishop Shahan's Rectorate, he was Rector of the University and Shrine and everything else. When he left the University, he retained the Shrine and then the Shrine had nothing whatsoever to do with the University.[87]

Visibility in Stone

The decision to adopt a modernized Romanesque style for the National Shrine introduced a decisive change in campus architecture, which even at that early date was not uniform. In the beginning, at the first meeting of the university committee, Archbishop Ryan of Philadelphia had emphasized that the residence halls—"the different Colleges"—should not be in close proximity, at least to that for divinity students, but he wanted all to be "so situated as to form a moral unity."[88] The original manor house that was taken over by the Paulist Fathers was not such as to set an architectural style. The first new building, Divinity Hall, later named Caldwell, had been designed in a somewhat heavy Norman fashion, although one of its early residents was unduly harsh in likening it to "an asylum with a brewery attachment."[89] At this time, incidentally, when the trustees donated a plot of about two-thirds of an acre for a Baltimore and Ohio passenger station adjacent to the campus, the railroad cooperated by building in "blue Georgetown stone so as to harmonize with the handsome University building."[90] McMahon Hall, of course, was built to be compatible with the first building, but Albert Hall, first named Keane, was erected for lay students across the campus from the clergy in red brick and in narrow dimensions. Nearer to it, in still another mode, the Catholic Missionary Union erected in 1904 its Italianate stucco Apostolic Mission House (now used as the Administration Building) on a lot that it was leasing from the university. Shahan, who reportedly thought that the development of the physical plant was the greatest need of the university, wanted something more pleasing than all this.[91] Early in his administration, the board authorized the preparation by Murphy of a general plan to provide a "harmonious arrangement for the development of the University departments,"[92] but on its presentation action was postponed.[93]

Shahan's first building was dictated by necessity; it was the central

---

87. AAB, Curley Papers, M 1198, Curley to McNicholas, Baltimore, May 9, 1933 (copy).

88. BT, mm, Jan. 27, 1885.

89. Stoddard diaries, Oct. 9, 1892. The earliest use of the name Caldwell Hall appears in SSS, mm, Mar. 7, 1898.

90. OR, C. K. Ward to Keane, Baltimore, Jan. 13, 1890.

91. Deferrari, *Memoirs*, 398–400.

92. BT, mm, Nov. 16, 1910.

93. *Ibid.*, Oct. 12, 1911.

heating and power plant built on what was then "the new Boulevard Avenue" that the university had already requested should be renamed for Brookland, the subdivision adjacent to it.[94] He presented it as "the nucleus of a School of Applied Sciences" and when it was completed in 1910 it was known as the Engineering Building.[95] While this was under way, construction was begun on Gibbons Hall. Completed in 1912, it was intended to house laymen. For this purpose, Gibbons had put aside all other contributions to the celebration of the golden jubilee of his priesthood and the silver jubilee of his elevation to the cardinalate. The trustees appropriated $100,000 for it and the Ancient Order of Hibernians solicited small donations from its chapters.[96] A niche over the door was left for a statue of the cardinal (but filled three decades later by a statue of Mary, Queen of Students) and a trustee donated a large oil painting, "The Death of Leo XIII," for the interior.[97]

This building exemplified Shahan's preference for "the ancient Catholic collegiate architecture" that was gaining in popularity at the time. He was hoping, in fact, that the university would inaugurate "an architectural uplift that shall not cease until the Catholic Church in the United States has put on a rich and varied vesture of educational edifices worthy of the purest and loveliest traditions of medieval Catholic life and scholarship."[98] His plans were for a green ellipse surrounded by buildings in Tudor Gothic, with the main entrance to the campus where it is presently located but with the university church at the farthest point from it. So along the portion of Bunker Hill Road that became the extended Michigan Avenue there was also erected with Gibbons a companion building that would accommodate a dining hall for six hundred students and residential quarters for eighty. This opened in 1914, just in time to house the Knights of Columbus fellows who, with other graduate students, were to occupy this Graduate Hall until 1970 (since when it has been renamed twice). It was originally intended to

94. BT, mm, Jan. 28, 1904. By order of the mayor of the District of Columbia, the name Brookland Avenue was changed to John McCormack Road at the beginning of 1985, to commemorate the centennial of the Irish tenor's birth.

95. AR (1908–1909), 7, and BT, mm, Apr. 26, 1911, exh. Also, "Power Plant and Engineering Laboratory," CUB, XVII (Nov., 1911), 702–6.

96. "Cardinal Gibbons Memorial Hall," CUB, XVII (Dec., 1911), 771–82, presents the dedicatory proceedings.

97. CUB, XIX (Feb., March, Dec., 1913), 161, 351, 671. The statue, executed in limestone by Clare Fontanini, then head of the department of art, was given by the Class of 1949 and dedicated on May 29, 1952. The painting by the Marquise de Wentworth was donated by John D. Crimmins of New York. It now hangs on the third floor of Caldwell Hall.

98. AR (1911–12), in CUB, XVIII (Nov., 1912), 19. The inveterate Irish lecturer Shane Leslie characterized Shahan as "a man who might have found his life amongst the

The Cardinal Gibbons Memorial Hall, completed in 1912 to commemorate the golden anniversary of the priestly ordination and the silver anniversary of the elevation to the cardinalate of the first chancellor, built and used continuously as a residence for lay students, with basement space for a chapel and offices.

add a chapel to this building but eventually, in 1962, its dining and residential spaces were expanded instead. Along the same street, in the same style, but with the Apostolic Mission House intervening, the Martin Maloney Chemical Laboratory was built simultaneously. The donor, a papal marquis, gave $120,000 toward its completion by 1917; it had opened in October, 1914.[99] Later, during 1923–24, he provided an additional $100,000 for the construction of an adjacent auditorium.

As it turned out, no other university buildings were to be erected in collegiate Gothic. Attention first had to be diverted to several pressing needs. One was space for the Catholic Sisters College that, after involved discussions that had begun early in 1909, the trustees decided

Irish scribes or the medieval builders." *American Wonderland; Memories of Four Tours in the United States of America (1911–1935)* (London: Michael Joseph, 1936), 127–28.

99. A visiting vice chancellor of the University of London was shocked because the building was as fully equipped and nearly as large as any chemistry building in Great Britain. Arthur E. Shipley, *The Voyage of a Vice Chancellor* (New York: G. P. Putnam's Sons, 1919), 37.

to establish as a separate corporation. It opened during 1911–12 in a temporary building on the property of the Benedictine Sisters in Brookland, although it was not incorporated until early in 1914. Land was acquired through the purchase of a farm at some remove from the campus. The temporary building was moved there and construction of a central building was initiated with gifts of $25,000 each from Genevieve Garvan (Mrs. Nicholas F.) Brady of New York and her sister, Mrs. James C. Farrell of Albany in honor of Anthony Nicholas Brady, founder of a fortune in rapid transit, public utilities and oil.[100] Additional gifts of $250,000 from the former and $50,000 from the latter allowed the completion and equipment of two wings of the building in the early 1920s. To Curley, the training of teaching religious in this Brady Hall was "the real golden link between the Catholic University and the whole Catholic educational system in this country."[101] Sisters who were students lived in Brady Hall or in houses that were established by their communities in the immediate vicinity.

By 1916, additions to the campus had enlarged it to 144 acres. There were eight buildings. Seven religious houses of men had been established in the vicinity. Students numbered 554, of whom only 144 were ecclesiastics. Thus Shahan and the board had to be deeply engaged in planning for a gymnasium. Early in his first term, they had resorted to temporary expedients in a stucco building because "motives of necessary economy caused the Board to consign to the Greek Calends the desirability of a gymnasium, club and assembly rooms for the students" although it was recognized that these were "most attractive features of a University to American students."[102] After committee meetings, consultations with faculty, alumni, and friends, and the coming of World War I, "a temporary gymnasium" was authorized in April, 1918. Before the November meeting of the board in that year "a gymnasium, or drill hall" was being erected. It continued in use as a gymnasium until 1985. When it was completed, in 1919, Shahan reported that it lacked "no feature of such an edifice" and that a three-story annex provided by the Knights of Columbus was being used by "the large body of young soldiers on the grounds."[103] A financial statement later showed that $86,564 had been contributed by alumni and friends, of which Cardinal Gibbons alone

100. AAB, Gibbons Papers, 115-T-8, Shahan to Gibbons, Washington, June 5, 1915.
101. AAB, Curley Papers, B 1461, Curley to Brady, Baltimore, Oct. 14, 1922 (copy).
102. BT, mm, Apr. 17, 1912. In 1908, it had been proposed that "with a gymnasium, club house and social assembly building" the university "could keep many a student from even the knowledge of temptations that greet him during the winter months." Spensely Papers, "Additional note concerning a gymnasium."
103. AR (1918–19), 9.

had provided $35,000; $99,600 had been contributed by the Knights of
Columbus; and $42,860 had been applied from an estate left to the
university.[104] Nearby there was opened in May of 1919 a federally
assisted Soldiers' Rehabilitation Camp. The National Catholic War
Council erected for it a building to provide vocational training, and
when this was acquired by the university in 1923 it was named St.
John's Hall.

Soon, with Louis H. Crook, a prominent professor of engineering, as
the planner, construction of an athletic field and stadium was begun.
Arthur Maguire of Detroit chaired an alumni campaign that was to
finance the project. By early 1924, when a little more than $16,000
had been raised, more than $27,000 had been spent in draining and
grading the field. Shahan urged that the stadium should be completed
by diverting to it two gifts of $25,000 each that he had received from
Edward Cudahay of the Chicago packing family, which he had originally
intended to use for the library.[105] He expected that "the finished Bowl
would be our chief financial asset"[106] and even after the board had
authorized the completion of the stadium he professed to hope that the
alumni would somehow "devise means for making some return to the
general University fund."[107] President Calvin Coolidge was present for
the dedication on October 4, 1924.

The John K. Mullen of Denver Library became the first campus
building to be affected by the design of the Shrine. Even as early as
1901, Conaty had urged upon the trustees that the need of a separate
library building could not be "too strongly emphasized."[108] The permanent visiting committee had reported from its first meeting that it
was an "urgent necessity."[109] Reiteration of the need, however, could not
overcome the "want of funds" that was then postponing also the construction of the chemical laboratory and the gymnasium, both destined to
be built before the library. Shahan reported an early donation of "over
$100,000" from an unnamed benefactor[110] and then the two $25,000 gifts
from Cudahay. The offer of a gift from Mullen was announced in 1921;[111]
it would amount to $500,000. There were cost over-runs that did not have
the prior approval of the trustees, to the distress of the treasurer who knew

104. OR, "Financial Statement," June 30, 1921.
105. AR (1918–19), 4; AR (1919–20), 3.
106. AAB, Curley Papers, S 893, Shahan to Curley, Washington, Apr. 25, 1924.
107. AR (1924–25), 19.
108. AR (1900–1901), 7.
109. BT, mm, Apr. 21, 1909, exh.
110. Ibid., Nov. 20, 1918.
111. BT, mm, Apr. 1, 1921.

all too well that the use of endowment for building was not only poor practice but would reduce for current purposes "already meager income."[112] Moreover, after Mullen had remitted $400,000 of his pledge, he was reported as demanding "ten scholarships, five full scholarships and five tuition scholarships, in recognition of his donation," with power of appointment, all of which Shahan recommended and the board accepted, in the expectation not to be realized, that not only the remainder of the pledge but also the excess expenditures might be forthcoming from the donor or his children.[113] The full basement and the front and central portions of the superstructure were completed and opened in 1928, the remaining side portions not until 1958.

Three important collections were added to library resources during Shahan's terms. The first was the donation of the library and *objets d'art* of Manoel de Oliveira Lima, accepted by the trustees in 1916 but, because of the war, not delivered from London until 1921. An alumnus, Monsignor Joseph M. Gleason of Oakland, California, was instrumental in persuading Lima, who was concluding a long career in the Brazilian diplomatic service, to make the gift to the university. The donor, who was favorably impressed with Shahan, insisted upon the separate housing of the collection and became curator for life, "for the pleasure of it."[114] The university received also the personal library of over 10,000 volumes, some of them rare, of Archbishop Curley.[115] Then, during his last term, Shahan raised the money to purchase the library of the Albani family of Pesaro, Italy, better known as the Clementine Library because Pope Clement XI was of the family and had contributed to the collection. It was a Franciscan friend and one-time colleague of Shahan's successor who discovered the availability of the library, which was not delivered until after Shahan had left office.[116]

It is not difficult to understand why Shahan has been appraised as

112. AAB, Joseph J. Nelligan Papers, John J. Nelligan to Patrick Hayes, Baltimore, Nov. 24, 1925 (copy).

113. BT, mm, Sept. 14, 1926.

114. BT, mm, Nov. 15, 1916, with exh., Lima to Shahan, Rio de Janeiro, Oct. 2, 1916. See also, OR, Gleason to Joseph M. Corrigan, Oakland, Apr. 10, 1942, and Herbert Wright to Corrigan, Apr. 14, 1942. Lima had earlier hailed the university in his *Nos Estados Unidos, Impressões Politicas e Sociaes* (Leipzig: F. A. Brockhaus, 1899), Chap. VII, "Catholicismo e Educacao." See Manoel de S. S. Cardozo, "Manoel De Oliveira Lima, His Life and Library," *CUB*, N.S., XII, No. 3 (Nov. 1944), 6–8.

115. BT, mm, Apr. 11, 1923. AAB, Curley Papers, Shahan to Curley, Washington, Dec. 17, 1922 and Jan. 5, 1923.

116. OR, Edwin Auweiler, O.F.M., to J. H. Ryan, Florence, Dec. 11, 1925; Ludwig Pastor to Shahan, Innsbruck, Sept. 6, 1928. For an illustrated description, see Michael Olinert, "A Pope's Library Is Brought to Light after 200 Years," *Smithsonian*, VIII, No. 10 (Jan. 1978), 70–77.

"the Rector-builder." One who came to know him well and who afterward was a central figure serving his successors has evaluated him as
"destined not to advance the University in productive scholarship but
to give it the fundamental buildings so greatly needed."[117] Even with
such an important reservation, however, he did not hesitate to call
Shahan the "second founder" of the university.[118]

Visibility in Service

Shahan was not only a builder of physical plant. His administration
led to the extension of the young university's educational influence
nationally. Although, with exaggeration, he accorded primacy to the
service that was being accomplished by "the creation of a distinguished
Catholic professoriate at the National Capital, second to none in the
world,"[119] he liked to emphasize that the university had gradually become "a fertile source of general Catholic services, educational and
charitable."[120] This contribution had been foreshadowed in Leo XIII's
founding document and, after Keane's untiring effort to begin with
professorial strength, had been initiated by Conaty. As the latter's
college and seminary conferences developed into the Catholic Educational Association, the usefulness of the university as a coordinating
agency could no longer be successfully challenged. It was becoming an
instrument in the development of organization that was being seen as
"brought about not so much by the planning of the Hierarchy as by
force of circumstances and institution of American methods," to the
extent that it could be called "the greatest recent change in American
Catholicism."[121] Shahan's thrusts in service were in the direction of
training for teaching and institutional development, on the one hand,
and of national organization and media, on the other.

Shahan needed little urging to emphasize training for teaching but
he received it steadily from Pace and Shields who were convinced that
professional preparation of teachers was necessary if Catholic schools
were to compete successfully with the public schools and if, because
teacher training was not available under Catholic auspices, Catholic
schools were not to become "to all intents and purposes, annexes of the
public school system."[122] Pace and Shahan had visited Münster in 1906

117. Deferrari, *Memoirs*, 400.
118. Deferrari, *Layman*, 136.
119. AR (1909–10), in *CUB*, XVI (Nov., 1910), 7.
120. OR, draft, n.d.
121. Peter Guilday Papers, John F. Fenlon, S.S., to Guilday, Baltimore, Jan. 16,
1926.
122. BT, mm, Apr. 21, 1909, exh., Shields and Pace to O'Connell, Mar. 1, 1908,
and "Some Relations of Catholic to Non-Catholic Schools."

to see at first hand the institution for teaching sisters that the bishops of Germany had opened there in 1899.[123] Shields, traveling around the country, lecturing on education and conducting institutes, thought that "everywhere" there was "beginning to be a realization of the great need of the University's influence in uniting and uplifting all our Catholic schools."[124] He was already offering correspondence courses and had founded on his own in 1906 what became the Catholic Education Press, through which he published textbooks that used pedagogical advances and maintained the central place of religion in education. He withstood strong opposition for his departure from traditional catechetical forms. Under his leadership, the department of education began in 1911 the publication of the *Catholic Educational Review* and in this organ and the *Catholic University Bulletin* he was able to propagate his ideas. Also in this banner year for Catholic teachers there were inaugurated summer sessions for women, both religious and lay, and, in the fall, what was to become the Catholic Sisters College. The following year a national program for the affiliation of high schools and colleges was begun.

Teacher training was made an obvious necessity by the increasing momentum of the high school movement that had begun about the middle of the nineteenth century. Spalding had pointed to the need in 1890.[125] Pace had made an effort with summer offerings in New York, where Corrigan and his successor, Farley, had shown that they were concerned about the need.[126] But the trustees did not authorize the opening of a "Summer School of Pedagogy" until 1911. Its organization for the first year has been attributed to the psychologist Thomas Verner Moore, O.S.B., and the registrar, Charles F. Borden; Shields assumed direction in 1912.[127] Shahan was able to report with pleasure that thirty-one states and one foreign country (Quebec) were represented among the 255 religious and 29 lay women who were enrolled in the first session and that "plainly . . . the Summer School was a move in the right direction."[128] The success soon led to the organization of branches. The first was in Dubuque, where 233 sisters were enrolled in 1914. Then, after the conduct of one-week institutes in 1916 and 1917, a five-week session was offered in San Francisco in 1918. Of course, during the

123. Paul G. Gleis, "Die deutschstammige Klosterfrau im Studium an der Universität," in Timpe, *op. cit.*, 209.
124. OR, Shields to Shahan, Washington, June 24, 1909.
125. "Normal Schools for Catholics, CW, LI (April, 1890), 88–97.
126. OR, "The Proposed Summer School for Teachers in New York City," Feb. 20, 1902.
127. Roy J. Deferrari Papers, Deferrari to Bryan J. McEntegart, June 1, 1954 (copy).
128. AR (1910–112), in CUB, XVII (Nov., 1911), 14.

entire period when Shahan was in office, since the university was still closed to women, the summer session in Washington became "a part of the Sisters College migrating to the University campus for six weeks during July and August."[129] There was no university summer session until 1929.

The response to the summer offerings in 1911 confirmed the need for the teachers' college. According to his younger colleague and his successor in several of his positions, even Shields "never had thought that the urgency of the demand would be shown by the Sisters themselves."[130] Shahan had laid a plan before the board while he was still acting rector and the permanent visiting committee had recommended its consideration at its very first meeting. Coeducation was still so much feared, however, as was the possible mingling of religious with the laity and even the mingling of the congregations themselves, and resources were viewed as so limited, that it was thought necessary to establish the college as a "completely separate corporation," which was not accomplished until 1914, and to build a separate campus.[131] At Shields's urging, Shahan did not wait for the formalities to be completed. While the proposal was still under consideration, he circulated a questionnaire to which he received replies from sixty teaching communities, only five of which, and these chiefly cloistered, did not approve his project.[132]

When classes in the new college opened during the academic year 1911–12, twenty-nine sisters of eleven different communities were in attendance. A tract of fifty-seven acres was purchased by Shields. In 1912 the university's bachelor of arts degree was conferred on eighteen sisters; in 1913, in addition to the bachelor's, the master of arts degree upon twenty-five, and in 1914, for the first time, the doctor of philosophy degree upon two. Shahan explained, "The instruction, leading to

129. Deferrari, *Memoirs*, 26.

130. Patrick J. McCormick, "Introduction," in Ward, *op. cit.*, xiii.

131. BT, mm, Apr. 21 and Nov. 17, 1909; Apr. 6 and Nov. 16, 1910; Apr. 17 and Nov. 20, 1912; Apr. 2, 1913; Apr. 22, 1914; and OR, Walter George Smith to Shahan, Philadelphia, Sept. 24, 1909; June 9 and July 14, 1911; Michael J. Lavelle to Shahan, New York, Oct. 18, 1909; James H. Blenk to Shahan, New Orleans, Dec. 20, 1909; Regis Canevin to Farley, Pittsburgh, Oct. 14, 1912; Henry Moeller to Shahan, Norwood, Ohio, Apr. 7, 1913.

132. BT, mm, Apr. 6, 1910, exh. A summary was sent to the apostolic delegate. ASV, DA, XVII, No. 1a/2, Shahan to Falconio, Washington, Mar. 1, 1910. Ambivalence was shown, however, by such leaders as Francis W. Howard, secretary of the Catholic Educational Association, who saw the need for centralization but feared the possible effects upon religious life (*ibid.*, II, 105/2, Howard to Venerable Sister, Columbus Ohio, June 10, 1911), and Mother M. Cleophas of St. Mary of the Woods College, who reported to Archbishop John Bonzano, the apostolic delegate, that after sending sisters to Washington she found the religious spirit "exposed to many dangers" (*ibid*, XIX, 905, Terre Haute, Mar. 31, 1913).

The Catholic Sisters College, opened in 1911 and separately incorporated until its dissolution in 1964. During the 1970s the site came to be called the Varnum campus.

the degrees of the University, was given under the direction of the latter by its professors, but apart from the regular courses and outside the University," although it was "identical in content and method with the parallel courses given in other departments of the University."[133] Under the rules approved by the trustees, sisters were not "permitted to attend classes or lectures nor to visit in any of the University buildings without special permission from the Ecclesiastical Superior," nor were university students "permitted to visit students of the Teachers College, in the College, without special permission from the Chancellor of the University."[134] By June of 1923, when degrees were publicly conferred upon sisters for the first time, 3,206 sisters had been enrolled. It was reported that enrollment during the previous year had reached 1,621 students, of whom 807 were lay women.[135]

The success of the summer session and of the first year of the Catholic Sisters College paved the way for approval of the program of affiliation

133. AR (1911–12) in CUB, XVIII (Nov., 1912), 8.
134. BT, mm, Apr. 22, 1914, exh.
135. OR, NC press release, June 18, 1923.

of high schools and colleges in 1912.[136] State universities had developed such systems, but this was the first under Catholic auspices. It promoted standards through inspections and common examinations, among other means. It could be seen as "one part of a master plan to upgrade curricula, to improve instructional outcome, and to supplement university efforts in teacher training."[137] After Shields's death, when Father Leo McVay continued to serve as secretary of the university committee responsible for the program, Pace emphasized as "the essential point" that through affiliation there had been built up "a real Catholic educational system with the University as its centre."[138] Although the program became rather "static" after Shields's death, it was to be revived vigorously in 1939 under the direction of Roy J. Deferrari until, its usefulness undone by the progress that it had helped to spur, it was terminated by action of the trustees in 1968.[139]

The program established in 1912 was not related to the affiliation of seminaries that, although recognized as an institutional mandate, had been steadily resisted by the faculty charged with administering the examinations for university degrees. Excluding the institutions in the vicinity of the campus, the St. Paul Seminary was still the only seminary affiliate when Shahan took office. The minutes of the trustees' deliberations on the subject suggest that the bishops wanted a plan put into effect, not so much to achieve the coordination and standardization for which the early advocates of affiliation pleaded as to obtain the prestige that the university might lend to their diocesan institutions. In 1910, for example, the board had asked "to have the 4th year of Theology made at the University, the students receiving, if according to Regulations the Degree of S.T.B. at the end of the third year in the Seminary."[140] A year later it instructed the senate "to report to the Visiting Committee modified revised and more lenient conditions for the obtaining of degrees in the Faculty of Theology."[141] Seminarians taking advantage of arrange-

136. BT, mm, Apr. 17, 1912. For a comprehensive account, see Rita Watrin, *The Founding and Development of the Program of Affiliation of the Catholic University of America: 1912 to 1939* (Washington, D.C.: The Catholic University of America Press, 1966). It is interesting to note that in recent years the Carnegie Foundation for the Advancement of Teaching has proposed that secondary education in the United States would be improved if every college and university would establish "a comprehensive partnership" with one or more high schools. CHE, XXVII, No. 4 (Sept. 21, 1983), 1.

137. Harold A. Buetow, *Of Singular Benefit, The Story of Catholic Education in the United States* (New York: Macmillan, 1970), 187.

138. AR (1923–24), 83. For an example of how the university assisted teaching communities, see Sister Generosa Callahan, C.D.P., *Mother Angelique Ayres, Dreamer and Builder of Our Lady of the Lake University* (Austin: Jenkins Publishing, 1981).

139. AS, mm, Nov. 21. 1968; BT, mm, Dec. 7, 1968.

140. BT, mm, Apr. 6, 1910.

141. *Ibid.*, Apr. 26, 1911.

ments were urged, in a provision of the affiliation agreement, "to pursue higher studies at the University."[142] Within a decade, however, the visiting committee was recommending discontinuance of the plan because the university was deemed "not prepared to give the vital training needed for the last remaining year."[143] As late as 1923–24, although the Paulist, Marist, and Holy Cross Fathers in the immediate vicinity had accepted the conditions of the affiliation agreement at once, there were only four affiliated seminaries elsewhere—at St. Paul, Mount Saint Mary's of the West in Cincinnati, St. Francis in Milwaukee, and the Benedictine St. John's University in Minnesota. The seminary at Maryknoll was affiliated the next year.[144] Curley saw the problem in the light of a broader need to overhaul seminary education as a whole and he sought to have the seminaries and the university consider together "the present day demands of the young Priests going out in the world of work."[145]

Service of another kind was required of the university when the United States entered World War I. Even before, Shahan and others were participating in consultations on military education.[146] Shortly before the formal declaration of war, Shahan wrote to President Woodrow Wilson to offer the services of the university in the nation's cause.[147] Other institutions, too, were concerned, as Shahan's delegate to a meeting of the Association of American Universities explained, "to impress upon the National Government the fundamental importance of conserving and properly utilizing our institutions of higher education; and to mobilize all of our educational forces, not only for the service of the country throughout the war, but also for the difficult period after the war."[148] The campus was decimated by the mobilization although engineering students were given a deferred classification. Graduate instruction was reported as "diminished almost to nothing, because of the salaries paid by government to scientific men, especially to chemists."[149]

142. *Ibid.*, Nov. 19, 1913, exh.

143. *Ibid.*, Apr. 1, 1921, exh.

144. The founders of the Catholic Foreign Mission Society had met at the university and it was first thought that their Maryknoll seminary should be established at the university. See George C. Powers, M.M., *The Maryknoll Moment* (Maryknoll, N.Y.: Catholic Foreign Mission Society of America, 1920).

145. AAB, Curley Papers, D 1281, Curley to Dowling, Baltimore, Feb. 11, 1926 (copy).

146. OR, Shahan to Josephus Daniels, secretary of the navy, Washington, May 15, 1916; Shahan to Abbot Lawrence Lowell, president of Harvard University, Washington, Oct. 9, 1916 (copies).

147. *Ibid.*, Shahan to Wilson, Washington, Mar. 28, 1917 (copy), and Wilson's reply, Mar. 30, 1917.

148. *Ibid.*, Kerby to Shahan, Washington, May 10, 1917.

149. BT, mm, Apr. 10, 1918, exh.

After the conclusion of hostilities, Shahan reported to the trustees that more than eight hundred former students had entered military service, of whom thirteen had sacrificed their lives, that more than fifty priest alumni had served as chaplains, that some six hundred young paymasters had been commissioned from the training school operated by the paymaster general of the United States Navy in Gibbons and Albert Halls, that the Student Army Training Corps inaugurated during September, 1918, had had a unit at the university with about five hundred enrolled, that the new Maloney Chemical Laboratory had been turned over to the government for the research of some sixty chemists, and that Liberty Loan subscriptions were being successfully promoted on campus.[150] The famed chaplain Father Francis P. Duffy of the "Fighting Sixty-ninth" had attended the university from 1896 to 1898 and had received the Distinguished Service Cross. Maloney Hall, on the other hand, had been the scene of inhumane invention, since it was there, where research on gases had been conducted as early as 1904 by the head of the department, that the poisonous lewisite gas had been developed.[151]

Shahan and the university rendered a unique service to the American Church when the war prompted the formation of the National Catholic War Council.[152] Recognition of the importance of a national agency led thereafter to the successor National Catholic Welfare Conference that is now known as the United States Catholic Conference. The role of the university in American Catholic life had sometimes—even if infrequently—been the subject of deliberation during the annual meetings of the archbishops of the country that had been inaugurated in 1890. After their spring meeting in 1917, the episcopal trustees of the university discussed informally the anticipated needs of Catholic service personnel. Alumnus John J. Burke, C.S.P., editor of the *Catholic World*, took the initiative to organize a meeting of diocesan and organizational representatives on the campus during August, 1917. This became the origin of the National Catholic War Council. Burke's principal lieutenants were his personal friend Kerby, of the department of sociology and the National Conference of Catholic Charities; his fellow-Paulist, Lewis O'Hern, whom the archbishops had appointed in 1913 to head a chaplains' bureau; and Charles P. Neill, who had been the university's

---

150. *AR* (1918–19), 12.

151. W. Lee Lewis, "Chemical War Work at the Catholic University of America," *CUB*, XXV (Dec., 1919), 271–74. See also, Dixon, *op. cit.*, 155–56.

152. See Elizabeth McKeown, *War and Welfare; American Catholics and World War I* (New York: Garland Publishing, 1988), for a full account; John B. Sheerin, C.S.P., *Never Look Back: The Career and Concerns of John J. Burke* (New York: Paulist Press, 1975), on Burke, and Kauffman, *op. cit.*, 200–203, 217–19, on the organizational meetings.

first appointee in economics and who was serving on a national Commission on Training Camp Activities.

According to a contemporary observer who was close to Shahan, Kerby aroused Shahan's interest in these developments and Shahan in turn persuaded Gibbons to take the leadership in promoting the organization.[153] In any case, after the meeting of the university's trustees in November, 1917, Gibbons was able to report to all the bishops an informal "unanimous opinion that the Hierarchy should act in concert" and that "the Board of Archbishops should organize without delay as a Catholic War Council."[154] This was a result that Burke had sought by forming an executive council of archdiocesan delegates to the August meeting. Within a few months, the archbishops assumed control, made the council an official agency of the hierarchy, and appointed its administrative committee. Burke continued, first as chairman of the bishops' committee on special war activities and afterward as the first general secretary of the NCWC.

Subsequently, Shahan impressed upon a former auditor of the apostolic delegation in Washington, Archbishop (later Cardinal) Bonaventura Ceretti, whom Pope Benedict XV had sent as his representative to the golden jubilee celebration of Cardinal Gibbons's episcopacy, the need for annual meetings of all the bishops. After the archbishops decided in February, 1919, that the entire hierarchy should indeed meet annually, Shahan reportedly planned their fall meeting "single-handed and alone."[155] The annual meetings of the hierarchy were held on the campus until 1966, when the accommodations that could be provided were no longer adequate. The pastoral letter issued after the first world war was written by Pace. It was in 1919 also that the administrative committee of the War Council issued in its name a statement on social reconstruction written by John A. Ryan that placed the hierarchy in support of progressive social action.[156] Evidently Shahan, who recognized the importance of national movements, had hoped to utilize the national organization of the bishops for an appeal for the university and was thwarted in this objective only by the influence of one member of the hierarchy upon Gibbons, whom Shahan thought had earlier been convinced on the point.[157]

153. John O'Grady Papers, autobiography (manuscript).
154. OR, circular letter, Baltimore, Nov. 21, 1917.
155. O'Grady Papers, O'Grady to Henry J. Browne, Washington, May 5, 1950 (copy).
156. "Program of Social Reconstruction," in Nolan, *op. cit.*, I, 255–71. See Joseph M. McShane, S.J., *"Sufficiently Radical": Catholicism, Progressivism, and the Bishops' Program of 1919* (Washington, D.C.: The Catholic University of America Press, 1986).
157. O'Grady Papers, autobiography.

Individual members of the faculties had especially important roles in the launching of the NCWC. John A. Ryan was chosen to head a department of social action and carried on his new duties simultaneously with his teaching until his retirement from the university in 1940. He remained director of the department until his death in 1945. Pace was delegated to proceed with the organization of a department of education, for which James Hugh Ryan of the diocese of Indianapolis was recruited as secretary. Two years later Ryan was engaged also to teach philosophy at the university and he continued in the two positions until his appointment in 1928 to succeed Shahan. At that time, he was succeeded in turn at NCWC by George Johnson, a priest of the diocese of Toledo, who had been appointed to the department of education in 1921. As a bishop had written before the decisive organizational steps had been taken, the time was ripe "for having a representative agent and bureau of Catholic education in Washington, independent of the University, but of course affiliated with it, for the purpose of keeping track of every bill in the educational, social[,] moral, and religious spheres."[158] Similarly, Shahan was corresponding in some detail with O'Grady concerning the "so-called Americanization problem," to which popular attention and foundation funds were being devoted, often with "sinister reflections on the Church."[159]

Concern for the needs of the armed forces led to a pioneer project in social work education that, with the conduct of Trinity College and the Catholic Sisters College as precedents, utilized university personnel while remaining outside the university's formal structure. A National Service School for Women began on an estate known as Clifton under the auspices first of the National Catholic War Council and then of the bishops' special committee. A subcommittee on women's activities was being chaired by Kerby, who was assisted until 1920 by his colleague John Montgomery Cooper, already known as a religious educator and anthropologist. Clifton became, in 1921, at a new location in northwest Washington, a resident professional school chartered by the District of Columbia to which the name National Catholic School of Social Service was later given. Since the university did not then admit women, it could not establish the school, although five of the first thirteen members of the faculty were from its own ranks, as were many thereafter. The management and support of the school were entrusted officially to the National Council of Catholic Women that had been established

158. OVR, Louis B. Walsh to Pace, Portland, Me., Feb. 14, 1919.
159. OR, O'Grady to Shahan, Washington, Dec. 19, 1918, and Jan. 13, 1919.

under the NCWC in 1920. Charles P. Neill served as director of the school for the first year but did not remain when it became evident that an intended twin school for men would not materialize. In 1923 the school gained accreditation from the National Association of Schools of Social Work and was affiliated with the university, and the master's degrees earned within it were conferred by the university. This relationship became more involved as years passed until, in 1947, retaining its name, the NCSSS was merged with the school of social work that had been established on the campus in 1934.[160]

More controversial was the university's relationship to the Knights of Columbus Evening School, initiated in 1919, and especially to the Columbus University, which obtained a charter in 1922. Evening schools were a national project of the Knights after World War I and provided what came to be called adult education with a vocational and patriotic emphasis. At their peak in the spring of 1920, there were more than a hundred schools in the nation enrolling more than fifty thousand students.[161] The dean of the Washington school was Frank O'Hara of the university's department of economics, and twenty of the twenty-four teachers were from the university. The visiting committee of the board of trustees described the school, which was conducted at St. John's College on Vermont Avenue, as "practically under University control, though not officially so."[162] About 1,500 students were reported as registered during 1923–24. The university had affiliated the school for its collegiate offerings in 1921 and in 1924 it recognized its secondary school offerings to provide for "a large group of Catholic students who otherwise would go elsewhere to continue their studies."[163]

When O'Hara established the Columbus University, Shahan became alarmed "that such an institution would be a constant cause of confusion and embarrassment" to the university.[164] Formal difficulties were resolved by O'Hara's resignation from the presidency of the institution and from its board of trustees, but he and others continued to teach courses until Shahan's successor took measures to terminate such relationships. Appreciating the service being rendered to Catholics who were unable to attend regular university courses, Archbishop Curley

160. For the history, see Loretta R. Lawler, *Full Circle: The Story of the National Catholic School of Social Service, 1918–1947* (Washington, D.C.: The Catholic University of America Press, 1951). See also Sheerin, *op. cit.*, 39.

161. Kauffman, *op. cit.*, 226.

162. BT, mm, Apr. 14, 1920, exh.

163. AR (1923–24), 22.

164. BT, mm, Sept. 26, 1922. Pace was soon able to report that the supreme board of directors of the Knights of Columbus was dissociating itself from the Columbus University. AS, mm, Nov. 3, 1922.

nevertheless later conceded, "The thing in itself is absurd."[165] Programs limited to law and accountancy continued to be offered until 1954 when the assets of the institution were transferred to the university.

Shahan, following in this respect the precedent established by Conaty in 1904, continued as president of the Catholic Educational Association. American Education Week was observed annually. A national outlook in other fields of Catholic endeavor was promoted. In 1910, the National Conference of Catholic Charities was organized on the campus, largely through the initiative of Kerby, who became its first secretary, but with Shahan in the role of "the real founder" and the president until 1927.[166] As the new organization got under way, Shahan pointed to the university as no longer "only a corps of teachers and students" but "a natural center or forum for the largest and most important works of Holy Church in this favored land."[167] In 1916, he agreed to serve as director of the International Federation of Catholic Alumnae, assuming a role in which the rector and vice rector of the university continued as long as they were clerics. In 1919, he was able to encourage Guilday in the foundation of the American Catholic Historical Association, which still has its home on the campus, as does the American Catholic Philosophical Association that was founded in 1926.

The campus was also the setting for meetings of many other groups. The national convention of the Holy Name Society was held during September, 1924, and later the Dominican philosopher, Ignatius Smith, took the initiative of organizing it at the university. Under the direction of Cooper, the Missionary Anthropological Conference was established in 1926. The following year the organizing committee of the Catholic Association for International Peace met. Shahan himself undertook organizational responsibilities as well. After World War I, at the request of Gibbons, he headed a general appeal for the restoration of the sister institutions at Lille and Louvain that had been in the path of hostilities.[168] Similarly, after proposing a fund-raising effort for the restoration of the church of San Francesca at Ravenna, he served on the national committee that was organized.

Scholarly journals were especially encouraged by Shahan. Shields had already begun to produce the *Catholic Educational Review* in 1911

165. AAB, Curley Papers, R 1403, Curley to J. H. Ryan, Baltimore, Dec. 1, 1928 (copy).

166. Donald P. Gavin, *The National Conference of Catholic Charities, 1910–1960* (Milwaukee: Bruce Press, 1962), 15.

167. AR (1909–10), 4.

168. OR, circular, June 20, 1919; also, Duval to Shahan, New York, July 3, 1919. Duval was an important donor for the restoration of Louvain.

and Guilday the *Catholic Historical Review* in 1915. The *Catholic Charities Review,* edited by John A. Ryan, began to appear from the campus in 1917 as the organ of the NCCC. *The New Scholasticism,* the organ of the American Catholic Philosophical Association, began publication in 1927. Finally, although Shahan was unsuccessful in persuading the faculty of theology to accept responsibility for a theological review without remuneration therefor, during his final year in office the *American Ecclesiastical Review* that Heuser had founded in Philadelphia many years before and had continued to edit was transferred to the university.[169] During the same year there appeared the first issue of the anthropological quarterly, *Primitive Man* (now *Anthropological Quarterly*), edited by Cooper.

Supplementing these journals, dissertations and other reports of research were organized in series. There were, for example, Patristic Studies, Educational Research Monographs, Philosophical Studies, and Studies in Psychology and Psychiatry. Coordination of this publication program was attempted through a Catholic University Press which, however, remained "a title rather than an organization" until 1939.[170] Shields, of course, had his Catholic Education Press. Also, in 1912, the board authorized joint publication with the Catholic University of Louvain of the Corpus Scriptorum Christianorum Orientalium, a series of translations from the languages of the East which Shahan foresaw as "destined to render to Oriental studies a service similar to the Migne Collection of Christian writings in Greek and Latin."[171] This followed closely upon the project that Hyvernat undertook for J. P. Morgan, the publication of fifty-three volumes in the Coptic section of the CSCO based upon the manuscripts that Morgan had assembled.[172]

Something of the role that the university had in giving visibility not only to itself but to the Catholic community in the United States can be inferred simply by noting the organizations that met on the campus during the year 1929–30, the first after Shahan left the office of rector. Three were associations with devotional aims: the Holy Name Society of the Archdiocese of Baltimore, the Catholic Students Mission Crusade, and the Association of the Miraculous Medal. Three were scholarly groups, the American Catholic Philosophical Association, the Ameri-

---

169. ST, mm, Jan. 14 and 29, 1924; OR, agreement, Dec. 31, 1927, and Shahan to Heuser, Washington, Feb. 15, 1928 (copy).

170. OVR, Pace to John R. Hagan, Washington, Apr. 2, 1920.

171. AR (1912–13), 4; see A. Vaschalde, "Historical Sketch of the Corpus Scriptorum Christianorum Orientalium," *CUB,* XX (Mar., 1914), 248–57.

172. "The Pierpont Morgan Collection of Coptic Manuscripts," *CUB,* XVIII (Feb., 1912), 186–90, reprinting a report from the *New York Sun,* Dec. 31, 1911.

can Catholic Historical Association, and the Catholic Anthropological
Conference. And three were concerned with broad aspects of educational or national policy, the Catholic Association for International
Peace, the Superintendents Section of what had just become the National Catholic Educational Association, and the National Catholic
Action Federation. As Shahan had foreseen before he had assumed the
office of rector, the university had become "a great hopper, in and
through which, the better elements of the various nationalities (in so
far as they are of our faith) [would have to] pass; in order that Catholicism
[should] present to the government and society of the United States a
uniform front by intelligent loyalty, sincere patriotism, and consistent
devotion to the public need."[173]

The Visibility of Students and Alumni

The students who were still in the "hopper" and the alumni who had
passed through it during the university's early decades could follow with
their own eyes the construction on the campus and the organizational
contributions that the young institution was making to Catholic life in
the United States. When he became acting rector, Shahan had found
that the 140 ecclesiastics and the eighty-five laymen who were then
enrolled were "in general well-behaved and docile."[174] Student organizations had come into being even during the first year of the institution's
existence, when only clerics were enrolled, with the formation of a
literary society, but the admission of undergraduate laymen, even in the
small numbers of the early years, was bound to give rise to campus
activities as varied as their talents and interests. The subculture of
"college life" soon took root on the campus.[175] Tuition scholarships
offered by the university were making possible a slow increase in enrollment; eventually, beginning in 1922, loans became available through
the Harmon Foundation.[176] Although as the number of laymen thus
began to increase, "a steady tightening up of discipline" was declared to
be necessary,[177] the mingling of the lay youths with the student priests
was already being perceived as conducive to a "general correctness of
life."[178]

Then as now, of course, competition in sports was followed avidly.

173. Shahan Papers, Shahan to H. J. Barry, Washington, Dec. 12, 1903 (copy).
174. BT, mm, Apr. 21, 1909, exh.
175. See Helen Lefkowitz Horowitz, *Campus Life; Undergraduate Cultures from the End
of the Eighteenth Century to the Present* (New York: Alfred A. Knopf, 1987).
176. BD, Ethel L. Bedient to Kerby, New York, Mar. 15, 1923.
177. Spensley, in *AR* (1912–13), 23.
178. Shahan, *ibid.*, 6.

There had been friendly games of baseball among the aspiring clerics during the university's first years—in one of which the Paulist novices, taking a cue from a principal reform movement of the day, pitted the Total Abstainers against the Non-Totals[179]—and very soon after the admission of undergraduates a faculty committee on athletics had been appointed.[180] About the same time, it is interesting to note, the Washington Board of Trade had a committee that was discussing college athletics.[181] The faculty committee argued that athletics should be encouraged "as a means of satisfying the students already in residence and of attracting others to the University."[182] Its theme was repeated in one of the first reports that Shahan received, in which the priest-proctor of the only residence hall for laymen at the time reminded him that while the parents of a prospective student might ponder over the course of studies that the university was offering, the young man himself would be "conning athletic records."[183] The faculty committee was sponsoring annual athletic balls at downtown hotels and finding satisfaction in the attendance at them of representatives of Washington seminaries and colleges, social leaders, and lending "dignity to the affair"—"a good quota of the faculty."[184]

Limits had been made explicit when Shahan's predecessor had asked the chancellor to resolve campus differences about the support of travel for intercollegiate competition. Gibbons had withheld his approval in view of "the small number of students . . . the loss of study entailed and the crippled condition" of the institution's finances.[185] But when Shahan took office the baseball team was already performing so well against the local competition that it could be credited with "gaining a national reputation" while athletics in general were said to be assuming "the same prominence as in other universities."[186] After a few years, a student editor, reviewing the history, remarked that it was not until 1909, the first year of Shahan's incumbency, "that any branch of athletics began to make appreciable progress."[187] The board's approval of the use of the temporary gymnasium, "especially for winter," allowed basketball practice.[188] Although Shahan was presenting the students as "not very

179. ACSP, Students' Book, 1890–1906, May 18, 1895.
180. AS, mm, Apr. 11, 1905.
181. OR, W. H. Singleton to O'Connell, Washington, Dec. 1, 1905.
182. *Ibid.*, Shanahan to rector and academic senate, Washington, Feb 16, 1906.
183. Spensley, in AR (1910–11), 26.
184. "University Chronicle—Albert Hall," CUB, XVI (Mar., 1910), 314.
185. OR, Gibbons to O'Connell, Baltimore, Nov. 5, 1906.
186. Spensley, in AR (1910–11), 26.
187. *Cardinal* (1916), 105.
188. BT, mm, Apr. 6, 1910; Apr. 26, 1911, exh.

strong" in football, the usual problems of eligibility, hours for practice,
and the like were not long in arising. Before the end of his first term
the athletic council that he had appointed during the year 1912–13 was
being asked to develop a statement of reasons for and against retention
of the sport.[189] This was sent for discussion in the faculties, from which
there emerged a consensus in favor of retention with, at the same time,
requests for definite information about costs and for a summary of the
suggestions that had been submitted.[190]

Although athletic fees were being charged to students and a director
of athletics was appointed in 1914, the "enormous cost" of football
continued to be a problem for the rector, as did the organization of
the athletic council. Thomas MacKavanagh, an associate professor of
engineering, chaired the council from 1919 until it was abolished by
Shahan's successor in 1930. During his first years, the erection of the
gymnasium and the stadium improved conditions greatly. A new coach
turned out "a fighting football team" that, it was said, transformed the
student body "from one split by fraternity politics and small jealousies
to an enthusiastic unit which had only one idea—to stand behind the
team for all it was worth."[191] The registrar, incidentally, found this
coach to be an exception; most coaches, he thought, had been "imbued
with the idea that the only way to train a team is on profanity."[192] It
was a boon for the team when, after some deliberation, first year law
students were found to be eligible to play.

The esteemed moralist John A. Ryan expressed the view that intercollegiate athletics had come to be "an almost unmitigated evil."[193] MacKavanagh at the same time was making penetrating analyses of the friction
with alumni and the petitions of students to which athletic policies
were giving rise and he asked pointedly if the institution's "slender
purse" could carry it "to the heights of its ambition."[194] The assistant
treasurer was urging the vice rector to curb the travel of the teams in
order to save expenses.[195] When complaints were sent to him, Curley,
as chancellor, would comment only that, whatever the difficulties might
be, they should be "settled from within without bringing an Archbishop

189. OVR, athletic council, for faculty reports, etc.
190. OR, "Memorandum in re Football," Dec. 21, 1916.
191. Washington *Herald*, Nov. 20, 1920.
192. OVR, Borden to Shahan, n.d.
193. Letter to the editor, *America*, XXIX (Oct. 6, 1923), 589, reprinted in *Tower*, II
(Oct. 17, 1923), 1.
194. OR, MacKavanagh to G. Dougherty, Mar. 15, 1923, and OVR, MacKavanagh
to Pace, Dec. 2, 1926.
195. OVR, J. H. Cain to Miss Brawner (secretary to Pace), Washington, Apr. 26,
1927.

The Shahan Debating Society, founded in 1910, has been the university's vehicle for intercollegiate debate. Shown here are the officers from the 1916 yearbook, Cardinal.

in on a football situation."[196] Actually, with respect to athletics, not much was settled during Shahan's time.

Reports of athletic events and of other student activities appeared regularly in the *University Symposium*, a journal which Shahan "permitted" the lay students to undertake, beginning in 1911, as "an intermediary between the students and the Alumni."[197] It ceased publication soon after the appearance, in 1922, of *The Tower*, the weekly newspaper that is still published. A yearbook, *The Cardinal*, appeared for the first time in 1916, and, except for the years 1918 and 1919 and from 1944 to 1947, annually thereafter. A student council that assumed responsibility for controlling social activities was in existence some years before it received the approval of the rector, in 1924. Thus, there were developing means of communication about extra-curricular as well as curricular affairs.

Forensic and dramatic activities were among the first to take shape. In the fall of 1907 the Catholic University Literary and Debating Society had been organized as the predecessor of the Shahan Debating Society,

196. AAB, Curley Papers, G 1083, Curley to T. F. Gormley, Baltimore, Oct. 9, 1925 (copy).
197. AR (1910–11), 5.

founded in 1910.[198] The growth of the latter society led to the organization of a second, but short-lived, Spensley Debating Society, named for
the Gibbons Hall proctor, who had died. The first intercollegiate debate,
in 1916, was lost to a team from The George Washington University.
Plays were produced by groups that seem to have had brief lives, a
Dramatic Society organized in 1912, the Players Club in 1917, the
Dramatic Association of 1921 or 1922. An important group for some
years, which sometimes sponsored lectures and debates, was the Leo
XIII Lyceum, formed in 1913 for the study of social questions in the
light of *Rerum novarum,* the first of what are sometimes called the "social
encyclicals" of modern popes.

The decade after 1910 saw the formation of numerous student groups
that were associated with academic departments or schools. Their names
usually indicated their interest. Thus, there were the Law Club, the
German Club, the Plumb Bob Society, the Triangle and T-Square
Club that became the Architectural Society, the Electron Society, the
Newman Classical Club, the Chemical Society, the E-50 Society of
civil engineers, the Dynamics Society, and the Commerce Club. A St.
Thomas Aquinas Society for clerical students was inaugurated in 1912.
Like these but with an interdepartmental appeal was the Irish History
Study Club that was founded with faculty encouragement after the
Dublin Easter uprising of 1916. In the second decade of Shahan's
administration there were added a Spanish Club, an International Relations Club, the Paciolo Society that replaced an Accounting Club, and
Il Circolo Italiano. The department of electrical engineering, finding
that "communication without wires, over vast spaces" was "in vogue,"
obtained a license to operate a broadcasting station early in 1923[199] but
made no application for its renewal when it expired during June of 1924.

For those musically inclined, a university orchestra had a brief existence about 1913 and was rejuvenated during the year 1922–23. Similarly, a glee club organized in 1913 failed to endure. But in 1920 Leo
Behrendt, an associate professor of German, established one that grew
to have more than fifty members. It was supported by membership dues
and by the proceeds of an annual dance until Shahan was able to
supplement the funds raised in these ways with an annual appropriation
of one hundred dollars. Also in 1920, after a competition conducted by
the senior class, the present alma mater song of the university was
adopted. Its words and music were composed by a student at the Sulpi-

198. Until 1928 the debaters appeared in white tie and tails.
199. OR, Broadcasting Station, and *Tower,* III (Mar. 4, 1925).

cian Seminary, James MacLean, later a Massachusetts pastor, whose effort had been awarded the second prize. The first had gone to Robert H. Mahoney, who was to become superintendent of schools in Hartford, Connecticut, for whose more complicated poem Victor Herbert had written and donated a musical score.[200]

Undergraduates were not long in establishing social clubs. Some brought together students from particular geographical areas, as did the Dakota Club for westerners and the Connecticut Club for those from the Nutmeg State. There were the Calumet Club, which sponsored minstrels, the Beta Beta Society, and the Woof Woofs. The 1920s saw the formation of the social clubs that commanded loyalties until the late 1960s, the Dod-Noon Club formed in 1920, the Abbey Club, in 1922, the Senators and the Utopians, in 1923. The student handbooks of the time made it clear that membership in "secret fraternities" was "strictly forbidden"[201] and Shahan once informed the senate that an attempt to establish such a group had been "disbanded."[202] Both the Abbey and the Dod-Noon Clubs sought approval to establish houses, but it was not until after Shahan left office that the latter club was able to rent "the cottage" on campus that had been built for Dean Robinson and had long been the home of the university's first auditor, J. Fendall Cain, and his family. When this was done, the Dod-Noon Club became a chapter of the national Phi Kappa fraternity for Catholic students which, until then, had had chapters only in non-Catholic institutions.

The student handbook informed the students plainly that they were divided "into Freshmen and Upper Classmen" and that the seniors were "THE Class of the University." All students were expected to appear "in Chapel, in the Dining Hall, and at all University functions properly dressed," that is, wearing neckties and jackets, not sweaters. All but seniors wore class caps. Seniors were to appear in cap and gown at all academic and other formal functions "as a mark of superior distinction." No freshman could be admitted to any club.[203] The practice of hazing freshmen, which was to continue until the late 1970s, led the board of discipline to forbid "under pain of expulsion" any injurious form,[204] but in spite of the threatened severity Shahan later had to denounce bodily

---

200. *University Symposium*, IX (Oct., 1920), 5–7.
201. *Rules, Regulations and Information for the Guidance of Undergraduate Students* (1923), 8.
202. AS, mm, Dec. 4, 1919. The life of the clubs and secret societies in the early 1930s is described by Professor Anon [Nicholas Chase], "Clubs and Secret Societies Recalled," *Tower*, Mar. 27, 1987.
203. *Rules, Regulations*, 7–8, 13–14.
204. AS, mm, Oct. 25, 1916.

hazing as "utter insanity and inanity" and limit what was done to "the maintenance of the traditional distinctions."[205]

Student discipline received, as might be expected, continuous attention. A committee reporting to the rector and academic senate in 1915 learned "from some sources . . . that the situation was quite satisfactory if not ideal; from others, that it was about as bad as it could be in any student body."[206] Not long before there had been scandals of some sort that had led Pace to speak of "the need of investigating the moral quality of men admitted to the University and of having conditions of character as well as scholarship."[207] Moral character was assumed by everyone to be a criterion for admission. There were expulsions for drinking and gambling, but the board lamented more the continuing presence of those who, "hardly deserving of the stigma of dismissal," were nevertheless "a demoralizing influence among the other students by reason of their low scholarship." It was recommended that "the University should not receive any undergraduate students who live in lodgings, as they are too young for such a measure of independence."[208] But the senate was always reluctant to exercise the authority that Shahan believed it had. It did establish a permanent board of discipline in 1915 and, after board action in 1918, a dean of discipline.[209] Louis H. Motry, a priest of the diocese of Albany, who later was a member of the school of canon law, was the first to be appointed to the latter post. Shahan brought the dean of discipline into the senate to establish "closer relations between the disciplinary agencies of the University and the academic body,"[210] but this did not produce the expected changes in faculty attitudes.

Although some students presented problems of discipline, the religious life of the students in general was usually found to be edifying. Keane had recognized at the outset that it was not possible to leave "this all important element in the lives of young men entirely to the good sense and the good will of the young men themselves."[211] Years later, in a typical residence hall, "some few" were daily communicants but on Sundays there was always "a fair number of communicants" while on First Fridays "practically the entire house" received the sacrament."[212] Sermons were "plain, direct, practical"; there were compulsory annual

205. *Tower*, Feb. 5, 1924.
206. OVR, committee (Pace, chairman) to rector and academic senate, May 28, 1915.
207. AS, mm, Jan. 13, 1915.
208. BT, mm, Apr. 1, 1921, exh.
209. AS, mm, Jan. 13, Feb. 19 and May 28, 1915; Apr. 18, 1918; BT, mm, Apr. 10, 1918.
210. AS, mm, Oct. 14, 1920.
211. OR, Keane to Shahan, Cape May, July 22, 1895.
212. BT, mm, Apr. 26, 1911, exh., Spensley to Shahan, Mar. 27, 1911.

retreats; the general atmosphere was religious; the environment, in fact, each year turned "the thoughts of several toward the priesthood."[213]

Although the student body grew during the Shahan years, there was institutional retrogression when a racial criterion for admission began to be invoked. It is difficult to document its origins, since no formal record of the change in policy seems to have been made. The first instance of the registrar's refusal to accept an application on the ground of color appears to have occurred in 1914 in the case of Charles H. Wesley of Howard University.[214] By 1917, instances of discrimination had become known to Negro leaders[215] but a uniform policy seems not to have been enunciated. The last Negro to receive a degree during this period was George H. Lightfoot, head of the department of Latin at Howard University, who had been a student between 1898 and 1901 and whose application for a master's degree had been approved by the faculty of letters on March 9, 1921. Pace pointed out to Shahan that it was "of some importance to decide whether he is really a student of the University and whether his name should appear on our published list."[216] Deferrari, who was Lightfoot's major professor, was instructed by Pace to direct Lightfoot not to appear at the commencement exercises, in view of the decision of the university to stand with other local institutions and, like them, to bar Negroes completely.[217]

Although Deferrari and others have attributed the change in policy to Pace, in view of his Floridian origins, it should be noted that Pace, with Bouquillon and Shahan, had been one of those who had proposed the university's original policy of nondiscrimination, that in 1919 he was willing to admit to graduate study a teacher at Dunbar High School;[218] and that in 1919 and 1920, when a new section of the Catholic Educational Association was to be devoted to "education of the colored race," he wondered if the impression might not be given that Negroes were being treated "in the Association, just as they are treated on some railways, instead of allowing them to come in simply

213. Spensley, in AR (1911–12), 32. Possibly William Maguire, a lay student of the period just before World War I and later a chaplain in the United States Navy, was the first lay student to enter the diocesan priesthood. OR, Thomas J. Mackin to Joseph M. Murphy, Spartanburg, S.C., n.d. [1934].

214. Dixon, *op. cit.*, 142–43.

215. AAP, Thomas Hogues to Kerby, Brooklyn, N.Y., Apr. 18, 1917, quoted, *ibid.*, 211; ASV, DA, II, No. 160 b/2, Thomas W. Turner to Bonzano, Washington, Nov. 3, 1919.

216. OVR, Pace to Shahan, Nov. 16 and 26, 1921.

217. *Memoirs*, 281–83; see also the correspondence of Pace to Shahan; Dixon, *op. cit.*, 211–12; and C. Joseph Nuesse, "The Loss and Recovery of Virtue in the Interracial Policies of The Catholic University of America," forthcoming.

218. OVR, Pace to A. H. Glenn, Washington, Feb. 12, 1919 (copy).

as Catholics."[219] He characterized a current rumor that colored students would be admitted to both his own institution and Georgetown as "part of the larger scheme to make the University declare its intention," so that it seemed to him "quite possible" that it would be necessary "to have some definite statement issued by the Board of Trustees."[220] Needless to say, the exclusion of Negroes brought severe criticism of the university.[221] The whole decade saw increasing racial segregation in Washington. The race riots of July, 1919, may have been decisive. Catholic ecclesiastics apparently deferred to the prejudices of the faithful.

After graduation, those who had been students cherished their memories, which in turn fostered institutional loyalty. Membership lists of both clerical and lay alumni were in Shahan's files by 1910.[222] Organization had begun when all were priests, after the dedication of McMahon Hall on October 1, 1895. Articles of incorporation had been filed the next year, when eighty-eight members were on the rolls. Members of the faculties were prominent as leaders. In 1899 the alumni of the law school began their own association. At the seventh annual meeting and banquet of the general association, in 1901, the change in alumni ranks was signaled by a toast offered to "The Clergy and Laity," although the Paulist Joseph McSorley, in toasting "The Professors and the Alumni," complained that the alumni felt "almost wholly cut off from the University."[223]

By 1914 an alumnus of the law school, P. Carberry Ritchie (LL.B., 1899) of Lakewood, New Jersey, was elected to the university's board of trustees. Shahan was calling attention to the selection of six alumni for the episcopate either in the United States or abroad. Appeals to alumni were soon to be made to collect funds for the gymnasium and stadium after which the leading fund-raiser became discouraged at finding a seeming obsession "with the idea that the faculty would not cooperate" in athletic matters.[224] Alumni clubs were formed in New York, Boston, St. Louis, and Connecticut. In 1923, with lawyers taking the lead, a Lay Alumni Association was incorporated. In 1927, the univer-

219. *Ibid.*, Pace to O'Connell, Washington, Mar. 31, 1920 (copy).
220. *Ibid.*, July 19, 1920 (copy).
221. See Constance McLaughlin Green, *Washington: Capitol City, 1879–1950* (Princeton: Princeton University Press, 1963), 266–67, 499, and *The Secret City: A History of Race Relations in the Nation's Capitol* (Princeton: Princeton University Press, 1967), 241, 302, in which The Catholic University of America is included, not without inaccuracies, in a brief survey of opportunities for Negroes in higher education.
222. For the official list of lay alumni as of Jan. 1, 1920, see *University Symposium*, VIII (Feb., Mar.–Apr., May–June, 1920), 200–208, 265–77, 311–17.
223. AS, General to 1907, Alumni.
224. OR, Maguire to Shahan, Detroit, Feb. 21, 1923.

The Washington Alumni Chapter during Shahan's rectorship. Organization of alumni began in 1895. The present Alumni Association of The Catholic University of America was incorporated in 1941.

sity sponsored its first homecoming and the practice of holding an alumni reunion in New York City was inaugurated.

Although women had not as yet been admitted to the university, there was formed in 1911 or 1912 an Alumnae Association of the Sisters College of The Catholic University of America. In 1916 it became an affiliate of the International Federation of Catholic Alumnae.

In a judgment not tempered by an understanding of the time, "a ghetto insular mentality" has been attributed to Shahan.[225] When he assumed the office of rector, the walls of an American Catholic ghetto had indeed been raised by conservative ecclesiastics in the United States and in Rome. But Shahan, conscious of his charge to lead "the growth of the most promising educational center which the Catholic Church possesses today in the entire world,"[226] was determined to be positive. Early in his third year, he had written that the university was "at the turning of the tale of success even in our generation."[227] During the longest administration in the university's first century, he was able to

225. Dixon, *op. cit.*, 48.
226. OR, Shahan to Fallon, *op. cit.*
227. *Ibid.*, Shahan to Patrick Henry Callahan, Washington, June 22, 1911 (copy).

give American Catholicism significant elements of its structure. He built academically, physically, and organizationally upon a foundation that had been tested severely. In pursuing both consolidation and growth, he earned the tribute of the university's first professor of American church history who, acknowledging the cost of the rectorship to Shahan's scholarship, wrote admiringly, "Without you as Rector, we'd have been a desert."[228]

228. *Ibid.*, Guilday to Shahan, Washington, Oct. 18, 1926.

CHAPTER VI

The Problem of Identity in Scholarship

As he prepared to leave office at the end of his third term, Shahan could report that the land owned by the university had been increased from seventy acres in 1909 to 270 acres in 1928. The library building that had just been completed was holding 273,674 volumes, about five times as many as had been available to the faculties and students in the earlier year. There were 113 instructional officers, almost four times the number with which he had begun. The faculties were reaching, he estimated, nearly 3,500 persons annually. He was counting 838 matriculated students—these, too, had increased fourfold—but adding the students at the Catholic Sisters College (138) and its summer session (715), those at Trinity College (368) and at nearby religious houses (446), and the 900 or so who were enrolled in the Knights of Columbus Evening School and the Columbus University. His professors were teaching in all of these institutions as well as in the National Catholic School of Social Service.[1]

The evidence concerning the scholarship of these professors, had Shahan reviewed it, would not have been so positive. There were indeed first-rate minds and able leaders among them. The national higher education community, expanding rapidly but itself obviously diverse, was continuing to look to the university as the national focus of Catholic intellectual effort. On the campus and elsewhere, however, there were ambiguities about the university's mission that typically were subsumed under discussions of its need to serve the Church or of the wisdom of what was already an old decision to offer undergraduate programs. There was general knowledge of the handicapping effects of the low salary levels that were prevailing but as Shahan's successor, not at all like him in temperament, was to report, the institution had spent "too much

1. OR, handwritten notes for meeting of BT, Apr. 18, 1928.

money for upkeep of the physical plant, and too little for the support of our professors who are the University." "Second-rate, and at times even third-rate men," he was to allege, had been appointed to teaching positions "with sad results in almost every instance."[2] He was only confirming assessments that had been made earlier by Pace, Curley, and others.

What was, nonetheless, especially notable in the faculties during the first quarter of the twentieth century and later was the presence of priest professors whose professional and public influence was making a crucial difference in the development of American Catholicism and its standing in American society. Perhaps the most widely known was John A. Ryan, at whose funeral Bishop Francis J. Haas, who had been his student, was to say that it was through Ryan "more than through any other individual that the Catholic University during its first 50 years came to be known and recognized, here and abroad, as an institution of courageous scholarship and of service to humanity."[3] Pace, who was occupied with administration and professionally recognized in higher education—by election to the presidency of the American Council of Education in 1925, for example—had early established himself in psychology and in Catholic education. His student, Thomas Verner Moore, a Paulist missionary before he became a Benedictine monk, had been led into psychiatry and had become prominent. Shields, who had earlier associated himself with Pace, was breaking new ground in pedagogy at the time of his death in 1921. Historical study was being promoted both academically and popularly by Guilday. Kerby in sociology was spurring the professionalization of social work among Catholics and had in O'Grady an outstanding colleague whom he found personally difficult but more than able as his successor in the National Conference of Catholic Charities. And although almost alone among Catholics in anthropology, in which he was later called by one better known than he "more universally respected and beloved" than any living American in the field,[4] Cooper was deeply involved also in the development of collegiate religious education and in the organization of Catholic institutions. These priests and others were intellectual and organizational leaders among American Catholics and through them the univer-

2. AACi, Cöln Papers, Ryan to Trustees, Washington, Nov. 16, 1931 (copy). The assistant treasurer was telling the board at the same time, "As our older department heads pass out, the men to replace them must be paid double the salary they received." OR, J. Harvey Cain, "Statement Concerning Financial Condition with Suggestions for Improvement," Jan. 27, 1931.

3. St. Paul *Catholic Bulletin*, Sept. 22, 1945.

4. OR, Clyde Kluckhohn to McCormick, Cambridge, Mass., Oct. 9, 1947.

sity was making inestimable contributions to Catholic education at all levels.

Shahan's own leadership, of course, should not be discounted. As rector he was looked to for organizational initiative not only in education but in almost any field in which a Catholic interest was perceived. As a scholar himself, given to seeking ideals in the medieval past, sharing prevalent Catholic tendencies to isolation, and necessarily conscious of the limited Catholic resources being allocated to higher education, he may have neglected somewhat association with those who were leading other university institutions. It seems, for example, that he preferred to delegate to others attendance at the annual meetings of the Association of American Universities—Shea was elected to serve as the organization's president in 1913—and that he invited the AAU meeting to the campus in 1927 only because he felt that "at last" in the new library that was under construction he had "something to show."[5] But of his leadership role there could be no doubt.

The Initiative of the Chancellor

Shahan was completing his second term as rector when Curley became chancellor. Seven years earlier, newly appointed to St. Augustine, his first see, Curley had yearned "to see some day assembled in the halls or on the campus every Bishop of the States, there to give evidence of practical interest, there to pledge men and means to it."[6] Offering congratulations when Shahan was named a titular bishop, he had professed to consider the university "far more important than the work of ruling any diocese in America."[7] And, when it was Shahan's turn to congratulate him upon his appointment to Baltimore, Curley telegraphed in acknowledgment that the university, "the glory of the Church in America," had to go forward and that he would be "ever ready to serve its interests."[8]

Curley was not uninformed about the university's problems. He was ready to write to a fellow archbishop that "a great number interested in the welfare of the University" were of the opinion that a new rector was needed. "All effort," it seemed, was being "centered on the work of the Shrine" with the result that the university had been "going backward as an institution of learning." Out of respect for Shahan's dedication,

5. Deferrari, *Memoirs*, 399.
6. Shahan Papers, Curley to Shahan, De Land, Fla., Apr. 13, 1914.
7. *Ibid.*, Curley to Shahan, Athlone, Ireland, Nov. 11, 1914.
8. OR, Curley to Shahan, St. Augustine, Aug. 8, 1921. On Curley, see J. J. Gallagher, *NCE*, IV, 541–42.

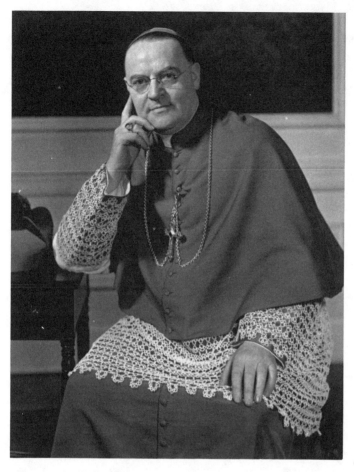

Michael Joseph Curley (1879–1947), bishop of St. Augustine (1914–21), archbishop of Baltimore (1921–39) and of Baltimore-Washington (1939–47), second chancellor of The Catholic University of America (1921–47).

however, he suggested that it might be wise to reappoint him "and allow him to resign after a year or so, then appoint a new incumbent." He mentioned, in this connection, that "quite a number of the professors" and "the delegation" were "in favor of putting Dr. Pace into Bishop Shahan's place."[9] When this preference was repeated at the end of Shahan's third term, although Pace himself had declined to be considered for the office, Curley explained to an inquiring pastor from Toledo that no matter who was rector it was Pace who regulated the intellectual

9. AAB, Curley Papers, D 1259, Curley to Dowling, Baltimore, Dec. 24, 1921 (copy).

side of the institution.[10] Although this may have been the case, there were a few on the campus who thought that Pace was "a disappointed man" and was "blockading progress."[11] He was accused by some of seeking the "laicization of the University."[12]

In later years, when the parish church in Pace's birthplace was named St. Edward's in his memory, Curley quipped that Pace had been "Starke's most brilliant son, although Starke never knew it."[13] Many had made a favorable appraisal before him. As early as 1901, Gibbons had inquired discreetly if Pace might consider appointment to the see of St. August-ine.[14] In 1913, Pace had been able to decline monsignorial rank for his work with Shahan on the *Catholic Encyclopedia* because, he felt, confer-ral of the title would have placed him with the rector "in a group apart" just when "something like unity" was being achieved on the campus and not without "considerable cost."[15] But in 1919 Gibbons thrust the higher rank of protonotary apostolic upon him to show publicly his gratitude for Pace's draft of the hierarchy's pastoral letter of that year.[16] On the campus, Shahan appointed him director of studies (1913–25) and also general secretary (1917–25). Curley himself took the initiative in 1924 to have Pace appointed vice rector *in academicis* and he held this position from 1925 until his retirement in 1936.

When, six years after its composition, Pace sent to Curley a copy of his comprehensive memorandum on the development of the university to 1917, he commented that, although "for some reason or other, its recommendations were not put into effect," he considered the needs of the institution to be still "substantially the same."[17] He had not been idle. Evidently through Cardinal Dougherty, he had been able to submit to Rome a draft of a proposed papal letter that was delayed by the deaths of first Gibbons and then Benedict XV, but that was soon issued in accord with Pace's purpose "to impress upon the Bishops the fact that the Holy Father is deeply concerned for the welfare of the University and, at the same time, secure some definite action in which they will all cooperate."[18] It was on April 25, 1922, that the new pope, Pius XI,

10. *Ibid.*, O 231, Curley to J. T. O'Connell, Baltimore, Apr. 16, 1928.

11. McNicholas Papers, Peter Guilday, "Memorandum for Bishop O'Hara," n.d. [1935].

12. *Ibid*, Report of Special Episcopal Committee, 1931, quoting Dean Cöln.

13. AAB, Curley Papers, M 291, Curley to McCormick, Baltimore, Oct. 14, 1941 (copy).

14. Shahan Papers, William T. Russell to Shahan, Baltimore, Sept. 3, 1901.

15. Pace Papers, Pace to Gibbons, Washington, June 13, 1913 (copy).

16. See Ellis, *Gibbons*, II, 169.

17. OVR, Pace to Curley, Washington, July 5, 1923 (copy).

18. Pace Papers, Pace to Cardinal Gaetano Bisleti, Washington, Dec. 6, 1921 (copy) and, earlier, Bonaventura Ceretti to Pace, Rome, Mar. 28, 1921.

coupled a request for a plan for development with a reminder to the bishops that "the whole thought and concern of the entire American Episcopate" was to be "centered on the University."[19]

Just a month earlier, on March 22, 1922, Curley had outlined his own plans before the permanent visiting committee. He was able to use the committee's report of this first meeting with him to advise Shahan that, although he was being reappointed to a third term, he should not continue "to concentrate much effort on the Shrine" because the university would "call for renewed work from now on."[20] To the trustees, just before the annual gathering of the bishops on the campus, Curley explained "how beneficial it would be if a complete survey of the University in all its activities could be made by a special committee appointed from the members of the Hierarchy."[21] Then, when he appeared before the bishops, he added that during his visit to Rome the previous summer he had been directed by the papal secretary of state, Cardinal Pietro Gasparri, to provide for the nomination of such a committee.[22]

Shahan was finding that since the responsibility for the university was being placed, as Curley put it, "where it was originally placed by Leo XIII, on the shoulders of the American Hierarchy," he was being asked only for "aid and advice" in an initiative that was neither in his hands nor even in the hands of the trustees.[23] Probably he knew of the part that his old friend was playing in these events so that in subsequent years, as Curley saw it, the man whom Pace had "always upheld and sustained was the man who forgot him most."[24] In any case, Cardinal William O'Connell, the senior American prelate at the time, became chairman of an ecclesiastically prestigious twelve-member committee of the hierarchy and Curley himself chaired a five-member subcommittee for conduct of the survey.

An Episcopal Assessment of Needs

The first task of the subcommittee was to solicit from members of the faculties their appraisals and suggestions. Curley found in all the letters that he received "a spirit of honesty and deep interest."[25] Only a few

19. *Dilecti filii Nostri, AAS,* XIV (July 25, 1922), 425 (in Latin).
20. AAB, Curley Papers, S 831, Curley to Shahan, Baltimore, Apr. 19, 1922 (copy).
21. BT, mm, Sept. 26, 1922.
22. AAB, Curley Papers, Fourth Annual Meeting of the American Hierarchy, mm, Sept. 27–28, 1922.
23. OVR, Curley to Shahan, Baltimore, Oct. 16, 1922 and Mar. 28, 1923.
24. AAB, Curley Papers, O 231, Curley to J. T. O'Connell, Baltimore, Oct. 14, 1941 (copy).
25. AAB, Curley Papers, D 1267, Curley to Dowling, Baltimore, Jan. 26, 1923

took the position of a veteran physicist and administrator who advised the chancellor that the university was "operating harmoniously and about as well as can be" so that "any considerable change, or reorganization, with the present resources, would be inadvisable."[26] Others pointed to a pervasive "fundamental reason for dissatisfaction" that was defined as "the impression, frequently the conviction, that the University has failed to realize the promises of its founders, and the hopes of its benefactors and friends."[27] Hyvernat pursued this theme specifically, alleging "that the Hierarchy took no interest in the University and that they left it entirely to a minority who, however well meaning, was not competent in University matters."[28]

There was frequent expression of concern that inadequate funding had led to a decline in standards. The holder of the Knights of Columbus chair of American history remarked that, "having at the outset required of all appointees a high degree of scholarship, so excellent a tradition could not have been ignored except under pressure of what seemed an imperious necessity."[29] The low level of professorial salaries that was requiring tolerance of off-campus employment was a frequent source of complaint. The need of a library building and of funds for its collections was presented as evident. Some again called into question the admission of undergraduates, more found fault with the nature of the undergraduate curriculum, and others pressed for some requirement of "gentlemanliness" on the part of students. Reorganization of the faculties into a distinct graduate school and college, which had been discussed since 1916, was generally perceived as needed. Although it was suggested that the university "could with immense advantage adopt, with local modifications, prevailing scholastic policies, which have been shaped by the tides of time,"[30] there were those who deplored what they thought was "too great a tendency to copy the aims and methods of non-Catholic institutions."[31] In one way or another, it was asserted by many that "personal rule" under a benevolent leader had taken the place of "constitutional government."[32]

(copy). In 1931, when a trustee committee was investigating the complaints of the faculty of theology, the dean, Cöln, remarked that Curley had asked the professors to write to him confidentially and had then turned over all the letters to Pace. McNicholas Papers, CUA: Investigation of Differences, mm.

26. *Ibid.*, Shea to Curley, Washington, Jan. 22, 1923.

27. *Ibid.*, "Present status of the University in the life of the Church in America, and its Internal Conditions," unsigned, n.d.

28. *Ibid.*, Hyvernat to Curley, Washington, Feb. 3, 1923 (Personal and Confidential).

29. *Ibid.*, Charles H. McCarthy to Curley, Washington, Jan. 13, 1923.

30. *Ibid.*

31. *Ibid.*, "Present Status . . ."

32. *Ibid.*

Receiving all these opinions, Curley mused, "If I had known the vast amount of work entailed in going into an examination of the University I would scarcely have had the courage to face it."[33] Trustees pressed him. A bishop who was an influential member of his subcommittee wrote to Pace that while "the University ought to be in truth the great centre of Catholic thought and learning," it had become in his opinion "a huge joke."[34] Another trustee urged that the university needed "three things in particular":

First, the cooperation of the Bishops. Secondly—*Much* money *soon*. Thirdly— Government by law, and not by caprice, or kitchen cabinet.[35]

Curley's response was that he was not going "to do any work with accompanying brass bands and fire works" and would not expect the trustees "to revolutionize the world in a couple of days or a couple of years."[36] But his pace did not slacken.

The subcommittee, after long meetings, presented a report to the full episcopal committee on April 10, 1923. In turn, after its own action on the report, the full committee submitted the requested "plan of development" to the pope on June 23. In Rome, it was the subject of consideration by the congregation of studies and of further correspondence between the cardinal prefect of the congregation and the chancellor.[37] Meanwhile, the committee's work was used as a basis for an appeal to each bishop "to increase, at least to double" the contribution of his diocese to the annual collection for the university in cooperation with "the Holy Father's design."[38] Reports of the Roman decisions and of steps taken to implement them were made to both the trustees and the bishops.[39] Just a month before, Pace had represented the university at the first international meeting of rectors of Catholic universities or their delegates that was held at Louvain during August of 1924.[40]

33. *Ibid.*, D 1267, Curley to Dowling, Baltimore, Jan. 26, 1923 (copy).

34. OVR, Joseph Schrembs to Pace, Cleveland, Feb. 26, 1923.

35. AAB, Curley Papers, L 232, Michael J. Lavelle to Curley, New York, Sept. 21, 1923.

36. *Ibid.*, L 231, Curley to Lavelle, Baltimore, Sept. 22, 1923 (copy).

37. OR, "Report of the Sub-Committee on the Catholic University of America" and "Letter Sent to the Holy Father by the Chancellor Outlining Plan of Development for the University . . ." (original in Latin). AAB, Curley Papers, Curley to Pope Pius XI, Baltimore, June 23, 1923 (copy); Gasparri to Curley, Rome, July 16, 1923; Curley to Pace, Baltimore, Feb. 11, 1924 (copy); Bisleti to Curley, Rome, July 31, 1924. Unless otherwise indicated, the quotations that follow from the reports and responses are from these documents.

38. NCWC Papers, William Cardinal O'Connell and Archbishops to Bishops of the United States, Washington, Oct. 26, 1923.

39. BT, mm, Sept. 23, 1924; NCWC Papers, Annual Meetings of the American Hierarchy, mm, Sept. 25, 1924.

40. OR, Exchange of Publications.

The final report that had been sent to the Holy Father had four principal divisions, devoted in order to the faculties, the administration, the resources, and the constitution of the university. At the outset of the subcommittee's deliberations, the old question of the scope of the institution—more specifically, its original graduate character—had been raised. The full committee, like the subcommittee, found itself divided and finally agreed on a compromise statement: "The original and primary scope of the University is postgraduate, the secondary purpose and scope is, by undergraduate work, to prepare for graduate work." This question was not referred to Rome.

As was to be expected, the principal emphasis in the report to the Holy See was upon the ecclesiastical fields. The full committee had approved without hesitation a recommendation that graduate work in the school of sacred sciences should be strengthened "by the appointment of the very best Professors to its chairs" and the congregation of studies approved as "quite in order" the establishment of new chairs in patrology, Christian archaeology, and liturgy while insisting "that the Course of Theology be really a higher or perfective course, and that everything center and converge on making it such." This recommendation it defined to require that "the problems . . . should be stated and solved not only in a thoroughly orthodox sense, but also in a truly scientific manner." The addition of the faculty of canon law, which had been accomplished in 1923 after two years of prodding from the congregation itself, was approved.[41] Also approved was a proposal for a "Higher School of Scholastic Philosophy" that the subcommittee had recommended "to prepare men for occupancy of chairs in seminaries."

A recommendation of the subcommittee that the university should arrange to offer seminary studies through the Sulpician Seminary that had been established across from the campus in 1919 was "put aside" in the full committee when O'Connell, whose attitude toward the Sulpicians was well known, objected that the proposal "might diminish the prestige of the University." The seminary question, therefore, was not referred to Rome until later, except in so far as the Basselin scholarships were involved.

Outside the ecclesiastical fields, the congregation, like the American bishops, was most interested in a proposal of the subcommittee for development of "a complete Department, and eventually a separate School, of Education, in which our Catholic teachers may be prepared,

41. OVR, Pace to Archbishops, Washington, Dec. 10, 1921, reporting summer interviews with Bisleti, brought to BT, mm, Apr. 26, 1922; approved Sept. 25, 1923.

Theological College, founded in 1918 as the Sulpician Seminary, continuing after 1934 for housing and spiritual direction of diocesan seminarians, expanded to its present size in 1964.

under Catholic auspices, for their work in parochial schools, high schools and colleges." The subcommittee thought that the university, as the center of Catholic education that it was established to be, had become "more necessary now" because non-Catholic systems had become "thoroughly united" and attempts were being made "to destroy our Catholic schools." A related recommendation of the subcommittee was for reorganization and extension of the program of affiliation. The congregation's response was that instruction in pedagogy "should be second to none of its kind."

The congregation found itself unable to decide upon the recommendation for the reorganization of the faculties of letters, philosophy, and science into a college and graduate school of arts and sciences. The question itself was, of course, uniquely American. It is doubtful if the bishops understood its implications and it remained unsolved throughout the Shahan administration. The full committee agreed readily that courses in engineering should be offered in a separate school that should stand "along with the School of Law as a professional school." With respect to the latter, the subcommittee had remarked, "Since we realize the necessity of having a University school of law with a really Catholic Faculty, it is felt that we should continue and strengthen, as far as possible, our present Law School."

The full committee was advised that the professors had expressed emphatically their dissatisfaction with the bishops' lack of interest in the university and it passed without comment recommendations for promptness in action on the part of the board. Noting that for years— since about 1903, actually—the appointments of instructors, "the future Associate Professors and Professors," had been made "almost exclusively by the Rector," the committee, "to prevent weakening of the Faculties," provided for departmental recommendations to the faculty and senate, and for appointments to be made by the senate subject to the rector's approval. The specifications for appointees reveal the mind of the academic leadership at the time and some of the problems with which it was contending:

(a) No person should be eligible to any teaching position in the University unless he is of known integrity of life and has a reputation for learning and teaching power in the subjects comprised in the department concerned.

(b) As a rule, only Catholics should be appointed Professors and Associate Professors.

(c) An Associate Professor ought to have the degree of Doctor or its equivalent.

(d) Every Professor doing graduate work must have that degree for which he is preparing candidates.

(e) A degree *honoris causa*, unless given by a standard university for exceptional learning, should have no weight in the matter of appointment.

(f) Graduates of the Catholic University, as a rule, should not be immediately appointed teachers in the University. This in-breeding has a bad effect academically. . . .

(g) A difference should be noted between qualifications for conducting graduate courses and qualifications for work with undergraduates. Candidates for positions in the undergraduate school should take a course in the principles and methods of education.

There was a clear recommendation that "as a rule, men should be promoted on the basis of productive scholarship." There were also interesting recommendations for faculty recruitment—"some plan by which the University would keep informed of Catholic students preparing for higher degrees in other universities"—and for a system of exchange professors.

The role of the academic senate was the pivotal issue of administration raised in the committee. It was resolved eventually through revision of the constitution. As the subcommittee stated, the senate, although properly "central in the life of the University," had "for some years past . . . not been functioning, as the Rector has done everything." In addition to the specific recognition of the senate's role in faculty appointments that the full committee had recommended, it proposed that in

any question of importance the rector should hear the senate "and give
its suggestions the attention that that important body merits." Further,
it proposed that if a majority in the senate should find a rector's decision
unacceptable, it might appeal to the chancellor or the board. When,
however, the committee urged "a return to the constitutional method"
of electing the rector, the Holy See replied that it had "never meant to
set aside the constitutional provisions." The congregation approved the
recommendation of the committee for the appointment of two vice
rectors, one, Pace, as vice rector *in academicis*, the other Dougherty,
who already held the title of vice rector, as vice rector *in temporalibus*,
or, later, procurator. In another administrative matter, the registrar—
whose *ratio agendi* Curley had found to be "distasteful to every member
of the Faculty"—was made subordinate to the general secretary.

There had been discussion in the committee of a recommendation that
the board should have attached to it in an advisory capacity "a group of
men representing the chief educational agencies." A respected layman of
wide experience had ventured to suggest to Curley the need of the bishops
for an advisory board of externs with powers exceeding those of the academic senate.[42] Although the subcommittee's recommendation for such
an advisory body met with general favor in the full committee, action on
it was neglected. It was decided that the Catholic Educational Association
was the proper instrument for the relation of dioceses and religious communities to the university, and, since Shahan was the president of the
association, it was left to him to "take the matter up."

In the matter of resources, the subcommittee, noting that "a fundamental difficulty" was "lack of funds," recommended a petition to the
Holy See for "a nation-wide drive in order to secure an adequate endowment." It was recognized that the university's salaries were "notoriously
low." The full committee took the course of asking the chancellor to
present to the hierarchy a financial statement showing departmental
costs per student, and forecasting the amount that would be needed for
continuance and for necessary improvements. It was pointed out that a
separate library building was "urgently needed," as were a residence
for priest professors, administrative buildings, and laboratories. Curley
reported these needs to the sixth annual meeting of the hierarchy on
September 25, 1924, at which the funding of the residence for clerical
faculty was given highest priority and approved through a resolution to
assess the dioceses according to the quotas assigned for their support of

42. AAB, Curley Papers, M 699, Constantine E. McGuire to Curley, Washington,
Nov. 6, 1923.

The Gymnasium, completed in 1919, used for its original purpose until the opening of the Raymond A. Dufour Center in 1985 and then strikingly renovated as the Edward M. Crough Center for Architectural Studies.

the NCWC. (The faculty residence, named Curley Hall, was not opened until 1939.) Curley reported, too, that it was agreed that the university's constitutions should be revised and that Shahan and Pace would soon leave for Rome to present the needs of the institution to the Holy See.[43]

The Revision of the Governing Documents

The constitutional revision that was then attempted was to be of its nature a time-consuming task. Probably neither the bishops nor the board in the mid-1920s appreciated its complexity or understood that the revision of the pontifical documents would require inevitably changes in the civil charter. The congregation of studies, in asking for a review of "the entire organization of the University," used characteristic Roman language pointing toward optimum conditions. Cardinal Bisleti counseled, "Let every Faculty be complete and well organized both within itself and in relation to the other Faculties; let each be provided with all indispensable elements and with whatever is needed for its perfect functioning."

43. NCWC Papers, Annual Meetings . . . , mm, Sept. 25, 1924.

It was of course the duty of the trustees to make the "thorough revision" that Curley explained to them was necessary. A committee to undertake the task was authorized. Curley, Shahan, and Pace were named as members and asked to add two others from the faculties.[44] They chose Monsignor Filippo Bernardini, founding dean of the school of canon law, who was a nephew of the papal secretary of state, and Aubrey Landry, who had been appointed as an instructor in mathematics in 1902 and was about to be elected by the academic senate to succeed Pace as general secretary. It was decided also that when the committee had formulated its recommendations it would give each member of the board no more than a month to respond before the results would be taken to Rome. But since it was thought to be expedient that the wishes of the congregation should be ascertained at the start, Shahan and Pace did not postpone their travel.[45]

Fifty conferences with officials of the congregation of studies were held from January through April. When agreement had been reached, Pace remained in Rome to supervise the translation and printing of the results, which presented in parallel columns the provisions of the existing constitution and the proposed modifications. Copies were sent to each trustee and each bishop.[46] Pace explained the draft to the board at its next meeting and a five-member committee chaired by Dowling was charged with its review and with a report of its findings to the bishops.[47] At Pace's urging, the schema was discussed in a series of meetings in each faculty and the results collated by the deans for presentation to the trustees on March 30, 1926. The board approved a revised general constitution on April 14. Pace took it to Rome and the approval of the Holy See for a trial period of seven years was given on July 24. The chancellor made a formal announcement at a general meeting of the faculties on October 13.

One of the significant features of the new constitution was its general applicability. Pace took the position that special constitutions were unnecessary and that a distinction should be made between what was constitutional in character and what was a matter of regulation subject to change by action of the constitutional authority.[48] In other matters,

44. BT, mm, Sept. 23, 1924.
45. OVR, notes on conference of Sept. 25, 1924; Curley to Pace, Baltimore, Sept. 27, 1924 (copy), and Curley to Hierarchy, Baltimore, Dec. 9, 1924.
46. BT, mm, Apr. 22, 1925; OR, Pace to Shahan, Rome, June 1, 1925; Curley to Hierarchy, June 24, 1925.
47. BT, mm, Sept. 15, 1925.
48. OVR, "Notes on Recommendations Submitted by Professors," probably prepared for Curley, and Pace to Dowling, Washington, May 11, 1926 (copy).

he was not satisfied that the authority given to the vice rector in the new document was adequately grounded with respect to discipline. A Catholic university, he maintained, could not "limit its treatment of students to purely academic training" and he considered that it should be the responsibility of the senate to enact the necessary regulations.[49] A particular question arose because mention of the Sulpician Fathers was omitted from the document. The provincial superior and his council wanted the original provisions for their authority over the student priests to be restored, while Pace held that the security of their position would lie only "in retaining the good-will of the Hierarchy and in doing their work so well that their place [could not] be filled by any one else."[50]

Differences between the original and the revised constitutions can be summarized briefly. In stating the institution's purpose, the new document was more clearly academic; students were to be enabled, "under the guidance of Catholic truth, to attain higher scholarship in every important branch of science" (Art. 1). The board of trustees was enlarged to include all cardinals and archbishops who were ordinaries, *de jure,* and ten bishops, ten priests, and ten laymen to be elected for five-year terms "either in a Plenary Council or in a general assembly of all the Bishops" (Art. 12). Provisions for consultation in the election of officers and enactment of regulations were made explicit (e.g., Art. 15, 28, 32). The principal officers were designated as the rector, vice rector, and procurator. The general secretary was made an appointee of the rector for a five-year term, with provision for consultation with the academic senate and subject to the approval of the board (Art. 44). There was a new provision for the "counsellors" to be chosen by the trustees who might, upon request by the trustees, "offer advice regarding anything [to] further the progress of the University" (Art. 18, 19). Pace hoped that, although the faculties had wanted to omit this provision, the "counsellors" would "interest all our Educators, especially teachers in Colleges and Seminaries, in the work of the University" so that it would be in truth "the center of our Catholic Educational system."[51]

Strange as it may seem now, the objections of the faculty, especially the faculty of sacred sciences, were strongest with respect to "the prominence given the *Department* as an element in the organization of the University, and the functions attributed to the Head of the Department." The constitution defined chair, department, and school rather clearly (Art. 10), and those who were heads of departments at the

49. *Ibid.,* "Notes. . . ."
50. *Ibid.,* Pace to Dowling.
51. *Ibid.,* "Notes. . . ."

time evidently felt that they needed more authority to insure proper functioning, while others saw the development as "autocratic."[52] Some took exception to the continued inclusion of philosophy as a department instead of its erection as a separate school. It was later argued that the mere mention of such a school in the document had been intended to give it independence since appointments of associate and ordinary professors in theology, canon law, and philosophy had to be approved by the Holy See, while appointments of others to these ranks were simply reported (Art. 79). All were to observe the provisions of canon law with respect to their duties and their recitation of the profession of faith and the oath against modernism (Art. 80).

Apparently little account was taken of American law when the revision of the pontifical constitution was drafted. Often enough, unfortunately, as counsel later remarked, it was reasoned "that religious, educational and charitable incorporations need not follow very closely the rules of law because they are seldom inquired into, and if any failure to observe the law were discovered, it would be overlooked because of the nature of the incorporation."[53] A layman on the board had raised the question when he had examined the proposed revisions and had advised the rector that he found clauses "in conflict with the present charter and the by-laws" which would "have to be reconciled."[54] Nothing seems to have been done at the time but after the approval of the Holy See was obtained the board was prompted by another lay member to seek the advice of counsel.[55] The latter's report of discrepancies was of some length, involving the expansion in the number of trustees beyond what the certificate of incorporation provided, the election of trustees by the bishops, the lodging of authority in agencies other than the board, and the like. Counsel pleaded that it was "most essential, especially at this time, that Catholic Institutions should live and be operated entirely according to the laws of our Country."

Counsel first advised and the board agreed that amendment of the original certificate of incorporation, which probably could have been acted upon only by the United States Congress in any case, would entail risks that it would be desirable to avoid. Therefore, it was decided that incorporation by a special act of Congress would be "not only the best practical method of procedure, but one that would accord more fully with the purpose and work of the institution."[56] A committee consisting

52. *Ibid.*
53. BT, mm, Apr. 27, 1927, exh., Hamilton to Shahan, Washington, Apr. 16, 1927.
54. OR, Nelligan to Shahan, Baltimore, Sept. 4, 1925.
55. BT, mm, Sept. 14, 1926. The member was Clarence Martin.
56. BT, mm, Apr. 27, 1927, exh., *op. cit.*

of Trustee Martin, Counsel Hamilton, Shahan, and Pace was appointed to draft a bill. As finally presented, however, the bill represented a reversal of counsel's original position. It confirmed the original certificate of incorporation and amended it, principally by providing for increases in the number of trustees, by specifying in greater detail their authority, and by authorizing the affiliation with the university of "any institutions of learning" inside or outside the District of Columbia. The bill was introduced into the Seventieth Congress on January 9, 1928, by Senator Thomas J. Walsh of Montana. After passing the senate on February 6 and after the rebuff of an attempt to reverse this action in the house of representatives, where the bill was introduced by Congressman Clarence McLeod of Detroit, the measure became law on April 3, 1928. The board, at its next meeting, adopted as the charter of the university Chapter XVIII of the Revised Statutes of the District of Columbia and Public Act 235 of the Seventieth Congress.[57]

The Sacred Sciences after Four Decades

The revision of the governing documents and the approaching retirement of Shahan pointed to a significant turn in the university's history. Unquestionably, the interest of the bishops as sponsors and of the trustees was still concentrated upon the state of the ecclesiastical faculties, that is, the school of sacred sciences, the school of canon law, and the department of philosophy. Of course, a Catholic university without a faculty of theology would have been, as a cardinal prefect of the congregation of studies had reminded the French hierarchy in 1875, a *corpus obtruncatum* (mutilated body).[58] In 1928, as earlier, the school of sacred sciences was easily the most amply staffed numerically of the several faculties, and it remained first not only in seniority and in the number of its endowed chairs but in the dignity that was ascribed to it. In academic respects, however, it had lost ground steadily.

Recruitment of ecclesiastical students had lagged from the beginning and the quality of those who enrolled was often disappointing. By Hyvernat's calculation, during the early decades only 46 per cent of those who matriculated remained for more than one year.[59] Responding to a fellow metropolitan who was urging "full stress" upon the graduate

57. BT, mm, Apr. 18, 1928.
58. Quoted in Alfred Baudrillart, *Vie de Mgr. Hulst* (2 vols.; Paris: Librarie Poussielgue, 1912), I, 366.
59. "Memoir," 17.

character of the school, Curley observed that "very few Priests are equipped for Post-graduate work in Theology."[60] The lack was symptomatic of the neglect of intellectual work among Catholics of the time. Some years later, when Archbishop John T. McNicholas of Cincinnati inquired of members of the theological faculty as to the reasons for the failure to grow, church historian Guilday cited his own twenty-year observation of a "quite evident . . . lack of interest on the part of our hierarchy in higher theological training."[61] Probably one reason for the persistent interest of the Holy See in the university was its perception of the need to remedy this lack. It was well known that Catholic theological literature was not yet being produced in the United States.[62]

To build enrollment, Shahan, toward the end of his administration, resorted to proposing the addition of a seminary course to the curriculum. The faculty's acceptance of Shahan's proposal was grounded in "the inadequacy of the number of well qualified students and the consequent apathy of both clergy and people at large towards our school."[63] The young Fulton John Sheen, who had been appointed to the faculty in 1926, was prompted partly by this development to transfer to the department of philosophy.[64] Curley resisted Shahan's proposal, considering it to be "a very advanced form of lunacy" for the university to establish "a second Seminary" across the street from the one established by the Sulpicians for diocesan candidates a decade before. Nor, contrary to what the German-born dean at the time apparently first suggested, did Curley expect the Sulpicians to be "such thorough-going simpletons as to take charge of a Seminary which would tend at least, to kill their own."[65] The university seminary program therefore was opened only to students of religious houses[66] until, a decade later, Roman intervention ended the academic offerings of the Sulpicians.

Except perhaps for the moralist Ryan and the historian Guilday, the faculty could not have been attractive to students. Central to the curriculum were the fields of dogma and morals and sacred scripture. But scholarship in these fields seemingly could not be maintained without difficulty. In dogmatic theology, Schroeder had had a competent successor, the metaphysician Shanahan, who had taught until 1920. He was

60. AAB Curley Papers, M 1251, Messmer to Curley, Milwaukee, Dec. 13, 1924, and M 1252, Curley to Messmer, Baltimore, Dec. 15, 1924 (copy).
61. McNicholas Papers, Guilday to McNicholas, Washington, Apr. 20, 1935.
62. Connell, in Deferrari, *Essays*, 220.
63. SSS, mm, Jan. 10, 1927; BT, mm, Apr. 27, 1927.
64. SSS, mm, Apr. 6, 1927. See Fulton J. Sheen, *Treasure in Clay* (Garden City: Doubleday, 1980), 43–46.
65. AAB, Curley Papers, P 40, Curley to Pace, Baltimore, Jan. 21, 1926.
66. AR (1926–27), 32.

followed by Daniel Joseph Kennedy, O.P., the first religious to hold faculty rank, who had been appointed as a lecturer in sacramental theology in 1908 and then, in 1909, when Shahan was new to his office, promoted to full professorial standing without previous consultation with the faculty and the senate.[67] When Kennedy became ill in 1924, he was replaced by another Dominican, Edward Fitzgerald, at the level of instructor. There was no specialist in dogma.

The position in moral theology left vacant by Bouquillon's death had been filled at first by temporary expedients and then by an alumnus, John Webster Melody, until the return to the campus in 1915 of Ryan, who had been a student under Bouquillon and a teaching fellow. Appointed originally as an associate professor of politics, he was transferred to moral theology with full professorial rank.[68] He brought frequent notice to the campus during succeeding decades, often in illustration of the university's outreach through his service to the National Catholic War Council and, from 1920 onward, as the director of the NCWC department of social action. To Cardinal O'Connell, indeed, he was one of the "irresponsible busybodies whose self-importance [had] turned their heads."[69] Curley, who usually disagreed with Ryan and did not hesitate to make the fact publicly known, often felt it necessary to defend Ryan's academic freedom.[70] A recent student, however, has remarked that Ryan should rank as one of only three deceased American Catholic theologians—the others being Orestes Brownson and John Courtney Murray—who are "still worth reading today for more than historic interest."[71]

In the field of sacred scripture, after having failed to defend and retain Poels, Shahan was soon relieved of an erratic stormy petrel when Grannan, one of the original twelve members of the pontifical biblical

67. See BT, mm, Apr. 21–22, 1909; AS, mm, Apr. 22 and May 12, 1909, for faculty protests.

68. AS, mm, Oct. 11, 1916.

69. AAB, M 28, O'Connell to Peter J. Muldoon, Boston, Oct. 24, 1924 (copy). Muldoon, bishop of Rockford, was episcopal chairman of the department of social action.

70. AAB, Curley Papers, R 1274, Curley to Ryan, Baltimore, Jan. 19, 1927, contains a facetious warning that O'Connell "might one day prevent [Ryan's] being appointed Archbishop of St. Paul" and also offers "congratulatory sympathy on [his] being perhaps the first of the Staff to form connection with the Holy Office." (Ryan had been delated by Cardinal Merry del Val.)

71. John A. Coleman, S.J., "Vision and Praxis in American Theology, Orestes Brownson, John A. Ryan, and John Courtney Murray," TS, XXXVII (March, 1976), 3. See also Charles E. Curran, *American Catholic Social Ethics: Twentieth-Century Approaches* (Notre Dame, Ind.: University of Notre Dame Press, 1982), Chap. II. For biographical data, see John A. Ryan, *Social Doctrine in Action: A Personal History* (New York: Harper and Bros., 1941), and Francis L. Broderick, *Right Reverend New Dealer: John A. Ryan* (New York: Macmillan, 1963), and NCE, XII, 767. See also Patrick W. Gearty, *The*

John Augustine Ryan (1869–1945), long-time professor of moral theology, pioneer in social ethics, first director of the department of social action of the National Catholic Welfare Conference (now United States Catholic Conference), with Supreme Court justices Hugo L. Black, Felix Frankfurter, and William O. Douglas on Ryan's seventieth birthday, May 25, 1939.

commission, resigned from the faculty in 1911 "to perform some service for the Holy See."[72] That same October, Franz Cöln, a priest of the diocese of Trier, was appointed as an instructor in the Old Testament to replace Poels. In 1913, another German priest, Heinrich Schumacher, of the diocese of Speyer, was appointed as an instructor in the New Testament to replace Grannan. An attempt was made to establish a biblical institute but this was doomed to failure because, even before a papal *motu proprio* on the teaching of scripture in 1924, the Holy See was maintaining that academic degrees in scripture "for the gravest of reasons, could be conferred only by the Biblical Commission and the

Economic Thought of Monsignor John A. Ryan (Washington, D.C.: The Catholic University of America Press, 1953).

72. BT, mm, Oct. 12, 1911, exh., Grannan to Gibbons and Trustees, Rome, July 6, 1911.

Biblical Institute."[73] Although the continuation of advanced courses in the field was explicitly approved by the prefect of the congregation of studies, Curley considered that the document was "a death-blow to Postgraduate work in Scripture done for the purpose of preparing Teachers in that department of Sacred Science."[74] Pace, after consulting on the point with Cardinal Mercier and the professors of Louvain and Paris and finding all agreed that the papal decree was "extreme," seemingly agreed with them also that protest was inadvisable.[75] Cöln and Schumacher, in any case, did not advance scriptural scholarship and Cöln's letters as dean of the faculty from 1925 until 1931 reveal pedantry in the extreme. More important contributions to scriptural studies were being made by the department of Semitic and Egyptian languages and literatures in the school of letters.

In auxiliary disciplines in the school of sacred sciences, church history was being taught by Patrick Joseph Healy, an Irish-born priest of the archdiocese of New York and an alumnus who always took an active interest in lay student activities. Healy, appointed in 1903 and to the Quinn chair in 1910, contributed numerous biographies to the *Catholic Encyclopedia* and longer articles on the Church's social contributions to the *Catholic University Bulletin*. Guilday, of the archdiocese of Philadelphia, who had been sent to prepare for what was to be a lifelong career on the campus, was appointed in 1914. He became the founding editor of the *Catholic Historical Review*, organizer of the American Catholic Historical Association, and author of, among other works, massive biographies of the American episcopal pioneers John Carroll and John England. His specialization in American Catholic church history brought him into conflict with members of the department of history, among whom he suspected he was "always running the danger of having anti-clerical minds act as judges."[76] He was to seek under Shahan and Shahan's successor, unsuccessfully, to have a separate department of American church history erected.[77] Toward the end of the Shahan period, in 1926, Joseph T. Barron was appointed in the field.

---

73. OR, "Letter from His Eminence Cardinal Bisleti regarding Degrees in Scripture," July 31, 1924.

74. AAB, Curley Papers, M 1252, Curley to Messmer, Baltimore, Dec. 15, 1924 (copy); also, S 608, Curley to Schumacher, Baltimore, Nov. 10, 1924 (copy).

75. *Ibid.*, P 32, Pace to Curley, Paris, Jan. 29, 1925.

76. OR, Guilday to Shahan, Washington, Nov. 14, 1925.

77. OR, Guilday to Shahan, Dec. 16, 1926; Shahan to Cöln, Dec. 20, 1926; Cöln to Shahan, Nov. 25, 1927. AAB, Curley Papers, R 1776, Curley to J. H. Ryan, Baltimore, Jan. 28, 1935 (copy); R 1776.1, Ryan to Curley, Washington, Jan. 29, 1935. Under Shahan's successor, Guilday was transferred to the graduate school of arts and sciences and was given there a division of American church history in the department of history.

Charles Aiken, who had received his doctorate in 1900, had been retained to teach apologetics. The chair in this field, which was not endowed, was named to honor Gibbons.[78] McKenna was added when he came to assist Shahan in the planning of the National Shrine. The careers of two appointees at junior rank, Roderick McEachern, who had been sent to Rome for training, and F. Sigourney Fay, who had been F. Scott Fitzgerald's headmaster at the Newman School, were cut short by death. The appointment of Sheen in 1926 was also cut short by his transfer to philosophy.

Religion was being taught to lay students for one hour a week for three years. It was Pace's thought, however, that it should have been given three hours a week to freshmen—who, he reasoned, would need grounding in fundamentals—and then three hours a week to seniors— to deepen their knowledge and treat problems that might have arisen during their collegiate studies.[79] The teaching of religion was most notably affected, in other Catholic colleges as well as on the campus, by Cooper's part-time appointment in 1909 and his appointment as a full-time instructor in 1920. He transferred to the department of sociology in 1923 but, apparently submitting to ecclesiastical counsel rather than his own preference, transferred back again in 1925.[80] The course outlines that he prepared set the pace in collegiate religious education for a generation. Alumni among the trustees such as Cardinal Patrick Hayes and Archbishop (later Cardinal) Glennon soon waxed enthusiastic in designating him "the head of all religious instruction at the university."[81] Maurice Sheehy, a priest of the archdiocese of Dubuque, who was to serve Shahan's successor as an assistant, came to the university in 1927 to join Cooper in teaching religion.

Supplementing the conventional subjects was instruction in ecclesiastical music, which had been introduced at the university's beginning but had been given academic status only in 1911, with the appointment of Abel Gabert, a priest of the diocese of Grenoble in France who was serving as choirmaster at Morristown, New Jersey. He was seen to be "after the heart of Pius X" and "in close personal touch with the great modern Benedictines."[82] In 1917 the board authorized conferral of the

---

OR, J. H. Ryan to J. A. Ryan, May 21, 1932 (copy). On Guilday, see John Tracy Ellis, *NCE*, VI, 844–45.

78. BT, mm, Sept. 20, 1921.

79. "Report of the General Secretary and Director of Studies," *AR* (1923–24), 45.

80. SSS, mm, Apr. 12, 1920; Jan 22, 1923; Oct. 5, 1925. See Regina F. Herzfeld, *NCE*, IV, 298.

81. BT, mm, Nov. 10, 1931.

82. BT, mm, Apr. 26, 1911, exh.; see also "Ecclesiastical Music at the University," *CUB*, XVII (Jan., 1911), 84–87.

John Montgomery Cooper (1881–1949), pioneer in religious education and anthropology, founder of the department of anthropology, president of the American Anthropological Association in 1940.

degree bachelor of music to serve particularly but not exclusively the needs of the Sisters College. Gabert was succeeded in 1925 by William J. DesLongchamps, a priest of the diocese of Detroit, who was to figure in an abortive attempt to establish a school of liturgical music at the beginning of the next administration.

Sometimes the board itself assumed initiative in the development of the faculty. In 1911, for example, it requested that pastoral and mystical theology should be taught. The Sulpicians John Fenlon and Anthony Vieban, who were in charge of the priest students, were called upon to offer the instruction. In 1919, the board approved the addition of a department of homiletics and the appointment of Hugh T. Henry to teach the subject. But no measure remedied the basic weakness in theology.

The School of Canon Law

The curriculum of the school of sacred sciences had included canon law almost continuously after Messmer had begun to teach it in 1890. Peries was his successor for a few years. The erection of a faculty in this subject in 1923, after steady pressure from the congregation of studies and after about two years of preliminary consideration, was the only change of its magnitude in academic organization made during Shahan's administration.[83] John T. Creagh, a Roman-trained priest of the archdiocese of Boston who had been appointed in 1897, was teaching the subject when Shahan became rector. After his resignation in 1913, received with regret, Bernardini had been brought from Italy, in 1914, to succeed him. He became the founding dean and, after 1933, a papal diplomat. Two recent alumni were selected for the faculty, Motry, the dean of discipline, in 1920, and Valentine Schaaf, of the Cincinnati province of the Order of Friars Minor, in 1923. Oliveira Lima, donor of his library, appointed professor of international law in 1923, and Francesco Lardone, appointed professor of Roman law in 1924, were lecturers. There were twenty major and thirteen minor students in the first year. Soon the chancellor was able to assure one of his priests who had studied in Rome that what the university was offering was "far better and far more practical than any Course given in Rome."[84] The school has since remained the only one of its kind in the United States and therefore a unique resource for bishops and diocesan chanceries.

The Arts and Sciences

At the end of the Shahan administration, although the scholarly attainments of the faculties of sacred sciences and of canon law were not even approached by those of any other American Catholic institution, they could not be regarded as satisfactory. Nor, for that matter, could the attainments of the faculties of arts and sciences be so regarded, even if they were generally expected to be in accord with current practice and, as John Gilmary Shea had remarked long before, "the real

83. BT, mm, Apr. 26, 1922, Sept. 25, 1923, and OR, Curley to Shahan, Rome, Aug. 2, 1922. AAB, Curley Papers, Varia, Pace to Curley, Washington, Dec. 10, 1921, and Bisleti to Curley, Rome, Aug. 15, 1922; D 1155, Denis P. Dougherty to Curley, Philadelphia, Dec. 27, 1921; P 15, Pace to Curley, Washington, Dec. 4, 1922; D 1268, Dowling to Curley, St. Paul, Jan. 23, 1923.

84. AAB, Curley Papers, M 251, Curley to Leo J. McCormick, Baltimore, Apr. 3, 1927 (copy).

and active part of the university."[85] Their staffing was less complete than in theology and their standing was extremely variable, either because Catholic scholars were not available, or because funds were lacking. Too few chairs had been endowed and of those that were funded not all were in essential fields. Since funding was a constant limiting factor, additions could be made only gradually. Moreover, the admission of lay students and of undergraduates required attention to problems of curriculum and of discipline that were different from those presented by ecclesiastics.

Neither the numbers of the students nor their quality were satisfactory. During the first world war, Kerby, then dean of the school of philosophy, remarked to the board on the loss of a "spirit of industry" among the students.[86] Some years later, in support of a proposal that admission to undergraduate study should be "carefully watched and drastically checked," a colleague reported that the administration of the relatively new intelligence tests "showed that our freshmen are far below the general college average."[87] Earlier, the board's visiting committee, sympathetic with an emphasis upon graduate work as more consonant with "the ideal upon which the University was founded," reported the "testimony of various professors" as showing that the undergraduates were "crowding to the University, overflowing the limited accomodation of the dormitories, and using the income derived from the revenue for courses in education which in many instances could be obtained elsewhere, and which were not originally contemplated as the proper sphere of educational activity by this University."[88]

Fortunately, so far as exposure to Catholic influence was concerned, in an institution of the small size of the university at the time, a student's experience in virtually any field was almost bound to be more coherent than the curriculum that was offered. Courses in religion were seemingly rather disorganized until Cooper's plan for reorganizing them was put into effect.[89] And although no one would have challenged Kerby's portrait of a Catholic university as in itself "a living, breathing Summa Theologica,"[90] and, granted that philosophy had been referred to from the start as "the central element" of the curriculum,[91] so that the board

85. ACQR, IX, 321.
86. BT, mm, Apr. 10, 1918, exh.
87. SP, mm, Dec. 7, 1926.
88. BT, mm, Apr. 1, 1921, exh.
89. OVR, "Suggestions for Reorganization of Religion Courses, May 15, 1918."
90. "Sermon on the Feast of the Immaculate Conception, Dec. 8," *Chronicle*, I (Nov.–Dec. 1897), 121.
91. *Year Book 1894–95*, 45.

had demanded that it be required of all,[92] strength in this vital and presumably integrating field was slow to develop. For this, Grannan blamed Pace because he had been for several years after Shanahan's transfer to theology the only professor of the subject.[93] Perhaps the three schools of letters, philosophy, and science were being administered somewhat as departments would be today, since what were then called departments often consisted only of the occupant of a chair.

The School of Letters

This was illustrated in the school of letters, which had ten departments—in Celtic, comparative philology, Egyptian and Semitic languages and literatures, English, French, German, Greek, Latin, Sanskrit, and Spanish—but in which staffing was uneven and enrollment even more so. In 1913, for example, the dean was reporting that there were five professors and eight instructors in the school and that they were teaching thirty graduate students and 295 undergraduates.[94] But only some of these students were pursuing major programs; the undergraduates especially were enrolled in courses such as English that were required by other schools. During 1927–28, only eighty were reported as registered in the school and more than half of these were graduate students.

The department that was able to maintain the most continuity and academic prestige was clearly that which Hyvernat had founded, and its standing was the direct result of his own scholarship and of his training of students in the ancient and medieval languages of the Christian Orient. Recognition of this standing could be seen in the cooperation of the department with the Catholic University of Louvain and in Hyvernat's selection to edit the Morgan collection of Coptic manuscripts. Students of Hyvernat who were appointed to faculty positions during Shahan's administration were the Canadian Basilian, Arthur Vaschalde, in 1911, and the Marist, Romanus Butin, in 1912. Hyvernat left them and later appointees to follow in the path that he had charted and, before his death in 1941, placed his personal funds in a small endowment for partial support of a research institute in the department of Semitic and Egyptian languages and literatures.

Since proficiency in the classics was still assumed to be a property of an educated man, Greek and Latin languages were studied by far more

92. BT, mm, Oct. 11, 1899; AS, mm, Mar. 14, Oct. 10, 1899; Mar. 13 and Oct. 15, 1900.
93. ADR, O'Connell Papers, [Grannan] to O'Connell, n.p., n.d. [1902].
94. OR, John D. Maguire to Shahan, Washington, June 10, 1913.

students than were the Oriental tongues. Originally, each enjoyed departmental status. A convert, George M. Bolling, was in charge of Greek and Sanskrit from 1895 until he left for Johns Hopkins and was succeeded in 1913 by John B. O'Connor, who had been impressively trained in his native Ireland and in England and the United States and had been teaching at Adelphi College. Beginning in 1901, Latin was being taught by John D. Maguire, a Philadelphia priest who had been a student on the campus during 1893–94 and had specialized in Latin at Bonn, Johns Hopkins, and finally the University of Pennsylvania. When Maguire died, O'Connor cared for both Greek and Latin administratively. His successor, in 1918, Roy J. Deferrari, obtained their formal merger. Deferrari, after obtaining his doctorate at Princeton, had been recommended to Shahan by a friend of Hyvernat and he soon led the department to a level that a Princeton luminary was to describe as "among the very best of all the Classical Departments in the country."[95]

Through Deferrari contacts were being maintained with the American Academy in Rome and the American School of Classical Studies at Athens and Deferrari was serving on the advisory council to the American committee on the latter. Of course, even in the sacred sciences, where dogmatic theology and canon law and some moral theology were being taught in Latin, it could be reported to a trustee visiting committee that "the Latin is bad, the Greek is worse."[96] And already undergraduates, as Deferrari remarked, were "ignoring the classics more and more."[97] Thomas J. McGourty, in 1912, and Joseph P. Christopher, in 1920, were added to the department. Deferrari was to become dean of the graduate school in 1930 and then secretary general in 1937 and to wield university-wide influence in academic matters. Colleagues whose appointments he recommended to Shahan, James Marshall Campbell in Greek, in 1920, and Martin Rawson Patrick McGuire in Latin, in 1924, first helped the department to maintain its reputation and then became his associates in administration.

The department of English, although it reached all undergraduates through its courses, did not maintain the lustre that Stoddard and Egan, both literary men, had given it originally. Upon the latter's resignation, during the O'Connell administration, Hyvernat had advised the rector that "it would be a good thing if the new man was more of a philologian than the new ambassador to Copenhagen."[98] Patrick Joseph Lennox of

---

95. AAB, Curley Papers, R 1585, Edward Capps to James Hugh Ryan, Princeton, Apr. 28, 1931 (copy).

96. BT, mm, Apr. 14, 1920, exh., John Fenlon, S.S., to visiting committee.

97. OR, Deferrari to Shahan, Nov. 7, 1921.

98. OR, Hyvernat to O'Connell, Rome, Aug. 2, 1907.

Dublin was appointed with high praise in 1908 and served on the campus until his retirement in 1938, but he was not known for scholarship and later was castigated by his deans for "incompetence in directing graduate work."[99] Francis J. Hemelt, who had studied under Egan and Pace, was with Lennox from 1912 to 1920 and was to return to the department in 1929, but also was not known as an outstanding scholar. Several junior colleagues remained in the department only for short periods until the appointment, in 1925, of Henry Edward Cain, son of J. Fendall Cain and brother of J. Harvey Cain, both in their time business officers of the university. Cain, valedictorian of the Class of 1925, later led the department to productivity.

During these early decades, instruction in modern languages was attracting but little support. Schroeder's early ambition to raise funds for a chair in German was a casualty of his case. It was a Cincinnati pastor who was at odds with prevailing German Catholic opinion who left a bequest to endow a chair.[100] Paul Gleis, who began teaching German in 1912, was appointed to occupy it. Leo Behrendt joined him, in 1926. Efforts to obtain support for instruction in French, first offered in 1906, were made during Shahan's third term by Jules Baisnée, S.S., later a member of the department of philosophy, and L'Institut Français de Washington, but without success.[101] At various times the rector or the trustees' visiting committee would recommend provision for regular instruction in Italian, Polish, or Spanish, but the board always found it necessary to defer such proposals for lack of funds. By 1917, the faculty, after long waiting, was able to propose successfully the organization of "a Department of Romance Languages and Literatures, with a view to a more rational grouping of courses and more advanced instruction in them."[102] At the time, French was chiefly and Spanish entirely undergraduate, while Old French, Low Latin, Provençal, Old Italian, and Romance Philology were all being offered in the remaining active department, Celtic.

This was indeed an unusual offering. The only other American institution that then had a department of Celtic was Harvard. Keane had persuaded the Ancient Order of Hibernians to endow a chair when it was under suspicion as a secret society.[103] Some members at least seem

---

99. OR, Deferrari and Campbell to Joseph M. Corrigan, Sept. 25, 1936.

100. OR, Shahan to Anthony H. Walburg, Washington, Aug. 6, 1910 (copy); BT, mm, Apr. 26 and Oct. 12, 1911.

101. *Ibid.*, Baisnée to Shahan, Sept. 20, 1926, and May 15, 1927.

102. *Ibid.*, Dunn to Shahan, Mar. 10, 1917.

103. McQuaid was expressing the view that "this new University Chair ought to be labeled the 'Murderers' Chair." ADR, O'Connell Papers, McQuaid to O'Connell, Rochester, Jan. 16, 1892.

to have thought that they were assisting "the spread and propagation of Irish as a living language"; at any rate, they disclaimed any "idea or knowledge or concern for the philology of Old Irish."[104] Also, the termination of the first appointee, Richard Henebry, a priest, aroused widespread controversy among Irish-Americans; a San Francisco alumnus, Peter Yorke, known later for his priestly work in social action, carried on a particularly vitriolic campaign against the university. Joseph Dunn was appointed to teach Celtic in 1899. Although he proposed that a comprehensive history of Gaelic literature should be undertaken in cooperation with Harvard, where he had been trained, Shahan's successor, many years later, still found puzzling this "very open field for this University." In thirty years' time, Dunn, with little teaching to do, had "produced very little."[105] James A. Geary was appointed to join him in 1913, and eventually succeeded to the chair.

The School of Philosophy

The faculty of philosophy had five times as many students as that of letters—427 during 1927–28—but the proportion of its students enrolled for graduate degrees—perhaps about 40 per cent—was smaller. Its departments of economics, philosophy, psychology, and sociology had been established in 1895. Departments of American history, education, and geology had been added, in 1903, 1907, and 1927, respectively.

In philosophy proper, which Pace continued to head, William Turner had been recruited from the St. Paul seminary in 1906. He had published a highly respected and widely used history of the field before his appointment to the see of Buffalo in 1919. The Dominican alumnus, Ignatius Smith, was appointed to the faculty in 1920 and became an exceedingly popular teacher of Thomism, a prominent campus figure, and afterwards a dean. Charles Hart of the diocese of Peoria, in 1921, Donald McLean of Nova Scotia, in 1923, and John T. Rolbiecki, of LaCrosse, Wisconsin, in 1922, were recruited for the faculty. In 1927, almost at the end of Shahan's administration, Sheen, who had pursued his advanced degrees at Louvain, transferred into the department. Just the year before, James Hugh Ryan, secretary of the NCWC department of education, who had been appointed to the department in 1922, had joined with Pace in founding the American Catholic Philosophical Association. Through its official organ, *The New Scholasticism,* and the publication

104. OR, Michael O'Reilly to O'Connell, New York, Mar. 17, 1904.
105. AAB, Curley Papers, R 1634, Ryan to Curley, Washington, Apr. 12, 1932.

Fulton John Sheen (1895–1979), professor first of apologetics, then of philosophy, internationally known radio and television apologist, auxiliary bishop of New York (1951–66), bishop of Rochester (1966–69), and titular archbishop of Newport (1969–79).

of its proceedings it became influential in the revival of Thomism that was underway. The trustees, in fact, were requesting the university to establish "a Graduate School of Scholastic Philosophy" in which priests could prepare for seminary teaching."[106] The next decade saw the organization of a separate faculty in the field.

Basic philosophical problems were certainly the deepest interest of Pace, but it was his continuous critical search for experimental data bearing on them that was crucial for the development of psychology on

106. BT, mm, Sept. 25, 1924, and Apr. 14, 1926; OR, Pace to Shahan, Washington, Sept. 14, 1925; OVR, "Outline of a Course in Scholastic Philosophy," Sept. 14, 1925.

the campus. He had in fact begun his European studies at the Sorbonne in chemistry and physiology but, after finding a second-hand copy of Wilhelm Wundt's *Grundzüge der physiologischen Psychologie* in a Paris book stall, he had decided to take his doctorate at Leipzig under Wundt and Carl Ludwig, a physiologist. The psychological laboratory that he had established in 1899 was a truly pioneer effort. When the American Psychological Association was organized in 1902 Pace had joined as a charter member and he presented papers at its first and second meetings that, like other publications of his, reported his experimental findings or utilized them.

Pace aroused the interest in psychology of Moore, then a Paulist, who took his doctorate in 1903 and then went to Germany to study with Wundt. He wrote that he thought the experience would make him "a far better missionary" than he could otherwise have expected to be but also that he knew that "the need for missionaries [was] more capable of being filled than the need for men who [would] do intellectual work."[107] While working with students in Berkeley, he continued his interest in psychology and, in 1910, returned to the department as an instructor. Soon, even as some of his confreres were asking, "When is Moore going to earn his living?" he was studying medicine at Georgetown, Munich, and Johns Hopkins, which conferred his medical degree upon him in 1915, in preparation for the establishment of a psychological clinic that was opened at Washington's Providence Hospital in 1916. Service in the medical corps of the United States Army during 1918–19 intensified his interest in psychopathology. His concern for the advancement of disciplinary knowledge was evident when he later wrote to Shahan, "A department of psychology in which no research is going on is a very dead affair."[108]

Finding a focus for his intellectual commitment in his spirituality, Moore left the Paulist congregation and, after a novitiate at Fort Augustus Abbey in Scotland, established with six others, in 1923, St. Anselm's Priory of the English Benedictine Congregation. Its location near the campus was not only a matter of convenience; it symbolized a desire for intellectual community that was abroad.[109] One member of

107. Pace Papers, Moore to Pace, Leipzig, Nov. 20, 1904.

108. OR, Moore to Shahan, Munich, Feb. 24, 1924. Moore's book, *The Driving Forces of Human Nature and Their Adjustment* (New York: Grune & Stratton, 1948), 38–49, includes his account of the founding of the department. On Moore, see Raphael Diamond, O.Cart., NCE, XVI, 300–301.

109. AAB, Curley Papers, B 2158, D 764, M 388–428, and M 1810–99, document the steps involved in this foundation as well as in Moore's foundation of St. Gertrude's School of Arts and Crafts for retarded girls.

Thomas Verner Moore (1877–1969), successively a Paulist priest, monk of St. Benedict, and Carthusian, professor of psychology and psychiatry and principal founder of St. Anselm's Abbey.

the new community, J. Edward Rauth, had been an assistant in the department. A Canadian layman in the department, Thomas G. Foran, who had come to the university as a Knights of Columbus fellow, became especially interested in intelligence and its measurement, and later became a professor of education. On his part, years later, having passed the age of retirement and not long before his withdrawal to a Carthusian monastery in Spain, Moore was proposing that the university should establish and staff a Catholic psychiatric hospital.[110]

110. BT, EC, mm, Oct. 11, 1944; OR, Magner to Moore, Oct. 26, 1944, and Moore to McCormick, n.d., handwritten, forwarding Magner's memorandum.

The departments of economics and sociology had been established in the school of the social sciences that had had a brief existence from 1895 to 1897. A department of politics established at the same time had never been staffed and had not survived.[111] In its earliest years, the department of economics had been led by men of broad interests. Frank O'Hara, whose doctorate was from the University of Berlin, and who was appointed to succeed David McCabe when the latter went to Princeton in 1909, seemed to want to transform the department into one of commerce, finance, and business administration. At first he persuaded the faculty to recommend opening a college of commerce downtown and he continued to press for such a college or, short of that, for "a commerce group" in the school of philosophy.[112] Until 1915, when O'Grady and John T. Drury were appointed as instructors, he was the only full-time appointee. O'Grady was later to vote against O'Hara's promotion to full professorial rank because, in his opinion, O'Hara had made no "contribution whatsoever to the field of economics."[113] William M. Deviny began teaching accounting in 1919. Paul J. FitzPatrick joined the department, in which he had received his doctorate, in 1922. O'Hara then was already serving as dean of the Knights of Columbus Evening School, and was expanding its activity by the establishment of Columbus University. Under him, the department, it was said later, had earned "the reputation of being a *refugium peccatorum.*"[114]

Happily, the situation in sociology was entirely different. Kerby was an outstanding figure, perhaps not so much for his scholarship, in which, however, he gave evidence of originality, as for his leadership in the National Conference of Catholic Charities, founded on the campus during Shahan's first year as rector. *The Social Mission of Charity*, published in 1921, became his best-known book. O'Grady, who began to offer courses in social work in 1914, found that the pioneer leaders of Catholic charities were looking upon the university as "a sort of shrine" and expecting it to produce those "who, by their scholarship and their crusading leadership would give Catholic charities a new position in the life of the Church and the nation."[115] Subsequently, O'Grady would establish a school of social work on the campus after succeeding Kerby

111. C. Joseph Nuesse, "The Introduction of the Social Sciences in the Catholic University of America, 1895–1909," *ST*, XII (Spring, 1986), 30–43, is an account of developments previous to the appointment of Shahan as rector.

112. SP, mm, Dec. 6 and 13, 1910; Mar. 6, 1911; Dec. 7, 1913; Jan. 11, Feb. 8, and Apr. 4, 1916; Jan. 20, 1919; AS, mm, Jan 11 and 18, Feb. 8, 1911; Jan. 12 and 27, Feb. 9 and Mar. 31, 1916.

113. AAB, Curley Papers, O 665, O'Grady to Curley, Washington, Mar. 8, 1929.

114. OR, Campbell and Deferrari to Ryan, May 29, 1935.

115. O'Grady Papers, autobiography.

William Joseph Kerby (1870–1936), first professor of sociology and head of the department (1897–1934), and first director of the National Conference of Catholic Charities.

as executive secretary of the National Conference. Cooper, of course, as an anthropologist was teaching in the department and a member of it briefly in the 1920s while he was still also deeply involved in the development of collegiate religious education. In 1925, toward the end of Shahan's tenure, Paul Hanly Furfey, who had been trained especially in the psychology and sociology of child life, joined the department, of which he was soon to become the leader.

The university's department of history had been inaugurated in 1903 with the appointment of Charles Hallan McCarthy to the Knights of Columbus chair in American history, but its extension into other fields was delayed. Nicholas A. Weber, a Marist priest, began service in 1909 by teaching "general history" to undergraduates. The board's visiting committee suggested development of graduate studies on a Louvain model in 1911[116] but a year later McCarthy was still deploring the lack of such subjects as English history and political science, although he seems to have been persuaded that he was offering "a somewhat better quality of work than is done in other universities."[117] A Franciscan who years later became the first apostolic nuncio to Ireland, Paschal Robinson, began to lecture on medieval institutions in 1914. In 1920, offerings in American history were augmented by two important appointments, of Leo Stock, who later resigned, remaining with the Carnegie Institution, and Richard J. Purcell, who was to succeed McCarthy in the Knights of Columbus chair.

Like the department of history, the department of education had been authorized before Shahan took office. After long importuning by Pace and Shahan, the trustees had established it in 1907. Shields was already offering courses in the field. Shahan could only be sympathetic because, as he was advising the trustees, he considered the training of teachers to be "one of the most important functions that any university can perform."[118] He had been interested from the first in the educational as distinct from the scientific purpose of the university, wanting the *Bulletin* to be "a high-class educational review."[119] So in 1910, McCormick, who was an alumnus and who had had experience as superintendent of schools of the diocese of Hartford, was brought back to the campus. McVay, who was to carry on the program of affiliation for many years, joined the department in the same year. Eleven years later, there were added George Johnson, a priest of the diocese of Toledo, who eventually became simultaneously director of the NCWC department of education and executive secretary of the National Catholic Educational Association, and Edward B. Jordan, later a dean of Catholic Sisters College and a vice rector of the university under McCormick. Francis P. Cassidy was appointed in 1922.

Pace, at an early date, recognized the need of a model school for the department but found Shields, who agreed with him about the need, unable to allocate the necessary funds. A pastor of St. Anthony's church in Brookland pressed for establishment of such a school in the parish facilities.[120] A Thomas E. Shields Memorial School materialized. When

---

116. AS, mm, Apr. 4, 1911; BT, mm, Apr. 26, 1911.
117. OR, McCarthy to Shahan, Nov. 13, 1912.
118. AR (1911–12), 14.
119. OVR, Pace to O'Connell, Jan. 13, 1906.
120. AAB, Curley Papers, P 1, Pace to Shahan, Dec. 12, 1921 (copy). The pastor was Pasquale Di Paolo.

the Dominican Sisters of Newburgh, New York, could no longer staff the school,[121] Johnson, who was the director, sought to establish it elsewhere in Brookland, but encountered the opposition of another pastor of St. Anthony's.[122] Its reestablishment did not become possible until 1935.

On the recommendation of the academic senate, at Shahan's request, the board established a department of geology late in his final term.[123] Fred L. Serviss was appointed as an instructor in the field and noted recognition of the university's work in geology in a report of the National Research Council. The department, however, was to have only a short life, since it was abolished within fifteen years.[124]

The School of Sciences

At the beginning of Shahan's administration, almost fifteen years after the establishment of scientific departments on the campus, there was still more than a little uncertainty about what these fields demanded and especially about what they demanded of Catholics. Provision had been made at the outset for botany, chemistry, mathematics, physics, and technology. The boast was made that the school of sciences that had been organized in 1906 had quickly become "the largest and most successful Catholic work of its kind in the United States."[125] Its progress, however, could be attributed more to the career aims of its students than to its participation in the controversies that were being stirred by scientific discoveries.

Most of these controversies were arising from developments in the biological sciences. Pace, from the beginning, had argued without effect that it was "almost impossible to teach Psychology unless the students [had] a fair knowledge of Biology."[126] Under financial pressures, the university had lost the beginning it had made with the outstanding botanist, Greene. One of his doctoral students, Theodor Holm, who had become a specialist in Arctic and Alpine flora while still a Danish explorer and who was at the time on the staff of the Smithsonian

---

121. OR, John J. Dunn to Shahan, New York, Mar. 19, 1928.

122. AAB, Curley Papers, C 1449, Patrick E. Conroy to Curley, Washington, June 16, 1928. For the subsequent history, see Edward B. Jordan, "The University Campus School," *CUB*, N.S., IX, No. 4 (May, 1942), 5ff.

123. AS, mm, Apr. 7, 1927; BT, mm, Apr. 27, 1927.

124. AB, mm, Dec. 9, 1942. The "variable success" of this field is described in G. S. Dunbar, "Geography in the Bellwether University of the United States," *Area*, XVIII (1986), 25–33.

125. "University Chronicle," *CUB*, XVI (May, 1910), 519.

126. AS, General to 1907, "Biology in the University" (manuscript signed by Pace, Oct. 18, 1897).

Institution, provided a nominal continuity for the department.[127] Shields, who had earned his doctorate in biology and evidently had been expected to found a department, was teaching some courses in the field, but was interested principally in education.

After about eighteen months in office, Shahan extended an offer of a "free hand" in organizing a department of biology to John B. Parker, an entomologist who had pursued graduate work at Ohio State University and was serving on the staff of Kansas State Agricultural College.[128] The department of botany was soon joined with the new department.[129] George J. Brilmyer became an instructor in 1914, to remain until 1942, but the load of undergraduate teaching for both liberal and premedical objectives and the cramped quarters of the department prevented attention to graduate students for some time.[130] William F. Simpson, whom the department had known as an undergraduate, was appointed in 1922 to teach bacteriology and, in 1925, John J. Clarke, who had been a Knights of Columbus fellow, was retained to teach physiology. Although a graduate course had been added specifically to meet the demands of priests and religious,[131] a priest-botanist who was appointed to the department in 1930 pointed out that such students who were preparing to teach in Catholic institutions had had to go to state colleges and universities where, in his estimation, "fully 95% of all non-Catholic biologists" were "frankly pantheistic or agnostic."[132]

The situation in chemistry was more stable because the original appointee, Griffin, served continuously until 1922. His efforts were supplemented by various members of the department or assistants who served for relatively short periods except for Henry L. Ward, appointed in 1920 and later head of the department, and Hardee Chambliss, appointed in 1922. The latter succeeded Griffin in the O'Brien chair.

Physics also maintained stability under the original appointee, Shea, who continued to head the department throughout the Shahan administration. His work was supplemented by that offered in mechanics, first by Zahm and then, from 1911 on, by Crook. Francis X. Burda was appointed to the department in 1914. George D. Rock, who had earned

127. OR, notes for meeting of BT [1904].
128. OR, Shahan to Parker, Washington, Oct. 21, 1910. See Edward G. Reinhard, "A History of the Department of Biology at the Catholic University of America," *CUB*, N.S., XX, No. 2 (Oct., 1952), 7–10.
129. BT, mm, Apr. 26, 1911, exh. and Parker to Shea, Nov. 26, 1912 (copy); AS, mm, Dec. 18, 1912; BT, mm, Apr. 2, 1913.
130. OR, Parker to Shahan, Dec. 7, 1916; Parker to Chambliss, Oct. 6, 1925, and May 17, 1926 (copies).
131. *Ibid.*, Parker to Landry, June 13, 1924.
132. OR, Hugh O'Neill to Ryan, Mar. 2, 1931.

his doctorate under Shea, was appointed to the faculty in 1923, and in later years served consecutively as head of the department, dean of the graduate school of arts and sciences, and secretary general. Leo F. Talbott, also trained in the department, joined the faculty in 1926.

Mathematics was taught at first by the Paulist Searle and René De-Saussure, an associate professor, with assistants, and also by Alfred F. Doolittle, who was listed as sole member of the department of astronomy until 1921. The department gained a lifelong professor when Landry was first appointed as a teaching fellow in 1902. He was joined in 1913 by Otto Ramler, and in 1918 by J. Nelson Rice, also products of the department, who remained in it until they retired. In 1924 and thereafter, J. Gardner O'Boyle, who also taught in mechanics, offered courses.

Courses in technology had presented a problem of classification in the early years but during Shahan's time they were listed as departments of the school of sciences. Shea offered electrical engineering until the coming of George F. Harbin in 1908. Ernest A. Valade, later a dean, joined him in 1917. Thomas McKavanagh succeeded Harbin in 1918.

In mechanical engineering, inaugurated under Zahm in 1903, George A. Weschler, appointed in 1910, became the mainstay of the department. Thomas J. Thompson, the first appointee in civil engineering, was succeeded after a few years by Fred Knight Merriman and then by Anthony J. Scullen, appointed to the faculty in 1914 and later dean of the school of engineering and architecture. Appointees to the department often began in a department of drawing, as did Scullen in 1913 and Harry Gallogly in 1921. Frank Biberstein joined the department in 1924.

Most acclaim was received, however, in the department of architecture that Murphy founded in 1911. His students were particularly successful in architectural competitions. Two, Thomas Locraft and Paul Goettelmann, were to succeed him in later years.

The School of Law

Although both engineering and law had been offered by the university since 1895, only law had been organized as a professional school, at the beginning of 1898. It remained the sole professional school throughout the Shahan administration, with problems of identity not only in scholarship but in its very claim to existence. The founding dean, Robinson, had begun with scholarly ambitions and had articulated hopes that neither he nor his successors for several decades had the resources to fulfill. Robinson had come expecting to receive graduate students only but had had to offer professional preparation to recent high school

graduates from the start. There were years when he was the only professor. He was already old when Shahan was appointed rector and he died
in the third year of the latter's first term. Enrollment remained a crucial
problem under the two successors whom Shahan appointed, Thomas
C. Carrigan from 1911 until his death in 1921 and Peter J. McLoughlin
from 1921 until his death soon after Shahan had left office. In some
years, when standards for admission were raised, there were no entering
students at all. The rector and the board could not avoid considering
dissolution of the school or abandonment of its so-called "undergraduate" program, but when they resolved to take these steps they failed to
implement them.[133]

Professional progress was made, however. Under Robinson, who had
begun with his brother John as a colleague, William H. DeLacy was
given a part-time appointment which he held for many years. In 1906,
Theodore Roosevelt appointed him to be the first judge of the juvenile
court of the District of Columbia, in which capacity he served until
1913. During Carrigan's first year, when Ammi Brown and Vincent L.
Toomey were already serving, Walter B. Kennedy and McLoughlin
were appointed to the faculty. Kennedy, who left in 1923, and Frederick
J. DeSloovere, who served from 1917 until 1922, were later to gain
national recognition as Catholic teachers of law, the former at Fordham,
the latter at New York University. Don Johnson, John Joseph Walsh,
John W. Curran, Raymond L. Carmody, and William O'Keefe were
others who served for short periods. During Shahan's last term there
were appointed James Condrick, who taught from 1923 until his retirement in 1957; James J. Hayden, appointed in 1924, and acting dean
from 1935 until 1937; and William Grogan, a member of the faculty
from 1927 until 1942. A combined six-year arts and law course had
been established in the school of philosophy in 1919 and in 1925 a pre-
legal curriculum was initiated. But the importance of the school was
signaled especially by its election to membership in the Association of
American Law Schools late in 1921. It thus became the first law school
in the District of Columbia to be recognized as in compliance with the
standards legislated by the American Bar Association.[134]

Of particular interest was the school's adherence to its Catholic
identity. What it was striving for was epitomized during the 1920s by
an alumnus among the trustees who was later to be elected president

133. See Nuesse, *CULR*, XXXV, 54–60.
134. The University had been urged to submit its application for membership several
years earlier when one of its prominent trustees was informed "that both Catholic schools
which now belong to the Association will be dropped from membership unless radical

of the American Bar Association. He proposed that "if the Catholic University would live up to its ideal" it would aim to "send to every state in the Union each year, a Catholic lawyer better trained than the average man in the science of the law."[135] Roscoe Pound of the Harvard law school before that had suggested an even more singular goal when he advised Catholic schools of law to begin "thoroughly at the bottom along some carefully chosen line," as Christopher Columbus Langdell had previously done in propagating the case method of teaching at Harvard, so that "instead of acquiescing in an inferior position and looking for their ideals and methods to the academic or proprietary law schools of the country," they would "set up an ideal and method of their own and become in that way a real force in the legal education of the country."[136]

The End of an Era

When Shahan retired in 1928, the university had been open for thirty-nine academic years. The nineteen of his administration might well have been called an "era of good feeling." Anyone with memories of the earlier time might have looked upon the prevailing harmony as a satisfaction of the institution's basic need. Undoubtedly, however, there were some in the faculties and in the larger Catholic community who were perceptive enough to anticipate that the end of the third term that Shahan was completing would be a point of transition. How the transition would come about or where it would lead could not have been so apparent. There were signs, to those aware of them, in Pace's early analysis and in Curley's initiatives. Beneath the surface, there was dissatisfaction with the identity that the university was projecting in the world of higher education. But the overt expression was, it seems, postponed. It was to erupt only a few years later in reaction to the administrative reorganization and academic upgrading that was begun by Shahan's successor.

What then became manifest were clearly divergent views about the university that were central to the question of its identity and to its concept of mission. The divergences were bound to be divisive when particular policies had to be judged. The most fundamental was on a

---

improvements are made." OVR, Walter George Smith to Carrigan, Philadelphia, Feb. 11, 1916, transmitting opinions of Roscoe Pound.

135. AAB, Curley Papers, M 588, Clarence E. Martin to Curley, Martinsburg, W. Va., Aug. 7, 1926.

136. OVR, Smith to Carrigan, Philadelphia, Feb. 11, 1916, and OR, J. M. Fox to Ryan, Aug. 30, 1930, quoting excerpts from letters of Pound to Smith, sent by Smith to Carrigan, Feb. 11 and 29, 1916.

perennial issue, one that continues to pervade all university education in the United States. It is presented popularly but misleadingly as teaching versus research. By the 1920s, of course, the modern American university, which does both, had taken definite shape. It had attained, as historians of knowledge have pointed out, an organizational structure "that would provide the United States with the ability to achieve a position of eminence in the intellectual world."[137]

Unfortunately, the issue was not to be understood by an episcopal commission of the next decade even after so distinguished a priest-professor as Cooper had explained to it that institutional status had become dependent "first and above all, less on teaching and on absorptive scholarship, and far less, than on productive scholarship of a technical order."[138] The university had been defined at its beginning as research-oriented. Not only Cooper but other veterans of the faculties such as Hyvernat, Moore, and Pace were determined to keep it so. Younger colleagues, including, for example, Deferrari in the classics, Furfey in sociology, Purcell and Aloysius K. Ziegler in history, were giving them support.

Had the matter been put to a vote, however, there is no way of knowing how the individual members of the faculties would have been counted. It is significant that some who were vocal made explicit their opinion that the university should be primarily a teaching institution. Smith, the future dean, put the question with seeming practicality: "Should not a man be rewarded for hard work in teaching classes and helping in other work about the university?"[139] His junior colleague, Sheen, who was already becoming the foremost American Catholic apologist through his use of radio, saw as a desideratum "a de-emphasis on research as an end and purpose of university education." Allowing for the need of research in the natural sciences, a Catholic university as he envisioned it existed primarily for the "organization and dissemination of truth in the natural and revealed order." With an idealizing backward look that Shahan and many other Catholics of the time might well have shared, he proclaimed that "the Middle Ages may have been poor in facts, but they were rich in principles; today we are rich in facts and poor in principles."[140]

Educational philosophy aside, there were circumstantial reasons for the preference of some for a teaching rather than a research institution.

137. Oleson and Voss, *op. cit.*, vii.
138. McNicholas Papers, memorandum of John M. Cooper, n.d. [ca. 1935].
139. *Ibid.*, Episcopal Visiting Committee, mm, Dec. 15, 1934.
140. *Ibid.*, Sheen to Gerald P. O'Hara, Washington, n.d. [ca. 1935].

One was in the ecclesiastical model that was current. It antedated research institutions and it carried the weight of ecclesiastical authority. Hyvernat had pointed to the problem at an early date. Archbishop McNicholas exemplified the mind-set some years later when he looked to the apostolic delegate to the United States as one who would know better than anyone in the country what a pontifical university should be.[141] A second reason undoubtedly arose from practical experience since in their day-to-day classroom work most professors were dealing with undergraduates. The effective presentation of matter rather than the advancement of scholarship had to be their main concern. The burdens carried by the most able professors were a third reason. Kerby, for example, was urging that there was little use in developing speculative statements of purpose "so long as the larger needs of the American Church demand time and energy from the Professors."[142] Fourth and less complimentary was the mix of minds of varying quality that Shahan had brought together. Although the first-rate professors were conspicuous, their mediocre colleagues would not have been capable of research.

Still another reason, less easy to specify, can be related to the composition of the faculties. The number of lay members had increased, so that a church historian could complain, probably quite unjustly, "Priests form but 30% of the staff, yet do 90% of the work."[143] To a future rector, McCormick, then dean of the Catholic Sisters College, there was evidence that "some of the lay professors seem to think that the university would do far better if priests were kept in the background."[144] Guilday, placing campus anticlericalism among his reasons for the lack of development of the faculty of theology, saw the ogre not in "a party or a clique" but in the appointments to "key positions" that Shahan's successor was making, in which the priesthood was not being "honored as it should be."[145]

The feeling of defensiveness that was revealed in relatively numerous statements such as these is somewhat surprising in view of the harmonious relations of clergy and laity that have been thought to characterize the university's history in more recent decades. The sources available

---

141. *Ibid.*, McNicholas to O'Hara, Cincinnati, Mar. 1, 1935 (copy). The rector at the time of the appointment of Archbishop (later Cardinal) Amleto Cicognani, noting that the latter had been a professor and had been associated with students of the University of Rome for a decade, was expecting the University to get "a good friend" who "really knows what a university ought to be." AAB, Curley Papers, R 1672, Ryan to Curley, Washington, Mar. 1, 1933.

142. *Ibid.*, Kerby to McNicholas, Washington, Mar. 10, 1935.

143. *Ibid.*, Healy to McNicholas, Washington, May 12, 1931.

144. *Ibid.*, Episcopal Visiting Committee, mm, Dec. 15, 1934.

145. *Ibid.*, Guilday to McNicholas, Washington, Apr. 20, 1935.

provide no evidence from the lay side. Given their calling, it would not have been unexpected that priest professors would retain pastoral outlooks and that some might even have neglected the stimulation of intellect in their students in favor of the development of character. But the drive toward academic excellence on the part of the most able priests was plainly evident. The clerical solidarity was perhaps supplying what one author, with religious institutes in mind, has described as a "religious founding group" that with Christian wisdom and *esprit de corps* is able to develop, and preserve a university community.[146] Guilday put it clerically, even while expressing the highest regard for a dean who had the dual handicaps "of being a layman and an Italian," when he argued that "the Catholic University of America is an institution governed by the hierarchy, manned mainly by the secular clergy, and should therefore be as far as possible in the hands of the secular clergy."[147]

After sixty years, it is possible to see that what was transpiring on the campus was indicative of changes that had begun in American Catholicism. The church as a whole was indeed in its "bricks and mortar" stage and would remain so for decades. Although the university that the bishops had founded had been conceived as a vehicle for the advancement of Catholics in American society, interest in its intellectual mission had lagged notably. There was lacking the "constituency of predominantly college-educated, middle-class Americans that was supporting non-Catholic institutions, both private and public."[148] But the number of lay Catholics who could provide such a constituency was beginning to increase. The appearance of *Commonweal* in 1924 could be taken as a kind of sign; Pace wrote to its founding editor that he thought that the idea of the periodical was "excellent, both as regards the character of the review and its management by laymen."[149] Shahan, of course, had earlier given national visibility to the university through organizations such as the National Catholic Educational Association and the National Conference of Catholic Charities. In his last term the foundation of the Catholic Association for International Peace by prominent professors from non-Catholic institutions, among others, demonstrated that Catholic interests were not merely clerical and parochial.

At about the same time, the university was assisting in the propaga-

---

146. David J. Hassel, S.J., *City of Wisdom: A Christian Vision of the American University* (Chicago: Loyola University Press, 1983), 371. See especially Chaps. XVII–XVIII for an elaboration of the concept.

147. McNicholas Papers, memorandum for Bishop O'Hara, n.d. [ca. 1935].

148. Oleson and Voss, *op. cit.*, ix.

149. OVR, Pace to Michael Williams, Washington, Jan. 2, 1923 (copy).

tion among American Catholics of the philosophical movement that its papal founder had earlier instituted officially. Pace was one of the first agents. While a student in Rome, he had followed Satolli's lectures and had been singled out by the future apostolic delegate as a candidate for the university's faculty.[150] Later, he was to be hailed as "the herald of the Thomistic revival in the United States."[151] The early catalogue material that he prepared made it plain that "the basis of all philosophic instruction" in the department that he headed would be "the system of St. Thomas Aquinas."[152] As one of the founders of the American Psychological Association, as well as in his later participation in academic and educational groups, he may have been exhibiting the "adventurous quality of mind" with which one author has credited the pioneers of the movement.[153] Fittingly, he was elected the first president of the American Catholic Philosophical Association.

The major impact of the Thomist revival was still to come. It was by no means to be confined to the department of philosophy. Indeed, what was expected was the fulfillment of what the convert Robinson had believed to be the mission of the university when he came to it in 1895 thinking that scholastic philosophy would be taught "as the basis of all scientific knowledge."[154] Into the 1960s, Thomism was to provide to a striking degree the basis for the formation of students in American Catholic colleges and universities. The number of such students, of course, was to grow rapidly. The places open to them in American society, which were still notably restricted in the 1920s, would also increase. Thus, Thomism became, as has been remarked, "a metaphysical component of the 'Americanization' of Catholicism."[155]

150. Pace Papers, Keane to Pace, Winchester, Va., Sept. 28, 1887, and Worcester, Mass., July 14, 1888.

151. *Ibid.*, by J. H. Ryan.

152. *Yearbook 1897–98*, 19.

153. Halsey, *op. cit.*, 140.

154. AS, General to 1907, memorandum to academic senate committee (ca. 1901–2).

155. Halsey, *op. cit.*, 150.

PART FOUR

The Assertion of Role, 1928-1953

. . . throughout the Catholic scene there still seems to be a lack of the proper understanding of the importance for the Church of true university facilities in all parts of the country. It seems that the work of Bishop Becker, Bishop Spalding, Bishop Keane and the rest must to some extent, at least, be done over again. Graduate studies need steady and substantial financial support, in part for buildings, but chiefly for men—professors and students. – *Roy J. Deferrari, "The Origin and Development of Graduate Studies under Catholic Auspices," in Roy J. Deferrari (ed.),* Essays on Catholic Education in the United States *(Washington, D.C.: The Catholic University of America Press, 1942), 211.*

CHAPTER VII

The Renewal of the
Graduate Thrust

The selection of a successor to Bishop Shahan proved to be anything
but a simple task. After the board had forwarded its recommendations
to Rome, the chancellor wrote to a brother bishop, "We have discovered
that it is infinitely easier to get an Archbishop for any See in the country
than to get a man qualified for the position of Rector of the Catholic
University."[1] Soon, however, he was to have reason to praise the fifth
rector, James Hugh Ryan (1886–1947), of whom he had had little
previous knowledge, as "not only a brilliant man intellectually, but . . .
an indefatigable worker and a splendid executive."[2] Seven years later,
delighted as he was at the progress that the university was making
under Ryan's vigorous leadership, which the trustees had endorsed by
unanimously recommending his reappointment as rector,[3] Curley could
only be profoundly shocked when, vacationing in his native Ireland,
he learned that Ryan would be prevented from completing his second
five-year term by his appointment to a diocesan see. He was not yet off
the pier when he exploded to those who met him in New York, "I can
get one hundred Bishops for Omaha—where can we get one Rector for
the Catholic University?"[4]

Before Ryan's initial appointment, believing that a mistaken choice
might mean "ruin to the University," Curley had suggested that "primarily an administrator" was needed.[5] The academic senate, it will be

1. AAB, Curley Papers, C 213, Curley to John J. Cantwell, bishop of Los Angeles,
Baltimore, Apr. 23, 1928 (copy).
2. *Ibid.*, G 216, Curley to Francis P. Garvan, Baltimore, Nov. 14, 1930.
3. BT, mm, Apr. 26, 1933.
4. AAO, James Hugh Ryan Papers, Peter L. Ireton to Ryan, Baltimore, Aug. 27,
1935. This and other items from the Ryan Papers have been supplied by courtesy of the
Reverend Eldon J. McKamy, chancellor of the archdiocese of Omaha.
5. AAB, Curley Papers, T 834, Curley to William Turner, bishop of Buffalo, Baltimore,
Apr. 6, 1928 (copy); also, Nelligan Papers, Nominating Committee for "Election of New
Rector."

James Hugh Ryan (1886–1947), fifth rector of The Catholic University of America, titular bishop of Modra (1933–35), bishop (1935–45) and archbishop (1945–47) of Omaha.

recalled, had reminded the board that the university's greatest need was money. Some at least in the senate and in the board were of the opinion that an outsider would be more effective in the situation than an appointee from within. The German-born scripture scholar who was then dean of the faculty of the sacred sciences wrote privately to the chancellor, "The University has been for so many years under the same overpowering influence that only a complete change of the Administration will allow an unbiased judgment as to our real condition and the improvements to be introduced."[6]

An outsider was in fact the favored candidate of many in the discus-

6. AAB, Nelligan Papers, Franz Cöln to Curley, Washington, Mar. 31, 1928.

sions that preceded the official steps that had to be taken and in the voting in the academic senate and the board. He was Francis Clement Kelley, bishop of Oklahoma City and Tulsa, who had become widely known earlier as a Chicago priest directing the development of the Catholic Church Extension Society.[7] There was support for him in faculty circles and among bishops in touch with professors, such as Turner of Buffalo and Hugh Boyle of Pittsburgh, a devoted alumnus. In a nominating committee that was appointed prematurely by the board's presiding officer, Cardinal O'Connell, Turner, who was a member, emphatically refused to be considered when he was told that he would be the best candidate. O'Connell reportedly objected to Kelley on the grounds that he was "too much inclined towards the use of political methods and was not always prudent in his utterances and did not possess the full confidence at least of the eastern bishops."[8] Curley, who was not present at the board meeting and who professed neutrality since he would have to work with any eventual appointee, supported Kelley's candidacy in the succeeding meeting of the board.[9]

In the committee, when Bishop Joseph Schrembs of Cleveland proposed consideration of Ryan, Turner and O'Connell both objected, Turner perhaps because he was aware of opposition to Ryan on the campus, mainly in the school of sacred sciences, and O'Connell perhaps because he remembered that Ryan had been an aide to Schrembs some years before in presenting successfully to the Holy See the case for the continuation of the National Catholic Welfare Council, which O'Connell had opposed.[10] Curley at the time was reporting that Ryan was "greatly distrusted by some members of the Hierarchy" and that he himself had doubts about his probable success as rector.[11]

Two other members of the professoriate, from the field of education, were seriously considered by the committee. One was Patrick J. McCormick, a later rector, about whom Curley commented that although he considered him to be his "very warm friend" he thought that McCormick did not have "the force needed in the man who has to take over the University with all its difficulties and problems." He found deficiencies also in George Johnson of the department of education, a second nominee of Schrembs, who became the preferred candidate of the committee, after an honorific nomination of Pace, the vice rector.[12] But then

---

7. See Gaffey, *Kelley*. For a brief biography, see E. A. Flasche, NCE, VIII, 144–45.
8. AAB, Curley Papers, S 562, Joseph Schrembs to Curley, Cleveland, Apr. 9, 1928.
9. AAB, Nelligan Papers, "Election of New Rector."
10. Sheerin, *op. cit.*, 70, 73.
11. AAB, Curley Papers, T 834, Curley to Turner, Baltimore, Apr. 6, 1928 (copy).
12. *Ibid.*, B 1343, Curley to Boyle, Baltimore, Apr. 6, 1928 (copy).

discussion was halted and it was agreed to maintain "absolute secrecy" because "the attention of Boston was called to the fact that the Academic Senate had a constitutional right to be heard on the subject."[13]

The senate reinforced its earlier message to the trustees by casting a majority vote to place Kelley's name as the first of the three on its *terna*. After him it recommended as its second choice Ryan and as its third Cooper.[14] In its turn, the board voted to recommend Kelley to the Holy See. It did so over the objections of Archbishop Hanna of San Francisco, who insisted that academic standing should be the primary desideratum in a candidate, and of Archbishop McNicholas of Cincinnati, who thought that respect for the Holy See should preclude the election of a bishop who had been appointed to his diocese not for a term but for life. Upon the latter's urging, a full explanation to Rome was agreed upon, so that the names of Kelley and Ryan were both forwarded.[15] Some bishops thought that in this action the board was derogating from the privilege—actually, the constitutional right—that the Holy See had extended to it in agreeing to accept on this occasion a single name. It was predicted that "if Kelly [*sic*] is passed over and Ryan is nominated, there will be unending trouble in the University."[16] Schrembs, with the others, deplored the publicity given to Kelley's candidacy and feared that it would be counter-productive in Rome.[17] Undoubtedly, such individual opinions were made known to the Holy See. Ryan's appointment was announced on July 12, 1928.

The Fifth Rector (1928–35)

Ryan was a priest of the diocese (now archdiocese) of Indianapolis and a native of the see city. After his preliminary preparation at Duquesne University and at Mount St. Mary's Seminary of the West, he had completed in Rome his studies for the priesthood and for the degrees of doctor of sacred theology and doctor of philosophy. From 1911 until 1920 he had taught at St. Mary of the Woods College in Terre Haute within his home diocese and he had just been chosen as president of that institution when he was asked to move to Washington to become the first executive secretary of the department of education of the National Catholic Welfare Conference (renamed in view of objections to the use of the word Council). After two years, in 1922, he had

---

13. *Ibid.*, S 562, Schrembs to Curley, Cleveland, Apr. 9, 1928.
14. AS, mm, Mar. 27, 1928.
15. BT, mm, Apr. 18, 1928.
16. AACi, Cöln Papers, Turner to Cöln, Buffalo, Apr. 23, 1928; also AAB, Curley Papers, T 835, Turner to Curley, Buffalo, Apr. 23, 1928.
17. AAB, Curley Papers, S 563, Schrembs to Curley, Cleveland, June 11, 1928.

The fifth rector greeting President Franklin Delano Roosevelt upon his arrival on campus to receive an honorary degree, June 14, 1933. Presidents Grover Cleveland, Benjamin Harrison, William McKinley, Theodore Roosevelt, Calvin Coolidge, Franklin Delano Roosevelt, Dwight Eisenhower, and Lyndon Baines Johnson have been visitors to the campus.

been given a concurrent position as an instructor in philosophy at the university. In 1926 he was promoted to the rank of associate professor, and in 1928, after his designation as rector, he was named the Elizabeth B. Caldwell professor of philosophy. Meanwhile, it will be remembered, he and Pace had founded the American Catholic Philosophical Association and its journal, *The New Scholasticism,* and Ryan had been invested, in 1927, as a domestic prelate of the papal household. At the time of his inauguration as rector, when President Calvin Coolidge received an honorary doctorate, he was only forty-two years of age. While in office, he was named, in 1933, titular bishop of Modra.[18]

Ryan began at once to do the things that every efficient executive

18. For other details, see Roy J. Deferrari, *NCE,* XII, 766–67, and Warren Willis, "The Reorganization of the Catholic University of America during the Rectorship of James H. Ryan (1928–1935)" (unpublished doctoral dissertation, The Catholic University of America, 1972), 16–18. The latter work provides a detailed account of the Ryan administration.

must do. "To assist and advise the administration in the solution of problems both of a curricular and extra-curricular nature," he appointed fifteen faculty committees.[19] The annual reports that he submitted to the trustees show that before his first year was out he had surveyed the strengths and weaknesses of all the academic units of the institution, had initiated a plan for their reorganization, and had set in motion planning for the fund-raising that would be necessary to realize the university's objectives. Contemporaries of his have attested that he "took his position seriously and worked hard to equip himself as an enlightened administrator" so that he might make the university, as he was heard to hope, "a Catholic Harvard."[20] He himself was elected to the council of the Medieval Academy of America. He gave the institution academic momentum for years well beyond his own presence in it, even if the onset of the great depression of the 1930s frustrated his financial plans.

Ryan's premises were not unlike those of the university's founding generation. His reading of modern history had convinced him "that every great movement directed against the Church has issued from the campus of a university."[21] Catholic universities were needed to be centers of counter-influence. He saw in "the sorry exhibition of hatred for everything Catholic" during the presidential campaign of 1928 the need to "train men, lay and cleric, for the specific purpose of creating a public opinion that will at least be just toward Catholics and the Catholic cause."[22] So effective was Ryan in explaining his purposes in Rome that he could report to trustees who were themselves well acquainted there that, as the third rector had once thought, the sacred congregation of seminaries and universities was looking to The Catholic University of America "to become a model university for the whole world," even for the "much older centers of learning in Europe."[23]

At the same time Ryan was ready to acknowledge that the institution had "not yet achieved, in the minds of many, first rank as a university," and that there should be "few if any illusions . . . concerning either the type or quality of scholarly work" being done. "It is," he apprised the board in confidence, "a matter of surprise to educators that the University is so undeveloped, given the immense resources of the Catholic

19. AR (1928–29), 12. See also OR, Committee on Committees. Some years later, a vice rector referred to the too numerous committees as "a fiasco." OVR, Edward B. Jordan to Mother Mary Bernard, O.S.B., Washington, July 19, 1944.
20. Ellis, *Catholic Bishops*, 26.
21. AR (1930–31), 2.
22. Shahan Papers, Letter to "Dear Reverend Fathers," n.d. [1928].
23. AR (1929–30), 2.

Church."[24] The ambivalence of some bishops toward Catholic higher education was reflected in a reply that he received to a circular letter sent during December of 1931 that reported not only "a growing tendency on the part of our catholic people to send their sons and daughters to secular colleges and universities," but "a sense of uncertainty regarding the 'returns' on the enormous investments, financial and human, tied up in our American Catholic educational system."[25] But a Catholic who had been a member of the Harvard faculty since 1911 and who had heard in his youth "the impassioned pleas" of John Lancaster Spalding expressed "a distinct shock" when he learned that the intervening decades had passed "without a general realization of what a sufficiently endowed university would mean."[26]

It did not take Ryan long to conclude that "the future of the University depends solely on getting the right type of men."[27] He canvassed Catholic scholars of reputation in a variety of fields: Karl Herzfeld, then at The Johns Hopkins University, in physics; Constantine McGuire, a consultant in economics who declined a faculty appointment; Albert Zahm in mechanical engineering. With some impatience, he wrote to the faculty of the sacred sciences that he had been "in communication with practically every important person in Europe who would know candidates" for appointment in theology and had visited, unsuccessfully, "a half dozen Universities the summer before last [i.e., immediately after his appointment] to obtain the names of candidates."[28] In his confidential communication to the board, Ryan reported that the most fundamental cause of criticism of the university was the lack of selectivity in faculty appointments. He explained, "A university is a society of men, not buildings, men working on the university level, animated by the same high scientific ideals, and devoted to the discovery and spread of truth and knowledge." What was of most importance in his estimation was "unity of purpose and high scholarly ideals, together with a devotion toward the truth and toward the Church which, when functioning in men of scholarly attainments and pursuits, will find us all together in a unified march toward the goal which the Catholic University has set for itself."[29]

24. OR, Ryan to BT, Mar. 16, 1931 (confidential).
25. *Ibid.*, Joseph F. Rummel, then bishop of Omaha and later archbishop of New Orleans, to Ryan, Omaha, Jan. 15, 1932.
26. *Ibid.*, Louis J. A. Mercier to Ryan, Cambridge, Nov. 5, 1932.
27. AAB, Curley Papers, R 1480, Ryan to Curley, Jan. 12, 1930.
28. AACi, Cöln Papers, Ryan to Bernard A. McKenna, acting secretary of the faculty, Sept. 27, 1930 (copy).
29. *Op. cit.*

Ryan saw the university's essential mission in its graduate work. He led the academic senate toward "a mentality" that would refuse promotion in rank to anyone who did not show "an interest in research by publication."[30] He reported that Pope Pius XI had been "particularly impressed by the type and quality of graduate work being done, having himself read a number of dissertations which had been presented to him by Sisters."[31] After he had succeeded in reorganizing the faculties, he informed the board that the new graduate school might "go a long way to justify the existence of the University in the eyes not only of the learned world but of the leaders of the church as well who look to us precisely, and it must be admitted somewhat impatiently, to prepare for ecclesiastical and civil life graduate students of the highest type."[32]

In the new Mullen Library Ryan found facilities for research work that few other institutions of the time could present[33] and in his view the city of Washington afforded to graduate students resources "which no university even with the largest endowment could supply."[34] Looking quizzically at the expansion of professional—"if it be not vocational"— education, he laid down the principle that "all existing professional work on this campus should be conducted in a graduate way and should follow and even be controlled somewhat by the standards laid down for the Graduate School."[35] In establishing as part of the university the summer session that until 1929 had been operated by the Catholic Sisters College, and to offer "greater assistance to our teaching Sisterhoods," Ryan encouraged "the hope of the Director gradually to alter the character of the Summer School so that, after a certain period of time, its work will be predominantly of a graduate character."[36]

To facilitate the attainment of such objectives and to allay the discontent on the campus—where the effects of inflation could be represented as having reduced the real value of salaries to "hardly two-thirds of the salaries paid in the year 1913"[37]—Ryan succeeded during his first year in establishing a faculty salary scale that he appraised as "at the level of colleges and universities of the same student attendance as the Catholic University." Group life insurance, toward which the university contributed, was made available as a benefit. Liberal sick leave grants were

---

30. AAB, Curley Papers, R 1634, Ryan to Curley, Washington, Apr. 12, 1932.
31. AR (1929–30), 1.
32. *Ibid.*, 11–12.
33. AR (1928–29), 11.
34. AR (1929–30), 3.
35. AR (1934–35), 4.
36. AR (1928–29), 11.
37. OR, Dunn to Trustees, *op. cit.*

made a matter of policy. Steps were taken toward the development of a pension plan.[38] These were obviously important measures, even if, as Curley thought, "no man living [would] ever see a contented Faculty at the Catholic University." "Outside the question of salaries," according to the chancellor's perception, "most of the things that annoy the Faculty are tiny trifles, air-like in their lightness."[39]

Academic Reorganization

The academic reorganization that was initiated during the first years of the Ryan administration was in the direction of prevailing American practice which, by 1920, had become more or less settled. In the arts and sciences, the three faculties of philosophy, letters, and science that had been established in 1906 were combined into the faculty of the graduate school of arts and sciences which served also the new college of arts and sciences. The relevant professional studies that were being offered in the school of science were placed in a school of engineering that embraced both graduate and undergraduate programs. Other faculties, those of theology, canon law, and civil law were not subject to reorganization. Ryan's work has been presented as an "Americanization" of an institution that had been organized largely along European lines and Ryan himself emphasized to the board, "This is not only a Catholic University but a Catholic University in America, and therefore should be organized and conducted along approved university lines."[40] He explained at some length why the assumptions underlying German university governance were not applicable in the United States, directing his remarks especially to the claims of clerics who seemed to be overlooking the differences. In general, he found beneficial the rise to importance of the accrediting agencies that were beginning to wield great power in American education, although this was not a popular position in Catholic circles at the time.[41]

Reorganization, of course, had been the subject of discussion at least since 1916, but progress had been stalled, first by failure of the board to act on the matter,[42] and later because the nature of the problem had not been understood in Rome.[43] Ryan acted quickly. Among the committees that he appointed were one on courses of study that was concerned with proposing undergraduate curricula and another on the graduate school.

38. AR (1928–29), 2, 3.
39. AAB, Curley Papers, T 836, Curley to Turner, Baltimore, Apr. 26, 1928 (copy).
40. OR, Ryan to BT, *op. cit.* See also, Deferrari, *Essays*, 206–7, and *Memoirs*, 26–27.
41. Deferrari, *Layman*, 139; Power, *op. cit.*, 369.
42. BT, mm, Apr. 10, 1918, exh.
43. OR, Bisleti to Curley, July 31, 1924, *supra*.

Reports of these committees were introduced into the senate on September 24, 1929. With slight amendments, the first was approved on the following December 12, and the second on January 16. By February 27, 1930, Ryan could announce that the executive committee, to which the board had delegated the necessary authority, had approved the reorganization. It was given full effect at the beginning of the next academic year.[44]

The reorganization embodied changes in academic leadership. Ryan advised the chancellor, "We must begin by getting active deans who will give all their time and thought to the Schools in their charge."[45] He had asked the deans themselves "to make it plain" that they were "in authority."[46] Deferrari, who had joined the department of Greek and Latin in 1918 and who was appointed acting dean of the graduate school of arts and sciences before his election as dean by the faculty, became in effect Ryan's right-hand man in academic matters.[47] In the law school, Ryan's first decanal appointee was taking a firm hold. But in addition to entrepreneurial deans, Ryan wanted to give "increasing authority" to heads of departments, acknowledging that in large institutions the departmental system might become isolating and unwieldy but believing, perhaps naively, that in an institution as small as The Catholic University of America such dangers did not exist.[48] His assessment was later incorporated into the university's governing documents.

Although it would seem that Ryan commanded widespread support for the measures that he was taking, he had to contend with significant and sometimes bitter opposition from members of the ecclesiastical faculties, from some other priest professors, and, before long, from a powerful archbishop. What he was attempting was perceived by the respected educator Johnson, among others, as shifting "the center of gravity . . . from the sacred sciences and philosophy to the arts and sciences."[49] The weakness of the theological faculty at the time went almost unmentioned. Philosophers such as Smith and Sheen were asking "Is this a teaching university or a research university?"[50] The future rector McCormick thought that the new graduate school was "an unwieldy thing" and that the "old method" was more desirable for sisters and laywomen.[51] Johnson, "looking back on the days gone by," could

44. AS, mm, Feb. 27, 1930.
45. AAB, Curley Papers, R 1480, Ryan to Curley, Washington, Jan. 12, 1930.
46. BD, mm, Oct. 19, 1928.
47. For a biographical sketch, see Thomas Halton, NCE, XVII, 179.
48. AR (1929–30), 6–7; AS, mm, Sept. 24, 1929.
49. McNicholas Papers, Johnson to McNicholas, Washington, Mar. 9, 1935.
50. *Ibid.*, Episcopal Visiting Committee, mm, Dec. 25, 1934, quoting Smith.
51. *Ibid.*, quoting McCormick.

not help but feel "that there was more of the real Catholic spirit and perhaps just as high standards of graduate work when things were not as well organized" as they were under Ryan.[52] Much of the blame for what was presumed to be happening was attributed ultimately to Pace, who was said to want the "laicization of the university," but placed immediately upon Deferrari, whom the dean of the school of sacred sciences called "the very worst of influences."[53] McNicholas, who was first to preside over a committee to investigate the differences that had arisen between the rector and the faculty of theology, but who, in 1934, became chairman of a Roman-appointed visiting committee for the ecclesiastical faculties, judged some of Deferrari's positions "to indicate that his philosophy of education is very secular and opposed to the mind of the Church."[54]

Diplomatic skill was not an outstanding characteristic of those whom Ryan selected as his principal lieutenants. Undoubtedly his own drive was found irritable by some, manifested as it reputedly was by his "rather abrasive manner, and his abrupt speech and his aristocratic and aloof way of life."[55] Managerially, viewed from the vantage point of the present, far too much crossed his desk. His assistant warned, "Every Tom, Dick and Harry on this campus can go to the Rector of this University with his troubles and there are so many details of administration heaped upon your office that it appears well nigh impossible for any man to handle it."[56] Curley, however, reported to Rome and to any number of Americans that Ryan was doing "ten years work in four, despite the bitterest and the most villainous kind of opposition from those from whom opposition should not be expected."[57] Unfortunately, some of Ryan's energy had to be spent upon problems of his own making, as when accepted standards of academic procedure were violated in abrupt terminations of faculty appointments.

One such case was the locally celebrated one of John J. Rolbiecki, who was at the time an associate professor of philosophy. At a preliminary meeting of what was to be the graduate school of arts and sciences, on May 27, 1930, Rolbiecki raised the question of the constitutionality of Ryan's reorganization, especially with reference to the inclusion of the school of philosophy in the graduate school, since the pontifical

52. *Op. cit.*
53. *Ibid.*, Episcopal Visiting Committee, mm, May 14, 1931, quoting Cöln.
54. *Ibid.*, McNicholas to O'Hara, Cincinnati, Mar. 1, 1935.
55. Ellis, *Catholic Bishops*, 26–27.
56. OR, Sheehy to Ryan, Oct. 20, 1931.
57. AAB, Curley Papers, B 818, Curley to Bernardini, Baltimore, Dec. 14, 1931 (copy).

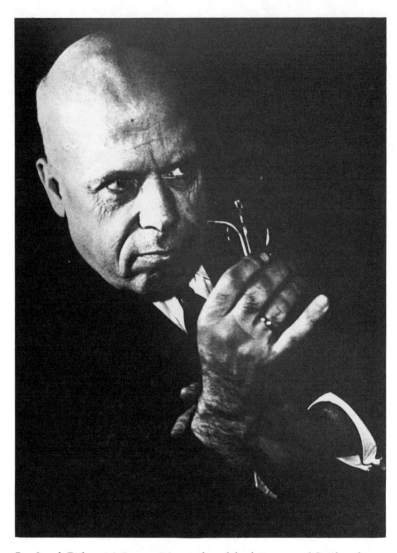

Roy Joseph Deferrari (1890–1969), member of the department of Greek and Latin (1918–60), director of summer sessions (1930–60), dean of the graduate school of arts and sciences (1930–37), secretary general (1937–60).

constitution under which the university was operating provided that the appointment of professors and associate professors in philosophy proper had to be approved by the Holy See. Rolbiecki seemed to Deferrari, who was presiding, to be defying authority and it was Deferrari's account of the meeting that was sent to all members of the board. The executive committee terminated Rolbiecki's appointment because "of his attitude towards the Board of Trustees," although Curley later was frank to admit "that there may have been something lacking in the form."[58] Rolbiecki appealed his case to the sacred congregation of seminaries and universities in November and early in 1931 circulated in pamphlet form his own argument, *A Statement of My Case.*[59] Meanwhile, a special trustee committee was appointed, with McNicholas as chairman, and this committee was instructed by the Roman authorities to find a solution to the case. The outcome was that Rolbiecki was reinstated after submitting a letter of apology for anything that might have been reprehensible in his action and after agreeing to withdraw his appeal.[60]

A second disturbing case followed within months after the decision in Rolbiecki's favor. It had desirable consequences for the reorganization that Ryan was instituting and the two German priests who were the principals and others also attributed its origins to this circumstance. At the beginning of the fall term in 1931, Ryan received from Franciscan priests charges of immoral conduct against Cöln, professor of Old Testament and then dean of the school of sacred sciences, and Schumacher, professor of New Testament. On October 19, Curley advised both that their resignations had been requested by the sacred congregation of seminaries and universities.[61] Both complied at once and then began actions for their vindication. The bishop of Buffalo, Schumacher's ordinary, regarded the accusations with skepticism from the first.[62] Both priests were accorded the rights associated with voluntary resignation and no publicity was given to their case. Eventually, in part with the assistance of McCormick, who by then had become vice rector, their case was settled administratively, as it had been begun, by recognition that they were resigned professors and by annual financial payments.[63] For the rest of their lives, Cöln resided in Cincinnati as a guest of the archdiocese, Schumacher in Buffalo.

The departure of Cöln and Schumacher was in effect if not in inten-

58. *Ibid.*, Mc 1186, Curley to McNicholas, Baltimore, June 8, 1931 (copy).
59. Privately printed [1931]. Other documents, including "My Rejoinder," mimeographed, are in Record Group 1-A, Historical-Miscellaneous, Box 3.
60. AAB, Curley Papers, Mc 1190, McNicholas to Trustees, Cincinnati, July 12, 1931.
61. OR, Pietro Fumasoni-Biondi to Curley, Washington, Oct. 19, 1931. Fumasoni-Biondi had become apostolic delegate in 1922.
62. ADB, William Turner Papers, Turner to Bisleti, Buffalo, Jan. 22, 1932, supplied by courtesy of the Reverend Walter Kern, assistant archivist; see also Louis H. Motry Papers, Turner to Schumacher, Buffalo, Jan. 24, 1932. Details may be found in OR, Case of Doctors Cöln and Schumacher; in AACi, Cöln Papers; and in the Motry Papers, for extensive correspondence with Schumacher.
63. OR, Corrigan to Cicognani, May 28, 1937 (copy).

tion a step in what Deferrari later portrayed as "bringing the School of Sacred Sciences, in spite of its strenuous protests, within the University family and subject to its Rector."[64] The "separatist" tendencies of the theological faculty had antedated the Ryan administration. Even under Shahan, Cöln had found the university to be "a kind of absolute autocracy."[65] He and the faculty had taken issue with various provisions proposed for the new constitution of 1926 and had objected especially to "the creation of a Seminary under the direct supervision of the University" instead of the school.[66] But the situation under Ryan seemed to Cöln "so confused, so strange and so critical" that he could not recall any parallel, thinking only that the difficulties could "surely be overcome, if and when the Faculty [had] the full and generous cooperation of the Vice Rector and the Rector Magnificus."[67]

When the meeting to elect officers of the graduate school was called, Cöln, with John A. Ryan, wrote to Deferrari to question the constitutional status of the school, supporting, among other things, the position that Rolbiecki had taken the previous spring.[68] Their faculty undertook an appeal to Rome, maintaining in it and in other documents that the constitution of 1926 "was not intended to abrogate the Constitutiones Propriae of the Schola Scientiarum Sacrarum."[69] In the board, apparently, Shahan and McKenna took up the cause; for this Curley had only "utter disgust,"[70] even if Archbishop John J. Glennon of St. Louis could look upon it all as "a splendid demonstration of Catholic liberty of thought."[71] In any case, the papal secretary of state, Cardinal Eugenio Pacelli, who was to become Pope Pius XII, cabled to the effect that the general constitution was applicable to all faculties.[72] Curley thought from the beginning that the theologians were acting like "little 'gossoons.' "[73] As the situation calmed, he declared, "Every Department in the University is in the finest kind of shape and going ahead with the utmost harmony except the one unblessed and unholy spot where only Priests are gathered."[74]

64. *Layman,* 139.
65. AACi, Cöln Papers, Cöln to Curley, Washington, Jan. 31, 1923 (copy).
66. *Ibid.,* memorandum, n.d. (copy).
67. *Ibid.,* Cöln to Faculty, Washington, Oct. 14, 1929 (copy).
68. OVR, Ryan and Cöln to Deferrari, Oct. 15, 1930.
69. AACi, Cöln Papers, Faculty to Curley, n.d. [after Dec. 1, 1930] (copy).
70. AAB, Curley Papers, R 1581, Curley to J. H. Ryan, Baltimore, Apr. 17, 1931 (copy).
71. BT, mm, Apr. 15, 1931.
72. AAB, Curley Papers, R 1590, Fumasoni-Biondi to McNicholas, Washington, May 7, 1931 (copy).
73. *Ibid.,* S 569, Curley to Schrembs, Baltimore, Dec. 29, 1930 (copy).
74. *Ibid.,* B 818, Curley to Bernardini, Baltimore, Dec. 14, 1931 (copy).

On May 24, 1931 Pope Pius XI issued an apostolic constitution, *Deus Scientiarum Dominus,* on universities and faculties of ecclesiastical studies. It was followed by regulations of the sacred congregation of seminaries and universities that were intended to promote common standards in ecclesiastical institutions.[75] Pace had reported to Curley some years earlier that there was in Rome "some vague idea of overhauling all Catholic universities."[76] When the papal document was issued, Ryan did not see "any reason to get excited about it" and was ready to use "the opportunity to revise our own constitution" in accord with a directive that all institutional documents had to be in conformity with the new regulations.[77] Separate committees of the board and the senate were appointed to propose revisions.[78] Since the term constitution was to be reserved for papal documents, the term statutes was prescribed to designate the result of their efforts.

One of the points at issue was the need for special statutes for the ecclesiastical faculties. This of course had just been debated during the academic reorganization that Ryan had effected. A host of questions was presented to the dean of the school of canon law for discussion with the Roman congregation.[79] In a draft of a revised governing document prepared early in 1932, an attempt was made to incorporate general provisions of the apostolic constitution "and at the same time include the statutes which deal more specifically with Theology, Canon Law and Philosophy."[80] Ryan and Pace brought the draft to Rome and were informed that, pending final action, the university was to be governed by what was being presented.[81] During the next two years, however, varying animadversions were received from Rome, the most important of which was a request for special statutes for the ecclesiastical faculties. The general statutes and the requested special statutes of the faculties of theology and canon law were approved on September 8, 1934. Approval of special statutes that had been submitted for the faculty of philosophy was being withheld, although they were declared to be entirely in conformity with the congregation's desires, since a new school of philosophy was in process of formation.

75. AAS, XXIII (July, 1931), 241–84 (in Latin).
76. AAB, Curley Papers, P 33, Pace to Curley, Rome, Feb. 15, 1925.
77. *Ibid.*, R 1602, Ryan to Curley, Washington, Aug. 6, 1931.
78. BT, mm, Nov. 10, 1931; AS, mm, Nov. 25, 1931.
79. OR, "Certain Questions and Doubts Concerning the Constitution *Deus Scientiarum Dominus* and Its Application to the Catholic University of America" (copy), for presentation Jan. 15, 1932.
80. *Ibid.*, "Revised Constitution of The Catholic University of America, March, 1932," *Notenda.*
81. AR (1932–33), 1–2, citing Bisleti to Curley, Rome, Sept. 5, 1932.

The promulgation of the new statutes, however, was not to be allowed to Ryan. The difficulties that led to postponement of the promulgation may have arisen from opposition to him within both the Roman congregation and the American episcopate. Curley had earlier informed Ryan that unfriendly agents were active in Rome.[82] The congregation's secretary, who seems to have been one of these, entertained a mistaken impression that Ryan would not accept the papal constitution.[83] Reportedly, he later told an American bishop that the provisions for a six-year program in theology that were in Ryan's drafts of new statutes did not correspond with the reality of what was being offered.[84] At home, in the board, McNicholas was expressing dissatisfaction that under the new draft "the Most Reverend Chancellor appeared to be the controlling factor, in fact, the whole thing."[85] And when the Roman congregation, in its letter of approval of the drafts in 1934, announced the appointment of the special episcopal visiting committee for the ecclesiastical faculties, it was significant that McNicholas was named as chairman.[86] Subsequently, Ryan was informed that still another draft of the statutes, including corrections or recommendations of the visiting committee, would be required.[87] McNicholas, meanwhile, seems to have been acting outside the board to obtain Ryan's removal from the university.

The Graduate Ascendancy

The Ryan years had brought a steady increase in enrollment despite the increasing seriousness of the national financial crisis that began late in 1929, during the second year of his incumbency. There were 1,644 students enrolled during the year after Ryan left office, some 70 per cent more than during his first year. The general secretary related this increase to what was happening everywhere when he explained, "Boys who would normally find work may enter college. Graduates of colleges will seek higher degrees in the hope of obtaining teaching or commercial

82. AAB, Curley Papers, R 1576, Curley to Ryan, Baltimore, Mar. 31, 1931 (copy).
83. *Ibid.*, R 1626, Ryan to Curley, Washington, Feb. 24, 1932. The secretary, Ernesto Ruffini, who later became a cardinal, expressed his surprise on the point to the apostolic delegate in Washington and was informed in turn that something was obviously wrong in his office. Ryan reported that a personal letter from the prefect was the only acknowledgment of his correspondence that he had received from the congregation in eighteen months.
84. OR, Gerald P. O'Hara to Corrigan, Savannah, Dec. 9, 1936.
85. BT, mm, Apr. 26, 1933.
86. AAB, Curley Papers, Roman Documents, Cicognani to Curley, Washington, Sept. 9, 1934. See an unpublished paper by Joseph M. White, "Archbishop John T. McNicholas and the Pontifical Commission of the Catholic University of America, 1934–50."
87. OR, Cicognani to Ryan, Washington, May 11, 1935.

The John K. Mullen of Denver Memorial Library, opened in 1928 and completed in 1958 to promote the "spirit of universal, literary, historic, philosophic and scientific inquiry and investigation" that a pioneer professor, Edward Lee Greene, rightly noted as characteristic of "the highest type of the modern university."

positions when economic conditions finally indicate a return to normalcy."[88]

What was especially notable, however, was the increase in the number and proportion of graduate students. During 1927–28, Shahan's last year, as will be recalled, undergraduates had comprised roughly two-thirds of the number enrolled for degrees. The proportion of graduate enrollment had been inching upward, but very slowly. In the first year after Ryan's reorganization, the number of graduate students almost doubled. By 1933–34, more than 50 per cent of the students had graduate standing. The graduate school of arts and sciences, with 640 students, had quickly become the largest school in the university.

The principal source of this increase was from the ranks of clerics and religious (of both sexes). Already in his first year, when lay students numbering more than 500 for the first time were still more than 50 per cent of the total, Ryan could "report with pleasure a large increase in the number of priest and sister graduate students."[89] During 1935–36,

88. Richard J. Purcell, in AR (1931–32), 27.
89. BT, mm, Nov. 5, 1929.

more than 60 per cent of the increased number of students were clerics and religious. Among the 382 full-time students in the graduate school of arts and sciences in that year, 162 were women religious, 146 were clerics. Even among the 448 part-time students there were 40 sisters and 166 clerics. There were other post-baccalaureate students in law and engineering and in the new professional schools of nursing education and social work. The general secretary was pointing to a "growing recognition on the part of religious teachers that they must pursue advanced studies in order to meet the requirements of national accrediting agencies."[90]

Evidence that the demand was even broader could be found in the searching of Catholic institutions for candidates for appointment and, by 1935, their "insistence on the *Catholic* training of those possessing the higher degrees."[91] The general secretary could observe that "Catholic students, whether lay or priests or nuns or teaching brothers," were "commencing to realize the intrinsic advantages of higher degrees from the sole Catholic institution in the Association of American Universities."[92]

The enrollment of sisters indicated the difference that had been made by the admission of women to graduate study. Originally, it may be recalled, the trustees had been unwilling to accede to the request of the faculty and women applicants had been turned away. Then, after the opening of Trinity College in 1900 and the founding of the Catholic Sisters College in 1911, women had been admitted to higher degrees while remaining at these neighboring institutions, so that a doctorate in philosophy had been conferred on women as early as 1914.[93] Ten years later, Sister Inez Hilger, O.S.B., of the College of St. Benedict in Minnesota, had been permitted to attend classes in sociology on the campus while pursuing her doctorate, the board having decided that it

90. Purcell, in AR (1932–33), 27.

91. Edward J. Farren, S.J., "The Department of Education of the National Catholic Welfare Conference, 1919–1938" (unpublished master's dissertation, St. Louis University, 1940), 92. See also, Francis M. Crowley, "Meeting the Shortage of Graduate Students," CA, XI, No. 4 (Sept. 1929), 29–31.

92. Purcell, in AR (1933–34), 27. Power, *op. cit.*, 368, assessing Catholic higher education of the period, points to the influence of The Catholic University of America in commenting, "If the colleges were to become universities, at least some of their religious faculty members should have advanced university degrees, and where could such students go unless they attended the Catholic University? Thus, coming from the school in Washington, graduates of the Catholic University introduced policies of wider university academic management with which they were only partially familiar. It is probably fair to say that prior to 1930 Catholic colleges working toward university standing were trial miniatures of the Catholic University of America."

93. AS, mm, May 28, 1915; Pace Papers, Pace to Edith E. Ware, Washington, Nov. 3, 1917.

was "best to leave the decision in each case to the Rector of the University."[94]

Although the academic senate was recommending that privileges for laywomen should be similar to those that had been extended to religious, Cardinal O'Connell for one "did not think it would add to the dignity of the University."[95] Sisters, for that matter, could obtain permission to follow graduate courses on the campus only if no graduate work in the subject was being offered at the Sisters College.[96] To Curley, who later remarked that he had not been "pleading for co-education or the admission of flappers into the University," the admission of sisters was a vital cause; the sisters, in his estimation, meant "more to the Church in America, in one sense, than all its hierarchy and its priests."[97]

Tiring of the topic, the board in 1928 unanimously left the decision to the chancellor and the new rector. The admission of women to graduate study was announced almost immediately thereafter.[98] Ryan gave "no publicity about women students, preferring to go slowly and let the fact of our accepting them become known gradually."[99] Later, even a layman who might have been expected to think otherwise was emphatic in holding that the university "should not have women teachers,"[100] although Regina Flannery in anthropology and Mary Elizabeth Walsh in sociology were already in charge of courses and the former was to become the first woman member of the faculty of arts and sciences, in 1935. Bishops found it difficult to accept women as teachers or even as students mingling with priests and seminarians.[101]

The graduate ascendancy was not merely numerical. Under the leadership of Deferrari, the graduate school made important qualitative strides, so that the general secretary could predict that "its increase in numbers should continue as its standards of admission, its requirements for degrees, and its teaching personnel are gradually improved."[102] Immediately visible to students were such measures as the specification of requirements; the publication of manuals; the renumbering of courses

94. BT, mm, Sept. 23, 1924.

95. BT, mm, Sept. 13, 1927.

96. OVR, Pace to Deans, Oct. 3, 1927.

97. AAB, Curley Papers, G 1362, Curley to Guilday, Baltimore, Oct. 10, 1934.

98. BT, mm, Nov. 13, 1928; AS, mm, Nov. 30, 1928.

99. BT, mm, Nov. 5, 1929.

100. Richard J. Purcell Papers, "Observations on the Catholic University of America," forwarded with Purcell to Francis J. Haas, Washington, Jan. 14, 1935.

101. McNicholas Papers, McNicholas to Karl J. Alter, bishop of Toledo and later archbishop of Cincinnati, Cincinnati, Mar. 2, 1935 (copy), and Alter to McNicholas, Toledo, Mar. 11, 1935.

102. Purcell, in AR (1933–34), 27.

to distinguish their levels as for undergraduates, for both undergraduates and graduates, or for graduate students only; and the scheduling of most graduate courses at afternoon hours and of some at late afternoon hours when they could be attended by part-time students who held regular employment. Many of the latter were teachers in the schools of the metropolitan area.

Three steps that were taken were of special importance to the administration and the faculties. One was the organization of a council of the graduate school. This body provided a means for exchange of information and for mutual understanding among the departments but it became also an instrument for the standardization of requirements and procedures. Second, as dean, Deferrari published a bulletin of the school through which the work of the council and expositions of the nature of graduate work could be circulated. Excerpts from this bulletin as well as outlines of requirements and the like were later published in a manual for graduate students. Third, criteria for faculty rank were defined. A committee of the academic senate attempted to define the "contribution to science" that might be expected of candidates for faculty appointments and promotions.[103] Ryan readily agreed that the consent of the faculty should be required for full professorial rank, but considered that only its advice to the rector was required at lower ranks. The arbitrariness of appointments by the rector had been a sore point for some during the O'Connell and Shahan administrations.

New departments were established within the graduate school of arts and sciences. During Ryan's first year, the department of religion was organized to train religious educators and French and Spanish were placed under a single department of romance languages. Meanwhile, astronomy was transferred to civil engineering, comparative philology was transferred to Greek and Latin, and Sanskrit was suppressed.[104] Soon Cooper became head of a new department of anthropology and he and Cornelius Connolly, a priest known for his work in physical anthropology, were promoted to full professorial rank. Sanskrit was revived at the same time in a department of Sanskrit and comparative philology but did not survive.[105] The *Washington Post* found encouragement in seeing in the new departments a "local reversal of the headlong dash of educational institutions toward commercialism."[106]

An instrument of the graduate ascendancy that was to gain in impor-

103. AS, mm, Mar. 10, 1932.
104. BT, mm, Apr. 10, 1929.
105. *Ibid.*, Nov. 13, 1934.
106. Editorial, Nov. 16, 1934.

tance during succeeding decades was summer instruction. The summer school that had been founded in the Catholic Sisters College in 1911 and conducted on the campus was being regarded as "an expensive luxury" which the university was maintaining at a severe loss.[107] It was immediately transferred to university control with Deferrari as director.[108] He proposed that graduate instruction should be offered, with the result that master's degree programs were authorized. The name was changed to "summer sessions"[109] and Ryan proposed that men should be allowed to enroll.[110] The "almost unhoped for success" of the venture indicated to him that the university was meeting "a real need" through this means of "helping to prepare teachers for their work in the field of Catholic higher education."[111] Branches were again authorized, first at San Rafael, California, then at Dubuque, Iowa, and San Antonio, Texas. Archbishop Francis J. Beckman of Dubuque argued typically that without a branch convenient to them many religious communities would be "compelled to send their Sisters and pupils to state universities."[112] When the university joined the Association of Deans and Directors of Summer Sessions as the only Catholic member, in 1935, Deferrari reported with satisfaction that the organization was not admitting summer sessions "which do not do a serious amount of good graduate work."[113]

Testimony to the leadership position of the university among Catholic institutions at this stage of their development was being renewed through attention to the need to encourage productive scholarship. In 1928, the year of Ryan's appointment, Catholic scientists and teachers of science had been brought together in the Catholic Round Table of Science. Cooper had chaired its organizational meeting in New York and an alumnus, the Reverend Anselm Keefe, O.Praem., had taken responsibility for coordination and publication.[114] Occasional articles began to appear that emphasized the intellectual and professional importance of Catholic participation in scientific work.[115] The outstanding

107. BT, mm, Apr. 18, 1928, exh., J. Harvey Cain, "Data for Meeting of Committee on Survey."

108. BT, EC, mm, Dec. 20, 1928.

109. AS, mm, May 29, June 7, and Nov. 5, 1929.

110. BT, mm, Nov. 5, 1929, exh.

111. AR (1929–30), 10.

112. BT, mm, Nov. 14, 1933.

113. OR, Deferrari to Ryan, Washington, Oct. 21, 1935.

114. OR, Corrigan to Ruffini, Washington, June 27, 1939 (copy), responding to a curial inquiry about the group.

115. See, for example, Karl F. Herzfeld, "Scientific Research and Religion," *Commonweal*, IX (Mar. 20, 1929), 560–62.

research universities of the country had by then been facilitating the advancement of science for two or three decades. In addressing the role that The Catholic University of America could assume, the editors of *Commonweal* noted the need for Catholics to realize that the Church had "always placed the accent on the person, not on the branch of knowledge or the topic under discussion," while holding at the same time, "on better grounds than [could] be formulated in a syllogism, that the end of the human mind is to know God through knowing a hierarchically ordered cosmos."[116]

Confirmation of the university's position was provided by the publication in 1934 of a report of a committee on graduate instruction of the American Council on Education.[117] Professor Raymond M. Hughes of the University of Iowa was its chairman; the educator Johnson was a member. This committee had had its origins in the protests of institutions that could claim some outstanding departments for graduate study but were nevertheless not being admitted to membership in the Association of American Universities. Scholars selected by the respective national learned societies were surveyed to ascertain the reputations of departments in thirty-five fields with respect to their capacity to offer doctoral work. The method employed aroused criticism but is still used today. Out of the twenty-three fields of the arts and sciences in which the university was offering doctoral work, it received ratings of adequacy in equipment and staff in five—in classics, history, philosophy, psychology, and sociology. In five other fields relatively large numbers of raters found the university's programs adequate. The only other department in a Catholic institution with a reputational rating of adequacy was that in chemistry at the University of Notre Dame. No department in any Catholic institution ranked among the highest twenty per cent in its field. It was misleading, therefore, to conclude from the report, as did Curley, that the five departments named were "doing first class graduate work,"[118] but there were grounds for the pleasure that the rector and the trustees took in the findings. Ryan was, as Deferrari reported, "greatly impressed with the thought of the ultimate effect upon Catholic schools generally" if Catholic institutions continued to neglect their graduate schools, thus forcing Catholic teachers and scholars "more and more to go to non-Catholic graduate schools for their training."[119] In its general

---

116. X (Oct. 7, 1933), 540.

117. Raymond M. Hughes, "Report of the Committee on Graduate Instruction," *ER*, XV (Apr., 1934), 192–234, also published separately by the Council. For a history of the development of this and other attempts to compare and measure academic quality, see Webster, *op. cit.*

118. BT, mm, Apr. 11, 1934.

119. Deferrari Papers, "Bishop Ryan and Universities" (copy), n.d.

effect, the Hughes report came to be credited with arousing Catholic graduate schools "out of a heavy lethargy."[120] Of course, in the original concept, although not in the practice that had followed its founding, The Catholic University of America had been intended as the graduate school for the entire American Catholic system.

The Professional Schools

After Ryan's basic academic reorganization, there were, outside the arts and sciences and the two ecclesiastical schools, two professional schools, the old school of law and the new school of engineering. An attempt early in his administration to add to these a school of liturgical music was to be frustrating. But two other new professional schools were organized subsequently, one in nursing education, in 1933, and the other in social work, in 1934. In each case, the influence of the national professional associations and the accrediting bodies related to them assumed an importance that was destined to grow during succeeding decades. Ryan, of course, was drawing upon the tradition of graduate education for his model of how these schools should be conducted.

The school of law, despite its age, had never gained a firm foothold in the university, even if under its second dean it had been accepted for membership in the Association of American Law Schools. Its third dean had died just before Ryan's appointment. Ryan was ready to recommend the dissolution of the school but took advice from a prestigious committee of externs that persuaded him otherwise. This committee insisted unanimously that there was a need for a Catholic graduate school of law and a majority of its members favored continuance of the professional program as well.[121] The search for another dean was protracted and eventually the board's executive committee left the choice to Ryan. John McDill Fox of Marquette University, a graduate of the University of Wisconsin and of Harvard Law School, was appointed on June 24, 1930.

For a time the outlook for the development of "a learned, scholarly, and cultured Catholic bar" seemed "very bright."[122] A chapter of Gamma Eta Gamma, the oldest national legal fraternity in the United States, was installed in 1931. A Legal Aid Society was proposed and in 1932

120. Deferrari, *Memoirs*, 116; also, McGuire, *op. cit.*, 109, and Gleason, *op. cit.* 43. (As late as 1933, some Catholic colleges were petitioning to have ordination to the priesthood recognized as equivalent to the Ph.D. degree. See "Proceedings of the Commission on Colleges and Universities," NCAQ, VIII (July, 1933), 44.)
121. AAB, Curley Papers, R 1433, Ryan to Curley, Washington, Mar. 5, 1929; BT, EC, mm, Mar. 11, 1929. See Nuesse, *CULR*, XXXV, 60.
122. AR (1929–30), 7.

Assertion of Role

Assertion of was established within the Council of Social Agencies of Washington.
Role Most important, undoubtedly, was the adoption in 1934 of a baccalaureate degree requirement for admission to the school, except for those applicants who were following the university's own arts and law program. Only about a dozen other schools in the country then had such a requirement for admission; none were in the District of Columbia. Fox, with other members of the faculty, promoted legal scholarship through the incorporation and activity of the Riccobono Seminar of Roman Law that had been organized the year before his arrival, after a series of lectures by Professor Salvatore Riccobono of the University of Palermo. His understanding of the mission of the university was shown in his emphasis upon the development of what he called a "theophilosophical" jurisprudence.[123] In many respects, therefore, his achievements as a dean were important for the university at large as well as for the law school. It was an institutional loss when his resignation had to be requested in 1935 after repeated incidents suggesting alcoholism.

Engineering, like law, had been offered since 1895. Ryan's reorganization erected a new school of engineering that included architecture and a part of chemistry as well as departments of architectural, chemical, civil, electrical, and mechanical engineering. Hardee Chambliss, professor of chemistry, who had been the dean of the school of science, was appointed acting dean and was soon elected as dean by the faculty. When he resigned, in 1934, Valade was appointed to succeed him. Meanwhile, in 1932, the academic senate had approved conferral of the degrees bachelor of engineering and bachelor of aeronautical engineering and, in 1933, doctor of engineering.

The funding of these departments had been a problem from their beginning. In 1920, Shahan had presented a proposal for their development, requesting unsuccessfully a million-dollar grant from the Carnegie Corporation.[124] The year before, a national qualification committee of the American Association of Engineers had assessed instruction in engineering as "rather weak."[125] Architecture, on the other hand, had gained recognition under Murphy, especially in Beaux Arts competition, in which students were unusually successful, so that the board's visiting committee had recommended special attention to that department's needs.[126] A basic problem, not uncommon in professional schools, was the engagement of faculty members in professional work

123. SL, Fox to Joseph W. Beale, Washington, Oct. 16, 1930.
124. OVR, Shahan to Carnegie Corporation, Washington, May 19, 1920 (copy).
125. *Ibid.*, Frederick C. Armstrong to Aubrey Landry, Chicago, Dec. 4, 1919.
126. BT, mm, Apr. 18, 1928.

outside the university. To clarify the duties and obligations of professors, among other things, Ryan secured the services of Professor Henry P. Hammond of the Brooklyn Polytechnic Institute for an exhaustive survey. At the same meeting at which his report was presented, the board voted to carry out his recommendations, but only "so far as funds [would] permit." At this meeting also, it changed the name of the school to include both engineering and architecture.[127]

Even before the reorganization of arts and sciences and engineering was accomplished, at the very beginning of his administration, Ryan had sought to seize what seemed to be an opportunity to establish a school of liturgical music on the campus. The opening of the Schola Cantorum had been announced in the spring of 1928. It included students of the university and of Sisters College, in which instruction in music was being offered. University students were enrolled through the faculty of theology, of which the director of the Schola, Father William J. DesLongchamps of Detroit, was a member. Curley, believing that the time was ripe, had given him permission "to take all necessary steps" toward building up a "fully equipped School of Ecclesiastical Music."[128]

That November, at his first meeting with the trustees, Ryan was able to present to the board an offer for the full support of the school, including the erection of a building to house it. The prospective donor was a convert, Justine Bayard Cutting Ward, a sister of Senator Bronson Cutting of New Mexico. Mrs. Ward had been a fervent admirer of the deceased Father Shields and with him had devised a method of teaching Gregorian chant to school children. Her offer was from the Dom Mocquereau Schola Cantorum Foundation, named for the monk of Solesmes under whom she had studied to further the reform of church music that Pope St. Pius X had initiated.[129] The funds, which would have amounted to about $1,500,000, were to be held in trust in New York. Construction of a building was begun in May of 1929 but in the next months, accusing DesLongchamps of having misrepresented himself as possessing a doctorate, Mrs. Ward demanded his immediate suspension and, failing to attain it, severed relations with the university in this matter as of January 5, 1930.[130] Both DesLongchamps and a French monk who had been

127. BT, mm, May 1, 1935.

128. AAB, Curley Papers, D 725, Curley to DesLongchamps, Baltimore, Apr. 21, 1928.

129. See Dom Pierre Marie Combe, O.S.B., *Justine Ward and Solesmes* (Washington, D.C.: The Catholic University of America Press, 1987).

130. OVR, Schrembs to Pace, Cleveland, June 6, 1930, notes that relations with Mrs. Ward had "so many delicate angles" that Schrembs as secretary of the board found difficulty in writing its minutes.

appointed to the faculty resigned and eventually a mutual release was signed by Mrs. Ward and the university. The name and the use of the building was the subject of inconclusive discussion in the board. In later decades, however, it came to house the present school of music and even to be named, in 1967, Ward Hall. A new wing was added in 1974.

The second floor of the completed building was first assigned to a more successful venture, an attempt, as Ryan later described it, to do for the nursing sisterhoods what had been done earlier for the teaching sisterhoods.[131] On the campus, the initiative came from Deferrari as dean of the graduate school and director of the summer session, and from Moore, head of the department of psychology, who was a doctor of medicine as well as of philosophy. They recognized that a movement toward collegiate schools of nursing had begun and that in the transition period hospital schools were to be staffed increasingly by nurse educators instead of physicians. Institutions such as Yale and Columbia had already developed influential departments of nursing education and had promoted standardizing agencies that were acquiring power. As Deferrari presented the matter, Catholic schools had either to send their prospective teachers to non-Catholic institutions in order to meet the new requirements or to close.[132] Experimentally, courses in nursing education were offered in the 1932 summer session. It became obvious that there was a demand for their continuance.

The development of the offerings became the responsibility of Sister M. Olivia Gowan, O.S.B., who had been a collaborator of Moore in the foundation of St. Gertrude's School of Arts and Crafts near St. Anselm's Priory. She became the first woman in academic administration at the university. There was some discussion of whether the nursing courses should be offered at the Sisters College or on the campus, since most students did not have baccalaureate degrees, but the view that prevailed was that, as Pace phrased it, it was "more important . . . to get this work done without waste of time or energy than to insist on the decision as regards place, of graduate and undergraduate subjects."[133] Moore argued that opening the courses to the lay women was "no essential departure from the . . . policy of allowing women to enter the University as graduate students."[134] The executive committee of the board agreed that the work should be carried on in the graduate school

131. OR, Ryan to Thomas A. Welch, Washington, Aug. 17, 1934 (copy).
132. AAB, Curley Papers, M 266, Deferrari to Ryan, Washington, Aug. 16, 1932. See Deferrari's own account, Deferrari Papers, "The Beginning of Instruction in Nursing at The Catholic University of America" [ca. 1960].
133. *Ibid.*, Pace to Curley, Washington, Oct. 3, 1932.
134. *Ibid.*, Moore to Ryan, Washington, Sept. 27, 1932 (copy).

Sister Maurice Sheehy, R.S.M., a member of the faculty, and Sister M. Olivia Gowan, O.S.B., dean of the school of nursing at a microphone of station WOL in 1942.

but turned over to the Catholic Sisters College when it was in a position to accept it and develop it.[135] The full board, however, authorized the establishment of instruction and its organization as a division "with the hope that its future development might earn for it full recognition as a School of the University."[136] That was not long in the future.

Training for social work had been undertaken by Kerby under the auspices of the department of sociology. As the first executive secretary of the National Conference of Catholic Charities, he had been in a position to link academic and professional concerns and to foster "the general recognition of the need of trained workers, of the value of expert direction and widely informed leadership" which was, he thought, "one of the most clearly defined results" of the organization's work.[137] Despite the reluctance of academicians to admit social work to their precincts, a movement toward special schools within universities had gained ground. Among Catholic institutions, Loyola University of Chicago had been

135. BT, EC, mm, Feb. 8, 1933.
136. BT, mm, Apr. 26, 1933, and Nov. 12, 1935. See Sister M. Olivia Gowan, O.S.B., "The History of the School of Nursing Education," *CUB*, N.S., XVIII, No. 6 (May, 1951), 2–4.
137. AAB, Curley Papers, K 704, Kerby to Curley, Washington, Feb. 16, 1925.

the first to establish, in 1914, a training program. By the early 1930s there was sufficient criticism of the failure of The Catholic University of America to establish such a school to disturb its administration. O'Grady, who was teaching in the department of sociology, seems to have peremptorily informed Ryan that he had agreed with the American Association of Social Workers "not to accept any more students for training until the Catholic University had set up a systematic training program."[138] Diocesan directors of Catholic charities, pointing to the output of the university's professors as their basic literature, exerted pressure upon the rector and the board. A school of social work was authorized in 1934.[139] O'Grady was appointed dean and gained provisional recognition from the American Association of Schools of Social Work.

Almost immediately, as O'Grady undoubtedly foresaw, there was presented the problem of coordination with the National Catholic School of Social Service which was, in some academic respects, already dependent upon the university. To protect its interests, lay women were not admitted to the new school in its first year. O'Grady reported to the trustees that the diocesan directors were demanding removal of the restriction. Father Burke, for the NCSSS, on the other hand, held that if the university school were to receive lay women, there would be "no place for another school of the same kind, doing the same work, in Washington."[140] Women were soon admitted but it was not until 1947 that the consolidation of the two schools was accomplished. O'Grady was sympathetic with Ryan's view that his new school should follow "the standards accepted by the Graduate School."[141] He was, however, increasingly critical of developments in the profession and later wrote that it was becoming "too mechanical" and "losing a lot of that life, that spirit for real Christian charity that should characterize the movement."[142]

Toward Excellence in the College

The renewal of the graduate thrust of the university and the expansion into new professional fields were not intended by Ryan or by any of his

---

138. O'Grady Papers, O'Grady to Corrigan, Washington, July 26, 1936 (copy). On O'Grady, see Thomas W. Tifft, "Toward a More Humane Social Policy: The Work and Influence of Monsignor John O'Grady" (unpublished doctoral dissertation, The Catholic University of America, 1979).

139. BT, mm, Nov. 13, 1934.

140. OR, memoranda of O'Grady and Burke.

141. AR (1934–35), 15.

142. O'Grady Papers, autobiography.

associates to denigrate undergraduate education but rather to improve it. Ryan advised the board that a university that would fully recognize its obligations to its constituency could not fail to build a strong college.[143] This was during a decade when Catholics were first beginning to enroll for higher education in truly significant numbers and when, simultaneously, the proportion of Catholic students attending Catholic institutions was beginning to decrease from the high point attained in the previous decade.[144] The committee first charged with reshaping the undergraduate curriculum saw its task as bringing the university offerings, so far as its facilities would permit, "into harmony with similar courses prescribed in other institutions representative of the Association of American Universities."[145] There was at the time a movement, rather far advanced, particularly in the older prestigious institutions of the northeast, toward what Ryan could describe as "a system which, though somewhat rigid, is yet plastic enough to meet the demands and needs of the individual."[146] The aspects that he was calling "somewhat rigid" involved the restoration of some of the requirements that had been abandoned when the elective system had been in vogue. At the time, critics of American higher education such as President Robert Maynard Hutchins and the philosopher Mortimer Adler of the University of Chicago were finding sympathetic audiences among Catholics whom they were chiding for neglecting their own heritage. But a resurgence of the ideals of liberal education on a more general scale was leading college educators to insist upon a common core in the curriculum, upon concentration instead of specialization, and upon a senior comprehensive examination to test understanding.

This movement was not universally favored. There were objections to it on the campus and among the constituencies of the university. Old resentments that undergraduate work was offered at all continued to be harbored. Thus, recounting his travels, Fox reported that he had found antagonism to the university among many clerics, some of whom "wanted to know rather belligerently why we didn't drop our undergraduate department instead of insisting upon competing with all of the other Catholic colleges."[147] Within the board at the time, some members still thought that an exclusively graduate institution was desirable.

---

143. AR (1934–35), 10.
144. David O. Levine, *The American College and the Culture of Aspiration, 1915–1940* (Ithaca: Cornell University Press, 1986), 203.
145. OVR, Report of Committee on Courses of Study, May 11, 1929.
146. AR (1934–35), 9.
147. OR, Fox to Ryan, Washington, May 5, 1931.

McNicholas, for example, "insisted that inasmuch as this University is a pontifical university, we ought to confine ourselves to our real work," by which he meant, clearly, graduate education. There was more general recognition, however, as Glennon for one was ready to admit, that "somehow in practice this did not succeed."[148] Time might have been saved if there had been deeper investigation into why this was so.

Since Ryan's plan for reorganization had separated engineering from the arts and sciences and, in the latter, had divided the administration of undergraduate and graduate offerings at the outset, the first task undertaken by the committee on courses of study had been confined to the curriculum of the college. The committee's basic proposal was to divide undergraduate studies between "tool courses" to be followed during the first two years and upper division work. The former were to help the student to make the transition from high school "but also to give him a fund of information and a training in methods of study and in habits of thought and industry such as will equip him for the more serious work of the third and fourth years of the course, in which a concentration of effort in some particular field is made possible for each student."[149] Only within the field of concentration were elective courses to be allowed. This distinction between courses for general education and those for concentration provided the groundwork for the development of the college program. It was to culminate in a senior comprehensive examination which, although taken in the field of concentration, was to test the student's power to integrate meaningfully all that he had learned.[150]

Not that nonacademic aspects of undergraduate life were to be ignored. Ryan was to tell the delegates to an annual meeting of the Association of American Colleges that their institutions had been retrograde in moral control through their policy of excluding "from the purview of university training all values other than the intellectual."[151] He reminded his own trustees later that "atmosphere is all-important in a university, and atmosphere is something that can be created."[152] To contribute to the goal of an undergraduate education that would be "both liberal and Catholic," as the catalog of the college was to put

148. BT, mm, Apr. 26, 1933.
149. *Op. cit.*
150. See Roy J. Deferrari (ed.), *The Curriculum of the Catholic College (Integration and Concentration)* (Washington, D.C.: The Catholic University of America Press, 1952), and *Theology, Philosophy and History as Integrating Disciplines in the Catholic College of Liberal Arts* (Washington, D.C.: The Catholic University of America Press, 1953), for detailed presentations of the program.
151. NC release, Feb. 1, 1935.
152. AR (1934–35), 6.

it,[153] and feeling that the move "would go a long way in meeting some of the criticism directed against the university,"[154] he made one of his first acts the appointment of a chaplain, the Dominican Edward Fitzgerald, who was a member of the faculty of theology. He inaugurated a new athletic policy, partly in view of "the feeling of prominent members of the Board of Trustees that more attention should be paid to athletics in general, and that, in particular, a sound program of physical training for every student should be developed."[155]

In the academic senate, even before Ryan's administrative reorganization was completed, the committee proposal to initiate one sequence for the degree of bachelor of arts and another for the bachelor of science was readily accepted.[156] Ryan thereupon urged that the action would be "meaningless without the adoption of the rest of the program" and thus persuaded an initially reluctant body to advance the effective date of the whole revised undergraduate program to February, 1930 instead of the following September.[157] A freshman week had been inaugurated in 1927 and now incoming freshmen were also to be subjected to tests of achievement and aptitude.[158]

The academic development was being led by James Marshall Campbell, a priest who was a member of the department of Greek and Latin and a close associate of Deferrari. Ryan was to appoint him as dean of the college of arts and sciences in October, 1934. The first meeting of the college—including "anyone teaching a subject listed in the curriculum"—had been held on May 26, 1930, with the vice rector, Pace, as the presiding officer.[159] After the elections in the fall, the vice dean, Nicholas Weber, S.M., a professor of history who had been dean of the former school of philosophy, became dean. In a reorganization preceding Campbell's appointment in 1934, the college was designated as an "institute" rather than a faculty in its own right, since it was "borrowing" all the instruction that it offered from other faculties. In most American institutions, in contrast, it was the college rather than the graduate school that constituted the faculty. Probably inadvertently, the arrangement that was adopted gave Campbell singular authority and influence during a long tenure that ended only with his retirement in 1966.

153. This formulation was used for the first time in the *Announcements* of the college for the academic year 1936–37 and was used annually thereafter until the consolidation of the college and graduate school in 1975.

154. AAB, Curley Papers, R 1384, Ryan to Curley, Washington, Oct. 1, 1928.

155. AR (1929–30), 14.

156. AS, mm, June 10, 1929.

157. *Ibid.*, Sept. 24, 1929.

158. OVR, Freshmen, Special Courses for.

159. *Ibid.*, "First Meeting of the Faculty of the College of Arts and Sciences, May 26, 1930."

James Marshall Campbell (1895–1977), member of the department of Greek and Latin (1920–66), dean of the college of arts and sciences (1945–66).

Symbolic of Ryan's effort for excellence in the college was the application of the university for installation of a chapter of Phi Beta Kappa.
An approach to the premier national honor society had been considered
as early as the academic year 1926–27.[160] It was recommended also by
one of Ryan's initial faculty committees.[161] The Associated Chapters
did not accept the first application when it was presented in 1930, at
the time that the College of St. Catherine became the first Catholic
institution to gain admission, perhaps because, as the rector reported,
except for The Johns Hopkins University and the University of Virginia,
"the Southern Schools" among which the university was listed registered

160. *Ibid.*, Martin to Pace, Martinsburg, W.Va., Jan. 25, 1927, and Pace to Martin,
Washington, Jan. 28, 1927 (copy).
161. *Ibid.*, Charles A. Hart to Pace and Committee on Committees, Nov. 9, 1928.

opposition.[162] Later the national secretary recalled as "among the most favorable considerations" the endeavor on Ryan's part to raise standards and the qualifications of the deans of arts and sciences that Ryan had appointed, but he mentioned also as unfavorable "the financial condition, the admissions requirements, the inbreeding of the faculty, and the rather liberal grading of students."[163] Campbell's administration of the college soon attended to the academic weaknesses. In 1934 the university was allowed to present eligible students for Phi Beta Kappa keys,[164] but the formation of a chapter was approved only in 1940. Fourteen members of the faculties became charter members at the formal installation on January 15, 1941, and Ryan was brought back from Omaha to be inducted, with his successor, as an honorary member.

Athletic Policy

Campbell, who was in many respects an instrument of Ryan's leadership, was not in sympathy with the decisions that Ryan made concerning athletic programs. Although the athletic council was in existence—there had been some kind of supervisory body since 1905—a committee on athletics was one of the fifteen faculty committees that Ryan had appointed soon after assuming the burdens of his office. MacKavanagh, who was its chairman and also still chairman of the athletic council, could not help but ask, "With the ushering in of the Faculty committee, where does the Council stand?"[165] Two or three years later, his question was answered by the abolition of both bodies to give a free hand to a new athletic director.[166] Meanwhile, however, Ryan had been the object of both external and internal pressures. Externally, first from alumni who were "thoroughly disgusted" with the existing athletic council and who protested because the athletic director who had served for sixteen years was being ousted.[167] Internally, on the principle expressed by the secretary of the faculty committee that "so long as an undergraduate department continues as an integral part of the University and under present conditions, it is absolutely necessary to have the representative athletic teams in the major sports if the University is to attract the better type of undergraduates and is to have that excess of applications

162. OR, Ryan to Martin, Washington, Sept. 29, 1933 (copy).
163. AAB, Curley Papers, R 1706, William A. Shimer to Deferrari, New York, Dec. 29, 1933 (copy).
164. OR, Ryan to Hart, Mar 23, 1934.
165. OVR, MacKavanagh to Pace, Oct. 15, 1928.
166. OR, Ryan to McKavanagh, Dec. 11, 1930, and Oct. 9, 1931.
167. *Ibid.*, James E. Woods to Martin, New York, Dec. 12, 1928 (copy).

over accommodations as to make greater selectivity possible."[168] Probably this was in accord with Ryan's own view.

Ryan's hope for an athletic fund that would provide an annual income of $50,000 was never realized. He was informed, too, that his athletic committee was finding it "difficult and in several specific cases impossible" to convince the old athletic director of its rulings on eligibility.[169] A new era, however, began with the appointment of Arthur J. ("Dutch") Bergman as athletic director.[170] He was a Notre Dame alumnus on the staff of the University of Minnesota. Ryan wrote to a trustee, "Either we must do the thing rightly or cut out athletics completely. If we cut out athletics, we might as well close the undergraduate work. I feel we have a very good man in charge."[171] Edmond R. La Fond, who was to succeed Bergman during the next administration, was named director of intramural sports. Soon Ryan, who was himself working out daily in the gymnasium, could report that three-fourths of the students were engaging in intramural competition of some sort during the year.[172]

"Big time" intercollegiate football became a prime objective of the university's athletic program. To Trustee Martin, who was pleased to note that his Alma Mater was "beginning to receive the local recognition it deserves," Ryan sent clippings that "for the first time"[173] put the university "among the major teams of the East."[174] In 1934, an annual Cardinals' Athletic Dinner was inaugurated. The crowning glories of the new policy in the Orange Bowl and the Sun Bowl were not to be attained until after Ryan had left his office. The costs, meanwhile, had not gone unnoticed. Financially, "the very considerable deficit" incurred by the intercollegiate program was to become an object of the board's attention.[175] Academically, when Campbell was appointed dean, he urged that if football was to be retained at all, intercollegiate competition should be restricted to institutions that did not emphasize the sport. "Money will not be saved by such a policy," he told Ryan, "but academic standards will be saved."[176]

Ryan maintained his confidence in Bergman and was pleased by favorable publicity in the sports section of the press. Responding to a telegram from Owen D. Young, who was chairman of President Herbert

168. OVR, Hart to Pace, Dec. 10, 1928.
169. *Ibid.*, Hart to Pace, Apr. 22, 1929.
170. BT, mm, Nov. 7, 1930.
171. OR, Ryan to Nelligan, Washington, Nov. 3, 1930.
172. AR (1931–32), 10.
173. OR, Martin to Ryan, Martinsburg, W.Va., Oct. 19, 1932.
174. *Ibid.*, Ryan to Martin, Washington, Nov. 22, 1932 (copy).
175. BT, mm, Apr. 22, 1936.
176. OR, Campbell to Ryan, Jan. 18, 1935.

The Cardinal Football Team of 1935, victors over the University of Mississippi in the Orange Bowl, New Year's Day, 1936.

Hoover's Committee on Mobilization of Unemployment Relief Sources, he agreed to participation, with the University of Alabama, George Washington University, and Georgetown University in a Charity Round Robin Football Game during December, 1931.[177] To evade a threatened move by accrediting agencies to drop all institutions offering athletic scholarships, he later insisted on the use of "some other phrase such as 'Student Loan.' "[178] Not only football was promoted. Under Dorsey Griffith, indoor track was revived; the university at the time offered "the only place in the city" that could accommodate a meet in which many high school and college students participated.[179] And Ryan defended intercollegiate boxing, in which La Fond's teams were to attain fame, "because it promotes fine sportsmanship and is developing desirable qualities in those who participate in it."[180]

Financing Excellence

When Ryan turned to the financial implications of his plans for the university, as he had to at once, he could only put in his own words a thought that had been expressed by every leader of the university cause before him. For the public as well as the board, he wrote, "Neither the Church nor Catholics as a group in the body politic can look forward to attaining the leadership our numbers and resources seem to imply until we are willing to invest, and heavily, in the production of scholars."[181] He was in office less than a year when he requested the board to recognize formally provisions in a letter of Pope Pius XI authorizing "a financial campaign over and above the Annual University Collection."[182] He was already consulting in the matter. So far as the university was concerned, in Ryan's opinion, it was lack of knowledge of it that was fundamental. The board, by unanimous vote, instructed its executive committee to draft a plan that could be presented to the hierarchy of the country.[183] Harvey J. Hill was employed as counsel; a campus "survey council" directed by Sheehy was put to work; a plan was prepared and approved by the board on April 15, 1931, and a university office for its execution was authorized.[184]

177. *Ibid.*, Young to Ryan, Hanover, N.H., Oct. 29, 1931.
178. *Ibid.*, Ryan to Cain, Washington, June 15, 1932.
179. *Ibid.*, Griffith to Staff, Feb. 20, 1930.
180. *Ibid.*, Ryan to Mary T. Norton, Washington, Apr. 7, 1932.
181. AR (1930–31), 21.
182. BT, mm, Apr. 10, 1929, exh. The papal letter was dated Oct. 10, 1928.
183. *Ibid.*, Apr. 30, 1930.
184. *Ibid.*, Apr. 15, 1931. AAD, Michael Gallagher Papers, Ryan to Gallagher, Washington, Apr. 11, 1931, forwarding "Executive Committee's Report to the Board of Trustees: History, Present Status and Future Needs of the University" (mimeo, 38 pp.

Two distinct financial goals were recognized from the beginning. As Ryan informed the board, $1,700,000 was needed "to put things in shape" and another $20,000,000 "to put everything in perfect working order over a period of twenty years."[185] These goals were projected to be realized in three phases, first, by increasing the proceeds of the annual diocesan collection to $600,000 in 1931 and $750,000 in 1932; second, by establishing a Bishops, Clergy and Laity Special Fund to raise $1,000,000 by June, 1932; and third, by establishing a Permanent Organization of Clergy and Laity to add $20,000,000 to the university's meager endowment, then less than one-tenth of this amount. Ryan knew that "a university without a substantial and adequate endowment is a university that tries to make progress under impossible conditions."[186] The average endowment of AAU institutions at the time was about $38,000,000.

Renewal of the Graduate Thrust

The plans were being laid, of course, when the national economy was sinking. Prior to a meeting held at Atlantic City on August 7, 1931, attended by Monsignor Paolo Marella of the apostolic delegation, Justice Pierce Butler, about twenty bishops, and others, Ryan was warned that Bishop Michael Gallagher of Detroit would propose that it was an inopportune time to appeal for funds. He confessed, "I do not know where we would turn, if we did not turn to the Bishops."[187] At the meeting, "in about as neat a speech" as Ryan had ever heard, Archbishop Glennon reminded the gathering "that there were moral and religious values over and above the material ones" and that these demanded episcopal support of the university. Justice Butler was said to have been "a tower of strength to the whole movement."[188]

The plan to increase the diocesan collections for the university included action already taken to have the first Sunday of Advent designated as "University Sunday," as the pope had suggested at the beginning of Ryan's tenure.[189] Five regional conferences of bishops and diocesan officials were held after the Atlantic City meeting. About sixty-five dioceses accepted targets for the collection that were based upon diocesan property evaluations.[190] When Hill's service was terminated, Sheehy was appointed assistant to the rector "for Univer-

---

and appendix); also, OR, "Synopsis of a Suggested Plan for Increasing University Income and Capital Resources" (n.d.).

185. BT, mm, Apr. 15, 1931.

186. AR (1933–34), 21.

187. AAB, Curley Papers, R 1602, Ryan to Curley, Washington, Aug. 6, 1931.

188. *Ibid.*, R 1603, Aug. 11, 1931.

189. AR (1928–29), 1–2; BT, mm, Nov. 5, 1929.

190. OR, "Special Report to the Board of Trustees on the Financial Campaign of the University," Nov. 10, 1931 (copy).

sity propaganda and drives."[191] The next year a program on the university was broadcast by the Columbia Broadcasting System in advance of the "University Sunday," and the use of the "Church of the Air" for this purpose became an annual project from 1934 to 1943.[192] The effort produced a 65 per cent increase in the collection from 1930 to 1931, but the proceeds of $409,189 were far short of the $600,000 goal. In the immediately succeeding year, the proceeds fell to $289,728 and they did not increase again until 1934.[193] In the view of many, there was ground for the rumor that the bishops who were "leading the way in this University program" were "complaining more bitterly about those doing nothing."[194]

In addition to the emphasis upon increasing the annual collection, there was the attempt to raise $1,000,000 to cover current needs, which included restoration of about this sum to the endowment fund from which it had been borrowed. Ryan had his priorities straight; he wrote to Curley, "the main thing is to get our finances on a sound basis. When this is done, we can go before the country asking for a substantial increase in our endowment fund."[195] What was first designated the Bishops, Clergy and Laity Special Fund was organized as the Friends of the Catholic University of America. Sixty-seven dioceses appointed diocesan chairmen. The constitution was modeled on a similar successful venture of the Catholic University of the Sacred Heart at Milan. A special papal blessing was received.[196] In practice, however, the Friends became chiefly an educational endeavor rather than a means for achieving a special fund.

Although it was decided at the Atlantic City conference that any general campaign or drive for the university should await economic recovery, hope was not lost. Curley, who knew he was "living in an atmosphere redolent of hunger, poverty and suffering," nevertheless saw ground for hope. "If times ever get back to normal," he wrote, "I think the University is going to make a regular plunge forward financially and every way."[197] Approval had been given at Atlantic City for the compilation of a "National Catholic Leadership List" that could be used when the $20,000,000 goal could be pursued. Consideration was given to the for-

191. BT, mm, Nov. 10, 1931.
192. OVR, Broadcasts, and OR, Catholic University Sunday Broadcasts.
193. AR (1931–32), 5; (1933–34), 2; (1934–35), 18.
194. AAB, Curley Papers, S 12081, Sheehy to Curley, Washington, Jan. 22, 1934.
195. AAB, Curley Papers, R 1561, Ryan to Curley, Washington, Jan. 20, 1931.
196. AR (1931–32), 8.
197. AAB, Curley Papers, S 1044 and S 1050, Curley to Sheehy, Baltimore, May 3 and June 2, 1932 (copies).

mation of a Pontifical Society for the Advancement of the Catholic University.[198] But economic recovery was not to occur during Ryan's administration. In fact, during the summer of 1932, when veterans and their families came to Washington, the university was to respond to calls from local Catholic leaders by supplying milk daily for the children in the encampment.[199]

By 1933, the university had to resort to drastic curtailments in operating costs and to reduction of its already low salaries. At the same time, the structure of its revenues changed. Income from the annual diocesan collection, which was supplying about 35 per cent of the revenues in 1932, was supplying only about 28 per cent in 1935. Dependence upon tuition income was increasing. Roughly, 55 per cent of all revenues were being derived from tuition in 1932; this proportion rose to 66 per cent in the immediately succeeding years. Ryan had initially seen an increase in enrollment as a means of obtaining additional revenues, but he could not have foreseen the trends with which he had to deal as the depression deepened. His thoughts about student aid remain of interest, nevertheless, since, especially for graduate students, he thought that it was "as important to be able to loan students sums of money to complete their education as it is to found scholarships for needy boys."[200]

The End of a Second Beginning

Ryan, from the beginning of his administration, was perceived throughout the country as an effective leader. An alumnus of the early years recalled, "I lived in the days (1903) when there were less than 100 students, when the public was talking of bankruptcy, when the Bishops were debating acknowledging failure, when the Faculty was torn asunder by interior strife. It is good to live today."[201] But Curley had already reported that there were unfriendly agents in Rome. Ryan was soon shocked by an "altogether unreasonable and vicious tirade" delivered at a meeting of the trustees by Shahan, perhaps with the prompting of McKenna.[202] Probably the conflicts with the school of theology and with clerics opposed to the academic reorganization that had taken place were behind the attack. But, later, when the ecclesiastically influential former dean of the school

198. OR, Sheehy to Ryan, Dec. 11, 1931.
199. *Ibid.*, William J. McGinley to Sheehy, New Haven, Aug. 4, 1932 and Sheehy to Ryan, Aug. 12, 1932.
200. AR (1929–30), 23.
201. OR, John B. Delauney, C.S.C., to Ryan, Washington, Nov. 16, 1930.
202. AAB, Curley Papers, R 1850, Ryan to Curley, Washington, Apr. 16, 1931.

of canon law, Bernardini, returned to the campus after an absence of a year and a half, he reported to Ryan that he was "very pleased with what [had] been done."[203]

The principal agent in the removal of Ryan by his transfer to Omaha seems to have been McNicholas, whom Curley labeled as "the juvenile Savanarola [sic] of Cincinnati."[204] More conclusive evidence than is now available may be revealed when the Vatican archives for the pontificate of Pope Pius XI are opened. That the removal was accomplished without the knowledge, let alone the consultation, of the chancellor was indeed, as Ryan wrote, "quite unforgivable."[205] Perhaps it was possible because the apostolic delegate, Archbishop (later Cardinal) Amleto Cicognani, did not trust Curley, as has been alleged.[206] In any case, the influence of McNicholas upon the delegate appears to have been sufficient.[207] McNicholas, an alumnus of the university, as chairman of the visiting committee for the ecclesiastical faculties seemed to be able to persuade easily the future cardinals, Edward Mooney, then bishop of Rochester, and Samuel A. Stritch, then archbishop of Milwaukee, and the other members, Bishop John B. Peterson of Manchester and Bishop Gerald P. O'Hara, then auxiliary bishop of Philadelphia, that the university was "a mess"[208] and that the committee would be unable to do anything about it "unless the Rector be changed."[209] To Peterson, who thought that his brother bishops were "for the most part either indifferent or ill-disposed," the problem was one of "unraveling the skein of a half-century's tragedy" without "a discouraging scandal."[210]

McNicholas felt that Ryan had "little if any concept of what a Pontifical university ought to be" and that "nobody in this country" would know as well as the apostolic delegate what it should be.[211] He had been informed that Stritch, who was "very strongly in favor of having a real Pontifical University at Washington and not merely a poor imitation of Harvard or Princeton," was "gathering considerable

203. *Ibid.*, R 1650, Ryan to Curley, Washington, Oct. 7, 1932.

204. *Ibid.*, M 404, Curley to Paolo Marella, apostolic delegate to Japan, Baltimore, Nov. 7, 1935 (copy). On McNicholas, see an unpublished paper by Steven M. Avella, S.D.S., who is preparing a biography of the prelate.

205. *Ibid.*, R 1779, Ryan to Curley, Washington, Aug. 14, 1935.

206. Sheerin, *op. cit.*, 169.

207. AAB, Curley Papers, M 404, Curley to Marella, Baltimore, Nov. 7, 1935 (copy), and Ellis, *Catholic Bishops*, 27, quoting a conversation of 1950 in which Bernardini, then apostolic nuncio to Switzerland, declared that the removal of Ryan "was a mistake and, in fact, Cicognani and I had a fight about it."

208. McNicholas Papers, McNicholas to O'Hara, Cincinnati, Apr. 22, 1935 (copy).

209. *Ibid.*, June 14, 1935 (copy).

210. *Ibid.*, Peterson to McNicholas, Manchester, Apr. 24, 1935.

211. *Ibid.*, Mar. 1, 1935 (copy).

information . . . on secular universities so far as they have been influencing our University at Washington."[212] McNicholas himself was "thoroughly fed up" with the emphasis on research.[213] In O'Hara's perception, what the bishops wanted in the university was "a class of priests who have a thorough knowledge of theology, even though they never produce a thing for publication." The school of theology, he thought, should be "the beginning and the end of every other school and department on the campus" and if this would be taken by some to be "clerical domination" it would serve the purpose of "smoking out" those who were failing to see "eye to eye" with the Church.[214]

This was an echo of a memorandum that O'Hara had requested from the church historian Healy[215] after the first hearings that the pontifical committee had begun late in 1934. Sheen wrote to O'Hara, "The fundamental problem is this: Is the Catholic University among other universities affiliated with the American Association of Universities [sic], or is it something apart and different in *kind* from all the others."[216] In all the rhetoric, however, there was no analysis of the factors to be considered in articulating the curricula of the university with the "queen of the sciences." There was not even a concrete suggestion that might have been the subject of discussion. Ryan went to Omaha with letters of regret from, among others, Cardinals Bisleti and Fumasoni-Biondi and Monsignor (later Cardinal) Alfredo Ottaviani in Rome, and numerous friends in the United States. Constantine McGuire summed up what many felt in writing to him, "For the time just ahead, we must see in your transfer a distinct set back to the process of strengthening, and modernizing the University."[217]

The Rise of Inter-Institutional Rivalry at the Graduate Level

There surfaced, during Ryan's penultimate year, a dismaying rivalry among American Catholic universities. The Hughes report of the Amer-

212. *Ibid.*, June 14, 1935 (copy).
213. *Ibid.*, Mar. 2, 1935 (copy).
214. *Ibid.*, "Memorandum," n.d. [1935].
215. *Ibid.*, "A Catholic University for the United States," Jan. 7, 1935.
216. *Ibid.*, Sheen to O'Hara, Washington, n.d. (1935). In his autobiography, Sheen, *op. cit.*, 46–47, presumes that he was blamed by Ryan for the transfer to Omaha, since Ryan had seen him leave the office of the papal secretary of state, the future Pope Pius XII, who was aware of the opposition to Ryan. Apparently Sheen always assumed that McNicholas was pro-Ryan!
217. AAB, Curley Papers, R 1793, Ryan to Curley, Washington, Sept. 14, 1935, quoted. For copies of other letters, see R 1782 (Coleman Nevils, S.J., former president of Georgetown University), R 1784 (Ottaviani), R 1785 (Theodore F. McManus, Detroit alumnus), R 1786 (Sister M. Rosa, St. Joseph's College), R 1787 (Bisleti), R 1788 (Fumasoni-Biondi). Acknowledging a personal letter from Ottaviani, without mentioning McNicholas by name, Ryan wrote of him, "The truth of the matter is (and this thought

ican Council on Education was seen by American Jesuits as "tantamount to an embarrassing accusation" against their not inconsiderable volume of graduate offerings.[218] Alphonse M. Schwitalla, S.J., who was then the dean of the graduate school of St. Louis University, tabulated the number of graduate degrees conferred by the thirty-three Catholic institutions that were offering them and found that the thirteen institutions controlled by Jesuits were awarding, during 1931–32 and 1932–33, more than half of the number, at both master's and doctor's levels.[219] His was of course a quantitative criterion. Apparently no attempt was made to refine the statistics by tabulating institutional differences by fields, which might have disclosed, for example, that there were important differences in the range of graduate work offered, or that there were differences among the clienteles that were being served, by nationally oriented institutions, on the one hand, and by urban or regionally oriented institutions, on the other. Instead, Schwitalla's efforts were directed "to secure public recognition for Jesuit institutions." The rationale was defensive; it was thought that there was "a move on the part of Catholic University to preempt the academic market in graduate education and so to garner the lion's share of publicity and acclaim before the eyes of the academic world."[220]

The rivalry that made its appearance in this fashion had been foreseen by a few when The Catholic University of America was founded. Little more than a decade after, in 1901, an alumnus who was a priest of the Congregation of Holy Cross and later a provincial superior, had outlined what was to become the historic issue. Representing at an alumni banquet the seminaries that were then associated with the university—which he did not hesitate to call "the greatest boon the Catholic Church and colleges of America had ever known"—he forecast what institutions operated by religious communities would do when he said, as reported:

The question which must now be seriously considered in view of the evolution in progress . . . is whether the Catholic colleges shall continue to send their

has been expressed to me by countless bishops) that he thinks he runs the Catholic church in the United States." OR, Washington, Aug. 26, 1935 (copy).

218. Paul A. Fitzgerald, S.J., *The Governance of Jesuit Colleges in the United States* (Notre Dame: University of Notre Dame Press, 1984), 37, citing Matthew J. Fitzsimmons, S.J., "The Instruction, 1934–1949," *Jesuit Education Quarterly*, XII (Oct., 1949), 69–78, for a subsequent allegation "that at least one hundred copies of the [latter's] article were sent to the General's Curia in Rome."

219. *Ibid.*, 35.

220. *Ibid.*, 34. Schwitalla had presented to the chairman of the Committee on Clarification of the Association of American Universities the unfavorable effects upon St. Louis

graduates to the Catholic University or whether they shall follow the example set by their neighbors and establish their own post-graduate courses. . . . Unless the Catholic colleges establish these courses they are in danger of being relegated to the class known as "small colleges" and become little short of high schools. [221]

In 1901, the conduct of small colleges of quality by Catholics would have been anything but a "danger." At the time, of course, American graduate schools in general, with few exceptions, were developing within institutions that had begun as undergraduate colleges. The Catholic University of America was, by intention, one of the exceptions, but its early experience was corroborating what a president of the University of Notre Dame was to observe some years later when he remarked that, among Catholics, few graduates were taking advanced work at all. [222] Catholic leaders were concerned nevertheless to prevent, so far as possible, recourse by Catholics to graduate study in non-Catholic institutions. In spite of their concern, during the 1920s, when the American bishops were still undecided about support of the Newman Club movement, [223] the alumnus who had succeeded Ireland as archbishop of St. Paul had asked his brethren pointedly if it was "advisable to condemn attendance at state universities, despite the fact that we have not been altogether successful in organizing one great Catholic university." [224] To officers of the university who were participating in meetings with representatives of other Catholic institutions, it had seemed that some were "fearful lest the University might get even a slight recognition" and were even "more anxious to prevent that than to accomplish anything practical." [225]

As Schwitalla's statistics showed, Catholic institutions conducted by religious congregations and orders were finding it expedient to more or less ignore the rescript that Keane had obtained from the Holy See when the university was founded, as well as the papal advice, often repeated, that while several Catholic universities might be needed eventually, it was necessary "to make certain the success of one before

---

University of a simplification of its "approved lists" that the AAU had attempted. OVR, Schwitalla to Adam Leroy Jones, St. Louis, Oct. 29, 1931, attached as an appendix to a memorandum, "The Action of the Association of American Universities with reference to its Approved Lists," submitted on behalf of St. Louis University (copies).

221. AS, General to 1907, James Burns, C.S.C., remarks at seventh annual meeting and banquet of the Alumni Association of the Catholic University of America, Washington, Apr. 23, 1901.

222. OVR, John Cavanaugh, C.S.C. to Pace, Notre Dame, Mar. 4, 1916.

223. Evans, *op. cit.*

224. OVR, National Catholic Welfare Conference, Department of Education, mm, Jan. 27, 1926, reporting remarks of Austin Dowling.

225. OR, [Pace?] to Shahan, Jan. 5, 1917.

starting another."[226] Attempting to hold to this course, Shahan and Pace had earlier earned Cardinal Mundelein's hostility by blocking his ambitions for a pontifical institution in Chicago, and near the end of his administration Shahan, when consulted by Cardinal Dougherty, had successfully interposed objections to the establishment of law schools at St. Joseph's and Villanova in Pennsylvania. Ryan was to withdraw such objections.[227]

Schwitalla led a movement of the late 1920s to organize a committee on graduate studies within the National Catholic Educational Association's department of colleges and secondary schools.[228] Acknowledging one of Schwitalla's letters for Ryan, who was out of the city, his assistant observed that some colleges that had "generously bestowed the Ph.D. and A.M. degrees [had] practically no men with graduate training recognized as such."[229] There was some hesitancy on the part of the university about "cooperation with a committee which considered all graduate schools in the Catholic institutions as established facts" but Ryan's trusted graduate dean and his own assistant agreed that there was "more to be gained through such cooperation than through ignoring [Schwitalla's] appeal."[230]

It was a period of institutional expansion. Ryan, informed that 60 per cent of all Catholic teaching in the country was either directly being done by graduates of the university or indirectly by priests and religious trained by graduates, and attributing "practically whatever intellectual life there is at Notre Dame" to The Catholic University of America, lapsed into parochialism in observing that the Holy Cross Fathers there were being "very disloyal, particularly since Father Burns went in as Provincial."[231] On their part, Jesuit representatives were passing a resolution to the effect "that the relationships between the Catholic University and our Universities, especially concerning graduate work, should be recalled to the Fathers Provincial of the American Assistancy since the situation is one which warrants serious consideration and action."[232] The Jesuit father general, however, in a landmark instruction issued in

226. John J. Keane, "The Catholic Universities of France," *CW*, XLVII, June, 1888), 293.
227. It was remarked at the time that the university had never protested against the foundation of the numerous Jesuit law schools elsewhere. BT, EC, mm, May 31, 1929.
228. OVR, Pace to Schwitalla, Washington, D.C., May 10, 1927 (copy); Schwitalla to Pace, St. Louis, Mo., July 7, 1927, and May 3, 1929.
229. OR, Sheehy to Schwitalla, Washington, D.C., Jan. 27, 1932 (copy).
230. *Ibid.*, Sheehy to Ryan, Aug. 12, 1932.
231. AAB, Curley Papers, R 1675, Ryan to Curley, Washington, Apr. 6, 1933.
232. BCA, Jesuit Educational Association file, abstract of *Proceedings* of NCEA, St. Paul, Minn., June 26–29, 1933, quoted in Fitzgerald, *op. cit.*, 35.

1934, asked his subjects in the United States to bring their graduate schools "to the level of the best in the country"[233] and appointed as his direct representative in the matter one who believed "that a truly representative graduate school was the key to academic prestige for a particular institution."[234] The latter's notes, written for a provincial superior, even posed the question: "As the Catholic University has a graduate school at Washington, is there need of a Graduate School at Georgetown, except for the M.A. in Philosophy at Woodstock, and possibly in the Law School?"[235]

In the light of subsequent developments, the eruption of this inter-institutional rivalry in the early 1930s can be interpreted positively as marking the rapid growth of American Catholic higher education. The foundation of The Catholic University of America had indeed been a major breakthrough, not only in the establishment of research-oriented study, but in the training of teachers at all levels from the elementary school to the university. Early in its history, an influential professor had portrayed it as a neutral center "where all religious orders might meet one another and the pastoral clergy, where all might teach, be mutually helpful, mutually corrective."[236] One of his colleagues had later remarked explicitly that the university had "opened a way to the higher education of men and women of religious orders devoted to teaching which would otherwise have been closed."[237] Shahan as rector had told the board that "the plain fact of the matter is that the training of teachers is one of the most important functions that any university can perform."[238] Now, during the Ryan administration, other Catholic institutions were maturing and were aspiring to offer advanced degrees. Changes in the university's role were being foreshadowed.

On the negative side, of course, the rivalry at the graduate level was evidence that Catholic institutions, no less than others, were acting according to their perceptions of their institutional interests, without the coordination or planning that might have served the Church. They were illustrating the thesis of the *Commonweal* editorial written earlier in support of the university, holding that "the Catholic body in the

233. Wlodimir Ledochowski, S.J., to Provincials of the American Assistancy, Rome, Aug. 15, 1934, quoted in Fitzgerald, *op. cit.*, 39.

234. Fitzgerald, *op. cit.*, 50.

235. BCA, Daniel M. O'Connell, S.J. File, "Notes on Georgetown," quoted, *ibid.*, 44–45.

236. Kerby, *Chronicle*, I, 113.

237. Egan, *Recollections*, 191–92.

238. AR (1911–12), 14.

United States [had] yet to solve the problem of adjustment to the national civilization" that in the view of the writer was reposing "more and more noticeably upon the especial kind of authority which modern universities possess." Although the Catholic advantage "seemed in other respects very great, it [had] not yet succeeded in investing its appeal to the nation—that is, in the strict sense, its whole missionary effort— with the new academic authoritativeness."[239]

239. XIV (Oct. 7, 1931), 539.

CHAPTER VIII

The Evidence of Momentum in Scholarship

The fruits of Ryan's leadership, in many ways, came to be recognized only after he had left the scene, when his work went on without him. In retrospect, it is clear enough that his continuing influence was bound to be exerted through the men whom he had tapped to assist him when he had begun the task of academic reorganization and also through the application of the standards that he had seen embodied in legislation of the faculties and of the academic senate. But that he had in fact initiated a kind of "second spring" in the university's history was to become evident only during succeeding, less vigorous administrations. The first, following an interim year under the veteran McCormick as acting rector, began in 1936 with the appointment to lead the university of Joseph Moran Corrigan (1879–1942), who had been rector of St. Charles Borromeo Seminary at Overbrook, a Philadelphia suburb. Corrigan was so little acquainted with academic life that, reportedly, he did not know until he came to Washington that a doctorate in philosophy could be earned in any field except the one from which the degree had been named.[1] Paradoxically, however, the corps of scholars at the university came to be augmented more auspiciously during his administration than during any other in the institution's first century.

Corrigan's appointment began with a constitutional irregularity. The chancellor of the university was instructed by the apostolic delegate that he should request each archbishop and bishop on the board to suggest "one or at most two names of men" who would be deemed qualified to "give new life to the Theological and Philosophical Studies" and to "continue the excellent traditions already established in the School of the Profane Sciences," while knowing at the same time "how to provide a Catholic foundation for the lay students." Even more

---

1. Deferrari, *Memoirs*, 412; Ellis, *Catholic Bishops*, 30.

Joseph Moran Corrigan (1879–1942), sixth rector of The Catholic University of America, titular bishop of Bilta (1940–42).

surprising was the delegate's instruction that the voting in the board was to be confined to the episcopal members, so that a recommendation to the Holy See would "not be made directly by the Board of Trustees."[2] This, Curley reported that he was told, "was the mind of the Holy See, meaning the Congregation of Studies."[3] Ryan, citing the various irregularities, wrote to a friend in the Roman curia, a future cardinal assessor of the holy office and prefect of its successor congregation, that there was "great dissatisfaction that the Statutes of the University have been set aside without good reason, and without a direct order from the Holy See."[4] The plain requirements of corporate standing in the United States seem to have been ignored by all concerned.

No consultation with the academic senate took place prior to the proceedings. Ryan, for that matter, had never grasped the importance of

2. McNicholas Papers, Curley to McNicholas, Baltimore, Oct. 14, 1935. For the original, AAB, Curley Papers, Roman Documents, Cicognani to Curley, Washington, Oct. 8, 1935.
3. AAB, Curley Papers, M 404, Curley to Marella, Baltimore, Nov. 7, 1935 (copy).
4. AAO, Ryan Papers, Ryan to Ottaviani, Washington, Nov. 1, 1935 (copy).

the procedure. The statutes of 1926, which had provided for consultation, had been approved only for seven years and were being revised. When Ryan's first term was expiring, in 1933, the dean of the school of theology had asked him if there would be a special meeting of the senate for the purpose of consultation and Ryan had replied that no provision for such consultation had been included in the new statutes that had been given effect provisionally.[5] Actually, it may well have been owed to McNicholas that the consultation of the senate in the selection of a rector and in other matters was eventually restored in the statutes that became effective in 1937.[6] Perhaps because there was no such consultation in this instance, the names that Curley received when he canvassed the bishops showed no convergence upon a favorite candidate.

An important organizational point was made, however, when a perspicacious bishop noted a systemic weakness in American Catholic higher education. There had been, he wrote, no "proper prevision and preparation of a qualified candidate in due time for this extremely important and responsible position."[7] Boston's cardinal archbishop cited problems that the trustees were not facing. He had sounded out two of his priests whom he had judged to be qualified for consideration and he had found that neither would allow his name to be put forward "for the reason, as they stated it, that they had no desire to subject themselves to the constant interference of meddlers in what they consider their duty; also because, as is evident from past history, no Rector seems to be secure in his tenure of Office."[8] Emphasizing the need for candidates conversant with the American scene, the alumnus who was bishop of Pittsburgh, finding himself unable to suggest any clerics who would be "at the same time good executives and possessed of scholarly habits and attainments," proposed that "the new Rector should know something of the methods and educational procedures which seem to be fruitful in the great secular universities."[9] There was a consciousness in the board that it would indeed "be hard to replace Bishop Ryan."[10]

The Sixth Rector (1936–42)

The promotion of Corrigan's candidacy was not a surprise. McNicholas had first suggested his name in 1928, before Ryan was appointed,

5. AS, mm, Mar. 30, 1933.

6. OR, McNicholas to Corrigan, Norwood, O., July 13, 1936. See also BT, mm, Apr. 15, 1931, in which, with respect to the appointment of deans, McNicholas proposed consultation while Ryan "saw no good reason" for it.

7. AAB, Nelligan Papers, Thomas Molloy to Curley, Brooklyn, Oct. 21, 1935.

8. *Ibid.*, O'Connell to Curley, Boston, Oct. 17, 1935.

9. *Ibid.*, Boyle to Curley, Pittsburgh, Oct. 27, 1935.

10. *Ibid.*, Francis Beckman, archbishop of Dubuque, to Curley, Dubuque, Nov. 6, 1935.

only to have a fellow trustee, a Philadelphia attorney—who seems to have changed his mind in 1935—remark that he had found the proposed nominee "a mere child in finances" and would "not care to tell of his own personal experiences with him along these lines."[11] Corrigan had been ordained for the archdiocese of Philadelphia after graduating from LaSalle College and studying at the Overbrook seminary and in Rome. He had been archdiocesan director of Catholic charities before he was appointed to the Overbrook faculty in 1918. He became rector of the seminary in 1925 and a domestic prelate of the papal household in 1929. After his appointment to the university, he was named first a protonotary apostolic in 1937 and then titular bishop of Bilta in 1940. He, however, had only begun the second year of a second term when he died unexpectedly. By 1941, as his first term of five years was drawing to a close, he had received honorary degrees from six American Catholic institutions and, as the first American to be so recognized, from the Catholic University of the Sacred Heart in Milan. Both the academic senate and the trustees had recommended him for reappointment.[12]

Before 1935, some of the most highly placed prelates among the trustees—Archbishops (later Cardinals) Mooney and Stritch in particular and Cardinal Mundelein less firmly—had been persuaded to support Corrigan. According to Curley, the visiting committee for the ecclesiastical faculties, of which McNicholas was chairman, undertook to summon Corrigan to "what was meant to be a secret meeting" at Spring Lake, New Jersey, and there "settled on his name."[13] In response to Curley's circular inquiry, Corrigan's ordinary, Cardinal Dougherty, had recommended his subject, not unjustly, as "a man of brilliant qualities, especially intellectual originality and eloquence."[14] Curley himself considered Corrigan to be a friend of thirty-five years standing, but he did not hesitate to inform the apostolic delegate, despite his knowledge of McNicholas' influence with the latter, that although he "would not know who to name," and thought that Corrigan would make a good bishop, he could not recommend him as "an efficient Rector of the University."[15] To others he mentioned Corrigan's persistent health problems, visible in his pathological obesity, describing him as the only man he ever knew "who could talk, sleep and smoke at the same time"

11. BT, mm, Apr. 18, 1928.
12. AS, mm, Mar. 8, 1941; BT, mm, Apr. 23, 1941. For a brief biographical account, see *CUB*, N.S., X, No. 1 (July, 1942), 1.
13. AAB, Curley Papers, M 404, *op. cit.*
14. AAB, Nelligan Papers, Dougherty to Curley, Philadelphia, Oct. 10, 1935.
15. *Ibid.*, Curley to Cicognani, Baltimore, Oct. 28, 1935 (copy).

or perhaps "fall asleep in a conversation at nine in the morning just as he might at twelve at night."[16]

When the board met on November 12, 1935, Bishop Turner moved that Ryan should be recommended to succeed himself, but Ryan immediately declined to be considered. Later in the meeting the board named him rector emeritus. Curley presented eighteen names that had been suggested by the episcopal trustees. According to a lengthy report of McNicholas that was requested by the apostolic delegate after the meeting, the presiding officer, Cardinal O'Connell, whom McNicholas regarded as "a most dangerous Prelate for the Church in this country," denounced "the whole new method of procedure," disparaged the Roman curia, referred to "traitors" in the board, and made "an impassioned plea" for the election of Robert H. Lord, who had been a professor of history at Harvard before his conversion and entry into the priesthood.[17] Lord was then teaching at the archdiocesan seminary of Boston. The minutes show that after general discussion a nominating committee was appointed to present three names to be voted upon. In the balloting, Corrigan received only eight of the twenty-six votes cast. Lord received fifteen votes. Francis A. Thill, the newly appointed chancellor of the archdiocese of Cincinnati who had been national secretary of the Catholic Students Mission Crusade and who was soon to be named bishop of Concordia in Kansas, was the choice of three trustees.[18] When the result became known on the campus, almost at once, the priest who had been Ryan's assistant wrote jubilantly to Curley that if there was truth in the rumor "the Holy Ghost [had] registered a great victory." He warned also that McNicholas was reported to be "most bitter."[19]

There was a general expectation among the bishops and trustees that Corrigan would be named despite his failure to obtain the vote of the episcopal trustees. The apostolic delegate reportedly said that when a new rector was appointed Curley would have to "leave the university alone."[20] When the appointment was made early in the spring of 1936,

16. *Ibid.*, Curley Papers, B 1304, Curley to Boyle, Baltimore, Oct. 29, 1935 (copy).
17. AACi, McNicholas to Cicognani, Cincinnati, n.d. (copy). McNicholas felt "that any man with Father Lord's antecedents and environments at a non-Catholic university cannot be expected to have completely a mens catholica." Moreover, he hoped "that before another election comes around we will have a new method of choosing [a rector], a method that will be definite and that will exclude all laymen and priests." Curley, also responding to a request from the apostolic delegate, reported that O'Connell had not mentioned Lord until after another bishop had placed his name in nomination. Curley himself voted for Corrigan. AAB, Curley Papers, Roman Documents, Curley to Cicognani, Washington, Nov. 20, 1935 (copy).
18. BT, mm, Nov. 12, 1935.
19. AAB, Curley Papers, S 1109–10, Sheehy to Curley, Washington, Nov. 15 and 18, 1935.
20. Sheerin, *op. cit.* 169. See also, Ellis, *Catholic Bishops*, 27.

Curley emphasized that Corrigan would get from him "exactly the same affectionate cooperation" that he had given to Ryan,[21] but he also remarked to the latter, undoubtedly referring to himself, "that a certain member of the Hierarchy, highly placed, [would] never get anything from the Holy See."[22] The board received Corrigan and elected him to membership at its spring meeting. Cardinal O'Connell welcomed him at length, having known him many years previously as a student at the North American College.[23] Curley subsequently announced the appointment formally to the faculties, at the same time that he thanked McCormick for his extended service as acting rector while announcing his appointment as vice rector.[24] Ryan wrote to Curley that he wished Corrigan "every possible success" but would wait to be asked before giving advice. Recalling a reference by William James to "university blackguards," he wondered if the university he had left did not "harbor more than its share of such animals."[25]

The Need of a Program

After his visit to the campus, Curley reported that its "atmosphere" was "quite calm."[26] As acting rector, for that matter, McCormick had found that despite some "disquietude" linked with questions about tenure, there was "a thoroughly satisfactory spirit of cooperation."[27] The new rector was hardly ready to announce a program for his administration, but he was aware that the world crisis of the 1930s required a response, he had a very good conception of what the university might do for the Church and the country, and he had a prospective event, the golden jubilee of the opening of classes, toward which he could point. Later, skilled rhetorically as he was, he could refer to his institution felicitously as "the utmost concentration of both the great ideas expressed by its name."[28] And after several years of the New Deal he could not help but note, with even "the most unobservant," that the "nationalization" of problems was "growing very fast." Accordingly, in the new statutes to which he had to give immediate attention, the university was to be given a mandate to be "the center of Catholic culture for the country." In the circumstances, it seemed to Corrigan

21. AAB, Curley Papers, S 1119, Curley to Sheehy, Baltimore, Apr. 13, 1936 (copy).
22. *Ibid.*, R 1813, Curley to Ryan, Baltimore, Apr. 20, 1936 (copy).
23. BT, mm, Apr. 22, 1936.
24. AAB, Archepiscopal Diary, May 5, 1936.
25. AAB, Curley Papers, R 1639, Ryan to Curley, Omaha, Apr. 19, 1936.
26. AACi, Cöln Papers, Curley to McNicholas, Washington, May 14, 1936 (copy).
27. BT, mm, Apr. 22, 1936.
28. *University and Universality* (Washington, D.C.: The Catholic University of America Press, 1940), 4, reprinted, *CUB*, VIII, No. 1 (Aug., 1940), 16.

that the departments over which he was presiding should be the re- sources from which the National Catholic Welfare Conference, the agency of the bishops, could "draw its power of action."[29]

The concept of the university as a national Catholic center was by no means novel. Catholic leaders had looked to the campus as the scene of the organization of the Catholic Educational Association, the National Conference of Catholic Charities, and the Catholic Association for International Peace, not to mention the establishment of the National Catholic War Council that had been transformed into the National Catholic Welfare Conference. Associations in academic disciplines had come into being, beginning with the American Catholic Historical Association, in 1919, and the American Catholic Philosophical Association, in 1926, both founded on the campus. There had been organized elsewhere, more loosely, but with the leadership of Cooper, the Catholic Anthropological Conference, in 1926, and the Catholic Round Table of Science, in 1928. During the period of Corrigan's administration there came into being the Catholic Biblical Association, in 1936, the American Catholic Sociological Society, in 1938, the Canon Law Society of America, in 1939, and the Catholic Economic Association, in 1941. After his death, but just after World War II, there were added the Catholic Theological Society, in 1946, and the American Catholic Psychological Association, in 1947. In most of these associations, scholars from the institution that Corrigan was appointed to lead were prominent participants if not organizers.

Soon after the opening of his first academic year, Corrigan was privileged to welcome to the campus the papal secretary of state who within less than three years would become Pope Pius XII. On the occasion, Cardinal Pacelli recalled that he had once hoped to be appointed to the university's faculty of canon law, but had been refused permission to leave the service of the Holy See by Pope St. Pius X.[30] Corrigan was inaugurated a little later, on November 18, and then left for Rome, with Lardone, later to be appointed director of ecclesiastical studies, assisting him, to prepare with the congregation of seminaries and universities the revised instrument under which the university was to be governed.

It is not yet possible to document satisfactorily the entire sequence of events that postponed until 1937 the ratification of what had begun as a revision of the statutes of 1926 to ensure their conformity with the

29. OR, Corrigan to Lardone, Mar. 26, 1938 (copy).
30. *Tower*, Oct. 29, 1936.

apostolic constitution of 1931. Ryan and Pace might have thought that they had completed the work. McNicholas and the pontifical commission on the sacred sciences had wanted to limit the power of the chancellor[31] and to extend privileges of consultation to the academic senate. Ryan had been notified hardly more than two months before he was transferred that the Roman congregation wanted the new draft of the statutes that it had requested to include the recommendations of McNicholas's committee "and other academic authorities."[32] One member of the committee at least understood the letter from the apostolic delegate transmitting the instructions to be "virtually a mandate" to complete work that had already in fact been begun by the committee; he called it "an important, delicate and difficult task."[33] McNicholas, incidentally, wrote that he could not think that the draft should be submitted to the trustees.[34] Corrigan assured the academic senate that copies would be distributed to the professors, but no record of the distribution appears in the minutes of that body.[35]

Meanwhile, Corrigan had acknowledged to the congregation that the documents prepared under Ryan had not been "fully approved," and that he felt it to be his "first duty" to devote himself "at once to the Schools of Sacred Sciences, and in a particular manner to the organization of a real School of Scholastic Philosophy."[36] During his several months in Rome he was received by Pope Pius XI and by Mussolini, finding as far as the university was concerned "that while nothing at all had been actually and definitely accomplished, still all the problems can be certainly be said to be moving apparently to a happy conclusion."[37] The revised statutes were approved on the feast of St. Thomas Aquinas, March 7, 1937, and were in fact the last work of the prefect of the congregation, Cardinal Bisleti, before his death. They omitted provisions of the 1926 document pertaining to counsellors, the director of the library, and institutional development. They incorporated, among other things, the much more specific criteria and procedures for faculty appointments, promotions, and tenure that had been developed under Ryan and provisions such as McNicholas had favored for appropriate consultation of the faculties and academic senate, not

31. BT, mm, Apr. 26, 1933; McNicholas Papers, O'Hara to McNicholas, Philadelphia, Feb. 27, 1935; McNicholas to Corrigan, Cincinnati, July 13, 1936 (copy).
32. McNicholas Papers, Cicognani to McNicholas, Washington, May 11, 1935 (copy).
33. *Ibid.*, Peterson to McNicholas, Manchester, May 21, 1935.
34. *Ibid.*, McNicholas to Corrigan, Cincinnati, Sept. 30, 1936 (copy).
35. AS, mm, Oct. 29, 1936. See OR, "Comments of Monsignor Pace," Dec. 9, 1936.
36. OR, Corrigan to Bisleti, Washington, Sept. 13, 1936 (copy).
37. *Ibid.*, Corrigan to McCormick, Rome, Feb. 23, 1937.

only for faculty rank and tenure, but for appointments to the offices of rector, vice rector, secretary general, dean, and head of department.

The promulgation of the new statutes required some new appointments in academic administration. Deferrari became secretary general, filling an office that Purcell, newly elected in 1930, had sought to enhance,[38] but that Ryan had discontinued in 1934 when revising the statutes. It is possible that Deferrari's appointment was intended deviously, since as dean of the graduate school he had made influential enemies; these may even have included the chancellor.[39] Although later, when his retirement was impending, in 1960, Deferrari could describe his office as entailing "not by any means a very burdensome set of duties,"[40] his power, if not his authority, made him the arbiter of virtually all things academic for many years. The power was buttressed especially by the respect in which he was held within the Association of American Universities and the Middle States Association of Colleges and Secondary Schools, by his revival and successful expansion of the university's program of affiliation, and by his direction of summer sessions. The appointment of his departmental colleague McGuire to replace him as dean of the graduate school of arts and sciences ensured continuity in policy and in concern for academic standards. His association with Campbell was close. Soon there was a quip in circulation to the effect that the university, thought to be a clerical institution, was in fact being run by two laymen and an anticlerical priest (all, it should be noted, from the same academic department).

Other specific initiatives of Corrigan can best be treated with related topics below. The theme that was interwoven with most of them was the university's contribution to what came to be called, following an unofficial English title of a papal encyclical, the reconstruction of the social order.[41] This was expressed in an elaborate program for the celebration of the university's golden jubilee. A year of commemoration was opened with a papal letter issued on September 21, 1938, calling upon the university "to bring to bear upon the most pressing problems of the day the full force of those principles of justice and charity in

38. OR, Purcell to Ryan, June 13, 1930; Ryan to Purcell, June 23, 1930 (copy).
39. AAB, Curley Papers, B 41, Jules A. Baisnée, S.S., to Curley, Washington, July 15, 1941; B 42, Curley to Baisnée, Baltimore, July 17, 1941 (copy).
40. OR, Deferrari to William J. McDonald, Mar. 8, 1960.
41. The reference is to *Quadragesimo anno*, issued by Pius XI, on May 15, 1941, to commemorate the fortieth anniversary of Leo XIII's pioneer *Rerum novarum*. For the original (in Latin), see *AAS*, XXIII (June 1, 1931), 177–228; trans., Sister Claudia Carlen, I.H.M. (ed.), *The Papal Encyclicals* (4 vols.; Raleigh, N.C.: McGrath, 1981), II, 415–43.

which alone they will find their solution."[42] A pastoral letter of the American hierarchy that followed announced a charge to the university "to compile at once a . . . comprehensive series of graded texts for all educational levels."[43] Responding to the alarm expressed by the bishops at "the spread of subversive teaching and the audacity of subversive action in the country," the rector proclaimed a National Crusade for God in Government that was announced on February 11, 1939, through stations of the National Broadcasting Company, in a program that was arranged to commemorate the anniversary of the coronation of Pius XI but became instead a posthumous tribute.[44] The Confraternity of Christian Doctrine made the subject the theme of its fifth national catechetical congress that was held in Cincinnati just before the final university celebration in Washington, November 11–13, 1939.

Among the other jubilee events that Corrigan announced were symposia at the college level, an essay contest on the theme "What the Catholic Colleges Can Do in Cooperation with The Catholic University of America to Promote Christian Democracy in Our Country," the commemoration of the accession of Pius XII to the papal throne, the annual presentation of children's greetings to the Holy Father, and the annual renewal on a selected day of the national crusade.[45] An address was presented to President Franklin Delano Roosevelt on August 3, 1939. On October 30, the apostolic delegate made the first presentation of papal *Benemerenti* medals to members of the faculties, honoring eighteen who had served for twenty-five years or more. The culminating events began with a corporate reception of the eucharist by members of the faculties on November 11. At the golden jubilee banquet, the rector presented the oration entitled "University and Universality." Jessica Dragonette, accepting no fee, sang. Eighteen of the "more than two-score" bishops in attendance were alumni of the university. For the final convocation on November 13, Pius XII broadcast in English his congratulatory message on the anniversary of the opening of classes.[46] A flag designed for the jubilee was later declared to be the university's official flag,[47] but remains virtually unknown. In a commemorative

42. *Sollemnia jubilaria*, AAS, XXX (Nov. 19, 1938), 340–43, trans., CUB, N.S., VII, No. 1 (Nov., 1938), 2–3.
43. "Catholic Crusade for Christian Democracy," CA, XX, No. 12 (Dec., 1938), 8.
44. OR, press release, Feb. 11, 1939. The New York *Times*, Sept. 25, 1939, subtly praised the purpose of the crusade "to lead the twenty-one [Catholic] millions in the United States to practice Christian principles in their everyday private and civic life."
45. BT, mm, Apr. 19, 1939.
46. "It is from a heart," AAS, XXXI (Nov. 25, 1939), 676–77. A photograph of the pope at the microphone is in CUB, VIII, No. 1 (Aug., 1940), 1.
47. BT, EC, mm, Apr. 3, 1940. See *Tower*, May 2, 1939.

The Fiftieth Anniversary Convocation, June 14, 1939, held in the university's gymnasium and attended by members of the hierarchy and Catholic leaders with members of the faculties and students, to which a personal message from the recently elected Pope Pius XII was broadcast.

publication, it was remarked that although the university was "a part of the Middle Ages"—then beginning to gain some admiration from historians—it was also "indigenous to the land whose Americanism it expounds to thousands of students, religious and lay, who go forth into monasteries, convents, academies, and dioceses of the land."[48]

The curriculum group established in response to the hierarchy's request was named, misleadingly, the Commission on American Citizenship. It had a rather remarkable and quick success, principally through

48. [Richard J. Purcell], *A Half Century of Progress* (Washington, D.C.: The Catholic University of America, 1939), 7. See the "Commemoration Days Issue," CUB, N.S., VIII, No. 1, *op. cit.*

publication of a three-volume curriculum guide entitled "Guiding Growth in Christian Social Living" and an accompanying series of eight "Faith and Freedom Readers" that were used in American Catholic elementary schools for more than two decades.[49] The first chairman of the executive committee, Monsignor (later Bishop) Francis J. Haas, dean of the school of social science that Corrigan had just established, reported to the trustees and the entire hierarchy that the commission was utilizing "the best elements of modern pedagogy as well as the basic truths of religion in order to instill principles of right and justice into the minds and souls of the Catholic youths of the nation."[50] Johnson of the department of education, who was preparing a policy statement under the title *Better Men for Better Times* (Washington, D.C.: The Catholic University of America Press, 1943), and Robert H. Connery, a political scientist who was the first director of the commission, were the other members of the first executive committee. A large advisory committee was enlisted. Mary Synon, as editorial consultant, and Sister Mary Joan Smith, O.P., as director of curriculum, were principally responsible for the progress of the work. The commission's activities included the sponsorship of civics clubs, the presentation of "Catholic Hour" broadcasts, and the preparation of materials for youth-oriented publications of the Pflaum Publishing Company of Cincinnati. Its efforts at the secondary level were not as successful as at the elementary. It continued in existence until 1969, when it became a curriculum materials development center of the school of education.[51]

Academic Developments

Soon after he became rector, Corrigan received from the deans of the graduate school and the college, Deferrari and Campbell, recommendations for the dismissal or retirement of twenty-three members of the faculty of arts and sciences, some of them professors of solid reputation. In five cases, it was noted that the affected parties were particular friends of the vice rector, McCormick, between whom and Deferrari there was reported to be "open friction."[52] Previous recommendations of this kind that the same deans had made to Ryan had been confined to junior appointees who had failed to "show promise of developing as full profes-

49. Mary Synon, "The University Builds a Curriculum for Elementary Catholic Schools," CUB, N.S., XII, No. 2 (Sept., 1944), 4–5.
50. OR, "Report of the Commission on American Citizenship," Nov. 5, 1942.
51. OVR, Brother Nivard Scheel, C.F.X., acting president, to C. Joseph Nuesse, executive vice president and provost, Sept. 26, 1968.
52. McNicholas Papers, CUA: Investigation of Differences, mm, May 14, 1931, testimony of Cöln.

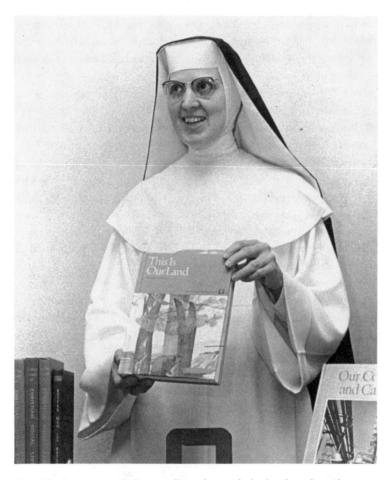

Sister M. Annunciata, O.P., a staff member, with the fourth-grade reader published in the Faith and Freedom series of the Commission on American Citizenship.

sors" and who would have had no claims to permanency.[53] An older professor and sometime dean reported rumors that the deans had been given "so much authority that they can do almost anything they decide to do."[54]

The recommendations sent to Corrigan for the dismissal of fourteen of the twenty-three would have affected eight who had been members of the faculty from seven to twenty-two years. The grounds for dismissal

53. BT, EC, mm, June 6, 1935.
54. OR, Hardee Chambliss to Curley, Washington, Mar. 9, 1936, transmitted through McCormick, who was then acting rector.

that were alleged included conduct of competing activities off-campus, unreliability, temperamental unfitness, lack of proper training for graduate teaching and for direction of dissertations, and disloyalty (apparently because children were being sent to a public instead of a parochial school).[55] When similar recommendations were made a year later it was proposed that a woman in junior rank should not be reappointed, not only because of low enrollment in her classes, but also because "students, especially Religious," were objecting to taking courses from her.[56] The rector, reporting the recommendations to the trustees, concurred in their judgment "that no drastic action should be taken" but he took the opportunity to point out also "that it would be necessary for the maintaining of the proper standards of the University, to engage men qualified to command the prestige which the University should enjoy, even though it meant carrying those who were dead wood until an opportune time for dispensing with them."[57]

In the years that followed, through his administration of the office of secretary general and in the role of chairman of the committee on coordination of the academic senate, Deferrari was able to extend to all schools the academic thrust of the Ryan administration. In the arts and sciences, McGuire was able to enforce high standards in the recruitment of faculty and in the formulation of recommendations for change. In general, of course, it was a time for "tightening up" rather than for expansion. The former departments of German, comparative philology, Celtic, and Slavic were combined to form a single department of German and comparative philology. The department of religion was renamed the department of religious education. Programs in art and music were introduced. Graduate work in biology and chemistry was strengthened. A department of library science was organized. The department of geology that had been established in 1927 was renamed the department of geology and geography, but then was recommended for abolition in 1941. The principle on which the latter action was based could logically have been generalized; it was "to husband our resources by developing only a few important fields for which adequate support is available."[58]

The organization of the department of library science in 1937 was concomitant with a much-needed upgrading of the university's library that had been initiated under Ryan. Courses had been offered since

55. OR, Deferrari and Campbell to Corrigan, Sept. 25, 1936.
56. *Ibid.*, Nov. 16, 1937.
57. BT, mm, Nov. 16, 1937.
58. OR, F. O. Rice, "Report on the Dept. of Geology," Dec. 19, 1940.

1930. Francis A. Mullin, a priest of Dubuque, became the first head of the department a year after his appointment as director of libraries in 1936. He was succeeded in 1941 as head of the department and acting director of libraries by James J. Kortendick, S.S., and, after his death in 1946, by Eugene P. Willging as director of libraries.[59]

The most prominent academic addition was the establishment of a program in speech and drama at the graduate level. Preparing the way for it were the dramatic associations that had been organized on the campus and that had become unusually active as the Harlequin Club, a Washington theater apostolate of the Dominican Fathers whose Blackfriars Guild had begun in 1932 to present productions at various places in the city, and the organization, in 1937, of the Catholic Theater Conference. In that summer of 1937, as "a scientific approach to Catholic Action through drama," courses in little theater work were offered.[60] In the fall, Gilbert V. Hartke, O.P., began a conspicuous service on campus that was to continue until his death early in 1986. He was joined in 1938 by Walter Kerr, who later became the drama critic of the *New York Times*. In 1939, an original production of "Brother Orchid" by a student, Leo Brady, was dedicated to the rector as the golden jubilee play and later in the year, during the run of another original production, "Yankee Doodle Boy," by Brady and Kerr, a scroll was presented to its subject, George M. Cohan. Brady became a member of the department and served until his death in 1984. The creative work in drama soon received wide acclaim, deserved all the more because it was accomplished in cramped quarters that were not intended to accommodate more than the music recitals to which they were later to be devoted. To extend the influence of the department, there was inaugurated in 1941 a speech and drama laboratory for high school students conducted during summer sessions. Departmental status was to be formalized in 1945.

A particularly noteworthy appointment made by Corrigan in 1937 after consultation of the faculty was that of Robert J. White as dean of the school of law. White, after graduation from Harvard College and Harvard Law School and successful practice in Massachusetts, had entered the Sulpician Seminary and had been appointed to the faculty after his ordination to the priesthood in 1931. His election as national chaplain of the American Legion in 1934 was an indication of his

---

59. See Peter Thomas Commy, "The Ultimate Professionalization of the Catholic University Library: Father Mullin and Eugene Willging," *CLW*, LVI (May–June, 1985), 416–18 ff.

60. OR, Deferrari to Corrigan, July 28, 1936.

widespread influence. Ecclesiastically, his doctoral dissertation on the legal effects of antenuptial promises in mixed marriages attracted favorable attention. Before accepting the deanship of a school that had never prospered, however, he persuaded Corrigan not only to retain the school but to limit its enrollment "to one hundred carefully chosen students, who, by their scholastic records and character, [would] give promise not only of success as lawyers, but [of] real Catholic influence in public affairs."[61] He scoured the country both for talent and for the scholarship funds to attract and support the talent. The baccalaureate degree was made a prerequisite for admission for all, appropriate curricular changes were introduced, appellate competition was enhanced, a Religious Round Table of Law Students and Lawyers was organized, outstanding lecturers were invited to the school, and an annual Red Mass was inaugurated. White's departure for the United States Navy in 1942 and later the ill health that prompted his resignation in 1948 deprived the university of genuine leadership in legal education.[62]

Corrigan's main concern nevertheless was like that of the American bishops who knew that the Holy See was "most insistent on the fullest development of the Schools of Theology, Canon Law, and Philosophy."[63] The task in philosophy was perceived more as one of organization than of faculty recruitment. After frequent discussion in the board, a faculty of scholastic philosophy had been established in 1934, but, although Pace and others were insisting that all philosophy should be taught in the new school, Deferrari had been able to resist the separation of the department from the graduate school. Ryan had maintained the department for the laity and had limited enrollment in the new faculty to priests, sisters, and brothers.[64] It was not until 1936, therefore, after Corrigan's accession to office, that the present school of philosophy was organized with the Dominican Smith as its acting dean. Prelates found it no easier than before to understand how doctorates in philosophy could be conferred upon those in whose studies philosophy itself had had "little if any place,"[65] but some years later Smith, perhaps with excessive optimism, could report that his school "naturally" had more relations with other schools than theology and that philosophy had become "in fact, the center of the university."[66]

61. OR, White to Corrigan, June 26, 1937.

62. See Nuesse, *CULR*, XXXV, 66–69.

63. BT, mm, Apr. 29, 1937.

64. McNicholas Papers, Episcopal Visiting Committee, mm, Dec. 15, 1934, and Deferrari to O'Hara, Washington, Dec. 29, 1934.

65. *Ibid.*, memorandum of Bishop Gerald P. O'Hara, n.d. [1935].

66. *Ibid.*, "Visitation of the Pontifical Commission for the Sacred Sciences of the Catholic University, May 20 and May 21, 1944" (copy).

Turning to theology, Corrigan found on his first visit to Rome, perhaps unexpectedly, that he would have to give priority to seminary instruction. The university seminary at the time was open only to religious who were castigated by a future cardinal as "for the most part, neither prepared nor disposed to follow a Course which leads to Theological Degrees."[67] In so far as Roman and episcopal concern had to do with requirements for ecclesiastical degrees, the ecclesiastical interest was of course akin to that of a professional accrediting agency. But to the Roman congregation it appeared that the entire organizational pattern in theology was irregular. It saw three separate units, the school of sacred theology, the university seminary, and the independent Sulpician Seminary across from the campus. To the papal curia, "the most practical solution" seemed to be "to take over the Sulpician Seminary."[68] Its position had been developed, no doubt, on the basis of opinions expressed in communications between the apostolic delegate, the chairman of the episcopal visiting committee, and the rector.[69] Cöln had proposed something like this at the beginning of the Ryan administration,[70] and Ryan had noted with concern that the diocesan students of the Sulpicians, who had formerly enrolled in numbers in the school of philosophy (not necessarily for courses in philosophy itself), were being enabled to earn the licentiate in theology from the seminary.[71] But the action that was being advised in Rome was drastic indeed.

Naturally, it could not be accomplished easily. Eventually, in what Corrigan felt was still "going to look very much like an unfriendly move" on his part, Pope Pius XI instructed Cardinal Bisleti as prefect of the sacred congregation of seminaries and universities to communicate the curial decision to the superior general of the Sulpicians, Cardinal Jean Verdier, archbishop of Paris.[72] The American provincial superior was believed to consider the order to be "a great blow to Sulpician prestige."[73] Since the Sulpician Fathers were retaining possession of the seminary property and were remaining in charge of the discipline of the house

67. *Ibid.*, "Statement of Monsignor Mooney, Archbishop-Bishop of Rochester," n.d. [1935–36].

68. *Ibid.*, Corrigan to McNicholas, Rome, Jan. 30, 1937.

69. AACi, Cicognani to McNicholas, Washington, Feb. 17 and 20, 1937, and McNicholas to Cicognani, Cincinnati, Feb. 23, 1937 (copy), indicate both the participation of Corrigan and the exclusion of Curley and John Fenlon, S.S., the provincial of the Sulpicions.

70. AACi, Cöln Papers, Cöln to Pace, Oct. 28, 1928 (copy).

71. AR (1928–29), 45.

72. *Ibid.*, Corrigan to McNicholas, Rome, Mar. 23, 1937.

73. AAB, Archepiscopal Diary, Sept. 1, 1937.

and the spiritual direction of the seminarians, agreements upon financial arrangements had to be made. Thus, although seminarians in the first year of theology began to attend classes on the campus in 1937, the first decennial agreement between the university and the Society of St. Sulpice was not signed until 1940.[74]

Another problem of seminary instruction with which Corrigan had to deal during his first visit to Rome concerned the affiliation of seminaries that were not part of the university. This had been a problem since the beginning of the institution. Corrigan reported that "after long explaining" he thought that he had succeeded in obtaining approval from the curial congregation for a proposal. This was to extend to seminaries the system of affiliation for high schools and colleges that Deferrari was reviving and to allow seminarians to transfer to the university no later than the beginning of their fourth year of theological study in order to become candidates for the licentiate from the university. The congregation apparently saw in the proposal an opportunity to promote unity in theological programs throughout the country.[75]

Nothing of course could be accomplished by fiat in the all-important task of recruiting scholars for the ecclesiastical faculties. Corrigan was told in Rome that Artur Landgraf of the Philosophische-Theologische Hochschule of Bamberg was considered to be "one of the two best dogmaticians in the world" and might be available for appointment.[76] Landgraf had known the university as a visiting professor during 1929–30 and accepted the position of professor of dogmatic theology and patrology when it was proferred, but after serving from 1937 to 1939 he returned to Germany and later became an auxiliary bishop of Bamberg. In 1938, however, there was added from the University of Münster a patrologist, Johannes Quasten, whose work was to gain international recognition. His influence was illustrated particularly in two series that he edited, one entitled "Ancient Christian Writers" and the other, consisting mostly of dissertations that he directed, "Studies in Christian Antiquity." Quasten served as a dean for two terms (1945–49). After his retirement in 1970, his services were retained in an adjunct capacity until he returned to Germany in 1979. Also in 1938, there was appointed Pascal P. Parente of the diocese of Trenton, a former Salvatorian who served as a professor of dogmatic and ascetical theology and briefly as a dean before his retirement in 1960.

74. BT, mm, Apr. 3, 1940. The congregation approved the agreement on July 1, 1940.
75. BT, mm, Apr. 29, 1937.
76. BT, mm, Apr. 26, 1938.

Two other appointments made by Corrigan were responsible for a "conservative" stamp that the school of theology was to bear for two decades or more. Joseph Clifford Fenton, of the diocese of Springfield, Massachusetts, who had taught previously at St. Ambrose College in Iowa and at the St. Bernard's Seminary that Bishop McQuaid had founded in Rochester, was appointed to the department of religious education in 1938 but transferred a year later to teach dogmatic theology. As a teacher and editor of the *American Ecclesiastical Review*, he became well known for his rejection of Newman's concept of the development of doctrine, for an extension to virtually all possible lengths of obligations that might be based upon papal encyclicals, and especially for his defense against John Courtney Murray, S.J., of the union of church and state as settled Catholic doctrine. He counted Cardinal Ottaviani as his influential friend in Rome. Fenton served as administrator of the school when John A. Ryan retired from the faculty and the deanship in 1940 and Corrigan chose to hold the reins himself. Upon Corrigan's death McCormick appointed him as the professor in charge and then as dean from 1943 until 1945. Ecclesiastical honors were given to him by his investiture as a domestic prelate in 1954 and as a protonotary apostolic in 1963. In the next year, after a severe heart attack, he resigned from the faculty to become a pastor in his diocese.

Both Fenton and Francis J. Connell, C.Ss.R., who was appointed as a moral theologian in 1940, were to find Vatican Council II almost beyond bearing. Although Connell was milder, far more kindly, and certainly more congenial than Fenton, his readiness to advance a formula for the solution of almost any real or speculative problem became all too evident. Both Connell and Fenton, as well as others in the faculty, encountered difficulties in obtaining advancement in professorial rank. Connell argued that any theological articles or pamphlets which would help the clergy and laity "to acquire a clearer and a deeper knowledge of the Catholic faith and to practice it more fervently" should be considered "scientific in the most correct sense of the term and quite worthy of the attention and the effort of a University professor."[77] After serving as dean of the faculty from 1949 until his retirement in 1958, he succeeded Ignatius Smith as dean of religious communities until his own death in 1967. (No further appointments to the office were made.)

Although changes in faculty personnel were not required in canon law, in which the inauguration in 1941 of *The Jurist* was a particularly

77. AAB, Nelligan Papers, Connell to Curley, Washington, Jan. 12, 1945. Curley's reply, Baltimore, Jan. 15, 1945 (copy), was in accord.

noteworthy development, the university received another outstanding German scholar when Stephan Kuttner was appointed to the school. He had emigrated from Germany in 1933 and had been occupied with research and teaching in medieval canon law in Rome. In 1940, after the entry of Italy into World War II, Vatican authorities recommended his move to Washington. He remained until 1964, when he became the first T. Lawrason Riggs professor of Catholic studies at Yale University. He took with him to New Haven and later to Berkeley an Institute of Research and Studies in the History of Medieval Canon Law that he had established and for which he had secured a handsome endowment. In 1943, soon after his arrival, he had become a founder and coeditor of the journal *Traditio.* During the 1950s he was the recipient of honorary degrees from the universities of Bologna, Louvain, and Paris, and of the annual award of the American Council of Learned Societies.

What proved to be an unsettling administrative development, however, occurred also in 1940 with the appointment by the Roman congregation of Lardone, professor of Roman law, to the position of director of studies for the ecclesiastical schools. Ryan, believing that the faculty of theology either did not understand the provisions of *Deus Scientiarum Dominus* or was determined not to put them into effect, had once foreshadowed the appointment by proposing the appointment of a dean by the Holy See.[78] The duties of the new position were seemingly among those that had belonged previously to the vice rector and the latter reported that he was told by the new appointee that he had "no authority in the Schools of the Sacred Sciences."[79]

Lardone encountered particular difficulties in seeking to enforce a directive of McNicholas's commission "that major subjects must be taught in Latin in *every* [ecclesiastical] school, even in Philosophy."[80] The rector, seeking to assist implementation of the directive, proposed establishment of an "Institute of Latin Practice." The board approved the proposal pending a budgetary appropriation that was never made because the faculties, as reported, "met the adverse condition that ecclesiastical students who come to the University not only can not

78. OR, Ryan to Cicognani, Washington, Feb. 11, 1935 (copy).

79. McNicholas Papers, "Visitation of . . . May 20 and May 21, 1944," quoting Monsignor Edward B. Jordan. The latter held both positions of vice rector and director after Lardone was appointed apostolic nuncio to Haiti in 1950.

80. OR, confidential memorandum, Nov. 14, 1940. Corrigan had earlier (on Nov. 29, 1938) communicated to heads of departments the insistence of the sacred congregation of seminaries and universities "that Theology and, for Seminarians, Philosophy must be taught exclusively in Latin" and that any students "unable to follow such courses because of lack of proficiency in Latin" were to be made known to him.

express themselves in Latin, but they cannot understand it in class."[81]
Smith, as dean of the school of philosophy, told the pontifical commission later that Lardone did not "know the university set up," was
"meddlesome," and insisted "on nonsensical measures," such as teaching
all philosophy in Latin.[82]

The School of Social Science

Corrigan's perception of the need for social reconstruction made him
especially receptive to proposals for emphasis upon the social sciences in
the university's offerings. In the 1930s, when these fields were relatively
young and still regarded skeptically everywhere, their development was
a notable feature of university life. At the same time, there was in
Catholic circles internationally a search for methods of Catholic Action.
One model was being exemplified popularly by the Jocist movement in
Belgium and France. The rector of the Catholic University of the Sacred
Heart at Milan had devised a papally praised curriculum for "the training
of leading men for social life."[83] It was a sign of the times, then, that
soon after he assumed office Corrigan should receive first a telephone
call and then a memorandum from O'Grady, who was both dean of the
school of social work and executive director of the National Conference
of Catholic Charities. He proposed that the university "should clarify
its aims in the whole field of social science" and "should bring the
School of Social Work, and the Departments of Economics, Sociology,
and Political Science of the Graduate School together in a School of
Social Science."[84]

Characteristically, O'Grady had a prospective leader in mind. He was
Haas, a former student of John A. Ryan, who had acquired a national
reputation as a mediator of labor disputes. Haas was then rector of St.
Francis Seminary in Milwaukee, but had been the director of the National Catholic School of Social Service from 1931 to 1935. In 1930,
the faculty of sacred theology had recommended him for a position in
moral theology, but Ryan had refused to make the appointment because

81. *Ibid.*, memorandum for BT, Apr. 23, 1941.
82. McNicholas Papers, "Visitation of . . . May 20 and May 21, 1944." Pace, long
before, had contended that one reason ecclesiastics were not writing on philosophical
questions was because they were "not familiar with the vernacular" and that if it was
desired to maintain the impression that philosophy was only for priests "a very practical
means" would be "to keep philosophy sealed up in Latin so that it will be safe from contact
with the world at large, like our Theology and Canon Law." OR, "Comments of Monsignor
Pace," *op. cit.*
83. SSoS, Agostino Gemmelli, O.F.M., "An Outline of Organization of a University
School for the Training of Leading Men in Social Life," n.d.
84. O'Grady Papers, O'Grady to Corrigan, Washington, July 25, 1936 (copy).

the doctorate that Haas had earned was not in the field.[85] In O'Grady's opinion, which was probably accurate on the point, there had never been a Catholic that had had "as good contact with our Federal Government" as Haas. He was entitled to ask, "Do we not have sufficient vision and ingenuity to profit by his contact?"[86] Haas himself, upon requests from Corrigan, wrote three memoranda, in the first of which he stated a guiding aim: "The broad purpose of a School of Social Science at The Catholic University would be, perhaps within the next ten or fifteen years, to imbue American economic and political thinking with Catholic social philosophy." He added appropriately, "Admittedly, the task is great."[87]

Corrigan quoted these words and several paragraphs almost verbatim in his inaugural address, envisioning "over a period of time, a great School of Social Science." There was, he said, "a great need for Catholic citizens who are well equipped, both in the basic principles of social science and in the *de facto* knowledge of methods and institutions."[88] He wrote to McNicholas that an institute of apologetics in which the latter had a particular interest and the new school being founded "should quickly come to prove the University's best levers for its work for the Church in America."[89] A recently issued papal encyclical on atheistic communism, with its emphasis upon social reform, seemed to support his plan.[90] Later, after the school of social science had been inaugurated, more specific encouragement was given when in his apostolic letter on the university's golden jubilee year, Pius XI wrote that in the fulfillment of its "traditional mission of guarding the natural and supernatural heritage of man" the university had to, "because of the exigencies of the present age, give special attention to the sciences of civics, sociology and economics."[91]

There were, unexpectedly, two sets of problems that were revealed at the start. The first set had to be resolved almost immediately. Corrigan

85. AACi, Cöln Papers, statement of faculty of sacred theology, Oct. 10, 1930; also, Sheen, *op. cit.*, 45.

86. O'Grady Papers, O'Grady to Corrigan, *op. cit.* See Thomas E. Blantz, C.S.C., *A Priest in Public Service: Francis J. Haas and the New Deal* (Notre Dame: University of Notre Dame Press, 1982).

87. OR, "Suggestions for a School of Social Science at The Catholic University of America," Washington, July 25, 1936. The subsequent memoranda, sent from Milwaukee, are dated October 22 (outlining curricular proposals) and October 26.

88. OR, press release, Nov. 18, 1936.

89. McNicholas Papers, Corrigan to McNicholas, Rome, Mar. 23, 1937. See Sheen, *op. cit.*, 52–53, on the proposed institute.

90. *Divini Redemptoris, AAS,* XXIX (Mar. 31, 1937), 65–106 (in Latin); trans., Carlen, *op cit.*, 537–54.

91. *Sollemnia jubilaria, op. cit.*, 342.

had no choice but to back down when the American Association of
Social Service Workers, as it was known then, took the position that
the plan for the school would make the school of social work "a segment
within a curriculum that is directed towards academic objectives rather
than towards professional objectives" and therefore would prompt automatic cancellation of the provisional membership in the association
that O'Grady had obtained.[92] Noting that Corrigan had laid his plans
in Rome, Curley remarked acidly to a diocesan director of charities that
the congregation of seminaries and universities, "meaning thereby the
dead Cardinal Bisletti [sic] and Monsignor Ruffini have made a study of
our University to a point where they seem to know more about it than
some of us on this side."[93] Corrigan used the occasion of the attempted
merger of the National Catholic School of Social Service with the
school of social science to dismiss O'Grady from his position as dean.
O'Grady appealed the action to Rome but, learning that a compromise
was being sought, accepted a sabbatical leave and pledged his support
for a newly appointed dean, Thomas E. Mitchell, a priest of the diocese
of Richmond.[94]

The second problem, a departmentalized conception of the school of
social science that effectively limited what it might attempt within the
resources allowed to it, was foreshadowed at the outset. There was
powerful opposition that was to persist until the school's eventual dissolution, in 1961, especially from Deferrari, who at first was still dean of
the graduate school, and from Campbell. The academic senate was not
consulted, apparently because it had to be reconstituted to conform to
the university's new statutes and was not called to meet until November.
Within the month before the school opened, there was still indecision
about the inclusion in it of the department of sociology.[95] O'Grady
feared, even after the opening, that nothing more than a change of the
name of his own school and the addition of some courses was being

92. OR, Corrigan to Margaret S. Lehle, Washington, Sept. 30, 1937 (copy of telegram); O'Grady Papers, Marion Hathaway to O'Grady, Pittsburgh, Oct. 7, 1937 (copy);
BT, mm, Nov. 16, 1937, exh.

93. AAB, Curley Papers, O 576, Curley to Thomas J. O'Dwyer, Baltimore, Sept. 15,
1937 (copy).

94. BT, mm, Oct. 11, 1938. See O'Grady Papers for O'Grady's extensive correspondence with his Roman representatives. Testimony of O'Grady's long-standing antipathy
to the National Catholic School of Social Service can be found in AAB, Curley Papers,
M 1878, T. V. Moore to Curley, Washington, June 19, 1934, enclosing a copy of M 1879,
Moore to O'Grady, of the same date, and in McNicholas Papers, Kerby to McNicholas,
Washington, Mar. 10, 1935.

95. SSoS, handwritten notes of Haas after conference with Deferrari, Sept. 7, 1937;
Deferrari to Haas, Washington, Sept. 8, 1937; also, Furfey to Deferrari, Aug. 10, 1937
(copy).

The celebration of the Sesquicentennial of the Constitution of the United States, bringing together (from left to right) Monsignor Patrick J. McCormick, vice rector; the Honorable Michael MacWhite, minister of the Irish Free State; Mrs. MacWhite; Monsignor Joseph M. Corrigan, rector; the Honorable Sol Bloom, member of Congress from New York, chairman of the national commission; and the Honorable Witold Wankowicz, counselor of the Polish embassy.

announced.[96] He was registering students in one office, Haas in another. "Nobody on campus," he complained, "could understand what the School of Social Science was going to do."[97] About six weeks later, the trustees approved the transfer of the departments of economics, politics, and sociology to the newly established school.[98]

Two effects of the establishment of the school were almost immediately visible. One was a thrust for attention to industrial relations that was attributable to the presence of Haas himself. Disliking administrative detail, he was inclined to leave it mostly to others. As head of the department of economics, he was able to bring to the campus to offer courses lecturers, prominent New Dealers among them, whom he had come to know during industrial disputes. He organized several institutes on specialized problems. Perhaps most importantly, he conducted a Sunday morning seminar in which he reviewed his mediatory activities

96. O'Grady Papers, memorandum, Oct. 1, 1937.
97. *Ibid.*, memorandum to Giovanni Battista Nicola, Washington, Oct. 5, 1937.
98. BT, mm, Nov. 18, 1937; SSoS, Corrigan to Haas, Nov. 22, 1937.

of the previous week—in an Allis-Chalmers strike, for example—and unfailingly presented in conclusion his application of the teaching of *Quadragesimo anno* to the resolution of the conflict.[99] The accent on labor economics brought many young priests to the school for graduate study. Some of them became "labor priests" in their home dioceses. One who became a national figure as a successor of John A. Ryan at the National Catholic Welfare Conference has recalled the campus of the time as "an exciting place to be for anyone interested in labor-management relations."[100]

With the entry of the United States into World War II, Haas was appointed by President Roosevelt, in 1943, to be the first director of the federal Fair Employment Practices Commission. Within a short time, in the same year, he was named bishop of Grand Rapids. Paul J. FitzPatrick, who had assisted him administratively, became head of the department of economics and remained "in charge" of the school until the appointment of C. Joseph Nuesse as dean in 1952. Beginning in 1941, however, the emphasis upon Catholic social teaching had found expression in an Institute of Catholic Social Studies, directed by John F. Cronin, S.S., that Corrigan had inaugurated as "a permanent feature of our Summer Session."[101] The school later maintained interdepartmental programs in Catholic social thought, which had received systematic emphasis in the department of sociology, and, briefly, in mission studies.

Sources of Renewal in Scholarship

When Corrigan came to the university, it had "first class men" by Ryan's rigorous definition in eight or ten departments outside the ecclesiastical schools. Several, among them Guilday, Hyvernat, Moore, and John A. Ryan, were nearing retirement. Others, Johnson and Purcell in particular, were to be lost by premature deaths. But, as the American Council of Education's survey of 1934 had shown, there was evidence of scholarly attainment or promise of it in various fields. Probably no one could have foreseen, however, that there would be, during the transition from the 1930s to the 1940s, a more or less simultaneous influx of outstanding scholars from four distinct sources. First, there were two eminent scientists recruited by the chancellor who, despite

99. See Francis J. Haas, *Man and Society* (2nd ed.; New York: Appleton-Century-Crofts, 1952), chaps. XIII–XIV.

100. George G. Higgins, *America*, CXLVII (Nov. 13, 1982), 294, reviewing Blantz, *op. cit.*

101. OR, Corrigan to Ordinaries, Washington, Apr. 16, 1941. See also, Deferrari to Corrigan, Aug. 2, 1940, and Roy J. Deferrari and John F. Cronin, "Institute of Social Studies Inaugurated," *CUB*, N.S., VIII, No. 4 (May, 1941), 4.

the blow that he had suffered in Ryan's removal, not only did not surrender but instead intensified his efforts in the university's cause. Second, the university benefited, as did many American institutions, from the immigration to the United States of German scholars who were seeking refuge from the Hitler regime. Third, the long-standing unwillingness of the Society of Jesus to allow any of its members to join the university faculties was finally overcome. Fourth, there was success in recruiting young American scholars who would strengthen academic programs.

The professors whom Curley recruited, Karl F. Herzfeld and Francis Owen Rice, were active participants in the Charles Carroll Club at The Johns Hopkins University in Baltimore and were influenced in some degree by the Benedictines of St. Anselm's Priory in Washington.[102] Herzfeld, of Viennese birth, was known internationally as a theoretical physicist. He had been at Hopkins since 1926, had given the commencement address to The Catholic University of America graduates in 1934, and had an offer to join the faculty of Princeton University. But when Shea retired in 1936, Curley recommended "very strongly" that Herzfeld should be appointed to head the department of physics. The trustees, despite the financial exigencies that were prompting them to deny all other appointments and promotions for the year, "decided not to lose this opportunity of obtaining the services of a distinguished scientist."[103] Years later, in 1960, a rector who was invited to present to Herzfeld the annual outstanding achievement award of the Washington Academy of Science could point to his "happy integration of deep religious faith and sacrificial devotion to science and scientific investigation."[104] In the same year, Herzfeld was elected to the National Academy of Sciences and received the Gibbons medal of the university's alumni association. What he accomplished in his department was illustrated by its representation in a meeting of the American Physical Society in 1952 to which six papers were contributed by colleagues or students.[105] He retired as head of the department in 1961 but by special action of the trustees was able to continue in service until 1968. Even after this date, as a professor emeritus, he remained active in an adjunct role until his death in 1978.

102. AAB, Curley Papers, H 866, Curley to Herzfeld, Baltimore, Apr. 27, 1936 (copy).

103. BT, EC, mm, Mar. 25, 1936. Corrigan later told the trustees that Herzfeld was "being mentioned as a Pontifical Academician." BT, mm, Apr. 26, 1938. A historical perspective is suggested by Daniel J. Kevles, *The Physicists: The History of a Scientific Community in Modern America* (New York: Alfred A. Knopf, 1978), 207–10.

104. OVR, William J. McDonald, typescript. See Herzfeld's own statement, *op. cit.*

105. *Ibid.*, Herzfeld to McCormick, May 26, 1952.

Herzfeld was followed to the campus by Rice, who had been at Hopkins since 1924. Before yielding to Curley's arguments, Rice outlined what would be needed in the department of chemistry that he was to head and he did the same for his prospective dean.[106] A year or so later, the dean could report that chemistry had been reorganized and could be considered "a first-class department."[107] Upon his retirement, in 1959, Rice himself felt "without exaggeration that the Chemistry Department is among the strongest in the country." He revealed both his personal zeal and his theological underpinnings in affirming that he regarded himself "as a member of the Lay Apostolate and would not want to make any decision that would adversely affect whatever work [he] could do in the time that is left."[108] He continued his research, first at Georgetown and then at Notre Dame. Curley, it should be said, never hesitated to reach into his own "education-charity account" for funds to assist Rice substantially (and, to a lesser extent, some other departments).

The German scholars, at least at first, could not have found the university an especially hospitable place. Its principal layman in academic administration was advising the rector that "foreign professors" would not "take hold and carry their share of the burden as regular members of the staff."[109] Efforts to place German Catholic scholars were being made by interested individuals, such as Constantine McGuire, and by agencies such as the Committee for Catholic Refugees from Germany that the American bishops had organized. Several academicians were given brief appointments on the campus before they accepted positions in other institutions, among them Ernst Stein, who had been a professor of Byzantine history at Berlin and was a visiting professor during 1934–35, and Goetz Briefs, formerly a professor of political economy at the Technische Hochschule in Berlin, who was a visiting professor of social economics in the school of social work from 1934 to 1937. Both Briefs and Stein received partial support from the Rockefeller Foundation, to which Corrigan reported that they had been "difficult subjects."[110] Ferdinand Hermens, who had a special interest in propor-

106. AAB, Nelligan Papers, "Considerations relating to scientific education with special reference to the Chemistry Department of the Catholic University," Mar. 28, 1938; OVR, Rice to McGuire, Baltimore, June 11, 1938.

107. OR, McGuire to Corrigan, Nov. 6, 1939.

108. OVR, Rice to McDonald, Feb. 4 and Mar. 5, 1959. Corrigan had described Rice as a "notable Catholic and internationally known for his work in chemistry." BT, mm, Apr. 26, 1938.

109. OR, Deferrari to Corrigan, Dec. 12, 1938.

110. *Ibid.*, Corrigan to Raymond B. Fosdick, Washington, Nov. 20, 1939 (copy).

tional representation, was a member of the department of economics from 1936 to 1938.

Five other Germans remained who, in the recollection of a commencement speaker four decades or more after their arrival, made basic contributions "to augment the University's scholarly reach and to redefine for the entire American community the scope and the centrality of crucial disciplines."[111] Two were Quasten and Kuttner. Another who came in 1938, Rudolph Allers, was one of four laymen who would have been considered by the Nazi regime racially tainted. Allers had been a student of Emil Kraepelin while gaining clinical experience after he had earned his medical degree at the University of Vienna, where from 1919 until 1938 he was head of the department of medical psychology. Although he was a brain surgeon during World War I, he was drawn more and more into psychiatry, in which his Adlerian position was modified and integrated into a Thomistic framework. Perhaps *The Psychology of Character* (trans. E. B. Strauss; London: Sheed & Ward, 1931) was his best-known work. He was a professor of the school of philosophy until he retired in 1948, after which he continued to teach at Georgetown University, where he died in 1963.[112]

Helmut A. Hatzfeld had been suspended from his professorial duties at the University of Heidelberg by the Nazis in 1935, and had fled to Louvain, where he had taught during the academic year 1939–40, and then from Belgium to the United States. He began as a visiting professor of romance languages in 1940, having already earned an international reputation in stylistics, and eventually, like Herzfeld, had his service extended by special action of the trustees until 1967, but remained in close association with his colleagues until his death in 1979. *Literature Through Art* (New York: Oxford University Press, 1952) became the most widely circulated work of his numerous publications.

Friedrich Engel-Janosi, Viennese by birth and education, also dismissed by the Nazis, had been a professor at the University of Vienna and had held visiting appointments at the universities of Rome and Cambridge before coming to the United States as a research associate at Johns Hopkins. He became a lecturer in the department of history in 1941, a visiting professor the next year, and then held a regular professorial appointment until his retirement in 1959. He returned to the University of Vienna and died there in 1978. Nineteenth-century

111. Elizabeth T. Kennan, May 11, 1985, AB, XVIII, No. 1 (Sept., 1985), 14.
112. See James Collins, "The Work of Rudolph Allers," NS, XXXVIII (July, 1964), 281–309, reprinted in Jesse Mann (ed.), *The Philosophical Work of Rudolph Allers: A Selection* (Washington, D.C.: Georgetown University, 1965), 1–19.

Austrian history, especially in relation to the papacy, was the principal field of his research, but his teaching probed modern intellectual developments in notable depth and subtlety.

It was in 1940 that the first Jesuit professor, Wilfrid Parsons, was appointed. In view of the history of Jesuit opposition to the founding of the university and the continuing disaffection that had been manifest, this was a milestone of progress. There had not been even a Jesuit student on the rolls until 1929, although at the very beginning of the century Pace had urged that quiet approaches to superiors should be made to "get just one of the S.J. younger men to take a course at the University."[113] Shahan had sought without result to persuade the superior of the New York province to allow one of his "distinguished men" to join the faculty, even temporarily, and thus to "help in a remarkable way the general interests of Catholicism in the United States."[114] Later, the Jesuit leader who had been associated with Pace and Shahan in the *Catholic Encyclopedia* project attempted to help confidentially, surmising that if all would go well a "hall" for Jesuit students would be established.[115] A confrere in Rome prepared the way for a favorable reception by the Jesuit father general of Archbishop Curley, and Wynne himself advised Curley on approaches to the provincial that might bring Jesuit students to the university.[116] Meanwhile, however, reports of faculty conflicts had caused at least one previously sympathetic Jesuit to wonder if the campus could be regarded as "a fit place" for young religious.[117]

A break had come early in the Ryan administration when a Detroit Jesuit, Louis G. Weitzman, enrolled as a graduate student in sociology.[118] Joseph F. Thorning, who in later years left the Society and became incardinated in the archdiocese of Baltimore, followed soon after. Both received doctorates in 1931. The president of the University of Detroit at the same time reported that consultors of the Missouri province "had been talking quite a bit about C.U. and felt that the Jesuits should cooperate and support it."[119] This confirmed earlier praise of a Detroit alumnus of The Catholic University of America by the

113. OR, Pace to Conaty, Starke, Fla., May 1, 1900.

114. OR, Shahan to Joseph F. Henselman, S.J., Washington, July 13, 1910. See also, Deferrari, *Laymen*, 102–3.

115. Pace Papers, John J. Wynne, S.J., to Pace, New York, Jan. 1, 1921.

116. AAB, Curley Papers, T 814, William Turner, S.J., to Curley, Rome, May 29, 1922; W 1121, Wynne to Curley, New York, Jan. 9, 1923; P 664, Curley to E. C. Phillips, S.J., Baltimore, June 18, 1934 (copy).

117. *Ibid.*, W 482, Louis J. Weber, S.J., to Shahan, n.p., Feb. 27, 1923 (copy).

118. *Ibid.*, R 1450, Ryan to Curley, Washington, May 13, 1929.

119. OR, J. M. Fox to Ryan, Detroit, Aug. 8, 1931.

Detroit president for the success that was being attributed to him "in the matter of unification"; this was portrayed as sealed by "the support of the Father General of the Jesuit Order expressed to the Jesuits of America to stand behind the Catholic University."[120]

Attempts to obtain a Jesuit for the faculty had been made early in 1930 when, upon the recommendation of the famed moralist, Arthur Vermeersch, S.J., after an inquiry to C. B. Moulinier, S.J., at the University of Detroit, and with Weitzman to some degree as an intermediary, Ryan sought to secure the services of T. Lincoln Bouscaren, S.J.[121] A few years later, after some prodding from his assistant, Ryan enlisted the help of Curley in an attempt to secure Thorning's services for the new school of social work, but was again unsuccessful.[122] Curley had expressed hope in spite of his earlier warning to Ryan that religious would be "interested primarily in themselves and their Community."[123]

When Corrigan laid plans for the university's celebration of the sesquicentennial of the United States Constitution in 1937, in cooperation with a national committee of which Representative Sol Bloom was chairman, he included in his committee on the project Fathers Wilfrid Parsons and Edmund Walsh of Georgetown.[124] Parsons, who had been an editor of *America,* was dean of the graduate school; Walsh was a widely known dean of the school of foreign service. It was soon thereafter that, when the Jesuit provincials communicated to the father general what they were perceiving as a "strained relationship" with the American bishops "arising from the alleged position of Catholic University," they were surprised to be advised that "since Catholic University enjoyed the prerogatives of a papal university, it had a pre-eminence that the Society should recognize" by continuing to send students and to assign professors upon request.[125] Although the first attempt to recruit Parsons for the new school of social science upon the retirement of John A. Ryan was unsuccessful, success was obtained in the next year. Parsons, whose appointment as a professor of sociology and politics became effective in the fall of 1940, became the first Jesuit member of a faculty. He became also the first superior of Carroll House, a residence for Jesuit students.[126]

120. *Ibid.*, Louis Brivard, S.J., to McManus, memorandum, Mar. 30, 1930.

121. *Ibid.*, Moulinier to Ryan, Detroit, Jan. 30, 1930; Weitzman to Ryan, Ridge, Md., May 26, 1930.

122. *Ibid.*, Sheehy to Ryan, Jan. 31, Mar. 24, and n.d., 1934; AAB, Curley Papers, R 1745, Ryan to Curley, June 15, 1934; P 664, Curley to Phillips, Baltimore, June 18, 1934 (copy).

123. AAB, Curley Papers, R 1676, Curley to Ryan, Baltimore, Apr. 7, 1933 (copy).

124. OR, program for Dec. 7, 1937.

125. Fitzgerald, *op. cit.*, 60.

126. Henri J. Wiesel, S.J., "Carroll House," *WL*, LXXX (1951), 45–49. A Father Kurt Patterson, S.J., had taught during the 1938 summer session.

Undoubtedly the ability of the university to attract outstanding scholars during these years was owed to its singular status as the national pontifical university and to its recognition as the leading—and at the time the only really broadly comprehensive—graduate school under Catholic auspices. Its power of attraction was felt by young lay Catholics trained in the United States as well as by ecclesiastics and scholars of foreign origin. All were, of course, conscious of membership in a Catholic academic world that was still more sharply defined in the 1940s than it has been since. Their consciousness was heightened by prevailing prejudices and by the virtual exclusion of Catholics from some fields at state or non-Catholic private institutions. But there were also Catholics who had attained standing in their fields outside the Catholic orbit who deliberately, sometimes at appreciable personal sacrifice, chose to offer their services to a church institution.

McGuire proved to be particularly adept in encouraging the recruitment of young talent. In some cases, he could depend upon outstanding professors to train successors. In anthropology, for example, Cooper was preparing his student, Regina Flannery Herzfeld, to assume the headship of the department after his death and the death of Connolly. Sometimes heads of departments could be encouraged to rebuild strength, as Cain did in English in recommending for appointment J. Kerby Neill, a son of the university's first appointee in economics; Giovanni Giovannini, a specialist in American literature; and J. Craig La Driere, who had been a member of the Society of Fellows at Harvard and who was to return there in 1964 to become chairman of the department of comparative literature. The influence of La Driere gave the department a cohesive Aristotelian-Thomistic orientation that marked it as unique in its region. In still other instances, resources that had been acquired were made more available than they had been, as in the appointment of Manoel Cardozo to be curator of the Lima Library as well as a member of the department of history.

The standards that were being employed in these appointments and that were subsequently developed and refined—sometimes, it may be, with excessive rigidity—were given permanency and force by their embodiment in the statutes of 1937 and in enactments of the academic senate. Although Ryan had been by no means inactive in faculty recruitment, he had renewed the role of the academic senate in this and other matters. The statutes of 1937 required the rector to have the consent of the faculty and the senate for appointments to the highest rank, the only one to which permanency of tenure was then attached. Departments thereafter had clear responsibility for faculty recruitment but their recommendations were subject to scrutiny by the faculty at large and its committee, and, when senior rank was involved, by a university-wide committee and the senate as well. The standards of evaluation that had first been given written form in 1932 were thus made progressively more comprehensive and precise.

The Transition in Financial Management

The momentum that the Ryan administration had given to the academic community could be maintained by decanal and departmental decisions in the development of the faculties in accord with the provisions of the statutes of 1937. Financial policies, on the other hand, had to be determined more directly by the trustees and the chief executive, the rector. Curley, not very long after learning of Corrigan's appointment, reminded the university's auditing firm that its work was "always to be sufficiently searching" to enable the university to retain "an unqualified certificate."[127] Also, he recommended for election to the board his own trusted financial advisor, William L. Galvin, who was chairman of the board of the Commonwealth Bank in Baltimore and a member of the Maryland bar.[128] Galvin was soon elected treasurer of the university and in this capacity attended diligently not only meetings of the trustees but weekly meetings of an administration and budget committee that became a central feature of university government during the early 1940s.

The effective and able business officer for many years had been J. Harvey Cain, whom the board had elected assistant treasurer and assistant secretary.[129] He could boast that his father, who had died in 1925, had, as auditor, "served the university before the first building was erected" and that his grandfather had "provided the lunches and banquets when the Bishops first met to discuss with prominent people the plans for the university."[130] Apparently Cain was always ready to express his opinion on any aspect of university life that came to his attention. He had, in consequence, earned enmities on campus. Curley, whose language was especially colorful, regarded Cain as an "animated tombstone" and felt that he had "altogether too much power."[131] Probably it was true, as Cain alleged, "that not one single word of complaint" had

---

127. AAB, Curley Papers, H 437, Curley to Haskins and Sells, Baltimore, June 9, 1936 (copy).

128. *Ibid.*, H 294, Curley to O. P. H. Johnson, Baltimore, Dec. 14, 1936 (copy).

129. BT, mm, Nov. 11, 1930.

130. OR, Cain to Cardinal William O'Connell, Washington, Nov. 11, 1937 (copy).

131. AAB, Curley Papers, R 1632, Curley to Ryan, Baltimore, Mar. 19, 1932 (copy); H 293, Curley to O. P. H. Johnson, Baltimore, Dec. 12, 1935 (copy).

ever been made to him by a university officer "about mismanagement in the business departments,"[132] but Corrigan dismissed him on May 1, 1937, on the ground that, according to the new statutes, it was necessary to appoint a priest to the position of procurator and that the university could not afford to retain his services as well.

Corrigan brought to the campus a Philadelphia priest, Joseph N. La Rue, to replace as procurator Monsignor David O'Dwyer, who had come to the university from Denver in 1927 to undertake what later became known as development. La Rue was instructed to "to make a complete survey of the material resources of the university" and to "investigate the management, personnel and methods of the business department."[133] La Rue's administration came under attack, in turn, especially, it would seem, from Galvin.[134] His resignation was accepted and Monsignor James A. Magner's appointment as procurator, assistant treasurer, and assistant secretary was approved by the trustees at the beginning of the academic year 1940–41.[135] Within a month, a recently appointed new archbishop of New York, Francis J. Spellman, was remarking that Magner was giving "evidence of a very high type of priestly and scholarly knowledge of what is going on."[136]

The university's financial situation during Corrigan's years changed but little. Its endowment of $3,672,676 in 1938 was the lowest of any member of the Association of American Universities, less than 3 per cent of that of Harvard at the time. It could be claimed, of course, that the $334,392 received from the diocesan collection was the equivalent of substantial endowment income. It was, in 1938, more than 27 per cent of the university's total income. About 40 per cent of the income, a little larger proportion than during Shahan's last year, but a smaller proportion than earlier in the 1930s, was being derived from student tuition and fees. When Corrigan began his financial appeals, a well-meaning provincial superior wrote that the "financial conditions" that he was revealing were "a rebuke to our Catholics who have been blessed with plenty."[137] One clerical trustee took "fleeting pleasure" in remarking, "If we were only as orthodox financially as the Jews, Episcopalians, Methodists and others, the Holy Father would pro rate the amount

132. *Ibid.*, C 66, Cain to Curley, Washington, Nov. 12, 1937.
133. OR, Corrigan to Curley, Washington, Oct. 23, 1936, with draft of letter to LaRue.
134. OR, Galvin to Corrigan, Washington, Sept. 6, 1940; Corrigan to Galvin, Washington, Sept. 16, 1940 (copy).
135. BT, EC, mm, Sept. 25, 1940.
136. *Ibid.*, Oct. 25, 1940.
137. OR, I. Lissner to Corrigan, Tenafly, N.J., Mar. 7, 1939.

James A. Magner (b. 1901), procurator, with Frank Biberstein (1900–1969), at the time head of the department of civil engineering.

needed for the University to each diocese in the country without a moment's hesitation."[138]

Although appeals had been made to foundations in earlier years, it could be said that the beginnings of the "grantsmanship" that was to become increasingly important in university finances were made during the Corrigan years. Moore obtained from the Rockefeller Foundation a grant of $85,000 to support teaching and research in psychiatry and child guidance from 1939 to 1943. World War II brought nursing into the limelight. Enrollment in the school increased dramatically. About $47,000 in federal funds was obtained for scholarships for students and small grants for the same purpose were received from Robert W. Johnson and the Kellogg Foundation. A federal grant for construction was soon to follow.

To raise funds, largely to retire the indebtedness of the university, including what had been borrowed from its own endowment fund during

138. *Ibid.*, Joseph F. Smith to Corrigan, Cleveland, Nov. 3, 1938.

Shahan's time, the trustees established in 1938 a Jubilee Fund. By the spring of 1940, returns approached only about one-half the goal.[139] Although contributions from some dioceses were notable, it was true that in others "the drive did not arouse much interest."[140] To the chagrin of Galvin, who moved immediately to prevent repetition of what had taken place, an operating deficit of $130,577 for the fiscal year 1939–40 was covered from the new fund.[141] After the repayment of other debts, the university borrowed $575,000 to restore what had been borrowed from its own endowment fund.[142]

Eventually, frustrated by budgets "put together in twenty-four hours,"[143] and finding that Corrigan was relying only upon "the Bishops' duty to supply the money," Curley wrote to Spellman that he regarded "the whole situation as absolutely hopeless" and could think of "only one solution and that is the elimination of the Rector either by means of self-elimination or a demand elimination."[144] To Corrigan's episcopal sponsor Curley wrote at the same time, with exasperation, "The Rector will not work, and I might add with all charity, that he cannot work." In reply he received only the "troubled" concern of one "brought face to face with friends who have serious differences."[145] Corrigan's death, only a few months later, changed the situation.

Student Life

An important change affecting the composition of the student body and, even more, the image of the Catholicity of the university occurred at the very beginning of the Corrigan administration. Ryan had maintained the policy of excluding Negro students that had become effective, without any clear documentation as to its origins, during the Shahan years. To the apostolic delegate Ryan had explained that although the university had begun to enroll "colored sisters" in 1932, the executive committee of the board had not made further exceptions and, hoping that the situation would change "at some later date," had voted "not to receive colored students, due to the peculiar conditions existing in

139. BT, mm, Apr. 3, 1940, exh.

140. James Michael Reardon, *The Catholic Church in the Diocese of St. Paul* (St. Paul: North Central Publishing, 1952), 540. The St. Paul quota was set at $150,000; $66,836.99 was subscribed.

141. OR, Galvin to Trustees, Washington, Nov. 8, 1940; BT, mm, Nov. 12, 1940.

142. BT, EC, mm, June 16, 1941.

143. OR, Galvin to Curley, Baltimore, June 13, 1941 (copy).

144. AAB, Curley Papers, N 1947, Curley to Spellman, Baltimore, Mar. 31, 1942 (copy).

145. McNicholas Papers, Curley to McNicholas, Baltimore, Mar. 30, 1942; McNicholas to Curley, Cincinnati, Apr. 11, 1942 (copy).

Washington."[146] Even when Mother Katharine Drexel, daughter of an appointee to the original university committee and foundress of the Sisters of the Blessed Sacrament, had complained against the university's policy, and Curley had reminded the board that no statutory exclusion, but only an action of the executive committee, was involved, the board had felt that "under present conditions" it was "not in a position to make any change in the practice of the University."[147] But when Corrigan followed the suggestion of the vice rector, McCormick, that he should confer with the chancellor before admitting a Negro applicant to the school of nursing,[148] he found that, as he wrote for his file, "the Archbishop said he has no objection; he approves of it."[149]

Word of the change of policy attracted comments both pro and con. Corrigan refused to make statements to the press and resented the "very unwise exploitation of every statement issuing from the University,"[150] but requested daily reports from the registrar on the number of Negroes enrolling during registration periods. There were thoughts at first of limiting their admission to graduate students and to those who were Catholic.[151] Within two years, in view of the international situation, the Holy See, citing the Christmas address of Pope Pius XI in 1937, called upon Catholic institutions "to reject validly and learnedly the absurd dogmas" of racism, eight of which were listed.[152] The university commissioned and published two books on the subject.[153] In May of 1939, the registrar was reporting that forty Negroes had been enrolled, thirty-one of them in the graduate school of arts and sciences. That fall, at the special convocation concluding the golden jubilee celebrations of the university, Mother Katharine Drexel became the first woman to receive an honorary degree from the university. It was not until about 1950, however, that integration of nonacademic aspects of student life was completed.

Another administrative change foreshadowed the expansion of what

146. OR, Ryan to Cicognani, Nov. 19, 1934 (copy).
147. BT, mm, May 1, 1935.
148. OR, McCormick to Corrigan, June 19, 1936.
149. *Ibid.*, memorandum, Aug. 28, 1936.
150. *Ibid.*, Corrigan to Edward C. Kramer, Director General, Catholic Board for Mission Work among Colored People, Washington, June 9, 1938 (copy).
151. *Ibid.*, Corrigan to W. F. Cleary, C.Ss.P., Washington, Apr. 8, 1938 (copy); Deferrari to Corrigan, Apr. 18, 1938.
152. *Ibid.*, Ruffini to Universities and Catholic Faculties, Rome, May 27, 1938, and read, AS, mm, Sept. 29, 1938.
153. H. S. Jennings *et al.*, *Scientific Aspects of the Race Problem* (Washington, D.C.: The Catholic University of America Press, 1941), and Joseph T. Delos, O.P., *et al.*, *Race: Person: Nation: Social Aspects of the Race Problem, A Symposium* (New York: Barnes & Noble, 1944).

are now called "student personnel services." The university had long had its dean of men, always a priest. But by 1936 there were not only women graduate students but women undergraduates in the Catholic Sisters College, the summer sessions, the school of law after 1928, and in nursing, beginning in 1932. As early as 1940, at Deferrari's urging, Eugenie Andruss Leonard, then with the United States Office of Education, was appointed to the department of education and to a new part-time position as the university's first dean of women. The position was made full-time at the beginning of 1942.[154] Curley clipped the issue of the *Tower* announcing the appointment and wrote in the margin in capital letters, for Corrigan's benefit, "For what purpose?"[155] McCormick, who was vice rector, later told the executive committee of the trustees that he had not had advance knowledge of the appointment and "lacked a comprehensive understanding" of what Leonard's duties were to be.[156] Leonard served until 1947, enjoying the confidence of Corrigan while he lived and pursuing with his confidential authorization the planning of the first women's residence hall, proposed for construction along Harewood Road but built along Brookland Avenue instead,[157] no doubt in deference to ecclesiastical considerations. Erected with federal funding, this became the first "nursing building." Later, used as a student residence, it was to be named Ryan Hall. Meanwhile, when Leonard found women graduate students difficult to organize, it was made clear that "so far as the social life is concerned, her main responsibility should be with the undergraduate students."[158]

The university at the time was still small—it had fewer than 1,500 students when Corrigan came to the campus—and it was almost homogeneous in religion, but it had its own unique complexity. Post-baccalaureate students were outnumbering the undergraduates, so that there were two distinct worlds. There were even more in reality, inasmuch as the numerous students who were clerics or religious were being kept by their respective rules at some remove from anything that was not curricular work. Also, within the graduate sector, those who were part-time students were on the campus only for classes. With respect to them, indeed, the secretary general, who was responsible for enrollment, was reminding the rector repeatedly that there was "a definite feeling among

154. OR, McGuire to Corrigan, Feb. 13, 1940, and Corrigan to Leonard, Jan. 2, 1942 (copy).
155. *Ibid.*, n.d., n.p.
156. BT, EC, mm, Sept. 9, 1942.
157. *Ibid.*, June 27, Sept. 9, 1942; Oct. 11, 1944; Jan. 12 and Mar. 22, 1945.
158. OR, Jordan to McCormick, Dec. 1, 1943.

the people downtown that the University is not interested in part-time students."[159]

Undergraduates, in the minority or not, were supplying for themselves and for others what is usually denominated as "student life." As an American institution, the university could hardly have been unaffected by those who on more typical campuses have always provided, in the words of an Irish observer, "lasting character, smell, feel, quality, tradition."[160] It was being affected, too, by the continuing rise in Catholic college and university enrollments during the 1920s and 1930s, derived partly from the general rise in college attendance that was under way, but also from the increasing proportion of Catholic college students that were enrolling in Catholic institutions during the first of these decades. According to some estimates, for example, about one-third of all Catholic college students had been in Catholic institutions in 1921, but from one-half to two-thirds were in such institutions in 1928.[161] Perhaps by the latter year, when Ryan was assuming office, most of the frivolity that had marked collegiate life nationally during the 1920s was already giving way.[162] Certainly, when Corrigan became rector in 1936, the impetus that Ryan had given to academic excellence in the college of arts and sciences was being expanded vigorously by the dean that he had selected.[163]

Actually, there is little to suggest that the pranks for which the collegians of the 1920s were known were ever prevalent on the campus. A report of the national chaplain of what was to become the Newman Club Federation names the particular disciplinary problem—not in itself new—that was associated with the prohibition era. There was, he had heard, "heavy drinking among all our students at Catholic and non-Catholic schools."[164] Students of architecture had already acquired a reputation for destructiveness. Their classrooms were said to reveal "a Bohemian atmosphere" and Cain as business officer of the university was ready to recommend that if they were "going to start in and batter up $1280 worth of chairs" the institution might find it more economical "to seat them on iron benches like convicts." He was complaining, too,

159. OR, Deferrari to Corrigan, Dec. 24, 1938; also, July 23, 1938; Feb. 17, 1939.
160. Sean O'Faolain, *Vive Moi!* (Boston: Little, Brown, 1963), 315.
161. Hennesey, *op. cit.*
162. See Paula I. Foss, *The Damned and the Beautiful; American Youth in the 1920's* (New York: Oxford University Press, 1955).
163. See James Marshall Campbell, "Report to the Alumni of the College," *CUB,* N.S., VIII, No. 4 (May, 1941), 5–6, 13.
164. OR, John W. Keough to Bishops of the United States, Philadelphia, Sept. 2, 1929.

that students were smoking, sometimes even with the permission of professors, in class.[165]

The fact was that Ryan's thrust toward excellence in the college was still not universally popular, even among those members of the faculties who were close to students. As late as 1941, when the chapter of Phi Beta Kappa was about to be installed on the campus, undergraduates who were stirred to protest the university's abandonment of its brief search for athletic glory could not resist the snide association of academic honor with bookworms. "Of course we have nothing against Phi Beta Kappa," they declared condescendingly in a passage of a petition that was censored before they could publish it, "we just think that it is more fun to get out in the open and do a little exercise once in a while."[166]

Social clubs that had been organized early in the 1920s continued to be important foci of undergraduate life until the late 1960s. The Dod Noon Club that had become the Omega chapter of the Phi Kappa fraternity was in the separate house that Ryan had authorized.[167] When Monsignor McKenna had complained that collegians housed so near would be a nuisance to the Shrine, Curley had held that no action should be taken "on presumption of misconduct that is feared from young Catholic men at some indefinite time in the near or far-off future."[168] A new club for "day hops," the Cave Dwellers, had been approved by Ryan.[169] Corrigan seems to have had no occasion to alter policies governing these clubs. It was not until 1952 that another chapter of a national fraternity, Sigma Beta Kappa, was given permission to have a house[170] and within the year after there was a reversion to the traditional reluctance to grant such permissions when a request of the Abbey Club to establish a house was denied. The general policy was then stated to be "to emphasize the benefits of residence on Campus and to work for the development of a community Campus spirit, particularly among undergraduate students."[171]

There was a somewhat distinctive organizational emphasis among undergraduates during the decade before World War II. Responses to varying student interests had been made from the beginning of the university. At the beginning of the Ryan administration, the student

165. *Ibid.*, Cain to Ryan, Feb. 13 and 20, 1932; Jan. 26, 1933.
166. OR, draft, Mar. 4, 1941.
167. BT, EC, mm, Mar. 11, 1929. The first petition on record is in OR, Charles A. Hart to Shahan, Dec. 15, 1925.
168. AAB, Curley Papers, M 825, Curley to McKenna, Baltimore, May 10, 1929 (copy).
169. *Tower*, Apr. 11, 1935.
170. OR, McCormick to Thomas G. Van Houten, June 6, 1952 (copy).
171. *Ibid.*, Magner to Constantine A. Courpass, Mar. 10, 1953 (copy).

council had taken credit for obtaining an infirmary in Albert Hall that opened during 1929–30. About the same time, when the problems associated with automobile traffic were still relatively new, the council had requested cooperation "in the movement to warn and stop motor vehicle drivers (both resident and day students including religious orders) from exceeding an excessive rate of speed while on campus roads."[172] The council had taken upon itself the publication of the student handbook for 1933–34. During Corrigan's administration, after the inauguration of Class Day ceremonies in 1938 and some proliferation of student organizations, there were complaints against restrictions on the council, censorship of the *Tower*, the quality of food served to lay residents, and the lack of student facilities.[173] The protest led to the first student assembly, in which Corrigan invited students to join in "the freedom of discussion which is rightfully yours."[174]

One aspect of the organizational emphasis was religious. A Spiritual Council that was organized in 1932 had begun by proposing to "plan" a tradition in emulation of one "long prevalent at Notre Dame University" that would have had the football team at corporate worship before each of its games.[175] But in its second year the council had begun to sponsor an annual celebration in honor of Mary, Seat of Wisdom, in the university stadium. Other Catholic college students of the Washington area had joined in the demonstrations, which continued until 1943. A Catholic Conference of Clerics and Religious, affiliated with the national Catholic Students Mission Crusade, had initiated in 1934 the annual celebration of the Church Unity Octave sponsored by the Friars of the Atonement. During Corrigan's time, there was a campus organization of the National Federation of Catholic College Students that had been founded at Manhattanville College of the Sacred Heart in 1937. Both news columns and editorials in the *Tower* assumed the wholehearted Catholicity of the campus.

Fame came to the undergraduates and the university through the Harlequin Club with its new moderator, Father Hartke, and in association with the new program in speech and drama. The productions of "Brother Orchid" and "Yankee Doodle Dandy" received wide acclaim. Within a few years the prospect of undergraduate concentration in the field, approved in 1944, attracted many freshmen. It led also to the dissolution of the Harlequins as drama became a curricular offering.

172. OVR, Student Council to Pace, ca. Feb., 1929.
173. OR, unsigned mimeographed bulletin, Mar. 10, 1941.
174. *Ibid.*, circular letter, May 26, 1941.
175. *Tower*, Oct. 6, 1932.

Gilbert Vincent Hartke, O.P. (1907–86), founder and long-time head of the department of speech and drama, for whom the university's handsome theatre was named when it was opened in 1970.

Fame on a wider scale came, for a part of a decade, as a result of the athletic policies that Ryan had initiated. He left the campus just as its football team was reaching its pinnacle of success. It was invited to play the University of Mississippi when the annual Orange Bowl game in Miami, Florida was still new. It won, 20–19, on New Year's Day, 1936.

Three thousand people were reported to have met the team at Union Station upon its return and to have led it in procession past the White House and back to the campus for a Sunday mass celebrated by Father Sheehy. A victory dinner with "the ladies invited and included as guests and participants" was arranged by the Washington alumni.[176] Four years later, the university's team played in the Sun Bowl at El Paso, Texas, in a game with Arizona State University that ended in a scoreless tie. But by 1941, after repeated expressions of concern, the trustees were deciding "to bring athletics more in line with the objectives of the University and with its financial capabilities."[177]

When Corrigan came to the campus, a sports reporter for the *Washington Times-Herald* had put to him the question of the avid fans, "Do you intend to pave a way to build up C.U. football? Or do you see fit to confine C.U.'s program to things scholastic?"[178] Long before, the watchful assistant treasurer of the university had warned that in subsidizing football Ryan was engaging in "a strictly professional, business proposition" and for that reason, "if for no other," his policy could not survive.[179] As Corrigan assumed office, the trustees requested a review of extramural athletics in view of "the very considerable deficit that was being incurred."[180] In subsequent meetings, however, the board usually found itself divided. Deferrari was pointing out to Corrigan that the university was undertaking "to finance a 'big-time' football program out of an available [lay] student body of 180 men."[181] Campbell, in a passage of his annual report that Corrigan omitted from the printed version, urged the de-emphasis of football "because it does not enjoy genuine support on the campus; it misrepresents the character of the College before the country; it has consistently failed to support, and has probably hurt, the lay enrollment of the College."[182] When the board's executive committee met early in 1941 and considered the deficits that were being incurred it adopted a proposal that had originated with Campbell to abolish all athletic scholarships and it suggested the resignation of the athletic director, who at the time had the highest salary on campus.[183] LaFond, who had been directing intramural athletics and coaching boxing, succeeded to the office. Noting the expected effects of the military conscription that was under way, the procurator reported the probability "that the reduction of the athletic program to intra-mural proportions [would] be more rapid than originally contemplated."[184]

LaFond's boxing teams were even more successful than those in

176. OR, Vincent L. Toomey to Washington Chapter, Jan. 10, 1936.
177. CUB, N.S., VIII, No. 4 (May, 1941), 11.
178. OR, Vincent X. Flaherty to Corrigan, Washington, May 20, 1936.
179. McNicholas Papers, Cain to Nelligan, Aug. 30, 1931 (copy).
180. BT, mm, Apr. 22, 1936.
181. OR, Deferrari to Corrigan, Apr. 5, 1939; also, Dec. 28, 1938.
182. *Ibid.*, Campbell to Corrigan, July 1, 1940.
183. BT, EC, mm, Jan. 9, 1941.
184. BT, mm, Apr. 23, 1941, exh.

football. Ryan had once defended intercollegiate boxing, it will be recalled. The university's team enjoyed repeated successes, winning forty of its fifty-four matches by 1940 and enjoying undefeated seasons during 1937–38 and 1939–40.

Track under Dorsey Griffith continued to be successful. In 1938, the coach could inform Corrigan that there would be "over three hundred athletes from twenty colleges, eighteen high schools and four clubs" in a meet that the university was sponsoring, which would be "the greatest indoor Meet in this section."[185] The meet in 1941 was moved to the Uline arena in the city and a featured race was named the Killion Mile for a member of the Class of 1916 who had been killed in World War I and for whom had been named the athletic field that was in use before the stadium was built.

Athletes or not, students who came to the university during the decade before World War II were participants in a dynamic phase of its history. Academic programs had been reorganized in a fashion that may now appear conventional but was then, on the campus, provocative of debate. The caliber of the programs had been strengthened immeasurably by the explication of standards and by the augmentation of the faculties with renowned scholars. The mixture of students, national and even international in representation and growing in number, and including religious of many communities, was colorful. The Catholic atmosphere was radical, in the best sense. Catholics in the country at large were gaining in confidence. Institutional aspirations could be high. The atmosphere could be open.

185. OR, Griffith to Corrigan, Mar. 2, 1938.

CHAPTER IX

The Introduction of the Postwar World

World War II marked a second watershed in American higher education, as World War I had marked a first. Although the basic organizational pattern of American universities had become more or less fixed by about 1920, it would have been impossible at the beginning of the 1940s to anticipate that during the next few decades there would be bulging enrollments and an unparalleled extension of educational opportunity, that federal funding would make possible both the swollen enrollments and the institutional expansion necessary for their accommodation, and that disciplinary differentiation would produce new relationships between academic and other national institutions, public and private, and new conflicts between disciplinary and educational goals within universities themselves. Corrigan's death, of course, antedated not only these developments but even the experience of the full impact of the war upon the campus.

The outbreak of hostilities in Europe on September 1, 1939, had heightened the pitch of the ongoing national debate on American foreign policy and had had reverberations within the university, too. There were visible on the campus students from other countries who had been delegates to a congress of the international Catholic student movement Pax Romana and who were prevented by the war from returning to their homelands.[1] During 1940, male students, both undergraduate and graduate, received the clear message that was conveyed nationally in the enactment by the Congress of unprecedented "peace-

---

1. OR, Edward J. Kirchener to Michael J. Ready, general secretary, National Catholic Welfare Conference, Washington, July 22, 1938 (copy), suggesting that the congress should be brought to the United States, especially since the bishops had prohibited attendance at the World Youth Congress that was being held at Vassar College, and Corrigan to Kirchener, July 30, 1938 (copy), authorizing the invitation for the meeting on the campus. Kirchener, then attached to the publicity office of the university, became the international president of Pax Romana.

time" military conscription. In the fall, also, space had to be found in Albert Hall and St. John's Hall for young American priests who in former years would have been pursuing graduate studies in Rome. Older members of the faculties could remember easily enough what the prelude to the previous world war, ended scarcely more than twenty years earlier, had meant to the institution.

To deal with the practical questions that were expected to arise, Corrigan, like his counterparts in other institutions, had been called upon to appoint various committees. There was a Council on National Defense, of which Dean McGuire was made chairman.[2] Two executive committees were established within it, one on military affairs, which eventually had to supervise precautions against possible air raids, and another on military training programs. Later there was a committee to promote the sale of war bonds and saving stamps; Herbert Wright, professor of politics, was its first chairman. From the beginning of the war, of course, particular attention was given to the pleas of Pope Pius XII for prayers for a just peace. A day of devotion to this purpose was sponsored officially on November 24, 1940.

Although there were at times uncertainties about the application of conscription policies to students in colleges and graduate schools, the effect upon lay enrollment became plain well before the Japanese attack on Pearl Harbor. When the United States Office of Education compiled statistics on graduate education for the academic year 1943–44, it found that enrollment in graduate schools nationally had declined from its "normal" level of about 100,000 students to the neighborhood of 30,000. Moreover, whereas the earlier figure had represented about seven per cent of the total attendance at colleges and universities, the proportion of graduate students to total attendance had fallen to about four per cent.[3] On the campus, however, the large proportion of clerics and religious in the student population was moderating the impact of national policies, since these students were not subject to conscription. Midway through the war, replying to an inquiry from the American Council on Education, Corrigan's successor was able to assert that "effective undergraduate and graduate instruction" had not been impaired, that the continued enrollment of the clerics and religious was expected, and that war projects and the university's location in the national capital were even providing partial compensation in the form

2. OR, Corrigan to AS, Oct. 29, 1940 (copy); McGuire to Corrigan, Feb. 27, 1941; BT, EC, mm, Jan. 13, 1942.
3. Henry G. Badger and Benjamin W. Frazier, "Effect of the War Upon Colleges and Universities, 1943–44," *AAUP*, XXX (June, 1944), 264–83.

*Patrick Joseph McCormick (1880–1953), seventh rector of The Catholic
University of America, titular bishop of Atenia and auxiliary bishop of Washington
(1950–53).*

of an increase in the number of part-time graduate students. In his
estimation, no far-reaching changes were likely to result from the war.
All that he anticipated—mistakenly—were the loosening of departmental boundaries and the integration of disciplines.[4]

Reports of the registrar for the period show that total enrollment,
after having grown steadily during the 1930s, had reached an all-time
high of 2,505 students in the fall of 1940. It fell to 2,075 in 1941, to
1,920 in 1942, and to 1,810 in 1943. In the latter year, some lost tuition
revenues were made up by the brief presence on campus of a unit of the
Army Specialized Training Program, which had from three to five
hundred trainees at any given time between August 1943 and March
15, 1944.[5] Special wartime instructional demands were being met upon
request. The school of nursing education, for example, upon selection
by the United States Public Health Service, was preparing teachers of

4. OR, McCormick to George F. Zook, Washington, May 25, 1943 (copy).
5. BT, EC, mm, May 5 and Sept. 9, 1943. For the accounts of those in charge, see
"Report of the Representative of the Rector for A.S.T.P.," AR (1943–44), 77–89. See
Louis A. Keefer, *Scholars in Foxholes* (Jefferson, N.C.: McFarland, 1988), for an account
of the short-lived ASTP program.

nursing cadets as well as teachers for the accelerated (*i.e.*, three-semester year) programs that institutions had been asked to schedule.[6] This change in the academic year was being adopted even in seminaries throughout the country. Bishops among the trustees supported its application to theological programs within the university.[7] Before the war was ended, thirty-six men who had once been students had given their lives in military service.[8]

The Seventh Rector (1942–53)

Corrigan died at a time when all the American bishops were presumably busy grappling with the effects of the war upon their dioceses and some, more farseeing than others, were estimating the international demands that would become urgent at the war's end. It was only to be expected that the trustees should turn for a successor to one whom they already knew well and whom they could accept by virtue of his seniority and of the offices that he had held, if by no other criteria, as someone thoroughly familiar with the institution for which they were responsible. The academic senate lightened their burden by its overwhelming recommendation for the office of rector of the incumbent vice rector and acting rector, Patrick Joseph McCormick (1880–1953). He received eleven of the fifteen votes cast in the body.[9]

There were some who had thought in 1928 that McCormick should have been appointed to succeed Shahan.[10] A junior member of the faculty at the time had the impression that he had been Shahan's personal choice.[11] On learning of Corrigan's death, a prominent archbishop wrote to McCormick quickly to express the hope that the university's trustees would have the "good sense and judgment" to elect him.[12] Curley, who in 1928 had thought that his personal friend was lacking in the "push and go" that a rector ought to have, this time let his brother bishops know before the board met that, despite his professed desire to be neutral, he did not think that they "could get a better man" than McCormick.[13] Probably he took some satisfaction in writing to the

6. ABC, mm, June 21, 1944.

7. OR, Ready to Ordinaries, Superiors, and Rectors, Washington, May 8, 1944; O'Hara to McCormick, Savannah, Apr. 3, 1944; Mooney to McCormick, Detroit, Apr. 3, 1944; Stritch to McCormick, Chicago, Apr. 8, 1944.

8. OR, "Members of the Catholic University Alumni, Faculty, and Students Who Are Serving in the Armed Forces of the United States," n.d., apparently prepared by the alumni office.

9. AS, mm, July 7, 1942.

10. McCormick Papers, Cain to McCormick, Washington, July 22, 1929.

11. OR, Speer Strahan to McCormick, Jackson, Miss., Aug. 21, 1943.

12. *Ibid.*, John J. Mitty to McCormick, San Francisco, June 17, 1942.

13. AAB, Nelligan Papers, Curley to Schrembs, Baltimore, July 27, 1942 (copy).

archbishop of Chicago, who had been one of Corrigan's supporters, that after the latter's death "in twelve days the brilliant young Dr. Magner and Dr. McCormick had done a piece of work which had not been done in six years before."[14]

There is no evidence that in turning to McCormick the trustees were giving any thought to carrying forward the momentum that Ryan's administration had given the university in the preceding decade. How they voted does not appear in the record because the individual ballots were given to the chancellor in secrecy for tabulation and transmission to Rome.[15] A papal decree dated March 1, 1943, arrived from Rome on May 22 and was conveyed at once by Curley to McCormick to notify him of his appointment. In the fall, when the alumni invited the faculties to an inaugural dinner, it was remarked that McCormick's appointment had dramatized "the elevation of a former student to the very exalted position of rector."[16] It was indeed the first such elevation. Two terms later, upon his death, McCormick could be eulogized just as fittingly as the last of the university's pioneers.[17] He was the last chief executive to have been closely associated with such figures as Pace, Shahan, and Shields.

McCormick, whose birthplace was Norwich, Connecticut, had been ordained for the diocese of Hartford in 1904 and then sent to the university for two years to prepare for the position of diocesan superintendent of schools, which he filled from 1906 until 1910 while assisting in a parish in Bridgeport. His earlier philosophical and theological studies had been pursued at St. Joseph's Seminary of the archdiocese of New York. The famed Father Duffy, who was then leading Dunwoodie's short-lived intellectual advance before the condemnation of modernism, had taken enough notice of the young alumnus to correspond with him for a time. Other ties to various pioneer Catholic efforts had been mediated through a relative, the well-known Father John Talbot Smith, whose estate McCormick would later administer. Smith had been a close friend of Brother Azarias, had been president of the Catholic Summer School, and had founded the Catholic Actors' Guild and the Catholic Writers' Guild in New York. When Shahan had invited McCormick to join the department of education to prepare diocesan superintendents

14. *Ibid.*, Curley to Stritch, Baltimore, Aug. 7, 1942 (copy).
15. BT, mm, Nov. 10, 1942.
16. OR, Vincent L. Toomey to Faculty, Washington, Oct. 22, 1943.
17. Francis J. Connell, C.Ss.R., "Eulogy of Most Reverend Patrick J. McCormick, D.D.," *CUB*, N.S., XXI, No. 1 (July, 1953), 2–4.

"according to the best methods,"[18] Smith had advised him to "accept on the spot."[19]

Upon joining the faculty, McCormick had quickly published, first his doctoral dissertation, *The Education of the Laity in the Middle Ages*, which he had completed in 1912, and then, in 1914, his *History of Education*, which gained wide acceptance as the first comprehensive work in the field by a Catholic author. He had been promoted to the rank of associate professor in 1914 and to full professorial rank in 1918. When Shields died in 1921, McCormick had become head of the department and therefore also dean of the Catholic Sisters College and director of its summer session, as well as editor of the *Catholic Educational Review*. Reportedly, he always opposed moves to amalgamate the Sisters College with the university or, for that matter, to admit women to any of the resources of the university outside it.[20] But, having served to general satisfaction as acting rector during the hiatus between the Ryan and Corrigan administrations and again after Corrigan's death, he was indeed in a logical position to be chosen rector. His imperturbable manner, handsome dignity, measured speech, and reputation as an avid golfer had endeared him to many both within and outside the academy. Years before, when he had celebrated the silver anniversary of his ordination, his academic service had been given ecclesiastical recognition through his investiture as a domestic prelate, and he was later, in 1950, to be ordained titular bishop of Atenia and auxiliary bishop of Washington.

No more than the trustees did McCormick give recognition to the rejuvenation of the university that had taken place under Ryan. He had been among those who had resisted Ryan's reorganization and he had not had previously a record for supporting progressive measures. He retained his identification with colleagues whom he may not have known too well but with whose causes he sympathized during the controversies of the Ryan years.[21] As one who was perhaps his severest

18. OR, Shahan to John J. Nilan, bishop of Hartford, Washington, May 19, 1910.
19. McCormick Papers, "Mary Ellen Ryan" to "Eugenius," Dobbs Ferry, N.Y., May 23, 1910 (Smith seems to have had a penchant for pseudonyms).
20. Deferrari, *Memoirs*, 418.
21. For example, in the proceedings following the dismissal of Rolbiecki, McCormick had responded to the apostolic delegate's request for his opinion by reviewing cautiously the legality of the action and then noting that the penalty imposed appeared to be too severe "in the judgment of the older Professors of the University." McCormick Papers, McCormick to Fumasoni-Biondi, Washington, Jan. 8, 1931 (copy). Similarly, he was considered by Cöln to have been his "truest friend in those bad days." OR, Carola Kopf-Seitz to McCormick, Fayetteville, O., July 8, 1949. See also, OVR, Cöln to McCormick, Bonn, Oct. 10, 1932; McCormick to Cöln, Washington, Dec. 17, 1932 (copy); and Cöln to McCormick, Lanham, Md., Nov. 11, 1933. McCormick figured in the settlement of the case. AACi, Cöln Papers, McCormick to Cöln, Washington, Jan. 5, Feb. 8, and May 7, 1938.

Commencement exercises, held annually in the university's gymnasium until their relocation out-of-doors in 1962.

critic has pointed out, however, McCormick made no attempt to undo the work of his predecessors but instead "maintained the *status quo* rigidly," as the trustees may have wanted him to do. More to the point for many, "he did not interfere with the decisions made by the faculties and deans, and he had a high respect for academic freedom in the best sense."[22] In this way, consciously or not, he facilitated the change from personal rule to bureaucratic administration that proceeded rapidly after World War II.

Bureaucratization was of course developing in all sectors of society and more rapidly than on the campus. McCormick, who had hardly known anything other than personal rule, benevolent as it might have been, had had some contacts with federal agencies. While associated with the *Catholic Educational Review*, for example, he had prepared reports of Catholic educational activity for the biennial surveys of the United States Office of Education. As rector he was called upon to assess the emphasis upon international organization that marked the

22. Deferrari, *Memoirs*, 419, 420.

immediate postwar years. Even during the war, he expressed the interest of the institution in cooperating with the Universities Committee on Post-War International Problems.[23] He was a signer of a document that urged American participation in what was to become the United Nations Organization for Education, Science, and Culture (UNESCO).[24] He had a larger part in the revival of contacts among Catholic institutions through the International Federation of Catholic Universities, which, after papal approval, held its organizational meeting in Rome in 1949 and elected McCormick to be its first vice president.[25] By that time, two sister Catholic universities had already conferred honorary doctorates upon him, those of Chile in 1942 and Louvain in 1949. In 1950, when the vice rector felt that he could not travel to the organizational meeting of the International Association of Universities held at Nice, France, McCormick delegated an assistant professor of sociology who was in Europe to represent the university in the signing of the constitution.

Upon his appointment to the rector's office, McCormick selected as vice rector Monsignor Edward B. Jordan, who had succeeded him as head of the department of education and dean of the Catholic Sisters College. When Jordan died in 1951, Monsignor Jerome D. Hannan of the diocese of Pittsburgh, a professor of canon law, was named to the position. Earlier, however, before the required statutory consultation of the academic senate in 1948, opposition to McCormick's reappointment for a second term had been organized by Deferrari and Campbell, who were then promoting for the first time the candidacy of William J. McDonald, a priest of the archdiocese of San Francisco and a professor of philosophy who was to become later the university's ninth rector. When the senate met, a tie on the first ballot was broken by a single vote on the second, without a change in the results for the two others who received a single vote each.[26] But an unrecorded secret ballot of the trustees again made McCormick "the choice of the Body to be presented to the Holy See" and his reappointment followed.[27] As this second term was expiring, McCormick declined to be considered for

23. OR, Ralph Barton Perry to McCormick, Boston, Oct. 22, 1943; McCormick to Perry, Washington, Oct. 29, 1943 (copy).

24. OR, George N. Shuster, William P. Tolley, and Guy B. Snavely to McCormick, New York, Feb. 28, 1945.

25. OR, Agostino Gemelli, O.F.M., to Rectors of Catholic Universities, Milan, Italy, Sept. 4, 1946; McCormick to Gemelli, Washington, Nov. 4, 1946 and, approving proposed statutes, Apr. 21, 1948 (copies). Pace had represented the university at the first similar international meeting, held at Louvain in 1924.

26. AS, mm, Feb. 26, 1948.

27. BT, mm, Apr. 7, 1948.

continuation in office and in fact died before the selection of his successor was completed.[28]

Managerial Changes

One sign of administrative improvement after McCormick's entrance
into office was his immediate resumption of the policy of former rectors
who had published annual reports to the trustees.[29] The practice, common in institutions of higher education, had been allowed to lapse after
1937–38. By campus tradition, reports of deans of faculties and other
officers were included. Although McCormick, like most of his predecessors, was not as frank as Keane had been at the beginning, and although
caustic or perhaps even simply unfavorable remarks were sometimes
omitted when reports of subordinates were published, the annual report
was recognized as a convenient device for recording events and promoting institutional aims. Beginning in 1944–45, the publications and
university activities of each member of a faculty were also listed.

A similar and even more significant advance, highlighting the importance of institutional records, was made during 1948 with the establishment of a department of archives and manuscripts as an independent
administrative unit.[30] Henry J. Browne, then a priest of the archdiocese
of New York who was a member of the department of history, organized
a model department.[31] Unfortunately, McCormick's successors proved
to be less supportive than he was, so that the archives soon became
understaffed. After Browne's departure in 1956, appointees were assigned to the dual role of archivist of the university and director of the
library's department of archives and manuscripts.

Under Corrigan, on a motion of Spellman, who had taken the trouble
to do some consulting and reading on the subject, the trustees had
ordered a survey to determine "the status of each department with
reference to the ratio of instructional personnel and students, income
and expense, safeguarding the requirements of academic standards."[32]
Faculty members were quick to point to the difficulties, one of the most
important being noted by the dean of the graduate school of arts and
sciences who, in submitting budget requests for the next academic year,

28. AS, mm, Feb. 26 and June 4, 1953.
29. BT, mm, Nov. 9, 1943.
30. OR, memorandum, Dec. 13, 1948; BT, mm, Nov. 15, 1949, exh.; ABC, mm,
May 10, 1950. The step had been recommended by the director of libraries, Eugene P.
Willging, June 25, 1948.
31. Henry J. Browne, "A Plan of Organization for a University Archives," AA, XII
(Oct., 1949), 355–58.
32. BT, mm, July 3, 1941.

reminded the administration that "an academic survey in a research university is misleading unless dissertation direction, laboratory and clinical work—which are not measurable—are remembered."[33] McCormick organized general, planning and executive committees;[34] appointed Professor Foran, a specialist in educational measurement, as director; and conducted serious detailed surveys annually throughout his administration.

The survey committees had to wrestle with the effects of distinctions between full-time and part-time teaching, between teaching and service loads, and between loads that were sometimes "ridiculously high" and sometimes "absurdly low." The inadequacies of the survey method could never be completely surmounted and the planning committee soon acknowledged that the value of an academic man was "primarily a question of his competence rather than of the number of hours he [might] be teaching or the number of students enrolled in his classes."[35] The trustees, however, eventually decreed unanimously, after a detailed presentation by Archbishop (later Cardinal) John F. O'Hara, C.S.C., of Philadelphia, a former president of the University of Notre Dame, "that teaching and service loads should be adjusted upward to the level of 15 hours per week on the undergraduate level and 12 hours per week on the graduate level."[36]

A faculty committee, noting from the published annual financial reports that more than 48 per cent of the university's total expenses were for instruction and research, made the important point that, no matter what survey method was employed, it was still true "that a much larger proportion of expenses is offset by income from tuition and fees than generally prevails in other universities."[37] There is no indication that the significance of this precise point was appreciated. Neither the trustees nor the administration seems to have addressed it. Serious planning for the desperately needed increase of the university's endowment had ceased with the Ryan administration.

33. OR, memorandum, n.d.
34. BT, EC, mm, Sept. 9, 1942.
35. OR, "A Survey of the Academic Load of Members of the Faculty," Mar., 1944.
36. BT, mm, Apr. 23, 1952, exh., "Minutes of Meeting, Budget Committee of the Board of Trustees," Mar. 14, 1952. It may be recalled that originally professors had been expected to lecture for four hours and that in 1896 that number had been increased to five. In 1908, the four-hour standard was being maintained in the sacred sciences but in other fields the loads were from six to twelve hours per week (BT, mm, Nov. 18, 1908). In 1922, ten hours were reported to constitute a full teaching load (SP, Pace to Arthur C. L. Brown, Jan. 15, 1922), but in 1928 Shahan was describing five hours as the minimum load for professors and ten hours as the maximum for those below full professorial rank (AACi, Cöln Papers, Shahan to Cöln, Feb. 17, 1928).
37. *Ibid.*, "Costs of Instruction 1941–42," Mar. 1943.

Unquestionably, the principal and also the most visible instrument of bureaucratic administration in the university—for nearly the next three decades—was what became known as the administration and budget committee. The name—soon shortened on campus to A and B committee—was used for the first time on September 25, 1942, after Corrigan's death, although administrative conferences in which the rector, vice rector, procurator, auditor, and treasurer participated had been begun on November 20, 1940. Magner had initiated them as a coordinating device. Meetings were to be held weekly but during the early years, even after McCormick became rector, there were lapses. The participation of the treasurer, Galvin, not only accented strongly the fiscal role of the committee but provided direct liaison with the trustees and informal access to the chancellor. Beginning with the meeting of October 2, 1942, minutes were circulated continuously.

A description of the functions of the committee that was later prepared for McCormick's successor and incorporated into the minutes summarizes well the membership and the scope that the committee attained:

This Committee was designed by the Executive Committee of the Board of Trustees specifically to deal with problems of the Budget throughout the year and had been further authorized and directed by the Executive Committee to consider special problems from time to time. In addition to these functions, the Committee had acted as a regular meeting place for the administrative officers to discuss problems of common concern, to secure advice, and, where desirable, to arrive at a common authority in the solution of any particular problem involved. The Committee as designed by the Executive Committee includes the Rector, the Treasurer and the Procurator-Assistant Treasurer, with the Vice Rector participating.[38]

Issues with fiscal implications and some without were sure to be brought before the committee. Two kinds of advantages ensued. One followed from the administrative coordination that was achieved, not least on the informational level. The committee meetings and the minutes that were disseminated to the principal officers of the university made available to all whatever information on a topic any single officer possessed. The minutes were written by the procurator, who had a manifest capacity for careful statement of the proceedings. A second advantage was fiscal. The committee device allowed continuous control of budgeted expenditures. Business officers and external auditors were particularly grateful for the authority that the minutes provided for appropriations and outlays. Disadvantages were perceived, however,

38. ABC, mm, July 15, 1953.

especially by the faculties and sometimes by students. The advantage of coordination was often thought to be offset by the slowing of the pace of decision and by a seeming "facelessness" in the rendering of negative decisions. The functioning of the committee, of course, was incompatible with personal rule.

What the administration and budget committee made increasingly visible was that the university had arrived, well before the committee was organized, at the point at which bureaucratic administration had to be joined with academic decentralization. The expansion of the institution in size and functions and its concomitant internal differentiation were calling for new forms of management. Yet the successful performance of its central academic mission could not be accomplished bureaucratically. In confronting the impasse, the university was not alone. No institution has as yet arrived at an entirely happy reconciliation of the opposed necessities.

Evidence of the new managerial situation emerged in virtually all sectors of the university. Financially, on Magner's initiative, the reorganized endowment and annuity funds were pooled; a category of restricted revenues functioning as endowment was established to include operating surpluses, unrestricted benefactions, legacies and bequests; and a plant fund was segregated.[39] Administratively, with the growth in size of the institution, the registrar's office was separated from that of the secretary general. Catherine R. Rich was appointed registrar in 1943 and served until her retirement in 1974.

Heads of academic departments began to receive financial compensation for their administrative work during the fiscal year 1948–49 and their duties were outlined in detail. It was becoming apparent, too, that lay members of the faculties who once could have been assumed to reside in the vicinity of the university were living in various places within the metropolitan area and for this reason, among others, expected to be assigned to office space on the campus. The need for secretarial assistance grew. A simplistic distinction between academic and supporting personnel was disputed, eventually with success, by the staff of the library which had academic, not secretarial, functions.[40] The influx of veterans required special attention, to federal regulations among other things, and in response to the campus veterans' organization. A veterans' counseling service was established in 1946 and continued until 1952.[41] Old problems such as fundraising that too often had

39. BT, mm, Nov. 9, 1943; Apr. 19, 1944; Sept. 19, 1945; Nov. 16, 1948.
40. ABC, mm, Jan. 31, 1945.
41. *Ibid.*, Apr. 25 and Dec. 19, 1945; Mar. 26, 1952.

Aerial view of the central campus in the 1940s, before the erection of Shahan and Keane halls, of residence halls across Michigan Avenue, and of the superstructure of the National Shrine of the Immaculate Conception, and before the demolition of Albert and St. Thomas halls.

been approached by ad hoc measures now had to be viewed more systematically, as when the trustees authorized the rector to study plans for administrative offices that would be charged with "financial and general promotion."[42]

Postwar Enrollment, 1945–53

The expansion of the student body of the university during the immediate postwar period, attributable in great part to the influx of veterans benefiting from the universally acclaimed "G.I. Bill of Rights," could hardly be regarded as normal growth, but it had lasting effects. Nationally, in the spring of 1946 it was estimated that 36 per cent of all students enrolled were veterans of World War II.[43] On campus, the peak was reached during the first semester of the academic year 1949–50, when the total enrollment of 4,757 students was about 90 per cent above that for the pre-war peak year, 1940–41. It was difficult to provide

42. BT, mm, Apr. 23, 1952.
43. *END*, Bull. 100 (May 2, 1946).

accommodations, either academic or residential. Housing for married students had never had to be provided before. Attempts to limit enrollment were only partially successful. For example, even after "it was agreed that the total enrollment for the year 1947–48 should not be allowed to exceed approximately 3,900 students,"[44] 4,276 found their way on to the rolls for the fall term. Undergraduate enrollment peaked a year earlier than total enrollment. During 1948–49, the 954 students of the college of arts and sciences represented an increase of almost 375 per cent from the 260 that had been enrolled for the first postwar years. Meanwhile, graduate enrollment in arts and sciences (including the school of social science) was only doubling, from 623 during 1945–46 to 1,291 during 1949–50. Students of foreign origin increased to roughly 10 per cent of the total enrollment, so that a foreign student advisor was appointed. Dean McGuire was the first to hold the office.

Adjustments in the opposite direction soon had to be made, beginning even during the peak year of 1949–50, because the budget for that year had been based upon an anticipated enrollment of 5,000 students, roughly 250 more than actually enrolled. Thereafter, although many students indeed continued to benefit from their "G.I." entitlements by pursuing graduate work, total enrollment declined each year, so that in McCormick's final year the 3,455 students registered were only a little more than 38 per cent more numerous than during 1940–41. Undergraduate enrollment declined at a faster rate than graduate. In addition to the graduation of the veterans, a partial explanation could be found in the relative stability of the number of ecclesiastical students enrolled during these years. They usually constituted about 30 per cent of the total enrollment, but declined in proportion as lay students increased and then rose again as lay enrollment decreased. Of more immediate but also of lasting significance, however, was the increase in the proportion of part-time graduate students after the peak year. During 1949–50 they were 40 per cent of the graduate students in the arts and sciences; during the three succeeding years their proportion rose successively to 44 per cent, 57 per cent, and 59 per cent.

Changes in enrollment required attention to policies affecting fellowships and scholarships. The Knights of Columbus fellowships, for example, were opened to married men,[45] but continued to be restricted to citizens of the United States and Canada because a proposal to extend eligibility for them to Latin Americans had been found not to be

44. ABC, mm, Jan. 29, 1947.
45. BT, mm, Apr. 19, 1950; ABC, mm, Dec. 14, 1949.

feasible.[46] As enrollment began to decline, the need for student recruitment led first to the offering of a tuition scholarship for undergraduate study, to be awarded competitively, to each ecclesiastical province each year.[47] Soon, full tuition scholarships for graduate study were awarded annually to ten sisters, ten brothers, and ten laymen or laywomen.[48] Additional half-tuition scholarships, to be awarded on the basis of need and ability, were authorized for selected departments.[49] An annual College Day for high school students and their counselors was inaugurated in the spring of 1953.

Although, beginning in 1936, enrollment had been reopened to qualified applicants without respect to race, the elimination of invidious discrimination in the use of campus facilities and in extracurricular activities was not accomplished until near the end of the McCormick administration. At first, it was official policy not to admit "colored students . . . to residence on the Campus or to residents' dining halls."[50] Problems that were not new arose in the use of athletic facilities. In 1947, the university rented its gymnasium to the Amateur Athletic Union of the District of Columbia for a Golden Gloves tournament in which Negroes were not allowed to participate.[51] That same year student leaders reported their concern that, although a Negro couple had been in attendance, a threatened appearance of an interracial couple at the junior prom might have provoked a "scene with the Hotel officials."[52]

The guideline that officers of the university seem to have followed was revealed in their advice to the director of libraries that the application of a Negro for employment "should be regarded from [the] practical standpoint of the reaction of the other members of the staff"[53] and, later, in their admonition to a director of student residences that a precedent in the assignment of a room to a Negro should not be set until they had discussed with the dean of men means of "securing the views of the other student residents."[54] In 1949, graduate students thought it necessary to report that in contacting all but three residents

46. ABC, mm, Jan. 29, 1947.
47. BT, mm, Apr. 19, 1950.
48. *Ibid.*, Nov. 11, 1952.
49. *Ibid.*, Apr. 15, 1953.
50. ABC, mm, Dec. 18, 1946.
51. ABC, mm, Feb. 12, 1947. For letters of protest see OR, John J. O'Connor, president, Catholic Interracial Council of Washington, to McCormick, Washington, Feb. 7, 1947; E. B. Henderson, vice chairman, Committee for Racial Democracy, to McCormick, Washington, Mar. 4 and 14, 1947.
52. OR, Fred W. Taylor and Stephen J. O'Reilly, "Report on the Junior Prom of the Class of 1948," Apr. 16, 1947.
53. ABC, mm, Dec. 18, 1946.
54. *Ibid.*, Oct. 20, 1948.

of Graduate Hall they had found sixty-one in favor and only three opposed to the assignment of Negroes to rooms in the building.[55] An assurance that official policy was nondiscriminatory throughout the institution was given in 1950,[56] but as late as 1953 the *Tower* made something of an issue about alleged segregationist practices.[57]

Undoubtedly, the movement of the university toward the full practice of Catholic principles in race relations was affected by the appointment, late in 1947, of Patrick A. O'Boyle (1896–1987) as archbishop of Washington and third chancellor of the university.[58] He allowed no doubt as to the position of the Church. Public attention was drawn also in an unanticipated way to the fact that the university's practice, if not above criticism, was well in advance of traditional community standards and of what other universities in the District of Columbia were doing. For a period of four years, from 1948 to 1952, the National Theatre, then the only professional stage in Washington, closed its doors rather than submit to demands that its audiences should be desegregated. The university's theater and that of Howard University became for the period the only legitimate theaters for lovers of drama in the metropolitan area.[59]

The admission of women to undergraduate study, begun but not completed under McCormick, presented issues of a different order. One issue was ecclesiastical, another, although considered within an ecclesiastical context, was inter-institutional. On the ecclesiastical side, serious objection had been expressed to the enrollment of priests and seminarians, obligated to celibacy, at a coeducational university. When the "schools for the laity" were first opened, in 1895, the trustees had rejected a faculty recommendation for the admission of women, who at the time would have been graduate students only. The establishment of the Sisters College and its summer session was viewed as a kind of solution of the problem for undergraduates as it appeared in the early years. Laywomen could be enrolled in it. But in 1928 the trustees had been still so evenly divided on the admission of women even to graduate study that the decision, in effect, had been left to the rector.

During the immediate postwar years, even the advisability of allowing women to attend mass in the Gibbons Hall chapel had to be discussed with the chaplain;[60] the use of the lounges in the residence halls of

55. OR, petition, Oct. 13, 1949.
56. *Ibid.*, Magner to Pearl Buck, Washington, Sept. 29, 1950 (copy).
57. *Ibid.*, Thomas P. Melady to McCormick, Feb. 25, 1953.
58. On O'Boyle, see John T. Donoghue, *NCE*, XVIII, 330–31.
59. Green, *Washington, Capital City*, 506; Richard L. Coe, "When Washington Theater Crossed the Color Line," *Washington Post*, Mar. 1, 1987.
60. ABC, mm, Jan. 23, 1946.

laymen was "strictly forbidden" to women;[61] and women had a separate glee club.[62] There were separate chaplains for men and women. For other reasons, namely inadequate facilities, women had to be excused from requirements in physical education.[63] The dean of women found her duties demanding enough.[64]

Inter-institutional considerations came to the fore when admission of undergraduate women to particular fields other than nursing became an issue. Proposals for the admission of women public school teachers desiring to obtain baccalaureate degrees had not been received favorably during the 1930s, even when they had been urged by Deferrari.[65] As a wartime measure, enrollment of undergraduate women in engineering and architecture had been allowed temporarily in 1942. And in order to avoid duplication, when enrollment in a course at Sisters College was small and the same course was being given at the university, it was agreed that the former should be consolidated with the latter.[66] Such an "arrangement based upon present need" was approved to allow lay-women "following college courses in pre-medical, pre-dental, speech and drama, special biology, and other courses not provided in local Catholic women's colleges" to enroll in the college of arts and sciences rather than in either the Sisters College or the school of nursing education.[67] Art was soon included.[68] The academic senate's committee on coordination, undertaking to grapple with the inconsistencies, asked for a definite statement of policy.[69]

The key consideration was always the effect that the admission of undergraduate women might have upon other Catholic institutions, especially women's colleges. Even when the board of governors of the Alumni Association urged that women should be admitted in any "field in which instruction was not available in a Catholic college . . . local to the students' residences," the administration and budget committee simply "agreed to take no action."[70] By the spring of 1950 the executive committee of the trustees was recommending to the board "serious

61. *Ibid.*, Feb. 20, 1946; Apr. 17, 1946.
62. *Ibid.*, Mar. 13, 1946.
63. AS, mm, Jan. 30, 1947.
64. Eugenie A. Leonard, "Women of The Catholic University of America," CUB, N.S., X, No. 5 (Mar., 1943), 7–8.
65. OR, Ryan to Deferrari and Borden, Dec. 11, 1930 (copies); Deferrari to Ryan, Sept. 11, 14, and 28, 1933.
66. BT, mm, Nov. 13, 1945, exh.
67. BT, mm, May 1, 1946.
68. *Ibid.*, Nov. 12, 1946.
69. AS, mm, Jan. 31, 1946.
70. OR, Andrew P. Maloney to McCormick, New York, July 7, 1949; ABC, mm, July 13, 1949.

consideration" of opening admission to women undergraduates generally, but its recommendation was promptly rejected on a motion by
Cardinal Stritch that was seconded by Cardinal Spellman.[71] That year,
however, when it was decided to suspend courses in education at Sisters
College, the board allowed women to enroll in bachelor's degree programs in education offered on the campus.[72]

The Inward Academic Look

It may be that, so far as academic initiative was concerned, the
McCormick decade was, as Deferrari was to call it, "lustreless and
stagnant."[73] The mere burgeoning of enrollment in the postwar period
was not a criterion of progress. It would be a serious mistake, however,
to assume that the professors and students of the time were intellectually
inert. Indeed, when the Middle States Association of Colleges and
Secondary Schools conducted its regular decennial visitation of the
campus, in 1947, its team was unequivocal in concluding that within its
"temporal" limitations "the University was accomplishing its announced
purposes exceedingly well."[74] If this was not the common opinion internally, it was perhaps because a standard of measurement derived from
different sources was being applied.

There was, it seems, little emphasis upon the changes that were
occurring in American society and, specifically, in the American Catholic community. The mission of the University was, in such circumstances, hardly likely to be rethought collectively. Inherited assumptions
about the centrality of the mission were not yet being challenged effectively from the outside. The implications of what the mission might
require of the university's sponsors or of its faculties were pursued by
some individuals or special groups, sometimes with keen insight, but
not with any supporting consensus. There was not a distinctive note
even in the reformulation of the mission attempted by Deferrari, who
represented the continuity of leadership from the Ryan regime. The
university should serve the Church, he maintained, "very much as the
state university serves its state, giving it every educational facility on
the higher level which Catholic education needs."[75] What Catholic
higher education needed, alas, was what was not agreed upon. Rectors
had once thought that the university's service to the Church was repre-

71. BT, EC, mm, Mar. 23, 1950; BT, mm, Apr. 19, 1950.
72. ABC, mm, May 10, 1950, see also Dec. 17, 1952; BT, mm, Nov. 14, 1950.
73. *Memoirs*, 420.
74. OR, "Pilot Study of The Catholic University of America, Washington, D.C.," 3.
75. "The Formative Years of The Catholic University of America," *CUB*, N.S., XIV,
No. 4 (Jan., 1947), 9.

sented in concurrent full-time appointments to a faculty and to the National Catholic Welfare Conference, but the death of Monsignor George Johnson in 1944 marked the end of such arrangements. The administration of a department charged with serving the American episcopate was being deemed incompatible with what professorial duties demanded.

To academicians, the test was the university's standing among its sister institutions in the Association of American Universities. Although this prestigious body was soon to renounce accreditation as one of its functions, its rating of graduate capabilities was presented to McCormick as "the one and great responsibility of the A.A.U."[76] After reputational ratings obtained just before American entry into World War II, Deferrari had informed McCormick's predecessor that, among AAU institutions, "Clark University is at the bottom, Virginia is next from the bottom, and the Catholic University, Indiana University, Kansas University, and Missouri University are tied in the third place from the bottom."[77] A few years later, when five departments were classified by the Association as capable of doctoral work, Deferrari and his successor in the dean's office urged that at least eight or ten should be brought to the standard "to maintain our membership."[78] Two years later they felt that eight departments would qualify but the association's committee on membership rated only five as satisfactory, sometimes with sharp differences from internal expectations.[79] Reputational surveys, of course, often may be out of date or based merely upon "halos" associated with individual institutions or with "stars" in individual departments.

It was to the university's credit that usually it did not shrink from comparison with the best. Ryan had insisted upon cooperation with the accrediting associations that were gaining power during his administration in spite of feelings "on the part of some that Catholic education ought to lead a ghetto-like existence so as not to be contaminated by the thinking of secular education."[80] The National Catholic Educational Association had been urged to discontinue its own program of accreditation.[81] Deferrari, when he assumed direction of the university's program of affiliation, had not only revived it but began to refashion it by

76. OR, Deferrari to McCormick, Feb. 19, 1945.
77. OR, Deferrari to Corrigan, Nov. 6, 1941.
78. OR, Deferrari and McGuire to McCormick, Oct. 30, 1944.
79. *Ibid.*, Deferrari and McGuire to McCormick, Oct. 30, 1946; "Report to the Rector on the Meeting of the A.A.U. Held at Princeton University, October 22–24, 1946" (copy); McGuire to McCormick, Oct. 27, 1947.
80. Deferrari, *Layman*, 139.
81. OR, Deferrari to Corrigan, Dec. 1, 1937.

discontinuing its accrediting functions and emphasizing the accreditation of Catholic institutions by their national, regional, and state agencies.[82] To him, even the National Commission on Accreditation, organized in 1950, was simply a "come-lately group" that, in spite of its support by the Association of American Universities and other groups, would never be able to control the voluntary regional associations through which accreditation, in his opinion, was being accomplished more than satisfactorily.[83] Difficulties were sometimes created by professions, such as law and chemistry, which maintained accrediting systems in which professional rather than academic interests were given primacy, or by state departments of education which imposed superfluous specific requirements for the licensing of teachers.[84] And the university would have been grossly remiss if it had forgotten, as McNicholas emphasized with respect to the training of priests, that it could be almost "hopeless" to attempt to correct "a wrong twist" away from Catholic values that might be received under secular auspices.[85]

There was support from other than reputational ratings for the critical self-evaluation that was becoming prevalent in Catholic higher education and that was to be expressed most eloquently by the university's Monsignor John Tracy Ellis before the Catholic Commission on Intellectual and Cultural Affairs in 1955.[86] Various studies of the institutional origins of academic achievement in the United States were appearing in which Catholic colleges and universities were found to be "among the least productive 10 per cent of all institutions."[87] More inclusive investigations under the auspices of the National Academy of Sciences and National Research Council were confirming that graduates of Catholic institutions were notably underrepresented among those who had earned doctorates from American institutions during the period from 1936 to 1950. During this period, interestingly, The Catholic University of America was found to have conferred about 40 per cent of all the doctorates conferred by Catholic institutions and to have ranked among the first ten American institutions in the number of doctorates that it

82. *Ibid.*, Corrigan, circular letter, Aug. 5, 1938.
83. OR, Cloyd H. Marvin to McCormick, Washington, June 12, 1950; Deferrari to McEntegart, Nov. 22, 1954.
84. *Ibid.*, Deferrari to McEntegart, Apr. 15, 1954.
85. OR, McNicholas to McCormick, Norwood, O., Aug. 5, 1945.
86. "American Catholics and the Intellectual Life," *Thought*, XXX (Autumn, 1955), 351–88, reprinted, Chicago: Heritage Foundation, 1969.
87. Robert H. Knapp and H. B. Goodrich, *Origins of American Scientists* (Chicago: University of Chicago Press, 1952), 24. See also, Robert H. Knapp and Joseph J. Greenbaum, *The Younger American Scholar: His Collegiate Origins* (Chicago: University of Chicago Press, 1953).

had awarded in philosophy, sociology, jurisprudence, and classical and foreign languages, and only just below this in history. It was thirteenth among all 113 institutions conferring doctorates in the arts, humanities, and social sciences. More than eight percent—actually about 12 per cent in the arts, humanities, and social sciences—of all those receiving doctorates from Catholic institutions had earned their baccalaureate degrees on its campus.[88]

To promote Catholic scholarship, the university had in these years not only its outstanding veterans but the eminent professors and able younger faculty who had come to it during the five or six years immediately preceding McCormick's succession to office. The academic senate, moreover, was continuing to develop and, with the individual faculties or departments, to apply formal standards for the recruitment and promotion of candidates of recognized ability. The caliber of some received public attention later, as when Kerr was invited to become the drama critic of the *New York Times* and when the rise of the Washington color school of painting reminded the campus that Kenneth Noland had once been an instructor in the department of art. In spite of low salary levels, the university was able to attract and retain dedicated Catholic scholars in basic disciplines by virtue of its reputation. Some assistance was derived temporarily from an unrealistically generous pension plan that had been approved after the revision of the pontifical statutes in 1937;[89] this was eventually modified when the university joined the Teachers Insurance and Annuity Association and again when faculty were included under the provisions of the Social Security Act of 1936.[90] A policy governing sabbatical leaves was approved in 1948.[91] A family allowance plan of extremely modest proportions was approved in 1951.[92] But in the same year the administration, while not prohibiting the formation of a credit union on the campus, declined to assign space to its office or to appear to sponsor it in any way.[93] Later administrations provided for the facility.

Organizationally, although there was little change in existing aca-

88. *The Baccalaureate Origins of the Science Doctorates Awarded in the United States from 1936 to 1950 Inclusive* (Publication 382; Washington: 1955) and *The Baccalaureate Origins of Doctorates in the Arts, Humanities, and Social Sciences Awarded in the United States from 1936 to 1950 Inclusive* (Publication 460; Washington: 1956). The data for Catholic institutions were extracted by the present author for presentation in an unpublished paper, "Catholic Institutions as Sources of Doctorates."
89. BT, mm, Apr. 19, 1939.
90. BT, EC, mm, Jan. 13, 1949.
91. BT, EC, mm, June 30, 1948.
92. BT, mm, Apr. 4, 1951.
93. OVR, Jerome D. Hannan to John T. Croteau, Dec. 15, 1951.

demic structures, the admission of new fields to departmental status confirmed a broadening of instructional scope that was under way. There was a signal of a sort when academic rank, that of assistant professor, was accorded to LaFond, the director of physical education and athletics.[94] Instruction in library science and in speech and drama that had been given for several years was recognized in the establishment of departments in these fields.[95] The department of geography was reopened.[96] In 1950, a division of music was organized by the transfer of offerings from the Catholic Sisters College and the appointment of John Paul as associate professor and head.[97] And, after some vacillation, the university accepted a unit of the Air Force Reserve Officers Training Corps in which physical education requirements could be fulfilled and gave its staff academic status in a department of air science and tactics.[98]

The most complex academic reorganization was the consolidation of the National Catholic School of Social Service with the school of social work of the university. The name of the former was retained when the consolidation was completed in 1947. The idea of a single school was hardly new. When the committee of diocesan directors of Catholic charities appointed to advise the university's school unanimously recommended a merger,[99] McCormick asked the vice rector and the two deans to study the matter and report. They determined that amalgamation would be desirable, outlined the several legal problems that would have to be solved, and recommended the appointment of a joint committee.[100] The negotiations required three years. Bishop Bryan J. McEntegart of Ogdensburg, a former president of the National Conference of Catholic Charities, who was to succeed McCormick as rector, and Monsignor John J. McClafferty, a fellow New Yorker who was to become the first dean of the consolidated school, had especially important roles in the preparatory work. When it was completed, the American Association of Schools of Social Work, since renamed the Council on Social Work Education, extended full accreditation to the new school.[101] New buildings on campus were required. Shahan Hall, dedicated in 1950, was built for offices and classrooms, the latter to serve not only the school but the university in general. The Agnes Regan

94. AS, mm, Oct. 30, 1942.
95. BT, mm, Nov. 13, 1945.
96. ABC, mm, Jan. 16 and 30, 1946.
97. ABC, mm, June 8, 1949; Apr. 26, May 24, and July 19, 1950.
98. *Ibid.*, Sept. 27, Oct. 12, Dec. 20, 1950; Jan. 10 and 17, Mar. 3, May 23, 1951.
99. BT, EC, mm, Sept. 9, 1943, Thomas E. Mitchell to McCormick, Aug. 18, 1943 (copy).
100. *Ibid.*, Jan. 12, 1944.
101. ABC, mm, Feb. 18, 1948.

Memorial Hall was built for residential purposes to match Ryan Hall and the St. Vincent de Paul chapel was built between the two.[102]

During these postwar years, after the beginnings made in the preceding decade, there was quiet but unusually solid progress in undergraduate education in the arts and sciences, primarily because of the leadership of the priest whom Ryan had appointed as dean in 1934. It was not that Campbell cared at all for the popular view that identifies academic institutions with their undergraduates. So far as he could control the situation, he gave no quarter whatever to those who had been called "rakes, rapscallions and idlers" and made no pretense of not preferring "scholars, sloggers, and bright stars."[103] He was interested, as the catalogue of the college was proclaiming and as the mission of the university could not but require, in an education that was both liberal, in the classical, not the political, sense, and Catholic. As he saw it, if the university was to maintain a college at all, "that college must be a small, highly-selected school, emphasizing undergraduate scholarship in the best current meaning of the phrases"; it would have no right "to spend part of the annual collection in supporting 'just another Catholic college.' "[104] Circumstances allowed the achievement of the aim.

The surge of enrollment and the serious application of veterans to study had marked effects. Even in McCormick's last year, when veteran enrollment was no longer statistically significant, the college alone had about one-fifth of the student body and more than a quarter of the university's full-time students. Not only the maintenance of academic standards but increasing selectivity in admissions was being facilitated. Undergraduate admissions came to be centralized in a committee of the deans of schools admitting undergraduates and the registrar, who served as director of admissions.

Even before the influx of veterans was felt the administration of the Graduate Record Examination, beginning in 1941, had shown the students of the college to be "far above [the] average as established by the results achieved in the leading colleges of the United States."[105] General requirements were made to include about one-half the courses taken by a student in arts and sciences. Among them was the history of Western civilization (which since has been replaced by a choice of more specialized courses), natural science, English literature, proficiency in a modern foreign language, four courses in philosophy and four in

102. BT, EC, mm, Jan. 7, 1948.
103. O'Faolain, *op. cit.*, 315.
104. SL, Campbell to James J. Hayden, Mar. 22, 1937.
105. OR, Deferrari to McCormick, Feb. 17, 1945.

religion, and, until 1967, what the dean liked to call the "intellectual
hurdle," namely, proficiency in Greek or Latin or in mathematics
through the calculus. Concentration was organized around a "reading
list" and a "coordinating seminar," unsatisfactory names for small group
instruction during each semester of the junior and senior years. A senior
comprehensive examination in the field of concentration was the final
requirement. It is a tribute to Campbell's leadership that this pattern
survived even the cacophony of the 1960s and 1970s and the narrowing
of interests common among newer faculty members. The recognition of
merit that had been achieved in 1940 by the inauguration of a chapter
of Phi Beta Kappa was followed in 1945 by one of Sigma Xi, the national
science fraternity.[106]

The two professional schools that were then serving undergraduates
presented contrasting records. In the case of the school of nursing
education, an "A" rating assigned by the National Committee for Nursing Service signified the national reputation in the field that the university enjoyed.[107] The way had not been entirely smooth. The staffing of
hospital schools by nurse-educators was leading to the closing of some
in favor of collegiate schools. In assisting this movement by the establishment of extension centers in many hospital schools and in other
ways, the university had incurred the displeasure of some hospital administrators. Father Schwitalla, the former dean of the graduate school of
St. Louis University, in a new capacity was said to want "to club the
secular agencies into recognizing the Catholic Hospital Association as
an accrediting agency for the nation as a whole," much as others had
"tried to do the same for Catholic education in general, but [had]
failed."[108] During the war and immediately thereafter, prolonged attention had to be given to the academic integration of the Providence
Hospital school in Washington, which became for a time the undergraduate division of the university's school.[109] Later, when a building for the
school was being planned, Magner, as procurator, proposed that it
should be named distinctively for the founding dean, who by that time
had served the university for more than twenty years. The suggestion
was followed eventually in the naming of Olivia Gowan Hall, but only
after another quarter century had passed.[110]

106. W. Gardner Lynn, "The Catholic University of America Chapter of the Sigma
Xi," *CUB*, N.S., XIII, No. 2 (Sept., 1945), 6–7.
107. ABC, mm, Sept. 28, 1949.
108. OR, Deferrari to Corrigan, July 8, 1939.
109. BT, EC, mm, May 21, 1942, and Jan. 14, 1943; ABC, mm, Mar. 23 and Apr.
6, 1949.
110. ABC, mm, Feb. 11, 1953; BT, mm, Jan. 31, 1981.

The situation in the school of engineering and architecture was not so favorable. What was perhaps the major persistent problem had been identified years earlier when an invited consultant, noting that "many men [had] various kinds of outside work," had advised the trustees that it was necessary to make clear to this faculty "what the duties are and what the obligations are."[111] Beginning in 1940, the Engineers Council for Professional Development, the accrediting body, had pointed to problems that, ten years later, led it to extend only provisional accreditation and to schedule a re-inspection of the engineering departments in 1952.[112] Also in 1950, the Architectural Accrediting Board withdrew accreditation from the department of architecture (which it restored in 1953 after departmental corrective measures had been taken).[113] The trustees, surprised by the difficulties, delegated power to act to the administration and budget committee. It was agreed to appoint an advisory committee which apparently trusted the dean's earlier report that "the outstanding need of the school was a separate engineering building."[114] In 1952 the Engineers Council withdrew its accreditation of all engineering programs except that in architectural engineering.[115]

When the board met there was discussion by Cardinal Stritch of "whether or not a school or department of engineering was a necessary adjunct to the primary purpose of [the] University,"[116] but the view that carried the day was expressed by Archbishop O'Hara, who remarked, "Our purpose is to educate engineers, not merely to train technicians."[117] McCormick appointed a committee. As its chairman, Deferrari declared, "There is definitely such a thing as a Catholic School of Engineering."[118] Upon the resignation of Dean Scullen, Francis Fox, O.S.F.S., was appointed acting dean, a new committee was appointed, and it was agreed that students of the school should be enrolled in the college of arts and sciences for the first two years.[119] McCormick's death just before the expiration of his second term left the problems to his successor.

111. BT, EC, mm, June 12, 1935, in the report by Ryan of the findings of Hammond.
112. OR, George T. Seabury to Corrigan, New York, Oct. 25, 1940; Albert B. Newman to Corrigan, New York, Nov. 20, 1940; H. H. Harkins to Corrigan, New York, Oct. 30, 1942; ABC, mm, July 26 and Oct. 25, 1950.
113. ABC, mm, June 21, 1950; July 1, 1953.
114. BT, mm, Nov. 14, 1950.
115. ABC, mm, Dec. 13, 1950; Jan. 10, May 9, Nov. 13, Dec. 5, 12, and 19, 1951; Jan. 30, Mar. 5, July 30, 1952.
116. BT, EC, mm, Oct. 15, 1952.
117. BT, mm, Nov. 11, 1952.
118. ABC, mm, Feb. 4 and 18, 1953; BT, mm, Apr. 15, 1953, exh., "Summary of Report on School of Enginering and Architecture dated March 14th, and a Supplementary Report dated April 9th, 1953, both made to the Most Reverend Rector."
119. BT, mm, Apr. 15, 1953; ABC, mm, May 6, Aug. 8, Nov. 4, 1953.

These were complicated by the unexpected death of Fox. A committee of externs was utilized to identify a new dean, first Thomas J. Kilian, who resigned after only a year in the office, and then Donald E. Marlowe, who served from 1955 to 1970, when he was appointed vice president for administration. What was named Thomas Pangborn Hall, after a generous donor, was dedicated for the school in 1961. Meanwhile, in 1957, accreditation had been restored to the departments of civil, electrical, and mechanical engineering.[120]

A proposal for the establishment of another professional school—in medicine—was not made known in university circles. Thought of a medical school was not new,[121] but in 1947, together with a prominent pastor and the national president of the alumni association, several Washington physicians characterizing themselves as "alumni and friends" submitted to the trustees a petition for the opening of a school of medicine as part of a Catholic medical center. They saw a threefold need, arising partly in medical education, which appeared to be separating itself from moral considerations; partly from practice, inasmuch as Catholic patients were often finding it necessary to consult physicians alleged to be lacking in "the proper ethical training and standards"; and partly from the dominance of Catholic institutions in the hospital field that were thought to need "a working model" that would present "possible solutions to their many problems."[122] The university agreed that the proposal was "a worthy project" but noted that "a great deal of thought would have to be given to all aspects of the problem."[123] Although the possible addition of a medical school continued to be mentioned occasionally in later years, financial exigencies continued to forestall any serious discussion of the matter.

The university's outward thrust was not abandoned during the McCormick years. Such massive bodies as the National Catholic Educational Association and the National Conference of Catholic Charities were no longer formally dependent upon it. It was still, however, as it remains, the seat of scholarly associations in anthropology, biblical studies, canon law, history, and other fields. In 1946, it was one of thirteen institutions to found the Oak Ridge Institute of Nuclear Studies.[124] On the campus, six members of scientific departments formed a committee for research in radioactive isotopes, then a new field.[125] An

120. OR, W. D. Hooven to McEntegart, New York, Oct. 31, 1957.
121. OR, Agenda for conference, Deferrari and McCormick, Aug. 10, 1943.
122. *Ibid.*, Petition of Edward P. McAdams *et al.*, June 1, 1947.
123. ABC, mm, July 9, 1947.
124. ABC, mm, Oct. 11, 1946.
125. *Ibid.*, Nov. 24, 1948.

exchange of professors in literature was arranged with the Catholic University of Louvain.[126] Community service was expanded with the opening of an extension of the school of engineering and architecture at Fort Belvoir, Virginia, in 1947. In 1949 a division of adult education was inaugurated under Father Sebastian Miklas, O.F.M.Cap.[127] And in 1953 the university became a member of the Greater Washington Educational Television Association, the local sponsor of public television.[128]

Broader educational influence was being disseminated through the Commission on American Citizenship, particularly at the elementary level, and through the university's program of affiliation and extension at the secondary and collegiate levels. Deferrari's revival of the latter program was evident in its steady growth. There was, for example, an increase of about 50 per cent in the total number of institutions affiliated, from 369 in 1944 to 553 in 1953. In 1953 there were 128 secondary schools affiliated and the university was administering 16,614 examinations to students enrolled in them, 35 per cent more than in 1944. Since the rate of increase for secondary schools was only a little more than 32 per cent, it was in postsecondary affiliations that the statistical growth was most noted. Jesuit institutions were, for the most part, opposed to the system and colleges under other auspices dropped affiliation after they achieved accreditation by their respective regional associations. This was, however, a mark of the contribution that the system was making. By 1950–51, the interest of minor seminaries in regional accreditation could be reported as growing and earlier in the preceding decade it had been noted that the number of novitiates affiliated as secondary institutions had been declining because the religious institutes involved were admitting only high school graduates.

Since Deferrari was not only director of affiliation but also director of the summer session and workshops, provision could be made for intensive exploration of possibilities for improvement of Catholic college programs. Annual workshops in higher education were devoted to philosophical and theological foundations and then to practical applications. Those in the early 1950s examined the college curriculum in detail. Proceedings of the workshops were disseminated through The

126. BT, mm, Apr. 7, 1948.
127. AS, mm, Dec. 12, 1946; Mar. 23, 1948; ABC, mm, Aug. 31, 1949. OR, McCormick to Deferrari, Sept. 1, 1949. See Sebastian F. Miklas, O.F.M. Cap., "A Look at Adult Education," CUB, N.S., XXIII, No. 1 (July, 1955), 6 ff.; "Profile of Adult Education," *ibid.*, XXVI, No. 1 (July, 1958), 3 ff.; "Pioneering in Adult Education," *ibid.*, XXXII, No. 4 (Apr., 1965), 7–9.
128. BT, mm, Apr. 15, 1953.

Catholic University of America Press. Institutes on these and related subjects were held in various Catholic institutions. In this way, what was being done for undergraduate education in the college of arts and sciences was given wide influence.

Integration as a Goal

Interest in intellectual integration seemed to peak during the postwar period. It was to be found among students—perhaps because of the maturity of the veterans—as much as among faculty members and educated Catholics generally. There was a consciousness of a social crisis that, uniquely, as the renowned Jesuit theologian John Courtney Murray pointed out, was "fundamentally the same the world over" and therefore "a challenge to the Church to assert in a new way her own unity and catholicity."[129] He was introducing the English translation of a penetrating pastoral letter published early in 1947 by the wartime archbishop of Paris that became the basis of countless discussions. For scholars, it was particularly noteworthy that the author was urging them to "integrate the conclusions of [their] several fields of specialization in order to try and form a cosmic vision of the universe."[130]

Undoubtedly one basis of the concern for integration was in a general reaction against the academic specialization that had already gained dominance and was not to be halted. Under the departmental system of American universities, new specialties could always be accommodated. By the beginning of the twentieth century the trend was transforming the institutional matrix of higher education. As a historian of the phenomenon has put it, "The American assembly line with its minute subdivision of labor and the American university with its cafeteria style of education were becoming emblems of the future."[131] On the campus, a popular professor of philosophy was castigating emphatically the "pluriversity" that was the result.[132]

Neo-Thomism was providing the framework for the search for intellectual integration. The university itself had begun only after Leo XIII had given official impetus to the scholastic revival. By the time that McCormick became rector the scholarship of such French luminaries as Etienne Gilson and Jacques Maritain and of numerous American lesser lights as well had gained widespread respect. Even at the popular level,

129. "Preface" to Emmanuel Cardinal Suhard, *Growth or Decline? The Church Today* (South Bend: Fides Publishers, 1948), v.
130. *Ibid.*, 82.
131. John Higham, "The Matrix of Specialization," in Oleson and Voss, *op. cit.*, 5.
132. Charles A. Hart, "The Significance of Thomism for Our Times," CUB, N.S., XIV, No. 6 (May, 1947), 7–9.

the "Americanized Thomism" of the nation's foremost apologist, the professor of philosophy Fulton Sheen, was captivating media audiences by bringing together "pre-World War I American innocence and certain aspects of the Catholic tradition."[133]

As the name of the university proclaimed, the spiritual aims of integration were being pursued in an unabashedly Catholic mode. When a tabulation of the religious affiliations of the students was made in the fall of 1950, apparently at the request of the chancellor, about 80 per cent were found to be Catholics, 17 per cent Protestants, and 3 per cent Jews. Among schools, the proportion of non-Catholics was somewhat less among undergraduates, somewhat more among graduate and professional students.[134] Of the students, the chaplain was able to report with some elation that numerous influences upon their spiritual formation were being exercised by priest proctors in men's residence halls, by priest-members of the faculties, by moderators of organizations, by special devotions, by small groups studying and practicing Catholic Action (then papally defined as "the participation of the laity in the apostolate of the hierarchy"[135]), and by the houses of study of religious communities in the vicinity of the campus, often through student affiliation with "third orders." On the other hand, he had to mention with regret "a decreasing interest and a declining attendance" of students at the solemn masses celebrated on five occasions during the academic year and to report the response of the students to the retreat conducted for them each year as not good.[136] Probably, however, these delinquencies were not portents.

So far as the undergraduate curriculum was concerned, the program of concentration that Campbell was fostering in the college of arts and sciences had been designed to stimulate integration in the individual. The general requirements that were ordinarily discharged during the freshman and sophomore years were expected to provide the breadth and background that was once called by psychologists the "apperceptive mass." Among these, the requirements in philosophy and in religion were to provide motives and intellectual tools. The senior "coordinating seminar" and the senior comprehensive examinations virtually com-

133. Halsey, *op. cit.*, 158. See Philip Gleason, "Neoscholasticism as Preconciliar Ideology," *CCICA* (1988), 15–25, and *USCH*, VII (Fall, 1988), 401–11. On Sheen, see John Tracy Ellis, *NCE*, XVIII, 474–75.

134. ABC, mm, Nov. 22, 1950.

135. See the encyclical *Ubi arcano Dei consilio, AAS*, XIV (Dec., 1922), 673–700 (in Latin), trans. Carlen, *op. cit.*, III, 225–39, and Dennis J. Geaney, O.S.A., "Catholic Action," *NCE*, III, 262–63.

136. John J. O'Sullivan, "Report of the Chaplain," *AR* (1952–53), 78; see also OR, James J. McPadden, dean of men, to McCormick, Mar. 5, 1952.

pelled students to relate the field of concentration to their entire academic experience.

To carry the discussion beyond the curriculum there arose a somewhat loosely organized Albertus Magnus Club that attracted hundreds to evening discussions in which representatives of disciplines defined their fields, outlined their philosophical underpinnings, and sometimes crossed swords.[137] With the assistance of a grant from a foundation honoring the pioneer professor Kerby, William J. Rooney, a Chicago priest and member of the department of English, organized seminars in which younger academics and graduate students pursued integrating themes. Assuming leadership in the name of the institution, administrators and professors joined in encouraging the organization of the Catholic Commission on Intellectual and Cultural Affairs, which Rooney served as executive director from 1953 until 1981. Through annual meetings of a restricted membership, the Commission sought to promote Catholic scholarship and interchange.[138]

Postwar Student Life

Developments in student affairs only partly served the cause of integration. Bureaucratization in an expanding institution had effects that tended to be centripetal. There was, in the first place, a proliferation of new student organizations, few of which were to endure, since the conventional student needs were already being addressed by groups that had been formed in previous decades. Organized in the immediate postwar period, for example, were the Allied Veterans, the Association of Students of French, the Association of Women Students, the Economics Club, the Graduate Hall Club, the Pan-American Students Club, and the Political Affairs Club. A new social club, the Clippers, came into existence in 1947. But juniors in the same year, bewailing lack of cooperation from other classes in the conduct of their prom, complained that "an impersonal mass educational program" was in effect.[139]

The International Relations Club, a postwar foundation, became the local vehicle for participation in the National Student Association when it was organized in 1947. Beginning in 1948, upon a proposal by Magner, an annual student activities banquet was sponsored by the

---

137. See, for example, reports in the *Tower*, Jan. 16, Feb. 13, Mar. 6, Apr. 17, May 1 and 22, 1953.

138. ABC, mm, Apr. 10 and Oct. 23, 1946, Mar. 21, 1947; OR, Edwin V. Stanford, O.S.A., to McCormick, Washington, Jan. 28, 1947.

139. OR, Taylor and O'Reilly, *op. cit.*

university and in the following year the Father Boniface Stratemeier Award was awarded for the first time to invite excellence in activities as well as scholarship.[140] A particularly innovative and outstanding edition of the yearbook, *The Cardinal*, appeared in 1950 when Fred J. Maroon, who has since become preeminent in photography, was editor-in-chief.

An enduring innovation was the Graduate Student Council, organized in 1950 through the leadership of Thomas P. Melady, a graduate student in politics who in later years was to become the Ambassador of the United States to Burundi and Ruanda and then to Uganda, then president of Sacred Heart University in Bridgeport, Connecticut, and in 1989 Ambassador to the Holy See. When the Council's constitution was approved in 1951, at its request Monsignor Magner was appointed the first moderator.[141] The Undergraduate Student Council, in its turn, was pointing to so many student needs that the rector assured it that all "available facilities" were being used to respond to "the growth of the student body, the multiplication of the student social groups, and the increased cost of facilities in town."[142] The proposal for an Alumni Memorial Hall that would serve as a student center was discussed throughout the 1940s but without practical effect.[143] Restaurant facilities supplementing university dining halls were still confined to the Dugout that had been opened under Graduate Hall with exaggerated acclaim twenty some years earlier.[144] Magner urged immediate consideration of expanded restaurant and recreational facilities and the board approved a project that was, however, not undertaken until after Mc-Cormick's death.[145]

Student interest in athletics was revived when World War II ended, but the director of athletics, returning to the campus, recognized that any expansion "would have to be on a very modest scale."[146] Permission was given for the resumption of intercollegiate football in 1947. Since the university had discontinued athletic scholarships, however, "practi-

140. ABC, mm, Feb. 25, 1948; May 18, 1949.

141. OR, McCormick to Melady, Jan. 24, 1951.

142. *Ibid.*, McCormick to Joseph M. Kolmacic, president, Jan. 5, 1951.

143. OR, Andrew P. Maloney, president, Alumni Association, to Corrigan, New York, Dec. 12, 1940; Maloney to Spellman, New York, Nov. 6, 1941; NC press release, Mar. 23, 1942; Maloney to McCormick, Feb. 16, 1945; Magner to McCormick, Mar. 12, 1948; Maloney to McCormick, New York, Mar. 17 and June 23, 1948; ABC, mm, Nov. 1 and 24, 1948; BT, mm, Nov. 16, 1948.

144. Shahan Papers, University Affairs, 1929–32.

145. ABC, mm, Feb. 18 and Apr. 14, 1948; BT, mm, Apr. 27, 1949; ABC, mm, Nov. 29, 1950; Jan. 6 and 31, 1951.

146. ABC, mm, Nov. 21, 1945.

cal interest" in the sport could be reported as "lost." It was reported further that the university's athletic policies had had no observable impact on enrollment and that there had been no regret over the earlier decision.[147] LaFond continued to coach successful boxing teams, even after the death of a boxer from another institution had prompted Moore to question the morality of the sport. Replying to Moore's objection, Curley questioned his analogy between boxing and dueling, which the German bishops had forbidden to Catholics, and refrained from a decision in the matter.[148] Track continued to be an intercollegiate sport and soccer also, in view of its popularity among international students who made up the teams. But the emphasis in athletics was shifted to intramural participation.

Administrative response to the postwar expansion in enrollment and in student activities prompted the development, slow at first, of student personnel services. Of course, the chaplain and the deans of men and women already had recognized positions. In 1944, the graduate school of arts and sciences recommended that the university establish a standing committee to serve as a clearing house for problems of student life, but on a poll of the faculties the three ecclesiastical schools were found to be opposed.[149] The counseling center established for veterans was placed under the supervision of the department of psychology and psychiatry.[150] By the beginning of the academic year 1948–49, what soon became the university counseling center was inaugurated "on an experimental scale,"[151] although neither the dean of men nor the dean of women appears to have been consulted in the matter.[152] A placement division of the center was organized in November, but given independent status the next year.[153] Then, as the clientele of the veterans' counseling center began to diminish, and a year before it was closed, it was proposed that the university's center should combine with the campus center for the veterans.[154]

In 1949, when overlapping responsibilities of the counseling center and the personnel deans were brought to the attention of the administration, a council for student personnel services was approved.[155] By 1952,

147. ABC, mm, Oct. 23, 1946; OR, Magner to Charles F. Phillips, Washington, Nov. 20, 1952 (copy).
148. AAB, Nelligan Papers, T. V. Moore to McCormick, Mar. 11, 1946 (copy); Curley to Moore, Baltimore, Mar. 12, 1946 (copy).
149. ABC, mm, Mar. 30 and Apr. 27, 1944.
150. *Ibid.*, May 7, 1947.
151. *Ibid.*, May 7, 1947; Apr. 9, 1948.
152. OVR, Marie Corrigan to Jordan, May 28, 1948.
153. ABC, mm, Oct. 19, 1948.
154. OVR, John Stafford, C.S.V., to McCormick, Feb. 28, 1951 (copy).
155. *Ibid.*, June 8, 1949.

however, the president of the undergraduate council was complaining that the administration was showing "no cooperation and lack of interest in student affairs."[156] A committee chairman supported the complaint with an eight-page memorandum detailing what he referred to as "a few surface problems on the Undergraduate-Lay level which could be strong indications of a much deeper origin."[157] Meanwhile, the graduate council was recommending the formation of a student-faculty-administration advisory board.[158] Late in 1952 an advisory council in student relations was appointed with Frank Biberstein, professor of civil engineering, as chairman.[159] It met monthly during the remainder of the year and continued in being under McCormick's successors until 1959.

Alumni Affairs

The decade of the 1940s was marked by an active presidency of the university's alumni association. Andrew P. Maloney, an officer of a New York bank and a nephew of the papal marquis who was the donor of the chemical laboratories and who later himself became a trustee, had begun attempts to increase the effectiveness of the association in 1938.[160] Annual reunions were begun and then, in 1942, an annual forum in New York. A national constitution was drafted and ratified during 1940[161] and was followed by incorporation in the District of Columbia during 1941. Efforts, only partially successful, were made to increase chapters of the association throughout the country.[162] In 1949 the association awarded for the first time its Cardinal Gibbons Medal, originally proposed by Maloney. The historian, Carlton J. H. Hayes of Columbia University, was the first recipient.[163]

A problem arose in the attempt to include in the national association women alumnae who were organizing on their own. It should be noted that when the national association had planned its dinner in New York in 1938 "the question of inviting alumnae [was] discussed and it was decided to omit the ladies at this affair."[164] A Catholic University of America Alumnae Association had been incorporated in 1944. Its Washington members claimed authority from the Ryan administration.

156. OR, James M. Bosilevas, president, to McCormick *et al.*, Apr. 29, 1952 (draft).
157. *Ibid.*, Earl Reum to McCormick, May 12, 1952.
158. *Ibid.*, Melady to McCormick, Apr. 10, 1952.
159. *Ibid.*, Biberstein to McCormick, Dec. 1, 1952.
160. OR, Corrigan to Maloney, May 10, 1938 (copy).
161. *Ibid.*, James J. Bowe to Corrigan, Feb. 19, Apr. 17, July 15, 1940.
162. OR, Maloney to McCormick, New York, Nov. 24, 1948; Mar. 15, 1949.
163. *Ibid.*, A. P. Maloney to Charles P. Maloney, New York, Nov. 30, 1939 (copy);
A. P. Maloney to McCormick, New York, June 9, 1949.
164. OR, AA, mm, May 19, 1938.

A chapter was formed also in New York.[165] The affiliation of the association with the International Federation of Catholic Alumnae and the
American Association of University Women was noted. McCormick
eventually appointed Joseph B. McAllister, later vice rector, to serve
as chaplain of the alumnae association.[166]

The alumni relations office on the campus presented another, internal
problem. It was staffed by an executive secretary of the association,
whose members paid dues and considered the office to be their own.
They assumed, for example, the right to increase the salary of the
incumbent or the right to decide upon means for fund-raising.[167] The
executive secretary, on his part, assisted the association in expressing
dissatisfaction about undergraduate admissions, tuition payments, athletic policies, and the like.[168] The thrust was expressed typically in
Maloney's plea to Cardinal Spellman "that the advantages of Catholic
University, and especially its 'college' or undergraduate department,
should be made available to the *average Catholic youth*"[169] and in his
further unwillingness "to establish a precedent of being obliged to make
any report" to any officer other than the rector.[170] It was not until 1951
that the office was placed "under the direct supervision and immediate
control of the University Administration."[171] The association's governing board considered that the resulting "misunderstandings" brought the
university's relations with its alumni to a "low point in our history."[172]
The competing claims of loyalty to Alma Mater and autonomy for the
association were difficult for the active alumni who had been undergraduates in a different era.

For alumni of the university's department of speech and drama, there
was an auspicious development in the organization, in 1949, of Players,
Incorporated, the forerunner of the present National Players, through

165. OR, Maloney to McCormick, New York, Oct. 7, 1946; McCormick to Maloney,
Washington, Oct. 10, 1946; Jordan to McCormick, Oct. 15, 1946, suggesting that the
issues be left *in statu quo*; Rosella Linskie to McCormick, New York, Oct. 31, 1946,
submitting a proposed chapter constitution; McCormick to Maloney, Washington, Nov.
9, 1946; McCormick to Linskie, Washington, Nov. 9, 1946; Margaret Smith Wasilifsky
to whom it may concern, Emmitsburg, Md., Dec. 10, 1946; Winifred MacNeill to
McCormick, Washington, Jan. 14, 1947 (copy).

166. *Ibid.*, McCormick to Marion E. Wolberg, Washington, Nov. 4, 1948.

167. OR, Maloney to Corrigan, New York, Jan. 7, 1942; OR, Maloney to McCormick,
New York, Dec. 8, 1942; AAB, Nelligan Papers, Curley to McCormick, Baltimore, Nov.
21, 1946; McCormick to Curley, Washington, Nov. 26, 1946; Maloney to Curley, New
York, Dec. 11, 1946; ABC, mm, Jan. 17, Feb. 18, Mar. 24, 1948.

168. OR, Maloney circular letter to alumni, n.d. [Mar., 1941].

169. *Ibid.*, Maloney to Spellman, New York, Nov. 6, 1941.

170. *Ibid.*, Maloney to Corrigan, New York, Jan. 7, 1942.

171. OR, Magner to Martin, Washington, Oct. 2, 1951.

172. *Ibid.*, Raymond DuFour to McCormick, Washington, Dec. 11, 1952.

which young graduates still obtain experience in a touring company. In 1952, for the first time, the company performed for American troops in Korea.[173] Such international tours have continued annually. Also at this time, the department began a relationship with the Olney Theatre, which has become the official summer theater of the state of Maryland.

Signs of Transition

When McCormick died, twenty-five years after the accession of Ryan in 1928, the university was completing its sixty-fourth academic year. During the twenty-five years that had just passed, despite depression and war and internal divisions, it had been able to reassert its role in a manner that was clearly consistent with what had been intended for it originally and with developed American university practice as well. Its renewed graduate thrust was presenting to undergraduates as well as to graduate students a goal of academic excellence. On the broader scene, no other American Catholic institution, even if better known, could have claimed among its central purposes maintenance of standing as a "national center of Catholic culture," as the pontifical statutes of 1937 put it.[174] A transition, however, was already under way. The campus in 1953 was a different place than would have been remembered by any who had known it during the Shahan years. The changes to come were to be even more far reaching. There were signs in academic affairs, administrative organization, finances, and public relations, even if they were hardly recognized for what they were.

Not as perceptible as might have been expected were the signs in finances, the field in which changes that take place in other realms are often revealed most concretely but somewhat after the fact. The revenues of the university during McCormick's administration were being obtained from the familiar sources in roughly the same proportions as in preceding years. From 1945–46 to 1952–53, inclusive, during the postwar expansion of the student body and the faculties, total revenues increased by 47 per cent. After the first of these years, however, the proportion supplied by tuition and fees varied only between 40 and 48 per cent, although total income from this source was increasing by about one-third. Similarly, the proportion from the annual diocesan collection (which had increased in amount by 90 per cent in ten years) varied between 25 and 30 per cent. What was new but not yet very significant was revenue from the administration of projects funded by the federal

173. *Tower*, Mar. 6, 1952.
174. Art. 2.

government. This was only $51,721 during 1952–53, but was more than four times the comparable amount for 1943–44 and more than three times that for 1948–49, when the annual income from these grants first began to grow. Income from endowment and funds functioning as endowment had never been large, but the principal of $6,538,623 for the year ending June 30, 1953, was 79 per cent larger than it had been ten years earlier.

The trends in expenditures would have been more informative if they had been examined more closely. Educational and general expenditures, which do not include those for auxiliary enterprises such as dining and residence halls and the like, increased by about 157 per cent from 1945–46 to 1952–53. From 61 to 65 per cent of these expenditures were costs of instruction. For two postwar years of swollen enrollment, 1946–47 and 1947–48, the income from tuition and fees was equivalent to about three-quarters of all educational and general expenses, but thereafter to only from 50 to 66 per cent, with the trend in the direction of decline. But income from the diocesan collection, which during 1946–47 was equivalent to 58 per cent of all educational and general expenses, was equivalent to only 35 per cent by 1952–53. Warning signals might have been found in these trends even if there had not been shortfalls of about three and five per cent respectively during the last two years of the McCormick administration. Measures to avoid operating deficits had to be devised by his successor.

Signs of change in public relations were noted more explicitly, but with rather specific reference to financial problems and to self–perceptions of shortcomings in imagery that were of long standing. Making the institution better known to American Catholics was an old theme. Curley had once remarked, "We cannot do too much advertising."[175] Professionalization had been recognized as a necessary goal but had usually been thwarted by financial considerations. The consultant that Ryan had employed at the beginning of his administration had left an outline for a public relations department that could not be funded.[176] Corrigan had established a bureau and, after its first director had resigned to accept a position at Columbia University, had appointed a second who served throughout McCormick's administration. Limited to a single professional, however, the concern of the bureau was principally with publicity in the press.

Professionalization of this limited scope did not target and certainly

175. OVR, Curley to Pace, Baltimore, Nov. 20, 1922.
176. OR, Ryan to Teaching Staff, Oct. 8, 1928.

did not affect deeper perennial or emerging problems. Among the former were the continuing scattered hazards that affected the annual collections in the dioceses. A bishop of a sizeable midwestern diocese, for example, declined to distribute the envelopes that the university had offered to send to him, surrendered all the scholarships that had been designated for seminarians or priests from his diocese, and took "compensation" from the collection when it was taken up.[177] Another, whose see city and surrounding territory in the east had a large Catholic population, consolidated the collections for the university and the National Shrine.[178] Still another, from a rapidly growing diocese in the west, found reason to omit the collection altogether.[179]

A specific emerging public relations problem was the distinction of the university's role from that of other Catholic universities. Deferrari, assessing the institution's relative position in 1941 as "not so strong academically" as it had been fifteen years previously, had warned Corrigan that there were "at least three very good graduate schools under Catholic auspices" that might qualify for membership in the Association of American Universities.[180] Not only Deferrari but others had used the rise of these schools to argue against tuition increases for clerics and religious.[181] Word had been passed on that the Rockefeller Foundation and perhaps others had the impression "that the Catholic University no longer [held] its unique central position for the training of priests and religious."[182] McGuire was later to echo Deferrari in urging that the university should not be "thought of in terms of other private universities, Catholic or secular . . . but should be regarded as standing in relation to our Catholic people throughout the nation as the great state universities stand in relation to their respective states."[183] From Harvard, a Catholic scholar who was then dean of the graduate school, commenting on the ambitions of some other Catholic institutions to be invited to join the Association of American Universities, expressed the opinion that they "should strive to be of the very highest order and thereby merit election."[184] The initiative among Catholics was being seized by such vigorous new presidents as the university's alumnus, Theodore M. Hesburgh, C.S.C., who was beginning a thirty-five year presidency of

177. ABC, mm, Oct. 9, 1946.
178. *Ibid.*, Feb. 26, 1947.
179. *Ibid.*, June 2, 1948.
180. OR, Deferrari to Corrigan, July 10, 1941.
181. *Ibid.*, Herbert Wright to the Rector and Board of Trustees, Nov. 7, 1941 (copy).
182. BT, mm, Apr. 15, 1942, exh.
183. OR, McGuire to McCormick, Apr. 16, 1946.
184. *Ibid.*, Francis M. Rogers to McCormick, Cambridge, Mar. 16, 1953 (*Personal and confidential*).

the University of Notre Dame with less endowment than his doctoral Alma Mater, and by the Jesuits Lawrence J. McGinley at Fordham and Paul Reinert at St. Louis. Members of the faculties were increasingly aware that the virtual monopoly in graduate education under Catholic auspices that the university had once enjoyed had disappeared and that the dominant position that it still held was being challenged.

More visible and tangible, and probably for that reason more provocative, were the signs of transition in administrative organization. There was reason enough in the expansion of the institution for the internal differentiation and bureaucratization that were under way. It is even probable that the processes should have been carried further, as they were to be, belatedly, into such areas as fund-raising, public relations, and student recruitment. It was well known, however, that the processes could be self-propelling. With many academic needs unfulfilled, bureaucratic growth inevitably produced suspicion. The seeming decline in academic deference that was accompanying the increase in bureaucratic staffs had both psychological and organizational repercussions. Although the protests of the professoriate were the most vociferous, they remained largely unrecorded. The point can be illustrated, however, by the dispute that had resulted from the placement among clerical employees of the staff of the library. Members of nonacademic supporting staffs, moreover, were beginning to claim benefits equal to those attached to faculty appointments on the ground that all were employees.

In the central academic realm, sights seem to have been focussed mainly upon the basic standardizing measures in organization and procedures that had developed from the initiatives of the Ryan administration. The conformity of the university more clearly with American, as distinguished from ecclesiastical or European, institutional practice had led to the standardization of both criteria and procedures for appointments and promotions in faculty rank. The academic senate, which had regained collegial vigor, was the principal agent of the process, although the standards upheld in a particular department or school were sometimes more rigorous than those of the senate committee. Unmistakable deference was being paid to the research orientation of the institution. Membership in the Association of American Universities continued to provide reminders of what was being achieved in the best American institutions. Institutional aims could be easily articulated for accrediting bodies, especially the Middle States Association of Colleges and Secondary Schools. Instruction was being enhanced not only at the graduate, but also at the undergraduate and professional levels. Barriers to enrollment based upon race and sex either had been eliminated or, with respect to women at the undergraduate level, were being removed.

Within disciplinary fields, the probable course of continuing specialization should have been discerned. Specialization had been embraced with the research orientation when the university began. Its consequences in theology had been the subject of memoranda by Hyvernat and Cooper.[185] McCarthy, the historian, had warned in 1921 that "the infinite subdivision of a science" was an achilles' heel and, in fact, the basic "structural weakness" of graduate instruction.[186] McCormick had had some vague hope for a counter-tendency. But American universities generally had long since gone farther in accommodating both disciplinary specialization and professional education. World War II had only highlighted what was being recognized as "the dependence of an expanding, modernizing society on scientific and technological expertise."[187] The strains were not being so keenly felt at The Catholic University of America as in some other institutions because the institution was not large and because it was relatively homogeneous. All the same, activities in behalf of intellectual and spiritual integration were being provoked. Also, those concerned with academic administration could have begun to notice conflicts between individual disciplinary and professional interest and institutional loyalty.

Nationally, portents of another kind were being obscured temporarily by the seeming success of American Catholic higher education, at least in statistical terms, and by the widespread interest in neo-Thomism and integration. What was beginning to disturb departmental chairmen and deans was that student enrollment in Catholic institutions was increasing more rapidly than the availability of Catholics qualified for appointments to the faculties. Even efforts to raise salary levels and so-called "fringe benefits" could not reverse the trend. In consequence, faculties were beginning to be more heterogeneous religiously. Students also, on their part, were coming from more diverse backgrounds than formerly. The pace of differentiation and mobility in the larger society was partly responsible. Just as significantly from a national point of view, within institutions under other than Catholic auspices, barriers to the

185. Hyvernat Papers, "Memoir," 41; McNicholas Papers, Memorandum of Cooper on department of religion, Jan. 7, 1935.

186. OR, op. cit.

187. Oleson and Voss, "Preface," *Organization of Knowledge*, x. The developments of the period are portrayed in their complexity in John Patrick Diggins, *The Proud Decades; America in War and Peace, 1941–1960* (New York: Norton, 1988). See also William L. O'Neill, *American High: The Years of Confidence, 1945–1960* (Glencoe, Ill.: Free Press, 1987).

appointment of Catholics to faculty positions were beginning to break down. Before long, McCormick's second successor would feel compelled to describe the emerging predicament of the university to the trustees with alarm as well as realism:

There is a short supply of good teachers, and a highly competitive market with a rapidly growing student body. Secular as well as Catholic colleges and universities are willing to bid for qualified Catholic teachers, including priests. The situation has become critical and even desperate.[188]

In short, the challenge of the 1950s was to discern the trends that were changing the face of higher education in America and to formulate institutional responses to them that would continue to demonstrate the compatibility of learning and scholarship with religious faith.

188. BT, mm, Apr. 28, 1965.

PART FIVE

The Assessment of Change, 1953-1989

. . . diversity among universities is largely owing to the fact that the American institutions, especially the more recent, have been organized to meet actual needs, rather than to perpetuate traditions; and since these needs are constantly changing, it is quite intelligible that new forms of university organization should appear and that the older forms should be frequently readjusted. – *Edward A. Pace, "Universities," CE, XV, 197.*

CHAPTER X

Challenges from within American Catholicism

Before it had reached its half-century mark The Catholic University of America had accomplished what its most prominent lay alumnus and trustee of the time had been able to call "a work of stupendous importance," even as he was pointing to limitations that he was finding in comparing it with other institutions in "the amount of its endowment, the encouragement it has received, and the opposition which has been ever present to most of its activities."[1] The limitations were to remain during the decades after he wrote, even while the university's academic role was being revivified. All the strengths that the institution could draw from its uniting values, accumulating tradition, and—in Ryan's case—vigorous leadership came to be needed to contend with the numerous controversies and contradictions that were bound to be introduced from the Catholic community of the United States. During the earlier decades, no matter how deeply the divisions ran, the consciousness that the university was a project of the national Catholic body could always have been clearly discerned. In the decades after World War II, this consciousness seemed to become progressively dimmed.

A university's role, of course, is necessarily subject to revision in a dynamic American society. Materially, soon after World War II, such innovations as television, jet air travel, air conditioning, antibiotic medicine, and the contraceptive pill were to introduce dramatically new conditions of life. Life expectancy itself was continuing to be prolonged. Students could take the advancing technology for granted. Their elders, also, soon became accustomed to all the presumed advances and could look upon an expanded social security system, pension plans, and health insurance as their own "entitlements." A business columnist has made the point well:

1. OR, C. E. Martin to Michael Williams, Martinsburg, W.Va., Apr. 9, 1930 (copy).

373

The Great Depression and World War II are a huge ravine in the American experience; they arrested normal change and were followed by a great burst of progress. The result is a society of greater individual choice and mobility without many of history's wants and discomforts.[2]

American Catholics, during the decades after the crossing of the "huge ravine," began to perceive more and more that collectively they too were, as social investigators among them had been reporting, upwardly mobile. Education for them had been, as it had been for others in American society, their most important channel of ascent. With others, of course, they had always found opportunities for individual advancement. Those from families of nineteenth and twentieth century immigrant origins—who were in the overwhelming proportion by far—could attribute to such opportunities the original attraction of the country for their ancestors. If bigotry, never completely dispelled, had delayed their rise, it had not prevented it and, ironically, it had served even to promote their solidarity. With Catholics already occupying leadership positions in numerous fields, the nomination of a Catholic for the presidency in 1928 and the subsequent election of a Catholic in 1960 could easily be taken to symbolize social advancement. There were signs of assimilation in Catholic education, too.

It would be hard to exaggerate the importance of higher education as an agency of assimilation and a channel of mobility. By 1960, 38 per cent of the eighteen- and nineteen-year-old population of the United States was in school. By 1969 the proportion would reach 50 per cent, its high point to date. College enrollments would increase by 350 per cent from 1950 to 1970. The proportion of high school graduates entering degree-granting institutions of some kind, ranging from 50 to 55 per cent during most of the 1970s and early 1980s, would reach a record 58 per cent in 1985.[3] For purposes of contrast, it is useful to recall that at the beginning of the century not one American youth in twenty-five was going to college.

So far as Catholic institutions were concerned, as already noted, until the 1920s the typical college was probably no better academically than it had been when The Catholic University of America was founded. A recent student has portrayed it as "a rather curious combination of strict discipline and rigid religious and doctrinal requirements, run on a very limited budget and in business to produce

2. Robert J. Samuelson, "Ten Triumphs of Consumption That Have Shaped Our Age," *Washington Post*, Oct. 1, 1986.
3. Sharon R. Cohany, "What Happened to the High School Class of 1985?" *MLR*, CIX (Oct., 1986), 28–30.

only good, moral men."[4] Many institutions were still operating both collegiate and secondary departments. "Feeders" for graduate schools the Catholic colleges had not yet become. A survey of selected institutions in 1923, for example, had disclosed that almost 50 per cent of the male graduates were entering either business or the priesthood. The number electing to pursue graduate study was then too small to be noted.[5]

The preference for business careers could be taken as symptomatic, for in no small part the steady growth of college enrollment in the United States—Catholic or other—was already following the expansion of college curricula into fields that had not been embraced previously. As has been remarked, "particularly in the light of traditional intellectual values, there is no better example of American higher education's entrance into the mainstream of American life than its responsiveness to the interests of the business sector and business oriented, ambitious young men."[6] More than might have been realized, however, The Catholic University of America, while not unaffected by the trend, was standing apart. That this was the source of discontent for some can be surmised. The renewal of the graduate thrust that had begun with the Ryan administration, while benefiting from the expansion of the changing Catholic colleges, had become also a renewal of commitment to the "traditional intellectual values" that had been in the minds of the founders, even if influential ecclesiastics, among others, were sometimes failing to recognize the fact.

Two accompaniments of the assimilative process were coming to the fore. One was a broad, many-sided intellectual result that was partly old and partly new. It was manifest in a widespread resurgence of concern for the lack of Catholic attainments in scholarship. Brownson and Spalding had expressed such concern in the nineteenth century. Monsignor Ellis, professor of church history at The Catholic University of America, provided what became the new keynote address on the theme in 1955. There was conspicuous, also, the search for the integration of disciplinary subject matter with Catholic philosophical and theological tradition. Cardinal Stritch was advising the rector that lay persons associated with Catholic higher education were "anxious for a deepening

4. David L. Salvaterra, "The Apostolate of the Intellect: Development and Diffusion of an Academic Ethos among American Catholics in the Early Twentieth Century" (unpublished Ph.D. dissertation, University of Notre Dame, 1983), 58.

5. "Occupations of Graduates of Catholic Colleges, A Survey by the N.C.W.C. Bureau of Education Discloses Interesting Facts," NCWC, IV (Mar., 1923), 29.

6. David O. Levine, *The American College and the Culture of Aspiration, 1915–1940* (Ithaca: Cornell University Press, 1986), 46.

knowledge of Catholic doctrine and Catholic teaching on certain problems in their own fields of learning." He thought that opportunities for
the acquisition of such knowledge were essential if there were to be
"Catholic universities in the real sense of the word."[7]

These currents of self-appraisal, mutually reinforcing as they were,
tended to heighten dissatisfaction with what Catholic institutions of
higher education were doing. Moreover, Catholics were seen to be
reminded, in the aftermath of Vatican Council II, that the Church
was confronting new conditions everywhere, both geographically and
intellectually. To many it seemed that The Catholic University of
America was not participating in the rapid forward movement of the
postwar educational world. Although the advantages of its institutional
tradition and of the comprehensive range of its offerings were still plainly
evident to unbiased observers, it was becoming evident also that the
momentum that Ryan had initiated had run down. Meanwhile, other
Catholic graduate schools appeared to be improving in quality and
expanding in size.

The New Situation of Catholic Graduate Schools

Accidental symbolism confirming the changing situation was introduced unwittingly by McCormick's successor who, almost immediately
after his appointment as rector, arranged to visit the University of Notre
Dame. A wag in Curley Hall quickly compared him to his disadvantage
with the first rector, who had looked for models in institutions with the
highest established academic reputations. In all probability, the object
of the new rector's interest was really Notre Dame's public relations
program, which was already acknowledged to be successful. But the
impression had become general that neither the administration nor the
trustees nor the episcopal sponsors of the university were *au courant*
with what was happening in American higher education. Although the
administration had recently proposed that Laval, for its strength in the
professional schools, and Notre Dame, for its strength in the physical
and social sciences, should be admitted to the Association of American
Universities,[8] it seemed to have assumed that on its part it could be
complacent in its charter membership in the prestigious group.

Of course, the same trends in enrollment that were bringing graduate
students to The Catholic University of America had been affecting
other Catholic institutions as well. More of these institutions than

7. OVR, Stritch to McDonald, Chicago, June 14, 1957.
8. OVR, Edward B. Jordan to Deane W. Mallott, Washington, Oct. 5, 1949.

ever before were following the virtually universal American pattern of building graduate programs upon their older collegiate foundations. They were perceiving "the need for greater excellence in our pursuit of education and professionalism and culture" to which their outstanding leader was later to attribute the origin of graduate schools in general.[9] Some Catholic institutions were still showing competitive intentions with respect to The Catholic University of America. Almost no attention was being given to the papal advice that one Catholic university should be developed to superior standing in all its branches before another should be established.

Nor was attention being paid to another Roman prohibition requiring the permission of the congregation of seminaries and universities for the enrollment of an ecclesiastic in a secular university.[10] Even if data for statistical compilations could not be assembled, it was well known that Catholic scholars and teachers, including priests and religious, were gaining access to institutions that in many cases would not have done so much as to consider them before World War II. Jesuit provincial superiors, having been instructed by their father general to develop scholarship in their faculties,"[11] were sending their most promising subjects for graduate study at Harvard, Chicago, Cornell, and North Carolina, among other non-Catholic institutions, even while the executive secretary of the Jesuit Educational Association was complaining to the university's rector that inspectors for its program of affiliation were "casting aspersions on other Catholic educational institutions" and— in a charge vigorously denied—recommending graduate study in departments at non-Catholic institutions.[12] There was developing the situation that the ninth rector would later describe as "critical and even desperate."[13] More than ever before, the mundane need for adequate funding was looming as a precondition for the achievement of the sublime aims that the founders and their successors had projected for the university.

The trend was related to both the progressive assimilation of Catholics and the financial realities within religious communities. The effect could be seen on the campus within the central faculty of arts and sciences, in which the proportion of full-time graduate students, al-

9. Theodore M. Hesburgh, C.S.C., "Social Responsibility of Graduate Education," CGSC, XII, No. 2 (Feb., 1985), 1.

10. OR, NC dispatch, Vatican City, Sept. 21, 1942.

11. Fitzgerald, *op. cit.*, 25.

12. OR, Edward B. Rooney, S.J., to Corrigan, New York, Apr. 20, 1940; Corrigan to Rooney, Oklahoma City, Okla., Apr. 29, 1940 (copy).

13. *Supra*, 369.

though it was to remain relatively stable for some years, was never again to be as high as it had been during the McCormick administration. Among the full-time students, clerics and religious were continuing to maintain a larger proportion than they constituted among students generally. Thus, although the university had been founded to exemplify to the whole country the congenial compatibility of simple faith with advanced scholarship, its declining appeal to graduate students—or, more realistically, its inability to offer them fellowships in substantial number—was confining graduate enrollment more and more either to clerics and religious subsidized by their dioceses and communities, or to part-time students employed in the metropolitan region.

What can be seen as most telling, so far as the position of the university in American Catholicism was concerned, was the seeming preoccupation of its trustees with their statistical measures of faculty service. The annual surveys that had been conducted for a decade or more were providing data of a sort. Their interpretation, however, was proving difficult. At one extreme, the former president of the University of Notre Dame, who had recently become archbishop of Philadelphia and would later become a cardinal, had proposed that "it should be possible to effect great savings by hiring on a part-time basis those whose service to the University have [sic] been consistently below the normal standard of fifteen hours of teaching a week."[14]

In 1953, just after McCormick's death, when the chancellor circulated to the trustees a committee's tabulations of income and costs by departments, Cardinal Spellman in New York, who was an active and interested trustee, asked for comments from President McGinley at Fordham. This referral itself was significant. Even more revealing, however, was McGinley's reply. First, he put his finger on a crucial question of judgment. Using the department of Semitic and Egyptian languages and literatures as an example of one that was consistently enrolling few students, he asked "whether the welfare of the Church justifies subsidizing the education of a few scholars in this field at the very high cost indicated." He was citing, of course, the per capita cost, not the department's expenditures, which are among the lowest in its school. His criterion was seemingly quantitative. One more conscious of the aims of the founders would have had to note that the department remains the only one in the country that concentrates upon Christian Arabic studies and that it has been able to render signal service to modern biblical research. Perhaps irony can be found in its vulnerability, since it was established by the first professor

14. AAB, Francis P. Keough Papers, John F. O'Hara, C.S.C., to Keough, Philadelphia, Pa., Mar. 11, 1952.

appointed to the university. What was really being called into question, indeed, was the university's aim.

In this respect, McGinley's further comments were indicative of the changed situation in which the university was operating. He was forthright:

> Unless Catholic University has the funds to continue all the graduate courses it now provides, it should face the fact that some graduate students may well have to attend non-Catholic institutions. The principle involved here would seem to me to be: to make the sacrifice required for those graduate courses which Catholic University has a special obligation to provide. I would think such a special obligation would refer to two types of courses: (a) subjects in which the general welfare of the Church is specially at stake and (b) subjects in which other Catholic universities are not already providing courses."[15]

This statement, if it had been examined at all analytically, would have been found to pose with more than ordinary clarity issues of depth that were to grow, not diminish, in importance during the ensuing years. Other Catholic institutions, most of them administered by religious institutes, had become large and well adapted to American academic patterns. Their graduate schools were serving, for the most part, local and regional clienteles. McGinley seems to have been assuming that the bishops' interest in a university, even in one of their own foundation, could be in large part no more than residual, an interest based upon a need to supply what other Catholic institutions were not undertaking to do. He was leaving unanswered questions of elucidation, of the definition of need, for example, and of the methods for its determination.

Underneath them all, however, were prior questions: What is a university? What must a university embrace to deserve the name? What makes a university Catholic? What is the relation of an ecclesiastical hierarchy to the conduct of a Catholic university? Others in succeeding decades would raise these questions, not only about the rise of graduate schools, but about American Catholic higher education in general. Thus, it can be said that the development of Catholic higher education after World War II was to bring a challenge to the university's self-understanding from within American Catholicism itself.

The Eighth Rector (1953–57)

McCormick's successor, Bryan Joseph McEntegart (1893–1968), was, like his predecessor, an alumnus of the university, but he had spent only

15. OR, O'Boyle to trustees, Washington, May 26, 1953; McGinley to Spellman, New York, June 18, 1953; Spellman to McEntegart, New York, Aug. 20, 1953; McEntegart to O'Boyle and McEntegart to Galvin, Washington, Aug. 26, 1953.

Bryan Joseph McEntegart (1893–1968), eighth rector of The Catholic University of America, viewing projected additions to the campus with James A. Magner, procurator, and John J. McClafferty, assistant to the rector for university development.

the first year after his ordination on the campus. His undergraduate work had been at Manhattan College, his theological studies at St. Joseph's Seminary, Dunwoodie. It was to obtain a master's degree in sociology in preparation for assignments in Catholic charities of his native New York that he was sent to Washington in the fall of 1917. A knowledgeable source has reported that, like others among the reputedly "brighter students" in the field, he may have been advised by Kerby to transfer to the New York School of Social Work for further professional training.[16] However this may be, he became director of the division of child care in the extensive archdiocesan charities organization. There for a time during the 1930s he had as an assistant director the priest who was to precede him to Washington as archbishop and third chancellor of the university.

McEntegart's experience in social work had included ten years of

16. O'Grady Papers, autobiography.

part-time teaching at Fordham University, the presidency of the New York State Conference on Social Work and of the National Conference of Catholic Charities, and membership on the boards of directors of the National Catholic Community Service and the United Service Organization. In 1942, he had been appointed national secretary of the Catholic Near East Welfare Association but soon thereafter had been selected to be the first executive director of the War Relief Services of the National Catholic Welfare Conference and then, within a year, bishop of Ogdensburg. It was after ten years on the banks of the St. Lawrence, as he liked to recall during Washington's humid summers, that he became the university's eighth rector. His administration was relatively short. Less than four years after his inauguration, during the spring of 1957, he became bishop of Brooklyn. The title of archbishop *ad personam* was conferred upon him in 1966, the year before the golden jubilee of his ordination to the priesthood and two years before his death.[17]

McEntegart's appointment, announced during the 1953 summer session, was a surprise on the campus. His name had not been among those for whom votes had been cast when the senate had decided upon its *terna*. In advance of the senate's meeting, Deferrari and Campbell had sought to solicit votes for McDonald, as they had done five years before. A countermovement had put in nomination the name of Bishop John J. Wright of Worcester, Massachusetts (subsequently bishop of Pittsburgh and later cardinal prefect of the congregation of the clergy in Rome). After three ballots, McDonald's name had been entered in first place. He had received eleven votes, Wright ten; one had been cast for McCormick, who had declared that he was not a candidate. Wright's name was placed second. Campbell was listed in third place after he had won a simple plurality of votes on three ballots.[18] How the bishops or trustees evaluated the senate's *terna* and whom they included in their own do not appear in the record.[19] McEntegart was installed on November 19, 1953, at a joint convocation with the National Catholic Educational Association that was marking the fiftieth anniversary of its founding at the university. President Dwight D. Eisenhower received an honorary doctorate and addressed the assembly. Meanwhile, the vice rector, Hannan, was continued in office and, a year later, when he left to become bishop of Scranton, McDonald was named to the university's second highest administrative position.

17. See entry by J. P. King, *NCE*, XVI, 268–69.
18. AS, mm, Feb. 26, 1953.
19. BT, mm, Apr. 15, 1953.

During his four years in the rector's office, McEntegart had to give most of his time to building projects to care for needs of the physical plant that in some instances had been recognized for many years. The erection of the superstructure of the National Shrine of the Immaculate Conception between 1954 and 1959 was also among his responsibilities. In all matters, including academic affairs, he was characteristically discriminating, systematic, and thorough. On his arrival, for example, there was on his desk a *cause célèbre* in the form of a lengthy report of an investigation that Campbell had conducted into a student petition that had offended the moderator of the International Relations Club. McEntegart placed the student leaders on probation instead of dismissing them as had been recommended and then suppressed the club.[20] A less controversial development that he could approve was the elevation of the division of music to departmental status and the authorization of a doctorate in the field.[21] During his first year, he appointed a faculty committee "for the study of University scholarly research, its achievements and policies,"[22] but its chairman, Ellis, was to provoke his ire the next year when his unflattering paper on Catholic scholarship was resented by some members of the hierarchy. During McEntegart's administration, the Ford Foundation distributed substantial grants to universities, from which The Catholic University of America received $300,000 that was restricted for a ten-year period to the increase of the endowment fund and another $300,000 as an "accomplishment grant" that was used to revise upward the faculty salary scale.[23]

In general, McEntegart was cautious in relations with academicians. Upon taking office, however, he reversed a previous decision of the administration and the trustees' executive committee that would have required the university to decline a renewal of the grant that it was receiving from the Agnes and Eugene Meyer Scholarship Fund of Washington. McEntegart held that Mrs. Meyer's notorious hostility to Catholic schools should not be allowed to deprive "worthy students" of aid.[24] He did pay attention to anonymous complaints on which his predecessor had not acted by requesting the vice rector to inquire if there was any "element of truth in them." That the inquiries were undertaken ponderously was not his fault.[25] When participation in the National

20. ABC, mm, Sept. 24, 1953.
21. BT, mm, Nov. 17, 1953.
22. *Ibid.*, Apr. 8, 1954.
23. *Ibid.*, Nov. 13, 1956.
24. ABC, mm, July 13, 1953; BT, EC, mm, Oct. 16, 1953.
25. OR, "Your faithful and humble servants" to Pope Pius XII, Washington, Oct. 11, 1952 (copy); Hannan to McEntegart, Dec. 2, 1953, enclosing replies to inquiries.

Student Association was called into question, he accepted recommendations in its favor but was anxious "that the representative of our University should be alert and able to safeguard Catholic interests."[26] He was himself alert to aspersions that might be cast upon the university, even if they appeared in book reviews intended only for scholars.[27]

Relations of Catholic institutions with the National Education Association were cool and when the university's membership in a newly organized affiliate, the Higher Education Association, was solicited, McEntegart was "not inclined to favorable action."[28] When the parent association celebrated its centennial and the university was invited to participate, a member of the department of education advised that nothing should be done because (as probably would have been the case) "many members of the hierarchy would ask a lot of questions."[29] McDonald, as vice rector, had earlier told the rector that the university would have little to gain even by celebrating the annual American Education Week, but that it could simply "give assurance of cooperation lest we may be accused again of maintaining a position of 'splendid isolation.' "[30]

At the outset of his administration, McEntegart recognized the long-standing need of the university for a "recruitment and development program."[31] The major problem, he told the trustees, was the decline in the number of full-time students that had set in after 1950. Male students especially were declining in number while women students were increasing.[32] The scholarship programs that had been adopted in 1950 and 1953 to attract students were augmented, but then reduced when retrenchment seemed necessary.[33] Later, looking toward the good will of the religious communities who then were maintaining eighty-six Washington houses of study, the new position of dean of religious communities was established.

With a building program looming, McEntegart was able to appoint Monsignor McClafferty, the dean of the school of social service, as assistant to the rector for university development.[34] Meanwhile, the

26. *Ibid.*, McEntegart to Hannan, Mar. 5, 1954.

27. *Ibid.*, Thomas T. McAvoy, C.S.C., to McEntegart, Notre Dame, Jan. 27, 1955.

28. *Ibid.*, G. Kerry Smith to McEntegart, Washington, Oct. 19, 1955, referred to Deferrari with the notation.

29. *Ibid.*, Smith and Paul Street to McEntegart, Washington, Apr. 16, 1956, with note from Francis J. Houlahan to McEntegart, Apr. 24, 1956.

30. *Ibid.*, McDonald to McEntegart, Oct. 12, 1954.

31. BT, mm, Apr. 28, 1954.

32. *Ibid.*, Nov. 16, 1954, exh.

33. Ibid., Nov. 16, 1954; Nov. 15, 1955.

34. BT, EC, mm, Oct. 20, 1955.

acquisition of the former Columbus University had to be completed, its building renovated, and the school of law moved downtown.[35] Also, property owned by the Sulpician Fathers across Michigan Avenue—on which residence halls were later to be constructed—was to become available for purchase when its use for wartime and postwar temporary housing could be discontinued, as was property across from it at Monroe and Seventh Streets, Northeast.[36]

The building program that was developed by McEntegart was divided into four phases, the first three of which were scheduled to be completed before 1962, the seventy-fifth anniversary of the university's founding.[37] Only allusion was made to a fourth phase to include possible construction of buildings for academic administration and liberal arts and for speech and drama and the fine arts. The first phase called for the immediate construction of a building, later named Keane Hall, for the department of physics. McEntegart gave highest priority to this project, which was planned to match Shahan Hall and to give symmetry to the space before Mullen Library as it faced the Shrine.[38] Second priority but with immediate construction in mind was given to completion of the wings of the library, which had been requested, at least since 1946, in representations from the director and in conferences of the procurator, Monsignor Magner, with the director and with prospective architects.[39] This phase, estimated to cost more than $1,900,000, could be funded from restricted reserves that the university had accumulated.

The second phase of the building program, scheduled to be undertaken during 1957 and 1958, was focussed upon student needs. It resulted in the construction of Conaty Hall as a residence for about two hundred undergraduate men, and of a student center, both financed through a loan of $1,350,000 from the federal Housing and Home Finance Agency and an appropriation of $200,000 from restricted reserves.[40] In 1950 the trustees had actually appropriated $900,000 for a center only to find that all bids that were received were in excess of this amount.[41]

The completion of the first phase and the execution of the second and third phases—projected for the years 1959 to 1962—were left to

35. BT, mm, Nov. 17, 1953; Apr. 28, 1954; Nov. 6, 1954.

36. *Ibid.*, Apr. 28 and June 30, 1954.

37. BT, mm, Nov. 13, 1956; OR, McEntegart to John J. Russell, Washington, Nov. 21, 1956, with edited copy of rector's report to hierarchy.

38. BT, mm, Nov. 15, 1955; BT, EC, mm, Jan. 16, 1958.

39. ABC, mm, Oct. 2, 1946; Feb. 4, 1948; Nov. 2, 1949; Sept. 30, 1953.

40. BT, mm, Nov. 12, 1957; Nov. 11, 1958; BT, EC, mm, Mar. 19, 1959.

41. *Ibid.*, Feb. 18 and Apr. 14, 1948; Nov. 29, 1950; Jan. 6 and 31, 1951.

McEntegart's successor. Included in plans for the third phase were the renovation of Caldwell Hall and the construction of a south wing to provide an auditorium and additional rooms for priest students;[42] the Thomas W. Pangborn Building for the school of engineering and architecture (to which McEntegart had earlier accorded third highest priority);[43] and a building for the school of nursing, the present Gowan Hall. A projected north wing of Curley Hall, to provide for additional priest members of the faculties, was never begun. For the construction in this third phase $3,600,000 was requested from the bishops. McEntegart had warned the trustees at an earlier date that the university would need not only the support received in the form of the annual diocesan collections but, every five or ten years, "periodical supplemental financing for building purposes."[44]

Just before his departure for Brooklyn, however, he and the faculties received from an unexpected source rude evidence that the position of the university among American Catholics was indeed no longer viewed as unique, even in Rome. Almost twenty years before, the same prominent alumnus and trustee who had recognized what had been accomplished under the university's perennial limitations had reiterated his concern that the university was "being run on a shoe string" and had expressed the opinion that "the argument that the University is the only papal institution in the country" was "not only threadbare" but had "gotten us nowhere."[45] The singularity of pontifical status, nevertheless, had continued to be a matter of pride. But when the *Annuario Pontificio* for 1957 arrived on campus the executive officers learned for the first time that a decree of the canonical erection of Niagara University had been issued by the congregation of seminaries and universities on the previous June 21.[46] McEntegart was so disturbed by the information that after arriving in Brooklyn he assigned an assistant chancellor to investigate the facts in the case.[47] Five years later, however, various other Catholic institutions were reported to be under consideration for pontifical standing. Action seems to have been averted only when attention was called to potential undesirable effects of such a move upon American political controversies of the time.[48] As late as 1966, when

42. This south wing was named the St. Elizabeth Seton Wing when its residential quarters were assigned to sisters in 1979. BT, mm, Dec. 16, 1978.
43. BT, mm, Nov. 14, 1961.
44. BT, mm, Nov. 15, 1955.
45. OR, C. E. Martin to Corrigan, Martinsburg, May 24, 1938.
46. AAS, XLVIII (June 16, 1956), 446–47, 846 (in Latin).
47. OR, McEntegart to McDonald, Brooklyn, Oct. 9, 1957.
48. *Ibid.*, O'Boyle to Egidio Vagnozzi, Washington, June 28, 1962. Archbishop Vagnozzi was apostolic delegate at the time and was later elevated to the college of cardinals.

Cardinal Joseph Ritter inquired if the university would object if St. Louis University petitioned Rome for authority to grant undergraduate degrees in sacred sciences to non-Jesuits, the executive committee of the board was unanimous in its opposition.[49] After subsequent developments beginning in the late 1960s, however, the university's pontifical status seemed no longer to be envied and was, in fact, to become more restricted in its meaning.

The Ninth Rector (1957–1967)

Challenges directed nearer to the heart of the university's mission were to confront McEntegart's successors. The first of these was William Joseph McDonald (1904–89) who probably entered upon the office of rector, which he was to occupy for ten years, with more good will than any of his predecessors had ever enjoyed at a comparable moment. When McEntegart's translation to Brooklyn was announced, it was taken for granted that McDonald would be appointed to succeed him. He received sixteen of the twenty-one votes that were cast on the first ballot for the first place on the terna that the academic senate sent to the chancellor.[50] Although the votes of the episcopal trustees were given in confidence to the latter and were not recorded in the board's minutes, McDonald's nomination to the Holy See can be assumed.

McDonald, a native of County Kilkenny in Ireland, had studied for the priesthood at the diocesan St. Kieran's College and had been ordained in the see city in 1928 for the archdiocese of San Francisco. From 1928 until 1936 he had served as a chaplain of Newman clubs, an associate editor of the archdiocesan newspaper, and a curate. Then, after his assignment for graduate studies and the conferral of his doctorate in 1939, he had been invited to join the faculty of philosophy, beginning in 1940. He had become vice rector in 1954. Soon after his appointment as rector and then as editor-in-chief of the *New Catholic Encyclopedia*, the honorary degree of doctor of science was conferred upon him by St. John's University of Brooklyn, in 1959. Other honorary doctorates followed. The International Federation of Catholic Universities elected him as its president for one term, from 1960 to 1963. Meanwhile, although controversies concerning his policies and his Roman allies had already erupted, both the senate and the trustees gave him overwhelming support for reappointment to a second term as rector.[51] Ecclesiastical promotion followed when, in 1964, he was named

49. BT, mm, Nov. 13, 1966.
50. AS, mm, May 29, 1957.
51. *Ibid.*, May 17, 1962; BT, mm, Oct. 14, 1962.

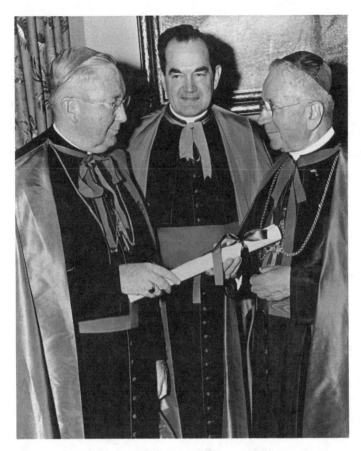

William Joseph McDonald (1904–89), ninth rector of The Catholic University of America, with Patrick Aloysius O'Boyle (1896–1987), archbishop of Washington and third chancellor of the university, and Amleto Cicognani (1883–1973), titular archbishop of Laodicea and apostolic delegate to the United States.

to the titular bishopric of Aquae Regiae and appointed an auxiliary bishop of Washington. When he left the university three years later, he became an auxiliary bishop of San Francisco.

The McDonald decade, which was to end in an academic debacle, was a period of notable expansion in the number of students enrolling and in the buildings comprising the physical plant. Total enrollment (of both full-time and part-time students) grew from 3,858 students during McDonald's first year, 1957–58, to 6,779 during his last, 1966–67. This was an increase of 75 per cent. Early in his second term McDonald estimated that if classes in adult education, summer sessions, workshops, and the like were included, the number of persons that the university was reaching annually would be about 14,000. This numerical growth could be cited by him in his defense against what he later called "certain manifestations of dissatisfaction"[52] and it may well have been accepted trustingly, since success often enough is equated with mere size. Changes that were occurring in the composition of the student body and that were mentioned occasionally were worthy of more analysis than they seem to have received.

Two trends had set in early in the postwar period. One was visible in the continuing increase in the number and proportion of part-time students, mostly at the graduate or professional level. They were about 90 per cent more numerous in the fall of 1966 than they had been in 1957, while full-time students had increased by only a little more than 69 per cent. Probably faculty were more concerned about a second trend shown in a faster rate of increase in undergraduate than in graduate or professional enrollment. In the college of arts and sciences, the total number enrolled doubled while McDonald was in office. The presence of the undergraduates on campus was particularly apparent and also particularly significant because most by far were full-time students.

Even more visible, perhaps, in a period when clerics and religious could still be distinguished by dress, was the increase in the number of lay students in relation to those with ecclesiastical status. The latter increased by only 39 per cent from 1957 to 1966 and whereas in the former year they had constituted about 33 per cent of the student body, in the latter they were only about 26 per cent. Confining the comparisons to full-time students makes the trend more marked. In 1957, clerics and religious were accounting for 41 percent of all full-time students, but by 1966 for only 29 per cent. The trend was not to be reversed. Within the category, enrollment of sisters had already peaked in 1963, when their number was 51 per cent more than in 1957; it was their subsequent decline that reduced their gain for the decade to about 22 per cent.

These trends did not change very much the relative proportions of students in the three conventional academic groupings of schools, the arts and sciences, the ecclesiastical, and the professional, if allowance is made for the inclusion in the former of professional departments that became schools in 1965 or later. About 52 per cent of all students were in the arts and sciences in 1957 and almost 57 per cent in 1966. Ecclesiastical students remained in about the same proportion—nearly 13 per cent—during the period. The proportion of enrollment in profes-

52. BT, mm, Apr. 20, 1966.

sional schools therefore declined in about the same degree as that in the arts and sciences gained.

Much of the rector's energy had to be devoted to the expansion of the physical plant required to accommodate the increasing enrollment. Some of the needed building had been long delayed. In some instances, too, as bids often exceeded estimates and the authorizations that had been obtained, the course that the university took, which with hindsight seems to have been consistently short-sighted, was "to try by every means possible to pull the project back to the original estimated costs" even when this required "foregoing some parts of the work to compensate for the rise in the cost index."[53] A whole floor of the student center was sacrificed, for example. Initially, McDonald had been responsible for the completion of the first phase of the program that McEntegart had begun, and for the entire construction planned for the second and third phases. The continued expansion that followed the completion of the program was for both academic and residential purposes, although expansion of the power plant had to be undertaken to serve both.

A building for the department of biology was named for Sarah McCort Ward, who had left a substantial bequest to the university. The William E. Leahy Memorial Hall, for the school of law, honored the deceased chairman of the board of Columbus University, who had been instrumental in the transfer of its property to the university. A grant from the National Science Foundation facilitated the renovation of Maloney Hall. An extension serving both biology and nursing was erected to join the buildings occupied by these units. The bishops of the United States were persuaded to fund an addition to Theological College, the former Sulpician Seminary, through a system of quotas.[54] Finally, on the academic side, the board approved the rector's recommendation to raise funds for a university theater, but a stipulation that construction could not begin until at least $500,000 was on hand proved to be an insuperable obstacle, even after a fund-raising firm was employed and after Jerry Wolman, a real estate entrepreneur, offered to contribute $1,000,000 in five annual installments (which he became unable to provide).[55]

53. OVR, conference at regional office of Housing and Home Finance Administration, Philadelphia, mm, July 17, 1958.

54. BT, mm, Nov. 14, 1961, May 2, 1962. The addition had been outlined to the EC, Apr. 7, 1960, and proposed to the BT, Apr. 27, 1960. Archbishop William O. Brady of St. Paul, who had been a student of the Sulpicians and knew the history, looked ahead to urge that "the situation should now be regularized so that the Theological College will become truly a part of the University and its development will become a University project." BT, mm, Nov. 15, 1960. The subsequent decision of a special trustee committee to purchase the seminary property seems to have been reversed by an intervention from McEntegart.

55. *Ibid.*, Oct. 14, 1962; Nov. 10, 1963; Nov. 14, 1965.

New residential accommodations were the principal need of students. When Gowan Hall was completed, the former "nursing building" was given over entirely to rooms for women and named in honor of James Hugh Ryan, the fifth rector. Later, a pioneer member of the faculties was honored in the naming of Shields Hall for sisters. A new residence hall for men was named to honor John Lancaster Spalding, one for women (later assigned to men) in acknowledgment of a bequest by Mary Flather. An addition was built to add to both residential and dining facilities in Graduate Hall. Benefactors were commemorated in the naming of two smaller halls, Joseph P. Reardon for men, and Frances Zimmerman for women. Two additional dining halls for women were built, one near their residential halls on what was still Brookland Avenue, one for sisters on the Sisters College campus. Also, the university undertook to acquire apartment buildings in nearby Brookland, the Donald and Oak Terrace Apartments on Twelfth Street, and the Perry Apartments at the intersection of Michigan Avenue and Perry Street, all three of which were to be sold during the 1970s.

The construction of Shields Hall prompted the dissolution of the Catholic Sisters College and its incorporation within the university. This was a condition for the loan to the university from the Housing and Home Finance Agency through which the construction was financed. The step was not radical. Administrative and instructional duplication entailed in the separate existence of the college had been recognized at least as early as the Ryan administration. Under disciplinary rules for religious in effect, however, it had not been until 1947 that permission to use Mullen Library had been extended generally to sister students.[56] By 1949 the trustees had been inquiring more seriously than ever before into "the necessity of continuing the separate organization of the College."[57] Registration had been taken over by the university and separate classes had been reduced to the fields of education and religion.[58] Although some communities continued to favor the university as the locale for the training of their members,[59] the enrollment of sisters for undergraduate work had long since declined. The rise of the Sister Formation Movement was introducing new considerations.[60]

56. ABC, mm, Oct. 15, 1947.

57. AAB, Keough Papers, O'Hara to McCormick, Buffalo, Apr. 13, 1949 (copy).

58. ABC, mm, Dec. 7, 1949; Mar. 8, 1950.

59. OVR, Sister Mary Robert Falls, O.S.U., to McAllister, Washington, Nov. 27, 1962.

60. OR, Sister M. Gertrude, C.R., to McEntegart, Port Chester, N.Y., Aug. 2, 1954; Deferrari to McEntegart, Nov. 10, 1954; McEntegart to Joseph Gorham, Aug. 30, 1955 (copy); Sister Mary Emil, I.H.M., to National Consultation Committee, Detroit, Oct. 6, 1956 (mimeo.); Deferrari to Ewald Nyquist, Washington, Apr. 20, 1959 (copy). OVR,

Incorporation into the university was completed by 1964.[61] As the last dean reported, the functioning of the college had been reorganized "into its realistic situation as Sisters Residences."[62] Soon the sister students were petitioning for administration of their residence halls under the dean of women.[63] By 1967, there was evidence of continuing decline in the enrollment of sisters and thought of assigning Brady Hall as a residence for lay women.[64]

There was little change in the university's pattern of governance and administration under McDonald. The civil charter documents and the pontifical statutes of 1937 were still controlling, even if for some reason it was maintained that "since these statutes were given to the University by the Sacred Congregation of Seminaries and Universities they have always been treated in a confidential way."[65] It took action by the academic senate to obtain a new edition of the papal documents, which had been amended with respect to procedures for the appointment of deans and the like.[66] The most important legal development was the election of the university in 1964 to accept the provisions of the District of Columbia Non-Profit Corporation Act, through which the corporate powers of the institution were broadened and the merger of the Catholic Sisters College into the university was facilitated.[67]

McDonald seems to have perceived from the beginning that the university had outgrown its inherited administrative structure, but his attempts at its revision were characterized by fear that his authority might be compromised. During his first year in office, he appointed not only Monsignor Joseph B. McAllister as vice rector and as director of studies for ecclesiastical schools, but, to newly established positions, assistants for academic affairs and for student personnel services, a coordinator of research, and an adviser to the dean of the school of law. There were subsequent realignments, but clear definitions of responsibility seem not to have followed even a more far-reaching reorganization in 1966 when McDonald announced that the trustees and the Roman

---

memorandum for file, Apr. 6, 1962. Deferrari portrayed the movement as exaggerating the existing deficiencies in teacher-training for sisters, as overstressing professional training in education, and as removing sisters unwisely to "college centers" from their own communities of formation.

61. *Ibid.*, Magner to John L. Hamilton, Washington, Apr. 24, 1964 (copy); BT, mm, Mar. 19, 1964.

62. OR, Robert McCall, S.S.J., to McAllister, Feb. 10, 1966.

63. *Ibid.*, Sister Ancilla Marie Petricone *et al.* to McDonald, Mar. 2, 1966.

64. *Ibid.*, McDonald to Reverend Mothers, Washington, July 6, 1967.

65. OVR, McAllister to Chrysologus Allaire, S.J., Washington, Dec. 18, 1957 (copy).

66. AS, mm, Dec. 17, 1963; Jan. 30, 1964.

67. BT, mm, Mar. 31, 1964.

congregation had approved the elevation of McAllister to be executive
vice rector and the designation of four other vice rectors—for academic
affairs, for business and finance, for development, and for research.[68]
The historian Robert Trisco was appointed to the first of these positions,
Magner to the second (with a change of title but not of duties). The
latter two offices remained unfilled during what proved to be McDonald's
last year in office.

Organizational ambiguities and problems that cannot be traced in
detail characterized also the first years of what may be the most enduring
contribution of the McDonald administration, that is, the production
and publication of the *New Catholic Encyclopedia*. It was initiated in
1958 by a proposal of the publisher, the McGraw-Hill Book Company,
to the university's librarian of a work that would have been based upon
the Italian *Enciclopedia Cattolica*. When the Catholic Commission for
Intellectual and Cultural Affairs expressed an interest in undertaking a
completely new work, its representatives and the rector met with Cardinal Stritch in Chicago, with the result that the work was placed solely
under the university.[69] Interests of the first *Catholic Encyclopedia* residing
in the Gilmary Society of New York were satisfied through the good
offices of Cardinal Spellman.[70] Although the rector's position as editor-
in-chief and a key editorial role for Professor McGuire were determined
at an early date,[71] the effective organization of the work began with the
appointments of Magner as assistant editor-in-chief, in 1962, and of
John P. Whalen, a priest of the diocese of Albany who had been
appointed an associate professor of theology, as editorial operations
director, in 1963.[72]

The Challenge of Traditional Academic Values

McDonald's administration was marked particularly by the beginning
phase of a development in American Catholicism that was not simply
one of expanding institutions but eventually one of theological import.
Although he had earned his doctorate on the campus and had served
in the faculty of philosophy for a decade and a half before he assumed
administrative responsibilities, McDonald as rector found himself being
challenged repeatedly by actions that were based upon what members
of the faculties were taking to be long-accepted academic values. What

68. AS, mm, Oct. 27, 1966.
69. BT, mm, Apr. 16 and Nov. 11, 1958.
70. *Ibid.*, Apr. 8 and Nov. 17, 1959.
71. *Ibid.*, Nov. 17, 1959.
72. *Ibid.*, Oct. 14, 1962; Apr. 24, 1963.

he on the other hand was appearing to define as the defense of orthodoxy or of ecclesiastical prerogative was often perceived by his colleagues as interference on a less lofty level. It was not that anyone then was putting any truth whatever in the widely quoted quip that a Catholic university is a contradiction in terms. The challenges that were arising from within the faculties were not even directed against ecclesiastical leadership as such. Protests, private and public, followed only what were considered to be violations of an implicit academic compact by the head of an institution who, statutorily at the time, had to be a priest. One instrument of protest was a newly organized Faculty Assembly that functioned until the mid-1970s.

Members of the faculties were all the more sensitive to apparent violations because the postwar developments in American Catholicism had put into sharp relief their historic aspiration for a university of the highest academic quality. The rising prominence of other Catholic institutions was producing deepening embarrassment and resentment when administrative policies seemed to be hindering academic progress. That the fears were not imaginary was revealed when, in contrast to its findings in 1934, a reputational survey of the American Council on Education in 1966 rated seven departments at the University of Notre Dame but only three at The Catholic University of America as adequate or better in the quality of their doctoral offerings.[73] Untoward incidents of academic significance were occurring more frequently than can be cited in detail.

Conflicts between academic and ostensibly ecclesiastical values could have been found in McDonald's discharge of his duties as vice rector, but the first that was somewhat open occurred during his first term as rector when preparations for Vatican Council II were begun. McDonald had announced the formation of a relatively elaborate committee and had charged it with formulating a response for the university to an invitation from a preparatory commission to propose items for consideration in Rome. But when the resulting report was submitted, he explained to the academic senate that the committee "had been in the nature of advisory to him and the official comments of the University had been sent by letter, copies of which were not available for distribution."[74] There was immediate suspicion that ecclesiastical authority was being invoked to suppress a product of faculty effort. Later, professors of canon law learned in Rome that what had been proposed in their

73. Allan M. Cartter, *An Assessment of Quality in Graduate Education* (Washington: American Council on Education, 1966).

74. AS, mm, Apr. 26, 1960.

faculty indeed had not been included in the report for the university. The rector's replies to their questions in the senate seemed to be evasive and cloaked behind a solemn oath of secrecy.[75] Earlier suspicions that the "official comments of the University" were his alone were confirmed.

More widespread conflicts developed over policies pertaining to extern speakers on campus. While vice rector, McDonald had insisted upon prior approval of speakers invited for public lectures by the campus chapter of the American Association of University Professors. Previous administrations, relying upon the good sense of the chapter's officers, had simply noted that the chapter was "an independent entity not officially representative of the university."[76] As rector, citing the supremacy of theology in the university, McDonald sought and obtained from the trustees a requirement of prior approval.[77] On several occasions he refused to allow the AAUP chapter and the honorary science fraternity Sigma Xi to cosponsor a symposium on "Evolution: An Evaluation," probably because an eminent biologist who was proposed as a participant had been associated with left-wing positions on political issues.[78] When the AAUP chapter invited the distinguished historical scholar, Dom Jean Leclerq, O.S.B., of Luxemburg to lecture on the "Use and Interpretation of Scripture from the Time of St. Gregory the Great to St. Bernard," three scholars in disparate ecclesiastical disciplines were consulted for assurance that the speaker would be "safe."[79] A little earlier, the appointment of Charles Malik of Lebanon as a visiting scholar in the school of philosophy had been approved only with the understanding that any collaborators he might bring to the campus had first to be "cleared" with the vice rector.[80]

Similar controversies developed in relations with the students. When the Catholic Students Mission Crusade, with a large membership of seminarians, requested permission to invite the Ceylonese ambassador to lecture on the United Nations, the vice rector was instructed to reply that McDonald would "not approve of a Buddhist lecturing on the missions."[81] A thick file of correspondence resulted from a student's

---

75. *Ibid.*, Mar. 28 and Apr. 25, 1963.

76. OVR, Browne to McDonald, May 21, 1955. McDonald had complained that approval had not been obtained for a lecture by Isaac Fein of Baltimore Hebrew College on "Three Hundred Years of Jewish History," and had noted in penciled comments that the university had been embarrassed by a lecture on church–state relations given by John Courtney Murray, S.J., in 1954 under auspices of the chapter.

77. BT, mm, Apr. 16, 1958.

78. OR, Helen E. Peixotto and Malcolm Henderson to McDonald, Jan. 8, 1959.

79. OVR, memorandum for file, Oct. 24, 1962.

80. BT, EC, mm, June 21, 1962.

81. *Ibid.*, Joseph F. O'Donnell, C.S.C., to McDonald, Jan. 23, 1958.

article in the *Tower* that seemingly led to suspicions of heterodox teaching by professors of biblical studies.[82] And when several priests who were graduate students, acting on their own, invited the notorious James Hoffa of the Teamsters' union to the campus for an unpublicized informal discussion of labor relations, McDonald felt it necessary to express regrets to Attorney General Robert Kennedy and to "dissociate the University administration from any responsibility" for Hoffa's appearance.[83]

Early in 1963 the issue broke into the public press when, from a list of thirteen possible speakers whom the Graduate Student Council was proposing to invite to the campus, the names of four well-known Catholic theologians were struck. They were Godfrey Diekman, O.S.B., John Courtney Murray, S.J., Hans Kung, and Gustave Weigel, S.J. The explanation given *ex post facto* was that "they all represented a particular point of view on issues still under study and unresolved by the Fathers of the Second Vatican Council, and that until these issues were officially settled, the University wanted to be impartial."[84] The rector was quoted as saying that "a prudential judgement was required on a problem without precedent in the history of our University."[85]

In the board, Cardinal Ritter expressed his disagreement with the ban on the speakers, commented that it was indicative of "troubles between the faculty and administration," and asked for "an objective investigation by an outside board." Archbishop Paul J. Hallinan of Atlanta, unable to be present, asked in a letter for public assurance "that reputable men will not be excluded from the University platform because of their views" and requested circulation to the bishops of the proposals to the Vatican Council that had been developed in the school of canon law. Disagreement was expressed also by Archbishop Karl J. Alter of Cincinnati, and in the cases of two of the speakers rejected, by Cardinal O'Boyle, the chancellor of the university. Cardinal Lawrence Shehan of Baltimore, while upholding the rector's authority, took the occasion to urge "an investigation of the forces responsible for suspicion and fear," excoriating specifically the *American Ecclesiastical Review* that was being edited by Monsignor Fenton, who was believed to be close to Cardinal Ottaviani of the holy office. The board, after discussion, decided to issue a statement supporting the rector.[86]

82. Hugh Maloney, "Penumbric Protection," *Tower*, Mar. 24, 1961; OVR, Confidential, The Maloney Article.
83. OR, McDonald to Kennedy, Washington, Dec. 9, 1963.
84. BT, mm, Apr. 24, 1963, exh.
85. NC release, Feb. 16, 1963.
86. BT, mm, Apr. 24, 1963.

McDonald had to defend his position on more than this "speakers' issue" in his presentation to the trustees. Issues had arisen one by one, but a report of a committee on proper academic procedure in the graduate school of arts and sciences had outlined the linkage between them and its significance.[87] McDonald later read to the senate a lengthy statement that he had presented to the board and the board's resolution of support for him. In this statement he attempted to explain his position or refute allegations with respect to deprecations of the course of university policy that had been made by Monsignor Ellis, whom McEntegart wanted the board to reprimand; to his veto of the proposed symposium on evolution; to his omission from the university's proposals for the Vatican Council of those from the faculty of canon law; and to his termination of the appointment of Edward Siegman, C.PP.S., an associate professor of scripture in the school of sacred theology.[88]

Biblical studies were a field of particular controversy at the time, only partly because the findings of scripture scholars were being reviewed critically as they were being incorporated into theology. Soon after his arrival as apostolic delegate in 1959, Archbishop Vagnozzi had delivered an unusually blunt speech at Marquette University in Milwaukee, in which he had included biblical studies with other aspects of American Catholicism that he singled out as particularly dangerous. The student article in the *Tower* had been read by Siegman before its publication and it was used also to place under suspicion Christian Ceroke, O.Carm., whose course in the department of religion and religious education the student had followed.[89] Siegman, who had suffered two heart attacks, was "replaced" for reasons of health, although his salary was continued for the year remaining of his term as an associate professor. He was precluded from returning on the ground that the pontifical statutes assured permanent tenure only for ordinary professors, although the university was in fact observing the more usual standards. The faculty of the school of sacred theology adopted a resolution of protest that gained wide circulation on campus.[90]

87. GSAS, "Report of a special committee on Departure from Proper Academic Procedure," Apr. 23, 1963.

88. AS, mm, Apr. 25, 1963.

89. OVR, McDonald to Vagnozzi, Washington, Mar. 24, 1961 (copy), dissociating the university from the views expressed, and Ceroke to McDonald, Apr. 23, 1961, noting McDonald's allusion to "high ecclesiastical authority" in a discussion of Apr. 10, 1961.

90. *Ibid.*, McDonald to John E. Byrne, C.PP.S., Washington, Apr. 18, 1962 (copy); Byrne to McDonald, Rensselaer, Ind., May 1, 1962 (telegram); McDonald to Byrne, Washington, May 2, 1962 (copy); Byrne to McDonald, Rensselaer, May 3, 1962 (copy); Siegman to McDonald, Rensselaer, May 8, 1962; McDonald to Walter J. Schmitz, S.S., May 15, 1962; Schmitz to McDonald, May 18, 1962. See Fogarty, *Biblical Scholarship*, Chaps. XII–XIV, for a fuller account that includes Siegman's scholarly contributions.

Changes in academic organization made during McDonald's adminis- tration also presented some difficulties. The first was a revision of the program by which seminaries were affiliated with the university. The norms of the Corrigan period that had allowed fourth-year theological students to become candidates for the licentiate had been abrogated in 1955. The sacred congregation of seminaries and universities, however, had desired that the degree of bachelor of sacred theology should be conferred by the university upon superior students from seminaries affiliated with it and the first of these degrees were conferred in 1958. The faculty was finding the program embarrassing because it had neither control of the seminary programs nor records of the work of the candidates. Its repeated resolutions were to lead to the termination of the program in 1970.[91]

Non-controversial changes included the shortening of the name of the school of nursing education to what had been intended originally— school of nursing.[92] An interdepartmental master's degree program in mission studies was approved.[93] The departments of romance languages and of German and comparative philology were combined to form the department of modern languages and literatures.[94] A division of applied physics and space science in the school of engineering and architecture was raised to departmental status.[95] The university joined with other institutions of the District of Columbia in forming the Consortium of Universities, through which joint action could be taken and through which students were to obtain the advantages of cross-registration among the member institutions.[96] The department of music was elevated to become a school.[97]

Three organizational changes, two of them undertaken without prior

91. OVR, John Rogg Schmidt to Nuesse, Apr. 24, 1968; Catherine R. Rich to Nuesse, Aug. 13, 1968; Walter J. Schmitz, S.S., to Nuesse, May 14, 1969; Nuesse to BT, Committee on Academic Affairs, Aug. 28, 1969 (copy); Clarence C. Walton to Cardinal Gabriel Garonne, prefect of the sacred congregation for Catholic education, Washington, Feb. 2, 1970 (copy); Nuesse to Rectors of Seminaries Affiliated with The Catholic University of America, Washington, Feb. 20, 1970 (copy).

92. AS, mm, Dec. 19, 1957; Jan. 30, 1958.

93. *Ibid.*, Mar. 25, 1958. A proposal for a program in missiology had been urged by Cooper as early as 1938. See OR, Cooper to Corrigan, Sept. 15, 1938; McGuire to Corrigan, Nov. 7, 1940; Thomas J. McDonnell to McCormick, New York, Dec. 17, 1948; Fulton J. Sheen to McEntegart, New York, Aug. 10, 1953; Nuesse to McEntegart, Feb. 11, 1957; Nuesse to McDonald, Jan. 16, 1958.

94. AS, mm, Oct. 30, 1958.

95. AS, mm, Dec. 17, 1963; BT, mm, Apr. 24, 1963; Nov. 10, 1963.

96. AS, mm, Jan. 28, 1965; BT, mm, Apr. 8, 1965; Apr. 20, 1966. For an earlier attempt at interuniversity cooperation, see OVR, McCormick to Corrigan, Dec. 7, 1938; and "Minutes of the Meeting of the Inter-University Seminar," Feb. 16, 1939.

97. AS, mm, Oct. 26 and Nov. 21, 1961; Nov. 25, 1965; BT, mm, Apr. 28, 1965.

consultation of the academic senate and the third blocked and reconsidered, became subjects of serious controversies. The first arose in 1965 when the department of education was elevated to the status of a school upon the request of its dean, who had been appointed to the position in 1963. His predecessor had made what seems to have been the first request for this action in 1957. It was now presented to the trustees as having the approval of the dean of the graduate school of arts and sciences, of which the department of education was a part. This approval was contested. The stated objectives were to place the new school "in a better position in seeking funds for research" and to enable it to promote more effectively than it otherwise could "advance into specialized fields." These objectives, it was anticipated, could be accomplished with "no increase in costs."[98] Although the realism of the move might have been questioned on this ground alone, it was principally the lack of prior consultation that gave rise to controversy.[99]

This was accentuated by a second action when, probably in an effort to bypass conflicts that were paralyzing the small department of politics, McDonald established an institute of international law and relations as an independent unit that would report directly to the vice rector but be unrepresented in the senate.[100] If his intent was pacification, the effect was the opposite. The institute was terminated by the succeeding interim administration in 1968, but the director had already brought suits against the university and its officers that were not dismissed in the courts until 1976.

A third controversial change was attempted but never completed. It had a longer history than the others. Ostensibly, its justification was in a statutory provision that the faculty of theology should embrace "the courses in Religion in all the Schools."[101] There had been little or no controversy after the organization of the department of religious education as long as its focus was upon the apologetic and moral instruction of undergraduates in the tradition that Cooper had established. During the early postwar period, however, there had developed a nationwide movement for the reorientation of undergraduate instruction in a stricter, more critical, disciplinary direction. The product, often known as "college theology," was not immediately accepted on the campus. It was so suspect, in fact, that the secretary general of the university had

98. BT, mm, Nov. 9, 1964.

99. AS, mm, Feb. 25, 1965.

100. BT, mm, Jan. 21, 1965; AS, mm, Jan. 25 and Nov. 25, 1965; OR, Middle States Association, Evaluation Document No. 15.

101. "The Statutes of the Catholic University of America Approved by the Holy See" (reprinted; Washington, D.C.: The Catholic University of America, 1964), Art. 86.

been authorized to attend a meeting of the Society of College Teachers of Sacred Doctrine only if he felt that the association would explicitly record a "policy of admitting to membership teachers of variant views regarding the relative values of giving instruction along theological lines or in accordance with the usual religion courses."[102]

The situation had changed abruptly in 1957. Gerard Sloyan, a priest of the diocese of Trenton who was an alumnus of the university and who had been serving as assistant dean of the college of arts and sciences, was appointed to head the department of religious education. The retirement of Sheehy and the death of William Russell had left him a department to rebuild. He took it out of the older tradition and in the direction of the new. Controversies ensued, such as the one that the *Tower* article was to provoke in 1961. McDonald reported to the board in 1966 that the department was duplicating the work of the faculty of theology, that he had discussed the problem with the executive committee in January, 1965, and had obtained "clearance" from the congregation of seminaries and universities during the next October,[103] and that he had then secured the approval of the academic senate for the transfer of the department from the faculty of arts and sciences to the faculty of theology. Before his presentation, however, the senate had voted to reconsider its action and to refer the question to a special committe. A joint report of the graduate school of arts and sciences and the school of theology opposing the move was, by vote of the senate, transmitted to the trustees.[104] Although the rector maintained that the senate really had no competence in the matter and that Sloyan had improperly approached the prefect of the congregation for Catholic education, who was visiting in the United States, the trustees refrained from immediate action and appointed a special committee to make recommendations.[105]

These developments were the prelude to nationwide publicity in the press and on television that resulted from a halt to instruction in the university that began in the faculty of theology. When Charles E. Curran, a priest of the diocese of Rochester, had been appointed to the faculty in 1965, Archbishop Vagnozzi had called the attention of the administration to an article in a Rochester paper that had described him

---

102. OR, Hannan to Deferrari, Feb. 23, 1954 (copy). The *Tower*, Nov. 27, 1951 had reported that the head of the department at the time "conceded that perhaps some students would benefit from a greater exposure to Theology, but he maintained that these would be greatly in the minority."

103. OVR, excerpt from *L'attività dolla Sancta Sode nel 1965*, 700, reporting positive action by the congregation approving the transfer.

104. AS, mm, Jan. 27, Feb. 24, Oct. 27, 1966.

105. BT, mm, Nov. 13, 1966; and, for earlier discussion, Apr. 20, 1966. The *Washington Post* had reported faculty actions on Feb. 19 and 22, 1966.

"as advocating a change in the Church's position on birth control and a review of its whole teaching on the subject." The reply of the vice rector had noted only that the appointment had been recommended by the dean and, unanimously, by the faculty, and had been delayed for a year until Curran could be replaced in the seminary in which he was teaching.[106] Curran's positions in moral theology had soon become so controversial that when an article reporting them appeared in the *National Catholic Reporter* the vice rector and the dean had discussed it with him. Curran, in turn, had requested to see the rector personally, had repudiated the article, and had given the rector a copy of his *Christian Morality Today*, which bore the *imprimatur* of the bishop of Fort Wayne. He had followed this interview, however, with a letter of October 21, 1966, in which he indicated that he was a member of a newly established Institute for Freedom in the Church.

When McDonald narrated these events and reported that the faculty of theology was requesting a full presentation of its views, the board appointed a committee consisting of Philip M. Hannan, archbishop of New Orleans, John Krol, archbishop of Philadelphia, and McDonald "to determine, in whatever way the Committee deems feasible, the exact views of Father Curran, and to recommend appropriate action."[107] At its next meeting, on a motion of Krol, seconded by Hannan, the board voted to inform Curran that his appointment as an assistant professor of theology would be terminated on August 31, 1967. There seems to have been no advertence to what proper academic procedure might have required. Archbishop Hallinan asked to be recorded in opposition and declared that Curran should be given reasons for the board's action. The committee that had recommended termination maintained that it was unnecessary to give reasons. McDonald, however, warned the board that "serious Campus repercussions" could be expected, since the faculty of theology had earlier voted to recommend Curran's promotion to the rank of associate professor.[108]

When notice of the board's intervention was given, the faculty of theology, followed by the other faculties of the university, declared itself unable to teach. There were no classes but many meetings during the ensuing week. Probably most of the tension had little to do with the Curran action specifically. It had merely touched off the explosion. The protest was ended only after a week when the chancellor of the univer-

106. OVR, Vagnozzi to McAllister, Washington, [Sept. 17, 1965]; McAllister to Vagnozzi, Washington, Sept. 24, 1965 (copy).
107. BT, mm, Nov. 13, 1966.
108. *Ibid.*, Apr. 10, 1967.

sity, having polled the trustees, reported that the board's action had been nullified and that Curran would be retained and promoted.

A clue to one aspect of McDonald's action in these cases was in the anxiety to please constituents that marked his concern for the public relations of the university. Sources of ecclesiastical influence have already been indicated. The apostolic delegate, of course, was as near as the telephone.[109] In other academic matters, McDonald sought exception to admissions standards, complaining in one case of the rejection of a foreign applicant who had been supported by "a letter from the second highest Prelate in his country" and in others of the rejection of applicants referred by high school counselors. He even went so far as to threaten "to invoke the statutes and admit people himself in such cases."[110] A few months earlier he had established an office for student recruitment, which was undoubtedly a desirable move, but it was to lead to tensions with the registrar, who remained chairman of the committee on admissions.[111] In efforts to please alumni, also, he followed a "policy of giving as many of our graduates as possible an opportunity to do some work for their Alma Mater."[112] Five alumni architects were working on university projects when he wrote. Earlier, he had followed the same policy in awarding contracts for insurance.[113] The susceptibility to influence suggested in these relations with various publics was indicative neither of administrative strength nor of appreciation for traditional academic values.

Academic Freedom and Dissent from Papal Teaching

Dissent from traditional Catholic teaching on the morality of contraception, which had been the occasion for the attempt of the trustees to refuse reappointment to Father Curran, became an issue of worldwide proportions when Pope Paul VI, on July 29, 1968, published the encycli-

109. OVR, McDonald to Vagnozzi, *op. cit.*, dissociating the university from the *Tower* article; Ceroke to McDonald, *op. cit.*, noting the latter's allusion to "high ecclesiastical authority" in the conference of April 10; also, Vagnozzi to McAllister, *op. cit.*, concerning the appointment of Curran; and OR, Vagnozzi to McDonald, Washington, Apr. 11, 1966, acknowledging a report of recent developments at the university, and Sept. 22, 1966, acknowledging a report of "a certain project in inter-confessional theological studies," copies of which are not in the file.
110. OR, special meeting, mm, Apr. 1, 1965.
111. OVR, Robert Comstock to McAllister, Jan. 13, 1965; Theodore McCarrick to McAllister, Jan. 15, 1965; Comstock to McCarrick, Feb. 25, 1965; McCarrick to McAllister, Mar. 1, 1965; Comstock to McAllister, Apr. 15, 1965.
112. OR, McDonald to Donald S. Johnson, Washington, May 31, 1965 (copy); McDonald to George Edward Beatty, Washington, May 31, 1965 (copy).
113. *Ibid.*, Raymond DuFour to McDonald, Washington, Jan. 17, 1961; Dolan Donohue to Roy Bode, Washington, n.d. [1961]; Donohue to McDonald, Washington, Sept. 20, 1962.

cal *Humanae Vitae*, reaffirming the traditional teaching.[114] By this time, of course, Father Whalen was completing the one-year appointment as acting rector that the trustees had asked him to accept when McDonald had left for San Francisco. There had been some expectation that the pope might accept the report of the majority of a papally appointed study commission that had found grounds for a change in Catholic teaching, since this report had been leaked to the press. Reportedly, in the press conference held at the Vatican when the encyclical was released, it had been emphasized that the papal position, while authoritative, was not infallible.[115] These circumstances, however, only made bolder the unprecedented immediate public dissent of many priests to the papal teaching in the encyclical.

Cardinal Shehan later recorded his impression that no solemn proclamation of a pope had ever been received "by any group of Catholic people with so much disrespect and contempt."[116] The campus was the first center of organization. Theologians had been prepared by several developments. After the "Curran affair" of 1967, at the request of the theological faculty, members had met with a special committee of the trustees to explore issues that seemed to be at stake. A report on the relationship of the offices of bishop and theologian had been requested from the faculty and delivered by it, but neither this report nor a specific critique of a draft of the episcopate's forthcoming pastoral letter had produced the modification in the latter that the theologians had proposed.[117] Late in June, 1968, Cardinals O'Boyle and Shehan had issued jointly guidelines for the teaching of religion in their adjacent archdioceses. These guidelines, which were intended to maintain traditional discipline, were released to the press on July 28 by the Association of Priests of the Archdiocese of Washington. On July 30, the day after the papal encyclical was released, the association held a previously scheduled press conference at which there was issued the statement of dissent from the encyclical teaching that Curran and other theologians had drafted the night before.

At the time there were eighty-seven signatories to the document; eventually there were about one thousand. Obviously, a conflict between the *magisterium* of the church, the pope and bishops, and the

114. AAS, LX (Sept. 30, 1968), 481–503 (in Latin), trans. Carlen, *op. cit.*, V, 223–36.

115. Ferdinando Lambruschini, professor of moral theology, Pontifical Lateran University, quoted in stipulation of facts to AS, Board of Inquiry, Eth. 8 of the record.

116. *A Blessing of Years; The Memoirs of Lawrence Cardinal Shehan* (Notre Dame: University of Notre Dame Press, 1982), 249.

117. "The Church in Our Day," in Nolan, *op. cit.*, III, 98–154.

signatories was in the public domain. To many it appeared that the theologians were usurping pastoral functions. Cardinal O'Boyle as chancellor met with the faculty of theology to hear the positions of the dissenters. On September 5, at a special meeting, the trustees reaffirmed that in theological controversies they would acknowledge the "competence and responsibility" of the *magisterium* and at the same time would follow the "accepted norms of academic freedom in the work of teaching" and "the due process protective of such freedom." They directed the acting rector "to institute through due academic process an immediate inquiry as to whether the teachers at this University who signed the recent statement of dissent have violated by their declarations or actions with respect to the encyclical *Humanae Vitae* their responsibilities to the University under existing statutes and under their commitments as teachers in the University and specifically as teachers of theology and/ or other sacred sciences."[118]

The ensuing inquiry was entrusted to the academic senate.[119] Its elected special committee proceeded with utmost care through twenty meetings, eight days of hearings, and about three thousand pages of testimony, exhibits, and background material. The committee was chaired by Dean Marlowe. Other members were E. Catherine Dunn, professor of English, Frederick R. McManus, dean of the school of canon law, Antanas Suziedelis, professor of psychology, and Eugene Van Antwerp, S.S., then director of the seminary department of the National Catholic Educational Association. Walter J. Schmitz, S.S., dean of the school of sacred theology, was elected as an alternate. Robert Trisco, professor of history and formerly academic vice rector, was designated an observer to represent the acting rector Brother Niuard Scheel, C.F.X., who had succeeded Whalen. Bishop James Shannon was designated to represent the trustees in attending the hearings, and Joseph P. Williman was designated as faculty representative. There were observers also from the American Association of University Professors and the American Association of Theological Schools.

The twenty-one "subject professors," as they were called by their counsel, presented extensive submissions, both theological and professional in content.[120] On the ecclesiological side, *Humanae Vitae* was

118. BT, mm, Sept. 15, 1968.
119. See AS, mm, Sept. 12, 1968, for the assertion, "It is the responsibility of the Senate to supervise any succeeding inquiry to assure that due academic process is assured."
120. The quotations used here are from the documents submitted in the inquiry. These have been published in Charles E. Curran *et al.*, *Dissent in and for the Church* (New York: Sheed & Ward, 1969), and John F. Hunt *et al.*, *The Responsibility of Dissent* (New York: Sheed & Ward, 1969).

labeled at the outset as pre-conciliar and "decisively hierarchial" in its approach, and neglectful of the conclusions of separated ecclesial communities and of the experience of Catholic spouses. Its teaching was presented as, like all moral teaching on which doctrine has not been infallibly defined, presumptively reformable. In support, theological manuals could be cited as consistently providing for private dissent from such teaching. Probing into the theology employed in the encyclical, the professors maintained that, in view of the diversity of philosophical systems, extending even to those employing natural-law reasoning, "Catholic moral teaching cannot be said to be based on *the* natural law."[121] They maintained further that theological data ought to be obtained from the contemporary situation by an inductive as well as a deductive method if the theologian is to fulfill the function of "interpreting the Christian tradition in the light of present day reality."[122]

The necessity for further development of the right of dissent was the burden of their argument. Such development was presented as justified "for the good of the church." First, it was maintained that "the changing ideal of science in general and the changing theological methodology require the greatest possible dissemination and discussion of theological interpretations."[123] The fact that contemporary collaboration for the theological enterprise necessarily involves many individuals was taken to preclude the restriction of dissent to private opinion. Second, the legitimacy of public dissent was defended on the premise that circumstances should be decisive in a choice of means. Under contemporary circumstances, in which the teaching of the Church on the morality of contraception is a crucial matter for millions of people, it was deemed necessary to inform priests that there was widespread dissent from papal teaching among theologians. Forestalling journalists from polarizing Catholic views was advanced as a related motive. Third, a juridical foundation for public dissent was found in the argument that teaching on the right to dissent would be meaningless unless known to those having the right, who were held to be "coextensive with every person who would have access to and be dependent upon the ordinary means of mass social communications media."[124]

These arguments pertained, of course, to the status of the dissenting theologians in the Church. Defense of the legitimacy of public dissent to the encyclical was a necessary prelude to their claim to have acted

---

121. "Submissions . . . ," Part I (Jan. 27, 1969), IV–2.
122. *Ibid.*, Part II (Feb. 18, 1969), I–2.
123. *Ibid.*
124. *Ibid.*, Part I, IV–63d.

responsibly within the academic context. On this point, they and their counsel took the position from the outset that the action of the trustees in requesting the inquiry was "an alien intervention in the workings of our American university committed to American principles of academic freedom and due process."[125] Their appeal in the first instance was to the codifications of the American Association of University Professors.[126] They could cite also in their behalf the so-called Land O' Lakes statement of American Catholic educators that had been issued the year before as a kind of declaration of freedom from ecclesiastical control.[127]

In its classic "Statement of Principles on Academic Freedom and Tenure," formulated in 1940 jointly with the Association of American Colleges, the AAUP had elaborated the position that "the common good depends upon the free search for truth and its free exposition."[128] It had allowed "limitations of academic freedom because of religious or other aims" of an institution only if they were "clearly stated in writing at the time of the appointment of a member of a faculty."[129] The necessity for this provision became a matter of dispute. In the proceedings under review, "the *general* concept of academic freedom" was maintained to be "perfectly consistent with fundamental religious objectives of the university." Specifically, it was held that "if one purports to be a professor of Roman Catholic theology but is not in fact a Roman Catholic theologian, he need not be retained in the theology department of a Roman Catholic university—not because the university may restrict his academic freedom, but because the university may determine that he lacks the requisite professional competence."[130] This position was consistent with a recently issued "Report and Draft Recommendation of a Special Committee on Academic Freedom in Church-Related Colleges and Universities" that became a part of AAUP policy in 1970 in the form of an "interpretive comment," as follows: "Most church-related institutions no longer need or desire the departure from the principle of academic freedom implied in the 1940 Statement, and we do not now endorse such a departure."[131]

125. OR, Hunt to Scheel, New York, Jan. 16, 1969.

126. Louis Joughin (ed.), *Academic Freedom and Tenure: A Handbook of the American Association of University Professors* (Madison: University of Wisconsin Press, 1967), provides the compilation then current.

127. Theodore M. Hesburgh, C.S.C., *et al.*, *The Idea of the Catholic University*, July 23, 1967. See also Neil McCluskey, S.J., *The Catholic University: A Modern Appraisal* (Notre Dame: University of Notre Dame Press, 1970).

128. Joughin, *op. cit.*, 34.

129. *Ibid.*, 36.

130. "Submission . . . ," Part II, II–40.

131. *Policy Documents and Reports* (Washington, D.C.: American Association of University Professors, 1977), 3.

The Land O' Lakes statement had no official standing but was presented as indicative of the views of prominent Catholic educators. It had emanated from a conference called in preparation for a meeting of the International Federation of Catholic Universities that was to take place in Kinshasa, Zaire, in 1968. Father Hesburgh was president of the IFCU at the time. In its key provision, the statement declared that "to perform its teaching and research functions effectively the Catholic university must have a true autonomy and academic freedom in the face of authority of whatever kind, lay or clerical, external to the academic community itself." Although there was also insistence that in a Catholic university Catholicism had to be "*perceptibly present and effectively operative,*" its manifestation was restricted by the statement to the influence of believers in the faculties, the teaching of theology, and liturgical celebrations. [132] In prefatory remarks, one of the participants, presenting the active participation of non-Catholics in the campus community as "most desirable and, indeed, even necessary to bring authentic universality to the Catholic university itself," hailed the anticipated product as "a Catholic sponsored pluralistic society."[133] On the campus, the senate was to urge adoption of the AAUP statements and to resolve that a university should be "free of arbitrary and extrinsic constraints, be they civil or ecclesiastical."[134]

The subject professors could hardly have asked for a more favorable verdict than was rendered unanimously in the report of the academic senate's board of inquiry. The senate approved the report without a dissenting vote. Its conclusions appeared to be derived from the principles of the AAUP and the views expressed in the Land O' Lakes statement. Controversies comparable to the one under review, it was remarked, would arise "rather frequently, in any university worthy of the name." Perhaps the key to the findings was in the position that any restriction imposed by the distinction between public and private dissent would be "objectively invalid and a disservice to truth, which the theologian should express freely and without reservation, even though aware of his own fallibility and careful to respect the rights of others, especially the role of the hierarchial magisterium." Thus, the dissent in question was judged to be responsible, to be within the bounds of academic propriety, to be the expression only of individual commitments, and to be compatible with the profession of faith made by the dissenters at the time of appointment. Even the judgment of a public

132. See Hesburgh, *Idea.*
133. Neil McCluskey, S.J., *ibid.*, Preface.
134. AS, mm, June 26, 1969.

ecclesiastical tribunal, it was maintained, could not supplant the right of the academic community "to render judgment concerning competency to teach." After its numerous conclusions on the conduct of the professors and the norms of licit dissent, the board of inquiry undertook to recommend that the university should "proceed quickly to incorporate in its statutes, bylaws and regulations, those norms of academic freedom and academic due process" recommended in the report.[135]

The trustees who had mandated the inquiry appointed a special committee to study the report that they received. On the recommendation of this committee, of which Cardinal Krol was chairman, they accepted the report insofar as it pertained to "academic propriety," but not insofar as there might be in it any implications of "agreement that all findings are supported in the record" or of "approval of the theological position expressed."[136] The trustees had recognized throughout that only the pope and the bishops could speak for the Church. They had found unprecedented the new situation in which dissent could be disseminated virtually universally because of advances in technology. Eventually, a new president, in his first year of office, believing that "solutions would not be achieved through confrontations with individuals, but rather through working with the Faculty at large,"[137] made public the conclusion of an unofficial panel of three bishop-theologians "that the dissent manifested by the theologians . . . was not sufficiently sensitive to the pastoral implications of their action."[138] Advocacy of a sterner posture than that adopted by the trustees was, however, rebuffed.[139]

The status of the subject professors was not further called into question. It was to be noted, however, that of the twenty who were clerics, fourteen were to leave the university and, in at least five cases, the priesthood. With the teaching of *Humanae Vitae* disputed, the way was prepared for the extension of dissent to other questions of sexual ethics and of the nature of Christian marriage itself. Perhaps the most pertinent comment concerning the dispute with which the board of inquiry had been charged to deal was made in the private notes of its chairman. Although he personally was ready to ask "Who can say, today, what constitutes the bounds of legitimate dissent?" he perceived also that while the university was being pressed to take sides "the greatest contri-

135. AS, mm, Apr. 1, 1969.
136. BT, mm, June 15–16, 1969.
137. Ibid., Dec. 6, 1969.
138. Ibid., Nov. 8, 1969, exh.
139. Ibid., Sept. 12–13; Dec. 6, 1969; BT, mm, EC, mm, Feb. 17, 1970.

bution it could make would be to define the proper roles of each contender."[140]

Academic Autonomy and Ecclesiastical Authority

The dissent from the teaching of *Humanae Vitae* was but one manifestation of the changes in thought and feeling that were beginning to sweep through the Roman Catholic Church and through Western societies generally at the time that the encyclical was issued. The roots of the changes and the reasons for their sudden appearance have not yet been satisfactorily explored. For present purposes, it can be remarked only in very general terms that American Catholics, confused and to some extent divided by what was happening in the Church that they had too superficially looked upon as unchangeable, were finding themselves arriving unexpectedly at new and sometimes unsettling perceptions in their own individual spiritual lives and in their collective identification.

Those Catholics who were in higher education were bringing out into the open, not always tactfully, views of the relationship between Catholic institutions and the Church that followed the Land O' Lakes assertion of 1967 that a university should maintain its autonomy "in the face of authority of whatever kind, lay or clerical." The role of ecclesiastical authority in higher education thus became in time the central issue of professional interest. As it began to be debated, the congregation for Catholic education issued for the guidance of ecclesiastical institutions provisional norms modifying the apostolic constitution, *Deus Scientiarum Dominus*, of 1931.[141] Such modifications had become appropriate in view of the decrees of Vatican Council II, in particular its declaration on Christian education.[142]

But Catholic institutions generally, represented in the International Federation of Catholic Universities, which under Hesburgh's leadership was being transformed from an ecclesiastical into a voluntary, self-governing association, were finding themselves split. Not all members were ready to concede that, in an institution declaring itself to be Catholic, ecclesiastical authority, even when grossly mistaken, could ever be regarded as wholly external. Some, in fact, were able to point to protection from anti-religious governments as one of the advantages of ecclesiastical status. The Roman congregation itself convened inter-

140. AS, Board of Inquiry, Donald E. Marlowe, "Ruminations on an Inaugural Weekend."

141. *Normae quaedam*, issued May 20, 1968, trans. Frederick R. McManus, for internal circulation (mimeo.), Sept. 9, 1968.

142. *Gravissimum educationis*, AAS, LVII (Oct. 8, 1966), 728–39 (in Latin), trans. Walter M. Abbott, S.J., and John Joseph Gallagher, *The Documents of Vatican II* (New York: America Press, 1966), 637–51.

national meetings in 1969 and 1972 and undertook unusually extensive correspondence in its efforts to clarify what was at stake. There were local results of some importance, as when there was established in the United States a joint committee of representatives of the National Conference of Catholic Bishops and of presidents of American Catholic universities. But two decades after the first debates at Kinshasa the issue of autonomy remains in dispute.[143]

The Catholic University of America, for easily ascertainable reasons, could not have been and was not in fact a conspicuous participant in these early American and international developments. At the outset, as an ecclesiastical institution, its relationship with the Holy See was different from that of any other American Catholic university. It had been represented at Land O' Lakes in 1967 by a subordinate administrative officer. True enough, in the course of its adoption of new bylaws it was already changing its own ecclesiastical status and becoming, according to the classification used by the Holy See, a Catholic university with ecclesiastical faculties. But, after its campus crisis only weeks subsequent to the Land O' Lakes meeting and in the years immediately following, it had to be preoccupied with the revision of its governing documents and with internal problems. Further, from 1967 until 1969 it was in a two-year interval between chief executives.

While it was engaged in redefining its own objectives, however, the university was able to find confirmation of its sense of direction in a concept of a Catholic university that emerged from the Roman congress of 1969 and that was incorporated into the final version of the statement, "The Catholic University in the Modern World," that was issued after the second congress, in 1972. This concept outlined the unique purpose of a Catholic university as "to assure in an institutional manner a Christian presence in the university world confronting the great problems of contemporary society" and it specified as "essential" four characteristics:

(1) Christian inspiration not only of individuals but of the university as such; (2) continuing reflection in the light of the Catholic faith upon the growing treasury of human knowledge, to which it seeks to contribute by its own research; (3) fidelity to the Christian message as it comes to us through the Church; (4) an institutional commitment to the service of the people of God and of the human family in their pilgrimage to the transcendent goal which gives meaning to life.

For other Catholic institutions but also for The Catholic University of America in its own way, the Roman congresses provided a counterpoint

143. Sister Ann Ida Gannon, B.V.M., "Some Aspects of Catholic Higher Education Since Vatican II," *CCICA* (1987), 11–32, provides a helpful chronological account of developments.

to what had been a historic claim of pontifical standing in the explicit recognition that all universities satisfying the stated conditions were to be regarded as "Catholic universities whether canonically erected or not."[144]

The revised definition of the university's ecclesiastical status was formalized a few months after the arrival on campus for the academic year 1969–70 of its first lay president. During Walton's administration from 1969 until 1978, and during the administrations of his successors, Edmund Daniel Pellegrino (b. 1920), from 1978 until 1982, and the Reverend William James Byron, S.J. (b. 1927), since the latter date, attention has been focused at various times upon claims of academic freedom, collegiality in governance, financial need, rights to tenure, student rights and freedoms, and similar issues. Until the 1980s, challenges to ecclesiastical authority seemingly tended to be more implicit than direct in the framing of these problems. Inheriting, for example, the bitter controversy provoked by the dissent from *Humanae Vitae*, Walton sought with the trustees to walk the fine line of respect for both academic propriety and magisterial authority.

An immediate problem was waiting for him because the faculty of theology was proposing for appointment to its vacant deanship the Reverend Roland Murphy, O. Carm., a professor and distinguished biblical scholar who was one of the signatories to the statement of dissent from *Humanae Vitae*. After what seemed to be amicable discussions, Walton chose not to appoint Murphy, named instead a search committee to propose candidates, and asked Schmitz, the previous dean, to continue in service until a successor could be found.[145] Murphy left the faculty for Duke University. The outcome was seen by some as ambiguous. Father Andrew Greeley, for example, in his syndicated column, expressed his suspicion, but refrained from asserting directly, that Walton was a "lay fink."[146]

A more explicit but also an unsuccessful challenge to ecclesiastical authority was presented in the case of Daniel C. Maguire, then a priest of the archdiocese of Philadelphia, who was a member of the department of religion and religious education.[147] Maguire, believing that he held a tenured appointment, applied for an ecclesiastical dispensation that would allow him to return to the lay state. His archbishop, in accord

---

144. "The Modern Catholic University / Its Thrust," *Origins*, II, (Feb. 8, 1973), 517.
145. BT, mm, Sept. 12–13, 1969.
146. St. Louis *Review*, Oct. 15, l969, reprinted in *Tower*, Oct. 24, 1969.
147. The departmental name had been changed on the recommendation of the council on religious studies. AS, mm, Dec. 11, 1969.

with Roman conditions for such dispensations, demanded his resignation from the university. If Maguire's claim to tenure had been valid,
his might have been a test case. The administration, however, discovering that Maguire's claim to tenure was based upon a faulty statement of
his service at other institutions that had been submitted when he was
appointed, found Maguire ineligible for tenure. Maguire's appeal to
the academic senate resulted in a recommendation from its special
committee, made after four days of hearings with counsel and observers
for each side, which, while appearing to favor Maguire, conceded that
he could not be considered as tenured. His resignation from the university followed.[148]

A consequence of the dispute in the Maguire case led to the inclusion
in the faculty manual, by action of the academic senate in the first
instance, of a provision intended to recognize the public ecclesiastical
obligations of clerical and religious appointees and to prevent future
controversies about issues related to laicization. Thus, the manual now
provides that the university's contractual obligations cease in any case
in which "the appointee resigns from the priesthood without seeking
laicization or is laicized under any canonical condition that requires his
resignation from the university."[149]

At length, years after Vatican Council II, on April 15, 1979, Pope
John Paul II issued a new apostolic constitution, *Sapientia Christiana*,[150]
applying to ecclesiastical universities and faculties. His first travel to
the United States in his capacity as pope followed in the fall. Certainly
his visit to the campus on October 6, 1979, was the highest ecclesiastical
honor received by the university in its history. Immediately after speaking to a national assembly of women religious in the National Shrine
of the Immaculate Conception, he spoke informally and endearingly to
groups of enthusiastic students on his way to what was then still the
university's gymnasium.[151] There he addressed members of the faculties
and representatives of Catholic colleges and universities from the entire
country. The burden of his message, not new, was to remind educators
that "the deepest and noblest aspiration of the human person" is "the
desire to come to the knowledge of truth" and that this had been the

148. AS, mm, Oct. 22, 1970; May 5, 1971. Sec. BT, EC, mm, June 7, 1971, and
BT, mm, Sept. 18, 1971, for authorization and dissolution by mutual agreement of a
joint committee of the trustees and academic senate to review the president's refusal to
recommend tenure for Maguire.

149. "Faculty Manual," Part II, Art. 23.

150. AAS, LXXI (May 15, 1979), 469–521 (in Latin), trans. *On Ecclesiastical Universities and Faculties* (Washington, D.C.: United States Catholic Conference, 1979).

151. *Tower*, Oct. 12, 1979.

basis for the historic relationship between the academy and the Church. Made plain, however, was the corollary that in this relationship institutions considering themselves to be institutionally committed—that is, both enlightened and bound in faith—would be in "an essential relationship to the hierarchy of the Church." Addressing theologians particularly, the pope depicted their contribution as "enriching for the Church only if it takes into account the proper function of the Bishops and the rights of the faithful."[152]

Two developments affecting the university subsequent to the papal visit, each with roots independent of the other, have been interpreted as challenges to the papal admonitions. One that affects all Catholic colleges and universities nationally is represented by resistance to provisions for higher education in the revised code of canon law, which became effective in 1983, and to a schema for the application of the provisions that is still under consideration by the Roman congregation for Catholic education. The other that in its specific aspects is peculiar to the campus is associated with the responses to the finding of the sister congregation for the doctrine of the faith that Father Curran must be considered "not suitable nor eligible to teach Catholic Theology."

The Association of Catholic Colleges and Universities, a department of the National Catholic Educational Association in which the university holds membership, has been the coordinating agency for expressions of opposition to Roman developments. These began during 1977 and 1978 when Catholic colleges and universities received for comment portions of the first draft of proposed revisions in the code of canon law of 1917. Objection continues to be taken, however, to the published revised code, principally to the provision that "those who teach theological subjects in any institute of higher studies [must] have a mandate from the competent ecclesiastical authority."[153] The enforcement of this provision is dependent for the most part upon the cognizant diocesan bishop and it may be that there is ground for the opinion that its practical effect in the United States will be minimal.[154] In principle, however, it establishes the right and responsibility of the Church to ensure that Catholic theology is taught consistently with Catholic faith.

More recently, Catholics in higher education have voiced publicly their concern that a "Proposed Schema for a Pontifical Document on

152. "Excellence, Truth and Freedom in Catholic Universities," *Origins*, IX (Oct. 18, 1979), 307, 308.
153. Canon 812. Canon Law Society of America, Code of Canon Law; Latin-English Edition (Washington, D.C.: Canon Law Society of America, 1983).
154. CHE, XXX, No. 15 (Dec. 7, 1983), 15.

Catholic Universities" would be a more serious threat to their autonomy.[155] When the first draft was issued, in the fall of 1985, President Byron joined with fourteen other college and university presidents to protest that, as drafted, the document "would actually cripple the present efforts of our North American universities to fulfill the mission the *Schema* describes." In their fears that the credibility of American Catholic higher education might be eroded, the presidents singled out for emphasis as "the single most important problem" presented by the document its "recurring insistence that any authentic Catholic university must be under the jurisdictional control of ecclesiastical authorities."[156] The editors of the Jesuit weekly *America* noted specifically that "the bishops have not sought such control, the standards of the academic community would not tolerate it, and governmental grants would probably be suspended" if the independence of Catholic higher education were compromised by the document.[157] Perhaps in response to these American critics and to the mixed response otherwise accorded to the document, another conference of some 230 delegates of Catholic colleges and universities around the world was convened in Rome during April, 1989, for further discussion of the proposed schema, of which a new draft has since been circulated.

In principle, the same claim for academic autonomy that is being made by many Catholic educators was made in the case of Father Curran, although two levels of the argument that he presented must be distinguished. One level is theological. It is Curran's contention that the stand he has taken on the morality of contraception and his nuanced positions allowing in some cases masturbation, sterilization, abortion, homosexual relations, and the dissolution of marriage represent only "faithful dissent" from teachings of the Church that have never been formulated infallibly, if indeed they could be.[158] He presents his views on these matters as based upon a "theology of compromise" that he has developed.[159] The other level of his argument is that proper academic procedure in his case requires, as was affirmed in the judgment of the

155. CHE, XXXII, No.⁴ (Mar. 26, 1986), 1, 16–24, reports the concern and provides the text of the draft and of responses from the Association of Catholic Colleges and Universities and, synthesized, from ten individual institutions.

156. Quoted, *ibid.* No. 18 (July 2, 1986), 2.

157. CLIV (Apr. 19, 1986), 313.

158. *Faithful Dissent* (Kansas City, Mo.: Sheed & Ward, 1986) presents the correspondence between Cardinal Josef Ratzinger, prefect of the congregation for the doctrine of the faith, and Curran. See also Curran's article, "On Dissent in the Church," *Commonweal*, CXIII (Sept. 12, 1986), 461–70.

159. "How My Mind Has Changed, 1960–1975," *Horizons*, II, No. 1 (Spring, 1975), 187–205.

special committee of the academic senate with respect to Curran and other dissenting professors in 1969, that only the academic community can "render judgment concerning competence to teach."

The consequences of the action of the Roman congregation that, in 1986, denied to Curran continued standing as a Catholic theologian eligible to teach became the subject of proceedings in the academic senate and in the civil courts.[160] In these proceedings, Curran appealed to the standards of academic freedom and tenure of the American Association of University Professors to protect the membership in his faculty that he had enjoyed since 1965. Support for him became widespread. It had to be recalled, nevertheless, that in 1969 Curran and his colleagues had declared that if a purported professor of Roman Catholic theology was not in fact a Roman Catholic theologian, the university could determine him to be lacking in the requisite *professional competence*. Put this way, the question became one of determining who could make the authoritative finding. Curran has maintained that "the ultimate decision with juridical effects must be made by peers in the academy."[161] To the Roman congregation and the bishops charged with fidelity to the faith the "ultimate decision" is necessarily the prerogative of the Church.

Inasmuch as the question presented in these terms is plainly ecclesiastical, its resolution, by long-established judicial precedents, would not be attempted in American civil courts. Although the university's motions for dismissal on this ground were not definitively rejected, Curran's suit, initiated in 1987, was allowed to proceed. It had been brought and was eventually decided under contract law. What Curran alleged was that the university, by giving effect to the papally approved finding that he was no longer eligible to teach as a Catholic theologian, was violating his contractual right to academic freedom as a tenured professor. He had been barred from teaching in the department of theology without a canonical mission from the chancellor and he had declined the university's offer to allow him to teach Christian ethics in another department on the ground that he would have to teach theology, his only competence, and this the university would not allow him to do. Five graduate students filed a separate suit, alleging that in its actions depriving them of Curran's tutelage, the university had breached their contractual right also. Both suits were joined by the court for the trial, which took place during December, 1988.[162]

160. See CHE, XXXIII, No. 1 (Sept. 3, 1986), 44–47; No. 6 (Oct. 8, 1986), 1 ff.; No. 19 (Jan. 21, 1987), 13 ff.; No. 41 (June 24, 1987), 4–6.

161. "On Dissent in the Church," *op. cit.*, 470.

162. *The Reverend Charles E. Curran and Julia Fleming et al. v. The Catholic University*

Rejecting Curran's claims after a careful legal analysis, the court found that "much as he may have wished it otherwise, he could not reasonably have expected that the University would defy a definitive judgement of the Holy See that he was 'unsuitable' and 'ineligible' to teach Catholic Theology." Further, the court acknowledged that, even if Curran's contractual claims had been found to be valid, it would have been "virtually unthinkable" for the court to have ordered specific performance, because "if plaintiff [had] had his way," the court would have had to order the university to teach Catholic theology "in open defiance of the Holy See."[163] This, it would seem, had been Curran's purpose and the purpose of some of his supporters. What was being challenged was indeed the competence of the Holy See to define authoritatively the boundaries of Catholic teaching in matters not infallibly taught, including some that can be regarded as presumptively reformable.

Issues of ecclesiastical polity were thus imposed upon the university. The proceedings and the outcome in the Curran case were disturbing to many to whom the academic freedom of a Catholic theologian should allow, as a canonist and former academic vice president has put it, "in addition to an honest presentation of integral official doctrine . . . legitimate critique and dissent."[164] A resolution adopted by the ordinary professors of the school of arts and sciences (16–4, with one abstention) noted "with grave concern" the testimony of university officials at the trial, deplored "the effective denial of academic freedom to Father Curran," and declared that the individual adherents would teach under protest "until the board of trustees reaffirms the university's commitment to full academic freedom."[165] At the same time, the university, in the final year of its first century of instruction, was made the object of an investigation by a committee of the American Association of University Professors that concluded that Curran had been deprived of his academic freedom and tenure without due process and without adequate cause.[166] Clearly, Curran's suit and the reaction to its outcome, not just disagree-

---

of America, Civil Action No. 1562-87, Superior Court of the District of Columbia, Civil Division.

163. Judge Frederick H. Weisberg, "Opinion and Order," 26, 28. For the full opinion, see *Origins*, 18, No. 40 (March 16, 1989) 664–672, or *CUAM*, I, No. 2 (Summer, 1989), 19–25.

164. Frederick R. McManus, "Academic Freedom and The Catholic University of America," *America*, CLX (May 27, 1989), 507.

165. The resolution is reprinted in *Commonweal*, CXVI (May 5, 1989), 274, with discussion of the issues by James H. Provost, Raymond H. Potvin, and Mary Collins, O.S.B., "In Rejoinder: What Next at Catholic U?" *Ibid.*, 270–75.

166. *Academe*, 75, 5, (Sept.–Oct. 1989), 27–40.

ing with papal teaching but challenging its authority, could be seen as symptomatic of pressures for change in American Catholic higher education.

The Catholic University of America in a Changed Environment

Unfamiliar or simply extreme as the positions of some contemporary Catholic educators may seem to be, they cannot be dismissed as merely rash. Catholic institutions of higher education are facing the fundamental question of the degree to which they can be assimilated into the dominating academic ethos without compromise to the faith of their founders. Specific developments of recent decades may not have been foreseeable. New legal questions are being presented. Some positions may be difficult to reconcile with Catholic tradition. The outcome of current approaches will surely be complex. But in the perspective of Catholic faith itself the challenges of the time are best interpreted as crises of maturity. They are manifestations of the continuous universal need of the Church for enculturation, not only in the developing world that is the focus of current thought and discussion of the problem, but also in the western world in which "ages of faith" have been superseded by steadily advancing secularization.

The founders of The Catholic University of America did not use the term enculturation—anthropology and sociology were no more than infant sciences in their day—but their central concern with implanting Catholic faith in American society was evident. They looked to the foundation of a university as the best means of demonstrating the compatibility of faith with the advancement of secular knowledge. Like them, their successors and colleagues in Catholic institutions, more numerous than they would have thought possible, necessarily look upon assimilation as a counterpart of enculturation. Taken as a whole, the course of American Catholic higher education has exemplified assimilation indeed. The Catholic University of America, by introducing the modern university movement into the Catholic community, had a pioneer role in the process. When it is recalled that it began in a faculty of theology, its more specific role in leading the way by which American theological scholarship has become a university enterprise can also be discerned. In turn, of course, the theological dissent within its faculty has become a university matter.

What the debates of the present are about can be defined as the determination of the point at which assimilation in higher education ceases to serve the purpose of enculturation and serves instead as surrender. Catholicism is a supranational and supracultural as well as a supernatural religion. There is evidence enough in the history of The Catholic University of America that the judgments of Catholic leaders can be mistaken. Certainly those who have viewed Catholic higher education solely as an agency of the Catholic subculture have been found to be shortsighted. Their identification of "Americanization" with "laicization" and "secularization" during the Ryan administration provides a conspicuous unfortunate example. But those who might be called assimilationists must also recognize that some degree of marginality is required of Catholics who live in a pluralistic society. The underlying problem is accentuated more and more as secularization advances and as core values of Catholic Christianity come to be challenged. The institutional forms in which the appropriate marginality can be expressed are not so clear. Creativity is called for if there is to be produced the desirable situation that Walton thought he found in arriving at The Catholic University of America, a situation consciously creating "an intellectual tension by adding to empirical knowledge and to rational knowledge a third dimension: supernatural knowledge."[167]

Concern about the feasibility of this goal is not new. In the generation of the founders, the ultra-orthodox Bishop McQuaid disclosed confidentially to the archbishops of the country his personal conclusion that American Catholics would never adequately support institutions that would be both truly Catholic and truly universities. During the academic revival that marked the administration of the fifth rector, a member of a faculty with his doctorate from Yale asked a related question that was already familiar, "Should Catholic universities learn a lesson from the experience of other denominational colleges which sacrificed their orthodoxy for endowment, prestige, recognition and membership in various associations?" That this professor, occupying the Knights of Columbus chair in American history, was regarded by a colleague or two to be anticlerical and by his deans to be disloyal because he was enrolling his children in public schools only adds point to the concern that he showed in writing, "Unless it has something to offer in addition to secular scholarship, The Catholic University fills no need."[168]

More than a generation later, but before the more highly visible secularizing developments of the 1970s and 1980s, an eminent metaphysician, who was joining the faculty of philosophy after retiring from the Sterling chair at Yale, posed the same question. Prodding his new

167. Clarence C. Walton, *The President's Reflections on The Catholic University of America* (Washington, D.C.: The Catholic University of America, 1972), 6.

168. Richard J. Purcell Papers, "Observations on the Catholic University of America," forwarded, Purcell to Francis J. Haas, Washington, Jan. 14, 1935.

Pryzbyla Plaza, between Keane and Shahan halls and before Mullen Library, is a gift of Edward Pryzbyla, Class of 1925. His annual contributions to the university have been dedicated to plantings that are enhancing the campus landscape.

Catholic colleagues, he voiced doubts as to how long their universities would be able to retain "the idea of a tradition, the importance of religion, and the studies of value in a philosophy." For a short while, he thought, these emphases might afford a kind of Catholic advantage in higher education by providing the "opportunity to maintain a position in the American educational system which was once possessed by leading institutions."[169] His reference, of course, was to the fate of the earlier colleges and universities founded by Protestants. The renunciation of their ties with the churches—from which, significantly, they had not been receiving adequate support—led to their rapid secularization. His suggestion was that this, too, might be the fate of Catholic institutions.

The views of contemporary Catholic educators, which seem in some respects so different from those of their forbears, have been formed, necessarily, in their experience of grappling with concrete institutional realities. These, too, have changed. The diversity of Catholic views

169. *Tower*, Mar. 6, 1970, quoting Paul Weiss.

that is to be found at the end of the 1980s is in no small part owed to the pursuit of institutional opportunities opened by the expansion of American higher education that began after the second world war. The entrance of government promoted this expansion nationally, first through federal support of the education of veterans of the war, but then, more deeply, in federal programs launched in reaction to the Soviet *sputnik* of 1957 and under the umbrella of the "Great Society" portrayed by President Lyndon B. Johnson. Educational opportunities were widely extended and graduate education was markedly changed by these programs.

By 1970, federal funding of programs and scholarships had been begun, degree programs had been multiplied, enrollments at both under-graduate and graduate levels had been stimulated, and the conduct of sponsored research and instruction had assumed unforseen proportions. Some presidents of Catholic institutions had become national figures. A "youth revolution" was in progress and was erupting in protest against the war being conducted by the United States in Vietnam. Under the pressures of the time, with points of view seemingly unleashed by the Vatican Council of the early 1960s, and often because of financial incentives or, in a few cases, because financial exigencies allowed no choice, some institutions went so far as to surrender their Catholic identity. More seemingly undertook to rely for their identity solely upon the influence of a "religious founding group."[170]

Such diminution of institutional marginality could not proceed as rapidly and as far at The Catholic University of America as at some sister institutions with graduate schools. Its name, its pontifical founda-tion and episcopal sponsorship, its institutional tradition, and the con-tinued pontifical standing of its ecclesiastical faculties still remain as deterrents. The loss of its flagship status, however, is testimony to the progress of other institutions, as is their greater success in attracting financial support. All Catholic institutions share both the problems that are presented by current challenges and the obligation to search cooperatively for solutions.

---

170. In studying forty church-related or single-sex colleges, Richard E. Harrison found that those that had broken their ties with the Catholic Church had experienced greater growth in enrollment than the others, but had shown also a more marked decline in morale and community spirit and less increase in scholarship than those that had remained Catholic. *Strategic Policy Changes of Private Colleges* (New York: Teachers College Press, 1978).

CHAPTER XI

Change and Continuity in Governance and Leadership

When the Alumni Association looked ahead to the fall of 1967 to plan its annual reunion—which had been moved from New York to Washington in 1948—it announced as the topic for the forum that it was still conducting "The Catholic University at the Crossroads." No previous forum had ever invited discussion of the university itself. The title would hardly have been selected if the time had been considered to be normal. But a nationwide audience had seen on television the events of the previous spring and some had concluded that what they were viewing was the culminating breakdown of a structure that had become dated. University policy had been made a public issue. There was awareness on all sides that decisions of major import were being demanded. Events were hoped for that would give promise of brighter days.

The first signs of change were given before the forum. Late in the summer of 1967 it had been announced that Bishop McDonald had resigned as rector and would become an auxiliary bishop of San Francisco and that Father Whalen would serve as acting rector for one year. Whalen had been engaged in seminary teaching before coming to the university in 1961 to assist in the production of the *New Catholic Encyclopedia*. He had assumed effective control of the project when there was danger that it might fail, and, after its successful conclusion, he had left the campus to manage a new venture in scholarly publishing under the name of Corpus Instrumentorum. He chose as his immediate assistants former staff editors of the encyclopedia. Brother Nivard Scheel, C.F.X., became his executive assistant and later succeeded him as acting rector. C. Joseph Nuesse, then head of the department of sociology, became acting executive vice rector, since the former incumbent, Monsignor McAllister, had resigned simultaneously with McDonald. Within the year, there followed a restructuring of the central administration of the university that was based to a great extent upon recommendations made by Heald, Hobson and Associates, an academic consulting firm that had been engaged by the trustees. The firm of Peat, Marwick and Mitchell had been engaged also for consultation in business and financial affairs.

The employment of the consultants had been authorized even before the explosive events of the spring. At the same April meeting at which the trustees had made their fateful decision not to renew Curran's appointment, they had authorized the organization of a survey and objectives committee that soon became the instrument for a thorough evaluation and restructuring of the university. The meeting had been informed by the rector of a resolution of the academic senate requesting regular liaison between representatives of the faculties and of the trustees.[1] The rector had presented preliminary recommendations to respond to the resolution, but a relatively new trustee, Carroll A. Hochwalt (1899–1988), a former vice president of Monsanto Corporation, believing that Catholic higher education was in need of "overhauling and renewal," suggested that a committee should be appointed to "determine the function and place of The Catholic University of America as a national University" and that it should be authorized to engage consultants to help it in its appraisal. He was immediately elected as chairman of the committee with four archbishops and five laymen as other members.[2] The National Conference of Catholic Bishops appropriated $100,000 for the study, the university $50,000, and two members of the committee and a family foundation the remaining $29,500.[3] At a special meeting in July, the academic senate elected representatives of the arts and sciences, the ecclesiastical schools, and the professional schools to serve with the committee.[4]

The acting rector and the trustee committee had only begun their tasks when the university received a previously scheduled decennial visitation from its regional accrediting agency, the Middle States Association of Colleges and Secondary Schools. In an experimental approach that was then being tried, a five-member team of externs was charged with reviewing the university's self-evaluation report and with apprais-

---

1. AS, mm, Jan. 26, 1967.
2. BT, mm, Apr. 10, 1967. The other members were Cardinal John Krol, Archbishop of Philadelphia, and Archbishops John P. Cody of Chicago, Philip M. Hannan of New Orleans, and Patrick A. O'Boyle of Washington, and Messrs. John Clarke of Chicago, Leo Daly of Omaha, Daniel J. Donohue of Los Angeles, Stephen Jackson and Charles P. Maloney of Washington.
3. *Ibid.*, Nov. 12, 1967, exh.
4. AS, mm, July 6, 1967. The representatives were, respectively, James P. O'Connor, the Reverend Frederick R. McManus, and Donald E. Marlowe, all deans.

ing the necessity of a full-scale investigation by representatives of academic disciplines as well as administrators. Certain comments in the report that this team submitted probably reflected the thinking of its two members from Catholic institutions, Father McGinley of Fordham and Norbert Hruby, president of Aquinas College in Grand Rapids, Michigan, but all members were in accord in rejecting as "totally inadequate" the institutional self-evaluation that had been submitted. Note was made that implementation of recommendations made by the Middle States team in 1957 had been "greatly limited by action of the Rector." The university was portrayed as in a "critical condition" and a full-scale revisit by the Association in 1970 was recommended.[5]

Issues that were being seen as confronting Catholic higher education in general were introduced and even highlighted in the report. The necessity of institutional autonomy was given particular emphasis. The university was advised that, even as a pontifical institution, it should follow American rather than European exemplars and should undertake to obtain "the sympathetic understanding and freedom to act which it needs from the pertinent Roman congregation." The trustees, because they were then overwhelmingly episcopal, were represented as having "always tended to be conservative in nature" and as being likely to subordinate the university's interest to their individual diocesan concerns. Moreover, in the wake of Vatican Council II, it was alleged that the university had failed to attract lay leaders to its governing and administrative bodies.[6] Scattered throughout, significantly, were recommendations that the historic claim of the university to be a "flagship" for other Catholic institutions should be abandoned. The claim had come to be resented. It was termed "'an albatross' around the University's neck." Any effort to maintain it was rejected as "counter-productive."

Independently, under the vigorous leadership of Hochwalt, the survey and objectives committee moved expeditiously to accomplish what it defined as its principal tasks, the development of a statement of the university's aims and the revision of its governing documents in accord with the statement. It left the appraisal of specific activities to the consultants. The latter, especially Jesse Hobson, a former director of

5. OVR, "Evaluation Report for the Commission on Institutions of Higher Education of the Middle States Association of Colleges and Secondary Schools" (Confidential). The visitation reported occurred Oct. 22–25, 1967.

6. At the meeting of the trustees in April, McDonald had pointed out "that he strongly favored the idea of increasing the lay membership of the Board" and that in order to do so—all archbishops, for example, being members *ex officio*—the limit of a total of fifty trustees "should be revised upward." BT, mm, Apr. 10, 1967.

the Stanford Research Institute, conducted their work in constant dialogue with officers of administration and members of faculties as well as trustees. The academic year 1967–68 was therefore stimulating to an exceptional degree.

The Statement of Objectives

Proceeding logically, the Hochwalt committee asked for assistance from the faculties and from the American hierarchy in the development of the statement of the university's objectives.[7] As the committee was using the term, its reference was to broad rather than specific purposes. Understandably, agreement upon what the university should aim to accomplish was viewed as a prerequisite for meaningful work. A preliminary report from a committee of bishops was received by September 10. The acting rector was asked to coordinate the reports from the faculties. This led to the drafting of two documents, only one of which, that of broader scope, received the board's attention at the time. This document, as a tentative working paper, was developed by a faculty committee chaired by Dean Marlowe.[8]

Review of the committee's working paper was undertaken, among other ways, in a faculty forum. Four university-wide hearings were scheduled but only three were held. Much of the discussion both in the forum and outside it was concentrated on the relevance of a model that was being advanced by some members of faculties and by the consultants, a model of a medium-sized, graduate, research-oriented institution that could be compared with several other American universities of distinction.[9] Perhaps the most pointed criticism of the approach was that being "another good private university" would not be enough. It was held, rather, that the university should "reflect in a special manner, the orientations, concerns and interests of the American Catholic community."[10] The text that was eventually adopted and that is now printed in the announcements of the university was endorsed by the consultants for providing "a new and more open concept of service to the church" and "a new and more open framework for realizing . . . ambitions as a university." It was approved by the trustees in a vote of seventeen to two.[11]

7. AS, mm, Aug. 1, 1967; BT, mm, Nov. 12, 1967.
8. AS, mm, Nov. 2, 1967.
9. Heald, Hobson and Associates, "Future Prospects for The Catholic University of America; Report to the Survey and Objectives Committee of the Board of Trustees, September 20, 1968," 3–4.
10. OVR, Charles E. Dechert, "Critical Comments . . ."
11. BT, mm, July 26–27, 1968.

A reading of the text of the statement suggests that what the consultants had referred to as the institution's "ambitions as a university" had been uppermost in the minds of the preparers. In the context of the preceding events, it could hardly have been otherwise. Fundamentally, however, it was being taken for granted by everyone who had thought about it that fitting "intellectual and academic witness to Christian faith and humanism" could not be given by an institution of inferior status. The received tradition of the university from the founders' day onward had been clear on this point. Therefore, the emphases upon institutional autonomy, academic freedom, research orientation, national outlook, and service—all of them features common to distinguished institutions in "the American academic community"—were far from new or surprising.

Much more difficulty was encountered in attempting to specify the significance of the broad objectives for the varied academic fields represented in the university. Dean O'Connor of the graduate school of arts and sciences, who was in charge of drafting a second statement to accomplish this purpose, presented a final draft at a special meeting of the academic senate at which, while giving its approval, the senate rejected an amendment to emphasize the centrality of theology and philosophy.[12] It soon became necessary to refer to this second statement as setting forth "goals" because of the semantic confusion that had been introduced by the previous appropriation of the term "objectives."[13]

The "multi-purpose" character of the university was reaffirmed by the senate a year after the statement was first approved, at a special meeting that was convened to consider the implications of the Heald, Hobson report. When a motion was passed to rank broad fields according to the priority that they should have, the senate placed in descending order religious studies, the humanities, the natural sciences, the social sciences, the social professions, the arts, and the applied sciences. This ordering by numerical vote was more significant in revealing how the concerns of the university were being perceived than in promoting agreement.[14] Despite opinions of the trustees that were voiced from time to time on the priorities of the various fields, the statement of "goals" was not seriously discussed in meetings of the board and was withdrawn after passage of a resolution categorizing it as an administrative document.[15] After more than a decade had passed, however, a

12. AS, mm, May 21, 1968.
13. Ibid., Dec. 5, 1968.
14. Ibid., May 15, 1969. The ordering was revoked in 1973. Ibid., Oct. 18, 1973.
15. BT, mm, Dec. 6, 1969.

revised statement that was almost as general as the first was presented by the academic senate and approved by the board after amendments were agreed upon.[16] Meanwhile, setting priorities had become the subject of seemingly never-ending internal discussions in which the leadership of successive presidents came to be tested.

Guiding the recommendations of the university's consultants in 1968 was the conviction that the statement of objectives had pointed in the right direction. Aware as they were of the financial problems of most private institutions at the time, problems that were in fact to loom larger during the next decade, they maintained that the only course that would offer the appropriate "potential for service, quality and financial support" would be the development of "a multi-purpose modern Catholic university with emphasis upon graduate work and specializing in areas closely related to the Catholic Church's history, culture and needs." A decision to move in this direction, they did not hesitate to remark, "would bring a great increase in operating and capital expenses with the corresponding need to greatly increase income."[17] This was in fact the statement of a challenge.

That acceptance of the challenge would enhance the service of the university to the Church seemed to be somewhat difficult for the sponsors of the institution to understand, even when the recommendations of the consultants were being discussed. Trustees, with the bishops generally, it seemed, were apt to define service in immediate, tangible forms. Yet, as Scheel, when he was acting rector, attempted to show, using the criterion of training alone, the university had prepared great numbers of the personnel of the Church: 28 per cent of the bishops at the time, 51 per cent of the chancellors of dioceses, 47 per cent of the assistant chancellors, 38 per cent of the diocesan superintendents of schools, and 48 per cent of the diocesan directors of charities.[18] There was irony indeed, therefore, in what a fund-raising consultant would soon report, that in seeking to estimate the feasibility of a financial campaign he had found that the university was not enjoying "the prestige or recognition it deserves and needs," especially in "its very important constituency—The Catholic Clergy in America."[19]

The New Governing Documents

Developing a new instrument of governance that would respond to changing needs and at the same time preserve university traditions was

16. AS, mm, May 7, 1980; BT, mm, June 21, 1980.
17. *Op. cit.*, 81, 80.
18. BT, mm, Dec. 7, 1968, exh.
19. *Ibid.*, Dec. 6, 1969, exh., report of Robert Kidera for Tamblyn and Brown.

a more complex task than deciding upon broad guidelines for policy. The problem had to be approached by the trustees in two stages. Certain needs had to be addressed immediately. For this reason, various revisions of the existing pontifical statutes were enacted piecemeal, as they were recommended by the survey and objectives committee and approved by the Roman congregation for seminaries and universities (soon to be renamed the congregation for Catholic education). The most important revisions accomplished in this way affected the size and composition of the board, the representation of the faculties in meetings of the trustees, and the representation of the faculties in the academic senate.[20]

The longer task was the revision or replacement of the ecclesiastical statutes that were in effect. To undertake this, the survey and objectives committee appointed a special committee with Cardinal Shehan as chairman.[21] A faculty committee chaired by Dean McManus of the school of canon law was elected by the academic senate to assist the Shehan committee.[22] "Ultimately," as Shehan was to report, "it was determined to write a succinct but comprehensive set of By-Laws, to write new statutes for the Ecclesiastical Schools, repealing all other statutes, and to recommend a set of Resolutions of first priority to the Board of Trustees."[23] The consequence of this decision was the enactment of a single set of civil bylaws, supplemented by special statutes to be applied "where the authority of the Roman Pontiff may be involved and where the appropriate Pontifical Congregations may properly be consulted."[24] The institution, of course, in spite of its official reclassification for curial purposes, remains pontifical by virtue of its charter, its juridical recognition in canon law, and its relationship to the hierarchy of the church.

The change was intended, as the chairman stated, to bring the governing documents "into conformity with the requirements of civil law and with the standards of the Middle States Association." Discrepancies between the civil and the ecclesiastical documents had often

20. BT, EC, mm, Oct. 19, 1967; BT, mm, Nov. 12, 1967; OR, Cardinal Giuseppe Pizzardo to O'Boyle, Rome, Nov. 28, 1967 (copy).

21. NC press release, Jan. 12, 1968; BT, mm, Apr. 21, 1968. Serving with Shehan were Cardinal Cody; Francis X. Gallagher, counsel for the archdiocese of Baltimore and principal draftsman; John J. Budds, chancellor of the University of Connecticut and president-elect of the Association of Governing Boards; Father McGinley; Stefan Kuttner, former professor of canon law, who had become the first professor of Catholic studies at Yale University; and Father Whalen.

22. The other members were Professors Albert Broderick, O.P., Karl Herzfeld, Edward D. Jordan, and John K. Zeender. BT, mm, Apr. 21, 1968.

23. *Ibid.*, Apr. 12–13, 1969.

24. *Ibid.*, July 26–27, 1968.

been cited in meetings of the board, as has been noted, but remedial
action had never been taken. The Shehan committee was proposing that the new instrument should be a civil document but that it should "specify that the University will be publicly identified as Catholic sponsored, that the University will be motivated by the spiritual, moral and religious inspiration and values of the Judeo-Christian tradition, that the University, through the fulfillment of its corporate purposes by teaching, research and public service, is dedicated to the education of man and to the temporal and eternal well-being of all men."[25]

Differences of opinion about the necessity of linkage between Catholic purpose and hierarchical control were aired in the board. Cardinals Krol and O'Boyle especially doubted that the former could be preserved without the latter. Shehan, concerned about the university's legal position, asserted "that as long as there is an authority outside the Board of Trustees which has control over the Board, there may be serious problems."[26] After opportunity for study, the bylaws proposed by the Shehan committee were approved by a vote of fifteen to seven. At the same meeting at which approval was voted, there was established a permanent committee on revision of which Krol was named chairman.[27] The Holy See gave its approval a few months later.[28]

Shehan's purpose in his committee, which became the purpose of the board, was to maintain the public identification of the university with the Roman Catholic Church through means that would be recognized and supported in American law. At first, it seems to have been thought that the generalities in the charter documents would have to be replaced with a new and more specific act of incorporation.[29] The committee, however, concluded early in its deliberations that this was unnecessary. Five principal means of maintaining Catholic identity were being incorporated into the bylaws: (1) the publication with the bylaws and in the catalogues of all the schools of the official statement of objectives that was then being considered; (2) the adoption of a historical preface to the bylaws identifying the university with the Catholic hierarchy of the United States and with the Holy See; (3) provision for the numerical equality of clerical and nonclerical members of the board, with voting requirements on crucial issues that would assure the maintenance of

25. OVR, Shehan to Whalen, Baltimore, June 21, 1968 (copy).

26. BT, mm, Apr. 5, 1968.

27. *Ibid.*, Sept. 13, 1969. The other members appointed were William S. Abell, Bishop (later Cardinal) William W. Baum, and Vincent C. Burke.

28. BT, EC, mm, Feb. 17, 1970, exh., Luigi Raimondi to Walton, Washington, Jan. 23, 1970. See Shehan, *Blessing of Years*, 265.

29. BT, mm, July 26–27, 1968.

ecclesiastical interests; (4) recognition of the *ex-officio* membership of the chancellor as the archbishop of Washington; and (5) the enactment of special statutes for the ecclesiastical faculties requiring approval by the Holy See. Historically, the Roman congregations always had been interested primarily in the ecclesiastical faculties and, as had been illustrated specifically during Shahan's administration, had found it difficult to pass upon proposals applying to other faculties.

To make ecclesiastical continuity explicit, the preface to the bylaws, in its original form, had ended with the statement that "the Holy See desires that the Catholic University of America remain the responsibility of the American Hierarchy and the whole of the people of God in the United States of America."[30] When, however, it was learned that Krol had maintained, in an annual meeting of the hierarchy over which he had presided, that the juridical relationship of the university to the hierarchy had been severed by the enactment of the bylaws,[31] there was added to the preface in 1975 the sentence, "Therefore, the relationship between the University and the Bishops can be dissolved only with the approval of the Holy See."[32] It was reported that the university's interpretation, as embodied in this sentence, had received the unanimous support of the administrative committee of the National Conference of Catholic Bishops.[33] Cardinal Shehan remained insistent on the need that he had expressed earlier to "permeate the By-Laws with a sense of sponsorship of the University on the part of the hierarchy and an acknowledgment of the debt of the University to the Catholic Church in the United States." At the same time, he placed on record "the continuing desire of the Trustees to make the Catholic University the pre-eminent seat of learning among Catholic institutions in this nation."[34]

There was little or no opposition in the board or elsewhere to the particular changes in its size and composition that were introduced before the first draft of the bylaws was attempted. The former board of fifty members was considered to be too large to be effective, especially since most of its members, as archbishops, were serving *ex officio* and often had only minimal interest in university affairs, and since the elected lay members were few. A board of thirty, all but two of whom would be elected, was thought to be large enough, and the even division

30. *Documents of The Catholic University of America* (1970), 2.
31. AS, mm, July 23, 1974.
32. *Charter and By-Laws of The Catholic University of America* (1976), 2; BT, mm, Nov. 22, 1975.
33. AS, mm, Sept. 11, 1975.
34. BT, mm, July 26–27, 1968.

between clerical and lay members was thought to be an advantage. By an amendment, it was later stipulated that of the fifteen clerics on the board, twelve were to be members of the National Conference of Catholic Bishops.[35] This strengthened an original provision that any alienation of property or cessation of university operations or the dissolution of the corporation would require the approval of three-fourths of the full board membership. Ultimate episcopal control was thus assured. The enlargement of the board to forty-two members at a later date did not introduce changes in these respects.[36]

In keeping with long-standing requests and the participatory movements of the 1960s and 1970s, provision was made at the outset for the attendance without right to vote of an elected representative of each of the three groups of faculties that were being recognized, the arts and sciences, the ecclesiastical schools, and the professional schools. One of the three representatives was authorized to attend meetings of the executive committee. Members of administrative staffs and of the faculties were appointed also to standing committees of the board on academic affairs, development and university relations, financial affairs, physical plant, and student affairs.[37] Student representation through selection by undergraduate and graduate organizations was authorized only after initial opposition.[38] The addition of one undergraduate and one graduate student member to each standing committee was first authorized.[39] Nonvoting participation in meetings of the board followed a little more than a year later.[40] Subsequently, nonvoting participation of the president of the Alumni Association was also approved.[41]

Particularly noteworthy, from the point of view of the faculties, was not only their representation in meetings of the board, but the protection or, even more, the recognition given in the bylaws to the academic tradition of the university. The academic senate, it was provided, was to share with the president "the immediate responsibility for the academic governing of the University by establishing, maintaining, supervising and in general being responsible for the academic policies of the university."[42] Although the approval of the president continued to be a condition of the validity of enactments of the senate, the possibility of an

35. *Ibid.*, mm, Nov. 22, 1975.
36. See revised bylaws circulated with *AB*, XVIII, No. 1 (Sept. 1985).
37. BT, mm, Nov. 12, 1967.
38. *Ibid.*, June 15–16 and Sept. 12–13, 1969; June 6, exh., and Sept. 26, 1970.
39. BT, EC, mm, Mar. 6, 1971.
40. *Ibid.*, Nov. 2, 1972; BT, mm, Nov. 18, 1972.
41. BT, mm, Sept. 21–22, 1973.
42. Sec. II, Par. 6.

Clarence Cyril Walton (b. 1915), tenth chief executive of The Catholic University of America, first to hold the title of president instead of rector, and first lay person in the office.

appeal to the board in the event of differences between the senate and the president was outlined, as were representation of the senate in presidential search committees, consultation of the senate by the board in the establishment or the dissolution of departments and schools, and consultations of the faculties by the president prior to the appointment of deans or departmental chairmen according to procedures determined by the senate.

Further, the constitution of the senate and a faculty manual, upon approval by the board, were declared to be "in full force and effect binding to the same extent as if incorporated *in toto*" in the bylaws.[43] These latter documents were not produced and approved until 1970 and 1980, respectively, although in the case of the faculty manual essential parts pertaining to faculty appointments and tenure had been enacted much earlier.[44] The enactments were in fact developments of practices inaugurated during the Ryan administration. They came to include formal reviews of all candidates for tenured appointments to be presented to the board, initiated in the fall of 1969.[45]

It should be noted that in these matters the faculties and the trustees were not always heeding the advice of the consultants. The perceptions of the latter were, in fact, at odds with members of the faculties in the finding that, despite appearances, "little authority" had been vested in the faculties.[46] It was proposed that the academic senate should be transformed into a faculty senate and that deans and heads of departments should be considered to be administrative officers so that they could be appointed without the locally required consultation and serve at the pleasure of the president, not for fixed terms.[47] The elective system, it was maintained, had "perpetuated mediocrity" where it had existed.[48] These recommendations were not accepted, however.

The "special statutes for Pontifical Schools," enacted by the board at the same time as the bylaws, were made applicable to the ecclesiastical faculties of theology, canon law, and philosophy, not by way of exception to the provisions of the bylaws, but to ensure that "those courses, programs, and degrees having canonical effects" would be conducted "according to norms and regulations promulgated by the Holy See."[49] Those who successfully complete the requirements of the ecclesiastical programs therefore receive pontifical degrees, but the ecclesiastical faculties offer academic and professional programs for conventional doctoral and master's degrees as well. And, although the faculties of theology and canon law are now departments of the school of religious studies, established in 1973, the ecclesiastical faculties remain those named in 1968.

43. *Ibid.*
44. AS, mm, Dec. 5, 1968 and Mar 1, 1973; BT, mm, Mar. 22, 1975.
45. BT, mm, June 15–16, 1969.
46. *Op. cit.*, 69.
47. *Ibid.*, 65–66.
48. *Ibid.*, 69.
49. Sec. II.

When the special statutes were enacted, the pontifical requirements in effect were those specified in the apostolic constitution *Deus Scientiarum Dominus* and accompanying norms, as modified by the *Normae quaedam* of 1968. Since the new special statutes were brief, the congregation sought from the beginning to obtain their elaboration, in part by the addition of materials that in American institutions are ordinarily outlined in catalogues or similar publications.[50] The new apostolic constitution of 1979, *Sapientia Christiana*, and the norms therewith published by the congregation for Catholic education, required further revision of the special statutes. It is this revision that includes more specific provisions applying not only to curricular matters but to the status of members of the faculties that is currently in effect.[51]

Administrative and Academic Reorganization

Changing the titles of the executive officers of the university from those of ecclesiastical origin to those prevailing in American usage was substantively a minor result of the recommendations submitted by the Heald, Hobson firm. Symbolically, it was more. The consultants were recommending nothing less than "a complete reorganization of the University."[52] The existing structure, of course, had been the subject of criticism from the Middle States Association in 1957 and of scorn from its team in 1967. In reality, however, improvement could be and was in fact sought and accomplished mainly through the clarification of lines of authority and responsibility, not by departure from the institution's academic traditions.

The board of trustees had already been reorganized by the special enactments adopted before the consultants reported and before the new bylaws were completed. Hochwalt had been elected the first chairman of the reorganized board. When the consultants reported, they proposed that there should be also an auxiliary body to advise and support the board but not to exercise authority. The proposal was reminiscent of one that had been incorporated in the constitution of 1926 without effect. It was for a board of visitors, sizeable, varied in composition, primarily lay, that would be nominated by the archbishops of the country, appointed by the trustees, and presided over by the university's chancellor.[53] Although subsequently the organization of such a body

50. BT, EC, mm, Jan. 29, 1971; BT, mm, May 16, 1971.
51. AB, XV, No. 1 (Nov. 23, 1982), appendix, noting approval by the AS, Jan. 22, 1981; BT, Jan. 31, 1981; and congregation for Catholic education, Dec. 21, 1981.
52. *Op. cit.*, 55.
53. *Ibid.*, 55–57.

was discussed from time to time, usually with enlistment of ecclesiastical support as a principal object, action was long in coming. During the 1970s particularly, Presidents Walton and Pellegrino gave considerable thought to the establishment of a group of this type that would be given papal recognition. What was to come into being eventually, in 1986, was a board of regents oriented broadly and frankly toward institutional advancement.[54]

The focus of attention was, as always, upon the presidency. Under the new bylaws, appointment to the office became the board's to make, after consideration of the report of a search committee instead of, as formerly, that of a *terna* recommended by the academic senate. To forestall possible conflicts with the requirements of apostolic constitutions, however, agreement was presumed that the final list of candidates being considered by the board would be submitted to the Holy See before decision was made.[55]

The presidency was no longer to be confined to priests. It transpired that the first two presidents to be chosen under the new bylaws were laymen. Walton, a native of Scranton, Pennsylvania, had earned his baccalaureate degree at the University of Scranton and his doctorate, in history, from The Catholic University of America. After teaching at Marywood College and the University of Scranton, he had served as dean of the school of business administration at Duquesne University and as associate dean of the school of business at Columbia University before becoming dean of the latter institution's school of general studies. Pellegrino had graduated from St. John's University, Brooklyn, had obtained his degree in medicine from New York University, and had served in administrative positions at the State University of New York at Stony Brook and in the state of Tennessee and then had become professor of medicine at Yale University and president of the Yale–New Haven Medical Center. The current incumbent of the office, Byron, a Jesuit priest, had earned his doctorate in economics at the University of Maryland and had been president of the University of Scranton at the time of his appointment.

When the bylaws were developed, there was recognition that the functions of the presidency were not the same as they had been before the university had grown in size and become bureaucratized. In the

54. *Envoy*, XIV, No. 4 (Summer, 1986), 2. Walton had obtained board approval for the organization of a Charter Society of Regents of The Catholic University of America, BT, mm, Sept. 23, 1972. A trustee committee later proposed an Order of *Sapientia Christiana* to recognize support of the pontifical faculties, BT, mm, July 7, 1979; Jan. 31 and Mar. 28, 1981.
55. BT, mm, Apr. 1, 1968; Apr. 1, 1978.

Edmund Daniel Pellegrino (b. 1920), eleventh head of The Catholic University of America, whose presidency of four years was the shortest in the university's first century.

consultant's view, the president's concern was to be chiefly "with the University's outside relationships, with planning for its future and with its over-all general academic and financial health."[56] Their further recommendation that the president should not serve for a fixed term but at the pleasure of the trustees had been incorporated into the bylaws. Also incorporated was the recommendation that all vice presidents should report directly to the president. A further recommendation that the vice presidents and a newly recommended officer, a director of institutional research and planning, should constitute an executive group advisory to the president was not made a bylaw. During the

56. *Op. cit.*, 55.

Walton and Pellegrino presidencies, however, the president's council consisting of these officers was, in some respects, a continuation under another name of the former administration and budget committee. At times, when the president did not convene the council weekly, the other members met to coordinate policies and procedures as required.

The recommended organization at the vice-presidential level was to recognize commonly defined university divisions in a pattern that was followed from 1968 until a subsequent administrative reorganization in 1983. Administrative structure must usually accommodate the individual talents and preferences of presidents and the requirements of particular situations. Following the Heald, Hobson recommendations, academic affairs, the central concern of a university, became the responsibility of the executive vice president and provost, "the principal subordinate executive and academic officer" in the consultant's concept.[57] The object was to retain the identity of academic purpose in the highest ranking position under the president in a bureaucratized institution. Three additional vice presidencies, for business and finance, development, and student affairs, were authorized in 1968. With Walton's coming, some of the responsibilities that had been discharged by Monsignor Magner—whose retirement at the end of 1968 was marked by an accolade from the academic senate for "resolute leadership in matters not only fiscal but also, in some instances, academic"[58]—were transferred in 1970 to a vice president for administration. Pellegrino modified the pattern in 1979 by separating the offices of executive vice president and provost and eliminating the former office two years later. In 1983, however, Byron introduced a new administrative chart in which an executive vice president was assigned authority in internal matters over other vice presidents—for academic affairs, administration, finance, student life, and university relations.[59] The first woman to serve in a vice-presidential capacity, Sister Rosemary Donley, S.C., who had been dean of the school of nursing, was appointed executive vice president in 1986.

Two major reorganizations of faculties were accomplished during the Walton presidency. The first was the organization of a school of religious studies. As the consultants emphasized, this was viewed as the area of "highest priority for development" and also as the area in which distinction could be attained with a lesser financial investment than other areas might require.[60] On their recommendation, a faculty task force to

57. *Ibid.*, 57.
58. AS, mm, Jan. 16, 1969.
59. AB, XV, No. 3 (Sept. 9, 1983), appendix.
60. *Op. cit.*, 81.

435

develop proposals was appointed in 1968. After initial hesitancies in considering conflicting reports of the task force and of the academic administrators affected by the proposal, the academic senate formed a council on religious studies to promote coordination and to develop proposals.[61] Eventually, a joint committee of the president and the academic senate was able to present a plan that obtained approval.[62]

With the reorganization that became effective in the fall of 1973, the former schools of canon law and theology and the department of religion and religious education in arts and sciences became departments of the new school. Two new departments, in biblical studies and in church history, were added. On the recommendation of a trustee–faculty search committee, the Reverend Colman J. Barry, O.S.B., former president of St. John's University in Minnesota, was appointed the first dean.

This reorganization had important effects. In the first place, it represented, as the consultants had proposed that it should, "a commitment to concentrate all existing efforts in religion and theology, to coordinate programs and to eliminate duplication and competition."[63] Former controversies concerning the relation of the department of religion and religious education to the school of theology could be submerged. Secondly, the resources of the school could be expanded modestly—but significantly. The new departments supplied dimensions of biblical and historical scholarship that had sometimes been neglected in the instructional programs of previous years. Walton was able to augment the faculty, especially by the appointment of several distinguished Jesuits, two of whom had formerly served in the theologate of Woodstock College. This was assisted by substantial additions to the endowment fund for the new school from the bishops of the United States and from the Catholic Daughters of America, and later from the Blanding Foundation of Oneonta, New York. Professional preparation that was being demanded, such as that in clinical pastoral education, could be incorporated into the school and many of the controversial issues and ambiguities that had marked the university's concern for the diocesan seminarians forming Theological College could be resolved.

Probably the consolidation of the graduate school and the college of arts and sciences into a single school, also recommended by the consultants,[64] did not attract as much attention as the organization of the school of religious studies. It was in fact resisted by faculty votes in

---

61. BT, mm, June 15–16, 1969; AS, mm, July 17, 1969.
62. AS, mm, July 15, 1969, May 24 and June 1, 1971; BT, mm, Sept. 23, 1972.
63. *Op. cit.*, 25.
64. *Op. cit.*, 35.

1971,[65] but accepted in 1974 to be effective at the beginning of the 1975–76 academic year.[66] As previously noted, the university's maintenance of the graduate school as the faculty of arts and sciences, an outgrowth of its own history, had been at variance with American practice and had sometimes brought the deans of the graduate school and the college into conflict. Although the needs of graduate students and of undergraduates are quite different, they can be provided for administratively by the staffing of a single office, as is in fact done in professional schools, which have, admittedly, a quite different purpose. This had been brought to the attention of the rector as early as the 1930s, when the deans of the college and graduate school, then quite new in their positions, observed that their operations had "almost of necessity to be conducted jointly both academically and financially" because they were "essentially the undergraduate and graduate divisions of one school, possessing practically a common faculty."[67]

Another change in academic administration introduced during the Walton administration was the establishment in 1972 of a center for continuing education and service to take account of the expanding interest of part-time students in university courses related to their career advancement—nationally, students over twenty-five years of age are now about 45 percent of the enrolled population—and to coordinate administratively the university's offerings, not only in continuing education, but in adult education and summer sessions as well. John J. Gilheany, an associate professor of mechanical engineering, was appointed to direct the center. Adult education had been begun in 1949 by Father Sebastian and he continued to direct the offerings until his retirement in 1974. Father Robert Paul Mohan, professor of philosophy, who had directed summer sessions since Deferrari's retirement in 1960 until 1972, was resigning from the office. Later, in 1975, Gilheany was appointed assistant provost to supervise also the offices of registrar, director of admissions, and director of financial aid. In 1979, in accord with a trend in nomenclature and for curricular reasons, the center was reorganized as a university college with divisions for adult education, continuing education and service, general studies, and summer sessions.[68] It was, of course, not a faculty in its own right.

Two other organizational developments had important institutional effects. One that was undertaken in the interest of efficiency and com-

65. BT, mm, May 16, 1971.
66. AS, mm, Dec. 5 and 19, 1974; BT, EC, mm, Feb. 3, 1975.
67. OR, Campbell and Deferrari to Corrigan, Sept. 25, 1936.
68. AB, XI, No. 20 (Aug. 6, 1979), 1.

pleted despite serious difficulties was the consolidation of what had become two separate units for electronic data processing. The registrar had begun to use the once familiar Hollerith "punch cards" during the summer of 1947. It was not long before the International Business Machines equipment that had been purchased was being used by members of the faculties engaged in quantitative research and, later, by the business offices of the university. It was replaced during the academic year 1961–62 with the installation of a computer. By the end of the decade, professors desiring more advanced equipment for their work had developed a proposal to the National Science Foundation that assisted the university to put into place, in 1969, an installation of the Digital Equipment Corporation for academic work.[69] In 1971, after new IBM equipment had been purchased for administrative use, the decision was made to combine the two units, then known as the data processing center and the computer center, to use the DEC equipment. There were serious practical problems in the translation of programs and also problems of administration, so that the dissolution of the data processing center was not completed until 1973. Since 1974, a single computer center has served both academic and administrative clienteles with more than ordinary satisfaction.

Another achievement, but one with a curious subsequent denouement, was the establishment of the Boys Town center for the study of youth development. Early in 1972, the trustees of Father Flanagan's Boys Town of Nebraska, who were being criticized in the press for failing to use their accumulating assets appropriately, resolved to establish research facilities of national significance at Boys Town and at selected universities. The Catholic University of America and Stanford University became the institutions invited to submit proposals for regional centers that would "conduct studies and train personnel in the area of youth development." An agreement with The Catholic University of America was signed late in 1973. A handsome building to house the center was designed by the Omaha firm of Leo A. Daly, an alumnus, and dedicated in 1977. Funding for interdisciplinary research was to be provided for a twenty-five year period at an annual level equivalent to the $450,000 appropriated for 1977–78. O'Connor, who had become vice provost and dean of graduate studies in 1968 and in that capacity had been instrumental in developing plans for the center, was appointed to be the first director. Apparently, however, administrative problems at Boys Town and failure to understand what could be expected from

69. BT, mm, Sept. 27–28, 1968.

research led the board of that institution to conclude that research had never been a legitimate objective for it. The agreement was terminated in a settlement reached in 1982 requiring removal of the name of Boys Town from the center.[70]

During the Pellegrino administration, also, as of January 1, 1981, the department of library and information science was elevated to the status of a school, as professional accrediting agencies had urged for some time.[71] Instruction in the field had first been offered during the summer session of 1929. Departmental status had been authorized in 1945, and accreditation of the master of library science degree achieved in 1957. Elizabeth Stone, who had chaired the department since succeeding Father James J. Kortendick, S.S., in 1972, and who was enjoying a national reputation for leadership in the field, became the first dean. On the other hand, during the Byron administration, in 1985, the school of education that had been given independent status twenty years earlier elected to return to its former departmental status in the school of arts and sciences.[72] Declining enrollment and national trends in teacher education were among the factors prompting the decision.

Some reorganization, necessarily, took the form of retrenchment. During the 1970s it was no longer possible to postpone response to a long-standing need to adjust academic offerings to depressing fiscal realities. At the outset it became apparent that the goal of annual receipts of $4,500,000 from the diocesan collections—set after Whalen's appearance before the American hierarchy in 1967—would not be reached. Reliance upon this goal in budgeting and the previous exhaustion of reserve funds had resulted in severe annual deficits that could be accommodated only by loans. A balanced budget policy, of course, requires that expenditures be limited to projections of income to be received. Thus, policies of retrenchment were imposed upon the Walton administration from the beginning. The number of full-time faculty positions was reduced by 5 per cent from 1969–70 to 1970–71 and by an additional 7.6 per cent from 1970–71 to 1971–72. Part-time positions were reduced immediately by 19 per cent. The number of graduate assistants was reduced by 11 per cent in the first year and by an additional 14 per cent in the second. Faculty salaries, already substantially lower than in comparable Catholic and local institutions, were frozen for the next year at 1970–71 levels except in the school of

70. *Ibid.*, Mar. 28, 1981; June 26, 1982.
71. *Ibid.*, Nov. 22, 1980. The extended name had been authorized earlier. *Ibid.*, Jan. 29, 1977.
72. *Ibid.*, Jan. 31, 1985.

law and in individual cases in which outstanding merit or considerations of equity required adjustments.[73]

Inevitably, perennial tensions of academic life were accentuated. As enrollment trends became more important, for example, offerings of long standing or of outstanding quality were sometimes placed at a disadvantage. Priorities had to be set and respected, even when their recognition was resisted by claims of academic autonomy against administrative decisions or when high quality was found in fields of low priority.[74] The central faculty of the arts and sciences, facing declining enrollment, found itself pitted against professional fields in which enrollment was growing. Litigation increased as, in accord with national trends, members of faculties and others resorted to it as a means of resistance. There was little support on campus for collective bargaining, which had become widespread nationally, but petitions to the National Labor Relations Board from the law faculty were filed twice, by opposing sides in faculty disputes, as weapons against the dean and against current policies.[75] Their eventual failure was due not only to lack of merit but to a decision of the Supreme Court of the United States in *National Labor Relations Board v. Yeshiva University* that upheld the opinion that authentic faculty participation in academic management, such as was prevailing at The Catholic University of America, rendered faculty ineligible for collective bargaining.

To protect its own role as well as that of the faculties in the termination of departments and tenured professors, the academic senate adopted, in 1972, a statement of procedures to be followed when program terminations were proposed. Reductions in programs had begun earlier. Questions affecting tenure had not arisen when units such as the child center of the department of psychology and the statistical laboratory of the department of mathematics, both academically significant, were closed. Similarly, in 1972, it had been agreed by all members of the Consortium of Universities that doctoral programs in German and in mathematics, in which enrollment was low in every member institution, would be offered only jointly. Subsequently, although the procedures that the senate adopted prolonged the process considerably, three academic departments were terminated. That of aerospace and

73. See OVR, C. Joseph Nuesse, "The 1972–73 Budget for Instruction and Departmental Research" (mimeo.).

74. On the criteria employed, see C. Joseph Nuesse, "Academic Priorities: Criteria for Assessment," AB, IV, No. 3 (Oct. 15, 1971), Suppl.

75. AS, mm, Mar. 1 and 15, Apr. 12, 19, 26, 1973; Mar. 17, Apr. 28, May 3 and 5, Sept. 8, Nov. 17, Dec. 1, 1977; BT, mm, Apr. 20, 1972, Mar. 26, 1977; Oct. 28, 1978.

atmospheric science in the school of engineering, in which enrollment had been declining steadily in spite of the outstanding quality of the faculty, was terminated by a reorganization of the school of engineering and architecture in 1975.[76] In the school of arts and sciences, geography was terminated in 1975[77] and speech pathology and audiology in 1979.[78]

Retrenchment was only one side—the dramatic one perhaps—of the changes that were occurring in academic programs during the 1970s. As is well known, even in times of adversity, and sometimes especially then, departments must inaugurate new programs and revise old ones in response to demands that are made upon them or in response to new opportunities. In 1971, for example, black studies was introduced at the undergraduate level as a supplement to regular disciplinary concentrations. Individualized experimental programs were begun in the same year. The traditional requirement in physical education was abrogated. Subsequently, there were added programs in managerial accounting in 1972; environmental science in 1976; and computer science in 1978. In 1979 programs in general studies were authorized to allow students somewhat beyond college age to pursue baccalaureate degrees without all the constraining requirements otherwise imposed upon undergraduates. Among new post-baccalaureate programs, perhaps the most noteworthy were those in clinical-pastoral education offered in the school of religious studies and in early Christian studies offered in the school of arts and sciences. The latter, begun with a grant from the Andrew W. Mellon Foundation, could utilize the unique resources of the university and of the Washington area in this field.

Underlying some of the tensions and contributing markedly to widespread uncertainties in the Church during the 1970s were the decline in the number of clerics and religious and the seeming ambivalence of so many about their roles. Within the university two effects—not the only ones, to be sure—were plainly identified. One was in student enrollment, the other in faculty expectations for compensation. The effect of the sharp decline in clerics and religious upon schools other than that of religious studies, particularly upon the school of arts and sciences, could not be other than marked. Summer sessions also, which from their beginning had been especially important in teacher education for religious, were no less affected. A peak in summer enrollment of 5,113 students, both ecclesiastical and lay, had been attained in 1965. During the summer of 1987 only 1,946 students were registered.

76. AS, mm, Jan. 17 and 31, Mar. 28, Apr. 11 and 25, May 16 and 21, July 24, Sept. 12, 1974, and Feb. 13 and 27, 1975; BT, mm, Mar., 21–22, 1975.

77. AS, mm, Sept. 12, 1974; Jan. 16 and 30, 1975; BT, mm, Mar. 22, 1975.

78. AS, mm, Mar. 30, Apr. 6, 13, 20, May 4, 1978; BT, mm, June 23, 1978.

More vexing at the time, however, was the issue of "parity" between the salaries of clerics and religious in administrative or faculty positions and those of the laity. Demands for "parity" were not new. McCormick in the last year of the second world war had sought to reduce the differential between salary scales that had been aggravated by emergency measures during the depression years of the 1930s. Trustees then took exception, as their minutes showed, "to the principal [sic] of raising the salaries of the clerical members to the same levels as those of the lay members, inasmuch as the living expenses of the clergy, particularly those living at the University, are considerably less than those of the laity, and also because the clergy are by the nature of their calling expected to make certain material sacrifices in pursuit of their works."[79] These remained the standard reasons for the reluctance of the board to accede to requests that were often repeated during the 1960s and 1970s. To them was added only the fear that if the requests were granted similar ones might arise in Catholic high schools and even in Catholic elementary schools.[80]

Responses from the faculties in general probably were based, for the most part, upon the familiar principle of equal pay for equal work. Diocesan priests arguing for "parity" tended to assert their individual rights to dispose of their own funds responsibly. Demands came also from religious, as McDonald had once noted,[81] but perhaps with more urgency than before in view of the needs of their communities, affected as they were by declining numbers. When Walton first proposed a plan for movement toward "parity" over a three-year period, the board would affirm only the "principle of just compensation and retirement provision."[82] Two religious, members of the law faculty, brought suits against the university in 1971 on both contractual and constitutional grounds but were unsuccessful in federal district and appellate courts. In disallowing their constitutional arguments, in 1976, the appellate court held that "the salary scale for priests in a church-related institution clearly appears to be an internal matter of the religious institution affected."[83] Meanwhile, "parity" had been approved by the board in 1973.[84]

In spite of changes such as these in governance and internal adminis-

79. BT, EC, mm, Jan. 12, 1945.
80. BT, mm, Nov. 13, 1966.
81. Ibid., Nov. 10, 1963.
82. Ibid., June 6 and Dec. 12, 1970.
83. Joseph A. Broderick v. The Catholic University of America and David J. K. Granfield v. The Catholic University of America, Civil Actions 1534-71 and 1535-71, U.S. District Court for the District of Columbia, affirmed by U.S. Court of Appeals, Jan. 29, 1976.
84. BT, mm, Sept. 22, 1973.

tration, continuity in the mission of the university and of its offerings was being maintained, as it had been in previous periods of rapid change, by a long-established institutional tradition. The founders and the first faculties had laid firm foundations, even if what had been built upon them had sometimes reflected what the trustees consulting firm was singling out as "weak leadership." The same consultants, knowledgable about other institutions, were quick to point out that "in reality, the University is far better than most people consider it to be, including its own faculty and staff."[85] Idealistic expectations and bleak fiscal realities had undoubtedly affected institutional self-esteem through the years. The consultant's judgment of academic quality, however, was soon confirmed by the visiting team of the Middle States Association in 1970 which, seemingly without reference to the forebodings of the visiting committee of 1967, found sufficient "insight, courage and dedication . . . at all levels of the university" to predict a bright future for it.[86]

Student Roles in Transition

The revision of the university's governing documents and other changes that were becoming visible within it at the end of the 1960s were occuring concomitantly with the rise of new social movements of national and in some respects international scope. As yet, the decade of the 1960s can hardly be said to be understood satisfactorily. It was hailed at first as the dawn of a new age. Popularly it became known for the social changes that in the United States began in the civil rights movement and then took strange counter-cultural forms before erupting in protests against American foreign policy and the war in Vietnam and then giving rise to the conflicting political tendencies of the 1970s and 1980s. The various movements have been described sympathetically as assaults on the American center that were "liberal in values, reformist in character, disciplined in tactics, persuasive in approach and [produc-tive of] most of the positive changes in policies that were associated with the 1960's activism."[87] Not all would agree with this judgment, but one of the visible formal effects of the emphasis upon participatory democracy in the activism of the time was the admission of students to participation in meetings of committees, departments, faculties, the academic senate, and the board of trustees, as already noted.

This participation emerged as an aspect of a seemingly new student

85. *Op. cit.*, 4, 7.
86. OR, "Report . . . ," 11.
87. Curtis B. Gans, "Looking Back at the Sixties: Rock 'n' Roll and Revolution," *Washington Post*, Dec. 20, 1987.

ethos. For all the attention that has been given to it by alumni, parents, and the public generally—no doubt with their own false dawns in mind—it remains as elusive of definition as the decade in which it became manifest. Undoubtedly the ethos was derived from a broader cultural change that began to give priority to individual expectations over social obligations. One student, for example, supporting "entirely" the new mood, expressed it well in remarking, "People aren't feeling the constrictions of social roles anymore. . . . More and more, in all the happenings of life—people are going to do as they please."[88] His elders could hardly help but contrast his statement with the admonition that they had heard Fulton Sheen repeat often that "right is right if nobody is right, and wrong is wrong if everybody is wrong."[89] Nor could they fail to note that both idealistic talk of commitment and reluctance to undertake it in practice were increasing. But in 1968, the Association of American Colleges, the American Association of University Professors, the National Association of Women Deans and Counselors, and the National Student Association had adopted a joint statement on students' rights and freedoms that they were recommending for adoption also by individual institutions.[90]

The new ethos could emerge, of course, because, however involved individual students had become in social causes, it was to their advantage that campuses should remain, as they always had been, in the words of a historian, "oases, sharply set off from the surrounding society in many of their fundamental qualities and frequently the objects of deep-seated suspicion."[91] Universities almost everywhere were to become targets of radical action. The Catholic University of America would not have been such a target in the early 1960s, when, for example, the Undergraduate Student Council passed several resolutions to "support President Kennedy in his desires to drive from this hemisphere the Communist movement."[92] The council was to sponsor a project in which twelve students were trained for apostolic activity in Mexico.[93] It later terminated its membership in the National Student Association because it objected to an NSA "policy of adopting political resolutions" that was alleged to overstep "the legitimate bounds of a student government organization."[94]

88. Michael Meng '75, interviewed in "The Collegiate Quest," *Momentum*, V, No. 3 (Oct. 1974), 12.

89. *Old Errors and New Labels* (New York: Century, 1931), 115.

90. BT, EC, mm, Jan. 18, 1968.

91. Veysey, *op. cit.*, x.

92. OR, resolution passed May 2, 1962; see also those of Oct. 23 and 29, 1962.

93. *Ibid.*, William Murphy to McDonald, Mar. 25, 1964.

94. *Ibid.*, James R. Lothian to U.S. National Student Association, Washington, Oct. 28, 1965 (copy).

In contrast, the student demands of the late 1960s were such as to produce shock effects. Those on campus were undoubtedly relatively conservative by the standards of activist leaders. What they led to, nevertheless, was consistent with national trends. Perhaps the most revealing outward change, symbolic in its way, was the decline almost to the point of disappearance of the social clubs and fraternities that once had been powerful in the student body. In their place, there was a rise in importance of avowedly governmental and political groups, in particular Undergraduate Student Government (formerly Council) and the Graduate Student Association. These became the accepted agencies of participation in the academic senate and the board of trustees and in the formation of policies affecting students. The advance of legalism in campus affairs was in accord with trends in American society. It was consistent also with the advancing bureaucratization of student personnel services. It is likely that on the campus as well as in other institutions, as a recent author has suggested, "new outsiders" were taking over and were influencing even the proponents of the traditional "college life."[95]

Some signs of impending change might have been discerned earlier in developments that were to lead to the bureaucratic expansion of student personnel services. In men's residence halls, it had become necessary to appoint young laymen as proctors. Until the academic year 1959–60, priests had virtually always had the responsibility. An attempt of the administration in 1953 to contract with religious brothers to provide this service[96] was probably motivated by the desire to gain more regularity than was being provided by priest students, who had long since replaced the priest members of the faculties who had lived in the residence halls in earlier years. Actually, since both De La Salle College of the Christian Brothers and Xaverian College of the Xaverian Brothers were to close in 1970, success in the negotiations might have been short-lived at best. As it was, Marist brothers could undertake the task only briefly. An effect of lay staffing, naturally, was to place in positions of responsibility for the supervision of student conduct persons not much older than the students and, before long, as "resident advisers," students themselves. Meanwhile, increasing demands for decisive roles in the formation of policies, sometimes even of academic policies, could be made by the student personnel staff. At the outset, there had been disappointment on the part of the still small staff because of feelings

95. Horowitz, *op. cit.*, 20.
96. ABC, mm, Aug. 29, 1953.

Centennial Village, the most recent addition to the campus, opened in 1988, with a central circle named for Silvio O. Conte and residence halls named for Charles A. and Anne D. Camalier, Jr., Jane B. Engelhard, James A. Magner, William J. McDonald, George J. Quinn, Joseph P. Reardon, Joseph Unanue, and Clarence C. Walton.

that it had been given too little attention by the Heald, Hobson firm during 1967–68, in spite of the establishment, on the consultant's recommendation, of the office of vice president for student affairs.[97]

At the heart of the demands made by the students and by those who were sympathetic with them was a revolt against policies that could be assailed as based in one way or another upon the formerly accepted principle that colleges and universities act with respect to students *in loco parentis*.[98] Colleges generally had withdrawn or were withdrawing their oversight not only of student morals but of propriety. There were reinforcing national movements such as that for the reduction of the minimum age for voting from twenty-one to eighteen years. Particularly insistent were student demands for "parietal" hours or "inter-dormitory visitation." These received popular attention because of their implications for youthful sexual codes. Without acceding to such student demands, but seeking nevertheless to placate them, Walton, whose experience with student protests had been gained at Columbia University, hailed the disappearance of the *in loco parentis* concept as traditionally

97. BT, mm, Sept. 27–28, 1968.
98. BT, EC, mm, Feb. 17, 1970.

understood and practiced while he scorned at the same time academic "indifference to student needs."[99]

Calls for "relevance" stirred the campuses. They often came from leaders who had emerged from the civil rights movement. Community involvement was emphasized by student activists, especially after the murder of Martin Luther King on April 4, 1968. Even before, the Consortium of Universities had begun, somewhat hesitantly, to prepare for discussions with governmental representatives about "the involvement of the universities in public problems."[100] During weekend disturbances in Washington after King's murder, when the administration seemed to be in disarray, the editor of the *Tower* wrote privately to inform the acting rector that "a number of students [had] cooperated above and beyond the call of duty to make the situation much calmer and safer than it might well have been."[101] But a perplexed parent, responding to a circular letter intended to allay fears, could inquire if it was "absolutely imperative for the students to be subjected to the possibility of . . . emergencies."[102]

As part of a Poor People's Campaign organized by the Southern Christian Leadership Conference early in 1968, it was announced that a Poor People's University was being planned. When the Consortium, on the premise that "it would be too dangerous to use on-campus University facilities," proposed to assist the Poor People's University in downtown locations,[103] the sponsoring Conference expressed serious disappointment[104] and later announced that it would initiate a university reform movement itself. Its agenda proved to be wide-ranging indeed and was intended, it was declared, "to destroy the vestiges of middle-class dominance" in higher education.[105]

Although the Poor People's University did not materialize, the agitation for "relevance" was heeded in many places by curricular revision that could have been interpreted as restoring the elective system. At The Catholic University of America, although the faculties were losing their grasp of the curricular principles that had been developed in the college of arts and sciences under Campbell's leadership, the undergraduate curriculum was not to be restructured significantly. As has been

---

99. *Op. cit.*, 13.
100. OR, Nuesse to Faculty, Dec. 6, 1967 (mimeo).
101. *Ibid.*, James L. Rowe, Jr., to Whalen, Apr. 9, 1968.
102. *Ibid.*, James D. Krull to Whalen, West Hempstead, N.Y., n.d.
103. AS, mm, May 16, 1968.
104. OR, memorandum of telephone call, Joseph N. Moody to Whalen, May 21, 1968.
105. *Ibid.*, memorandum, June, 1968.

noted, courses, but not programs of concentration, were introduced in black studies. More important for the social purpose that was in the forefront were half-tuition scholarships for disadvantaged students that were inaugurated in 1969 in a Partnership Program in which local business was expected to provide funding for the other half of tuition charges. After the first year, the university became the only contributor. The participants and other students from the black minority formed a club named Black Organization of Students at The Catholic University of America (BOSACUA).

Since, according to the traditional academic calendar that was to remain in effect until the fall of 1970, there were still two months between the rioting that followed King's murder and the annual commencement, the academic senate prudently undertook to devise procedures for use "if student protests should interfere with the conduct of academic affairs."[106] Demonstrations soon became so much a part of campus life that before the end of the next year the senate charged an ad hoc committee with consideration of campus disorders.[107] Protest activity peaked during the year 1969–70. In the fall, when a "moratorium" to protest the Vietnam war was organized nationally, the campus accommodated about three thousand visiting students, "not in support of the Moratorium," as Walton, beginning his administration, reported to the senate and trustees, "but to extend Christian hospitality."[108] That winter, improvement of campus security, already acknowledged to be necessary, became urgent after the murder of a student.[109] Only a little later, around-the-clock demonstrations required administrative and faculty readiness for virtually continuous discussion through two nights with the five hundred or so students who participated to present grievances and demands.[110]

Actually, the councils and students generally were divided on the issues and on the wisdom of the strike goals that were being declared by national leaders, but there was no serious challenge to the relatively small number of activist leaders on the campus. The influence of the activists was to wane, however, as the end of the Vietnam war came in sight. As early as the fall of 1970, incoming freshmen were reported to be unimpressed by what activist leaders were proposing to them during the orientation programs conducted by upperclassmen.

106. AS, mm, May 16, 1968. Under the "early semester" schedule adopted in 1970 the first semester ends before Christmas and the second begins by mid-January. A majority of American institutions now follow this plan.
107. *Ibid.*, May 22, 1969.
108. *Ibid.*, Nov. 25, 1969; BT, mm, Dec. 6, 1969.
109. BT, EC, mm, Feb. 17, 1970.
110. BT, mm, Mar. 14, 1970.

The persistence of student activism made a so-called "speakers' policy" a source of contention. In September, 1969, it had been declared that sponsorship of a speaker by a student organization would not be taken to imply approval or endorsement of any opinions that might be presented. Procedures would require only previous consultation with a moderator or an assistant dean of students. Both restraints on freedom of expression and conduct disrupting such freedom would be excluded.[111] In 1970, however, the trustees directed preparation of a policy for their approval after they had defeated a resolution that would have forbidden the appearance on campus of William Kunstler, the activist attorney.[112] What became an unseemly incident followed in the spring when the president, after conferences with student leaders and a supporting vote in the academic senate, sought to prevent the appearance of Ti-Grace Atkinson, a radical feminist who was reported to have made religiously offensive remarks a prominent feature of a talk that she had given at the University of Notre Dame. The Graduate Student Association, which had contracted for her appearance, sought and obtained injunctive relief.[113] Not only this action but a slap administered to Atkinson by a member of the audience ensured publicity.[114]

Beginning with a policy approved by the trustees in 1973,[115] there was put into effect what is now embodied in a somewhat elaborate statement entitled "Policy and Procedures for Presentations Sponsored by Registered Student Organizations."[116] Recognition is given to the commitment of the university, on the one hand, to academic freedom, freedom of expression, and the right of peaceful assembly, and on the other, to the avoidance of blasphemy, pornography, calumny, and advocacy of violence and disorder. Provision is made for a review board with equal representation of administrative officers, faculty, and students to assist in consideration of controversial cases. Final determination is left with the president, however.

Something like a return to "normalcy" might be suggested by student acquiescence in the development of this policy. Indeed, outward signs of student conservatism were to become visible enough in the 1970s and 1980s. Students returned to more conventional modes of dress,

111. OVR, see file labeled Counseling and Services.
112. BT, EC, mm, Nov. 4, 1970.
113. *Ibid.*, Apr. 1, 1971.
114. *Tower*, Mar. 12, 1971.
115. BT, mm, May 8, 1973, exh.
116. CUA Student Handbook 1988–89, 202–5. The current statement is dated December 12, 1980. See also, "Guidelines on Freedom of Expression and Dissent," approved by vice president for student life, July 1, 1987, *ibid.*, 182–83.

refrained from demonstrations, offered pleasant greetings to professors and administrators, and acknowledged pursuit of conventional career goals. They expressed moderate and sometimes conservative opinions on current issues in signed columns of the weekly *Tower*. President Walton, although with the hope of attracting students from metropolitan centers of the northeast, even went so far as to place the university in Division I competition in basketball;[117] an action that his successor was to retract.[118] On some campuses there was to come even a revival of Greek-letter fraternities and sororities. What future historians are likely to note, however, is that the independence—or isolation—of students from parents and professors that had been declared in the 1960s was not altered. The lasting consequences of the changes in student roles that began in that decade must be left to such historians to trace.

The Expansion of the Federal Role

An external source of change in the university's daily operations that would not have been envisioned before its entry into the second half of its first century was the expansion of the federal role in higher education that began after the second world war. Rectors and members of the faculties had usually been among the opponents of the occasional congressional efforts to provide federal aid for public schools or to establish a cabinet department of education. Federal activities had been limited for the most part to the collection of statistics or to emergency measures, such as the support of research and training during wartime or temporary assistance to students through agencies such as the National Youth Administration of the 1930s. During World War II, when many Catholic institutions were responding to a questionnaire that was being circulated by the American Council on Education, Deferrari as secretary general was confidently warning the rector that these institutions were in effect requesting federal subsidies and were thus contravening the will of the majority of the hierarchy that was known to be "strongly opposed to having our institutions of higher learning receive any subsidy for general purposes from the Government."[119]

Some forty years later, however, Catholic institutions, like others, having shared what a president of the Association of American Universities was recalling as the "expansive optimism" of the postwar period, were sharing also "the imminent prospect of greatly increased competition for a smaller amount of money." He was noting for American

---

117. ABC, mm, Apr. 17, 1975.
118. OR, PC, June 26, 1979; Mar. 3, 24, and 31, 1980; BT mm, Mar. 29, 1980.
119. OR, Deferrari to McCormick, Aug. 31, 1944.

higher education generally the "high degree of institutional dependency on the government for the support of important academic functions."[120] During the year 1986–87, for example, The Catholic University of America was receiving $8,390,311, a little more than 13 per cent of its total educational and general revenues, for federally sponsored programs of research and instruction, and another $865,222, a little more than 1 per cent of these revenues, for federal support of student aid. In addition, it was paying interest on loans from federal agencies for construction or renovation of classroom facilities, on which the unpaid balance was in excess of $2,000,000, and was refinancing four federal college housing loans, on which balances prior to retirement then amounted to $5,816,074. It was at the same time borrowing from the same agency an additional $3,500,000 for partial funding of construction and renovation of residence halls.[121] Moreover, having received by special legislation a federal grant of $15,000,000 for its construction, the university was preparing to open Hannan Hall for its vitreous state laboratory and department of physics. On a different side, the federal government was exercising through its legislation for equality of opportunity and affirmative action a restrictive role affecting faculty and staff appointments and tenure. Clearly, much had changed during the postwar decades.

Undoubtedly the university was well down the list of beneficiaries nationally in the contract and grant support that it was receiving for instruction and research. The Johns Hopkins University with its applied physics laboratory had received $445,718,000 during 1985–86 and Massachusetts Institute of Technology, the next institution in volume of support, $188,120,000. Significant federally supported research on the campus had begun in 1942 when Herzfeld and his associates had become involved in wartime projects.[122] At the time, as the dean of the graduate school of arts and sciences had emphasized only a little earlier in a passage of his annual report that the rector had omitted from the printed version, the "scholarly productivity" of the faculties, in spite of the institution's historic research orientation, was in his judgment far below what it should have been.[123] The university was still foremost in research so far as Catholic institutions were concerned, but it was lagging well behind the trend in other institutions with which it was seeking to be

120. Robert M. Rosenzweig, "The Politics of Having Less," *CGS*, XIX, No. 3 (Mar., 1986), 2.
121. AR (1986–87), 117–19, 122, 127.
122. AR (1945–46), 6–10.
123. OR, McGuire to Corrigan, Nov. 6, 1939.

Hannan Hall, opened in 1987 for the department of physics and its vitreous state laboratory, named for the retiring chairman of the board of trustees, Philip M. Hannan, J.C.D., 1950 (b. 1913), auxiliary bishop of Washington (1956–65) and archbishop of New Orleans (1965–89).

identified. Among the latter, the major research universities had found themselves well prepared for the wartime developments. Their resources had grown enormously because of what they had received from private donors during earlier decades. Already, in 1934, Hughes was finding that 208 of the 226 graduate departments rated as distinguished in his study were in research universities. These institutions were ready to utilize federal funds when they became available.[124]

As already noted, postwar federal support for instruction and research had first appeared in the rector's report for the year 1948–49, when $38,771 was received. By the tenth year thereafter the amount was $751,336.[125] In this latter year a coordinator of research was appointed "to centralize the planning and organizational aspects of the University's growing number of research projects."[126] According to the appointee's tabulation, only $196,000 was being received for research; the remainder of the grant monies provided were for instruction or for recovery of indirect costs.[127] In his view, the "potential" for research support was

124. Geiger, *op. cit.*, 262 and *passim*.
125. AR (1948–49 to 1957–58).
126. OR, McDonald to Faculty, Sept. 4, 1958 (mimeo.).
127. *Ibid.*, Francis de Bettencourt to McDonald, Oct. 13, 1958.

"at least four times the amount actually obtained."[128] After another ten years, during 1967–68, the volume of federal support for instruction and research had reached $3,035,283 or a little more than 18 per cent of all educational and general revenues at the time.[129] Relative to other sources of university income, this was the high point of contract and grant support. Although the dollar amounts of federal funds were to continue to increase steadily—to $8,390,311 during 1986–87—an effect of the retrenchments of the 1970s was to reduce the proportion of these funds to about 13 percent of all educational and general revenues in each year after 1981.

Faculty critics and the coordinator himself sometimes found themselves unhappy with administrative processes for reviewing research proposals.[130] The administration was perceived as viewing the coordinator's work as entirely "one of promotion."[131] There were complaints "that segments of the administrative staff . . . whose support for contracts is either required by the government or by internal procedures . . . have little enthusiasm for their work and have no sympathy for 'odd type professors' who are working on unintelligible projects of dubious value."[132] Some but not all of such administrative difficulties were overcome after 1968 when responsibility for research administration was given to the vice provost for graduate studies. Since the administrative reorganization of 1983, officers reporting to the academic vice president have exercised the responsibility.

Although government support has been given mainly to research and instruction in the physical sciences, departments in other fields receive it as well. As early as 1953, contracts were in force for work in eight departments.[133] During the year 1986–87, twenty-one departments were receiving support for sponsored research, in all but one or two cases from federal sources.[134] Support is being received also from quasi-independent agencies such as the National Endowment for the Humanities—notably in the case of early Christian studies—that are funded by the federal government. In general, the sponsorship of research by governmental and by private agencies and the administrative procedures that receipt

128. *Ibid.*, June 3, 1959.
129. *Report of the Treasurer, Fiscal Year Ended June 30, 1968* (Washington, D.C.: The Catholic University of America, 1968), 10.
130. OVR, de Bettencourt to McDonald, Mar. 6, June 3, Dec. 22, 1959; Feb. 25, 1966.
131. *Ibid.*, Marlowe to Magner, June 29, 1959, forwarded to McAllister.
132. OR, C. Steward Bowyer and Peter M. Livingston to McDonald *et al.*, July 11, 1966.
133. OVR, Magner to Hannan, Dec. 18, 1953.
134. AR (1986–87), 124.

of such support requires have come to be integrated into the functioning of the institution.

Federal support of student aid has been less reliable. Immediately after World War II, of course, many students were able to use to advantage the well-known "G.I. Bill of Rights." But it was only after the launching of *sputnik* in 1957 that student aid became a regular purpose of federal legislation. The university's first receipt of federal funds for the purpose was reported for the year 1958–59 when grants from the National Institutes of Health and the National Science Foundation were acknowledged.[135] Fellowships became a prominent feature of the National Defense Education Act of 1958, through which American graduate programs were expanded enormously. The importance for the institution of these grants and of those that followed for both undergraduates and graduates can be inferred from the fact that during the 1960s almost two-thirds of all annual expenditures for student aid— which amounted to $3,459,064 by 1969–70—were funded from federal grants. The university's total expenditure for student aid during these years was about 15 or 16 per cent of its total educational and general expenditures.

Federal support declined steadily and drastically during the 1980s, even as the volume of the university's expenditures for student aid– currently about 13 per cent of its total educational and general expenditures—was increasing, from $5,458,267 during 1980–81 to $8,291,866 during 1986–87. Annual increases are required both because of the steady rise in tuition and because of student needs. The dollar increase in outlays during the 1980s has been above 50 per cent. During the longer term of two decades, from 1966–67 to 1986–87, the increase was above 39 percent. But in the short term, the proportion of the total expenditure covered by federal grants has fallen from about 34 per cent during 1980–81 to about 10 per cent during 1986–87. The problem of funding that is represented in this decline is self-evident.

Federal assistance for construction on the campus has been through both grants and loans. It had begun with the grant to the university's young but highly regarded program in nursing education that provided $156,000 toward the construction, begun in 1945, of what is now known as Ryan Hall.[136] Grants from the National Science Foundation had assisted the renovation of Maloney Hall in 1962 and the purchase of new computer equipment in 1969.[137] In 1957, the university had

135. AR (1958–59), 10.
136. AR (1944–45), 7–8.
137. BT, mm, May 2, 1962; BT, EC, mm, Jan. 18 and Sept. 27–28, 1968.

begun to take advantage of loans that were made available for the construction of student housing. In this instance $1,350,000 was bor- rowed from the Housing and Home Finance Agency to assist in the construction of Conaty Hall and the student center (currently named University Center–East).[138] Most recently, a $3,500,000 federal college housing mortgage loan has been applied toward the construction of the eight new halls that constitute the Centennial Village, opened in 1988.[139]

The university's largest federal grant by far, for the construction of Hannan Hall, providing handsome new facilities for the department of physics and its prestigious vitreous state laboratory, was obtained by special legislation in the United States Congress. Although it was not the first to receive assistance by this route, the university shared in the widespread criticism that educators directed against the evasion of the peer review process that is customarily used to pass on the merits of proposed research projects[140] (peer reviews have not been prescribed for building projects). Subsequently it was found that in the federal budget for 1987–88 the Congress had appropriated $225,000,000 for similar projects and had ordered the department of defense not to grant more than 14 per cent of its $85,000,000 fund for university research programs to institutions in any one state.[141] As *The Wall Street Journal* remarked, the Congress was "well along in turning the American university system into its own political plum."[142] Reporters were suggesting that "academic pork" could be regarded as a type of "post-industrial pork" that was replacing more traditional forms.[143] Subsequently, however, the Congress was to go even farther in including in a trade bill "a grab bag" of education and training programs costing annually $1,700,000,000.[144] It can be assumed that the end is not yet in sight.

The Extension of Rights on the Campus

Somewhat the same mixed motives—scientific, ethical, benevolent, and crassly political—that earlier led the Congress to initiate and in-

138. BT, mm, Nov. 12, 1957.
139. AR (1986–87), 119.
140. CHE, XXXII, No. 16 (June 18, 1986), 1 ff.; No. 17 (June 25, 1986), 1 ff.
141. *Ibid.*, XXXIV, No. 18 (Jan 13, 1988), 15 ff. and No. 20 (Jan. 27, 1988), 1 ff.
142. Editorial, "Porky Goes to College," Feb. 1, 1988.
143. Paul Blustein, "U.S. Budget Increasingly Free of Pork-Barrel Spending," *Washington Post*, Mar. 20, 1988; Judith Havemann, "'Academic Pork' Proliferates as Traditional Form Lags," *ibid.*, Mar. 22, 1988.
144. CHE, XXXIV, No. 48 (Aug. 10, 1988), A19; see also Colleen Cordes, "Colleges Received About $289-Million in Earmarked Funds," *ibid.*, XXXV, No. 21 (Feb. 1, 1989), 1 ff.

crease support of research and student aid, to the extent that American higher education has come to be supported materially by federal funding, led the Congress also, increasingly after the 1960s, to expect colleges and universities to become exemplars of national efforts for societal reform. Federal expectations often were extended by state and local legislation. At all levels, of course, administration and enforcement of policies had required bureaucratic growth, certainly in governmental but also in academic institutions. During the 1970s and 1980s, the principal emphasis of the new governmental objectives, so far as universities were concerned, was to require affirmative action to guarantee and promote civil rights. That the arm of the federal government could reach farther was suggested, however, by the introduction into the Congress, in 1988, of the "Student-Athlete Right-to-Know Act" intended to redress recruitment of educationally unqualified athletes for intercollegiate competition.[145] Some state governments had already undertaken to expand control over private colleges by forbidding them to offer new academic programs without governmental permission.[146]

Traditionally, educational institutions had been objects of social legislation only in their individual capacities as corporate employers. By the 1960s, the university was sharing in the administration of workmen's compensation laws, unemployment insurance, social security, the withholding of income taxes, and the like. Business and finance offices had been expanded as a result but normal academic procedures had hardly been affected.

Similarly, not much had been changed on campus when, in 1970, the National Labor Relations Board first asserted jurisdiction in faculty bargaining. Previously, collective bargaining had been confined largely to nonacademic employees. The first such units of The Catholic University of America to be organized for bargaining purposes had been those of housekeeping and maintenance, which had become affiliated with the International Union of Firemen and Oilers in 1967.[147] Well before, the university had adhered to a policy of contracting only for union labor in its construction projects, inasmuch as such a policy was considered to be an application of Catholic social teaching on the right of labor to organize. As has been seen, however, the organization of the law faculty bargaining committees failed to persuade members of the faculties generally that collective bargaining would be desirable for them.

---

145. Jonathan Yardley, "Colleges & Athletes: Don't Make a Federal Case of It," *Washington Post*, June 27, 1988.
146. "Md. Proposes Rein on Private Colleges," *ibid.*, Dec. 3, 1987.
147. BT, EC, mm, Oct. 19, 1967.

The tactical resort of some professors of the law faculty to legal action was illustrative of new tendencies in dealing with grievances that could be noted by the early 1970s. For example, to provide for hearings by peers outside administrative channels, the academic senate, in 1969, established a faculty grievance committee authorized to hear complaints of individuals and, if disposed to do so, to recommend corrective action in any matter not affecting faculty tenure.[148] On its part, responding to characteristic demands for explicit written regulations as a basis for any administrative action as well as to demands for privacy, the administration, in 1970, after consultations concerning the implications of the so-called "Buckley amendment" in federal legislation, promulgated regulations to protect the privacy and confidentiality of student records and to guarantee access by students to their own official records.[149] Litigation as a means of pursuing claims of one kind or another against the university became common. As it grew, and because the administration had begun to distribute among different firms the several types of litigation in which the university was involved, instead of relying solely upon the firm of Hamilton and Hamilton, which had provided legal counsel through most of its history, an "in-house" general counsel eventually was appointed.[150]

The cases of litigation that began to multiply in the 1970s were of varying degrees of seriousness. Some were attempts to further claims that were plainly of no more than individual interest, serious as they might have been for the parties concerned. Others had significant institutional implications, especially as they affected faculty salary scales or tenure policies. Undoubtedly measures that were taken to accomplish the fiscal retrenchment that was necessary at the time provoked some of the litigation. Threats to institutional autonomy loomed, however, when attempts, successful or not, were made to apply public law in the campus arena.

For example, in 1971, when the Graduate Student Association and Undergraduate Student Government petitioned for the injunction that was to prevent the president—on contractual grounds—from cancelling the scheduled appearance of Ti-Grace Atkinson, it was alleged that the attempt to cancel the lecture was an infringement upon the students' "constitutionally protected rights of free speech and freedom of assembly."[151] Not long after, the two lawyer priests who brought suit to obtain

148. AS, mm, May 22, 1969.
149. AB, II, No. 16 (Feb. 19, 1970), 1–3.
150. *Ibid.*, XII, No. 1 (Sept. 10, 1979).
151. *Tower, op. cit.*

"parity" of salaries pressed constitutional claims under the first and fifth amendments, asserting, among other things, that the university's receipt of federal funds had transformed its salary policies and its partial tuition grants to seminarians into inadmissible "state action."[152] In the civil suit that he brought in 1987, Father Curran maintained that to respect his right to permanent tenure, the university had to allow him to teach Catholic theology despite the finding of the Holy See that he was neither "suitable nor eligible" to exercise the function of a professor of Catholic theology.

More explicit and immediately relevant judicial or administrative limits upon institutional autonomy and customary collegial processes were to be found in applications of the Civil Rights Act of 1964 and related legislation and executive orders. In what seems to some the extreme that has been reached thus far, in a case at another institution, a court has granted conditional tenure at an institution to a plaintiff who was found to be the victim of discrimination because of her sex.[153] Of course, there has not been in academe any significant opposition to the elimination of invidious racial or sexual discrimination from American life. On the contrary, support for the objective of the Civil Rights Act remains overwhelming. The administration of the law, on the other hand, has given rise to various kinds of difficulties. Sometimes virtual quotas or preferred treatment appear to be required by law. Often bureaucratic procedures have resulted in rigidity or have allowed harassment of administrators. The deep philosophical differences between those who interpret the goal as equality of opportunity and others who expect equality of results have emerged frequently enough. In some places, moreover, local enactments have extended the protected categories of citizens in ways to which objection has been taken.

It was the Walton administration that had the task of initiating and developing university policies for compliance with the federal directives of the 1970s. At the outset, by executive order, colleges and universities holding federal contracts had been prohibited from discriminating on the basis of race, color, religion, sex, or national origin. Late in 1971 there were issued regulations under which contracting universities were required to present written programs for affirmative action to ensure compliance with the executive order. Guidelines for the application of the order were issued in 1972 and a format for the presentation of the required affirmative action plans was distributed in 1975.

152. *Op. cit.*
153. *Kunda v. Muhlenberg College*, 621 F.2d 532 (3d. Cir. 1980). William A. Kaplin, *The Law of Higher Education*, (2d ed.; San Francisco: Jossey-Bass Publishers, 1985), 125–

On the campus, meanwhile, committees for the development of an institutional affirmative action plan had been appointed as early as 1972. In 1975, Mrs. Karen Greenwalt was named the university's first equal opportunity officer. Since that year the university has identified itself in its advertisements as "an equal opportunity employer" and, utilizing a document from Vatican Council II, has published in all its announcements its commitment to the belief that "with respect to the fundamental rights of the person, every type of discrimination, whether social or cultural, whether based on sex, race, color, social conditions, language, or religion, is to be overcome and eradicated as contrary to God's intent."[154] The university indicates necessarily, however, in its affirmative action plan, that with respect to positions for which a Catholic background may be required, "religion may be a factor in determining suitability."[155]

The experience of the university in beginning the administration of its affirmative action plan has been relatively favorable. Perhaps the most serious negative effect of governmental requirements has been unintended. In complying with procedures for advertising positions as they become available, academic departments seemingly have tended to restrict their searches for the best available candidates to those responding to the advertisements. The limitation would, of course, be normal in most nonacademic searches, but recruitment of members of faculties has usually been more searching. Otherwise, in a few minor cases before courts or administrative bodies, the university has had to defend itself against allegations of ethnic or sex discrimination made by unsuccessful applicants for appointment or continuation in positions. Expenditures of time and funds have been required in such cases as well as others. Moreover, successful defenses have seldom if ever received publicity comparable to that given to the initial accusations. It is the latter that are remembered. But, although academic departments may often have found themselves at a notable financial disadvantage in bidding for the services of the most qualified applicants, there has been on campus no significant movement to transform the objectives for the appointment of those from protected minorities, as stated in the

---

31, finds the court's holding as "actually narrow and its reasoning sensitive to the academic community's needs and the relative competencies of college and court" (131).

154. *Gaudium et spes*, No. 29.

155. "The Affirmative Action Program of The Catholic University of America (Revised 1978)," 3. In *Corporation of the Presiding Bishop of the Church of Jesus Christ of Latter Day Saints v. Amos* (Case No. 86-179) and *United States v. Amos* (Case No. 86-401), both decided in 1987, the United States Supreme Court has upheld a broad interpretation of the Civil Rights Act of 1964 that allows religiously affiliated institutions to exercise religious preference even when the employment in question is not related to religion.

affirmative action plan, into quotas. In academic matters, it is still presumed that appointments ought not to be made on grounds other than qualifications.

University leaders, of course, must give attention not only to developments within their own institutions but to what is happening elsewhere as well, especially, in the case of The Catholic University of America, in view of what may be a growing opposition to the consideration of religion as a factor in academic appointments and promotions.[156] In one seemingly extreme case, charges of religious discrimination have been filed against a Catholic college because, allegedly, preference in the appointment of a president was given to a Catholic over a Jewish applicant for the position. Several Catholic institutions have been the subjects of complaints by Catholics because they have given preference in the filling of positions to members of sponsoring religious orders. In Washington, at the conclusion of an eight-year dispute, Georgetown University has been required, under the District of Columbia Human Rights Act of 1977, which prohibits discrimination on the basis of sexual orientation, among other things, to accord to two "gay-rights" groups on its campus all the privileges associated with the institution's official recognition of student associations, although it has not been compelled to accord such recognition itself.

The Planning Imperative

Well before the expansion of the federal role in higher education and the student rebellions of the 1960s, the complexity of university administration had become plainly visible to trustees and to interested lay persons. Calls for institutional planning that were made from time to time were certainly in order. Brief attention had been given to physical planning at an early date when, in 1910, the trustees had authorized the preparation of a campus plan that, upon receipt, they failed to implement. It will be remembered that in his memorandum of 1917 Pace had gone much further, singling out the lack of comprehensive planning as the principal weakness of the university, which then had completed little more than its first quarter-century. Five years later he had been instrumental in obtaining a letter of Pope Pius XI to the American bishops that urged their support of the university and requested from them a plan for its development. At the end of the 1920s and the beginning of the 1930s, the Ryan administration, without producing a planning document of general scope, had given evidence

156. Zoe Ingalls, "Church-Related Colleges Come Under Increased Fire for Basing Faculty Hiring and Promotion Decisions on Candidates' Religion," *CHE*, XXXI, No. 13 (Nov. 27, 1985), 1 ff.

of what could be accomplished with systematic foresight, although even then the university's business officer could express disappointment[157] at the board's failure to adopt his proposal for a committee "to study the University's future course."

Every administration, of course, has had to propose—and, with luck, to execute—short-range building and financial plans. During the middle 1960s, in response to the demands of trustees, the rector was promising that "a long-range plan for growth and development" would be presented imminently.[158] In spite of his later reluctance to support the chancellor's proposal for an "over-all study" by consultants, the executive committee of the board soon proceeded to approve establishment of a planning committee.[159] Then, before a year had elapsed, the survey and objectives committee came into being. On the recommendation of its consultants, provision for continuous institutional research and planning was included in the university's table of organization.

Two administrative units devoted to planning were established near the end of Whalen's year as acting rector. Edward D. Jordan, a professor of nuclear science and engineering, was appointed to be the first director of a new office of institutional research and planning, reporting to the president. He was appointed to serve at the same time as secretary *ex officio* of an advisory committee on university planning of which the executive vice president and provost was made chairman. Six members of faculties and a graduate and an undergraduate student were appointed as other members. The committee began by assigning task forces composed of appointees from all parts of the university to investigate and make recommendations on disparate topics of current concern, such as the campus school, human rights and intergroup relations on the campus, physical planning, physical sciences and technology in the curriculum, religious studies, student life, and urban affairs.[160]

Although the committee was not continued, the new office became the source of projections of enrollment, assessments of the "cost–benefit" efficiency of departments, analyses of budget data, and assistance in the development of criteria for the determination of academic priorities. With changes in its name and personnel, and sometimes in its functions, the office has continued to serve successive administrations in compiling and analyzing data. Currently its detailed statistical compilations are issued to accompany the annual report of the president.

157. OR, Cain to Ryan, Oct. 23, 1931.
158. BT, mm, Nov. 9, 1964.
159. *Ibid.*, Apr. 20 and Nov. 13, 1966.
160. *Ibid.*, Dec. 7, 1968, exh.

The president is, by virtue of his office, the chief planning officer of an institution. Walton, pressed by financial exigencies, sought to appraise the quality and significance of the work being done in the faculties and enlisted to assist him individual professors representing the humanities, the professional schools, science and engineering, and the social sciences. His conclusion was that, although savings might be achieved in some places, there should be no "drastic surgery" of the university's programs. In reporting this conclusion to the board, he had to add that in still another of the reputational surveys sponsored by the American Council on Education no graduate department of the university had been rated by colleagues in other institutions as distinguished or even superior.[161] Then, partly in response to requirements of the District of Columbia, preparation of a new master plan for the physical development of the campus was authorized and, upon its completion, approved by the board.[162]

Experience has shown that realistic planning is a continuous process. Planners—whose membership in the Society for College and University Planning grew by more than 30 per cent during the 1980s—must be prepared to deal with contingencies and with rapid change. Nationally, in consequence, the earlier emphasis upon "long-range" planning, such as Pace had in mind, began to give way to what has come to be called "strategic" planning.[163] This is, indeed, the rubric preferred by the Byron administration.[164] Strategic planning is for objectives that are set for shorter time periods than are implied in long-range planning. Careful account is taken of changing external factors that affect enrollment, financing, and technology. Budgets are constructed to give effect to plans.

Of course, institutional drift would be the inevitable result, even with short-range planning, if decisions about current activities and proposals were not made in the light of well-defined purposes. That at the most general level the university was founded to be "the nursery of the higher life," as Spalding called it, has been clear throughout its century of existence. That its planning would have to be circumscribed by the limitations of its resources was to become equally clear soon after its

---

161. *Ibid.*, Dec. 12, 1970. The survey was that of Kenneth D. Roose and Charles J. Andersen, *A Rating of Graduate Programs* (Washington, D.C.: American Council on Education, 1970).

162. BT, mm, Nov. 17, 1973; Nov. 23, 1974.

163. CHE, XXXIV, No. 20 (Jan. 27, 1988), 15–17.

164. William J. Byron, S.J., "Planning to Plan," *Tower*, Sept. 17, 1982, and memorandum to committee on planning and budget of the academic senate, "On Choosing Between and Among the Children," May 14, 1984; also draft, "Strategic Plan for the Catholic University of America, 1983–1988," BT, mm, June 18, 1983, exh.

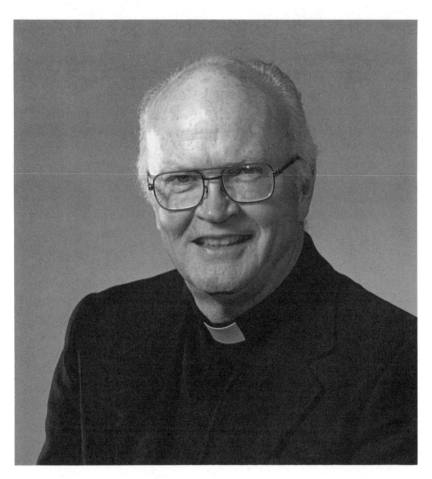

William James Byron, S.J. (b. 1927), current president of The Catholic University of America, inaugurated in 1982, the first religious to be appointed as chief executive.

beginning. Not unexpectedly, therefore, tension has arisen when the aims of graduate education have not been supported by the funding provided for their achievement. It follows that it has been manifest also when there have been differences about the appropriate means for achieving aims within the commonly recognized limitations. The logic of the survey and objectives committee in 1967 in undertaking to develop a general statement of contemporary aims as a prelude to its further work could not be denied.

The statement that was adopted by the academic senate and the trustees during the following year has provided parameters for all subsequent attempts to order academic activities. There have been presidents' committees on university planning, in 1976; on university priorities, in 1981; and on strategic planning, in 1985. In addition, during the academic year 1978–79, the senate conducted a review by the several faculties of the approved statement of 1968. In no instance, of course, have the committees or the academic senate or the responsible officers of the university fully resolved the tensions inherent in the task of adapting programs to the scale permitted by the available resources.

Historically, members of the faculties often have tended to view the problem of adaptation on the campus as one of conflict between the respective aims of graduate and undergraduate education. The "great expense normal to graduate studies" has been a subject of frequent discussion in administrative and trustee circles,[165] since, in accord with the university's mission, sometimes as many as two-thirds of its students during the past fifty or more years have been pursuing post-baccalaureate work. But perhaps more important have been the differing points of view associated with the several fields of subject matter that are represented in the university. The effects of such differences are magnified when enrollment trends and opportunities for funding from without prompt deviations from accepted aims. As the credentialing functions of colleges and universities have multiplied, emphasis upon professional education has increased. Distinction in professional fields has been attained, as when the school of nursing, for example, received a ranking of ninth in the nation from a professional journal.[166] But, although the distinctive functions of the university in ecclesiastical and religious studies are acknowledged by virtually everyone, the centrality of the basic disciplines represented in the arts and sciences may not always be appreciated by the ecclesiastical and the professional faculties or by lay observers.

Illustrations of the point can be found in reports from the faculties to the academic senate in 1978 during the review by the latter of the university's statement of objectives. Explaining that most members of the law faculty were still in general agreement that legal education should include concern for values, the dean at the time added that "there was no agreement on the values, or value systems, to be explored or introduced." Some members of the faculty, he reported, believed that "it might be sufficient merely to give students the opportunity to recognize and confront the value choices that inhere in the disci-

165. E.g., ABC, mm, Oct. 7, 1953; BT, mm, Nov. 10, 1963; OR, McDonald to Robert J. Lageman, Washington, Feb. 8, 1965.
166. Patricia A. Chamings, "Ranking the Nursing Schools," NO, XXXII (Sept.–Oct., 1984), 238–39, reported to BT, mm, Jan. 31, 1985.

pline."[167] The faculty of another professional school found ground for criticism of what it deemed to be "overemphasis on Research, inadequate emphasis on Professional Education, and unclear statement of the service function." Its thrust was further elaborated in a suggestion that a revised statement should acknowledge that the university "originally was conceived as a center for graduate study" but that it had "evolved purposefully into a modern American university committed to outstanding academic and professional education and service to the community."[168] In contrast, the faculty of arts and sciences was to declare its research mission so "central to all its programs and activities" that without research it could "neither aspire to nor claim excellence and distinctiveness for its programs "either graduate or undergraduate."[169]

As these statements reveal, underlying the evident problems of complexity in institutional life are more basic problems of values. With the increase of complexity, especially since the second world war, planning for the future has come to require more formality and technical expertise than formerly. The values that are served remain fundamental, however. In a period when the values of American higher education and of western society itself appear to be in disarray, the consistent manifestation of Catholic values in a university would give it particularity, indeed. Thus it can be said that the planning imperative for The Catholic University of America will demand continued recognition of the intellectual tradition that it has inherited and of the academic tradition that has given particular expression to the heritage.

167. OVR, John L. Garvey to James Dornan, May 9, 1978 (copy).
168. *Ibid.*, Joan W. Mullaney to Dornan, Mar. 29, 1978 (copy).
169. *Ibid.*, E. R. Kennedy to Dornan, Oct. 25, 1978 (copy).

CHAPTER XII

Perspectives and Prospects

Realistic planning for the future of the Catholic University of America can begin only with recognition of the changes in its position and in its functioning that have occurred during its first century. That there have been such changes is not in itself remarkable. It is a truism that change is inevitable, that in the life of an institution as in that of a person, "to live is to change," as Cardinal Newman once remarked.[1] But no one recounting the history of an institution or of a time can any longer view entirely with optimism what another Victorian, Alfred Lord Tennyson welcomed as "the ringing grooves of change."[2] Even on an impressionistic level, alumni of a university, for example, may well prefer what they remember to what they hear about the campus life of the present. But they and, not less, those officers who must plan for the institution's future, can never know with certainty what may be in store. The best informed will seldom attempt forecasts. They will rely rather on their knowledge of how the institution has coped with change in its past to find a basis for confidence that it will cope with the challenges to come. The historical change that has already occurred will provide perspectives for their judgment.

In the case of The Catholic University of America, the broadest perspective, no doubt, is centuries old and purposive. It reaches back to the faith of the founders and, before them, to the faith of the early Christians. With all academic institutions that profess a corporate Catholic identity, its underlying purpose remains that of uniting its pursuit of the knowledge that can be attained by human reason with Catholic faith. This purpose is stated succinctly in the opening sentence of the apostolic constitution *Sapientia Christiana*: "Christian wisdom, which the Church teaches by divine authority, continuously inspires the faithful of Christ zealously to endeavor to relate human affairs

---

1. *An Essay on the Development of Christian Doctrine* (London: Longmans, Green, 1875), Chap. I, Sec. 1, Par. 7.
2. "Locksley Hall," 1842.

and activities with religious values in a single living synthesis."[3] This document, it may be noted, while formally prescriptive only for ecclesiastical faculties, provides a link to the institution's tradition. It is well to recall that it expresses the intent of the declaration on Christian education of Vatican Council II[4] and that it was shaped in part by conclusions emanating from meetings of the International Federation of Catholic Universities and of those convened by the congregation for Catholic education.[5] The bishops of the United States also, in their pastoral letter of 1980, proffered their official encouragement of American Catholic higher education.[6]

Historically, as already noted, and as a member of the present faculty of philosophy has reminded his readers, it was during the so-called "ages of faith" that "the harmony that Christians expect between faith and reason was at the source of the establishment of the university as a peculiarly Christian institution."[7] The American churchmen who established The Catholic University of America were witnessing to this harmony in the tradition that was their heritage, even when they differed, as they did, sharply and publicly, in their perceptions and in their practical judgments about the readiness of American Catholics for the foundation and conduct of a university as they understood it. Any attempt to maintain the enterprise that they established without fidelity to their faith would belie the name that they attached to it. Differences would seem to be admissible only with respect to views as to what corporate fidelity requires.

Among more immediate institutional perspectives, two academic developments of national scope have been presented as clearly determinative of the university's understanding of itself and of its position in American society. The first in time, taking shape during the institution's formative years, was the general American university movement of the late nineteenth and early twentieth centuries. It was as the new university was seeking to define its own institutional character in pursuit of its universal Catholic aim that it committed itself internally to the academic ethos that was then emerging in the United States. The second development, more recent and more particular in scope, has been marked by the arrival of sister Catholic institutions at maturity in the

---

3. *Op. cit.*, Foreword.
4. *Op. cit.*, 738.
5. See Gannon, *op. cit.*,
6. "Catholic Higher Education and the Pastoral Mission of the Church," in Nolan, *op. cit.*, IV, 401–416.
7. Robert Sokolowski, *The God of Faith and Reason: Foundations of Christian Theology* (Notre Dame: University of Notre Dame Press, 1982), 162.

same movement in which The Catholic University of America was among the pioneers.[8] The ascent of these sister institutions has affected to a notable degree the singularity that the founders and their successors for a generation or two were able to claim for their achievement. The redefinition of this singularity is the broadest and perhaps the principal present challenge to the sponsors of the university.

The earlier development, it is important to recall, was one of which the founders, even in their somewhat unusual corporate act of foundation, were hardly aware. It was during the short period between the decision of the bishops in 1884 to found the university and the opening of classes in 1889 that the enduring academic mission of the university was specified. Although what is now known as graduate work was then only beginning to be defined, the university's commitment to it already had been internalized in the original concept of the founders, on which the first faculty could build. It was not displaced when, in 1904, it was decided to offer undergraduate programs as well. Subsequently, even if the funding that the university would receive would never be enough to enable it to rank with the great research universities of the country, so that it would come to be classified rather among the more numerous institutions offering doctorates, it would be bound by an orientation toward research that was firmly planted during its earliest years.[9] The commitment was renewed and strengthened after 1928. It endures in campus culture.

What practical-minded Catholic leaders, even those who were academics, saw quickly during the university's first years was that their troubled institution could provide an organizational focus for efforts in various fields that without it might not have been united. The aspirations of the scholars recruited to the faculties were hardly being shared by the Catholic body at large. Even the particular objective that the bishops had most frequently and fervently articulated, the preparation of an educated clergy, was never to receive from them the attention that might have been expected. Perhaps more recognition of what could be produced by scholarship within a community of faith was actually being accorded by the academic world outside the Church. But, as the

8. See Andrew M. Greeley, *From Backwater to Mainstream; A Profile of Catholic Higher Education* (New York: McGraw-Hill, 1969).

9. The 1987 Carnegie Classification of Higher Education, prepared by the Carnegie Foundation for the Advancement of Teaching, groups institutions into ten categories. The Catholic University of America is included among "Doctorate granting universities I" which, in addition to offering a full range of baccalaureate programs, incorporate in their mission a commitment to graduate education through the doctorate and award at least forty Ph.D. degrees annually in five or more academic disciplines. CHE, XXXIII, No. 43 (July 8, 1987), 22–23.

founder of the university's department of sociology was to observe, the institution was "forced to take on a rather practical character . . . distinct from technical research although of very great value in the life of the Church."[10] Of course, neither he nor the successors of the founders nor any administrators or professors as late as the mid-twentieth century could have foreseen the extent to which the upward mobility of Catholics in American society would alter profoundly the perspectives of their national pontifical university.

It is an aspect of this mobility that the more recent major current of change affecting the university can best be seen. There are now several American Catholic universities that are dedicated to the scholarship that advances as well as transmits knowledge. And, in its way, perhaps, the change in the ecclesiastical status of the university that occurred with the promulgation of its new bylaws in 1970 was a culminating recognition of the integration of Catholic institutions generally into American higher education. Some of these institutions, indeed, have been notably more successful than The Catholic University of America in obtaining endowment to fund their development. As President Byron has remarked, noting the loss of the "invisible subsidy" that was once provided by dioceses and religious communities when clerical and religious enrollment was five or six times what it is at present, to maintain the university's "commitment to graduate education and research is not an issue at the theoretical level," although it is "difficult to do as a practical matter, given our small endowment and the virtual absence of meaningful federal support for graduate study, especially in the humanities."[11]

Funding in Perspective

Undoubtedly, as the president has thus recognized, funding is one of the pressing problems that The Catholic University of America and Catholic institutions generally share with virtually all other institutions of higher education in the United States. It remains true for all that while adequate funding cannot guarantee the attainment of quality in higher education, quality cannot be achieved and maintained without it. If at the outset, as a historian of the university movement has recalled, "it was the absence of the cash ingredient, the lack of financial support from the American public, which did more than all else to delay the American university,"[12] much was to change during the twentieth

10. Kerby Papers, Kerby to Curley, Washington, Jan. 19, 1923 (copy).
11. "Contemporary Issues and Historical Identity," *USCH*, VII (Fall, 1988), 468.
12. Pierson, in Clapp, *op. cit.*, 79.

century, so that some research universities now can be called "corporations of the education industry."[13] So far as Catholic institutions are concerned, the upward mobility of Catholics has given the lie to the doubts of bishops and prominent laymen of their ability to support higher education.

The support that is being given to sister Catholic institutions is a particular manifestation of this mobility. In current compilations, for example, the University of Notre Dame is found to rank among the first twenty-five American universities in the amount of its endowment, $463,502,000 in 1988.[14] When Father Hesburgh became its president in 1952, its endowment was less than that of The Catholic University of America, which then had a market value of $7,583,279.[15] In the intervening years, the latter figure has grown only to $35,430,098,[16] much less still than the endowments of Loyola University of Chicago, Georgetown University, and Boston College, which rank among the first fifty-six institutions with endowments in excess of $200,000,000 in 1988.[17] Moreover, the placement of relatively numerous Catholic institutions among colleges popularly regarded as current leaders in undergraduate education can be taken as further confirmation of American Catholic mobility.[18]

Whether for all institutions together, for Catholic institutions as a category, or for any institution singly, a major aspect of the problem of funding is necessarily that of rising costs. Asking his audience in 1986 during Harvard University's celebration of its three hundred and fiftieth anniversary whether these costs could be matched by "the value of the education received in exchange," Secretary of Education William J. Bennett reported that "gross national spending on higher education in the nation has gone, in constant 1985–86 dollars, from $12 billion in 1950 to $53 billion in 1965 to over $100 billion." Some of this spending, of course, can be accounted for by the increase in the number of institutions, which the Secretary cited as 1,852 in 1950, 2,230 in 1965, and 3,231 in 1980.[19]

What is adequate or proper funding for any given institution must, naturally enough, be decided in the light of its own purpose, history,

---

13. Geiger, *op. cit.*, 1.

14. "Fact File: Value of 315 Endowments on June 30, 1988," *CHE*, XXXV, No. 23 (Feb. 15, 1989), A 29.

15. "Report of the Procurator," *AR* (1951–52), 88.

16. *AR* (1987–88), 114.

17. *CHE*, *op. cit.*

18. *USNWR*, CV, No. 14 (Oct. 10, 1988), C 6, 15, 20, 22, 24.

19. "Text of Secretary Bennett's Address Last Week at a Harvard University Anniversary Celebration," *CHE*, XXXVI, No. 7 (Oct. 15, 1986), 29.

and circumstances. That the institutional experience will reflect the national trend can, however, almost be taken for granted. At The Catholic University of America, using Secretary Bennett's years for comparison, annual operating expenditures, without adjustments for inflation, have increased from $3,751,000 during fiscal year 1950–51 to $15,714,000 during 1965–66 to $65,761,000 during 1985–86.[20] It is plain that even at present levels of operation the pursuit of the mission of the institution requires very substantial outlays of funds.

About 41 per cent of the total operating expenditures of the university during the fiscal year 1985–86 were in the category designated as for instruction and departmental research (exclusive of externally funded research). Twenty years earlier the proportion had been about 35 per cent. The increase is not a mark of institutional health, as might too readily be assumed, for the most munificently funded institutions are able to reduce the proportion in order to enrich extra-academic aspects of institutional life. When inter-institutional comparisons are made within the general category of educational and general expenses, which excludes auxiliary enterprises (principally the feeding and housing of students), the proportion of the university's expenditures for instruction and departmental research rises to 47 per cent. Among private member institutions of the Association of American Universities, this proportion is near the upper limit of the range from 20 to 49 per cent of educational and general expenses that prevailed during 1985–86.[21]

Professorial salaries have always been by far the major item of cost in the calculation of expenditures for instruction and departmental research. In the past clerics and religious and dedicated lay persons could be relied upon to supply talent that otherwise could not have been afforded. As circumstances and policies have changed, the Catholic environment of the campus and the attractive features of its Washington location have continued to be advantages. In 1980 the evaluating team of the Middle States Association was finding the institution to command "the affection and loyalty of an extraordinarily dedicated, enthusiastic group of faculty and students" with a commitment that seemed "far to exceed the tangible rewards" they were receiving.[22] Commitment of such an order, however, requires renewal if it is not to become more tenuous with each generation at successive removes from the founders.

20. See annual reports of the treasurer.

21. Julie A. Conlin, "Institutional Profiles; Association of American Universities, HEGIS Data: 1985–1986" (mimeo.).

22. OR, "Report to the Catholic University of America by an Evaluation Team representing the Commission on Higher Education of the Middle States Association of Colleges and Schools" (typescript), 7.

According to tables published annually by the American Association of University Professors, the average salary in full professorial rank at the university during the academic year 1987–88 was $45,800. This average was the lowest of all institutions in the District of Columbia. Nationwide, at this rank, the university was found to be in the next to lowest quartile among institutions conferring the doctorate. At lower ranks, it was in the lowest quartile.[23] Data from surveys collected by the National Center for Educational Statistics showed the university's average salaries in all professorial ranks during the academic year 1985–86 to be the lowest among the private member institutions of the Association of American Universities. The highest comparable average salary in full professorial rank among these institutions was then $68,545.[24]

The sources of the funds that are needed for salaries and other operating expenses of a university are necessarily of prime importance in any investigation of its quality. Bishop Keane, when the university was new, made repeated declarations that all institutional costs would be met by income from endowment. Deficits that were incurred in the early years were attributed to failure to obtain similar income for administrative costs. Even if the assumptions underlying this approach to the university's finances had been less naive, however, the loss in 1904 of a major portion of the endowment funds that had been obtained by then would have been a crippling blow. Although the loss could be presented as temporary and although the university in later years was to receive additions to its endowment from time to time, the effect of the Waggaman bankruptcy upon its progress in the early years was telling.

Distinguished institutions have always had to seek endowment continuously for professorial chairs and for the support of students through fellowships and scholarships as well as for other purposes. At one end of the scale, Harvard University's endowment, the largest in the country, with a market value of $3,435,006,000, supplied it with income of $125,280,596 during fiscal year 1985–86. In the same year, the $29,771,109 endowment of The Catholic University of America was the lowest among the private institutions of the Association of American Universities. At Harvard, not surprisingly, the income from endowment represented 17.5 per cent of all institutional revenues for the year. Only Rice University, uniquely positioned, could report a higher proportion; it was receiving 39.9 per cent of its total revenues as income from

23. "Average Salaries of Full-Time Faculty Members at 1,700 Colleges and Universities," *CHE*, XXXIV, No. 34 (May 4, 1988), A 15.
24. Conlin, *op. cit.*

endowment. At The Catholic University of America in the same year only 2.0 per cent of total revenues were being received from this source.[25]

The timeliness of recent efforts to restore an emphasis upon endowment can hardly be in question. Benjamin T. Rome, a trustee emeritus and thus far the university's most generous alumnus, has set an example first by his funding of annual concerts of the school of music at the John F. Kennedy Center for the Performing Arts and of the Cardinal Patrick O'Boyle scholarships for study in Europe by students of the department of architecture, and more recently by the establishment of the Hyman Foundation endowment fund that led the university to attach his name to its school of music in 1984. The organization of the board of regents in 1986 represented a further important step in securing support for the university that, in a hundred-million dollar campaign inaugurated at the beginning of its centennial celebration in 1987, was expected to increase endowment as well as provide for current needs. Among the gifts received at an early date, that of the Doris B. and Edmund M. Reggie Forum Endowment Fund has added most substantially to the institution's resources.

The most unique feature of the university's funding has been its reliance upon the annual collection for its operation that is taken up in the dioceses of the United States. It was the introduction of this collection, in 1903, that enabled the institution to survive the loss of sixty per cent of its endowment in the following year. Currently, the collection provides somewhat more than four million dollars annually, which is a little more than six per cent of the university's total revenues. Sometimes, unfortunately, this income has been regarded not as a supplement to endowment but as a substitute for it. It can be acknowledged, of course, that when categories of revenue are combined to add income from private contracts, gifts, and grants—with which accountants would classify the collection receipts—to income from endowment, the university's receipt of 14.4 per cent of its revenues during 1985–86 from these two sources combined places it just below the median in this respect among private institutions of the Association of American Universities.[26]

For most of its history the university could rely upon the diocesan collections to provide a major portion of its revenues. Between the fiscal years 1948–49 and 1960–61, for example, the collections were supplying each year from 33 to 45 per cent of educational and general revenues.

25. *Ibid.*
26. *Ibid.*

Assessment
of Change

The downward movement in this proportion to the present level began during fiscal year 1957–58 when 39 per cent of educational and general revenues was still being derived from this source. The decline was interrupted briefly during 1968–69 when, in response to Father Whalen's appeal before the annual meeting of the hierarchy in the previous year, the collections represented almost 22 per cent of educational and general revenues. It is evident that the increase in the dollar value of the contributions, from $3,382,039 during 1968–69 to $4,527,896 during 1985–86 is woefully less than would be needed to restore the collections to the place that they once held as a source of revenue.

It may be, as has sometimes been suggested, that the expectation of revenue from the annual collections became a deterrent to the search for endowment. On the university's side, caution could be preferred to initiative, on assumptions of dependence upon the bishops; on the side of the bishops themselves, fund-raising efforts other than for the collections could be fended off as intrusions from the outside. Each year, indeed, some disaffected bishops have omitted remittances of any kind to the university. Apparently, however, until recent decades, institutional leaders did not foresee that the episcopal sponsors of the university, presumed to be zealous for its mission, would allow their financial contributions to decline so drastically in proportion to the university's needs. The beginning of the downward trend may have been obscured somewhat by increases in enrollment and by new sources of revenue from governmental funding of research and instructional programs. In any case, as late as 1965–66, when the collections were supplying less than 19 per cent of the university's educational and general revenues, they covered more than 40 per cent of university-funded expenditures for instruction and departmental research. Twenty years later they were supplying less than seven per cent of the revenues and less than 19 per cent of the expenditures in this category.

The virtually inevitable result of lack of income from endowment and of the diminution in the proportion of the university's revenues received from the diocesan collections has been increasing dependence upon the tuition and fees paid by students. During the fiscal year 1986–87, more than 67 per cent of educational and general revenues were being obtained from this source. In the Association of American Universities, only Clark University, Syracuse University, and the University of Southern California were at all comparably tuition-dependent. After 1950, when enrollment was no longer swollen by veterans of World War II, the proportion of revenues being received from tuition and fees fluctuated within rather narrow ranges. From 1951 until 1964 the range was only from 50 to 53 per cent; during the next decade it was from 48 to 55 per cent. Even these ranges were markedly above those of most private institutions in the Association of American Universities.[27] In 1974 there began the steady rise to the present level of dependence.

It is in this setting that the Byron administration has undertaken its financial campaign to provide for the needs of the institution's second century. Probably because of the unique source of its funding through the annual collections, the university was late in turning to the organization of development activity. At various times in the past, rectors appointed assistants whose duties were directed toward development. Alumni and friends were solicited. The advice of consultants was sought. Campaigns were planned and sometimes begun. Only after the change in the university's bylaws in 1970, however, was a vice president appointed for this area. Father Whalen, the first to be appointed vice president for university relations, remained in the position only during 1970. He was succeeded by the Reverend Monsignor John F. Murphy, who had been president of St. Thomas More College in Covington, Kentucky, who remained for three years. Occupants of the position supervise alumni relations, development and fund-raising, public information, and public relations. The importance of the office in a modern university is obvious.

Enrollment in Perspective

Enrollment is an important source of revenue in virtually all institutions, but especially in those that have been allowed to become tuition-dependent. It is not by any means, however, the most significant fact about the university that it has become a larger place by far than it was, say, at the end of the Shahan administration in 1928, when undergraduates still constituted the majority of students. During the first semester of its hundredth year, a few more than seven thousand students, both full-time and part-time, enrolled for courses. Thus, with only some five thousand "full-time equivalent" students, graduate and undergraduate, it remains a relatively small institution in comparison with most American universities. It is the smallest of the six universities within the District of Columbia and much smaller than the nearby state universities in Maryland and Virginia.[28]

The peak for the century in total enrollment, inclusive of both full-

27. *Ibid.*
28. Statistical data are from the office of the registrar and from AR (1987–88) and other compilations of the office of planning and institutional research.

time and part-time students, was reached during the first semester of the academic year 1979–80, when 8,595 individuals were registered for instruction. Roughly, total enrollment had increased by more than 150 per cent since 1953, which was the year of its lowest level following the second world war, when only 3,385 students were on hand. It was in fact more than 75 per cent higher than it had been in 1949, the peak year of the immediate postwar period and 240 per cent higher than it had been in 1940, before military conscription had affected enrollment. The period from 1953 to 1966 had been marked by steady increases; a falling-off had occurred from 1966 to 1971; then steady increases had followed until 1979.

Many factors can be operative in periodic fluctuations in enrollment like these—rising costs of tuition and living expenses; changes in birth rates; in ecclesiastical policies; in the effectiveness of efforts to recruit students; and in the relative popularity of fields of study; and publicized controversies. With respect to the first of these factors, for example, costs during the 1980s, rising at about twice the rate of inflation, have been moderated by the greater availability of student aid and by changes in parental income levels. Some economists, in fact, maintain that "the vast majority of families with children in college do not face an appreciably higher burden relative to income" than they did during the 1970s.[29] In so far as changing birth rates are a factor, it is argued that the national increase in undergraduate enrollment during the late 1980s has paralleled an actual increase in the college-age population for the period from 1987 to 1989 and that decreases must be expected during the immediately succeeding years when the college-age population will decline in numbers.[30] The effect of such trends upon an individual institution requires attention to many other factors, of course.

Undoubtedly the most conspicuous change in the student body of The Catholic University of America during the past quarter-century has been its loss in both numbers and proportion of clerical and religious members. As already noted, this proportion, which as recently as the early 1960s was characteristically about 30 per cent of all students enrolled, has fallen to about six per cent. Among the visible results in what was sometimes known as Washington's "little Rome" has been the closing of houses of study of religious communities. Those for women religious have been most seriously but perhaps not as conspicuously

29. Terry W. Hartle, "The Rising Cost of College: The Conventional Wisdom is More Complicated than You Think," *AEIM*, No. 51 (Fall, 1986), 4.

30. John Kraus, "Colleges Must Prepare Now for the Enrollment Crash of 1990," *CHE*, XXXIV, No. 17 (Jan. 6, 1988), B2; see also Jean Evangelauf, "Record College Enrollments

affected. Among men's communities, some houses that had been only recently built, such as those of the New York province of the Carmelite Fathers and those of the Claretians, the Viatorians, and the Society of African Missions, were among the first to be sold. Holy Name College of the Order of Friars Minor, opened in 1930, now houses Howard University's school of divinity. The university has acquired for its own use the former Holy Cross College, Marist College, St. Bonaventure College, and the Vincentian house of studies. Since its quasi-monopolistic position in graduate education under Catholic auspices is no longer enjoyed, restoration of the former prominence of houses of study in its vicinity can hardly be expected.

Relations between the houses of study and the university were in fact sometimes strained. In the past, small seminaries were maintained in some religious houses, not only to inculcate distinctive forms of community life, which were to be valued, but often to effect seeming economies and in some instances to accommodate students who could not gain admittance to the university. During the past two decades, several communities have joined in cooperative arrangements of their own. The Washington Theological Union (originally named Coalition of Seminaries) operates as a separate institution enrolling students of the member seminaries, first of all, but also other students.[31] The Cluster of Independent Theological Schools, on the other hand, is a consortium arrangement constituted originally by three communities. Through membership of the Cluster and the Union as well as the university in the interdenominational Washington Theological Consortium, students from both these competing theological enterprises sometimes have access to courses in the university's school of religious studies.

It can be inferred correctly that the replacement of clerical and religious students by lay students was a prerequisite of the university's growth in enrollment after 1970. Largely because the Brothers of Christian Schools and the Xaverian Brothers have changed their policies for admission to their respective communities and closed their large scholasticates, enrollment of undergraduate clerics and religious is now almost negligible. And whereas during the academic year 1961–62 there were almost as many clerics and religious enrolled in the graduate school of arts and sciences as in all other graduate and professional fields

Mask Serious Flaws in Student-Admissions System, Experts Warn," *ibid.*, XXXV, No. 22 (Feb. 8, 1989), A 1 ff.

31. See BT, mm, Sept. 26, 1970, for note of the formation of the Coalition and mention of its probable effect upon university enrollment.

combined, those now enrolled are found overwhelmingly—in the proportion of 70 per cent—in the school of religious studies.

Given the university's history, the proportion of its students enrolled for graduate study has always been of particular interest. Terminologically, reference should be made to post-baccalaureate rather than graduate students, since students in law, for example, although since 1934 they have had to have a baccalaureate degree upon admission, are enrolled for a first professional, not a graduate, degree in their field. Post-baccalaureate students at the beginning of the 1960s were 59 per cent of total enrollment. By 1975–76 they constituted 68 per cent, but during the next decade declined to the previous level or just below it. Of more significance than their proportion, however, is their distribution among academic and professional fields.

At the beginning of the 1960s, the graduate school of arts and sciences alone had 55 per cent of all post-baccalaureate students. At the time, to be sure, it contained three departments that were later elevated into professional schools. But its other departments, as well as the school of philosophy and the school of theology, were offering primarily academic, as distinguished from professional, instruction. When the measure of "full-time equivalent" enrollment is applied, it is clear that, after some reorganization, the three schools that now offer primarily academic programs—arts and sciences, philosophy, and religious studies–are currently enrolling less than one-third of all post-baccalaureate students. The change in the position of these schools may be seen even more sharply when it is noted that 58 per cent of all current post-baccalaureate students but more than 70 per cent of those in the academic fields are enrolled as part-time students. The effect of the lack of fellowship support for graduate students is apparent. In its impact upon the character of the institution the shift to professional education at the post-baccalaureate level that is revealed in these changes is more significant than the growth in undergraduate numbers that is more often the subject of comment.

Two aspects of education for the professions especially tend to lead professional faculties toward separatism within academic communities. One is the specialized orientation to practice of professional school curricula. To the extent that professional education begins in the undergraduate years—as in the schools of engineering and architecture, music, and nursing—some liberal content, too often merely minimal, can be included among general requirements. But recognition of the likely narrowing effects of professional education was implied when, during the first major expansion of the university's originally limited professional offerings, early in the 1930s, the rector at the time observed that all *Perspectives* professional education in a university ought to have a graduate—by *and* which he seems to have meant, intellectually liberalizing—character. *Prospects* Instead, antipathy toward such a concept has tended to prevail in rivalries between academic and professional schools.[32]

What was to happen, as Bishop McEntegart had noted during the 1950s,[33] was that there would be a continuing increase in emphasis upon professional services in American higher education. A later head of the institution also emphasized that professional schools were "making important contributions to Catholic life."[34] Career orientations were bound to change as the proportion of youth enrolling in academic institutions increased. That enrollment in professional schools, there-fore, as in academic departments, would fluctuate in accord with na-tional trends was to be expected. Only in the school of law during the most recent twenty years has there been consistency of enrollment at capacity levels. But aspirations for higher education in general and the placement of professional training within universities of the United States have given the professions and their accrediting bodies increasing leverage within academic institutions. As a study of the phenomenon has shown, professional agencies "seek to assure equity for (and give bargaining strength to) the programs and schools they accredit and to protect them from pressures from the overall system in which they exist."[35] That this, perhaps even more than a specialized curriculum, is a source of separatism is not surprising.

So far as the proportion of undergraduates in the student body is concerned, it can be argued that it is its increase that is sustaining the academic departments. Enrollment in academic courses is maintained by the liberal objectives and requirements of undergraduate programs in the arts and sciences and by the general and preprofessional require-ments in engineering and architecture, music, and nursing. Moreover, although the 3,246 undergraduates enrolled in the fall of 1988 were outnumbered by the 3,774 post-baccalaureate students, since 90 per cent of all undergraduates are enrolled as full-time students, they easily tip the balance in "full-time equivalent" enrollment. To an appreciable degree, therefore, the university's student profile now resembles more

32. E.g., AS, Board of Inquiry, Vernon X. Miller to Charles E. Curran, Aug. 22, 1968, deploring "the graduate school orientation in the new dispensation."
33. OR, address to Alumni Association in response to its award of Gibbons medal, 1957.
34. BT, mm, Jan. 23, 1982, reporting remarks of President Pellegrino.
35. Eliot Freidson, *Professional Powers: A Study of the Institutionalization of Formal Knowledge* (Chicago: University of Chicago Press, 1986), 80.

than ever before what would be regarded as the typical American institution, in which the undergraduate component would be considered to be the heart of the university and in which students in professional schools would be numerous.

That The Catholic University of America was founded in a different tradition hardly needs to be emphasized. Older members of the faculties may sometimes still protest what they consider to be a disproportionate growth in the number of undergraduates. But when the fear is expressed that changes in the student population are diverting resources from the institution's commitment to graduate instruction and research, it is important to remember, as the board was once reminded, that "quality is not related to a particular value of the graduate to undergraduate ratio."[36] The most prestigious institutions for graduate study enroll far fewer graduate than undergraduate students. Departments may indeed seek undergraduate enrollment to provide a "teaching base" that will enable them to support more numerous and more diversified faculty appointments for their graduate programs. It is the viability of the institution as a whole that must be assured if its particular mission is to be attained. In this respect, a policy that makes a balanced budget the first priority of an institution may risk obscuring the fact that the basic requirements of graduate education presuppose a level of funding that is independent of tuition income. Reliance upon such income from undergraduate enrollment and assignment of priorities for professional schools inevitably diminish the distinctiveness of the university.

Although efforts to recruit students have been made to some extent in every phase of the university's history, a separate office of admissions and financial aid was not established until the appointment in 1968 of Raymond J. Steimel, an associate professor of psychology, as its first dean. As the so-called G.I. students began to complete their degree programs after World War II, the university, as has been seen, had sought to maintain higher levels of enrollment than before by offering new scholarships or other financial aid. But a decline in freshman enrollment and the recommendation of the Heald, Hobson consultants prompted new attention to student recruitment. The office established in 1968 has been maintained since with consistent results. Actually, recruitment activities are aimed for the most part at reaching prospective undergraduate students. For the first semester of the academic year 1988–89, for example, about 2,700 applications for admission as freshmen were received, about 1,800 were accepted, and about 850 young

36. BT, mm, Jan. 23, 1982, quoting remarks of President Pellegrino.

men and women came to enroll. Graduate students, on the other hand,
with specialized objectives, usually select institutions for study on the
basis of the reputations of the departments in which they are interested
and of the stipends that are offered to them. Centralized recruitment
efforts at the graduate level are therefore necessarily limited.

Until 1958 and even later, responsibility for recruitment was assumed
to be primarily that of the registrar, who reported to the secretary
general. Of a registrar of the 1920s and 1930s, it was said that in
recruitment matters he had "no equal."[37] Sometimes alumni or benefactors seeking the admission of individuals might complain, as when an
irate pastor threatened to leave the university's "list of friends" because
a conscientious registrar seemed to be exercising "absolute and unlimited
power."[38] After an accrediting team raised a question about the lack of
a recruitment program, in 1957, a part-time director of recruitment was
appointed. The rector at the time argued, however, that the clerics
and religious among the university's alumni and its affiliation program
enabled it to maintain a "wide geographic distribution" that other
institutions could equal "only with considerable effort and expense."[39]
In 1962, when a full-time position of admissions advisor was established,
the incumbent, evidently seeking quantifiable results and recalling instructions that had been given to him by administrators when he was
appointed, complained that the committee on undergraduate admissions
was being too restrictive in order "to keep the errors of admission at a
low minimum." He asked of the vice rector, "Are we to be so selective
that we enroll only the most brilliant?"[40]

A particular problem of student recruitment that then seemed to
demand attention was the changing sex ratio among undergraduates. In
the early 1960s, when enrollment in engineering was falling off and
women had been admitted to undergraduate study generally, an alarmed
assistant to the vice rector thought it "impossible to estimate the damage
done to the prestige and the morale at this University by the growing
imbalance between male and female undergraduates."[41] Actually, the
sex ratios of applicants and of enrolled students were to become fairly
constant. About 45 per cent of undergraduates currently enrolled are
males. There are, of course, important differences by schools: few fe-
males study engineering, few males study nursing.

37. J. H. Cain to J. H. Ryan, Oct. 20, 1931, referring to Charles F. Borden.
38. Henry F. Graebenstein to McCormick, Washington, Oct. 10, 1947.
39. OVR, "Progress Report to the Middle States Association of Colleges and Secondary
Schools," Mar. 19, 1959.
40. OVR, William F. Moran to McAllister, June 13, 1963.
41. OVR, Daniel M. Nolan, O.P., to McAllister, Dec. 10, 1963.

During the first years after 1968, which coincided with the rise of student radicalism, recruiters sympathizing with student causes were sometimes inclined to downplay the name of the institution and general requirements in philosophy and religion. Prospective students from Catholic high schools, it was said, wanted "the experience of a coeducational college where religion [was] not compulsory." Occasionally recruiters assured them that at The Catholic University of America religion really made "no difference." In response to the remarks of a student panelist in this vein, it was emphasized to the director of admissions at the time that the requirements to which objection was being taken were "not imposed on the basis of any assumption of catechesis or conversion" but "on the basis of assumptions that religion is an extremely important part of the cultural heritage, that religious questions are inescapable in personal life, and that students of an institution with a religious commitment should gain some knowledge of the foundations and implications of the commitment."[42] Interestingly, a graduate student during the period was finding that "at C.U. what is so unique is the totally Christian atmosphere of the entire university."[43]

The Institutional Aim in Perspective

In the final analysis, assessments of change in the life of any institution necessarily lead back to its aim. Indeed, an outstanding analyst of management has identified as the first task of leadership that of "thinking through the organization's mission, defining it and establishing it, clearly and visibly."[44] Fortunately, in addressing its current challenges from within the Church and from the larger society in which it lives, The Catholic University of America can draw upon a century's experience of an enviable continuity in perceptions of its institutional mission.

Within a fully Catholic perspective, the duality that is often seen between the university's religious and its academic aims is dissolved. The commitment of the university to the ethos of academe that was taking shape at its beginning did not extend to the secularizing tendencies that had already become dominant. Rather, it seemed to the founders, on truly traditional grounds, that the compatibility of academic and religious purposes could be assumed. Nevertheless, any Catholic university in a pluralistic society expects to be evaluated both as Catholic

42. OVR, Nuesse to John Flato, Oct. 18, 1974 (copy).
43. OVR, Estelle Gearon to Eugene R. Kennedy, Takoma Park, Md., Jan. 14, 1976 (copy).
44. Peter F. Drucker, "Leadership: More Doing Than Dash," *Wall Street Journal*, Jan. 6, 1988.

and as a university. The academic evaluation can become somewhat complex, given the scope that American universities have come to claim, but the criteria that are applied in the process are familiar enough in academic circles. For a Catholic institution, essentially, the ultimate test is its degree of success in conducting integrally an academic enterprise within the context of Catholic faith. Disciplines naturally vary widely in the opportunities that they offer for reference to the context. What the Church seeks is a corporate commitment to its universal aim. Tensions in American Catholic higher education arise in consideration of the feasibility of such a corporate commitment or of what it might entail.

Fidelity to both the faith of the founders and the ends of higher education is officially proclaimed in the statement of aims of the university that was approved by the academic senate and the trustees in 1968 and that remains in effect. Undeniably, however, institutional adherence to Catholic faith is being challenged more often than in the past. The relation of the financial support of the institution to its capacity to cope with such challenges seems to be poorly understood. Pressures are both external and internal. Externally, the secularization of American society that has affected all Catholic institutions is proceeding rapidly. The emergence of American Catholics from what was sometimes characterized as their "ghetto" has removed protective sociological walls. New governmental and other societal interventions are having secularizing effects. Internally, the university, like every other institution under Catholic auspices, is contending with pressures toward secularization in unresolved dilemmas that are presented by the increasing pluralism in its faculties and students. Not the least of the pressures, indeed, have their origin in its corporate search for academic excellence. As Father Hesburgh has remarked of his own institution, as it has become "better" as a university, it has encountered an "overhanging weight of secularism" that has become "heavier and more menacing to the core Catholicism of the University."[45]

Perhaps ultimately because striving for perfection is inculcated in Christian spiritual teaching, as Catholic institutions of higher education define their approach to the Church's worldwide evangelical problem of presenting the faith in terms appropriate to the increasingly differentiated but universally rising educational levels of national populations, it is their character as models that comes to the fore. This is a character that is thrust upon them. In the United States, all Catholic institutions

45. "Contemporary Issues and Historical Identity," *USCH*, VII, (Fall, 1988), 471.

together serve only a minority of the national student population, somewhat more than half a million of the twelve and a half million who are enrolled in colleges and universities. They reach, obviously, only a minority of Catholic students. Given the rise of the university institution to centrality in modern societies, Catholic universities of manifest strength would seem to have special importance for the Church. Their weakness or their absence, where resources would support them, would be telling. Significantly, although The Catholic University of America can no longer assert that it is a "flagship" for other American Catholic institutions, it has an evident contemporary challenge to refashion the commitment to serve as a model that was enunciated when it was named, that was intended in the singularity that was so long claimed for it, and that was expressed in the aspirations for it that were voiced from time to time in its first century. Faithfulness to its intended uniqueness is indeed a condition of its survival.

To refashion the university's commitment in the light of new academic, ecclesiastical, and social developments is a many-sided task. On an academic plane, it was logical to begin with the reorganization that resulted in the opening of the school of religious studies in 1973. The renewed strength in ecclesiastical studies that was gained would seem to have been an obvious requirement of any aspiration toward a Catholic institutional model. That this is officially recognized in the status of the departments of canon law and theology and the school of philosophy as ecclesiastical faculties subject to the Holy See has come to be seen by some Catholic educators as a disadvantage. Catholic theology as a university enterprise, however, which has been acclaimed by some of the same educators as an achievement, had begun in the United States with the founding of the university under pontifical auspices. Concern to provide for the advanced study of theology in relation to developments in other disciplines was expressed in the first rector's favorite project, the series that his successors were to call "culture lectures," and in his anxiety to expedite the addition of what he himself called the "faculties for the laity" to augment the initial faculty of the sacred sciences.

It is with respect to theological research and teaching in a university setting that issues of academic freedom have sometimes been presented. The Poels and Siegman cases in biblical studies have been especially regrettable. The record, of course, discloses that there was greater agreement in the earlier decades than during the 1970s and 1980s upon the identification of relevant restraints and upon submission to ecclesiastical authority. It has been in fact only during the 1980s that the university has been formally accused of violating the academic freedom of a professor. It is Father Curran who has gone so far as to ask, "Is a Catholic university an oxymoron?"[46] To this question President Byron has made the obvious response. In his words, to "proclaim a Catholic identity without accepting an ecclesial limit on theological explanation and communication is to misunderstand not only the nature of church-relatedness, but also the idea of a university and the meaning of academic freedom."[47]

Freedom from irrelevant restraints is of course a basic right of a member of a faculty in any university. It follows that the definition of the issues in any controversy is of prime importance. There is no possibility of bridging the chasm on the point between those who accept willingly doctrinal and disciplinary restraints as relevant and those who believe that truth, if can be said to be attainable at all, can be determined only in "the marketplace of ideas." Short of the latter absolutistic position, the tradition of The Catholic University of America in defense of academic freedom—even if sullied—provides a perspective of prime importance for its future. Throughout the institution's history, beginning in its earliest years, it has not been uncommon for non-Catholic professors to remark that, respecting the philosophical and theological boundaries of Catholic doctrine, they have been able to enjoy greater freedom than colleagues at other institutions who have been subject to the private whims of benefactors or to state legislatures. In the celebrated instance of John A. Ryan, the university's stance was made a matter of public knowledge, since he was being protected in his views on social and economic policies by the same chancellor who was publicly known to find his views repugnant.

Its experience of controversies, almost always bound to be confusing, should not be allowed to obscure the unique opportunities that have been afforded to the university for the clarification of how academic freedom, collegiality, pluralism, and other features of academic life can be operative in an institution conducted under Catholic auspices. Considerations introduced by the examination of what is required by both Catholic and academic norms have provided a lively context for the discussion of institutional priorities. Some changes in the university's academic profile have occurred in interaction with developments in the Church. The university has been near the center of most ecclesiastical controversies, usually with all the major contending parties represented

46. Letter to Editor, *Washington Post*, May 29, 1988.
47. *Ibid.*, June 5, 1988.

in it. Sometimes the sponsorship of the hierarchy of the United States has exposed the university peculiarly to misunderstanding and criticism. No experience of controversy, however, has lessened the need for the center of Catholic thought that the university has been.

In all probability, when the university was founded not even its foremost proponents could have foreseen the place that disciplinary research would come to have in its service to the Church. At the end of its first century, however, the university is noting challenges not only to its Catholicity but also to its research ideal. These do not arise only from its expansion in professional fields. Rather, the perennial tension between the research and teaching functions of a university has been aggravated by the progress of specialization arising from the inherent development of the research ideal itself. In contrast with European practice, requiring leading professors to be responsible for entire disciplinary fields, subdivision of disciplines was to become continuous in large institutions of the United States. In this way, a fundamental institutional problem "became that of finding the means for providing every faculty member with some chance to contribute to the advancement of knowledge—not to mention the advancement of his own professional career."[48] Specialization accelerated after World War II. Even at The Catholic University of America, the trend can be personified by contrasting the scholars of earlier generations, known for breadth, and the more recent products of graduate departments, trained within a narrower compass.[49]

Specialization is, as has been recognized, essential for the progress of research. It may be, at the same time, counter-productive for teaching and for the maintenance of community in academic life. There is as yet no clear vision of how the opposing effects can be reconciled. Meanwhile, continuing specialization is being encouraged by various developments in higher education that would seem to be desirable in themselves. Within universities, it is not only the mode of training offered in graduate schools that is a factor; of even greater importance are the typical policies of institutions that govern faculty rank and tenure. Within disciplines, pressures are exerted by professional organizations that are subdividing endlessly in response to specialized and occupational interests. The research sponsored by governmental and private agencies

48. Geiger, *op. cit.*, 74.
49. On the point in general, see Burton R. Clark, *The Academic Life: Small Worlds, Different Worlds* (New York: Carnegie Foundation for the Advancement of Teaching, 1988), and Russell Jacoby, *The Last Intellectuals; American Culture in the Age of Academe* (New York: Basic Books, 1988).

has become an important stimulus for specialization. Ultimately, it must even be asked if mass education in pursuit of equality of opportunity is not also a factor. If undergraduate instruction focused upon career objectives does not lead to cultivation of mind, the increase of graduate student populations inevitably places a premium upon the acquisition of specialized knowledge, which can be gained much more easily than scholarly breadth.

Problems of higher education such as these affect all universities but they arouse special concerns in an institution that seeks to pursue academic disciplines in a community inspired by Catholic faith. Often specialists are too narrowly prepared to present a discipline in any adequate context. Specialization by its nature lends itself readily to the separation of academic from evangelical aims. When, moreover, there are too few Catholic scholars in a specialization or when financial support to obtain the scholars is lacking, religious pluralism in the faculties is likely to be increased to a point hardly conducive to the communication of a Catholic interest. Not a few observers of the process have predicted that the secularization of Catholic universities will follow. The challenge to the Catholic University of America is to utilize its traditional strengths to refashion its historic commitment to the pursuit of knowledge.

Indeed, at the beginning of its second century, the university can look forward to the revitalization of the aims that brought it into being originally. The American university movement of which it became a part has assumed unparalleled intellectual and physical proportions. There are calls for its self-renewal. Participation in the process will offer new opportunities to an institution that has experienced the vicissitudes and the rewards of a century-old attempt to enlist the culture of mind in the service of religion.

Index

American Catholic Psychological Association, 293

American Catholic Sociological Society, 293

American Council on Education, 195, 262, 281–82, 311, 331, 391, 450, 462

American Council of Learned Societies, 306

American Ecclesiastical Review, 182, 305

American Education Week, 181

American Legion, 301

American Psychological Association, 224, 237

American School of Classical Studies, Athens, 220

"Americanism," condemnation of, xviii, 73, 75–78, 79, 94, 95, 127

Amherst College, 115

Ancient Order of Hibernians, 166, 221–22

Anderson, Charles J., 462n

Andrews, Thomas Francis, chair, 90

Anselm, St., 4

Anthropology, offerings in, 195, 216, 260

Antioch College, 112n

Apologetics, 215, 308

Apostolic activity abroad, 444

Apostolic delegate to United States, 75, 77, 235, 287–88, 296, 401

Apostolic Mission House, 165, 167

Applied physics and space science: department of, 397; termination of, as aerospace and atmospheric science, 440–41

Architectural Accrediting Board, 354

Architectural Society, 187

Architecture, department of, 163, 231, 264, 473

Archives and manuscripts, department of, 338

Arizona State University, 328

Armstrong, Frederick C., 264n

Army Specialized Training Program, 332

Art, department of, 300

Arts and sciences, 72, 108, 109–10, 217–31, 249; school of, 436–37, 440, 464–65

Assimilation of American Catholics, 374–76, 416–19

Association of American Colleges, 270, 405, 444

Association of American Law Schools, 232, 263

Association of American Universities, 121–22, 143–44, 176, 196, 258, 262, 269, 277, 280, 295, 319, 348, 349, 366, 367, 376, 450, 471, 472, 473, 474, 475

Association of Catholic Colleges, 119–20

Association of Catholic Colleges and Universities, 412, 413n

Association of Colleges of the Middle States and Maryland, 119

Association of Deans and Directors of Summer Sessions, 261

Association of the Miraculous Medal, 182

Association of Priests of the Archdiocese of Washington, 402

Association of Students of French, 359

Association of Women Students, 359

Astronomy, offerings in, 59, 231, 260

Athletics: beginnings, 183–86; director of, 273, 274, 328, 360–61; faculty committees, 184, 273–74; funding, 185, 274, 328; intramural, 328, 361

Athletics, intercollegiate, 271; baseball, 184; basketball, 450; boxing, 276, 328–29, 361; football, 184–85, 274–76, 327–28; soccer, 361; track, 276, 329, 361

Atkinson, Ti-Grace, 449, 457

Atonement Friars, 326

Auweiler, Edwin, O.F.M., 170n

Avella, Steven M., S.D.S., 280n

Ayers, Robert C., 74n, 94n, 127n

Babcock, Kendrick C., 153n

Badger, Henry G., 331n

Baisnée, Jules, S.S., 221, 295n

Baldwin, E. J., 52

Baltimore and Ohio Railroad, 165

Banigan, Joseph, 115

Bamberg Philosophische-Theologische Hochschule, 304

Barger, Robert N., 28n

Barron, Joseph T., 214

Barry, Colman J., O.S.B., xv, 70n, 77–78n, 92n, 125n, 126n, 139n, 436

Barry, H. J., 183n

Basselin, Theodore B., 157, 161; scholarships, 202

Baudrillart, Alfred, 148–49, 210n

Baum, William W., 427n

Baumert, W. A., 155n

Beale, Joseph W., 264n

Beatty, George Edward, 401n

Becker, Thomas Andrew, 12, 16, 21, 23, 24n, 26, 27, 31, 44, 50n, 62, 63, 91, 239

Beckman, Francis J., 261, 289n

Bedient, Ethel L., 183n

Behrendt, Leo, 187, 221

Benedict XV, Pope, xvi, 163, 164, 178, 198

Benedictine Sisters, 168

Bennett, William J., 470, 471

Berelson, Bernard, 69n

Bergman, Arthur J., 274

Berlin Technische Hochschule, 313

Berlin, University of, 92, 113, 313

Bernardin, C. W., 112n

Bernardini, Filippo, 207, 217, 251n, 254n, 280

Beta Beta Society, 188

Biberstein, Frank, 231, 320, 362

Biblical studies, 54, 57, 86, 95, 96, 213–14, 378, 396, 436, 484

Biology, offerings in, 110, 113, 114, 130, 229, 300, 389

Bisleti, Gaetano, 198n, 201n, 202n, 206, 214n, 217n, 249n, 253n, 281n, 294, 303, 309